The Institute of Transportation Engineers (ITE) is an international educational and scientific association of transportation and traffic engineers and other professionals who are responsible for meeting mobility and safety needs. The Institute facilitates the application of technology and scientific principles to research, planning, functional design, implementation, operation, policy development and management for any mode of transportation by promoting professional development of members, supporting and encouraging education, stimulating research, developing public awareness and exchanging professional information; and by maintaining a central point of reference and action.

Founded in 1930, the Institute serves as a gateway to knowledge and advancement through meetings, seminars and publications; and through our network of more than 15,000 members working in some 80 countries. The Institute also has more than 70 local and regional chapters and more than 90 student chapters that provide additional opportunities for information exchange, participation and networking.

This document is disseminated under the sponsorship of the Department of Transportation in the interest of information exchange. The United States Government assumes no liability for its contents or the use there-of. This report does not constitute a standard, specification, or regulation. The United States Government and ITE do not endorse products or manufacturers. Trade and manufacturers' names appear in this report only because they are considered essential to the object of the document.

Library of Congress Cataloging-in-Publication Data

Intelligent transportation primer/U.S. Department of Transportation,
Federal Highway Administration; Institute of Transportation Engineers.
     p. cm.
   Includes bibliographic references.
   ISBN 0–935403–45–0 (alk. paper)
     1. Intelligent Vehicle Highway Systems—United States.
I. United States. Federal Highway Administration. II. Institute of
Transportation Engineers.

TE228.3.I576 2000
388.3'12–dc21

Institute of Transportation Engineers
1099 14th Street, NW • Suite 300 West • Washington, D.C. 20005-3438 USA
Telephone: +1 (202) 289-0222
Facsimile: +1 (202) 289-7722
ITE on the Web: www.ite.org

3000/PMR/CPC/1000/TB-014/ISBN: 0–935403–45–0

Intelligent Transportation Primer

This project was developed in partnership with:

The Center for Advanced Transportation Technology
at the University of Maryland

Institute of Transportation Engineers

ITS America

Intelligent Transportation Systems Joint Program Office
of the U.S. Department of Transportation

Institute of Transportation Engineers
1099 14th Street, NW • Suite 300 West • Washington, D.C. 20005

Contents

Chapter 6: The Role of ITS in the Emergency Management and Emergency Services Community

Chapter 7: Public Transit and ITS

Chapter 8: Electronic Toll and Traffic Management

Chapter 9: Commercial Vehicle Operations and Freight Movement

Acknowledgments

Intelligent Transportation Primer

This text has been developed as a collaborative effort of the Institute of Transportation Engineers (ITE), ITS America, The University of Maryland Center for Advanced Transportation, the Intelligent Transportation Systems (ITS) Joint Program Office of the U.S. Department of Transportation (U.S. DOT) and the chapter authors. Donna C. Nelson of the Center for Advanced Transportation at the University of Maryland served as the text senior editor. Appreciation is expressed to William J. Harris for his preliminary efforts in drafting the book's content and encouraging the collaborative effort. The development and production of the text was funded through a contract with the ITS Joint Program Office of the U.S. DOT (DTFH61-95-C-00171 Task 16).

The efforts of the ITE headquarters staff in overseeing the administration and production of the text is appreciated. Those who worked on the project include: Agneta Melén-Wilmot, Ann O'Neill, Mark R. Norman, Thomas W. Brahms, Jane A. Wetz, Edward R. Stollof, Erin K. Grady, Russell W. Houston and Larry A. Woldt.

Chapter reviews were coordinated by Fredrick D. Cwik for ITS America , by William S. Jones for the ITS Joint Program Office and by Tom Brahms for ITE.

Production management: Agneta Melén-Wilmot, Manager of Special
Publications Production, ITE

Copy editing and book design: Michelle V. Peña, Capitol Publishing Corporation

Printing and binding: PMR Printing Company, Inc.

BY Francis B. Francois • Executive Director Emeritus •
American Association of State Highway and Transportation Officials

INTRODUCTION

This book is concerned with intelligent transportation systems (ITS), a discipline that emerged in the last few decades of the 20th century, which provides a family of unconventional solutions for improving the safety and performance of surface transportation in nations worldwide. While the acronym ITS has come to be accepted in the United States, in some other nations telematics is the term used to identify this discipline. The purpose of this introduction is to explore the reasons ITS has emerged as an important transportation discipline; provide an overview of what is included in the discipline; and examine some of the issues that will face those who choose to practice in this increasingly important field, whether for a private-sector industrial enterprise, in an engineering consultant practice, as a member of a governmental entity, in academia, or elsewhere. The following chapters will then develop and explain many facets of ITS, as the discipline continues to evolve.

Transportation challenges and solutions

Is the discipline of ITS a solution looking for a problem, or a timely solution that when properly applied can address existing transportation challenges that heretofore have been partially or entirely unsolvable? This question has been debated worldwide in the transportation community, and the result among the great majority of transportation professionals is that ITS is a solution that when properly applied can address or at least relieve some of the growing surface transportation problems facing the United States and many other industrialized nations in Europe and Asia.

Transportation problems—nature and magnitude

The discipline of ITS as explored in this book concentrates on the surface transportation system, (including highways, roads and streets) and the different classes of vehicles that operate on them. Among those vehicles are automobiles; light, medium and heavy trucks; vans; motorcycles; and rubber-tired transit vehicles. This book does not specifically treat the other modes of transportation, such as airplanes and airports, harbors and inland waterways, or the railroads. But ITS does often draw on and borrow technology used in these other transportation modes. Beyond this, it must be recognized that the surface transportation system is critical to the effective utilization of airports and seaports, to move goods and people to and away from them. Thus ITS often affects the other modes; and by making the highway, road and street system and the nation's transit systems more effective and efficient, they increase the effectiveness and efficiency of these other modes as well.

What are the transportation problems facing the surface transportation system, as we enter the 21st century? There are many, and they are similar across the world in industrial nations. One set of problems centers on the growing congestion of highways and roads. It is common knowledge that the U.S. surface transportation system is increasingly congested, and that many hours are lost simply sitting in slow or nonmoving traffic. This congestion results in a waste of energy, contributes to the air pollution associated with the burning of fossil fuels, causes disruption to scheduled public transportation services and generates untold thousands of unproductive hours that negatively affect the nation's economy and the personal activity time of drivers and passengers alike. Another set of problems relates to safety. Each year there are thousands of vehicle crashes on U.S. highways and streets that cause injuries, deaths and property damage and that can result in incidents that slow or stop the orderly flow of traffic. These same conditions are increasingly present in France, Germany, the United Kingdom, Japan, Korea and other nations; and even such relatively less motorized nations as China are concerned about surface transportation problems and are exploring ITS applications. In this chapter the surface transportation problems of the United States will be discussed as an example, with the understanding that many of the same or at least similar problems exist elsewhere in the world.

The U.S. highway system has been designed and constructed and is maintained and operated primarily by the states and their local governments. The federal government owns and is responsible for some limited mileage, primarily in national forests, parks and on military bases. But the federal government's major and most important role in America's highways is in its capacity as part of a state–federal highway partnership that began when the U.S. Congress enacted the first federal-aid highway program in 1916. A similar federal role in public transportation emerged in the last four decades of the 20th century.

Considerable funding for constructing the nation's major highways has come from the federal government, through the state–federal partnership that began in 1916. The responsibility for operation and maintenance of the system has rested with the state and their local governments, although this has been eased to a degree in recent transportation reauthorization legislation enacted by the Congress, beginning in 1981 when an Interstate resurfacing, restoration, rehabilitation and reconstruction (4R) program was enacted. Rising from a 50–50 funding arrangement for dividing capital costs between the federal and state governments that was in place for decades, under the federal-aid highway act of 1956 the federal government provided 90 percent of capital funding for the 40,000 plus miles of the National System of Interstate and Defense Highways (commonly called the Interstate system) authorized by that act. The enactment of the Intermodal Surface Transportation Efficiency Act (ISTEA) in 1991 called for establishment of a new National Highway System (NHS) of some 155,000 miles (plus or minus 15 percent, and including the Interstate system), and among many new provisions ISTEA established the normal federal share of funding for affected highways and transit systems at 80 percent.

Over the years since 1916, under the state–federal highway program partnership, the federal government has provided technical assistance and guidance to the states and their local governments in the use of federal dollars, which has helped produce a nationwide system of highways of a high, uniform quality that among other benefits made possible the development of today's motor carrier industry. The Interstates in particular served to connect all fifty states of the nation, often running where the railroad system never reached and making possible economic growth in all states. The NHS expands upon the Interstate system to provide more quality highways to the nation.

Local roads and streets in the United States are normally the responsibility of local government entities that exceed 30,000 in number, including municipalities and counties, and in some instances special purpose districts. These local entities usually receive little or no federal financial aid for the construction and operation of the local roads and streets for which they are responsible, and the extent of state fiscal aid varies. There are exceptions to this pattern, as in North Carolina and Virginia, where the state has assumed most local road responsibilities; but in nearly all states the reality is that local elected officials make decisions on local roads.

This great number of governmental entities with road and street responsibility requires cooperation and coordination if area or region-wide decisions on the construction and management of the road system are to be made. While this widespread responsibility can be a problem in rural areas, it can create significant difficulties in urban areas when there is a desire to effectively coordinate traffic signals and system operating procedures among many units of local government. These institutional issues can be especially challenging when efforts to implement ITS activities are undertaken.

Turning to public transit, this industry was essentially in the private sector until after World War II, when a sharp fall in ridership caused many private-sector transit companies to go out of business. As a result, local municipalities and counties established transit agencies to provide needed publication transportation services, and in some areas state and local governments created special transit agencies. These new transit agencies often functioned independently of the officials responsible for local roads and bridges and the state transportation agencies. As a result, it has often proved difficult to coordinate the scheduling and other needs of public transportation vehicles with the operation of the roads and streets, sometimes resulting in less than desirable transit services. In the 1980s more cooperation developed in many parts of the nation between transit agencies, state transportation agencies, and local elected officials, especially as the need for funding to subsidize transit operations grew.

The federal role in transit was largely confined to providing grants directly to transit agencies, until the enactment of ISTEA in 1991. Under ISTEA a new transportation planning process was put in place that required consideration of both highway and transit needs and the participation of both road and transit agencies in the process, and which provided for the transferability of certain federal funds between highways and transit. The ISTEA also established new roles for the Federal Transit Administration (FTA), in research and elsewhere, and encouraged cooperation between the FTA and the Federal Highway Administration (FHWA). The subsequent Transportation Equity Act for the 21st Century (TEA-21), enacted by Congress in 1998, continued and expanded upon these key provisions.

States have long provided funding for highways; and increasingly they are also funding public transportation, to the level that when viewed nationwide by the end of the 20th century the states were collectively expending more on transit than the federal government. But the extent of state fiscal support for transit varies, and in some states there is minimal if any funding provided. The fare box remains an essential component of transit funding, supplemented by grants from the federal and state governments, and often the local governments whose needs are being served.

Over the last four decades of the 20th century there was growing recognition that better planning and coordination of the transportation system was necessary, both in urban areas and across the states. In some metropolitan areas transportation planning bodies were put in place by local governments, often with state and federal assistance, in an effort to improve planning and coordination. The author was an elected official in Prince George's County, Maryland from 1966 to 1980 and in that capacity served on the Board of Directors of the Metropolitan Washington Council of Governments (WASHCOG). In those years he helped establish such a transportation planning board for the metropolitan Washington area, which included the major local governments and the Maryland and Virginia Departments of Transportation (DOTs). But the local transit agency, the Washington Metropolitan Area Transit Authority (WMATA), which was responsible for building and operating the Washington Metro system and operation of a metropolitan-wide bus system, was not a member of this transportation planning board. Similar arrangements were established in those years in many other states.

Recognizing the need for more effective regional planning and coordination, in enacting the 1991 ISTEA the Congress established a requirement for metropolitan planning organizations (MPOs) in urban areas, including not just highways and roads but also transit agencies, and charged them with preparation of plans for the use of federal transportation funding for both highways and transit in their geographic area. The plans were subject to review by the state transportation agencies, and thus a new era of state and local transportation decision-making was launched nationwide. Congress reinforced and strengthened the MPO process in 1998 with passage of the TEA-21.

What are the type and extent of the challenges facing the surface transportation system of the United States? The selected data of the following tables illustrate the situation in the late 1990s.

Table 1–1
Extent and Jurisdictional Control of America's Roads and Streets, 1998
SOURCE: *Highway Statistics 1998* (Washington, D.C.: Federal Highway Administration, 1998).

Jurisdiction	Rural Mileage	Urban Mileage	Total Miles	% of System
State	660,834	110,017	770,851	19.7
Local	2,285,447	730,152	3,015,599	77.2
Federal	118,369	1,485	119,854	3.1
Total	3,064,650	841,654	3,906,304	100.0

The 3.9 million miles of road shown in table 1–1 are by no measure of uniform construction and design. Some are multilane, limited access highways; others are unpaved rural roads with little daily traffic. As late as 1976 more than one-half of the total mileage of roads and streets in the United States was unpaved. By 1996, continuing road improvement programs by the states and local entities had increased paved roads to 60.5 percent of the total. As of 1996, the road and street system of the United States also included 581,863 bridges, of which 101,518 or 17.4 percent were classified as structurally deficient and another 81,208 or 14.0 percent as functionally obsolete. These statistics illustrate that the road and street system of the nation, while including some excellent facilities, is of varying quality and that a continuing road and bridge improvement program is necessary to maintain mobility.

Table 1–2
Total Road Mileage and Travel by Functional System, 1998
SOURCE: *Highway Statistics 1998* (Washington, D.C.: Federal Highway Administration, 1998).

System	Total Mileage	% of All Miles	Travel - Millions of Vehicle Miles	% of All Travel Miles
Interstate	46,084	1.2	625,469	23.8
Other Arterials	387,957	9.9	1,266,029	48.3
Collectors	792,619	20.3	388,930	14.8
Locals	2,679,632	68.6	344,939	13.1

The data of tables 1–1 and 1–2 show that while the local roads and other collectors constitute extensive mileage in the United States, the bulk of vehicle miles of travel occur on the Interstate system and other arterials. The Interstate system, while comprising only 1.2 percent of the mileage, carries 23.8 percent of vehicle miles of travel. The Interstate system and most of the other arterials are under the jurisdictional control of the states, which means that the state DOTs bear much of the burden for dealing with total vehicle miles of travel. At the same time, the fact that 730,152 miles of urban roads (86.75 percent) are under the jurisdictional control of local governments makes clear the importance of local government involvement in such issues as urban traffic management and urban congestion issues.

Table 1–3
Changes in Key Indicators for the Nation's Roads and
Highways Over Twenty Years, 1978–1998
SOURCES: *Highway Statistics 1998* (Washington, D.C.: Federal Highway Administration, 1998).
Highway Statistics Summary to 1995 (Washington, D.C.: Federal Highway Administration, 1995).

Indicator	Percent Change
Total road and street mileage	0.6% increase
Population of nation	21.4% increase
Number of licensed drivers	31.3% increase
Number of motor vehicle registrations	42.6% increase
Total vehicle miles of travel	70.0% increase
Capital outlay in constant dollars (Based on 1997 $)	92.9% increase
Total motor fuel use	23.8% increase
Gallons of motor fuel use per mile	27.1% decrease

The indicator data of table 1–3 help explain the problems found on America's highways and streets. While capital outlay increased over the 20-year period, only 0.6 percent was added to the nation's total road and street mileage. During the same period the number of registered vehicles increased by 42.6 percent, and the total vehicle miles of travel increased by 70.0 percent. The result is an increased number of vehicles on the road at any given time and more congestion, especially in urban areas.

Part of the use of the road and street system is attributable to Americans traveling by personal motor vehicle (e.g., automobile, light truck, van, motorcycle). According to FHWA's *Our Nation's Highways,* this is the predominate form of personal transportation in the United States, accounting for a total of 90.8 percent of all such travel in 1995, a number that grows each year. By contrast, the same publication states that public transportation accounts for only 2.13 percent of personal travel, or 3.4 percent if school buses are added in.

The situation is similar for freight. According to *Our Nation's Highways,* the nation's highway system carried 25 percent of the total revenue ton-miles of freight in 1995, compared to 19 percent in 1960. More significant, according to the FHWA, is that almost 93 percent of the total dollars of freight in 1993 was transported on the nation's highways. The motor carrier industry is the key component of the increasing reliance of industry on the just-in-time (JIT) principle for receiving components and retail goods, and the efficient movement of trucks is thus important to all aspects of the American economy.

Turning now to traffic safety, despite the sharp rise in vehicle miles driven in the United States over the past twenty years, table 1–3 shows that the highway fatality rate (i.e., fatalities per 100 million vehicle miles of travel) trended downwardly, reaching 1.69 in 1996—a 48-percent decrease since 1976. This drop is attributed to several causes, including improved road conditions, safer vehicles, enforcement of driving under the influence of alcohol laws and other factors. But the number of accidents, or crashes as they are increasingly being called, is still high.

In 1996, the total number of deaths on U.S. highways was 41,907, with 35,580 being vehicle occupants and the other 6,327 being pedestrians. Of the deaths 21,265 occurred at night and the others during the day. Rural areas of the United States accounted for 24,600 of the deaths, and urban areas for 17,307. Beyond deaths, it also needs to be remembered that many crashes result in injuries to vehicle occupants and pedestrians that are far in excess of deaths. For example, the U.S. DOT estimated that injuries from highway and street crashes reached more than 3,215,000 in 1994. Added to this must be the property damage claims and the lost wages and productivity resulting from vehicle crashes. Clearly, increasing the safety of America's highways is important in all areas of the nation. ITS can offer help in reaching this goal.

Turning now to public transportation, while the total percentage of personal transportation trips taken by transit is low, it needs to be remembered that in much of urban America transit use is far greater than the national average, reaching 30 percent or more of work trips in some places. And transit use will need to increase in future years if urban congestion is to be relieved and air pollution problems abated. Table 1–4 provides some data on transit in the United States.

Table 1–4
Transit in the United States, 1997
SOURCE: Bureau of Transportation Statistics, *Pocket Guide to Transportation*
(Washington, D.C.: U.S. Department of Transportation, 1999).

Mode	Route Miles Serviced	Number of Vehicles	Vehicle Miles (Millions)	Passenger Miles (Millions)
Bus	155,817	697,548	6,800	144,900
Commuter Rail	4,417	4,943	251	8,000
Transit Rail	2,186	11,471	599	13,139

The bus data in table 1–4 include commercial, federal, school and transit buses; and transit rail includes both light and heavy rail. The data make clear that travel by bus—rubber-tired vehicles that travel on America's roads and streets—is far and away the largest component of America's public transportation systems. Thus, when congestion is present on the roads, as is common in many urban areas at the end of the 20th century, the operation of a fleet of transit buses is directly affected. The transit industry knows that reliable schedules are vital to attracting customers, together with providing riders with accurate information. The tools offered by ITS are increasingly being recognized and relied upon by the leaders of the transit industry to provide the better service that customers expect and want.

This discussion by no means exhausts the review of current problems with the transportation system in the United States and other nations. One subject not addressed to any extent to this point is the need for more funding being faced by public agencies everywhere, which can sometimes grow worse in response to other things growing better. A good example of this is illustrated by the data of table 1–3 regarding motor fuel use. For energy conservation and to reduce air pollution, a 27.1-percent decrease in the amount of fuel used per mile is an important achievement. But this increased efficiency means that the total number of gallons of motor fuel is reduced, which in turn reduces the revenue derived from a per-gallon motor fuel tax. To compensate for this revenue reduction, either the fuel tax must be increased, the agency's program reduced, or another source of revenue found—all of which can be politically difficult to achieve. Clearly, there are many problems, all of which present challenges for the discipline of ITS to help meet.

National transportation goals

Given the transportation problems faced by the United States, what are the transportation goals of the nation? There are in fact many goals, coming from different public agencies and a host of private-sector entities. On the public-sector side, the federal government has the need for goals to guide its involvement in the nation's surface transportation system and to help it carry out the traditional commerce and public safety responsibilities it must discharge. States need goals to guide their expenditures and plans; and municipalities, counties and transportation agencies also need goals.

Beyond the public sector, different areas of the nation's private sector also hold transportation goals. The nation's motor carrier industry has goals set at the national, state, regional and individual company levels that will further its operations and increase the possibility of profits. Those goals are sometimes in conflict with goals adopted individually and collectively by the nation's railroads. Other operators of transportation services, including intercity bus service providers and local taxi services, also have goals. Those industries that need transportation for efficient operations, such as manufacturers who today are often dependent upon JIT deliveries of parts and equipment, have their transportation goals. And such industries as tourism and recreation that depend on transportation also have goals. Given this array of sometimes competing goals, it is difficult to state a specific set of national transportation goals that are all inclusive.

At the federal level, in recent times each incoming president's administration and DOT have undertaken development of transportation goals for the federal government, which commonly are changed when a new administration takes office. The Clinton administration was especially dedicated to this process and developed comprehensive goals that they distributed widely using the Internet, meetings across the nation and other means. And of course Congress periodically enacts major transportation bills, such as the 1991 ISTEA and the 1998 TEA-21, with the intent of identifying a set of national goals to be implemented by the administration, the states and their local governments, and the private sector, as appropriate.

Typically, the states also develop transportation goals, with one eye on the actions and proposals of Congress and the administration and the other on the state's need to further the economy and lifestyle of its residents. Local governments, which normally have land use planning and zoning responsibilities, also must develop transportation goals. And since the enactment of ISTEA and TEA-21, the strengthened MPOs typically engage in setting regional transportation goals as part of their process in producing the required Transportation Improvement Program called for by Congress.

All of the goals resulting from this array of activity are important to those producing them, and collectively they more or less guide transportation programs in the United States. Without getting into great detail, what is the overall thrust of this array of transportation goals? The following goals are commonly included on any such listing for the United States, and other nations have similar goals of their own:

- achieve and maintain an acceptable mobility level to satisfy local, regional, and national needs for the movement of people and things to their desired destinations;
- minimize the time delays caused by congestion, and the accompanying waste of fuel, addition of pollutants to the atmosphere and loss in productivity;
- maximize the safety of surface transportation by reducing the opportunities and propensities for crashes to a minimum and supporting rescue services to maximize their effectiveness;

- establish institutional relationships that will clear traffic incidents as rapidly as possible, so that normal traffic flow can be restored;
- consider traffic demand reduction techniques, to help reduce vehicle traffic;
- support intermodal connectivity, to maximize the movement of people and things from one mode of transportation to another;
- effectively manage public transportation vehicle movements, to minimize travel times and meet schedules;
- provide meaningful travel information to consumers, to help them better meet their mobility needs.

Approaches to these problems

What approaches are available to the United States, and other nations, to address their modern surface transportation problems and to achieve goals such as those set out above? There are several approaches, and among them are the following.

The traditional approach has been for the public sector to build and improve conventional transportation facilities, adding highway and road capacity in an effort to eliminate or at least reduce congestion. For decades this approach worked, but in the closing decades of the 20th century it failed to be as effective as in past years. There are several reasons for this failure:

- The fiscal and social cost of constructing new facilities and reconstructing existing highways and roads under traffic have risen to such an extent that available public-sector revenue cannot meet the demand. This does not mean that construction is not an answer in some instances, but it is no longer the universal tool it once seemed to be.
- As environmental awareness and concerns have risen, particularly in air quality and wetland preservation, it has become increasingly difficult, expensive and time consuming to obtain approvals to proceed with projects.
- In many urban areas, right-of-way acquisition for new or expanded road capacity has become difficult if not impossible, because of a combination of land cost, environmental constraints and citizen opposition to projects.

In some areas of the nation, local transit systems—both rail and bus—have been expanded in an effort to relieve personal travel on roads and streets. In cities like Washington, D.C.; Atlanta, Georgia; Los Angeles, California; and Portland, Oregon these expanded transit facilities are drawing many people off the roads and streets. But they have not solved the congestion problem, in part because of the widespread expansion of the metropolitan area into the suburbs and beyond and the difficulties transit faces in trying to serve people and location mobility needs in such widespread areas.

In the 1990s there was renewed interest in the adoption of techniques to reduce travel demand, and some seem to be working. In the Portland, Oregon area, a growth boundary was instituted to limit further expansion of development, growth management has been adopted, transit is being used to effectively move people throughout the city and along new development corridors and less reliance on new roads is required. The concept of value pricing, where the driver of a vehicle pays a fee related to the time of day or other factors, is under consideration in several jurisdictions, with the goal of encouraging off-peak travel and reducing total trips. It is probable that further travel reduction programs will be explored and launched in the next few decades, but as of this writing it is not clear how they might be instituted over whole states or regions without major changes in institutions and the attitude of the users.

Technology as part of the solution

Technology has been utilized for many decades to help manage road and street travel, often as the result of research carried out to seek solutions to specific problems. The use of technology has centered on the road-way, the vehicle and the driver, with the overall goal being to improve the interaction between these to improve the orderly and safe flow of traffic. Until about the 1980s, the technology in use was somewhat ele-mental, centered on the use of electrical equipment such as the stoplight invented by Garrett A. Morgan in the 1920s to improve traffic flow on city streets.

In recent decades, some signal systems have been networked and magnetic loop detectors have been utilized to adjust stop-and-go signals to accommodate the traffic flow. In many urban areas, radio advisory services were established to provide traffic information during rush hours. These services normally employ an aircraft and a reporter who periodically makes observations on one or more local radio or television station. While useful, the information is necessarily sketchy in response to the schedule demands of the transmitting station and the availability of sponsor revenue.

The advent of the space age in the 1960s, the development and widespread usage of the computer, the invention and increasingly widespread deployment of cellular telephone technology, the deployment of earth-circling satellite arrays that can be utilized to precisely determine the position of a vehicle or other object on the roadway, the development of microwave and fiber optic communication networks and many other technology advances have made a new array of technical possibilities available. Beginning mostly in the 1980s and especially in the 1990s, interest developed in applying these advanced technologies to solving or at least alleviating surface transportation problems, including reducing or managing congestion and improv-ing transportation safety. Some members of Congress took an interest in this area and provided funds to conduct research and undertake some deployments. The next chapter describes in detail how industry, acad-emia and the public sector came together with transportation experts to explore how advanced technology might be meaningfully used as part of the solution to meeting road and street problems being faced by the United States and other nations. The result of those efforts have made advanced technology one of the avail-able tools to address transportation needs as the world enters the 21st century.

Definition and concepts of ITS

There is no one accepted definition of ITS, or telematics, in part because the discipline is still young and evolving. The concepts included within ITS are also evolving, although there are now a number of them established that are giving definition to the discipline.

General definition

One definition of ITS was adopted in 1998 by the Intelligent Transportation Society of America for com-municating the ITS concept to the general public. It reads: "People using technology in transportation to save lives, time and money." The U.S. DOT's ITS Joint Program Office circulated a more formal definition in April 1999. It reads:

> Intelligent transportation systems collect, store, process and distribute information relating to the move-ment of people and goods. Examples include systems for traffic management, public transportation management, emergency management, traveler information, advanced vehicle control and safety, com-mercial vehicle operations, electronic payment and railroad grade crossing safety.

This U.S. DOT definition reflects the developments that have occurred in ITS up to this writing, and as further developments occur the definition will undoubtedly change. But generally, the ITS discipline is concerned with the collection, distribution and use of information to solve transportation problems.

Concepts central to ITS

There are several concepts that are central to the ITS discipline. The first concept is that there are items of information that, if gathered and distributed in a timely way, can positively affect how the transportation system functions and its safety. A second concept is that information collected and used in ITS can be of benefit to one or all of the following: the driver of a vehicle, the entity for whom a driver may work, pedestrians, transit riders, other members of the public and the public sector officials responsible for management of the transportation system.

A third concept is that ITS can only be truly effective nationally when a unified framework for integrating the many components of an ITS system, called a systems architecture, has been developed and put in place. As this is being written, much is being accomplished toward producing such a systems architecture for use by public agencies and private organizations alike.

A fourth concept is that ITS development and deployment requires expertise in a number of areas, including electronics, civil engineering, human factors, information management, satellite technology, public- and private-sector policy development and management practice and finance. It is not expected that each practitioner will have professional knowledge in all of these areas, and thus the assembly of a team is the usual approach to developing and implementing an ITS system. But it is important that those with electronic and computer skills be aware of the concerns of the civil and mechanical engineers who develop and build roads and vehicles, for example, and that all engineers be aware of and understand the human factor limitations that may be involved in use of a particular technology. There are a number of additional concepts that will be explained and developed in the following chapters.

Potential impacts of ITS

At the end of the 20th century, development and deployment of ITS technologies was only beginning. Given the many institutional and technical problems still to be solved, it is unclear now how widespread ITS will become in future decades. But given what is known from the work that has been completed and the ITS systems that are beginning to function, some measure of the potential for ITS is emerging.

In the public sector, it is understood that advanced traffic management systems are possible, and that they can work to significantly increase the throughput of vehicular traffic. A system in Sydney, Australia has been operating effectively for many years; and through signal coordination it produces near freeway capacity flows on arterial streets. Traffic engineers are now applying these concepts in some American cities. In addition to loop detectors, new equipment is used to identify traffic flow problems and to adjust the signal system to adapt to the changes, including television cameras and other sensing devices.

Japan has seen widespread use of in-vehicle equipment to help drivers navigate to a selected destination, and such equipment was tested a few years ago in the Orlando, Florida area in the United States. In-car equipment is now becoming available in the United States, based on the development of satellite global positioning system (GPS) equipment used with maps contained on CD-ROMs that are located in the vehicle. Different systems for transmitting the information to drivers have been developed, including different visual display devices or voice directions. This is an example of where human factors must be taken into account, so as not to overload the driver or make travel less safe.

In the safety arena, MAYDAY equipment is being developed and some is now in operation that can inform a central monitoring location that a vehicle has been engaged in a crash and that help is needed. The MAYDAY equipment pinpoints the location of the crash and can facilitate a rapid recovery operation. In an effort to reduce rear-end vehicle crashes or crashes of a vehicle into a tree or other immovable object, vehicle-mounted radar systems are under development that will warn the driver and brake the vehicle. Looking at the vehicle, the U.S. DOT and the American automobile industry are jointly working on what is currently termed the Intelligent Vehicle Initiative, which has as one of its goals the application of ITS technologies to improve highway safety.

One ITS technology that has been developed and deployed in several locations around the United States is automatic toll collection, whereby a vehicle carrying the proper equipment can move through a toll road or toll bridge entrance without stopping. It can be expected that wider use of this equipment lies ahead, with improvements in its operation flexibility and effectiveness.

In the private sector, ITS technologies that rely on GPS to locate motor trucks wherever they may be operating are now being considered by several and adopted by some major trucking companies in the United States. These technologies can be expected to be widely used in years to come. With this equipment, the motor carrier entity's management can increase the efficiency of its vehicle fleet and customers can receive up-to-the-minute information on where their load of freight is and when it will be delivered, a much desired goal in the JIT operational mode many manufacturers and retailers are now following.

Turning to the public transit industry, ITS technologies are now being deployed to better manage the vehicle fleet, including GPS equipment to track the movements of the vehicles, the adoption of new communication equipment to inform users of the system on the progress of their vehicle and if schedules will be met, and use of area-wide traffic information to make real-time adjustment to vehicle operations. In addition, the transit vehicle, because it is moving in the traffic flow, is used to gather information for use by a central traffic management center. New electronic fare equipment has been developed and is in operation, which simplifies and speeds fare collections. Systems are being put in place that will give a transit bus priority at stop lights, which can be operated by the bus driver or the central traffic management center. The new ITS systems are allowing transit buses across the city to operate much like the railroads, which have for years used advanced electronic systems to manage their trains.

Looking ahead, most observers believe that these ITS applications will thrive and expand—and still more can be anticipated. For example, studies are now underway on the possible use of the world's low-orbiting satellites to track all vehicles as they move on a nation's highways and roads, so that user fees might be collected based on miles driven, the roads used for travel and the time of day when travel occurs. The goal of these studies is to examine a new concept for collecting user fees and to replace motor fuel taxes and other levies. Instead of paying fuel taxes, the vehicle owner would receive an invoice periodically for use of the roads and streets, much like is done for electric, water and sewer utilities. It is also believed that because the time of day and the roads used would be a factor in charging fees, drivers might then make decisions that would result in a reduction in traffic congestion.

In the 1990s, considerable effort was expended in the United States by government and industry to determine the feasibility of what is perhaps the ultimate ITS technology—the operation of vehicles on a roadway without the intervention of a driver. In a massive experiment held in California, several different approaches to this concept were installed and tested, and the conclusion was that the concept appears feasible. But there are many hurdles to be overcome before the United States might expect to see such a system put in place.

Other nations are now conducting their own experiments in this area, and it is possible that an operational automatic highway for all vehicles or perhaps just for long-distance trucks might evolve in the first few decades of the 21st century.

All of these effects have an economic aspect. On the one hand, governments and individuals who are expected to use ITS equipment must expend funds to do so. Part of what will determine the rate of ITS deployment will be the availability of public funding—federal, state and local—for ITS projects and the willingness of the expected users to purchase the equipment. The possibility of employing private-sector funding for ITS deployment is also being examined, and new concepts of public–private partnerships are being proposed and examined. As of this writing, it is difficult to project what the deployment of ITS will be nationwide over the next ten years.

In January 1998, the FHWA published a report titled *Intelligent Transportation Systems—Real World Benefits*. The report summarized the benefits expected to occur because of ITS deployment in metropolitan areas and rural areas; because of commercial trucking and intelligent vehicle systems; and because of the positive effects of ITS, including enhanced public safety; reduced congestion; improved access to travel and transit information; cost savings to motor carriers, transit operators, toll authorities and government agencies; and reduced environmental effects. The FHWA report also discussed positive results in all of these areas. Similar studies can be expected over the coming years. In addition, studies have been carried out that demonstrate that the private-sector ITS industry can thrive over the coming decades, if current trends continue and mature.

Will ITS provide the solution to the congestion and safety problems facing the United States on the nation's streets and highways? The answer, unfortunately, is no. But there is general agreement in the public sector that ITS can help the situation by moving traffic more intelligently and helping to maximize usage of the road and street system. There is also agreement that the nation's public transportation system will operate more efficiently and with better service to the customer through the use of ITS technologies. And by increasing the use of transit and reducing traffic delays, the effect on the environment is expected to be favorable.

In summary, ITS technologies are expected to have a significant, and in some areas a major, effect on surface transportation in the United States and other nations over the next few decades. Time will determine if those expectations are met, but it is clear that they can only be met if certain issues are resolved and a strong cadre of ITS professionals is developed and employed in the public and private sectors.

Issues associated with ITS

As might be expected for any new discipline such as ITS, there are a number of associated issues that will affect the ultimate deployment of some or all ITS technologies. A partial summary is as follows, and the chapters to come will address these and other issues in depth.

Interoperability—standards and architecture

As mentioned above, one aspect of ITS is that a fully operational national system cannot be deployed in the absence of an agreed upon systems architecture. The reason is obvious. If many manufacturers produce equipment that is incompatible with the equipment of others, and if state and local governments install systems that are incompatible with other systems, then in an environment where vehicles move across regions, states and the nation, vehicles equipped in one location may find their equipment is useless in another state or metropolitan area. The U.S. DOT has thus taken the lead, with the encouragement of Congress, to develop and implement a systems architecture. To carry out this effort, an array of standards development organizations (SDOs) have come together to jointly develop a set of standard, in a host of areas.

Standards development is difficult, especially in an emerging area like ITS. The beginning point is usually to consider the equipment and practices already in use and to seek a common standard that will include as much of what exists as possible. Beyond this, in the still developing field of ITS, new concepts will be devised over time, some of which will undoubtedly be radically different from those now in use. The systems architecture must therefore be adaptable for such new equipment and concepts, or otherwise these new developments will not be employed and innovation will stop. At the same time, the standards developed must be adequate to assure interoperability.

Some have held that the federal government should simply develop and adopt standards for ITS and impose them. But history has shown that this approach has often not worked in surface transportation, for two main reasons:

- Given fifty different states having responsibility for their highway and road systems, which have taken different approaches in many instances as between states and sometimes within a state, development of a single standard by the federal government can conflict with state conditions and be unworkable.
- States and local governments commonly have much equipment in place that is useable for ITS applications, such as stoplights, controllers, sensing equipment and traffic management programs. They cannot afford to abandon this equipment, and thus any standard needs to take into account the legacy system problem if it is to succeed. Public agencies hold that the best way to develop standards, therefore, is to have the SDOs who have traditionally done this for state and local entities to lead the effort in those technical areas where they have the expertise.

The necessary standards for the United States are well along in development as the 21st century begins. But there are issues on the international scene that need resolution. There should be compatible standards worldwide, many argue, because vehicles, computers and other equipment are sold worldwide. Yet there are entities in some nations who would prefer to develop their own standards and convince other nations to use it, in an effort to monopolize a market. Resolution of these issues is being sought.

Financing and paying for ITS

The problem of how to finance installation of ITS systems will need to be addressed if full deployment is to occur and the full benefits of ITS are to be recognized. State and local transportation agencies have heavy conventional demands on their funding and ITS installations can be expensive. State governments usually have more flexibility in the source of funds than their local governments, but there are still difficulties in finding resources. Federal assistance for ITS has been and will continue to be important. In the 1990s the pattern has been for Congress to earmark federal dollars for specific ITS projects and activities. The TEA-21 legislation goes beyond this and it makes ITS activities an eligible item for use of federal highway and transit aid in almost all situations. But even with this opportunity, it may prove difficult to convince hard-pressed state and local officials to use federal funds for ITS activities, unless the merit of doing so is clearly demonstrated. It is expected that new arrangements will be developed in some areas where a blending of public- and private-sector funding will occur, in order to assure ITS deployment. Again, the TEA-21 legislation offers some opportunities for this and more concepts are under development.

Turning to the private sector, trucking companies and other ITS users are beginning to make investments in the technology. A key factor is to demonstrate that such investments will produce positive financial results, over time if not immediately. The private individual will also need to make an investment in ITS equipment for his or her vehicle and elsewhere to realize the benefits of ITS. Some equipment may become standard on all vehicles, which will probably increase their cost. Other equipment will be available separately to be installed later. Again, the benefits of ITS will need to be explained and accepted if consumers are to accept higher costs and invest in the technologies. ITS presents new marketing and business challenges that will need to be resolved before widespread usage can be expected.

Institutional changes

It has been emphasized earlier that ITS is a new discipline, which requires the collaboration of expertise from several areas to be successful. Within industry this is requiring new institutional arrangements, and the formation and staffing of new functional entities, to successfully develop and market an ITS product line. Engineering firms are finding it necessary to broaden the skills they employ so that they can comprehensively and adequately address the design and installation needs of an ITS system. In short, ITS is requiring restructuring in many private-sector entities.

The public sector also faces the need for institutional change, and often this is more difficult to achieve here than in the private sector. A typical U.S. urban pattern is a central city surrounded by many smaller incorporated areas, all of which have their own charters and elected governments. In addition, in most states there are county governments, which can and often do overlap the cities. In some of these urban area there exists strong feelings against cooperation among the governments. Yet if an area-wide ITS is to be deployed, cooperation across the region is necessary for success. The MPO planning process put in place by ISTEA and TEA-21 can help resolve these institutional problems, and in some instances the state government can help. The ITS practitioner should have an understanding of these governmental issues and the possible ways to resolve them.

Among other institutional issues there are legal questions that need to be resolved in many areas, from deciding who will be responsible for tort damages if incidents occur because of ITS installations, to developing new procurement regulations that make possible cooperative acquisitions of equipment and services in a competitive environment where many systems are proprietary. Because many ITS applications must involve a number of different governments to succeed, the institutional issues are important and exceed those found on most projects in the past.

Education and training

The ITS discipline is new and it is still developing. The public and private sectors both have a need for trained professionals and ways must be found to meet those needs. This has led to the development of education and training activities, which have been a major focus of the U.S. DOT and the academic community. A number of training courses have been devised and implemented and more will be needed. It is expected that long-distance learning by the Internet will become an important means for increasing levels of expertise.

The problem is especially acute in state and local transportation agencies, where recently there have been efforts to significantly reduce the size of the workforce. The typical highway agency employs mostly civil engineers, who usually have little or no expertise in the electronic and communication skills that are key to ITS installations. Many agencies are turning to consultants to meet their needs, at least until they can hire or develop the expertise they need. As ITS deployments occur, the need for education and training will expand. And more materials like this textbook will need to be developed.

Other issues

There are of course other issues beyond those discussed that will need to be addressed as ITS deployments move ahead. And new issues will arise. The ITS discipline is exciting and many issues lie ahead that cannot now be anticipated. What this means is that those who practice the ITS discipline will need to be resourceful and willing to move into and become expert in new areas as the need arises. The following chapters will make clear many of the current and possible issues that will be faced, but more will come.

BY Lyle Saxton • Retired • Federal Highway Administration

HISTORY OF ITS IN HIGHWAY OPERATIONS[1]

Precedents to intelligent transportation systems

Early traffic control

The origins of traffic control predate even the automobile and can be traced back to the 1860s in London where a semaphore-type signal was installed to protect the members of the Parliament when crossing a busy intersection near the House of Parliament. In the United States, some of the earliest forms of traffic control were various semaphore-type signals installed in several cities in the 1910s. The first three-color traffic signal head of the general form of today is acknowledged to have been installed in Detroit, Michigan, in 1920 (Mueller 1970).

From these simple beginnings, traffic control systems have evolved to include a range of active traffic control devices including intersection signal control, ramp metering for freeway access ramps, and variable message signs. The control of signalized networks has progressed from very simple fixed-pattern control strategies to those based on time of day and, currently, to more sophisticated traffic-adaptive control techniques. During this evolution, traffic signal systems in the 1960s had started to apply the newly evolving digital computer to the central control of area signal control systems. For example, by 1970 five locations in the United States (i.e., Wichita Falls, Texas; San Jose, California; Austin, Texas; Baltimore County, Maryland; and New York, New York) had systems designed around the IBM 1800 (Bermant 1970).

These various applications were intelligent traffic control systems for their day because they sought more systematized and advanced ways of controlling traffic. This history in the traffic profession of seeking new and innovative better ways of smoothing the flow of traffic, increasing the safety of the system user, and obtaining the most performance from the existing infrastructure was part of the stimulus for early highway traffic research.

The roots of intelligent transportation systems

The intelligent transportation system (ITS) program, which has become very visible in the 1990s, has specific roots that are directly traceable to research and development activities started in the early 1960s by the federal government, industry, and universities. Probably the most visible and robust of these early activities was that of the Bureau of Public Roads (BPR) of the Department of Commerce, the predecessor to the current Federal Highway Administration (FHWA). In this time period, BPR's Office of Research undertook a major new research and development initiative to improve the safety and efficiency of highway-based travel. The program was a dramatic change from past research activities sponsored by this organization in size, vision, and content. At the core of the this new effort was the premise that existing and evolving modern electronic communications and control systems could be applied to vehicle–highway operations in ways that would substantially benefit the nation and the user.

This major new initiative into advanced electronics and systems technology was part of the larger growing enthusiasm of the world and the United States in particular, with new electronics and system technology. Modern society was in the space age. For example, television audiences were seeing weather pictures from space since the launch of the first weather satellite in 1962. Similarly the United States had committed to put a man on the moon by the end of the 1960s, and this once science fiction fantasy now seemed attainable through our nation's engineering expertise.

And the world now had the transistor and modern semiconductors as a basic enabling technology. The transistor, with its fundamentally different characteristics and in contrast to the vacuum tube, had the small size and low power that made many new system concepts feasible. And its availability and performance was now growing at a dizzying pace. Large and powerful (for their time) transistor-based mainframe digital computers were available and the software sciences were evolving. The consumer had color television, microwave ovens (although expensive) and transistorized portable radios. Given this technology context, it seemed obvious that the nation should gear up a major program to realize projected benefits in highway transportation that would derive from the application of this same basic technology.

At the leadership focal point of this major new federal research program were a few key people. Robert Baker was the Director of Research for BPR and a prime mover in this initiative. Baker was a relatively recent employee of BPR, having come from Ohio State University in the early 1960s. Dr. William Wolman was another newcomer to the highway business who played a significant role in this advanced systems program in the late 1960s and 1970s. A mathematician recruited from the National Aeronautics and Space Administration (NASA), he was the Chief of the Traffic Systems Division, which was the organizational focal point of this program in BPR.

Probably the best known system to be remembered from this program is the electronic route guidance system (ERGS) (Rosen, Mammano, and Favout 1970). It projected a major leap forward in highway operational performance and driver assistance. It envisioned providing the individual driver with routing guidance that not only was based on the best physical route, but was also based on real-time traffic conditions (i.e., dynamic route guidance). Selected intersections, strategically located throughout the street network, would be instrumented with roadside hardware that included communications with vehicles when traveling over inductive loops, communications with a central computer via hard wire, and a limited buffer storage and processing capability. Vehicles would have on-board displays, possibly even a heads up display, an inductive loop-based two-way communication capability, and an encoder for inputting the driver's destination. Thus the 1960s ERGS was functionally designed to have essentially the same basic functional performance as the more recent TravTek operational test performed in Orlando, Florida, in the early 1990s. (It is interesting to note that a major participant in both the ERGS and TravTek projects was the General Motors Corporation [GM].) ERGS was expected to be initially tested as a static route guidance system in the Washington, D.C. area starting around 1970. It was to include approximately 100 roadside units and 50 vehicles.

But ERGS was only one of many visionary new systems. Another major activity included the urban traffic control system (UTCS), which would revolutionize network traffic signal control by interconnecting individual signalized intersections to a central control center. A mainframe digital computer would control the entire network by selecting the most appropriate timing pattern from a family of pre-computed timing plans that had been optimized for different sets of traffic conditions. Current traffic conditions would be determined by a surveillance system consisting primarily of a network of inductive loop traffic detectors. The detectors would be polled on a regular basis and the surveillance information transmitted back to the central computer over leased telephone lines. UTCS was thus the forerunner of modern, present day urban traffic signal control systems.

The passing aid system (PAS) was an additional project intended to bring a new level of safety and driver convenience to rural two-lane driving. It would provide a signal to the driver as to whether or not there was oncoming traffic and, thus, if it were safe to pull out of your lane and pass another vehicle in a two-lane road driving situation. PAS was tested at the engineering prototype level in a special rural laboratory located on approximately 15 miles of rural two-lane road in the state of Maine.

Other significant projects included a system of moving lights on freeway entrance ramps that the motorist would pace with to assist in freeway merging situations; FLASH, a system for motorists to signal when they observed a disabled motorist by flashing their bright lights three times when passing designated locations; a roadside radio motorist information system using low-power transmitters in the AM broadcast band; a major activity to model the overall processes and functions of highway travel; and a project to develop a fully automated highway system. An excellent summary of many of these technologies exists in a special issue published in 1970 by the Institute of Electrical and Electronics Engineers (IEEE 1970). The IEEE continued to support this area of advanced highway electronics with additional special issues on these topics in 1980 and 1991 (IEEE 1980 and 1991).

Substantial programs were mounted and resources applied to research, develop, and field test these various new systems. While the 100 intersection ERGS test was never performed due to lack of funding support from Congress, actual field testing was performed on prototypes at two Washington, D.C. area intersections. UTCS was more fortunate than ERGS as its operational test phase was funded and approximately 130 intersections in Washington, D.C., were brought under control in the early 1970s. The PAS experimentation was performed in cooperation with the state of Maine; the FLASH motorist aid system was evaluated along 50 miles of Interstate in central Florida; and the freeway merging aid system was tested in Tampa, Florida. During the 1970s, automated highway system experiments were performed on test tracks and unopened Interstate lanes as part of the program contracted to the Ohio State University.

It is also worthwhile to note that these programs in the late 1960s and 1970s brought in the systems and aerospace firms that had never before been active in highway transportation research. A sampling of these firms include Raytheon, Sperry, General Electric, Honeywell, TRW, and Booz-Allen. Industry and university, too, were involved in selected research aimed at using advanced electronics technology to enhance highway and motorist performance. GM, most notably, sponsored early research with the Radio Corporation of America on automated highways dating back to the 1950s. GM also was an early pioneer in in-vehicular motorist information and assistance systems. Robert Cosgriff, then with Ohio State University, was active in similar projects.

An example of a broad transportation program that would use ITS type systems was also considered by the newly established U.S. Department of Transportation (U.S. DOT) during this period. It focused on the needs of the Northeast Corridor and resulted in a plan published in May 1971 (U.S. DOT 1971). The proposed action program included development and implementation of a real-time highway information system to assist intercity drivers in making route choice decisions. The longer-term program was focused on automated highways and included two recommendations to provide alternatives to continued proliferation of conventional highways. The recommendations were:

1. Expansion of the automated highway research and development program to define and evaluate possible concepts
2. Preparation of proposed legislation for the Post Interstate Highway Program, which will permit highways to be planned and built in such a way that accommodation of automated capability will be possible

The intervening years

But necessary major policy and funding support for a full-blown national program did not develop. Many of these systems were seen as too advanced and unproven. Similarly, the gasoline shortage, appearing in the early 1970s, affected travel and helped create an environment that did not support the research and deployment of these advanced transportation systems.

During the remaining 1970s the FHWA's Traffic Systems Division continued a modest level of research in basic areas such as traffic operations, motorist information and communications, and automated highway systems. Some specific examples included preliminary work on in-vehicle safety hazard warning systems, initial development of a family of traffic simulation models, continued research in specific control systems for automated highways, a television-based wide area detection system, and advanced highway advisory radio. The FHWA research program also was instrumental in working with the Department of Interior and the Federal Communications Commission to establish the Traveler's Information Service, which provided for the operation of highway advisory radio stations on 530 and 1610 kHz. During these years, the U.S. DOT's Urban Mass Transportation Administration also supported development of advanced technology focusing on urban applications. Two important efforts directly related to ITS included a dual mode program (automated control of buses) and automated vehicle control.

The 1970s also saw growing international interest in ITS type systems. For example, around 1972 FHWA's research offices hosted a major delegation from Japan and discussed its research efforts with special emphasis on the ERGS program. These discussions contributed to Japan's important efforts from 1973 to 1978 to develop and evaluate their comprehensive automobile communication system (CACS), which had striking similarities to the ERGS. CACS was in turn the precursor of Japan's road/automobile communication system (Takada et al. 1989) and advanced mobile traffic information and communication system (Tsuzawa and Okamoto 1989) efforts. Similar activities were undertaken in Europe during the 1970s, especially in the United Kingdom and West Germany. For example, the Federal Republic of Germany developed and field evaluated a route guidance system known as ALI that was functionally very similar to ERGS and CACS.

Changing times and growing support

Starting in 1981, however, there was yet another downswing at the federal level in support for ITS type research. Ronald Reagan was elected president and with his administration came new policies and political appointees generally opposed to advanced research activities. Thus, the early 1980s became a low point in staff morale and agency productivity towards the development of more advanced motorist information systems and vehicle control technologies. This lack of advanced research program support on the part of this new administration also translated into minimal support for underlying research in supporting areas such as human factors and computer modeling.

But broader national and international events were occurring that would result in a resurgence of activity. ITS type research and development (R&D) projects were continuing in Europe and Japan. Rapid technological advances were also continuing in semiconductors, electronics, and computers. The-state-of-the-art had reached the stage where powerful and sophisticated devices were available for computer processing, storage, and display functions. Further, these devices provided for small packaging and affordable cost, which are essential market requirements. By contrast, the earlier 1960s' technology did not include microprocessors, integrated circuits (especially the very large-scale integration of today), CD-ROM storage, flat-screen displays, and so forth. Thus the resulting 1960s' systems were much, much less powerful (i.e., intelligent), packaging was much more bulky, and the system architecture favored centralized systems over distributed (e.g., to use large mainframe computers). On-board vehicle systems were much less robust in the services and features provided to the motorist. By the mid-1980s, however, highly sophisticated but relatively affordable consumer technologies were becoming commonplace, such as cellular telephone systems. The age of the personal computer and networking was emerging, and there was a growing realization by society that these advanced systems were, in fact, much more near-term than had been previously thought.

Congestion was also becoming a much more serious national concern. The Interstate Highway construction program was nearly complete and no major new construction was anticipated. The general transportation mindset and highway program philosophy was slowly shifting from that dominated by adding new capacity through new construction to that of achieving more efficient operation of the existing physical plant. This emphasis on operation raised to a much higher priority those technologies and systems such as ITS that held promise for benefits in efficiency and safety. By contrast in the 1960s, while good operations was an acknowledged desirable feature, it was generally not seen as a particularly important program priority.

The dominant national problem, which provided the interest in the FHWA in ITS-type systems, was congestion. While ITS forerunner systems had major safety emphasis, the mid-80s' resurgence of interest initially focused on congestion. Annual vehicle miles traveled in the United States had doubled since the late 1960s without similar increases in urban arterial and freeway capacity. Urban congestion was now quite serious and the percent of peak-hour traffic on urban Interstates, which was congested, had now exceeded fifty percent. FHWA's Traffic System Division had performed a staff research study published in 1986 that identified the top U.S. cities with the greatest congestion and also made estimates on total urban freeway delay for that year, as well as predictions for 2005 (Lindley 1986). The results were picked up by the national press and received wide publicity. Even major national weekly news magazines, such as Time Magazine, featured the growing public concern with traffic congestion.

The earlier BPR program had stimulated interest in the highway community for the potential benefits that advanced technologies and systems might bring to future traffic operations. Embedded in the program results was the recognition that modern electronic communication and control systems held tremendous promise for future highway operations and would someday achieve this potential. In this respect, the earlier program provided a level of expectation and opportunity waiting in the wings for the national need. This awareness became especially important in discussions associated with "beyond the Interstate construction era" and "how to deal with growing urban congestion."

Efforts had also been continuing to develop a much more aggressive traffic operations national research program. The FHWA's Traffic Systems Division had formulated a proposal for a major "R&D Program in Traffic Operations to Combat Urban Traffic Congestion," which emphasized seven major initiatives including navigation and vehicle control. This program was formally submitted to ten state DOTs for their comment. Also, in March 1986 the Transportation Research Board (TRB) hosted a workshop in Baltimore, Maryland, which would lead to a broad, multiyear traffic research effort conducted by the TRB as part of their National Cooperative Highway Research Program. Many of the subsequent leaders in Mobility 2000 and now ITS were participants in those deliberations.

How ITS started

National need and interest

The event that is broadly accepted as the pivotal meeting in triggering a resurgence of national interest and support for what has become ITS occurred in October 1986. The California DOT (CALTRANS) had been conducting a two-year planning study examining its needs for future capacity to deal with growing traffic congestion. Their studies had resulted in some very unnerving projections that no realistic and affordable construction program could maintain traffic flow at even the present levels of congestion. Further, state gasoline tax increases to support such efforts would be unacceptable; and environmental concerns and difficulties in acquiring new right-of-way were further major deterrents to a major construction program. Given this reality, CALTRANS was developing a substantial interest in new transportation technology as a major piece of a long-term department strategy and in 1986 established an Office of New Technology (Shladover, Bushey, and Parsons 1993).

As part of its commitment to this new initiative, CALTRANS sponsored a three-day conference for its mid- and senior-level managers entitled "Technology Options for Highway Transportation Operations" in Sacramento, California, on October 28–30, 1986 (Shladover, Bushey, and Parsons 1993). Over 100 attendees met to consider the role of advanced vehicle–highway technologies in meeting growing congestion including several outside experts who were invited as speakers and participants. John Vostrez of CALTRANS and William Garrison of the University of California at Berkeley were two of the principals in organizing this crucial event. The conference became a watershed for ITS as it established a new level of national credibility and interest in these systems. For example, Richard Morgan, then FHWA's executive director, was a participant and subsequently took various national and internal FHWA actions that were instrumental in this national reawakening of support for advanced transportation systems.

Following closely on the conference, ad hoc national efforts were initiated to follow up on this rekindled interest. For example, FHWA research hosted a small group in December 1986 that laid the foundation for the Pathfinder project as a joint cooperative undertaking between CALTRANS, GM, and the FHWA. William Spreitzer of GM, who had also been at the CALTRANS Conference, and Frank Mammano, an FHWA researcher, were principal leaders in this early effort to evaluate a motorist navigation system in the Los Angeles, California area. California also continued its national leadership efforts and followed up the conference with additional outreach efforts to find other states and universities that might partner with them in a broader-based national program to apply advanced technology to deal with congestion and safety needs.

On a broader front, there were beginning efforts to develop a national consensus group to set goals, scope, and a vision for this reemerging national interest. This activity quickly attracted a core group of 20 to 25 individuals from government, university, and industry. Their common denominator was a current involvement in highway transportation and a sense that a major national window of opportunity was now opening for what was to become known initially as the intelligent vehicle highway system (IVHS). Their mutual agenda recognized a need to articulate the national highway transportation needs that would benefit from this program, define broad program activities that should be undertaken and, most importantly, establish some form of permanent national program coordination.

These activities were occurring in a national environment that was becoming increasingly supportive for a new program. Considerable national effort was being focused on thinking and planning for an anticipated major change in the nation's highway program that would be occasioned by the next highway authorization legislation. This impending legislation was to define the post Interstate highway era, and there was almost universal support for programs with "vision" that would extend the efficiency and effectiveness of the existing physical highway system. FHWA was internally devoting considerable resources to a loosely structured process to develop position papers on an assortment of "futures" topics that would help describe the setting and needs for the future highway program. Several of the topics dealt directly with ITS areas.

In parallel, a national group known as Project 2020 was also engaged in broadly similar activities. Composed of key highway transportation organizations such as the American Association of State Highway and Transportation Officials (AASHTO) and the Highway Users Federation for Safety and Mobility (HUF-SAM), it would sponsor many activities. One would lead to a June 1988 conference organized under their sponsorship by the TRB. The conference topic would broadly discuss the opportunities presented by advanced electronics highway technology and systems.

In March 1988 thirty-nine participants, including most of those now pushing for a national program in ITS, met in a meeting at the University of California at Berkeley to further develop a national agenda and also search for a consensus on how to establish a permanent organizational structure. While the meeting did not achieve the latter objective, it did serve to further consolidate the sense of national need and commitment to further develop this advanced technology program.

Mobility 2000

Following the Berkeley meeting, a participant, Lyle Saxton, chief of FHWA's Traffic System Division in the Office of Research and Development, wrote a letter to the principals of this core group suggesting an interim ad hoc organization and offering to assist in staffing this activity until a more permanent organization was established. This offer was positively received and a meeting was scheduled for June 21, 1988 at the National Academy of Sciences in Washington, D.C. Nineteen individuals from government, industry, and university attended in what became a major step in the evolving ITS program. By consensus, it was decided to move forward with national planning, using this ad hoc management and coordination structure, and to name it Mobility 2000.

The following two days a TRB conference was held, sponsored by the Transportation Alliance Group and others who brought approximately 250 invited participants together to "Look Ahead to 2020" (TRB, NRC 1988). The previous decisions of the Mobility 2000 group were informally presented and discussed during the conference, which further served to give impetus and focus to those with this national interest.

With its national emergence, Mobility 2000 immediately started planning for a national workshop. Several of the core members volunteered their services, and plans were laid for a three-day meeting in San Antonio, Texas, in February 1989. At this time, two individuals stepped forward and took on the heavy burden of actually finding a location and providing all the mailing, registration, program, and logistical support that is essential for a successful national meeting. Dr. William Harris and Sadler Bridges of the Texas Transportation Institute (TTI) volunteered both themselves and TTI to this purpose. Their combined support leading to and during the workshop were invaluable. But perhaps even more important was their preparation of a subsequent workshop record that received broad national distribution and attention.

But again, several national supporting events were occurring. During the fall of 1988, two smaller two-day meetings of invited participants met to consider one of the dominant areas of interest—that of advanced driver information systems. Substantial national publicity for IVHS also resulted from a press event in held in Ann Arbor, Michigan, and organized by the University of Michigan Transportation Research Institute. Through the efforts of two early leaders, Dr. Kan Chen and Robert Ervin, several ITS type systems were displayed and demonstrated giving credence to the substance of this new program. It is also noteworthy that the original name IVHS was first used by Ervin and Chen.

The first Mobility 2000 National Workshop was attended by 57 invitees. Held in San Antonio, Texas, on February 15–17, 1989, it became the first major national event to bring together key decision-makers and the core group of those planning an ITS program. The workshop was cast around five breakout groups: advanced traffic management systems (ATMS), advanced driver information systems (ADIS), advanced vehicle control (AVC), commercial vehicle, and national organization and program issues (Texas A&M University 1989). In setting the objectives of the workshop, the moderator, Lyle Saxton, summarized the goal as getting down to specifics, including:

- Describing a vision of what the system (ITS) will look like and what it will do for the nation
- Describing the most promising plan of evolutionary stages that should be used to get there
- Putting special emphasis on identifying specifics of the program for the next five years

By the time of this workshop, the name IVHS had been embraced by this group and its content had been grouped into the four broad areas of ATMS, ADIS, heavy truck/commercial, and AVC. This program grouping had taken form in planning for the workshop during the fall of 1988 and was used as the basis for breakout groups during the workshop. Later, the titles would change slightly and ADIS would be broadened to advanced traveler information systems (ATIS); heavy truck/commercial would soon become commercial vehicle operations; and a fifth grouping for advanced public transportation systems (APTS) would be added, recognizing the inclusion of this important area.

A highlight of the first workshop was the attendance of James Pitz, then the director of the Michigan DOT and also that year's president of AASHTO. Pitz had become a strong champion of the program both in his state and nationally through his presidency of AASHTO. The workshop had been structured to provide for three speakers to give their "Evaluation of the Workshop" at the final session. Pitz was the lead-off speaker and strongly supported the IVHS program and encouraged Mobility 2000's continued national efforts to establish a firmer understanding of the program.

With the first workshop a national success, the leaders of Mobility 2000 scheduled a meeting in late March 1989 in Cambridge, Massachusetts, to be hosted by Professor Joseph Sussman of the Massachusetts Institute of Technology, who was also one of the early activists in Mobility 2000. The purpose of the meeting was to review the results and consider the next steps for further developing support for a national program. It was soon agreed that a second national workshop should be organized to further develop the program's scope, goals, and benefits. Also, each major meeting was proving very effective in bringing in new national participants and expanding the base of support. Planning and supporting activities for this next meeting was begun in earnest in late summer.

A cornerstone of this national workshop planning effort was to establish five committees that would work through the fall and early winter to each develop a working paper with substantive program content prior to the workshop. The committees were the now classical four system areas plus a new one on operational benefits. Already a firm philosophy of IVHS as a national partnership had been established and co-chairs were selected for each committee with one from the federal government and the other from a nonfederal organization. The chairs of these committees and their members met many times, and a more detailed consensus of the IVHS program rapidly emerged as they focused on their individual working papers.

In retrospect, one of the major legacies of Mobility 2000 is this foundation of consensus vision that has lead ITS program development for the intervening years up to the present. Indeed, even the ITS America Strategic Plan, developed later in 1991, reflects the definitions, scope, and milestones developed in these meetings during 1989.

While these workshop planning activities were underway, other noteworthy events were also focusing positive attention on IVHS. On June 7, the House Subcommittee on Transportation, Aviation, and Materials of the Committee on Science, Space, and Technology held a one-day hearing on Advanced Vehicle–Highway Technology and Human Factors Research. This was the first Congressional hearing on IVHS and served to further establish national program credibility; and, in this case, it nourished a developing congressional interest in the program.

Lyle Saxton, in his position as assistant for Advanced Technology Systems to then FHWA Executive Director Richard Morgan, testified on his behalf. Using slides and prepared testimony, he provided an overall summary and rationale of the evolving role of advanced technology in improving highway operations. In addition to describing the then four major IVHS user areas, he noted three fundamental development issues that would shape the ITS program throughout the 1990s as follows:

> Let me cite three examples of system design issues: (1) what is the overall system architecture that integrates the vehicle and highway elements of IVHS into the most cost-effective system; (2) what is the recommended communication link between the vehicle and highway consistent with the enormous numbers of vehicles, present radio frequency demands, and the state-of-the-art of technology; and (3) what are the necessary standards and specifications that will assure standard interfaces and commercial interchangeability while not limiting innovation or commercial opportunity (Saxton 1989).

The U.S. Congress continued its growing interest in IVHS and in its Conference Report on the DOT and Related Agencies Appropriations Act of 1989 directed the secretary to report to the Congress on IVHS. The report was to:

- Assess ongoing European, Japanese, and U.S. IVHS research initiatives
- Analyze the potential effects of foreign IVHS programs on the introduction of advanced technology for the benefit of U.S. highway users and on U.S. vehicle manufacturers and related industries
- Make appropriate legislative and programmatic recommendations

The U.S. DOT in its response issued a discussion paper in the Federal Register and solicited public comments. On March 14, 1990, the 63-page report was transmitted to the Honorable Robert C. Byrd, then Chairman of the House Committee on Appropriations (U.S. DOT 1990).

Another major event occurred at the HUFSAM annual meeting in Washington, D.C., in November 1989. At this meeting HUFSAM proposed that they and the U.S. DOT join as partners in sponsoring a National Leadership Conference on IVHS. The objective was to pull together 100 of the top leaders in industry and government to discuss the potential of IVHS. GM had been instrumental in making this proposal through HUFSAM and later assisted in the financing of the conference. Lester P. Lamm, then executive director of HUFSAM, had also become a very visible advocate of a national IVHS program and put his considerable contacts and personal commitment behind this proposal. In a subsequent informal, executive-level planning meeting between HUFSAM and the DOT, it was proposed that the primary focus of the conference should be the establishment of a permanent national IVHS organization to follow on the successful path charted by the ad hoc Mobility 2000. Further, that the major features of this proposed national organization should be prepared before the conference so it could be presented to the attendees of the planned Leadership Conference and be the primary focus of their discussions.

An important meeting with international implications also took place during this period. Hans Peter Glathe of the European Prometheus project visited the United States and met with key U.S. representatives and supporters of the IVHS program to share views on the status of the respective programs and to discuss opportunities for cooperation. Perhaps the most important byproduct was feeling out the mutual credibility and direction of the programs. To the U.S. representatives, it further confirmed the international commitment to ITS activities and the importance for a strong U.S. program.

Meanwhile, planning and supporting committee work for the second National Mobility 2000 workshop was very active. Bill Harris and Sadler Bridges of TTI had once again volunteered to organize the workshop; and Dallas, Texas, was selected as the site. The workshop was held on March 19–21, 1990 and was attended by over 200 listed participants. The working groups had each successfully prepared a detailed working paper that included sections on vision, objectives, milestones, and benefits (Texas A&M University 1990). The workshop was then organized around the five crosscutting groups:

- Program milestones
- Research and development needs
- Operational tests
- Program investment requirements
- Organizing for IVHS

The Dallas workshop served to cement the vision and major program features that had been evolving through the many prior meetings and national activities. Thus, there was a strong consensus that Mobility 2000 had established a sound basis justifying the undertaking of a major national IVHS effort. It's an interesting aside that much discussion and emotional energy was devoted during the workshop to developing an estimate of program cost—especially deployment costs. Richard Braun, a former commissioner of the Minnesota DOT had been assigned to chair this working group and labored late with his group to develop meaningful estimates. The debate centered on whether or not to publish the estimates or if they might seem so high that they scared off support for the program. In the end, the majority view was to openly display the estimates as it was strongly felt that the cost-benefits were substantial and certainly supported the estimated investment. These estimates projected that a $35 billion investment in IVHS R&D, field testing, engineering, and deployment over the next twenty years would achieve a substantial deployment of systems, which would have major operational benefits to the United States (TTI 1990).

Following this second Mobility 2000 national workshop, a flurry of activity occurred to produce a written record of the results and recommendations in time for the May National Leadership Conference. With considerable hard work from the principals involved in the workshop, and especially TTI, an excellent executive summary was prepared by late April (Texas A&M University 1990). This summary was updated and printed as a glossy twenty-page document entitled Mobility 2000 Presents Intelligent Vehicle Highway Systems. This document was widely distributed and was one of the most effective, succinct descriptions of IVHS that has been prepared. Its page on "Action Items" described eleven items that have become the main elements of the national program. Excerpts include: establish a strategic plan, determine appropriate architectures, create a national organizational structure, provide mechanisms for international cooperation, promote technical standards, and more.

Formation of a national ITS organization

On May 3–5, 1990, the National Leadership Conference was held in Orlando, Florida, with then U.S. DOT Secretary Samuel Skinner and Alan Smith, executive vice president of GM, as the co-chairmen.

Through the personal efforts of individuals such as Lester Lamm, executive director of the HUFSAM, and other key highway community leaders, the meeting was successful in attracting senior-level executives and international participation; and it set the stage for actually establishing a formal national organization to work in partnership with the U.S. government to plan and carry out an IVHS program. Towards that objective, Lamm in the closing session on May 5, presented *An Action Plan for Implementing IVHS,* which described a concept for an organization to be named Electronic Highway Transportation Association of America.

The meeting was quickly followed that summer by meetings hosted by HUFSAM to plan for the formal organization. Later that year IVHS America would be formally established with Lester Lamm, of HUFSAM, and Frank Francois, executive director of AASHTO, as the two principals.

Federal ITS legislation

No program can be successful without an adequate resource base and a level of national legitimacy. Continuing the rapid pace to establish a national ITS program, Congress in 1991 passed the Intermodal Surface Transportation Efficiency Act (ISTEA), which detailed a program in ITS. It stated "the Secretary shall conduct a program to research, develop, and operationally test intelligent vehicle–highway systems and promote implementation of such systems as a component of the nation's surface transportation systems." It contained specific objectives, requirements, and substantially increased funding for federal IVHS programs starting in the fiscal year 1992. Some of the major elements included a national clearing house, a strategic plan, reports to Congress, a national Corridors Program, a call for standards development, and the demonstration of an automated highway system. This landmark legislation clearly moved the ITS program onto the national stage and dominated the program's course over the next six years (Congress 1991). As part of the program's implementation and stewardship, the U.S. DOT would establish a formal IVHS program office and recognize IVHS America as a utilized federal advisory committee.

Federal support of the ITS program continued, and in 1998 the Congress passed its next major transportation authorization titled Transportation Equity Act for the 21st Century (TEA-21). ITS is distributed throughout many specific elements of the bill and a general characterization is that TEA-21 mainstreams ITS, removing it from the sense of a separate or isolated program. TEA-21 continues the funding support of ITS with approximately $1.3 billion projected over the six-year life of the authorization. However, the funding elements are changed over the previous ISTEA and are now roughly divided between research and deployment incentives. One stipulation of TEA-21 was to require the federal designation of critical ITS standards as well as the conformance of federally funded sites to the national ITS architecture and standards. Following in succession to the ISTEA of 1991, TEA-21 continues the federal support and momentum for ITS.

Lessons learned—comparison with earlier efforts

In conclusion to this look at the emergence and development of the IVHS and subsequent renamed ITS program, it is useful to compare it to the earlier efforts in the 1960s and early 1970s. While these earlier research and demonstration programs of the 1960s contributed to the establishment of ITS, except for computer traffic signal control, these early systems never made it beyond the prototype stage. Given the substantive program in the 1960s, what happened and why were they not further developed and deployed?

Briefly, there are at least six principal reasons supporting today's strong ITS program that did not exist earlier. First, there is a very serious congestion problem today that is recognized as affecting mobility, commerce, trip quality, and even our international competitiveness. Further, this problem is not stabilized but is continuing to grow in severity with no adequate traditional solutions available. In the 1960s the beginnings of this problem were recognized, but the problem was not particularly serious. Also, there were major highway construction programs underway, including the Interstate system, which were expected to forestall any significant urban traffic congestion well into the 21st century. Thus, the last fifteen years has seen a much more serious interest in advanced technology as a means of reducing growing traffic congestion and its negative societal effects.

Second, our society has become technologically sophisticated. Information, communications, and computer technology now pervade our business and personal lives. We accept and even demand technology such as cellular phones, cordless phones, personal computers, portable mini televisions, and so on, which have conditioned us to the capability and utility of state-of-the-art electronics-based technology. In the 1960s these types of personal and business devices did not exist and much of the technology envisioned for highway implementation was looked at by budget and program decision-makers as "Buck Rogers" and unrealistic.

Third, today's enabling technology is much more advanced compared to the early 1970s. The state-of-the-art had reached the stage where powerful and sophisticated devices were available for computer processing, storage, and display functions. Further, these devices provided for small packaging and affordable cost, which are essential market requirements. By contrast, the earlier 1960s' technology did not include microprocessors, integrated circuits (especially the very large-scale integration of today), CD-ROM storage, flat-screen displays, and so forth. Thus the resulting 1960s' systems were much, much less powerful (i.e., intelligent), packaging was much more bulky, and the system architecture favored centralized systems over distributed (e.g., to use large mainframe computers).

Fourth, today's program evolved from a newly found partnership between industry, university and state, local and federal government. This partnership recognized the different roles and objectives of each, but in doing so it built in the necessary features that have cemented this strong partnership foundation. Out of this partnership, key national figures have become program champions. In contrast, the earlier program in BPR was a standard federally run research program. The government was both setting design goals and developing prototype designs. A lack of true partnership with industry and other government almost guaranteed no buy-in or commitment to take these systems to production and operation.

Fifth, the present ITS program, while having a major research element, has deliberately and wisely focused on a balanced program that emphasizes operational testing and deployment of results. The federal, state, and local agencies have stepped forward with a strong commitment to the deployment of state-of-the-art systems with demonstrated operational benefits. While the earlier programs certainly intended eventual implementation, they were research activities that did not provide a sense of operational application in the near future.

And sixth, although not occurring until around 1991, the ITS program transitioned into a major national activity due to congressional support and funding provided by the ISTEA of 1991. This support was primarily the result of Senator Lautenberg of New Jersey, then chairman of the Transportation Subcommittee of the Senate's Appropriations Committee. Senator Lautenberg's championing of the ITS program was a critical factor that never occurred in earlier efforts in the 1960s and 1970s. However, the national visibility that developed in the late 1980s for the ITS program was clearly the springboard that brought the program to the senator's personal attention and led to his support.

These six primary characteristics of the mid- and late 1980s provided an environment very supportive of the research and application of advanced electronic highway systems and what has become the ITS program. But perhaps most of all, in the mid-1980s a core group of individuals from the public, private, and academic sectors bought into the national need and value of IVHS. Coming from divergent interests and backgrounds, they banded together and shaped a common vision and consensus that is now embodied in the present ITS program.

References

Bermant, O. I. 1970. "The Application of a Digital Computer for Traffic Control." *IEEE Transactions on Vehicular Technology* VT-19, no. 1 (February). New York, NY: Institute of Electrical and Electronic Engineers, 98–106.

Congress. 1991. Intermodal Surface Transportation Efficiency Act Of 1991 (December 18). Title VI-Research, Part B-Intelligent Vehicle-Highway Systems Act, Public Law 102–240.

Institute of Electrical and Electronic Engineers. 1970. *IEEE Transactions on Vehicular Technology, Special Issue on Highway Electronic Systems* VT-19, no. 1 (February). New York, NY: IEEE.

Institute of Electrical and Electronic Engineers. 1980. *IEEE Transactions on Vehicular Technology, Special Issue on Highway Electronic Systems* VT-29, no. 2 (May). New York, NY: IEEE.

Institute of Electrical and Electronic Engineers. 1991. *IEEE Transactions on Vehicular Technology, Special Issue on Intelligent Vehicle Highway Systems* 40, no. 1 (February). New York, NY: IEEE.

Lindley. 1986. *Quantification of Urban Freeway Congestion and Analysis of Remedial Measures* (October). Washington, D.C.: Federal Highway Administration.

Mueller, E. A. 1970. "Aspects of the History of Traffic Signals." *IEEE Transactions on Vehicular Technology* VT-19, no. 1 (February). New York, NY: Institute of Electrical and Electronic Engineers, 6–17.

Rosen, Mammano, and Favout. 1970. "An Electronic Route-Guidance System for Highway Vehicles." *IEEE Transactions on Vehicular Technology, Special Issue on Highway Electronics Systems* VT-19, no. 1 (February). New York, NY: Institute of Electrical and Electronic Engineers, 143–152.

Saxton, L. 1989. Statement by L. Saxton, Federal Highway Administration, before the Subcommittee on Transportation, Aviation, Materials; House Committee on Science, Space and Technology; on Advanced Vehicle-Highway Technology and Human Factors Research (June 7).

Shladover, Bushey, and Parsons. 1993. "California and the Roots of IVHS" (Spring). *IVHS Review.* Washington, D.C.: IVHS America.

Takada, Tanaka, Igarashi, and Fujita. 1989. "Road/Automobile Communication System (RACS) and Its Economic Effects." *Proceedings of IEEE Vehicle Navigation and Information Systems Conference.* New York, NY: Institute of Electrical and Electronic Engineers.

Texas A&M University. 1989. *Proceedings of a Workshop on Intelligent Vehicle Highway Systems by Mobility 2000* (February). Ed. Harris and Bridges. College Station, Texas: Texas A&M University.

Texas A&M University. 1990. *Mobility 2000 Presents Intelligent Vehicles and Highway Systems: 1990 Summary* (March). Ed. Harris and Bridges. College Station, Texas: Texas A&M University.

Texas Transportation Institute. 1990. *Proceedings of a National Workshop on IVHS* (March 19–21). Sponsored by Mobility 2000. College Station, Texas: Texas A&M University.

Transportation Research Board, National Research Council. 1988. "A Look Ahead: Year 2020." *Transportation Research Board, Special Report #220.* Washington, D.C.: TRB, NRC.

Tsuzawa and Okamoto. 1989. "Advanced Mobile Traffic Information and Communication System – AMTICS." *Proceedings of IEEE Vehicle Navigation and Information Systems Conference.* New York, NY: Institute of Electrical and Electronic Engineers.

U.S. Department of Transportation. 1971. *Recommendations for Northeast Corridor Transportation* (May). Washington, D.C.: Internal U.S. DOT report.

U.S. Department of Transportation. 1990. *Report to Congress on Intelligent Vehicle-Highway Systems* (March). Washington, D.C.: U.S. DOT.

Endnote

1.   Much of the material for this chapter is based on a previous paper by the author titled "Mobility 2000 and the Roots of IVHS," published in the Spring 1993 issue of *IVHS Review* by IVHS America (now ITS America).

BY Donna Nelson, Ph.D. • Director • Maryland Transportation Technology Center, University of Maryland

Introduction

Some aspects of intelligent transportation systems (ITS) have been in use for some time—certainly well before passage of the Intermodal Surface Transportation Efficiency Act in 1991 (ISTEA). Few would argue that ITS started with ISTEA, or even with the efforts of Mobility 2000. There is no clear consensus on when "ITS" started, and furthermore, on exactly what ITS is and what constitutes ITS.

The remaining sections of this book are centered around ITS systems (chapters 4 through 13), ITS technologies (chapters 14 through 18), standards and architecture (chapter 19 and 20) and ITS deployment (chapters 21 through 27).

The objective of this chapter is to provide an overview of the ways in which ITS systems and technologies are defined, and to describe some of the national initiatives and programs that are central to discussions of ITS.

Describing ITS applications

The 1992 Strategic Plan for Intelligent Vehicle Highway Systems (IVHS) in the United States is defined in terms of five functional areas (IVHS America 1992):

- Advanced traffic management systems (ATMS)
- Advanced vehicle control systems (AVCS)
- Commercial vehicle operations (CVO)
- Advanced public transportation systems (APTS)
- Advanced vehicle control and safety systems

While these functional areas provide a basic framework for discussing and planning the development of an ITS program in the United States, further detail was needed to more clearly define the potential of ITS and to create a national program. Advanced rural transportation systems (ARTS) was also added to this list.

Several other related yet distinct ways of discussing ITS technologies and applications have emerged through development of the National ITS Program Plan (U.S. DOT and Intelligent Vehicle Highway-Society of America 1995) and the National ITS Architecture. The lightly shaded boxes in figure 3–1 represent approaches to describing different aspects of ITS. While these various definitions are related, they serve different purposes.

Figure 3–1. Graphic view of the national ITS architecture.
Source: U.S. Department of Transportation, National System Architecture Hypertext View,
<http://www.itsa.org/archdocs/index.html>.

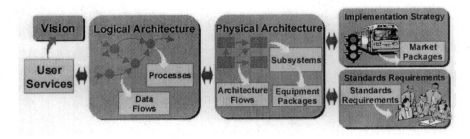

- Thirty-one *user services* were developed to provide a framework for identifying the high-level services that might be provided to address specific problems and needs. These services, grouped into seven bundles for convenience (table 3–1), illustrate the services that could be provided to users. The potential users of a particular user service include transportation system operators, incident responders, the general public, or anyone else involved in using, operating and maintaining surface transportation systems. User service requirements, processes and dataflows further define these services. User service requirements describe the functions required to implement each user service. Processes are the activities and functions required to provide the user services. Data flows identify the information shared by these processes.

- *Market packages* address specific transportation problems and needs. Sixty market packages, listed in table 3–2, build upon the user services to provide a more refined set of ITS service-building blocks that are implementation- or deployment-oriented.

- *Subsystems* correspond to the existing environment such as traffic operations centers, automobiles and roadside signal controllers. Nineteen subsystems are defined in the national ITS architecture. Subsystems are grouped into four classes: centers, roadside, vehicles and travelers. Figure 3–2 shows a few examples.

Figure 3–2. ITS subsystems.
Source: Federal Highway Administration, *National System Architecture CD Version 3.0.*

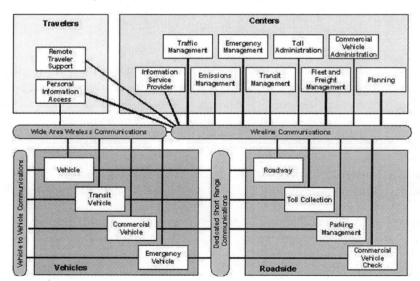

Table 3–1
ITS User Services
Source: Federal Highway Administration,
National System Architecture CD Version 3.0.

User Service Bundle	User Service
Travel and Transportation Management	En-Route Driver Information Route Guidance Traveler Services Information Traffic Control Incident Management Emissions Testing and Mitigation Highway-Rail Intersection
Travel Demand Management	Pre-Trip Travel Information Ride Matching and Reservation Demand Management and Operations
Public Transportation Operations	Public Transportation Management En-Route Transit Information Personalized Public Transit Public Travel Security
Electronic Payment Services	Electronic Payment Services
Commercial Vehicle Operations	Commercial Vehicle Electronic Clearance Automated Roadside Safety Inspection On-Board Safety Monitoring Commercial Vehicle Administrative Processes Hazardous Material Incident Response Commercial Fleet Management
Emergency Management	Emergency Notification and Personal Security Emergency Vehicle Management
Advanced Vehicle Control and Safety Systems	Longitudinal Collision Avoidance Lateral Collision Avoidance Intersection Collision Avoidance Vision Enhancement for Crash Avoidance Safety Readiness Pre-Crash Restraint Deployment Automated Highway Systems

- *Equipment packages* group the like functions (called P-specs) of a particular sub-system together into packages of hardware and software capabilities that can be implemented and that relate to the user services and their functional requirements. The national ITS architecture has defined approximately 110 equipment packages.

ITS applications are also often discussed as either metropolitan (urban) or rural.

ITS programs and initiatives

Since 1991, the U.S. Department of Transportation (U.S. DOT) initiated many programs that are now central to our concept of ITS. An understanding of these programs and how they are related will help put the following chapters in context.

Table 3–2
ITS Market Packages
Source: Federal Highway Administration,
National System Architecture CD Version 3.0.

Traffic Management	Network Surveillance
	Probe Surveillance
	Surface Street Control
	Freeway Control
	HOV Lane Management
	Traffic Information Dissemination
	Regional Traffic Control
	Incident Management System
	Traffic Prediction and Demand Management
	Electronic Toll Collection
	Emissions Monitoring and Management
	Virtual TMC and Smart Probe Data
	Standard Railroad Grade Crossing
	Advanced Railroad Grade Crossing
	Railroad Operations Coordination
	Parking Facility Management
	Reversible Lane Management
	Road Weather Information System
Transit Management	Transit Vehicle Tracking
	Transit Fixed-Route Operations
	Demand Response Transit Operations
	Transit Passenger and Fare Management
	Transit Security
	Transit Maintenance
	Multi-modal Coordination
	Transit Traveler Information
Traveler Information	Broadcast Traveler Information
	Interactive Traveler Information
	Autonomous Route Guidance
	Dynamic Route Guidance
	Information Service Provider (ISP) Based Route Guidance
	Integrated Transportation Management/Route Guidance
	Yellow Pages and Reservation
	Dynamic Ridesharing
	In-Vehicle Signing
Advanced Vehicles	Vehicle Safety Monitoring
	Driver Safety Monitoring
	Longitudinal Safety Warning
	Lateral Safety Warning
	Intersection Safety Warning
	Pre-Crash Restraint Deployment
	Driver Visibility Improvement
	Advanced Vehicle Longitudinal Control
	Advanced Vehicle Lateral Control
	Intersection Collision Avoidance
	Automated Highway System
ITS Planning	ITS Planning
Commercial Vehicles	Fleet Administration
	Freight Administration
	Electronic Clearance
	Commercial Vehicle Administrative Processes
	International Border Electronic Clearance
	Weigh-In-Motion
	Roadside CVO Safety
	On-board CVO Safety
	CVO Fleet Maintenance
	HAZMAT Management
Emergency Management	Emergency Response Emergency Routing MAYDAY Support

Field operational tests

The Field Operational Test (FOT) Program was initiated by the U.S. DOT in 1991 to demonstrate the potential benefits of ITS products, technologies and approaches on a limited scale under real-world operational conditions. These tests were an interim step, bridging the gap between conventional research and development and full-scale deployment (U.S. DOT, FHWA, and Vehicle Technology Group 1998). FOTs were sponsored and supported by several administrations of the U.S. DOT, including the Federal Highway Administration (FHWA), the Federal Transit Administration (FTA) and the National Highway Traffic Safety Administration (NHTSA). Partners in an FOT typically included a local or regional transportation agency, as well as the FHWA. The partners often included private-sector providers of the equipment, systems, and services interested in demonstrating their idea.

Early deployment plans

The FHWA funded the development of Early Deployment Plans (EDPs) in most of the 75 largest metropolitan areas. These EDPs serve as a tool that allows local and state agencies to systematically plan and implement ITS technologies as part of an integrated transportation system, and lead to a regional framework for each of the metropolitan areas in which they are developed (DeBlasio, Eichenbaum, Liu, and Skane 1997).

Priority corridors

The ITS Priority Corridors Program was established in ISTEA. The corridors were established according to a number of specific criteria set out in the act, with severe or extreme ozone nonattainment as the controlling ISTEA criterion (U.S. DOT 1997a). Corridor funds were available to eligible state and local entities in areas with severe or extreme ozone nonattainment for application of ITS and in corridors and areas where the application of ITS could demonstrate potential benefits related to improved operational efficiency, reduced regulatory burden, improved commercial productivity, improved safety and enhanced motorist and traveler performance.

The four corridors selected in this program were: I-95 (Maryland to Connecticut), Houston, Gary-Chicago-Milwaukee (GCM) and Southern California. Each of these corridors presented different challenges and opportunities. All, however, placed a heavy emphasis on public–public partnerships. Some of the characteristics of these corridors are shown in table 3–3.

National intelligent transportation infrastructure initiative

The national intelligent transportation infrastructure (NITI) initiative addresses the integrated electronics, communications and hardware and software elements needed to support ITS services and products. Three elements of NITI have been defined to address the needs of three specific types of users: metropolitan travelers, commercial carriers, and rural travelers (U.S. DOT 1997b).

- *Metropolitan ITS infrastructure.* The metropolitan ITS consists of nine components (U.S. DOT, FHWA 1997): freeway management, incident management, traffic signal control systems, electronic toll collection systems, electronic fare payment, transit management, highway–rail intersection, emergency management services and regional multimodal traveler information.

- *Commercial vehicle information systems and networks (CVISN).* The objective of CVISN is to link existing disparate information systems and databases to support a number of CVO-oriented ITS services including: commercial vehicle electronic clearance systems, automated roadside safety inspection

Table 3–3
Comparative Description of the Four Priority Corridors
Source: Federal Highway Administration,
National System Architecture CD Version 3.0.

	Houston	S. California	GCM	I-95
Geographic Scale	Small	Large	Med. To large	Very large
Management Complexity	Simple	Very Complex	Complex	Very Complex
Major System Elements	ATMS, ATIS, Transit	ATMS, ATIS, Emergency Response	ATMS, ATIS, Transit, Incident Management	CVP, Interregional travel, incident management, ATIS, ETTM, Intermodalism

systems, on-board safety monitoring, commercial vehicle administrative processes, freight mobility systems and hazardous materials incident response technologies (Orban, Brand, Amey, and Kinateder 1998).

- *Rural ITS infrastructure.* The rural ITS infrastructure identifies seven clusters of related technologies to enhance the safety of rural highways and that upgrade the transportation services systems in rural communities. These clusters include: traveler safety and security systems, emergency services, tourism and travel information services, public traveler services/public mobility services, infrastructure operation and maintenance technologies, fleet operation and maintenance systems and commercial vehicle operations systems for rural areas.

The elements of NITI closely parallel the ITS user services, and they can be linked to the ITS market packages and equipment packages defined in the national ITS architecture. The NITI service provides a high-level means of thinking about ITS that is relatively simple to convey to state and local transportation officials, as well as to the general public. It also provides a means of tracking the deployment of ITS. It also provides a framework for tracking ITS deployment and measuring improvements in the transportation system.

Model deployment initiatives

The U.S. DOT created the model deployment initiative (MDI) in 1996 to serve as a showcase for ITS. These MDIs were to demonstrate the benefits of an integrated transportation management and multimodal traveler information systems and to serve as "laboratories" for conducting rigorous evaluations of the benefits of integrating ITI infrastructure in a metropolitan area.

Four MDI sites were selected: Phoenix (AzTech), Seattle (SmarTrek), San Antonio (TransGuide) and New York City/New Jersey/Connecticut (iTravel). Phoenix focused on enhancing traffic and transit management operations and developing an extensive traveler information system. Seattle concentrated on enhancing traffic management and emergency response operations and creating a comprehensive traveler information system. San Antonio focused on implementing an innovative emergency medical services management system, enhancing traffic management operations, and creating a multimodal traveler information system. Finally, New York City/New Jersey/Connecticut focused on developing a highly integrated, multimodal traveler information system.

Sites selected as MDIs had many, but not all of the ITS components needed to create an integrated system. MDI funding was to allow these sites to deploy and integrate several ITS systems. Although the MDI program is nearly complete, all sites have funded future system expansions and enhancements.

The National Automated Highway System Consortium

ISTEA provided a legislative mandate to the U.S. DOT to "develop an automated highway and vehicle prototype from which future fully automated intelligent vehicle-highway systems can be developed." The approach taken by the US DOT was to develop a research program based on a consortium of government, academia, and the private sector. The National Automated Highway System Consortium (NAHSC) began work in October 1994 with nine core members: Bechtel Corporation, the California Department of Transportation, Carnegie Mellon University, Delco Electronics Company, General Motors Corporation, Hughes Electronics Corporation, Lockheed Martin Corporation, Parsons Brinckerhoff, Inc. and the University of California at Berkeley's Partners for Advanced Transit and Highways (PATH) Program (TRC, NRC, and National Academy Press 1998). This consortium was charged with evaluating alternative automated highway system concepts and specifying, prototyping and testing a "preferred" automated highway system that would serve as the basis for the development of future automated highway systems.

The NAHSC staged a successful public demonstration of automated vehicle and highway technologies in August 1997. Following the demonstration, the U.S. DOT's focus shifted instead on the development and deployment of nearer-term intelligent vehicle technologies, such as collision warning system through development of the intelligent vehicle initiative (IVI).

The IVI

The U.S. DOT launched the IVI in 1997 in an effort to develop a "human-centered" transportation system in the United States. The IVI advocates the creation of smart vehicles that fully consider the driver's requirements, capabilities, and limitations (U.S. DOT, FHWA, and Vehicle Technology Group 1998; U.S. DOT 1997c). The IVI is organized around four specific vehicle types: cars, transit buses, commercial trucks and special vehicles such as snowplows. The primary goal of the IVI is to work jointly with the motor vehicle and trucking industries, state and local DOTs and other stakeholders to accelerate the development, introduction and commercialization of driver assistance products to reduce motor vehicle crashes and incidents.

The IVI is a multi-agency research and development effort aimed at accelerating the development, availability and use of integrated in-vehicle systems. The IVI will emphasize the development of industry-wide architectures and standards, integrated system prototyping and field test evaluations so that the government and industry participants can assess benefits, define the performance requirements and accelerate the deployment of incremental driver-assistance products.

References

DeBlasio, A. J., H. M. Eichenbaum, M. M. Laube Tai-Kuo Liu, and A. R. Skane. 1997. *A Review of Metropolitan Area Early Deployment Plans and Congestion Management Systems for the Development of Intelligent Transportation Systems* (September). Washington, D.C.: U.S. Department of Transportation.

IVHS America. 1992. *Strategic Plan for Intelligent Vehicle Highway Systems in the United States* (May 20). Washington, D.C.: IVHA America.

Orban, J., D. Brand, S. Amey, and J. Kinateder. 1998. *Executive Summary: CVISN Model Deployment Initiative Summary Evaluation Plan* (July). Washington, D.C.: U.S. Department of Transportation.

Transportation Research Board, National Research Council, National Academy Press. 1998. *Special Report 253: Review of the National Automated Highway System Research Program.* Washington, D.C.: TRB, NRC.

U.S. Department of Transportation. 1997a. "Implementation of the National Intelligent Transportation Systems Program: 1996 Report to Congress." *Policy Review of ITS Priority Corridors: Executive Summary* (September 26). Washington, D.C.: U.S. DOT, <http://www.its.dot.gov>, appendix D.

U.S. Department of Transportation. 1997b. *The National Intelligent Transportation Information Infrastructure Initiative* (September 19). Washington, D.C.: U.S. DOT.

U.S. Department of Transportation. 1997c. *Intelligent Vehicle Initiative Business Plan* (November). Washington, D.C.: U.S. DOT.

U.S. Department of Transportation, Federal Highway Administration. 1997. *Tracking the Deployment of the Integrated Metropolitan Intelligent Transportation Systems Infrastructure in the USA: FY 1997 Results.* Washington, D.C.: U.S. DOT, FHWA, <http://www.its.dot.gov>.

U.S. Department of Transportation, Federal Highway Administration, and Vehicle Technology Group. 1998. *Intelligent Transportation Systems Field Operational Test Cross-Cutting Study Advanced Traveler Information Systems* (September). Washington, D.C.: U.S. DOT, FHWA, and Vehicle Technology Group, <http://www.its.fhwa.dot.gov/cyberdocs/welcome.htm>.

U.S. Department of Transportation and Intelligent Vehicle-Highway Society of America. 1995. *The National Program Plan for Intelligent Transportation Systems* (March). Washington, D.C.: U.S. DOT and Intelligent Vehicle-Highway Society of America.

BY Brian L. Smith • Assistant Professor • University of Virginia

Transportation management describes a broad set of systems developed and operated primarily by public-sector transportation agencies focused on the active operation and management of the surface transportation system. Most of these systems are not new, nor unique, to intelligent transportation systems (ITS). In fact, one could argue that transportation management has been around since Garrett Morgan patented the first traffic signal in 1923. However, as ITS has developed, transportation management systems have made extensive use of advances in technology.

Transportation management is considered to be a foundation for regional ITS because it serves as the "eyes" of the system. Transportation management systems collect extensive data describing the status of the surface transportation system. While transportation management uses this data to support operations, the data are also invaluable to other ITS functions, such as traveler information systems.

Objectives of transportation management

An understanding of transportation management hinges on the word "management." Management can be defined as the use of resources to influence the decisions of others. In this case, transportation management seeks to influence the decisions made by users of the surface transportation system. Given this fundamental definition, one can see that transportation management ranges from legally enforceable traffic control devices that assign right-of-way to motorists (e.g., traffic signals) to providing information on current traffic conditions in an attempt to influence mode, route, or travel-time choice. It is important to note that this latter form of management is not control. Travelers are in no way legally bound to change their behavior based on the management system. This adds to the challenge of effectively developing and operating such systems.

Before discussing the core functions of transportation management systems, it is important to examine the goals that these systems seek to achieve. The following three goals are the fundamental reasons for public agency investment in transportation management:

1. *Improve the safety of the transportation system.* Safety is of primary importance to the transportation profession. A central goal of transportation management is to improve safety. In the past, this has primarily been done using traffic signals and regulatory signs (e.g., STOP, YIELD) to control traffic in a safe fashion. With ITS transportation management systems, this goal is also addressed by providing detailed information to motorists that enable them to make decisions that result in safer travel. For example, dynamic message signs (DMSs) may be used to warn motorists of icy locations, or travelers may decide to use rail transportation to avoid hazardous driving conditions.
2. *Improve the use of the system's capacity.* The surface transportation system represents a significant societal investment. In order to realize the best return on this investment, it is necessary to actively manage the system. Other similar systems, such as telecommunications networks, use sophisticated technology to manage the system to ensure efficient use of capacity. The goal of transportation

management is to do the same for surface transportation. Achieving this goal is not trivial. Some control activities actually reduce capacity. For example, the use of an all-red interval at a signalized intersection to allow vehicles to clear the intersection will result in a small amount of delay, but it is considered essential to ensure safe operations. In addition, the definition of capacity is even debatable. Minimizing total vehicle delay in a signal system may be considered to be a way of measuring this objective, while another way may be to minimize delay per person in the system. The definition is important. For example, depending on the definition used, a region may or may not choose to operate a system that provides signal priority to high-occupancy transit vehicles.

3. *Provide predictable transportation services.* In this information age, people have come to expect complete, comprehensive information to be available to them at all times. For example, a wide variety of information is available on-demand on the Internet, or one can tune into any one of a number of 24-hour "news" stations on most cable television systems. People are coming to expect the same level of information for surface transportation, particularly because the system plays such an important role in their lives. People are used to making changes in their behavior when provided information about an event, even if they have no control over it. For example, people are very interested in weather forecasts, because it makes their upcoming days more predictable. A goal of transportation management is to make current and upcoming trips more predictable as well. Clearly, this goal can only be met in conjunction with traveler information systems, which are described further in chapter 5.

Core functions of transportation management

The implementation of transportation management can take numerous forms. In fact, all of the following systems can be classified as ITS transportation management: freeway management systems (FMSs), traffic signal systems, incident management systems and tunnel control systems. Although transportation management systems throughout the world tend to possess unique characteristics to respond to particular regional transportation needs, all transportation management systems share the same four core functions. These functions are described below:

- *System state estimation.* To actively operate the surface transportation system, it is necessary to understand, as fully as possible, the status of the system. For example, a basic home air conditioning system cannot function effectively without sensing the home's air temperature. Nor can a financial professional manage your investments without understanding the status of the markets and your personal state (e.g., age, income, debts). In both of these examples, it is clear that neither management system can determine the complete system status. For example, no one has yet been able to predict the behavior of the stock market, and the temperature in one room with the air conditioner's thermostat is not necessarily the same as that in another room of the home. As seen in these examples, a management system uses a limited number of sensors to test strategic locations in a system to estimate the overall system status. This is exactly the case in ITS transportation management. The system state estimate developed in this function is then used to allow for informed transportation management decisions.

- *Management strategy determination.* Once the status of the system has been estimated, a key, and often very difficult function is required: determining a management strategy. In other words, figuring out what should be done to make the transportation system operate more efficiently, safely and predictably. In addition, this includes determining when action should be taken. In many management systems, this is a relatively simple step. In the home air conditioning example above, the cooling system is activated if the temperature is above a certain threshold, and it is deactivated if the temperature is below another threshold. In ITS, this function is extremely difficult. The surface transportation system changes rapidly, and it is impossible to manage each individual entity traveling through the system. Traditionally, this function has been accomplished in a largely manual fashion. However, more and more tools are becoming available to supplement and enhance human judgment in this area.

- *Management strategy execution.* The concept of this function is quite simple. Once one has decided upon a strategy, he or she must execute the strategy. In ITS transportation management, this function usually relies on using a combination of control and management tools and resources varying from traffic signals to traveler information devices such as DMS and highway advisory radio (HAR).
- *Management strategy evaluation and feedback.* This function completes the "feedback loop" commonly seen in classic control and management systems. This is a particularly important function for ITS. Given that surface transportation is in no way deterministic, it is important to continually evaluate the effectiveness of management strategies that have been employed. Not only does this allow for immediate changes to refine the management strategy, but it also allows transportation managers to better understand how to use the management and control tools and resources at their disposal.

These four functions make up the core of ITS transportation management. As seen in figure 4–1, their relationship can be considered using the framework of classic feedback control. As stated earlier, transportation management systems have been classified in a number of ways. To structure the discussion in this chapter, we will consider two basic classes of transportation management systems: traffic signal systems and FMSs. Traffic signal systems are intended to operate arterial facilities, while FMSs are used to manage limited-access freeway facilities. While these classes of systems offer a convenient categorization for discussion purposes, these systems operate in tandem in ITS, working together to achieve the goals stated above.

Figure 4–1. Core functions of transportation management.
SOURCE: Brian L. Smith.

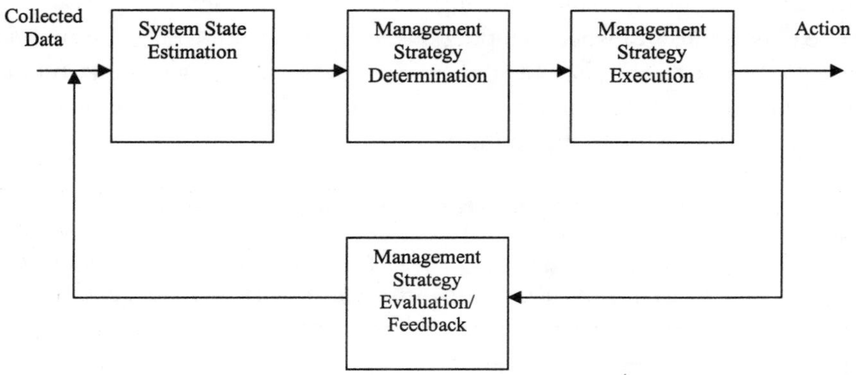

Traffic signal systems

Traffic signals have been used since the 1920s to assign right-of-way at intersections. Many of the signals in use today operate in "isolated" mode. This means that the operation of one signal does not consider conditions at any other signalized intersection. Isolated intersections are either controlled with fixed timing plans that do not change regardless of traffic demand, or in a traffic-actuated mode in which the fixed plan may be modified slightly if an immediate demand is sensed at the stop line of one approach to the intersection. In addition, isolated intersections include the ability to define multiple timing plans for use at different times of the day. A number of approaches and tools are available for engineers to develop timing plans for isolated signals. A complete discussion of these tools is contained in the *Traffic Control Systems Handbook* (reference listed at the end of this chapter).

As the use of traffic signals has grown due to growing traffic demand, it has become clear that efficient system operations cannot occur with signals functioning in an isolated mode. To address this, transportation engineers now operate network signal systems, in which signal control is coordinated among multiple intersections. Through the years, a number of different approaches have been developed for coordinated control. While each approach has distinguishing characteristics, they all share the same objective. This objective is to control traffic signals to allow for the efficient and safe flow of traffic throughout the system. This section of the chapter will focus on the essential elements of network signal systems. Individuals interested in details of particular implementations of network systems are encouraged to refer to the *Traffic Control Systems Handbook.*

System state estimation

In order to estimate the network's state, signal systems sample traffic conditions using basic vehicle presence detectors at strategic locations. The vast majority of these detectors are in-pavement inductive loops; however, alternative technologies are beginning to see more use (see chapter 14 for more information). Generally, all signal systems, whether isolated or networked, place detectors at or near the stop lines of intersections to allow for actuated control.

In network signal systems, system detectors are also used. While the purpose of detectors at stop lines is to determine if there is an immediate demand for right-of-way, the purpose of system detectors is to detect increases or decreases in overall demand level, shifts in directional demand, and changes in cross-street directional demand. Since these detectors attempt to measure overall demand, it is desirable that they should be placed outside the area of influence of intersections. In other words, they should be far enough downstream to be outside the acceleration zone of vehicles leaving the upstream intersection, and far enough upstream of an intersection to be outside the area where standing queues form from the downstream intersection. Figure 4–2 illustrates basic guidelines for the placement of system detectors. A rough rule-of-thumb developed by TTI researchers is that on arterials, system detectors be located every 800 meters to measure demand at points that are indicative of changing traffic conditions.

Figure 4–2. System detector placement guidelines.
SOURCE: K.N. Balke, R.S. Keithireddipalli, C.L. Brehmer, *Results of Simulation Studies Relating to the Operation of Closed-Loop Systems in a Traffic Responsive Mode,* Research Report 2929–2 (College Station, Texas: Texas Transportation Institute, January 1997, p. 38).

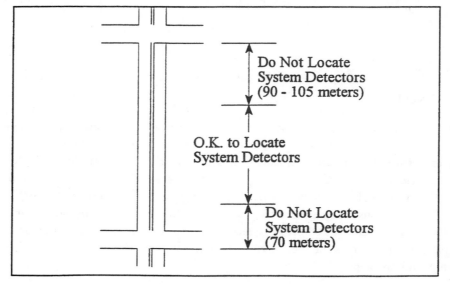

It is important to keep in mind that system detectors can only be used to collect samples of basic traffic data (generally volume and occupancy) to use in estimating the system's state. This is necessary to allow a timing plan to be selected that is best suited for current conditions. In other words, this function permits traffic-adaptive control to occur. In most cases, the samples from the system detectors are "input" into an optimization algorithm to determine signal timing parameters (these algorithms will be discussed in the next section). In newer adaptive signal control systems, such as RT-TRACS, it is expected that knowledge-based systems will be used to categorize the state of the system in an effort to choose the most effective optimization approach.

While the purpose of system detectors is to support the estimation of the overall demand that needs to be satisfied by signal system, at times special demands must be addressed. This is most often seen in signal pre-emption and priority in which certain vehicles, usually emergency response and transit, are provided preferential treatment at intersections. This demand is detected using transmitters mounted on the vehicle and receivers at or near the affected intersection. Once this demand is determined, the signal is controlled accordingly. An example of a signal preemption system is shown in figure 4–3.

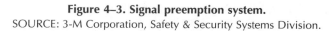

Figure 4–3. Signal preemption system.
SOURCE: 3-M Corporation, Safety & Security Systems Division.

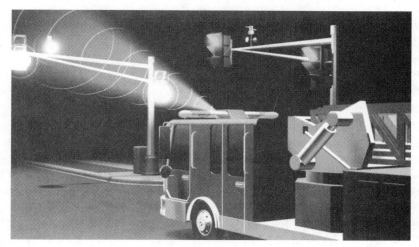

While preemption systems are in use today, it is likely that other types of data will be available to signal systems as ITS development and deployment advances. For example, as systems become more integrated, it is likely that signal systems will receive information from FMSs. This information may include a request for extended green-time in a particular corridor to meet anticipated arterial demands expected due to vehicle diversions that are occurring because of an active freeway incident.

Management strategy determination

Once the state of the system is estimated, this information is used to determine how to manage the system—in this case, through the timings of the system's traffic signals. The signal timing plan (i.e., the set of timings for each signal in the system) serves as the management strategy for network signal systems. The general goal of this function is to assign right-of-way at intersections in order to achieve the optimal system-wide flow of traffic. The basic parameters in a signal timing plan are:

- *Cycle length*—the time required for one complete sequence of signal phases at an intersection.
- *Split*—the percentages of a cycle length allocated to each of the various phases in a single cycle.
- *Offset*—used to provide a green-band progression along an arterial. The offset is the difference between the main street green phase at an intersection and the green interval start in the system's master intersection.

Considering these definitions, it is clear that there are a large number of control parameters to define in a signal timing plan for a system of many intersections. Given that these parameters can take on an infinite number of values, the process of searching through these for optimal values is a very difficult process. This is the challenge of developing signal timing plans.

In the past, traffic engineers have used manual techniques to develop timing plans. However, as the sizes of signal systems continue to grow, this becomes impractical. There are two basic approaches for developing signal timing plans for network signal systems. First, a set of different timing plans can be developed off-line that correspond to a set of prevailing traffic conditions. Second, timing plans can be developed in real-time in response to traffic conditions. This approach is referred to as traffic-adaptive.

The development of timing plans off-line requires transportation engineers to start with fairly intensive data collection. The basic data that must be collected include:

- System geometry
  - Spacing between intersections
  - Number (and types) of lanes and width
- Traffic demand
  - Volumes
  - Turning movement counts
  - Speed limitations

While this data collection may, at first glance, seem straightforward, this is often not the case. As stated earlier, the objective of network signal system control is generally to provide safe and efficient traffic flow through the system. A signal timing plan developed for morning peak traffic demand should provide efficient service at that time. But traffic demand during the afternoon peak is usually significantly different from morning peak. Therefore, this timing plan will not provide efficient service at this time. Thus, an effective network signal system will include a number of different timing plans that can be implemented for different classes of traffic demand. In general, these classes are defined by time of day and section of the system. It is not uncommon for a moderate-size city to develop hundreds of timing plans to account for various sections and time-of-day traffic patterns.

There are a number of software packages that a transportation engineer can use to develop signal timing plans off-line. These include PASSER, TRANSYT-7F, SYNCHRO and others. These packages differ in the way they define efficient traffic flow, and the method they use to search for optimal signal timings. Therefore, in practice, certain packages tend to be better suited for different signal system configurations or different traffic demand characteristics. For more information on these packages, refer to the *Traffic Control Systems Handbook*.

Traffic-adaptive signal systems are attractive in that they continually refine the signal timing plan to meet current traffic demands. In other words, rather than define a fixed number of timing plans using off-line techniques, and then attempting to use them at the time(s) most appropriate, an adaptive system adjusts the timing plan automatically at regular intervals (usually on the order of a few minutes). Conceptually, this works in exactly the same manner as developing off-line timing plans. The data collection effort (which often includes manual counts in developing off-line plans), simply involves polling the system detectors to ascertain the current system state. Obviously, given the need for complete system information, traffic-adaptive systems typically require significantly more detectors than traditional systems. Once these detectors are polled, the system searches for optimal signal timings in real-time. This process is repeated at regular intervals as the system operates.

Conceptually, this approach is clearly superior to off-line techniques. Why isn't it used in all systems? First, traffic-adaptive systems require a large number of system detectors. While one can use manual counts for minor movements in an off-line approach, this will not work in traffic-adaptive systems. Therefore, with more detectors (and therefore more communications), these systems are more expensive and more difficult to maintain. In addition, as stated earlier, the timing parameter search process is very challenging. In order for traffic-adaptive systems to perform in real-time, they require significantly greater computer power than off-line systems, or they require simplifying assumptions to reduce the search complexity. This has led to the prevailing opinion that a well-developed off-line timing plan will outperform a traffic-adaptive system under repeatable traffic conditions.

As with off-line signal timing software packages, the available traffic-adaptive systems vary slightly both in their definitions of efficient system operation and in how they search for signal timings. Examples of traffic-adaptive systems include SCOOT, SCATS, and RT-TRACS.

Management strategy execution

The execution of the management strategy in a signal system is very straightforward. The timing plan developed or selected is simply implemented at each signal in the system. The plan is generally selected from or downloaded to each local signal traffic controller, which then drives the signal until a new plan is activated.

The effectiveness of a traffic signal system is directly dependent on motorist compliance with the signals. A significant safety concern in such systems is individuals disregarding red (stop) commands. Photo enforcement systems are becoming widely used as a means to automate the enforcement of red lights and as a deterrent for future violators. These systems combine detectors located 6–8 feet past the stop line in each lane (within the intersection), a field processor, an industrial 35-millimeter or video camera and communications. When the signal turns red, the processor polls the detectors to see if a vehicle is in their area. If so, the processor then triggers the camera to capture a series of images of the offending vehicle. These images are imprinted with the date, time, intersection location and speed of the vehicle. Generally, these images are then forwarded to the police department, where they are verified and citations are issued.

Management strategy evaluation and feedback

A key advantage of using a traffic-adaptive signal system is that the evaluation and feedback function are largely automated. Traffic-adaptive systems continually refine timing plans automatically based on current traffic conditions. However, any adaptive system has limitations. Therefore, many of these systems also include an operations center where traffic operators monitor the system performance and can intervene when necessary. The control center for the Montgomery County, Maryland transportation management system is shown in figure 4–4. As seen in the figure, the centers typically include video surveillance of select intersections plus a map describing current system-wide conditions.

Figure 4–4. Montgomery County Maryland Operations Center.
SOURCE: ATMS website.

Figure 4–5. Signal system software user interface.
SOURCE: PB Farradyne, Inc.

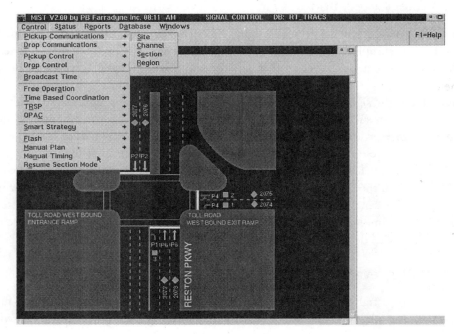

Traffic signal systems that use timing plans developed off-line for common traffic conditions require manual evaluation and feedback. Many of these systems include an operations center similar to Montgomery County's. As traffic operators monitor traffic conditions, using data from system detectors and sometimes closed circuit video, they attempt to determine if conditions have changed enough to justify employing a different stored timing plan. These systems typically employ a core software platform to facilitate these functions. In general, this signal system software polls, processes and stores system detector data; displays conditions using a graphical user interface; and stores multiple timing plans. An example user interface from such a system, in this case PB Farradyne's MIST system, is shown in figure 4–5.

It is important to remember that in a nontraffic-adaptive system, traffic operators can only choose from a set of timing plans developed off-line or manually adjust the timing at a selected intersection. If they identify traffic conditions for which no timing plan has been prepared, there is little that can be done. In addition, many nontraffic-adaptive systems do not incorporate a traffic operations center and they operate strictly on time-of-day. If conditions have changed since the time-of-day plans were developed, the system will perform poorly. The key point here is that effective system operation requires that transportation engineers regularly reassess the suite of timing plans that have been developed. If the suite does not adequately address the range of current traffic conditions, new plans must be developed using one of the standard off-line tools.

FMSs

The first FMSs appeared in Detroit, New York and Chicago in the early 1960s. While freeways are, conceptually, limited-access, free-flowing facilities, the tremendous demands placed on them, particularly in major metropolitan areas, have made it necessary for freeways to be actively managed. This active management is intended to ensure that freeway travel is as safe as possible, predictable and efficient.

While similarities exist, FMSs differ fundamentally from signal control systems due to the significant differences in each system's control mechanism. While the management of signal control systems is legally enforceable, this is generally not the case for freeway management tools. The effects of this fundamental difference become clear as we examine the core functions of freeway management, particularly when considering the tools available for management strategy execution.

System state estimation

System state estimation in FMSs consists of sampling traffic conditions and then classifying the system state based on the samples. The most common way of sampling traffic conditions on freeways is using vehicle presence detectors or closed circuit television (CCTV) cameras. Generally, detectors are placed every half mile to 1 mile in the freeway system to sample volume, speed and occupancy. CCTV cameras are generally placed in such a way that continuous coverage of the freeway is achieved. In other words, the full range of adjacent cameras are such that they just meet in the middle. While this sort of placement is common, it is not required, nor universally adopted. In general, more densely spaced detectors and cameras provide an FMS with more complete system condition information.

Vehicle presence detectors provide traffic condition samples at a point. To estimate system link status between points requires assumptions about the continuity of flow. Another approach to sampling traffic conditions of freeway links is to use transponder-equipped vehicles as probes. This approach samples a limited number of vehicles as they travel throughout the system, as opposed to counting all vehicles that cross a limited number of locations in the freeway system. The use of vehicle probes allows for the estimation of traffic flow, travel time and density on links of the freeway system. It is a practical method in areas in which electronic toll collection systems are in place and transponders are widely used. Tag readers are placed throughout the system to identify vehicles as they navigate the freeway system. As the percentage of vehicles that can be sampled as probes increases, the accuracy of system condition estimation improves.

A number of other sources of information, such as reports of incidents from citizens, the police, or the media, can provide significant system condition information in FMSs. These differ from sensor data or probes in that they do not provide a continuous stream of condition samples. Rather, these sources provide event information at unpredictable intervals. The sources of this event data are nearly endless. Beyond accident reports, FMSs receive reports of work zones from contractors, maintenance efforts by departments of transportation (DOTs) and special events from the event sponsors. While an FMS will at times be offered this form of information, it is also important for FMS operators to actively seek out this type of information from regional sources.

As seen in the previous description, a wide variety of data sources exist to support system state estimation. Furthermore, much of this data, such as the event reports and CCTV video, requires the active attention of a trained traffic operator to extract relevant information. This makes it very difficult to process this data, or fuse the data, to come up with a comprehensive description of freeway conditions. A number of approaches at data description and analysis have been developed. Two common approaches are described in the following section: system condition maps and incident detection algorithms.

System condition maps attempt to summarize and present all of the condition information by overlaying the information on a regional map. Generally, links of the system that include detectors or probe information are color-coded to indicate the level of congestion. In addition, event information, such as incident and work zone locations, is depicted using icons. The goal of such a condition map is to allow system operators and users of the transportation system to quickly scan the region for abnormal conditions or events. The challenge in creating effective system maps lies in presenting a comprehensive view of regional conditions, without creating an overly cluttered graphic.

Under the prevailing normal conditions, freeway traffic flows smoothly. Therefore, the manual monitoring of data returned by system detectors or images captured by CCTV becomes a very tedious task. It is desirable to use an automated process to continually scan detector data for abnormal conditions or an interruption in flow. Such a condition is considered a possible incident, triggering an alarm that will then prompt a traffic operator to use CCTV to examine the area in question. A number of approaches have been proposed and used to identify possible incidents. These approaches are generally referred to as incident detection algorithms.

While the development of incident detection algorithms continues to be an area that attracts a great deal of research, the basic premise is rather simple. Algorithms attempt to forecast what conditions should be at a particular location at a particular time. The method used to forecast differs widely, from considering upstream detectors, to using time series statistical models. Once this forecast is generated, the current condition is compared to the forecast. Once again, the exact method in which this comparison is executed differs widely. To learn more about specific incident detection algorithms, refer to the *Traffic Control Systems Handbook*.

A fundamental problem with incident detection algorithms lies in tuning the algorithm to quickly identify potential incidents without generating a large number of false alarms. In general, the more sensitive an algorithm is, the more false alarms it generates. As a result of this problem, many operators in FMSs do not feel that incident algorithms play a significant role in traffic state estimation. However, there is a consensus that as the size and scope of FMSs grow, the size of traffic operations staffs will not keep pace. This will force the further improvement and use of incident detection algorithms to supplement manual techniques.

Management strategy determination

Once the state of the freeway system is estimated, a significant challenge in freeway management is to develop viable management strategies. While signal systems can actually control traffic, FMSs have little ability to control traffic, and therefore they must attempt primarily to manage the system. The means used to manage the system will be discussed in the next section. As a result, management strategy determination for FMSs differs significantly from that for traffic signal systems.

A key objective of FMSs is to support incident management. An incident can be defined as a nonrecurrent event that reduces roadway capacity. Therefore, incident management strives to restore full capacity as soon as possible after an incident occurs. There are six basic phases in incident management:

1. Detection and verification
2. Response
3. Scene management
4. Traffic management
5. Incident clearance
6. Motorist information

While many agencies play many roles in incident management, an effective FMS supports each phase of incident management. The detection and verification phase has been described in the previous section. This section will focus on how an FMS works to support incident response, scene management and traffic management.

Once an incident is detected and verified, time is of the essence. An FMS's role is to determine the most effective response plan to restore roadway capacity. This response plan typically includes the identification of appropriate response personnel and equipment, plus the preferred communication links. In addition, the response plan includes determining how to use traveler information devices to provide details to travelers.

In the past, the operation of FMSs has been completely manual. Operators relied on their memories and experience to develop a response plan based on the current state of the freeway system. As FMSs have grown, a number of them have supplemented operator experience with rule-based (also referred to as expert systems) software. This software contains a number of predefined response plans that apply to a range of traffic conditions and incident characteristics. Once an incident has been detected, these systems attempt to match the incident with one in the rule base. The operator can then either use the response plan as is, or modify it slightly to better fit current conditions. The San Antonio FMS that manages 26 miles of freeways employs 34,000 rules in its incident response rule base. This ratio of freeway length to rule base size demonstrates the significant effort required to develop and operate a rule-based system effectively.

A management strategy that is used in many FMSs, both under incident and nonincident conditions, is known as ramp metering. Ramp metering systems regulate the number of vehicles entering the freeway, ensuring that the demand does not exceed capacity. By doing so, at times traffic desiring to enter the freeway mainline must wait in queues on the ramps. There are a number of ways to develop ramp metering strategies. In general, strategies are developed to either reduce congestion or to improve safety. In reducing congestion, a metering rate is determined to ensure that demand remains below capacity on the freeway mainline. In improving safety, metering rates are determined to break-up platoons of entering vehicles competing for gaps in the freeway traffic stream.

While many FMSs operate individual ramp meters in an isolated fashion (similar to isolated intersection control described earlier), it is becoming more common for ramp meters to be managed as a system. In doing so, the same fundamental problem must be addressed as traffic-adaptive signal systems. System demands must be collected using system detectors, and an overall objective function must be defined to allow for optimization.

Finally, an area of active research in freeway management strategy determination is known as dynamic traffic assignment (DTA). DTA continually attempts to identify the optimal (usually in terms of minimizing overall system delay) assignment of vehicles to sections of the transportation system. This process is extremely computer-intensive, requiring origin and destination matrices to be estimated and traffic assignments to be made, all in real-time. The concept behind DTA is to actively attempt to fine-tune the distribution of traffic on the overall transportation system, rather than trying to just respond quickly when something goes wrong (such as an incident). To date, a significant problem beyond the computational challenge of DTA lies in implementation. Even if optimal assignments are determined, there is no existing mechanism to ensure that drivers adhere to the preferred assignment. This is particularly true given the fact that a system optimal assignment may result in some individuals being assigned routes that are not optimal from an individual perspective.

Management strategy execution

FMSs, and to a lesser extent traffic signal systems, rely very heavily on the use of traveler information dissemination as a means to execute management strategies. In other words, FMSs use information in an attempt to modify the behavior of travelers as the primary tool for executing management strategies. There are a number of methods widely used in FMSs to provide traveler information—DMSs, HAR and others that will be discussed below. Regardless of the information delivery mechanism, the provision of traveler information imposes significant operational responsibilities on FMS operators. In order to have any hope of affecting the behavior of travelers, the information must be viewed as credible. To achieve credibility, the system must provide information that is:

- *Timely*—in this era of the Internet and cable television news coverage, people expect information on events (such as incidents) as soon as they occur. If and when this does not occur, people lose confidence in the source.
- *Accurate*—if a driver modifies her behavior based on inaccurate information, the source again loses credibility.
- *Reliable*—in order to be viewed as a credible, trusted source of information, the information must be reliable. If the information is timely and accurate for one out of every three incidents, drivers will quickly lose confidence.

As seen in the above discussion, people hold high expectations in this information age. In essence, information provided by an FMS is judged in the same light as news provided by major media outlets. These outlets expend significant levels of effort to "scoop" the competition and to provide thorough, in-depth information. As such, it must be clear that regardless of the technology employed, an FMS must place a high level of commitment to actively operating traveler information systems.

Finally, it is important to consider the range of objectives that providing traveler information may address. As alluded to earlier, many people view traveler information as a means to directly modify driver behavior (e.g., choose an alternate route, reduce vehicle speed). Another very important objective of traveler information is to make travelers aware of the overall state of the transportation system. This information may not be at all useful for modifying behavior, rather it is simply available to inform the driver. This concept is best presented comparing it to the provision of a different kind of information, weather forecasts. Most people watch local weather forecasts daily. There is very little (in fact nothing) that they can do to change the upcoming weather. However, the information allows them to be mentally prepared and make small adjustments to their daily lives (e.g., choosing a jacket, taking an umbrella). Providing a driver with information on bottlenecks or incidents, for which a viable alternative route may not exist, is very similar to a weather forecast. The driver will now know what to expect and can make small adjustments accordingly (e.g., make cellular phone calls to family or business associates). As road rage becomes a bigger and bigger problem, using traveler information to make trips more predictable, and drivers more informed, is an important function of FMSs.

The remainder of this section describes issues associated with providing traveler information using the most common approaches, including DMSs, HARs, and the broadcast media.

DMSs

DMSs are widely used in FMSs. A number of technologies (e.g., reflective flip-disk, light-emitting diode, fiber-optics) and configurations (i.e., permanent and portable) are discussed in this book. DMSs have an advantage in that they are an element of the infrastructure, and every driver has the opportunity to read and use the information provided on the DMS. In addition, they are unique (when compared to static signs) and tend to attract the attention of motorists. An example of a DMS used for incident management by the Virginia Department of Transportation (VDOT) is shown in figure 4–6.

Figure 4–6. Dynamic message sign.

The key consideration when using a DMS is to recognize the limited amount of information that can be delivered. When one considers that a driver is operating a vehicle at freeway speeds, and monitoring multiple lanes of traffic, it becomes quite clear that very little information can be presented via a DMS. Therefore, it is essential that DMS messages be well-crafted to provide just the essential information. A number of guidance documents have been developed to assist in the crafting of DMS messages. The material presented below is derived from the VDOT's DMS Operator's Manual.

First, one must recognize that the fundamental characteristic of a DMS is that it is dynamic. Therefore, VDOT has developed a training program for DMS operators, rather than develop a list of accepted, predefined messages. The general thought process defined in the guidelines is as follows:

1. *What is the purpose of the message?* It is essential to establish the message's purpose up-front in order to craft a message that meets the situation's needs in the limited amount of space available. Typical purposes of DMS messages are an incident or work zone advisory, an alternate route diversion message and guidance messages for special events.
2. *What is the message?* Different message purposes require different message components. For example, an incident message should clearly describe the incident, its location and instructions for motorists. On the other hand, a special event message should contain only two components: the intended audience of the message and the instruction to the audience.
3. *Evaluate the message display.* The presentation of a DMS message is very important. Given the technology's ability to flash and scroll messages, it is tempting to create long messages. However, the breaks between scrolled messages may confuse the motorist. Once a DMS message is created, it is essential that it be reconsidered in its entirety before it is displayed.

While the above represents a very short summary of VDOT's DMS operator's manual, it clearly illustrates the challenge of creating an effective message. The importance of this cannot be overstated, particularly given the credibility requirements of FMS information dissemination.

HAR

HAR is another widely used information dissemination tool for freeway management. HAR systems generally transmit low-power AM radio signals (with variable ranges, usually on the order of several miles). HARs must be licensed by the Federal Communications Commission; and they are not allowed to broadcast advertising, commercials, or entertainment. However, alternative approaches to HAR are being investigated. For example, the New York State Thruway is attempting to gain an FM signal allocation. Regardless of the technical approach taken, HAR provides FMSs with an audible dissemination tool with limited range. The advantage of using a HAR over a DMS is that it provides a significantly larger amount of information capacity. In other words, once a driver tunes to a station, he or she generally will have over a minute to receive traveler information (as opposed to a few seconds for reading a DMS). However, the drawback of using a HAR is convincing motorists to tune in. The motorist must actively tune his or her radio to the proper frequency. This requires effective signing to alert the motorist to the existence of a HAR and then convince the motorist that it is in his or her interest at this time to tune in. For this reason, many groups, such as the I-95 Corridor Coalition, are advocating joint use of DMS and HAR in FMSs. The DMS is used to provide very basic condition information and point motorists to the HAR for more detailed information.

The creation of a HAR message follows a similar process to that of a DMS described above. As an example, VDOT's HAR incident message elements are provided in table 4–1.

Coordination with broadcast media

Given that the provision of traveler information is a significant management tool for FMSs, it is important to maintain close coordination with the broadcast media. The broadcast media outlets (e.g., radio, television and Internet) are in business to reach people with timely information. By working with the media, an FMS can effectively reach a much larger audience.

Table 4–1
HAR Incident Message Elements
SOURCE: Virginia Transportation Research Council, 1995.

Statement	Purpose	Examples
Attention Statement	Indicates to whom message is intended; indicates start of message	"This is the Virginia Department of Transportation Traveler Advisory Radio. Attention (northbound I-81 traffic / Virginia Beach traffic / football traffic)."
Problem Statement	Briefly state the problem and its severity. Be explicit in telling motorists how it affects them, but do not elaborate beyond what indicates severity of situation.	"An accident causing heavy congestion" "A short detour because of road construction" "Right lane closed for maintenance" "A hurricane alert has been declared for the Tidewater area for Tuesday evening."
Location of Incident	This allows drivers to make educated decisions about where to expect the conditions, and whether to divert.	"Southbound on I-95 at mile 115" "Eastbound, after the Glebe Road Exit" "For 10 miles, beginning at milepost 144" "After Exit 155"
Reason to Follow Advisory	This may be delay associated with not following advisory, or some other consequence.	"To avoid heavy congestion, ..." "To avoid a one hour delay, ..." "For parking at The Diamond, ..." "Speeding in work zones carries a maximum fine of $250."
Give the Advisory	In many cases this is simply informational, while at other times some action is required on the part of the motorist. Sometimes the advisory is implied, given the problem statement.	"Use Route 29 south to Exit 49." "Use alternate routes." "Expect 30 minute delays." "Merge left."
Time Statement	Should indicate when message was last updated, or when future conditions will be in effect. Include time, day-of-week, and date.	"This message recorded 5:50 p.m., Monday, August 16."
FCC Call Letters	FCC rules require this to be broadcast at least every 30 minutes.	"This is WPDF 247" (or appropriate call sign). Say each letter or number individually.

There are a number of ways that an FMS may work with the media. Many systems share their video feeds from CCTV with local television stations. The stations broadcast video during news reports. Most FMSs have maintained control over which video signals are shared at any given time. This allows inappropriate video of accident scenes to be blocked from the media when needed. In addition to CCTV, FMSs often directly contact radio traffic reporters to provide information on major incidents. Cultivating a close relationship with these reporters provides significant long-term benefits.

Finally, sharing information with private traffic information services is becoming an important means of providing information to citizens. Services such as SmarTraveler in Boston, Massachusetts and Washington, D.C., combine information from FMSs with privately collected data to provide a regional traveler information service. An example of SmarTraveler's Internet information for the Washington, D.C. area is shown in figure 4–7. This resource also proves beneficial to FMSs, providing a new source of information to assess the state of the system.

Figure 4–7. SmarTraveler website.
SOURCE: ©SmartRoute Systems, Inc.

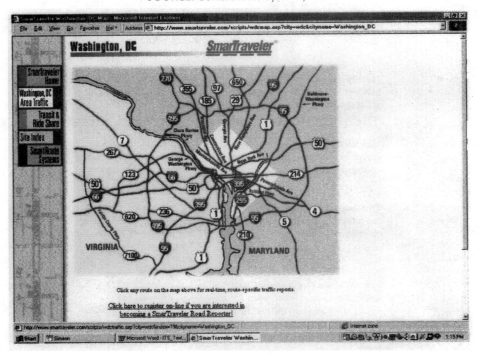

Management strategy evaluation and feedback

As seen in the other functions of freeway management, while a number of automated support tools exist, the ultimate development and implementation of management strategies remains a largely manual process. Therefore, the abilities of operators in an FMS dictate the effectiveness of the system's operation. This final function, evaluation and feedback, is an important aspect of refining and improving the decision-making abilities of operators.

One important activity of this function is to perform incident debriefs. After major regional incidents, responding agencies meet to discuss what went right and what went wrong in the course of managing the incident. This feedback allows freeway management personnel to make better decisions in the future.

Another important activity is to analyze incident data to look for trends. In the past, little data has been archived at FMSs. However, recent research has shown that by archiving condition data and incident logs, it is possible to identify trends. By understanding where and when incidents tend to take place, FMSs can better allocate resources, such as safety service patrol routes, to be able to more quickly respond to events in the future.

Conclusion

Transportation management systems provide the foundation for many ITS user services; they have been evolving for many decades, as transportation professionals have worked to improve the operations of the surface transportation system. While signal systems and FMSs have traditionally been operated as independent systems and presented as such in this chapter, this is rapidly changing. A future ITS challenge is to integrate these systems to perform the core transportation management functions described in a seamless manner across regional arterials and freeways.

For more information

Federal Highway Administration. 1997. *Freeway Traffic Operations: Participant Handbook* (January). Washington, D.C.: FHWA.

National Cooperative Highway Research Program. 1998. *Transportation Management Center Functions, NCHRP Synthesis 270.* Washington, D.C.: NCHRP.

Texas Transportation Institute. 1997. *Results of Simulation Studies Relating to the Operation of Closed-Loop Systems in a Traffic Responsive Mode* (January). Texas: TTI.

U.S. Department of Transportation. 1996. *Traffic Control Systems Handbook* (February). Washington, D.C.: U.S. DOT.

U.S. Department of Transportation. 1998. *Developing Traffic Signal Control Systems Using the National ITS Architecture* (February). Washington, D.C.: U.S. DOT.

U.S. Department of Transportation. 1998. *Developing Freeway and Incident Management Systems Using the National ITS Architecture* (August). Washington, D.C.: U.S. DOT.

Virginia Transportation Research Council. 1995. *Variable Message Sign Operator's Manual* (January). Virginia: VTRC.

Virginia Transportation Research Council. 1995. *Highway Advisory Radio Operational Guidelines* (September). Virginia: VTRC.

BY Carol Zimmerman • Vice President •
Battelle Memorial Institute

ADVANCED TRAVELER INFORMATION SYSTEMS

What are advanced traveler information systems?

Advanced traveler information systems (ATIS) are an integral component of intelligent transportation systems (ITS). ATIS can provide transportation system users with greater transportation options and travel efficiency. A person traveling to work, shop, or on a long-distance trip may want to know the best path to take in terms of distance, road or weather conditions, or points of interest along the way. Intermodal trips are facilitated when bus and train schedule and fare information is readily available. Prior knowledge of roadway congestion, incidents, and transit delays can reduce stress even if they cannot be entirely avoided. For consumer vehicle operators, such as truck and taxi drivers, traveler information can have direct impact on productivity and profitability, as it helps them avoid costly delays.

Traveler information can be provided before or during a trip. Pre-trip information provides a way to plan a path, the mode of travel, and identify stops along the way. Because travel conditions can change once a trip has started, the ability to access traveler information during the course of the journey (en-route information) will also be useful.

What distinguishes an ATIS from the low-tech approaches used to inform travelers in the past is how data are collected, processed, and delivered. In an advanced system, information is stored electronically in computer databases so it can be retrieved and delivered to the traveler when and where it is needed. Data are collected from sources as diverse as traffic and transit management systems (see chapters 4 and 8), weather services, Yellow Pages, and tourist organizations. Telecommunications, including voice, data, or video transmissions over wireline or wireless networks, are the means by which travelers access ATIS databases across the whole spectrum of rapidly expanding technologies, such as cellular phones, cable television, handheld computers, and in-vehicle devices. Many ATIS systems in place today are evolving from manual, labor-intensive operations with limited distribution to more highly automated processes that can serve travelers on demand.

Table 5–1 shows an extensive list of data of potential interest to the traveler. This information may originate from government agencies (e.g., departments of transportation [DOTs], transit operators) or from private sources (e.g., Yellow Pages). Figure 5–1 presents a system diagram illustrating the relation of various sources of information and their stakeholders in a typical real world ATIS from the Phoenix, Arizona, region.

What are the objectives of ATIS?

ATIS must provide information that satisfies the needs of multiple individuals and organizations. For travelers, which range from commuters, tourists, business travelers, and operators of commercial vehicles for local or long-distance purposes, ATIS translates to more efficient and less stressful travel. Knowing which routes are to be avoided because of traffic congestion, what bus and train routes are available, and what routes have truck weight and height restrictions are just some of the types of questions that travelers are looking to answer with ATIS. Public transportation agencies view ATIS as a transportation management tool that can help meet transportation policy objectives, such as managing traffic congestion or increasing transit use. By providing information to the users of the transportation network, agencies hope to effect travel behavior in a way that will benefit the system as a whole. Businesses involved in ATIS deployments are seeking profitable revenue opportunities for their ATIS products and services. Thus, they want to satisfy the needs of travelers and agencies that fund deployments.

Table 5–1
Potential Contents of ATIS
Source: *Developing Traveler Information Systems Using the National ITS Architecture*
(Washington, D.C.: U.S. Department of Transportation, 1998, pp. 2–3 and 2–4).

Static information—known in advance, changes infrequently	Planned construction and maintenance activities
	Special events, such as parades and sporting events
	Toll costs and payment options
	Transit fares, schedules, routes, and so forth
	Intermodal connections
	Commercial vehicle regulations, such as hazmat and height and weight restrictions
	Parking locations and costs
	Business listings, such as hotels and gas stations
	Tourist destinations
	Navigational instructions
Real-time information, which changes frequently	Roadway conditions, including congestion and incident information
	Alternate routes
	Road weather conditions, such as snow and fog
	Transit schedule adherence
	Parking lot space availability
	Travel time
	Identification of next stop on train or bus

The extent to which an ATIS can accommodate multiple objectives is an open question, but logic dictates that ATIS planners identify the most important objectives before a regional ATIS is developed. For example, if a public agency disseminates information for free to travelers, it may undercut the potential for the private sector to find paying customers for traveler information services. Similarly, an ATIS focusing on traffic congestion and incident reporting on major roads will be of limited value for travelers who wish to plan a multimodal trip. Finding the appropriate balance to competing objectives is the challenge for ATIS developers.

Figure 5–1. Example ATIS system diagram, Phoenix, Arizona.
Source: Pierre Pretorious.

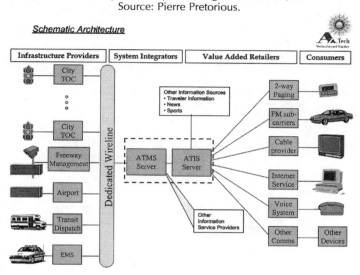

ATIS and the national ITS architecture

Typically, an ATIS for an area is not conceived as a standalone system. Rather, ATIS is part of a larger system of ITS that interacts with other ITS subsystems to collect data and disseminate information. The national ITS architecture (see chapter 19) addressed the interdependencies among ITS components. The architecture identifies linkages among the diverse elements of ITS and provides a framework for guiding the evolution of ITS in a logical and consistent fashion. Figure 5–2 illustrates the application of the some of the concepts of the national architecture to the ATIS project known as Partners In Motion in the Washington, D.C., region.

The concepts and processes embodied in the national ITS architecture help both public and private sector participants in ATIS to better understand how their system fits into the larger ITS for their geographic region. They can use the language of the architecture to communicate with parties who are building and operating other ITS elements, so that integration can be realized.

The development of ITS standards complements the national ITS architecture to ensure interoperability among products and systems and support the growth of national and international markets for ITS technologies. Several standards applicable to ATIS are emerging from the process of ITS standards development (see chapter 20), and they are listed in table 5–2. While a discussion of standards is beyond the scope of this chapter, it should be noted that ATIS standards will be a key component for traveler information products that can be used anywhere in the United States and beyond.

Technology platforms for delivering traveler information

Advanced technology is what distinguishes ATIS from earlier forms of traveler information. This section provides an overview of the technologies and the methods for delivering information to travelers to which those technologies have given rise.

**Figure 5–2. Example of ATIS application of national ITS architecture:
Partners In Motion, Washington, D.C., metropolitan region.**
Source: Battelle Memorial Institute.

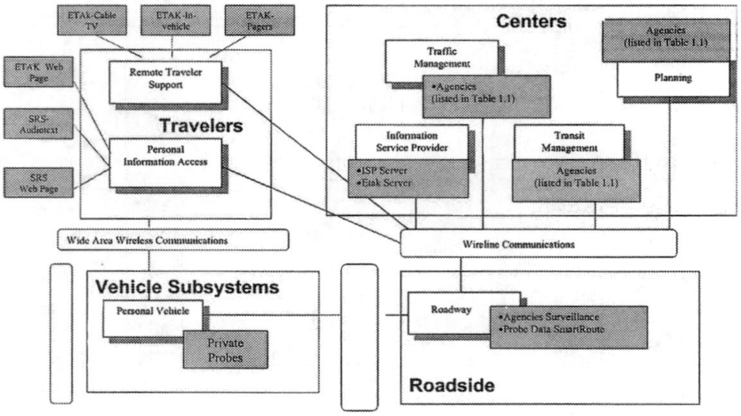

Enabling technologies

ATIS is the beneficiary of a number of technologies that have experienced rapid growth and evolution in recent years (Zimmerman et al. 1997). Although transportation was not the driving force behind the development of these enabling technologies, they provide the foundation on which ATIS applications can be built. Important enabling technologies include the following (many of these technologies are described in chapter 14 in more detail):

- *Information processing speed of computers*—enormous advances in the power of integrated circuits along with reductions in cost and size have helped to fuel the proliferation of equipment available for businesses and consumers alike.
- *Digitalization*—all types of information (i.e., voice, data, image) can be stored in digital form, enabling data to be transmitted, stored, and processed in a similar manner.
- *Wireless communications*—are exploding both technologically and in market demand. Digital cellular and PCS, two-way paging, FM-subcarrier, and other wireless services enable mobile information.
- *Speech technology*—examples of speech technology include voice recognition and synthesized speech. Voice-activated interface technologies are tools that enable a person to give the computer (or other appliance) a voice command, a key step toward hands-free human interfaces.
- *Global positioning system (GPS)*—the GPS constellation of 24 satellites provides location coordinates to GPS receivers, which can determine location to 30–100 meters accuracy using three satellite signals.
- *Miniaturization*—creates enormous opportunities to put things precisely where they are needed with minimal weight and size.

ATIS dissemination platforms

Technological advances have made more platforms for dissemination of traveler information available than ever before. Through the combined forces of technology push and market pull, electronic devices, information services, and new forms of communication have proliferated. For ATIS, the platforms can be characterized as those for pre-trip and those for en-route traveler information access. Pre-trip ATIS platforms are those that are primarily from a fixed (not mobile) location, for example:

Table 5–2
ATIS-Specific Standards Currently Under Development
Source: "Summary of Standards" (Washington, D.C.: U.S. Department
of Transportation, <http://www.its.dot.gov/standards>, 1998).

Standard	Standard Development Organization & Document Number	Description
ATIS Data Dictionary	SAE: J2353	A minimum set of medium-independent data elements needed by potential information service providers (ISPs) to deploy ATIS services and provide the basis of future interoperability of ATIS devices.
ATIS Message Set	SAE: J2354	A basic message set using data elements from the *ATIS Data Dictionary* needed by potential ISPs to deploy ATIS services and provide the basis of future interoperability of ATIS devices.
ATIS Message Structure for High-Speed FM Subcarrier	SAE: J2369	A general framework allowing transmission of traveler information via FM subcarrier. Creates a preliminary coding and message structure for link travel times using high-speed FM subcarrier.
High-Speed Subcarrier (HSSC) Layer 1	NRSC: HSSC1	A physical modulation scheme for delivery of data to mobile users, over FM subcarriers, to ITS applications.
In-vehicle Navigation and ATIS Communication Device Message Set Standard—Evaluation Project	SAE: J2256	A standard used to define the form and content of the messages sent between a traffic management center (TMC) or ISP and vehicles, including traffic information, emergency service, and route guidance information. Also used to test and evaluate key messages by implementing via AMPS cellular network.
Information Service Provider—Vehicle Location Referencing Standard	SAE: J1746	A standard location-referencing format for ISP-to-vehicle and vehicle-to-ISP references. This standard reflects the cross-streets profile of the current location reference message specification document as expressed in the *National Location Referencing Information Report* (SAE J2374).
TCIP—Passenger Information Objects	ITE: TCIP-PI	Data objects relating to providing passengers (and potential passengers) with information for planning and making public transportation trips. Includes schedules, fares, on-line services, trip planning, and facility information.

- Kiosks, placed in shopping malls, office lobbies, or other areas of high foot traffic, are built on a PC platform with ATIS software and databases and are equipped with communication links for accessing real-time traveler information. Kiosks equipped with touchscreen, video, and sound features can be user-friendly. Printers for dispensing hardcopies and telephones for contacting a live operator can also be supported from a kiosk.
- Web pages may be accessed anywhere an Internet connection is available, as illustrated in figure 5–3. Figure 5–4 shows a popular ATIS web page in the Seattle area. The proliferation of Internet access from both home and office has made web pages one of the most popular means for disseminating traveler information. Both real-time and static data can be easily displayed and accessed by the user, and links to video images from traffic cameras are also being added to many ATIS websites.

Figure 5–3. Regional ITS information backbone showing connection to ISPs in the Seattle region.
Source: System Overview Specification, Smart Trek Metropolitan Model
Deployment Initiative Project, Version 2.0 (October 2, 1998, p. 17).

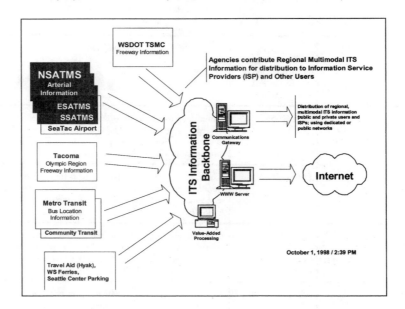

- Audiotext telephone service supplies traveler information over a wireline telephone connection. SmartRoute Systems of Cambridge, Massachusetts, has deployed menu-driven telephone ATIS in several metropolitan areas including Washington, D.C., Boston, Massachusetts; Cincinnati, Ohio; Minneapolis, Minnesota; and Philadelphia, Pennsylvania.

En-route ATIS platforms enable travelers to receive messages while traveling using wireless communications, such as shown in the following examples:

- Cellular phones can provide access to audiotext and live operator services. General Motor's Onstar service provides cellular callers with concierge services from a live operator, including directions and emergency road services.
- Portable computers, ranging from laptops to handhelds to palmtops, can incorporate GPS for location, wireless communications for receiving real-time traffic updates, CD-ROMs for storing geographic map databases, and interactive speech technology for handsfree use. The entire platform requires integration of several firms' products, including consumer electronics provided from firms such as Casio and Toshiba, wireless services from firms such as Cue or Ricochet, application software from companies such as TravRoute and Etak, and real-time traveler information from an ISP such as SmartRoute Systems or Metro Networks. Figure 5–5 illustrates the components of such a system offered by Fastline in Seattle, Washington.
- In-vehicle devices are platforms provided by either original equipment manufacturers or aftermarket suppliers. With their primary function being navigational assistance, real-time traffic information is a valuable enhancement that manufacturers are seeking to add. Siemens Automotive demonstrated navigation and traffic information as part of the Atlanta Traveler Information Showcase in 1996. More recently, Microsoft has given impetus to in-vehicle computing that can include traveler information with the development of the Windows CE operating system for portable devices. In January 1999, Clarion began a nationwide roll-out of its Auto PC device, which is capable of receiving traffic and other

Figure 5–4. Washington DOT web page for traveler real-time traffic information.
Source: Washington State Department of Transportation,
web-capture, <http://www.smarttrek.org> (January 22, 1999).

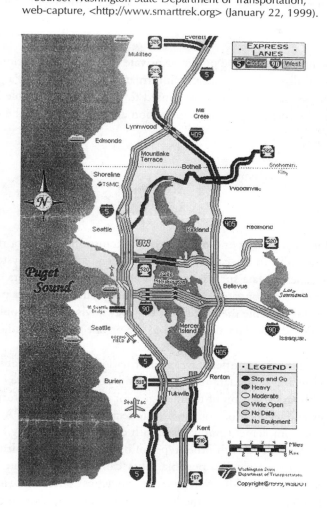

Figure 5–5. Traffic information services provided by Fastline in the Seattle region.
Source: System Overview Specification, Smart Trek Metropolitan Model
Deployment Initiative Project, Version 2.0 (October 2, 1998, p. 29).

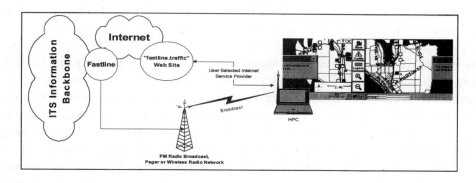

information; and many additional manufacturers are expected to follow suit in this family of products. Increasingly they will use the Internet as a means for accessing information, including ATIS.

The business of ATIS

ATIS does not naturally belong to either the public or private sector, because various combinations of roles for gathering, processing, and disseminating traveler information are possible. In a guide for ATIS deployment (ITS America 1998), five business models were used to illustrate the possible arrangements based on who performs and pays for the consolidation of information and who provides the information to travelers:

1. Public-centered operations
2. Contracted operations
3. Contract fusion with asset management
4. Franchise operations
5. Private, competitive operations

The public sector, as predominant owner and operator of the transportation infrastructure, generates much of the data on which ATIS is built. In the course of managing road and transit systems (see chapters 4 and 8), transportation agencies generate data such as traffic speed and volumes or data on transit delays and incident locations, which are the basic inputs to ATIS. Indeed, many public agencies provide traveler information directly to the public using variable message signs; highway advisory radio; public address systems; and, increasingly, their own websites. Public data are also fed to the private media for radio and television broadcast.

Although the public sector can and does offer traveler information services, options for involvement of the private sector increase as more and more data from public and private sources are consolidated. This richer source of data combined with an expansion of technologies for disseminating information to travelers represents an opportunity for revenue-generation for the private sector. Firms such as Arinc, Metro Networks, and SmartRoute Systems typically complement public data with data they collect (e.g., drivers acting as probes, aerial surveillance, private cameras) and with other types of data (e.g., weather, airline arrival and departure) in order to have the most comprehensive data possible. They can then disseminate information to travelers directly (e.g., by telephone, radio, television, web page) or can act as content providers and resell information to other firms. As technology expands the methods for disseminating data to travelers, a new ATIS role has emerged: that of the ISP. The ISP "obtains data, adds value to them through customization or packaging, and then provides that data to customers" (ITS America 1998, p. 74). An example of an ISP is Cue Paging, which acquires data from an ATIS content provider in each metropolitan area it serves and packages the data for sale to subscribers of its FM-subcarrier paging service. Similarly, website providers offering a broad range of content for a metropolitan area, such as Microsoft Sidewalk or AOL Digital Cities, act as ISPs by packaging traveler information among the content choices available to their customers.

The following example illustrates how some of the ATIS business models are being applied in the United States. Partners In Motion is an ATIS in the Washington, D.C., region, where a coalition of 26 public transportation agencies competitively awarded a six-year contract to a team of firms to build and operate a multimodal ATIS for the region. Data are provided by both the public and private sectors, but the data are fused and disseminated by the private team members. ISPs can obtain the data under commercial arrangements with the private sector, which owns the rights to the fused database. A mixture of public and private funding supports the program in the first three years, after which revenue generated through sale of the data are expected to make the ATIS self-supporting. The public sector will share in a portion of the revenues generated.

Figure 5–6. Locations of major ATIS deployments as of 1998.
Source: *Choosing the Route to Traveler Information Systems Deployment* (ITS America, 1998, p. 78).

Partners In Motion is just one example. The business models used vary from one region to the next, depending upon the market conditions and policy objectives of the governmental agencies of the area. Figure 5–6 shows the locations of major ATIS deployments in the United States.

ATIS in Europe and Japan

In comparison to North America, Europe and Japan are farther along in the ATIS deployment (Shibata and French 1997). In Europe progress has been aided by standard communication media available for the transmission of traveler information. As early as 1972, German drivers were able to receive traffic alerts over special radio signals, a system that has evolved into the RDS-TMC available in eleven European countries today. RDS-compatible car radios are commonly available throughout Europe from many manufacturers. Similarly, GSM, the standard for digital cellular adopted by European cellular operators, provides a mobile transport platform that can be used for ATIS or other ITS data transmissions. A different approach has been taken by Trafficmaster, a private company in the United Kingdom that collects real-time traffic data with infrared sensors and sends information to subscribers using a pager transmission to in-vehicle units. By 1996, Trafficmaster reported approximately 50,000 subscribers.

In Japan the availability of ATIS has been aided by deployment of ATMS for collection of traffic data dating back to the 1970s. Early experimentation with in-vehicle systems in the 1980s evolved to a system known as Vehicle Information and Communication System (VICS), which was established as a public–private partnership in mid-1995. Information is transmitted to in-vehicle units using a combination of FM broadcast and roadside beacons. Revenue for VICS is obtained at the time of purchase by means of a surcharge placed on the in-vehicle unit. In 1994 a for-profit operation known as ATIS Corporation began offering traveler information for the Tokyo area for a monthly usage fee, and information is displayed on a PC or in-vehicle unit.

Paying for ATIS: alternative approaches

Who should pay and how much are essential questions that must be addressed in ATIS. If the information has value to the traveler, should he or she not be willing to pay? How much and how should such payment be collected? If the public policy objectives are the driving force behind ATIS, such as congestion management or promotion of transit usage, should not ATIS be publicly funded? Should traveler information be available to every traveler regardless of the ability to pay?

Answers to these questions are being sorted out in each ATIS deployment. Table 5–3 outlines some of options that are available. In general, traveler information that is customized and pushed to the individual over the communications method of choice will tend to be privately paid, such as in paging-based traveler information services. On the other hand, the public sector has demonstrated willingness to subsidize ATIS to disseminate publicly collected data, as on transportation agency web pages; or to ensure universal access to all travelers through subsidized telephone-based services (e.g., in Washington, D.C.; San Francisco, California; Boston, Massachusetts).

Table 5–3
Paying for ATIS: Some Options

Who Pays	Payment Type	Example Usage
Public sector pays	Total or partial subsidy	Audiotext telephone service, kiosks, web page
Privately paid for	Advertising supported, free to user	Television, web page, radio, kiosks
	Subscription	Paging, personalized e-mail
	Fee for each use	Kiosks
	One time charge included in product purchase	In-vehicle navigation devices

Although a number of private payment options are available, travelers have yet to demonstrate a willingness to pay much money for traveler information. Some market research has indicated that consumers would pay prices as high as $36 per month, but no services to date have succeeded with those types of charges. Indeed, SmarTraveler service in Boston, Massachusets, showed a dramatic reduction in usage among cellular phone users when fees were imposed on cellular calls to a telephone-based ATIS following a free introductory period.

Marketing of ATIS

One of the most challenging issues facing ATIS is simply how to market it. As marketing specialists understand, ATIS involves positioning a new product in a new product category. Before travelers can try and potentially purchase a specific ATIS product, they must be aware of traveler information services in general and the benefits they can offer. ATIS faces formidable opponents in the competition for the attention of the typical consumer, who is bombarded with hundreds of marketing messages in the course of a week. Not typically armed with multimillion dollar marketing budgets, print and broadcast advertising in local media are simply not affordable for most firms engaged in ATIS. Consequently, ATIS marketers are forced to use such low-cost approaches as press releases and consumer fairs to promote their products (Zimmerman 1998).

Special markets for ATIS

While the daily commuter is the primary market for many ATIS products and services, there are other special market segments for which ATIS can be of value. Services have been tested for several special markets including operators of commercial vehicles, tourists, and transit users. While these markets can benefit from the same information on traffic and road conditions that most ATIS currently provide to commuters, traveler information services for these special markets also provide information unique to their needs and interests.

For example, height and weight restrictions and turning geometry of roads along a trucker's route are critical pieces of information in addition to the traffic speed or construction activities along those routes. To address these special needs, TranSmart Technologies and the American Trucking Associations (ATA) Foundation are partnering with public sector agencies in the Gary/Chicago/Milwaukee corridor (Connie 1998) and in the Phoenix, Arizona, (Inside ITS 1998a) region to implement a commercial vehicle operation (CVO) traveler information system that will incorporate trucking-related information. Along the east coast, a CVO service named FleetForward has been developed by a team of private sector partners headed by the ATA Foundation in conjunction with the I-95 Corridor Coalition of public agencies (Inside ITS 1998b). FleetForward takes the CVO ATIS a step further by integrating the information with routing and fleet management software used by trucking operators.

ATIS designed to serve tourists can have multiple objectives: to provide enhanced access and mobility for tourists; to relieve congestion at tourist destinations; and to stimulate economic development, especially in rural areas. In Arizona an ATIS targeting tourists along Interstate 40 in the heavily traveled corridor leading to the Grand Canyon was developed as a field operational test involving public and private sector participants. Using websites, kiosks, variable message signs, and a phone system, the I40 ATIS is able to provide both pre-trip and en-route information to visitors. Evaluation of the system showed that tourists especially like having comprehensive information on facilities, routes, weather, and attractions in one place (Orban 1998).

Size and growth of the ATIS market

Although proponents of ATIS regularly cite the benefits to be obtained by both travelers and policymakers, the demand for products has been slow to materialize. While perhaps not unusual when compared to the market growth patterns of other new consumer products, the size of the ATIS market has been modest to date, frustrating the profitability plans of many vendors. For example, from 1991 to 1995 one study showed a growth from $1.7M to $5.0M for in-vehicle navigation products (Owen, Frost, and Sullivan 1996). The same report forecasted high demand among rental car firms; but only one major rental company, Hertz, has shown a strong interest to date (Inside ITS 1998b). In a recent market study, SRI Consulting (1997) projected only 250,000 people in the United States (or 500,000 under the most optimistic assumptions) would be paying subscribers to real-time ATIS reporting services by the year 2001. Table 5–4 further characterizes SRI's perspective on the prospects for the ATIS market.

Because integrated driver information systems (IDIS) will be broad information platforms for handling all types of information, SRI expects "that eventually most, if not all, of the in-vehicle applications will be merged or integrated into some type of IDIS system within the next 10 to 15 years." Traveler information is to be one of many types of information services that IDIS will eventually incorporate.

Even considering the availability of free ATIS services that are available in some metropolitan areas thanks to government subsidies (e.g., Boston, Massachusets; Seattle, Washington; Washington, D.C.), only a small percentage of the population currently makes use of the services. Many factors can be cited to account for the slowness of growth. First, consumer awareness that these new products and services are available is currently quite low. Second, price is high, especially for in-vehicle products; and demand can be expected to climb as prices begin to drop. Third, quality and comprehensiveness of information needs to be improved in order for consumers to pay the kind of fees that suppliers need to collect for a viable business.

A market analysis by Hagler and Bailly (1998) echoed these findings. Factors considered critical for the success of traveler information services included raising consumer awareness, demonstrating reliability and significant time savings, and establishing partnerships with recognized travel brand names to promote consumer confidence (e.g., AAA). The same study identified critical risk factors, including the various states of completion of the public infrastructure that supports ATIS and the fact that ATIS is somewhat dependent on the success of complementary products, such as in-vehicle devices and map databases.

Table 5–4
Traveler Information Products and Services Forecast:
Sales in Units and Dollars in North America, 2001 to 2011
Source: David Benson, "SRI Market Forecast—Realistic Scenario" (SRI Consulting, 1997).

	2001		2006		2011	
	Units (M)	$ M	Units (M)	$ M	Units (M)	$ M
ATIS: reporting services	.25	10	.65	26	1.5	60
ATIS: software	1.0	9	5.2	15	7.5	17.5
ATIS: kiosks		30		17.5		11.5
ATIS: portable and in-vehicle dedicated devices	.06	19.5	.032	11.1	.008	4
In-vehicle navigation systems	.48	854	1.5	1950	3.5	2100
IDIS	.58		3.37		5.95	

User response to ATIS

While the market for advanced traveler information services and products is still in the early stages, attempts have been made to assess user response. Understanding user response is important not only for current and future vendors in this market, but it is also important to the public sector that has helped fund deployment of ATIS in many locations. Assessments generally seek to gauge users' perception of the benefits of ATIS, the features they want, the impact on travel behavior, and willingness to pay for the products and services.

One of the earliest assessments of user response to ATIS was performed in the Boston area on the original SmarTraveler telephone service initiated in 1993 (Englisher et al. 1996). In contrast to radio and television reports on traffic and transit conditions, callers to the SmarTraveler service were provided personalized information on their specific route on demand. A survey of users in 1994 showed a high level (80 percent) of overall satisfaction with the service, with relief of anxiety the most widely perceived benefit by two out of three respondents. Users also ranked the service higher than broadcast media (i.e., radio and television) on every attribute surveyed.

On the west coast, a survey of 105 callers to the TravInfo telephone-based traveler information service has also provided useful insight to the user's experience with ATIS (Yim et al. 1999). A variety of effects on the travel behavior of callers to the service are reported in table 5–5. The results indicate that information can have an impact on travel behavior, with 46.7 percent of the callers surveyed reporting some type of change. It is interesting to note that among all the possible types of behaviors reported, change in mode of travel occurred least frequently. Indeed, the researchers conducting the survey concluded that transit and traffic callers are distinctly different markets and that few people called seeking information on more than one mode.

Table 5–5
Traveler Information Impact on Travel Behavior of Telephone Service Callers
Source: Y.B. Yim et al., University of Berkley, PATH.

Travel Behavior Impact	Percent of Respondents
Change reported	46.7
Departure time and route change	4.8
Departure time change	10.5
Mode change	1.0
Cancellation of trip	3.8
Route change pre-trip	7.6
En-route change	20.0
No change reported	53.3

A study sponsored by U.S. DOT is seeking to understand the value placed on ATIS by users of in-vehicle devices equipped to deliver real-time traffic information (Mehndiratta et al. 1999). Drawing on users of devices from ATIS projects in Boston, Massachusetts; Seattle, Washington; and Chicago, Illinois, the research has shown that geographical coverage of routes and frequency of information updates are important attributes for in-vehicle information services. Moreover, the market appears to be split into two segments on whether they want to receive routing advice or simply advice about traffic delays to enable them to make their own decisions. This study, along with others that have investigated willingness to pay for traveler information, indicates that users will pay fees to receive real-time traveler information. However, as some of the earlier attempts at charging fees were not successful (Inside ITS 1998a), the potential for revenue generation for ATIS still bears watching. Recently, Cue announced a nationwide roll-out of an FM-paging-based traffic information service, TrafficNet, which is to be sold at an annual subscription basis at the rate of $60 per year, and includes free hourly weather forecasts and news alerts along with traffic updates (Cue 1999). Time will tell if travelers will find prices such as these acceptable in the ATIS market.

Conclusion

ATIS is here today in various parts of North America as well as Europe and Japan. Its proliferation has been fueled by the perceived demand of travelers for better and more immediate information on travel conditions and options and the increasing technological means for delivering that information. At the same time, better collection and fusion of real-time information on traffic and transit congestion, delays, and incidents by public transportation agencies and private sources makes feasible the establishment of operational centers that can service traveler demand for information. Users of existing ATIS perceive the benefits of the ATIS that are emerging over traditional traveler information sources, but tapping the revenue potential of this market is still a major challenge for ISPs.

References

American Trucking Association Foundation. 1998. "FleetForward, Real-time Traffic Information for Commercial Vehicle Operations" (December). *Technical Memorandum 1: Phase I Data Collection and Analysis, Phase II Preliminary Architecture, for the I-95 Corridor Coalition.* ATA Foundation.

Connie, L., R. Pritchard, P. DeCabooter, J. Hochmuth, and D. Sham. 1998. "Implementing a CVO Traveler Information System in the Gary-Chicago-Milwaukee Corridor." Submitted to 1999 ITS America Annual Meeting (September).

Cue Corporation. 1999. "Cue To Provide Wireless Messaging and Real-Time Traffic Information to the Clarion Autopc®" (January 7). Press release.

Englisher, L. S., R. D. Juster, S. Bregman, D. G. Koses, and A. Powell Wilson. 1996. "Consumer Response to the SmarTraveler ATIS: Findings from the Second Year Evaluation." *Proceedings of ITSA 1996 Annual Meeting, Houston, Texas* (April 15–18).

Hagler, and Bailly. 1998. "Consumer Spending Expectation for In-Vehicle Information Systems" (October 29). Presentation by Dr. Richard R. Mudge to the Integrated Traffic and Navigation Data: A Conference on In-Vehicle Information Services for the U.S. Market.

Hallenback, M. E. 1998. "Choosing the Route to Traveler Information Systems Deployment: Decision Factors for Creating Public/Private Business Plans." ITS America. U.S. Department of Transportation, Joint Program Office, and Washington State Transportation Center.

Mehndiratta, S. Raj, M. A. Kemp, J. E. Lappin, and D. Brand. 1999. "What ATIS Information Do Users Want: Evidence From In-vehicle Navigation Device Users." *Proceedings of Transportation Research Board 78th Annual Meeting, Washington, D.C.* (January 10–14).

Orban, J. E. 1998. "Evaluation of Advanced Traveler Information Systems in Rural Tourism Areas." Presentation to ITS Ohio Sixth Annual Meeting (October 15).

Owen, S., Frost, and Sullivan 1996. "Forecast of the U.S. Advanced Traveler Information Systems Market." *Proceedings of ITSA 1996 Annual Meeting, Houston, Texas* (April 15–16).

Shibata, J., and R. L. French. 1997. "A Comparison of Intelligent Transportation Systems: Progress Around the World Through 1996" (June). ITS America.

SRI Consulting. 1997. *Intelligent Transportation Systems Market Report: IVNS, ATIS, IDIS, and VSC* (March). Report three, part 1. SRI Consulting.

Transport Technology Publishing. 1998a. "TranSmart, ATA to Offer Real-time CVO Info in Midwest, Arizona Areas" (November 30). *Inside ITS:* 6–8.

Transport Technology Publishing. 1999. "Hertz, Magellan Say $50M Navigation Investment Responds to Demand" (January 11). *Inside ITS:* 2–4.

U.S. Department of Transportation. 1998. "Developing Traveler Information Systems Using the National ITS Architecture" (August). Washington, D.C.: U.S. DOT.

U.S. Department of Transportation. 1998. "Summary of Standards." Washington, D.C.: U.S. DOT, <http://www.its.dot.gov/standards>.

Youngbin, Y., R. Hall, R. Koo, and M. Miller. 1999. "Travinfo 817–1717 Caller Study." *Proceedings of Transportation Research Board 78th Annual Meeting, Washington, D.C.* (January 10–14).

Zimmerman, C. A. 1998. Panel on marketing. *Proceedings of ITS America Annual Meeting, Detroit, Michigan* (May).

Zimmerman, C. A., C. Cluett, J. H. Heerwagen, and C. J. Hostick. 1997. "Communication and Information Technologies and Their Effect On Transportation Supply And Demand" (January). Washington, D.C.: Transportation Research Board.

BY Thomas C. Lambert • Vice President and Chief of Police •
Metropolitan Transit Authority of Harris County, Houston, Texas

C H A P T E R

6

THE ROLE OF ITS IN THE EMERGENCY MANAGEMENT AND EMERGENCY SERVICES COMMUNITY

Introduction

We have had the opportunity throughout the reading of this book to gain a better understanding of intelligent transportation systems (ITS) and how these systems affect the quality of lives in our communities on a daily basis. We have seen how these systems allow us to access real-time traffic information before we ever leave our homes, how these systems assist us in better managing roadway traffic conditions through real-time management of traffic signal systems, and how these systems through various information sources keep us informed of travel conditions during our journey. We have seen how these systems ease our ability to pay to use toll facilities and how integrated smart cards have allowed us to use various regional transit services by means of the same fare card irrespective of the agency providing the service. In all respects, we have seen how ITS assists us on a daily basis and how it makes our travels safer and more efficient.

But we have not talked a lot about how ITS supports the emergency management and emergency services community in providing essential public safety services to our communities. This chapter will focus on these services and how ITS directly benefits the delivery of these services. We will not talk about a specific technology or a specific system. Rather, we will talk in terms of service delivery and how these systems cannot only assist emergency responders in their response to an emergency, but also how these systems can enhance the safety of these responders.

Emergency management and emergency services

Everyday in our communities a police officer, a firefighter, an emergency medical technician, or another emergency responder receives a call for service to assist someone in an emergency situation. There has been a major freeway accident with serious medical injuries, one of the vehicles is on fire and the other is leaking hazardous materials. The police officer cannot speak to the firefighter by radio while enroute because they are on different radio systems, the ambulance gets stuck in traffic attempting to arrive on the scene, the emergency medical staff at the emergency room estimates the severity of the injuries at the scene because they have no way to receive patient information and the emergency management center must determine what areas of the community to evacuate and how to get this information out to the public.

This story is repeated throughout our communities on a daily basis. But the same could be true as such relates to how we respond to natural disasters that confront our communities as well. This does not have to be the case, and ITS can assist our emergency service providers in their response, coordination, and management of these emergencies.

Lets revise our story as illustrated above by incorporating some ITS into our information process and how these systems might assist our emergency service responders in their response, coordination and management of this major accident. The 911 center receives notification that a vehicle has been involved in an accident and that severe structural damage has occurred. They are also notified that the vehicle's air bags have activated and that there are two occupants in the vehicle: the vehicle's driver and a front seat passenger. The 911 center also is notified of the vehicle's location. All of this notification is done automatically through the vehicle's automated collision notification system (an ITS).

The 911 center notifies all of the appropriate emergency service providers of this accident through their participation in a regional integrated computer-aided dispatch system. The regional traffic management center (TMC) is also a part of this system and provides real-time traffic information to all responders. Traffic managers use their closed circuit television (CCTV) cameras to monitor the accident scene and to report their observations to all responders. The CCTV is focused on the second vehicle involved in this accident to determine the vehicle's cargo and what substance may be leaking from the vehicle. The vehicle's placard is observed and notification is made to the hazardous materials unit prior to their arrival on the scene. The emergency management center activates contingency plans that have been coordinated and tested by all emergency responders. Weather information systems that have been incorporated into the regional emergency management center are monitored to determine wind conditions and how this information will be used to determine the areas to be evacuated. Further coordination occurs while information continues to be provided to all of the responders enroute to the accident scene.

Police, fire, and ambulance vehicles responding to the scene are provided with real-time traffic information to determine the best routes to take to expedite their response. Since they are operating under emergency conditions, they receive emergency preemption at signalized intersections that expedites their response to the scene while enhancing their safety and that of the public. Emergency service dispatchers track all on-duty vehicles to determine the closest vehicles to the scene based upon their actual location. This information to better manage available resources assists in expediting response to this emergency. Through direct communication with the TMC, alternative route plans are coordinated and implemented to assist with managing traffic around the accident scene. This information is communicated to the public by means of the dynamic message signs along the freeway corridor, through the news media that has video links to and from the TMC, through highway advisory radio systems that provide real-time traffic information to the public and through information service providers that receive traffic data from the TMC to keep the traveling public aware of traffic conditions. This information dissemination continues throughout the response, coordination and management of this accident.

Our responders have now arrived at the accident scene and begin the process of getting emergency medical attention to the injured, continue their coordinated response to managing this major incident and begin their investigation of this accident. The responding ambulance is equipped with video technology that is linked directly to the regional emergency room. Trauma doctors at the emergency room can visually monitor the accident victims to determine the actual severity of their injuries and to work with the emergency medical technicians on the appropriate treatment for their injuries while they are enroute to the hospital. Police officers work hand in hand with the traffic managers to keep traffic moving around this accident scene. Since their police vehicles are equipped with video systems that can transmit video back to the traffic center and can receive video from the traffic center, they have an overview of traffic conditions that are affected by this accident and what actions they need to take to manage this traffic. They have also established a command vehicle at the accident scene that is equipped to receive information from all responders to ensure that the scene is managed to expedite medical attention to the injured, manage traffic conditions to minimize secondary accidents and to expedite clearance and ensure that all steps required to accomplish the emergency management mission as a result of this accident are met. Accident investigators recognize the importance of getting traffic moving back to normal as soon as possible and thus they use photographic and surveying technology that allows them to get their accident measurements in an expedited manner. Since all responders are on a regional radio and computer-aided dispatch system, they can communicate with each other either verbally or by data.

Our revised illustration demonstrates how ITS can enhance the delivery of emergency management and emergency services to the community. Although a major accident was used to illustrate these applications, similar experiences will occur as our communities must address other emergencies that might range from a tornado to a hurricane, from an ice storm to a flash flood, or from an industrial accident to an act of terror. Each of these emergencies requires that information be provided to all responders on a real-time basis and that the information be accurate. ITS provides a framework to accomplish this requirement.

Conclusion

ITS can and does assist emergency management and emergency service professionals in providing essential public safety services to the community. These systems, if coordinated and planned properly, can also enhance the leveraging of funds to ensure that all stakeholders who can benefit from these systems share in not only the initial capital cost of these systems, but also system operating and maintenance costs. This approach to project funding also encourages the development of new partnerships that can ultimately benefit the delivery of services to the community.

The delivery of emergency services to our communities is a fundamental responsibility that must be met and one that requires us as emergency service providers to constantly look at new ways to enhance these services. We should look to ITS as another tool in our toolbox to enhance our delivery of these services. To do so will require us to expand our horizons to include more partners in our coordination and planning of these services and to look to the tools that they can bring to this most important effort. ITS can assist us in expanding our horizons and in building on these most important partnerships to prepare us to meet the challenges and opportunities that await us in the future.

**PUBLIC TRANSIT
AND ITS**

BY Larry Schulman • Principal Associate • LS Associates

Background

Transit agencies in the United States have been using various forms of advanced intelligent technology in the management of transit fleets for nearly three decades. Agencies in Canada and Europe have been using these technologies even longer. However, the technology has evolved significantly over the last decade; and the use of comprehensive integrated systems has rapidly increased in agencies of all sizes. Using a combination of automatic vehicle location (AVL), computer-aided dispatch (CAD), vehicle performance monitoring, automatic passenger counters and customer information systems, transit agencies have been able to significantly improve performance and levels of service provided to customers

One of the earliest demonstration systems was implemented in Hamburg, Germany, in 1964. In 1986, the Chicago Transit Authority (CTA) initiated the first major program in the United States. CTA used a signpost system developed by Motorola on 500 buses. The primary purpose was to assist the CTA in handling emergency responses. In 1972 the Toronto Transit Commission installed a microwave signpost system for the entire fleet using the new technology as a means of improving operations.

Throughout the 1970s and 1980s, transit properties followed the earlier examples using a combination of signpost and odometer navigational technologies, but adding additional functionality. In 1975, General Motor's Urban Transportation Laboratory demonstrated a system in Cincinnati, Ohio that provided information on passenger loads, run times and system-wide schedule adherence. In 1979, New York City Transit was the first system to transmit mechanical sensor information related to fare boxes and drive train performance. The digital messages reduced the need for audio communications.

In the late 1980s and early 1990s, transit agencies began to explore use of other radio-navigation methods, as the costs of these technologies became more reasonable than those of the signposts. Early demonstrations of Loran-C,[1] aided by dead reckoning sensors, proved unsuccessful. These systems did not provide sufficient accuracy and were soon abandoned. However, with the completion of the 24-satellite global positioning system (GPS) constellation in the mid-1990s, attention in the transportation industry turned quickly to this new technology.

Interestingly, while the use of GPS technology was growing rapidly in the general transportation community, the transit community remained very cautious. Even though transit had had experience with AVL systems, use of satellite-based systems raised questions. Today, GPS is clearly the technology of choice in the transit industry. Current GPS systems are augmented with differential GPS and dead-reckoning tools such as odometers, gyroscopes, or map matching to compensate for loss of coverage caused by tall buildings and underpasses in larger cities.

The entire ITS industry, along with transit, has grown relatively strong in the last decade in the United States. Many of the early operation tests have given enough positive results to move programs from demonstrations to the deployment stage. Specific funding for ITS activity has been increasing and shifting from research and demonstration to system deployment. Part of the increased funding for ITS has resulted from special legislation to provide target funding for all ITS endeavors including transit. Today, most U.S. transit agencies procuring new communication systems or new buses include some components of advanced ITS technologies. By the end of this century, we can anticipate seeing most small, medium and large transit agencies integrating advanced communication and fleet management systems into all their fixed-route and paratransit operations.

Architecture and functionality

While there is significant variation in the design and functionality of specific fleet management systems being initiated by transit properties, the basic system architecture of each remains the same. Figure 7–1 indicates the three main elements—the vehicle, the mobile communications backbone and the control center—and the relationship among the elements.

Figure 7–1. System architecture.
Source: Courtesy of Orbital TMS.

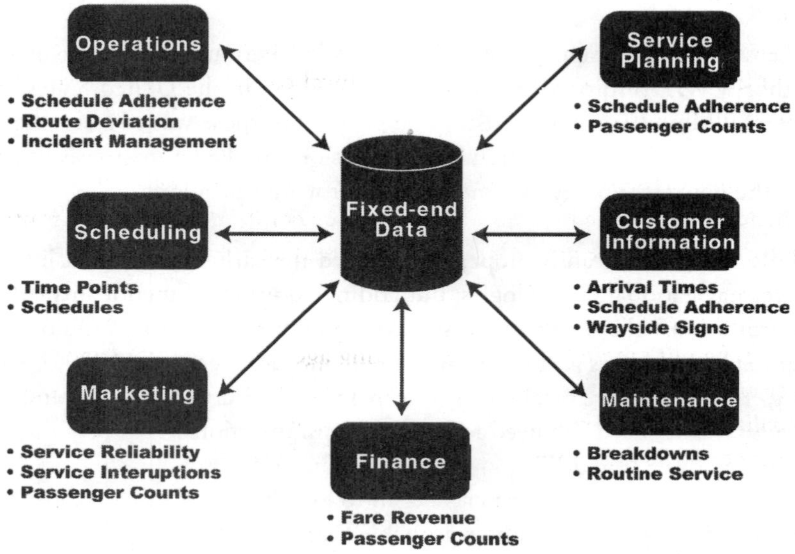

The vehicle is the mobile end of the system. It contains the system components that allow for the determination of the real-time location of the vehicle, the interface between the vehicle operator and the system, and the communication between the vehicle and the control center. Also, it may contain a number of sensors that allow for the collection of the various data elements that provide for the enhanced functionality of the system.

The communication system is the element that allows for the two-way, voice and data communication between the vehicle and the command or dispatch center. It provides the means for passing the real-time location data and other data collected on board the vehicle to the dispatch or command center. It also provides the means for passing information from the dispatcher to the vehicle operator.

The third element is the control or dispatch center—the fixed-end of the system. It is here that the major decisions are made to improve the operation of the system. Based on the information conveyed to the center from the vehicle, the dispatcher can make and transmit to the vehicle operator instructions to improve regular schedule adherence or make unscheduled adjustments in service such as detours. It is also through the control center that various data are transferred to other functional departments.

At the option of the transit properties, real-time data on vehicle arrival times can be transmitted from the vehicle or the control center to passengers desiring up-to-date information on the availability of services. This can be done at bus stops, transit terminals, or through Internet services to individual homes or the workplace.

In-vehicle system components

In-vehicle systems cover a wide variety of components, each of which provides different functions. The two main components on board the vehicle are the vehicle control head, which provides the operators interface to the system and the in-vehicle unit, which houses the electronics of the system.

The control head includes a keypad, a backlit liquid crystal display, a covert microphone and an audible alarm. The system may also include a removable memory card for data storage. The display shows vehicle status and GPS-based system time. It allows the operator to continuously view status with respect to schedule (i.e., early, late, on time) as well as any unusual mechanical conditions on board the vehicle. It also allows the control center to communicate directly with the operator. The keypad allows the operator to perform a number of functions. It allows for data messaging between the operator and the control center by allowing the operator to send various predetermined data messages to the control center that indicate certain events occurring on the vehicle. It allows the operator to access voice communication on a routine or priority basis. It serves as the operator log-on device and at minimum will replace the radio data head allowing for logging on the radio system. If the total system is designed properly it can also serve as the log-on device for other system components such as destination signs, voice annunciation systems, passenger counters and the fare box. To maximize this capability requires the implementing agency to carefully plan and integrate the total range of functionality anticipated in the system. This is especially important if available budgets require the total system functionality to be implemented in phases over time. Failure to do so will result in redundant technology, unnecessary expense and unnecessary system complexity.

The in-vehicle unit provides the brain of the vehicle system. It provides the platform for in-vehicle data collection, storage and processing; it integrates all the electronic functions on the vehicle. It contains a powerful computer, a GPS receiver, the radio modem interface and a covert microphone.

The in-vehicle unit keeps continuous position, speed and direction. The computer stores information on blocks, routes and schedules. It collects event data, tags the data with time and position and determines whether or not to send exception condition messages. It receives downloaded data from the garage and uploads collected data to the garage. It controls voice and data messaging and controls all vehicle equipment tied into the system.

The GPS receiver receives signals from three GPS satellites; and with differential corrections, odometer and route matching techniques, it computes the accurate location of the vehicle. The computer calculates the difference between actual location and time and schedule location and time; and it determines whether the vehicle is on time, ahead of schedule or late. It also determines whether the vehicle is on or off route. Information on status and location are continuously displayed on the vehicle control head and forwarded on an exception basis to the dispatcher in the control center.

The exception reports are based on locally determined parameters, which indicate whether a vehicle is considered to be off schedule. These parameters may indicate that a vehicle is to be considered off schedule if it is two minutes ahead of the scheduled time or five minutes behind the scheduled time. Only in those cases will a message be sent to the dispatcher to assist or instruct the operator. In all other circumstances, it is expected that the operator alone can correct the situation. This continuous data on schedule adherence greatly assists the operator in improving on-schedule performance. Previously, this type of information was only available on a periodic basis and was provided through street supervisors that were located along the route.

One of the important new features provided by an integrated AVL system is a covert microphone, which can be inconspicuously triggered by the operator when a distress situation occurs on the vehicle. As the operator activates the emergency silent alarm, a covert microphone is opened that provides one-way communication between the vehicle and the control center. The dispatcher can hear what is happening on the vehicle and, knowing the location, can immediately dispatch the appropriate response vehicle to the exact location of the vehicle. Some systems also include a direct connection to the video surveillance system (if available) that starts a real-time transmission of images from the vehicle to the control center.

Operator safety has always been a major concern to transit agencies. Most vehicles currently include a silent alarm that can be triggered by the operator. This provides information to the dispatcher that a distress situation is occurring on the vehicle, but the exact location of the vehicle is not known. Without knowing the exact location, there could be substantial delays in the arrival of a response vehicle. In the case of a medical emergency or a physical threat, the minutes saved could be the difference between life and death. Furthermore, if a highjacking were occurring on the vehicle, it could be very difficult or impossible to locate the vehicle. This safety feature has become a very important factor in vehicle operators accepting the use of these systems on the vehicle.

A fully integrated, comprehensive vehicle system can include a number of additional functional components that can be installed on the vehicle and integrated with the real-time location data. These include automatic passenger counters, video surveillance systems, voice annunciation, the fare box, exterior destination and route signs, interior next STOP signs and door opening and lift sensors. It can also include other sensors that indicate the status of various systems on the vehicle such as mechanical systems, electric systems, and fuel systems.

Passenger counters

Passenger counters automatically record data on persons entering and leaving the vehicle. Coupled with the route and location data, accurate information is provided on vehicle loading at individual bus stops. Several versions of the technology have been used on transit systems. The earlier treadle systems had numerous mechanical problems and turned out to be unacceptable to the industry. More recently, passive infrared systems have been used. Two variations are currently in use—horizontal beam systems record the passenger when the beam is cut by the passage of a body; and vertical beam technology looks down and records the passage of the person by thermal mass movement. This technology can record movements by direction and eliminates the problem caused by wide passageways. It can report passenger loading with a reported accuracy of 95 percent.

Generally, the passenger data is not needed on a real-time basis. In most applications, the data is recorded on the vehicle and transferred at the end of the day or at specified times. Based on system configuration, the data may be transferred via mobile radio, memory card, floppy disk, or a limited-distance radio system. The availability of this data on a daily basis is a significant improvement to the previous data collection method that involved periodic manual counts by a checker sitting on the bus. On major routes the data was only collected several times a year; on minor routes the data was collected annually or every second or third year. Automatic passenger counters, which record data on a continuous and repetitive basis, allow for the recording of weekday and seasonal variations of travel. Coupled with the data on schedule adherence and location, this information provides a valuable tool for schedule planning as well as schedule revisions. It also assists in the development of operator routing and assignments (e.g., run cutting).

Real-time data transmission over the mobile radio system can vary depending on desired applications. Data can be transmitted when a certain pre-determined threshold is reached, indicating an overloaded condition. Or data can be transmitted in conjunction with a signal priority request that would indicate not only that the vehicle is behind schedule, but also that the vehicle is partially or fully loaded. This data could be important in deciding whether or not to give priority to the transit vehicle.

Annunciation

Interior next stop and voice annunciation systems allow for the automatic announcement of the next stop and information about the stop. Interior signs visually display the next stop. Voice annunciation announces the next stop, and it can include information about the stop. This could be information on a transfer point to a connecting line or other transit mode, the location of a major transfer terminal, or a specific landmark attributed to the stop such as a municipal building, historical place, and so forth. The location of these announcements are predetermined, prerecorded and triggered by the AVL system at various points along the route. Another voice feature is an exterior route and destination announcement that can be made as the vehicle approaches the bus stop. These systems provide for the most basic elements of passenger information.

Video surveillance

Transit agencies are installing video surveillance camera systems on vehicles that can be integrated with the control system provided by the in-vehicle unit. These systems can record events that occur on the vehicle. Most systems record a predetermined number of frames per minute. This data can be transmitted on a real-time basis or stored for downloading at a later period. However, more recent systems will automatically begin a transmission of real-time images when the silent alarm is activated and enhance the number of frames per minute. Several transit agencies are exploring the use of video data to determine passenger counts and loading.

Fare boxes

Automatic fare boxes are also being installed that can be integrated with the in-vehicle control unit for logging purposes and for the recording of revenue collection by location (stop) and time. Normally, this data is stored on the vehicle and transferred at a later time; however, this data can be transferred on a real-time basis if desired by the agency.

Signal priority

Signal priority systems are being installed to allow a vehicle operating in mixed traffic to have priority as it arrives at a traffic signal. This priority may be a request to hold the green signal so that the bus can proceed throughout the intersection without stopping, or a request for a green signal as the vehicle is approaching the intersection with a red light. Generally, this request is made when the vehicle is behind schedule. This request can be coupled with information on the number of passengers on the vehicle to determine if priority should be given.

In case of express service, the request for priority treatment may be made as the vehicle approaches the intersection, regardless of whether it is behind schedule. The objective is to reduce the travel time for the vehicle as much as possible. The decision to give priority is not automatic, but it is a decision made based on the effect that the priority implementation would have on the total traffic in the system. A successful priority system requires careful coordination with the local traffic agency. The necessary coordination is to be realized in U.S. cities as integrated traffic and transit management centers are established.

Figure 7–2 displays the functionality that is currently available through the procurement of a comprehensive, fully integrated system. These include logging, fare collection, vehicle maintenance, customer information (e.g., on-board, wayside, and off-system), vehicle tracking, traffic signal priority, incident management and mechanical sensors.

Figure 7–2. In-vehicle system components.
Source: Courtesy of Orbital TMS.

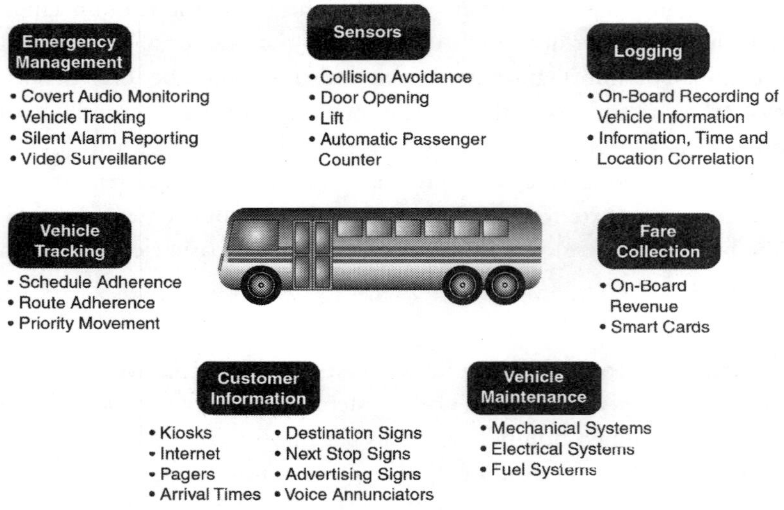

Fixed-end subsystem components

The fixed-end component or the control center is generally located in a garage or, in the case of large multiple garage transit agencies, located at a central headquarters. It is at this location that all data from the individual vehicles is aggregated and specific fleet operational management decisions can be made. It is also the location at which specific data can be transferred to other agency units to enhance their operations.

The core of the center is the central (host) computer that connects to individual dispatch workstations. The configuration allows for flexible, dynamic routing of messages from the host computer to individual dispatchers overseeing the operation of fixed-route or paratransit services. It stores all historic and real-time information and provides access to this data on an as-needed basis. It also provides for the transfer of data to other agency systems that will use the dynamic data available from the system for other management functions such as maintenance, schedule, planning and so forth. Most contemporary systems use a Window NT operating system.

The dispatch workstation is the heart of the fleet management operation. It is co-located with the radio control console that is the basic connection to the private radio system. The workstation usually contains two monitors. One monitor displays the various events occurring on the vehicles—schedule and route adherence, messages being sent by the vehicle operator to the dispatcher, instructions being given by the dispatcher, emergency calls, and the like. Incoming messages are recorded in time sequence; however, emergency messages are immediately posted to the top of the queue. The dispatcher has the option of viewing any message sent by a vehicle operator and responding by a data message through the console, or by a voice call through the headset or microphone. There is also the capability to send messages to groups of vehicles or the entire fleet. Some systems include a series of service management tools that can assist the dispatcher in making the appropriate response.

Generally, one dispatcher is able to handle 200 to 300 vehicles. The exact number will vary with the complexity of the system and the operating service at the time of day. The shift supervisor is able to oversee the operation of multiple dispatchers.

The second monitor is normally a map display, which shows the location of all vehicles in service on the route. Through color codes, the display can indicate the status of each vehicle. The map can be shown at various scales and with route overlays. In emergency situations where an alarm has been forwarded, the map will immediately center on the distressed vehicle and remain there until the situation has been resolved. A third monitor can be installed for reports and analysis; however, this information can be overlaid on either monitor.

Some agencies provide a direct connection of incoming data to emergency units such as transit police or even local police and emergency units. Immediate access to information on an incident, coupled with exact location of the vehicle, allows for more immediate response to incidents on the vehicle. Direct access to data from mechanical sensors on board the vehicle allow for better maintenance of the vehicle and the scheduling of required maintenance before a breakdown occurs. Management is able to get periodic standard reports or ad hoc reports on fleet performance. Data can also be sent directly to the telephone communication center providing information to the general public.

Figure 7–3 displays the various operation units within a transit agency that would have real-time access to the dynamic data available through a comprehensive CAD and AVL system. These divisions include service planning, customer service, maintenance, finance, marketing, scheduling and operations.

Mobile communication subsystem

The mobile communications system is the means of two-way data and voice communication between the vehicle and the control center. These systems vary widely between transit agencies depending on geographic area, site coverage, and fleet size. The process for installing a fleet management system varies with the type and condition of the existing radio system. As older radio systems are being replaced, many transit agencies are integrating the installation of the fleet management system with that new purchase. Where radio systems are still in good condition, the new system is piggybacked on the existing radio system.

A variety of mobile communication systems are currently being used in the transit industry. There appears to be no one solution for all properties. The basic elements of the system are the fixed-end equipment, the remote transmission site(s) and the radios located in the vehicle. Communication systems may include private or shared radios or public networks; may be analog or digital; single-site, multisite, or simulcast; and have conventional (untrunked), trunked, or pseudo-trunked channels. Radios systems can operate at

Figure 7–3. Fixed-end data usage.
Source: Courtesy of Orbital TMS.

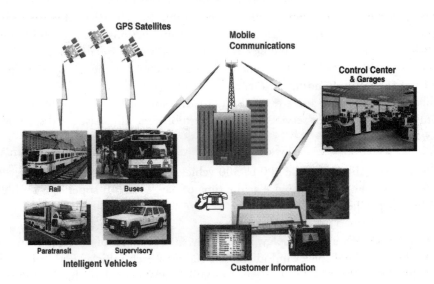

different frequencies ranging from 450 to 900 MHz. There are several radio systems suppliers with different system configurations. Each transit system application must be designed to accommodate the specific conditions required or desired by the property. One of the major advantages of the fleet management system is that it makes better use of the existing channels by moving the majority of the voice communication to data messaging.

Geographic information systems

One of the underlying elements necessary to implement a fleet management system is a complete and accurate geographic information system (GIS). The GIS system allows the transit agency to inventory and geographically locate all features of the transit system, bus shelters, bus stops, transfer facilities, signage and more on a base map. Information on each facility can be stored indicating the type of shelter, specific location (e.g., near side, far side, mid-block), maintenance records, or the street furniture located at the facility. The bus routes and time points are geocoded on GIS maps providing the basis for the schedule and route adherence information and automatic voice-annunciation messages.

Many transit agencies are beginning to develop such comprehensive mapping systems in conjunction with other municipal services. Where such GIS systems do not exist, they must be developed as part of the installation of an AVL system. Such data can be manually input into the GIS system; or, alternatively, new technology is being developed that uses voice-actuated GPS recording.

Passenger information systems

While major emphasis has been placed on the use of the advanced technology for improvements of system operations, these new systems provide great opportunity to convey information to the customer, opportunities that never existed before. The provision of in-vehicle, real-time information for the passenger has already been discussed in an earlier section. However, information on system status and vehicle arrival times can be provided to travelers waiting for a vehicle, seeking information on available service, or planning a trip from home or office.

Variable message signs at bus shelters along the route or at transfer terminals can provide real-time informa-tion on the time of arrival of the next vehicle. They also can provide information on the number of passen-gers on the vehicle. This allows the traveler to make a decision as to whether to take the next bus that may be crowded, or the following bus that may have a seat. Knowing the time of arrival of the bus removes a large portion of the stress caused by not knowing where the bus is or when it will arrive. It also allows the traveler to do some other things while waiting for the bus, such as buy a newspaper or a cup of coffee. It allows the traveler to decide whether to stroll leisurely or rush to the point of departure.

Interactive kiosks can be placed at key locations in a metropolitan area or at major transfer terminals, includ-ing airports or train stations. This provides travelers with real-time information on the status of vehicles in the system. Also, it can assist the traveler, who may not know the best way to reach their final destination, in developing an itinerary. Information can be provided on alternative routing and include information on fares, time of travel and the like. The system can also provide predetermined itineraries for key attractions or points of interest in the community.

Other off-route technologies are being used to assist travelers in obtaining up-to-date, real-time travel infor-mation. Dial-in telephone services are being used to provide transit users up-to-date real-time information on various options for point-to-point travel. While telephone customer service facilities have existed for some time, the availability of almost instantaneous route plans coupled with real-time information route sta-tus have greatly enhanced the provision of this service. The itinerary-planning feature replaces the manual process that depended on strip route maps and the operator's personal knowledge of the system.

Personal paging systems allow the transit rider to quickly check predetermined routes that are used on a recurring basis, or to be notified if there is some problem on a specific route that is used for the normal daily commute. The Internet has become an information mechanism for many travelers and potential transit users. If the routing is unknown, the Internet can provide an itinerary that best meets the traveler's needs. The Internet can combine the real-time transit data with real-time information on traffic conditions and provide the traveler with various options to complete the desired travel. The traveler can choose the travel mode that best suites his or her needs in terms of cost, convenience and total travel time.

Electronic fare payment systems

Electronic fare payment systems replace the current use of cash or tokens for the collection of transit fares. This greatly simplifies the payment system for the transit passenger and greatly reduces the financial burden on the transit agency.

In recent years the transit industry has migrated from the use of cash fares to weekly, monthly, or other flash passes. This has simplified the fare collection process. Others have gone to tokens or exact fare systems, again greatly simplifying the collection of revenues and the burdens on the vehicle operator of making change. However, these cash or token systems still require the agency to collect, count, distribute, or handle coins or tokens. These systems are time consuming and expensive to the transit agency. Also the handling of large sums of money require extensive and costly security systems, and the handling of large numbers of coins and bills invites shrinkage of revenue.

The electronic fare-collection system replaces the cash or token by an electronic card. This card records the transit transactions electronically by use of a magnetic strip or integrated circuit. It eliminates any actions by the vehicle operator and removes all the stress on the passenger by canceling the need for carrying cash or worrying about the exact fare. It greatly reduces or can eliminate costly collection and processing by the transit agency. Also, the collection and revenue functions and associated costs can be borne by a local financial institution, credit card company, or bank.

Electronic fare cards can be contact cards or proximity (contactless) cards. Proximity cards can work without being taken out of a wallet. Systems can operate on a credit or debit basis. The debit card would require the traveler to place a given amount of money on the card and each transit traction would be debited from the account. The credit card would record each transit transaction and bill the traveler at the end of the month or a specified period.

The use of smart cards or an electronic payment medium can greatly enhance and simplify the use of the total regional system. This would be accomplished by allowing the single card to be used on all bus and rail systems within the region, as well as transit-related parking at rail stations or express bus pick-up points. In the larger transportation context, the same card could be used on toll roads and for auto-related parking within the region.

Smart cards need not be limited to transportation purposes alone. As the country moves towards the cashless society, the same card could be used for simple retail purposes such as convenience purchases, snack foods, or newspapers—both within the transit arena or the larger community.

Standards and interoperability

With multiple subcomponents being integrated in a system or subsequently added to a vehicle, standardizing component interfaces and streamlining the installation of the systems has become a significant issue. With the encouragement of the U.S. Department of Transportation (U.S. DOT), the transit industry—including both the suppliers and the operating agencies—has developed a vehicle area network standard. This standard, J1708, has been adopted by the Society of Automotive Engineers (SAE) and is currently pending adoption by the International Standards Organization as an international standard. J1708 was one of the first national standards to be adopted in the ITS community. A parallel software standard, J1587, has also been adopted by the transit industry.

Most fleet management systems requiring specialized interfaces and customized software are using these standards, and most procurements are requiring J1708 compatibility. This has allowed for interoperability between various equipment suppliers and has allowed a robust competition within the supply side of the industry.

A second effort is that the Transit Communications Interface Profiles seeks to build a consensus for standard data definitions for interfaces and communication protocols. This will allow for more efficient sharing of information among multiple transit systems as well as promoting information-sharing among other transportation systems in the community. To be most effective in an urban community, data should be shared across multiple transportation modes and functions.

Support of regional transportation integration

In addition to the important use of data within the transit property, real-time AVL data supports various regional activities. At transportation information centers or multimodal terminals, AVL data can provide real-time status on bus arrival and departure. This can provide valuable information to travelers at transit transfer points and provide connection protection with other modes (e.g., hold vehicles for passenger making a change from one service to another).

In traffic management centers (TMCs), a transit vehicle acting as a "probe" can provide a valuable tool to measure congestion levels or report traffic incidents. Travel times and therefore congestion can be determined based on bus speed. Accidents or traffic problems can be reported via radio or data systems directly to traffic control centers. These can be used to adjust traffic signals or reroute traffic. Likewise traffic data relayed to the transit dispatch center can assist transit in restoring service that is interrupted due to an incident on the street or freeway.

Data can also be provided to operators of other transportation services such as fire, police, or emergency services, all of whom are interested in the latest information on roadway conditions. Ideally this data would be compiled through a TMC that would make this data available to all emergency services.

Real-time transit data is also a valuable commodity to those private companies that resell data for profit. These companies repackage the data and sell to third parties that disseminate information to the public. These could be various advisory services such as radios or television stations. This could be an ultimate source of revenue to the transit agency.

Other system opportunities

In the last decade, most emphasis on the installation of GPS-based CAD and AVL systems has been fleet management of fixed-route bus operations. More recently, transit agencies have been realizing the benefits of using similar technology on rail- and demand-responsive services and in various collision-avoidance systems.

Rail applications

Light-rail systems and commuter-rail systems operating at-grade on dedicated rights-of-way do not have the same severity of schedule adherence problems as buses. However, the uncertainty of time of arrival is an issue for waiting passengers on rail systems. Customer satisfaction can be greatly enhanced by providing real-time platform information on system delays and arrival and departure times. On-board announcement of next stop and station information is also a passenger convenience.

GPS technologies are being used to track trains and provide real-time train location. This real-time arrival data is now being used in place of static schedule information. Information can be displayed on variable message boards or periodically announced on platforms or in stations.

On commuter rail, systems are being developed to allow real-time arrival information to be accessed through interactive direct-dial telephone or to be accessed through the Internet or fax services. Pager systems are also being developed that automatically page a rider if there are delays on the line used for a daily commute.

On light-rail systems that generally operate in mixed traffic, one significant barrier to service enhancement is the time lost in waiting, along with regular traffic, for a light to change at an intersection. GPS-based vehicle-tracking technology is being used to develop signal priority systems that provide a green signal to the light rail vehicle as it approaches the intersection. Use of these systems is significantly improving the operation of light-rail systems. While granting priority for light-rail vehicles is beginning to be integrated in U.S. cities, it is already commonplace in European communities. Signal priority can be achieved by holding or advancing a green signal as the vehicle approaches the intersection. Implementation of these systems requires close coordination with local traffic departments to balance the effect of vehicle priority on the operation of the entire street network.

Specialized service applications

In addition to fixed-route services, several types of specialized services are provided that operate on variable routes. Demand response services provide a vehicle on a request basis. Generally these requests are made in advance, and individual trips are matched and batched into a routing that is assigned to a vehicle. Algorithms have been developed to allow the batching of the individual trips in a manner that maximizes the use of the vehicle and minimizes the travel times of the individual riders.

During the day there are usually cancellations or changes in requirements that would permit better use of vehicles. However, this requires the ability to know the actual location of all vehicles in the network and a re-batching of the remaining trips. GPS-based vehicle tracking systems, which provide real-time location data on each vehicle, provide the basis for this dynamic routing of vehicles.

It also allows for a more timely service by allowing individuals to call and request a same-day pick up. The ability to create new routings on an almost real-time basis improves the quality of service and reduces the total costs by allowing underused vehicles to be removed from operation.

Flex-route or route-deviation services is another type of service that is enhanced through the use of GPS-based vehicle-location systems. For this service, a traveler would call and request a special pick-up. A vehicle operating on the fixed route would go off route to pick up the passenger and then return to the route. To operate efficiently, this operation requires information on vehicle location, as well as the ability to notify the operator to deviate from the route to the pick-up point. It requires information on schedule adherence and the determination as to whether the vehicle has sufficient time to move off route without seriously affecting the arrival time for passengers waiting downstream on the fixed route. It also requires bus arrival information at stops along the route, allowing passengers to know when the vehicle is going to arrive.

Collision avoidance applications

GPS-based technology is being used to reduce accidents at railroad crossings. In lower density areas outside of the urban core, many commuter rail systems no longer operate in a grade-separated right of way. With advanced location technology, a signal can be sent to lower the gate as the train arrives at intersections. There is also technology being developed that indicates that an emergency vehicle is approaching a crossing and needs priority over the train. The appropriate signal would slow down the train, allowing the emergency vehicle to proceed safely through the intersection. Lastly, technology is being developed that would automatically brake or disengage the power on a vehicle approaching a grade crossing with an oncoming train that is not responding to the signal to stop.

Other types of sensors are being developed to avoid collisions between buses and other vehicles or objects. These technologies include systems that emit warnings or alerts to avoid rear-end collisions and lane-change collisions, and prevent lane or road departure. There are systems that can override operator control of the vehicle in the event of an impending collision, or they can provide totally automated operation of the vehicle.

Implementation

Various processes are currently being used by transit agencies to purchase advanced-technology fleet management systems. These purchases are generally done in conjunction with a new radio system procurement or as a special procurement using an existing radio system. Purchases can be made directly by a transit agency through a special procurement, or a more recent trend is to purchase various system components as part of the original bus purchase with a bus manufacturer (original equipment manufacturer [OEM]).

Three different models are being employed for procurement of fleet management systems:

- System-wide installation of a comprehensive system
- Phased installation of a comprehensive system
- Installation of stand-alone components

System-wide installation of a comprehensive system

The first model is a system-wide installation of a comprehensive CAD and AVL system. In this case, a suite of equipment comprised of multiple subsystem components is installed on all vehicles in the fleet. This model is generally used by larger properties that see more benefit to full installation than smaller properties.

By way of example, Portland, Oregon (Tri-Met) is an area of 1.2 million population. They operate 800 vehicles with an annual ridership of 65 million trips (Federal Transit Administration, U.S. DOT 1996). They have purchased a full CAD and AVL system for all fixed-route and paratransit vehicles.

Another area, the city of Oakland, California (outside of San Francisco), has a population of 2.2 million. They operate 700 vehicles with an annual ridership of 62 million trips. They have purchased a full CAD and AVL system for their property, which also includes passenger counters, voice annunciation and next-stop destination signs. Other systems that have followed a similar path are found in Denver, Colorado; Buffalo, New York; and Ann Arbor, Michigan.

Phased installation of a comprehensive system

The second model is a phased installation of a comprehensive system. In this case the equipment suite is installed on a portion of the fleet, typically using all vehicles out of one garage.

By way of example, New York City, the largest transit agency in the United States, with a population of 16 million, is following a phased implementation. New York City Transit operates about 4,500 vehicles with a ridership of 1.9 billion; however, they are proceeding with a pilot project covering 170 vehicles. The pilot also includes a passenger information system that sends information to bus shelters announcing arrival time.

Atlanta, Georgia, a city with a population of 2.2 million, operates 750 vehicles with a ridership of 143 million trips. They implemented a program of 250 vehicles in conjunction with the 1996 Winter Olympics. The program also included passenger counter and passenger information. Another large transit agency in Chicago, a city with a population of 7 million, operating a fleet of 1,300 vehicles with an annual ridership of 442 million trips, is using a combination of two processes. The incident management system is being installed on the total system. However, the fleet management system is being installed on only 300 vehicles in the first phase.

Installation of individual stand-alone components

The third model is installation of individual stand-alone components. In this case a stand-alone system (or systems) is initiated on the entire fleet or a portion of the fleet. These include systems such as voice annunciation or passenger counters, or a new radio system with CAD capability but no AVL. This appears to be a new procurement method developing in conjunction with the purchase of new buses through an OEM.

Procurement issues

A number of factors that affect the implementation of fleet management systems, such as availability of funding, agency procurement practices, acceptability of innovation within the agency, comfort level and adaptability of in-house staff to work with new technologies, previous experience with AVL demonstrations or pilot projects and numerous external forces.

While there is no right or wrong approach to implementing these systems, the agency should develop an overall plan specifying the full system functionality that eventually will be desired. This plan should be followed to ensure the cost-effective phased integration of the system. This is especially needed when individual system components are purchased over several years.

Each system component requires a control device, and most require GPS-based location data and a central processing computer. Therefore, it is most cost-effective for the transit agency to ensure that the first system component installed provides the flexibility to allow other components to be integrated using the same control head, location device and computer. Failure to do so will result in multiple pieces of equipment being installed, which will complicate the operation of the equipment and add unnecessary additional costs.

Table 7–4 illustrates the potential problem. Seven of the eight most used components require control displays, three require a computer, and three or four require GPS receivers and antenna. If not planned properly, separate and uncoordinated implementation will result in unnecessary cost and unnecessary complexity.

Table 7–1
Stand-Alone System Component Requirements
Source: Larry Schulman.

Component	Keypad/Display or Controls	AVL Computer	GPS Receiver and Antenna
Radio control	Yes		
AVL and two-way messaging	Yes	Yes	Yes
Public address	Yes		
Voice and visual annunciation	Yes	Yes	Yes
Destination sign	Yes	Shared	Shared
Automatic passenger counter	Yes	Yes	Yes
Video recording			Possibly
Farebox	Yes		
Summary	7 keypad/display units	3 AVL computers	3–4 GPS receivers and antennas

Unfortunately, some systems are proceeding incrementally and may be unnecessarily duplicating equipment and paying unnecessary dollars, or conversely may be installing equipment that will have to be subsequently replaced. The objective should be to procure an initial system that has the capacity to be incrementally upgraded and to embark on a path that allows for full system integration. Not every stand-alone system provides that flexibility. Not planning for the full system in advance will be a very costly mistake to a transit agency.

Benefits

There has been a very predictable outcome with respect to determining benefits within the transit industry. As always, the transit agency, as a public body, must justify its investments by explaining the benefits of the new technology. While rigorous data are still being collected, the efficiencies resulting from GPS-based AVL applications are being reported around the nation. The major benefits that have been reported from transit agencies are as follows:

- improved customer service in terms of increased service reliability, improved safety and security and improved bus status information;
- improved operational efficiency in terms of increased flexibility of assignments, faster response to emergency situations, improved efficiency in tracking on-time performance and increased capability in handling grievances;
- increased ridership.

In a study recently conducted by the Transportation Research Board (TRB) under the Transit Cooperative Research Program, transit agencies were asked their objectives in initiating an AVL system (TRB 1997). These objectives were as follows:

- Schedule adherence was reported by 56 percent of the respondents.
- Safety and security was reported by 48 percent of the respondents.
- Performance monitoring was reported by 40 percent of the respondents.
- Public information was reported by 40 percent of the respondents.
- Improved communications was reported by 20 percent of the respondents.
- Improved fleet management was reported by 20 percent of the respondents.
- Improved management systems was reported by 8 percent of the respondents.

Those objectives perceived to be most important to the agencies in implementing these systems are very similar to the benefits that agencies are reporting as resulting from the implementation of their systems. The goal of the transit industry is to better use the existing infrastructure and the current transportation network to serve the increased demand for transportation. Transit systems are employing innovative approaches and advanced technology to coordinate and enhance the existing transportation services. These services can be summarized in several categories:

- fleet management systems that improve the efficiency, reliability and safety of transit systems, thus making them more attractive to prospective riders, transit operators and the municipalities they serve;
- traveler information systems that facilitate traveler decision-making by providing information on multiple transportation modes through a variety of media, including telephones, monitors, cable television, variable message signs, kiosks and personal computers;
- electronic fare payment systems that employ electronic communication, data processing, and data storage techniques aimed at the use of smart cards for transit, parking and other potential uses;
- transportation priority systems that integrate fleet management systems and centralized traffic signal control systems to detect approaching buses or emergency vehicles and preempt traffic signal operation, allowing the vehicles to pass through intersections more efficiently.

While difficult to measure, a recent study conducted for the U.S. DOT indicated that implementation of these innovative systems is estimated to save the transit industry between $3.8 to $7.4 billion in the next 10 years (The Volpe Center 1996b). Approximately 44 percent of the total benefits are estimated to accrue from fleet management systems, 34 percent from electronic fare payment systems and 21 percent from traveler information systems. On an annualized basis it is estimated that transit will save between $550 million to $1.1 billion per year.

References

Federal Transit Administration, U.S. Department of Transportation. 1996. *Transit Profiles: The Thirty Largest Agencies* (December). Washington, D.C.: FTA, U.S. DOT.

Transportation Research Board. 1997. *AVL Systems for Bus Transit, TCRP Synthesis 24.* Washington, D.C.: TRB.

The Volpe Center. 1996a. *Advanced Public Transportation Systems Deployment in the U.S.* (August). Washington, D.C.: U.S. Department of Transportation.

The Volpe Center. 1996b. *Benefits Assessment of Advanced Public Transportation Systems* (June 30). Washington, D.C.: U.S. Department of Transportation.

Endnote

1. Loran-C was originally developed to provide radio navigation service for U.S. coastal waters and was later expanded to include complete coverage of the continental United States as well as most of Alaska. In the early days of land-based vehicle fleet tracking, it was adapted for bus vehicle tracking.

BY Lawrence Yermack • President • PB Farradyne Inc.
Robert E. Fielding • Managing Engineer • PB Farradyne Inc.
Phillip Leshinsky • Director of Toll Facilities • PB Farradyne Inc.

ELECTRONIC TOLL AND TRAFFIC MANAGEMENT

Introduction

Nomenclature is always a challenge in a technical field and especially so with emerging technology. This chapter could as easily be entitled automatic vehicle identification (AVI) or electronic toll collection (ETC) or even dedicated short-range communication (DSRC). Today the term "DSRC" is gaining acceptance because it refers to the idea of short-range communication but does so in a context that allows it to be seen as applicable to more than toll collection and to incorporate commercial vehicle applications as well. Instead this chapter is entitled "Electronic Toll and Traffic Management" (ETTM) because this is the term most widely used by toll operators to describe the application that allows vehicles to pass through a toll plaza, without stopping, but allowing for vehicle identification and the payment of the toll. It is also a term used interchangeably with ETC.

In the late 1980s when this technology was first deployed on toll facilities (first in Norway and then later in the United States), it was known as AVI. This is, in effect, what the technology does: automatically identify a vehicle. This term was eventually dropped by the International Bridge Tunnel and Turnpike Association, the worldwide association of toll operators. They felt that the word "identification" could imply an invasion of privacy. Thus they adopted the acronym ETTM to describe both the toll aspect of the technology as well as its applicability to traffic management. Before describing how ETTM works, lets review why ETTM is desirable. ETTM offers a range of benefits to patrons, toll operators and to society in general.

Reduced congestion

A typical toll lane operated by a toll collector accepting the patrons' toll in cash and making change as necessary can process on the order of 350 vehicles per hour. An automatic coin machine-equipped lane can process on the order of 600 vehicles per hour. This same rate can be achieved with an exact toll of say $1 and a toll collector. Prior to ETTM, the highest processing rate achieved was in the range of 900 vehicles an hour, which combines an automatic coin machine with a toll collector who stands in the lane slightly in advance of the machine, collects the toll, makes change if necessary and puts the toll in the coin machine. ETTM-dedicated lanes can process 1,200 vehicles an hours, or double the coin machine rate. Beyond that ETTM offers the ability to design a toll plaza without a tollbooth, allowing for nonstop traffic at open road speeds. Thus a lane of nonstop traffic can have tolls collected at the theoretic maximum capacity of a lane of traffic or more than 2,000 vehicles per hour. These increases in plaza throughput translate directly into reduced plaza congestions, as vehicles waiting to pay their toll pass through the plaza without stopping.

Less construction

Toll plazas are designed to provide sufficient tollbooths for the peak hours, usually the morning and evening travel times. As traffic increases, more tollbooths are needed. There are toll plazas with as many as 6 lanes of toll collection for each lane of highway traffic. Consequently the traditional toll plaza is quite wide, requiring considerable real estate and expense. ETTM allows for much smaller toll plazas, and reduced construction, as increased traffic is processed by ETTM. Traditionally toll plazas are built with the expectation that they will be enlarged over the years as traffic increases. Today toll plazas can be built with the expectation that they will not need to be expanded as the percentage of traffic using ETTM can be increased over time and the percentage of traffic paying conventionally is reduced.

Less pollution

While the science of truck and car emissions is best left to other texts, the basic principle can be articulated here. Vehicles at idle produce more emissions than vehicles in motion. ETTM by reducing congestion at the toll plaza consequently also can reduce vehicle emissions and thus reduce air pollution.

Improved customer convenience

The singularly most significant reason for the popularity of ETTM is the customer convenience it provides. In New York City, in the first year ETTM was available one million tags were sold. ETTM allows patrons to drive through a toll plaza without the need for cash, coin, tokens, or tickets; and without the need to roll down the window and without the need to stop. We can measure the time savings based on before and after queue times and can translate this time savings into dollars based on average wages for an area. This calculation will not explain the magnitude of the popularity of ETC. The two measurable savings to patrons are time and in some cases money through a discount program, however intangibles also enter into the consumer decision.

Improved revenue security

Toll facilities to the extent that they operate a cash business need to be concerned about leakage to dishonest employees. Even the best revenue control systems are subject to some losses of cash. ETTM simply takes the cash out of the process, replacing it with an electronic transaction that is settled for from the lane in a data processing facility. Toll operators can eliminate the nagging problem of cash losses with this application.

Better information

Prior to the advent of ETTM, toll collection was an aggregate or wholesale activity. What is meant by that is: tolls were collected from a number of anonymous patrons and deposited each night as a total dollar amount representing X transactions. While the total deposit represented a number of individual transactions, there was no real data on each individual transaction. ETTM has converted toll collection to a retail business with each patron identified by name and address with an account profile and a travel history. The toll operator now has a great deal of information on individual customers and their travel behavior. This information can be used to better plan the future activities of the operator.

There is another side to the availability of all this customer data and that is the potential for an invasion of privacy. Most toll operators have adopted policies to protect the privacy of their patrons and will not use the data for commercial purposes and even provide some protection from other government agency inquires.

Improved safety

The safety of patrons and employees on the toll plaza is of paramount significance. ETTM introduces new traffic patterns that could affect the safety profile of the facility, because it often mixes nonstop traffic with vehicles stopped and queued at the plaza. While the safety record for ETTM has been good, special attention is necessary. On the other hand, the data available from ETTM on traffic patterns will allow operators to more effectively deploy personnel for plaza operations.

Toll basics

Barrier vs. closed systems

Tolled roads and crossings have two generic toll collection techniques: open (barrier) systems collect tolls at one of the more discrete points along the roadway that allow the vehicle to proceed past that point and closed (ticket) systems collect tolls based on distance traveled when the vehicle leaves the tolled roadway. Without ETC, both forms require contact between the vehicle's driver and the staff or equipment of the road so that money can be paid, a charge card can be read, or a ticket can be taken and then surrendered. These actions slow traffic, inconvenience drivers, add to congestion and pollution, increase wear and tear on vehicles and stationary equipment and are labor-intensive. Also, because money is changing hands, security systems and auditing functions must be conducted to assure the correct flow of revenue from the users to the owners (authorities).

With ETC, no physical contact is required between the vehicle or its driver and the roadway staff or equipment and all these undesirable effects are eliminated or reduced. Users of the tolled roadways establish accounts with the owners. Then, at a barrier, the vehicle is identified and the toll is charged to its account. And in a "ticket" system the vehicle is identified both when it enters and when it leaves the roadway and an appropriate toll is recorded in the account. The technology that allows the vehicle to be identified in this contactless manner and that makes ETC possible is known as AVI. When augmented with other technologies such as automatic vehicle classification (AVC), video enforcement systems (VES) and modern data processing, ETC becomes practical.

Channeled vs. open highway systems

Likewise, tolled roads and crossings have two generic physical configurations in the locations where tolls are collected. In toll collection modes requiring contact, vehicles are guided (channeled) into lanes at which the toll is paid, a ticket is taken or surrendered, or a charge card is read. In contactless systems, channeling may still be used, but unrestricted travel on an open highway can still be tolled effectively, although the system architecture along the roadway becomes more complex to accommodate the higher vehicle speeds and the vehicles that straddle or are changing lanes when they pass a reader. Channeling is the most common arrangement because ETC and other contact toll collection methods are usually used on the same roadway and the mixture of channeled and unchanneled traffic creates unwanted traffic control and safety problems.

AVI

AVI technology is the key to ETC. Since ETC is based upon the charging of tolls to pre-existing accounts, accurate association of vehicles (and therefore the types of the vehicles) with accounts is mandatory. AVI works in conjunction with other toll collection devices and subsystems in a lane (channeled configuration) or along the open highway to provide this vehicle association.

Most modern AVI products comprise a radio frequency transponder (also known as a tag) mounted on a vehicle and a stationary electronics unit, usually called a reader, that activates the transponder when it appears in the reader's vicinity. The reader drives a radio frequency antenna that directly communicates with the tag. The transponder contains, at a minimum, a unique identification code that it transmits to the reader. The in-lane system (of which the reader is a part) attempts to match this code to a list of codes it has previously stored; and, upon achieving the match, it records the passage of the vehicle as normal, for which an appropriate toll is charged, or abnormal, for which other tolls are charged or other actions are taken. Similarly, a failure to match the tag code with a prestored code results in an abnormal passage. In most ETC systems, the charging of tolls and the taking of other actions is performed by the other devices with which the reader works, rather than by the reader itself. Figure 8–1 shows a typical architecture for an ETC lane.

Figure 8–1. ETC lane architecture.
Source: PB Farradyne Inc.

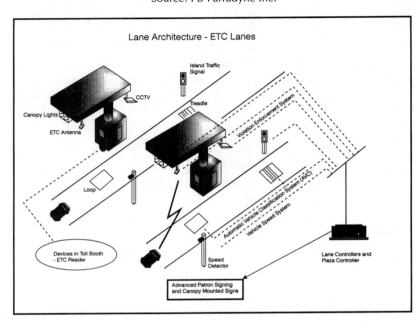

As described in the next section, an account may allow the use of more than one tag, each of which is associated with its own class of vehicle, and may allow the transfer of tags between vehicles of the same class. Because vehicle class is the primary determinant of the toll, accurate identification of the tag through its unique code (and therefore of the class of the corresponding vehicle) is the minimum requirement for AVI, although other information is typically stored in the tag and exchanged with the reader.

Functional requirements of transponders

Operating principles

Designs of equipment for contactless passage of ETC tag-equipped vehicles universally use radio frequency communication between tags and readers. At presently used frequencies (915 MHz in the United states and 2.5 GHz or 5.8 GHz elsewhere), the radiation pattern of the reader antennas is compact enough to screen out most unwanted radio frequency radiation, and the influence of extraneous radiation fields that penetrate the beam patterns has been largely eliminated by careful design of the devices. In addition, the power of the radiated field from the reader is quite low, because the distance from the antennas to the tag is short, and it does not interfere with other systems operating at the selected frequencies. Since tags only respond to interrogations from readers when the tag has arrived in the reader beam pattern, their radiated power levels are much lower than from the reader, they do not radiate at all when not in the pattern and they do not interfere with other systems either. Also, measurements of radiation power levels have been taken on tags and readers from several manufacturers and found to be well within the prescribed safety levels of the United States.

Transponder power sources

Transponders require power to communicate with readers and to perform any other internal operations. Two transponder power sources are in current use. Those known as Active have miniature batteries permanently embedded in the transponders, while those known as Backscatter derive their power from the radiation from the reader. These techniques are mutually exclusive in current product lines. The batteries currently in Active transponders have guaranteed lives of at least five years, after which the transponders become useless and must be replaced. The Backscatter transponders have tag-to-reader range limitations that require closer control of roadway equipment location and orientation than for Active transponders.

Readability and tag positioning

Because the beam pattern of the reader is narrow and its radiated power is low, the location of the tag in or on a vehicle must be controlled or communication may be unreliable. The conventional location for tags is inside the windshield on its centerline near its upper edge. The tag is mounted to the windshield with velcro-like strips. The location need not be precisely controlled because the designs are somewhat tolerant of translational and angular variations. However, some vehicle configurations and equipment prevent reliable communication, including vertical (rather than sloped) windshields and those coated to reduce solar heat transmission into the cabin. For such vehicles, tags designed for mounting at the front bumper are available. These tags are compatible with overhead antennas, but also work with antennas embedded in the lane. However, windshield tags do not work at all with embedded antennas. Systems can be configured using both types of antennas in a lane, but system logic is required to prevent unwanted antenna interaction or corruption of data.

In addition, some tags are mounted on the roofs of truck cabs to overcome incompatible windshield angles or coatings. Special brackets are used to properly orient the tags, which are compatible only with overhead antennas.

Transponder types

The earliest transponders were read-only devices that were permanently encoded with a minimum amount of data (including a unique identification number). Each time a transponder was interrogated by a reader, the tag would transmit all the encoded data. They are known as Type I transponders and they can be used for most ETC applications in conjunction with appropriate system logic and data processing.

Later transponder designs, known as Type II transponders, use read-write technology that allow a reader to "write" data into the transponder's scratch pad memory. Then, at the next interrogation by a reader, the entire contents of the tag (permanent data plus scratchpad contents) are transmitted to the reader. This cycle can be repeated continuously without limit. This type of transponder finds maximum usefulness in closed toll systems because the entrance point on a roadway can be stored in the tag upon entry onto the roadway and read out upon exit. Then, the system can compute the correct toll based on the distance traveled without the need for the entry and exit points to communicate with each other, thereby reducing the communication load on the system.

For each transponder type, compatible readers must be used. While tags of both types may be used on a given roadway, this is unusual. Currently, most toll collection applications use Type II transponders because they provide much greater freedom in system design and growth potential, but Type I transponders remain in operation in the field.

The most advanced form of transponders is Type III, which includes both the read-write capability and a data processing capability. This allows some of the back-office accounting functions to be performed "on the tag." While theoretically possible, practical considerations such as the need for the AVI subsystem to interact with the AVC and VES subsystems in the lane controller (the data processor associated with the toll collection lane that collects, correlates and transmits vehicle and toll transaction data upstream to a central data processing facility) and the need for assurance of and audibility of revenue-generating transaction information, has limited their use for these purposes.

For all transponder types and their corresponding readers, error avoidance (error detection) techniques are used to assure accurate data transmission. Various forms of data integrity encoding, multiple read cycles and read-write-read again cycles are some of the techniques employed in current products available in the market place. The readers embody the sophisticated error detection processing in Types I and II technologies, but Type III transponders may also have error detection capability.

Standardization

The mobility of modern societies assures that many transponder-equipped vehicles will travel roadways equipped with readers of other manufactures. Usually, such tags and readers are incompatible so no tag reading occurs. Public agencies, authorities, industry associations and public interests all encourage widespread compatibility for the convenience of the motoring public and efficiency of highway commerce. At least two organizations in the United States have undertaken effective AVI technology standardization strategies. In the northeast, the Interagency Group (IAG), a consortium of roadway and crossing operating authorities, has selected the Mark IV Industries product line for use on all IAG roadways and crossings. This is an active technology using Type II tags and enjoys widespread use on tolled roads and crossings from Massachusetts to Virginia and westward as far as Illinois, with millions of tags in use. In contrast, California has established an open standard known as Title 21 that is based on a backscatter Type II technology for use throughout the state. In each case, use of a common AVI technology has enhanced motorist mobility and convenience, as anticipated.

The economic advantages of standardization extend to:

- the lower tag and reader prices due to economies of scale,
- the stability and consistency of the performance of the AVI devices,
- the increased ease of integration of the AVI technology into roadway systems due to the familiarity of designers with the technical characteristics of the technology, and
- a more orderly evolution of the technology to more capable and advanced versions, although at the expense of the speed of evolution a more disorderly technical environment would enjoy in the absence of standardization.

Other applications

AVI technology provides other opportunities to enhance private or commercial travel. Since the windshield tags are both vehicle-mounted and removable from their velcro strips, obvious additional uses such as for fuel purchases, parking, car washing and miscellaneous purchases at convenience stores along streets and highways are frequently considered; but little if any of these have been implemented. A major impediment is that accounts with toll authorities must meet stringent revenue protection requirements established by bond-holders, and a variety of nontoll collection applications using a toll collection account might impair the security of the toll revenue.

A burgeoning application for AVI technology is for the preclearance of trucks, a system that avoids the need for trucks to be weighed at weighing stations along a highway. Trucks are weighed once and their weight and other data is entered into a Type II tag. Subsequently, when the truck passes a reader installed for that purpose along a highway, the system "clears" the truck to continue without stopping, thereby saving the driver and the truck time and the truck operator money. At least two such systems are in operation in different pats of the country and their use is spreading. AVI tags are usable for both ETC and preclearance applications, as long as the data storage requirements of each do not interfere with the operation of the other.

State highway and transportation departments can better manage the traffic in their area when better information regarding traffic density and speed and obstructions to traffic flow is available in real time. With many tags for ETC in circulation, they can be used as probes to sample the traffic at various points to provide the wanted information without interference with the ETC application.

Toll and vehicle classification

The are many reasons for charging different tolls for different vehicles on a roadway or at a crossing. The most common reason is to relate the toll to some measure of the damage or deterioration the vehicle causes to the road. Because heavier vehicles have greater effects, they are charged higher. Other reasons often used are cultural or political. In one state, recreational vehicles are charged a lower toll than comparable trucks; and in another, buses pay less than cars. Sometimes, place of residence determines the toll, in part. Usually, the damage and deterioration reason is combined with one or more cultural or political reasons in the assignment of tolls.

With the variety of tolling approaches and long before the advent of ETC, several authorities established individual, formal toll tables that relate tolls to physical vehicle characteristics, vehicle usage, or other cultural or political factors. The tables often required human toll collectors to make intelligent and sometimes subtle distinctions when assigning and collecting tolls in a lane. Once established and in use for a period of time, the toll tables become fixed elements in the society and have the force of law and are similarly hard to change. When ETC systems are deployed, they usually must incorporate the toll tables extant; it is unusual for the toll tables to be changed at those times.

Vehicle weight is universally agreed to be a major determinant of the rate at which roadways deteriorate in use. However, weighing a vehicle requires it to come to a stop on a truck scale, or that it be weighed while it is in motion. Weigh-in-motion devices (WIM) are relatively new, always expensive and are not used for routine toll collection purposes. Rather, over the years, the number of axles and the number of wheels on each axle have been used by most authorities as a reasonably accurate measure of weight.

Classification

The anticipated widespread use of ETC required that authorities formalize a vehicle classification formulation that would allow each authority to charge a correct toll to each vehicle using common vehicle features that could be observed by instrumentation and computer processed without requiring human participation. A leader in establishing such a formulation has been the aforementioned IAG; and other authorities use their own, comparable formulations. The IAG recognized that some vehicle features are easy to reliably detect by instrumentation, but others are harder. They also recognized that nonvehicle, political, or cultural features would be largely impossible to detect by instrumentation. Accordingly, the IAG's formulation concentrates on the vehicle characteristics that can be measured with devices and computer processing that may be either already field deployed or might be deployed in the foreseeable future.

Matching

When a patron enrolls in an ETC system, that person's vehicle(s) is described to the toll collection authority, which in turn assigns a vehicle class to each vehicle and adds that class to the record containing the transponder identification. A file of all such records (which is often voluminous because it contains information for every transponder in the ETC system) is stored in each ETC-capable lane in the authority's entire roadway and/or crossing system. Subsequently, when a vehicle appears in a toll collection lane, an AVC system installed there will take measurements of the vehicle and using programmed instructions it will convert these measurements into a vehicle class. In real time, the ETC system in the lane will read the transponder identification number, access the vehicle classification assigned to the transponder and compare it with the classification determined by the AVC. If they match, the toll corresponding to the classification is inserted into the patrons' records. If the classifications do not match, further action is needed because a mismatch may indicate misuse of the transponder (such as an attempt to use a transponder with a lower classification to pay a toll for a vehicle for which a higher toll is warranted).

Automatic vehicle classification

Most toll systems employ some form of AVC in order to determine the vehicle class and corresponding toll. AVC is typically comprised of one or more devices employed in the lane to gather information on the passing vehicle. AVC systems are deployed on a facility-by-facility basis and cannot be characterized by a standard configuration. AVC systems are selected to meet the needs of each individual agency.

For manual toll collection, typically some form of axle counting device is used to record vehicle axles as a check on the classification inputs entered by a toll collector. Generally any other vehicle characteristics that need to be recorded are done manually by the toll collector. For ETTM lanes, especially those with no toll collection personnel, these additional vehicle characteristics need to be determined and recorded in an automated fashion with no manual intervention. Various advanced techniques, employing complex algorithms receiving data from optical, acoustic, or video devices, have been used individually and in combination to meet the needs of individual agencies.

Two important elements must be determined by the AVC system: vehicle separation and vehicle axles. Vehicle separation allows the system to "frame" transactions, ensuring that collected vehicle characteristics are related to a single vehicle or physically attached combination for determination of the corresponding toll. Vehicle axles remain one of the most common determinants of a toll.

AVC state-of-the-art

Two common approaches for the determination of vehicle separation are inductive loops and optical sensors. Loops are cut into the roadway surface and detect inductance changes created in the magnetic field above the loop when a vehicle passes. Because loops sense an area of coverage, they can be satisfactorily employed in high-speed installations where vehicles are widely separated but are problematic for lower speed locations where vehicles are closely spaced. Micro-loop probes reduce the coverage area, but they remain susceptible on low-speed installations. Optical sensors, using infrared technology not visible to the human eye, offer true point detection and are advantageous in slow speed locations. Typically a diagonal beam or light curtain passes infrared light between a transmitter and receiver pair allowing any interruption or obstruction to be sensed as it is passed between the pair. The light curtain, by virtue of its multiple beams, provides accurate detection of trailer hitches and other connections of combination vehicles. Overhead optical sensors are also in use that employ a transmitter and receiver to reflect infrared light off surfaces below and based on the time of return determine the absence or presence of a passing vehicle. Acoustic sensor devices, transmitting sound waves, have been employed in a similar manner with less success due to the air turbulence created by passing vehicles.

There are numerous axle-counting devices available. The simplest forms are the pneumatic tube and piezo-electric sensor. While these can successfully count axles, neither has been able to sustain the wear and tear of the continuous stop-and-go toll lane environment. Inductive loops and logic algorithms have been used with limited success because they are unable to sense a point. In pavement full metal framed 2- and 4-strip treadles have become the most common and most accurate axle-counting devices. The multiple strips allow the treadle to sense both forward and reverse direction and provide redundancy if an individual strip fails. Alternative configurations of treadles can also be employed to detect dual tires on passing vehicles. Other nonintrusive (not in pavement) technologies are being advanced with some success. The overhead infrared sensors previously discussed can be used to infer number of axles (based on length and height of profile) and are also being developed for a "side-fired" application that may more readily be able determine vehicle axles. Lastly, video technologies are being experimented with in other ITS applications and may be available some-day for AVC. Images of vehicles can currently be captured for video enforcement, and as camera resolution and image recognition software improve, accurate vehicle classification may ultimately be possible at a reasonable cost.

Enforcement

The migration to ETTM lanes, both through toll plazas and open road type tolling, has increased the need for enforcement. No longer is it necessary to stop and complete the toll transaction in cash. The availability of cash-less, nonattended lanes provides an outlet for toll evasion that has never previously existed. Lanes may be equipped with the traditional violation light and buzzer to alert plaza-stationed police, but continuous 24-hour presence is not cost effective. An automated VES, or the appearance of one, is an effective means of reducing violations.

The choice and extent of VES to be deployed at a facility is dependent on the desired result of incorporating VES. Two major functions of VES emerge: violation deterrence and violation enforcement. Violation deterrence refers to the ability of the system to be "perceived" by drivers as a mechanism that will capture toll evasions and allow an agency to adjudicate the offense. Violation enforcement refers to the ability of the system to "actually" capture and adjudicate toll evasions. The chosen approach is based on a number of factors that each agency must address including legislative authority, capital costs, processing costs and adjudication costs. With an appropriate fine structure, "actual" violation enforcement can generate significant revenue.

A VES typically consists of an in-lane camera and computer to store captured images. It is the presence of the camera that provides part of the "perceived" violation deterrence. In-lane captures need to be closely timed to insure that the violating vehicle is the vehicle image captured. Some agencies provide images that capture an island traffic signal red indication or other violation notification within the image frame. Compressed images are then forwarded to a processing location for further analysis. At this location, images may be processed by Optical Character Recognition to discern the license plate numbers and then manually to append additional appropriate information about the violation or the evading vehicle registration, obtained from account records or the local Registry of Motor Vehicles. Systems can be configured to handle multiple processing (e.g., appeals, nonpayments), by tracking an individual toll evasion through to closeout.

Depending on legislative authority and the agencies' needs, back-end processing can vary dramatically. The system may be designed and employed only to record and track multiple offenders so that warning notices can be sent. This also can constitute a portion of the "perceived" violation deterrence. Habitual offenders that are not responsive to the warnings may be targeted at a particular plaza by the on-site police presence. Or the system may be designed and employed to fully process each violation to the maximum extent, by sending images of the infraction with administrative fees or fines attached. Legislation may permit the agency to adjudicate each violation or it may be a police function processed through the criminal court system. Figure 8–2 shows typical data flows in a violation enforcement system.

Figure 8–2. Violation enforcement system data flows.
Source: PB Farradyne Inc.

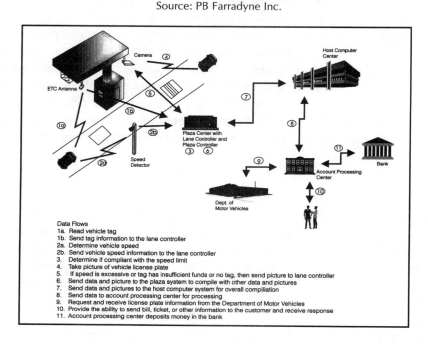

Data Flows
1a. Read vehicle tag
1b. Send tag information to the lane controller
2a. Determine vehicle speed
2b. Send vehicle speed information to the lane controller
3. Determine if compliant with the speed limit
4. Take picture of vehicle license plate
5. If speed is excessive or tag has insufficient funds or no tag, then send picture to lane controller
6. Send data and picture to the plaza system to compile with other data and pictures
7. Send data and pictures to the host computer system for overall compiliation
8. Send data to account processing center for processing
9. Request and receive license plate information from the Department of Motor Vehicles
10. Provide the ability to send bill, ticket, or other information to the customer and receive response
11. Account processing center deposits money in the bank

Nonreal-time processing

Large ETC systems have many patrons and transponders active at any time, and they process high volumes of traffic each day. As an example, in the New York City area, the ETC system of the Metropolitan Transportation Authority Bridges and Tunnels has over 2,000,000 transponders in circulation; and almost 500,000 ETC transactions occur daily. The resulting data that is generated each day, comprising the tolls being accrued, the violation images to be interpreted and the updating of the patrons accounts, requires powerful and sophisticated data-processing capabilities. This capability is provided in back-office operations that are often called customer service centers. These centers are networked with:

- each ETC-capable lane in the system to collect the data on each vehicle transit,
- the toll plazas to provide operating personnel with information to observe the system's operation and to maintain it,
- the banks that handle the checks or credit card debits that the patron uses to pay the authority for the tolls he or she has accrued,
- the various departments in the authority that are responsible for auditing the system and the flow of revenue, and
- the local department of motor vehicles so that license numbers of violating vehicles can be traced using sophisticated wide area and local area networks that include fall-back modes of operation to allow continuous operation and flow of traffic even in cases of communication failures.

Figure 8–3. Typical data flows for account processing.
Source: PB Farradyne Inc.

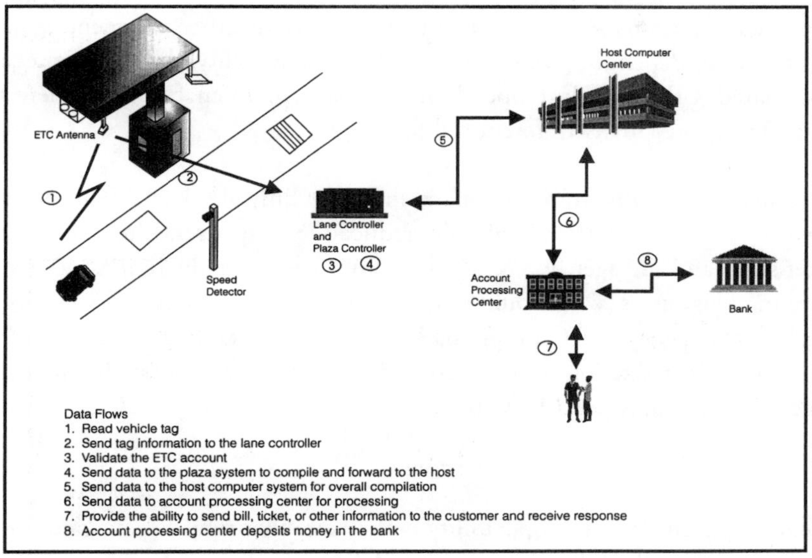
Host Computer Center
ETC Antenna
Lane Controller and Plaza Controller
Speed Detector
Account Processing Center
Bank
Data Flows
1. Read vehicle tag
2. Send tag information to the lane controller
3. Validate the ETC account
4. Send data to the plaza system to compile and forward to the host
5. Send data to the host computer system for overall compilation
6. Send data to account processing center for processing
7. Provide the ability to send bill, ticket, or other information to the customer and receive response
8. Account processing center deposits money in the bank

Interoperability

When two or more toll agencies have the same or compatible ETC technology (the ability to read the other agency's tags with your deployed readers), they have the ability to be interoperable. Interoperability occurs when customers from two or more toll agencies are able to use one tag to pay the various tolls at all of the agencies. This in turn creates a seamless transportation system for the drivers.

Degrees of interoperability

Once toll agencies have the same or compatible ETC technology, the implementation of interoperability depends on making their back office process reciprocal. There are four distinct degrees of interoperability, dependent on the proportion of integration of the back offices of the toll agencies. The degrees of interoperability are:

- *One tag*—Customers can use their tag at more than one agency, but they must open accounts (companion accounts) at each agency. They need to fund all of their accounts and they would receive separate statements. They would have to deal with each respective service center to conduct any business.
- *One service center*—In addition to the functionality under "one tag," customers would also be able to use the service centers of either toll agency to perform any activity on their account. This is without regard as to which agency the customer's account is with.
- *One account*—A customer would open an account with one toll agency and this is the only account that is needed. The opening of this account entitles the customer to all of the privileges of each toll agency. The customer will only have to fund this one account, as the tolls from all of the agencies would be charged to this account. The customer would receive a single statement that would list all of the toll charges without regard to the agency.
- *One back-end system*—While not necessarily noticeable to the customers, it is the next logical step for the toll agencies to take.

Benefits

The benefits of interoperability to the customers are obvious. They receive all of the benefits of ETC (e.g., saving of time, convenience, automatic replenishment, statements) at other toll agencies with little or no additional effort. In addition, depending on the degree of interoperability, these customers may also receive agency discounts associated with ETC. Interoperability is a particular benefit to commercial vehicles and commuters who often travel over many different toll facilities.

The toll agencies also receive benefits from interoperability. Not only are they able to offer additional service to their customers with little effort. They can actually reduce their expenses. Interoperability increases an agency's ETC market share and the agency receives the additional cost reduction associated with ETC. This is due to the increase in casual users, who would only occasionally use that agency's facilities and would probably not be part of that agency's ETC program. Additionally, depending on the degree of interoperability, the agency may receive cost reductions due to economies of scale. If they are sharing functions (and costs) with another toll agency, they can process ETC transactions less expensively.

The process

The toll agencies' main concern with interoperability is to insure that they will be paid for the toll. Toward that regard, they have developed the following interoperability process:

1. The toll agencies involved will sign an Memorandum of Understanding guaranteeing to pay each other for all toll transactions by each other's valid customers incurred on each other's facilities.
2. Each day the agencies' back offices will forward a file of all of their valid tags (tag validation file).
3. Each back office will incorporate the other agency's tag file into their own tag validation file and upload it to their plazas.
4. Each agency's plaza software treats the other agency's valid tags as valid and records the toll transactions.
5. The other agency's customer's transaction is downloaded to the back office with the regular transaction files.
6. Transactions by another agency's customers are segregated out, and a separate datafile of these transactions is created and sent to the other agency's back office.
7. The other agency's back office will process these transactions against their customer's accounts and create a report of how much revenue is due the first agency.
8. There will be a financial settlement done at agreed upon, specified intervals between the agencies and back offices (depending on where the toll revenue resides).

There are variations as to the system architecture within which these datafile (tag validation and transaction files) transfers take place. The E-ZPass Interagency Group has each agency's respective back office transfer these files to the other agency's back office. In California, the files are transferred to and downloaded from a central server. The advantage of the California model is that the agency's back office is only uploading and downloading once, to a single component. The E-ZPass can be particularly time consuming and cumbersome when there are more than three agencies that are interoperable.

Issues

Most of the more complicated issues in implementing interoperability involve the creation of policies and procedures on which all of the agencies can agree. Following are some of the more important issues.

Financial

- Deciding on how to handle transactions that agencies are unable to post.
- Deciding on a policy for the handling of disputed tolls.
- Creating the ability to determine the proper classification of a vehicle based on each agency's own classification system.
- Decisions have to be made on post-paid accounts. Should they be included in interoperability; if so, how should the financial settlement be handled?
- Decisions on the coordination of account policies (e.g., fees, discounts, tag deposits, minimums for account opening, replenishment parameters) have to be made.
- A revenue reconciliation process will have to be developed.
- An acceptable settlement process will have to be agreed to.
- The guaranteeing of each agency's toll revenue will have to be assured.

Technical

- The primary technical need is the ability to read each agency's tags.
- Mutually agreed upon file formats for all datafiles will have to be created.
- An agency's ETC system must be programmed to allow tag flexibility. This is the ability to recognize that tag types are agency-specific (e.g., a nonrevenue tag at one agency will be a revenue tag at the other agency).
- Scalability is very important. Interoperability greatly increases the size of the datafiles being processed, and if additional agencies are added, an agency's ETC system must be able to accommodate them.
- An agency's back office system will have to be modified to accept and record toll plazas from other agencies. An agency's lane and plaza system will have to be modified to accept and record out of agency tags.

Legal

- Interagency agreements and the settlement process cannot violate a toll agency's bond covenants.
- A mutually agreed upon confidentially policy must be agreed upon to protect the privacy of all agencies' customers.

Operations

- A decision on whether the violation enforcement process will be included in interoperability has to be made. If it is, policies and procedures on how to incorporate it have to be created.
- A decision has to be made as to whether to allow a customer to have commuter plans with more than one agency while maintaining only one account. If the decision is to allow it, then a great deal of programming will be required to accomplish it.
- Proper signage will be required so that drivers know that their tags can be used on the other agencies' toll plazas.
- To the extent possible, the in-lane feedback on each agency's toll plaza should be as similar as possible, so as not to confuse the drivers.

Most of these issues do not have a set solution or method of addressing them. Different toll agencies have resolved them differently. The important point is that toll agencies that want to implement interoperability will have to come to a mutual understanding on these issues before they can proceed.

Traffic management

The tag and reader technology used for ETC is also being used for traffic management. The ability to collect tolls and monitor traffic using essentially the same equipment truly maximizes its value.

This approach uses vehicles equipped with toll tags as "probes" to report abnormal traffic flow caused by highway incidents. To identify these probes, readers are installed at periodic intervals along important highways and arterial roads. Vehicles are recognized by these readers as they pass, and this information is transmitted to a central site where travel times are computed. The tag information is scrambled to ensure confidentiality. These times are then compared with historical information to alert system managers of disruptions in normal traffic flow.

Functions

The deployment of the tag and reader technology in this manner allows for several different traffic management functions. The most important ones are:

- *Monitor traffic flow*—Traffic volume, the traffic speed between different readers, the average travel time, the deviation from the historical traffic flow and the vehicle exit probability can all be determined and reported on.
- *Incident detection*—The system can determine the probability of an incident and alert the proper channels.
- *Origin/destination*—The system can record when a vehicle entered and exited its geographical boundaries and can report on origin and destination with time, date and location as specific parameters.
- *Path travel*—The system can determine the various times of trips based on origin and destination, time of day and date or location. It can also report on the deviation from the historical average.
- *Peak period*—The system can determine the peak traffic periods for individual locations.
- *Fleet management*—The system can locate individual vehicles (as long as they have tags) and project when they will reach their destination. TRANSMIT is using this function to determine when buses will reach their terminal.

Standards

Even though this is a unique approach, these systems are true traffic management systems. As such, they interface with various other systems and must conform to set standards. Among the standards that must be adhered to are: the Traffic Management Data Dictionary, the national ITS architecture, National Transportation Communications Interface Profile Center-to-Center protocol (ASN.1) and ASN.1 Message Sets.

Future applications

As the technology advances, the tag and reader technology can be used for more advanced traffic management functions. Because it is based on roadside-to-vehicle communication, it can be used for new and more advanced traffic management functions, such as:

- Automated motorist information
- In-vehicle messaging
- Bus priority
- Emergency fleet management
- Dynamic route guidance

BY Mr. Kim Richeson[1] • Transportation Systems
Program Area Manager • Johns Hopkins University,
Applied Physics Laboratory

Valerie B. Barnes[2] • CVISN Architect •
Johns Hopkins University, Applied Physics Laboratory

CHAPTER

9

COMMERCIAL VEHICLE OPERATIONS AND FREIGHT MOVEMENT

Introduction

Background

The commercial vehicle operations (CVO) element of intelligent transportation systems (ITS) includes the ITS technologies that uniquely support CVO. The scope of CVO includes the operations associated with moving goods and passengers over the North American highway system and the activities necessary to regulate those operations. These include activities related to freight movement, carrier operations, vehicle operation, safety assurance and credentials administration. This chapter is focused on the movement of goods, rather than on the movement of passengers. Most of the material applies, however, to both cargo and passenger CVO.

Figure 9–1. ITS/CVO.

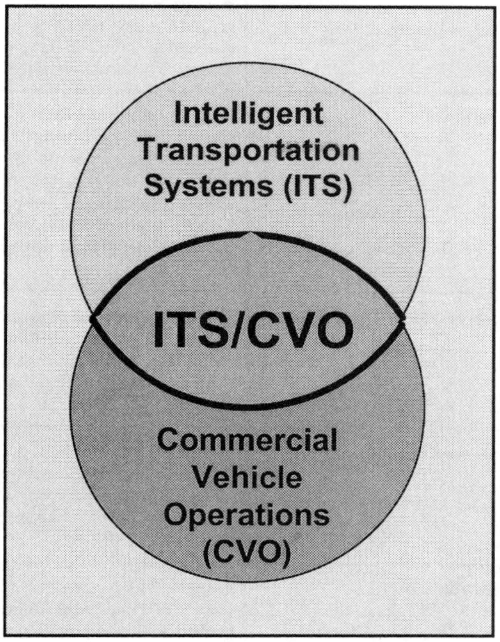

During the development of the National ITS Program Plan (ITS America 1995) in the early 1990s, the CVO stakeholder community's needs were categorized into CVO user services (table 9–1). Initially, these served as the fundamental requirements for the CVO portion of the ITS national architecture.

Table 9–1
ITS/CVO User Services

- Commercial vehicle electronic clearance
- Automated roadside safety inspection
- On-board safety monitoring
- Commercial vehicle administrative processes
- Hazardous materials incident response
- Freight mobility

As research and deployment activities increased in the mid-1990s, emphasis shifted away from the categorizations of requirements in the ITS/CVO user services, and priorities for ITS/CVO were placed on slightly different groupings of the business functions in the private and public sectors. This chapter is organized around those CVO business functions listed in table 9–2.

Table 9–2
CVO Functions

Freight movement	Moving goods from an origin to a destination. Planning for the acquisition and distribution of material goods. Purchasing and scheduling required transportation services. Tracking freight items and packages.
Carrier operations	Carrier business administration functions. Customer service. Managing safety. Scheduling, load matching, order processing. Dispatching, routing, and tracking equipment and shipments. Managing drivers and maintaining vehicles. Communications among commercial fleet managers, commercial drivers and intermodal operators.
Vehicle operation	Vehicle location and navigation. Controlling the vehicle and monitoring vehicle systems. Driver monitoring. Logging driver activities. Communications with the commercial fleet manager.
Safety assurance	Roadside safety monitoring, inspection and reporting. Providing carrier, vehicle and driver safety information to roadside enforcement personnel and other authorized users. Compliance reviews.
Credentials administration	Applying for and paying for credentials. Processing credential applications, collecting fees, issuing credentials and maintaining records about credentials. Supporting base state agreements. CVO tax filing and auditing.
Electronic screening	Sorting vehicles that pass a roadside check station, determining whether or not further inspection or verification of credentials is required, and taking appropriate actions. Fixed or mobile sites. At international borders or domestic locations.

Government-sponsored research and deployment in the mid-1990s put emphasis on safety assurance, credentials administration and electronic screening through the Commercial Vehicle Information Systems and Networks (CVISN) initiative (see Introduction to Commercial Vehicle Information Systems and Networks, listed in the "References" section at the end of this chapter, for a description of CVISN). Other Federal Highway Administration (FHWA) research projects focused on international border clearance, the intelligent vehicle initiative, automated inspection and hazardous materials incident response. Private industry continued to apply ITS technologies in the freight movement, carrier operations and vehicle operation areas.

CVO mission and vision

A mission statement briefly says why an activity exists. The purpose of commercial vehicle operations is to transport goods and people using trucks and buses on the North American highway system. It provides a service to its customers, shippers and travelers. The U.S. Department of Transportation's (U.S. DOT's) mission in CVO (Office of Motor Carriers 1997) is:

> To promote safe commercial vehicle operations through the development, communication and enforcement of effective and cost-beneficial safety regulations and practices; and to promote technological and operational advances which support an efficient and economical transportation system.

A vision statement says how the mission might be realized. The U.S. DOT's vision for CVO (Office of Motor Carriers 1997) is:

> The nation's need to move people and goods in commercial vehicles is met in an efficient, economical and crash-free manner.

Figures 9–2 and 9–3 illustrate the CVO vision. The figures show key functions performed by the CVO stakeholder community. To achieve the CVO vision, some existing systems are being modified and some new information systems are being developed. These must provide high quality and timely information to CVO stakeholders. Information technology is critical to achieving the vision of efficient and seamless operations. Information must flow quickly and reliably among governments and carriers to enable all stakeholders to perform their tasks effectively and efficiently. Checks that were originally done manually must be automated. This vision of CVO is supported by ITS technologies.

As shown in figure 9–2, safety and efficiency will be supported by ITS technologies such as electronic transponders (also known as "tags"), on-board computers, monitors and navigation equipment, mobile communications and safety equipment.

Figure 9–3 shows that electronic information exchange among various CVO stakeholder groups will support many business functions. The electronic business transactions will be supported primarily through wireline connections as shown in the figure, but wireless connections will also be used. The Internet will be used to support CVO business.

Chapter organization

This chapter on ITS/CVO is organized into sections corresponding to the major business elements of commercial vehicle operations and freight movement:

- Elements related to the business with goods to move and the receiver of those goods
  —Freight movement (shipper and consignee)

- Elements related to the motor carrier
  —Carrier operations
  —Vehicle operation
- Elements related to government and regulatory functions
  —Safety assurance
  —Credentials administration
  —Electronic screening
- And finally, a discussion of one of the key ITS/CVO initiatives
  —CVISN

As you read the chapter, keep figure 9–4 in mind. This figure illustrates the main functions in commercial vehicle operations and freight movement.

Figure 9–2. Vision: safe and efficient operations.

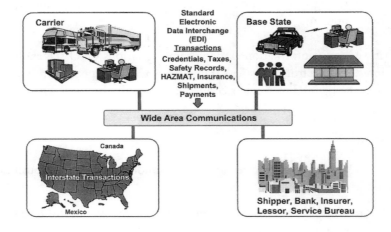

Figure 9–3. Vision: electronic business transactions.

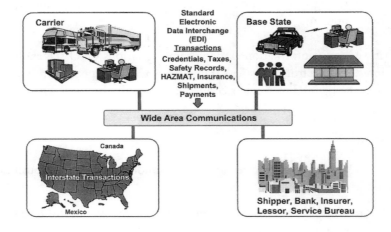

Figure 9–4. CVO and freight movement—operational functions.

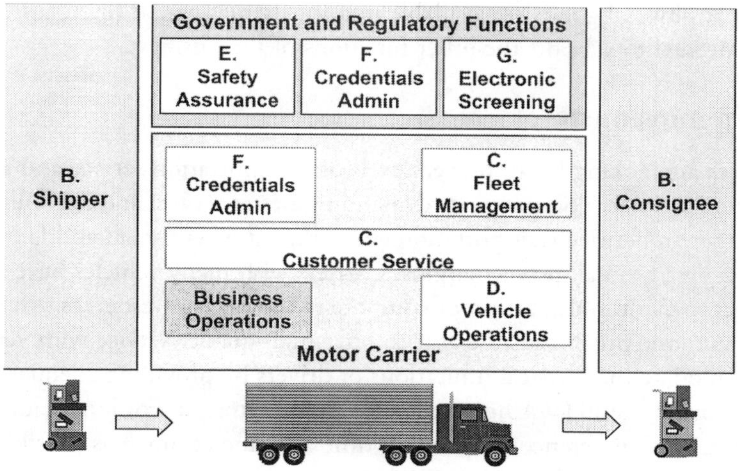

Freight movement—the shipper's and consignee's perspective

Freight movement refers to the transportation activity of moving goods from an origin to a destination. It involves a shipper, a carrier and a consignee. In modern freight movement, the movement of information about the freight is nearly as important as the freight movement itself. Without information about freight, businesses cannot operate effectively and efficiently. ITS offers the potential for dramatic improvement in the information flow associated with freight movement.

Shippers, carriers and consignees—roles and relationships

A shipper may be a manufacturer, wholesaler, retailer, professional-service company, or private individual. In fact, virtually everyone is a shipper at some time. The focus of this section is on large-scale shippers who move substantial quantities of freight and for which freight movement is a critical part of their business. Timely freight movement may be key to controlling costs and improving quality, customer responsiveness, or competitiveness.

The consignee is the person or organization that receives shipped items. A consignee may also be a manufacturer, wholesaler, or the like. In fact, the shipper and consignee may be different parts of the same company. For example, an engine manufacturing plant at one factory site may ship engines to a final vehicle assembly plant at another factory site owned by the same company.

The motor carrier is the company that operates one or more trucks to actually move the freight. In this discussion, we are taking the perspective that the shipper is a customer of a for-hire carrier, to clearly differentiate between the shipper and the carrier. The same principles apply to private carriers.

Business logistics

For the shipper and consignee, the freight movement problem is part of a larger logistics problem: as a business, how can I ensure that I always have the physical things I need where I need them? Physical things may include raw materials, components, and finished goods. In a broader sense, they may include in-process materials, maintenance parts, consumable supplies, tools and capital equipment. Logistics is the business activity that ensures that physical goods are available in a timely manner, at the required location, and in the required condition as needed to support the other functions of the business.

Problems in freight movement

Shippers and consignees are looking for improved levels of transportation service and are very cost conscious. As an anonymous carrier has said: "Shippers are demanding better service and are willing to pay less to get it." This creates a highly competitive transportation environment where small and large carriers alike must work hard to maintain already small profit margins. Carriers with many vehicles have a complex scheduling problem in order to get maximum utilization of equipment and human resources. An owner or operator with only one vehicle and one driver must be able to offer high-quality service with very limited resources. Schedules must accommodate the physical limitations of drivers by providing adequate rest times and must do this in a way that satisfies the FHWA hours-of-service requirements. For long haul routes, schedules should allow for most drivers' preference of spending time at home as much as possible. Ignoring this can lead to high driver dissatisfaction and turnover. Trade routes are often unbalanced with more freight flowing into a location or region than flowing out. This creates a situation of empty return trips and poor resource utilization. Finding and scheduling backhaul loads adds another dimension of complexity to the scheduling problem. Traffic congestion makes reliable scheduling difficult and traffic incidents can render even the best schedule useless.

ITS objectives for freight movement

Objectives for the freight movement aspects of ITS from the perspective of shippers and consignees are to:

- Improve planning for the acquisition and distribution of material goods
- Support the purchase and scheduling of required transportation services
- Identify freight items and packages, pallets and shipping containers to permit comprehensive in-transit visibility by motor carriers
- Improve the information flow at shipping and receiving docks
- Provide information to aid in selection of motor carriers and evaluation of their performance

Key operational concepts for freight movement

The term operational concept refers to an idea for how a technology or system can be used to accomplish a business process. Considering new operational concepts enabled by ITS may help shippers and consignees make decisions about how to invest in ITS technology to improve freight movement. Several key operational concepts are described in table 9–3. They are each related to a theme of integration of planning, scheduling and monitoring across business functions and systems within each shipper and consignee as well as across business boundaries up and down the supply chain.

Integrated logistics management

The scope of the logistics function varies greatly among businesses. Table 9–4 shows a list of possible functions that a corporation may consider to fall within the scope of business logistics.

Table 9–3
Key ITS/CVO Operational Concepts

- Integrated logistics management
- Just-in-time (JIT) manufacturing
- Enterprise resource planning

Table 9–4
Potential Scope of Business Logistics Activities
SOURCE: Donald J. Bowersox, Patricia J. Daugherty, Cornelia L. Droge,
Richard N. Germain and Dale S. Rogers, *Logistical Excellence* (Digital Press, 1992).

- Sales forecasting
- Purchasing
- Inbound transportation
- Intra-company transportation
- Outbound transportation
- Raw material/WIP inventory control
- Finished goods inventory
- Finished goods field warehousing
- Order processing
- Customer service
- Logistics systems planning
- Facilities design
- Materials management
- Logistics administration
- International logistics
- Capital equipment procurement
- Computer processing for distribution applications

Traditionally, logistics have focused on transportation, warehousing and inventory management. More recently, some companies are taking a broader view that includes at least some of the other elements listed in table 9–4. The objective remains the same: provide the physical resources necessary to support business activities when and where required. But now leading edge companies are integrating these logistics activities to a much higher degree than before. This may include putting these functions under a common organizational structure reporting to a common vice president. Or it may involve integrating information systems for each of these functions to make cross-functional management and coordination possible.

Just-in-time manufacturing
Just-in-time (JIT) manufacturing is the process of reducing inventories by having raw materials and components arrive at a manufacturing site directly from their source at exactly the time required to support contin-

uing manufacturing operations. The margin of error in delivery time is typically less than an hour. Clearly, this approach saves on inventory costs for the manufacturer; but it puts a much bigger stress on transportation.

Enterprise resource planning systems

The term "enterprise resource planning (ERP) system" refers to a group of closely integrated information systems, each of which supports a business function. ERP systems typically include the business functions of materials management, production planning, sales, distribution, accounting, controlling, finance and human resources. Manufacturing industries such as chemicals, pharmaceuticals and electronics were the primary early users of ERP systems. But their use is expanding to other manufacturing sectors, consumer packaged goods and other industries.

ITS technologies

ITS technologies used to support freight management operations of shippers and consignees include:

- Commercial-off-the-shelf (COTS) software packages—to support business logistics functions such as those listed in table 9–4
- Communication networks
- Electronic data interchange (EDI)
- Electronic funds transfer (EFT)
- Electronic commerce
- Shipment identification
    —Bar codes
    —Optical character recognition
    —Radio frequency identification
- ERP systems

A representative operational scenario

An operational scenario will be used to illustrate how ITS technologies are being used to implement some new operational concepts. Consider the example in figure 9–5.

Summary of ITS benefits

Shippers and consignees can use information system technologies such as ERP systems, EDI and EFT to directly benefit their operations. They are also indirect benefactors of the ITS technologies used by motor carriers. Even though shippers and consignees may never use ITS traffic management, traveler information, vehicle and other technologies, they benefit from hiring carriers who do. They can rely on such carriers to meet JIT schedules and to engage in cost-effective electronic commerce.

Carrier operations

Operational functions of a motor carrier

A motor carrier is a commercial business (or part of a business) that provides highway freight transportation services. The motor carrier industry is segmented in several ways. A primary differentiation is that the carrier may be a public or private carrier. Private carriers haul goods for their own corporation. For example, a grocery store may operate its own fleet of trucks. Public carriers are for hire to anyone who needs their services. Another basic distinction is based on whether the carrier handles only full truckloads, less-than-load shipments, packages, or a mix. Other distinctions are made by the type of freight carried and types of vehicles operated, for example refrigerated trucks, flatbed trucks, tank trucks, or hazardous material carriers.

**Figure 9–5. ITS technology integrates shipper, carrier, and
consignee operations to improve efficiency.**

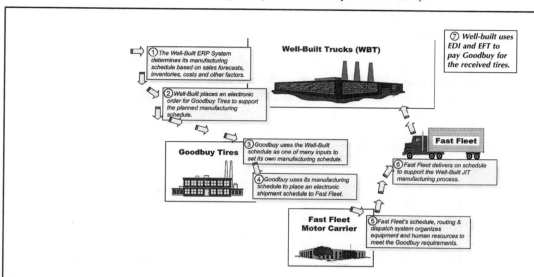

In this fictitious scenario, the shipper is Goodbuy Tires; the carrier is Fast Fleet, Inc.; and the consignee is Well-Built Trucks, Inc. Goodbuy, Fast Fleet, and Well-Built have all entered into contractual relationships to become EDI trading partners and have worked to make their information systems interoperable to their mutual benefit.

Well-Built has formed close partnerships with all its suppliers. It has implemented an ERP system that allows them to share data among their forecasting, procurement, receiving, manufacturing, accounting, sales, distribution and billing systems. Well-Built has interfaced its ERP system with a comparable system at Goodbuy Tires. The Well-Built system is used to generate a comprehensive manufacturing schedule based on sales forecasts, factory maintenance schedules, labor availability, and other inputs. The resulting schedule is used to prepare EDI transactions to order tires from Goodbuy.

The Goodbuy ordering system receives the EDI transactions from Well-Built and uses this as an input to its manufacturing and distribution systems. It schedules the manufacturing of the required tires and also generates shipping request EDI transactions, which it transmits to Fast Fleet.

Fast Fleet brings the EDI shipment requests into its scheduling, routing and dispatch systems. These systems prepare comprehensive schedules for tractors, trailers and drivers, specifying the exact times that each of these items is to be at specific loading docks at the shipper and consignee factories. The schedules are also provided to the Fast Fleet accounting system for accounting, billing and payment receipt purposes.

The Well-Built ERP system accounts for the number of vehicles manufactured. It knows how many tires of each type are used on each type of vehicle. It uses this information to generate an EDI transaction to Midland Bank to initiate payment for the tires it has used on a monthly basis. Midland uses EFT to pay Goodbuy for the tires. Similarly, Goodbuy pays Fast Fleet for delivery of tires using EDI and EFT.

According to the U.S. DOT's *Selected Office of Motor Carrier Statistics,* there are on the order of 500,000 interstate motor carriers operating in the United States and an estimated several hundred thousand more intrastate carriers. They range in size from owner-operators with a single vehicle to companies with thousands of vehicles.

Just as there is a great diversity of motor carriers, there is a great diversity in how they operate and how they are using ITS. Figure 9–6 shows a simple categorization of the operational functions of a generic, mid-sized, public motor carrier. By mid-sized we mean one with several hundred vehicles and employees.

Figure 9–6. Motor carrier—operational functions.

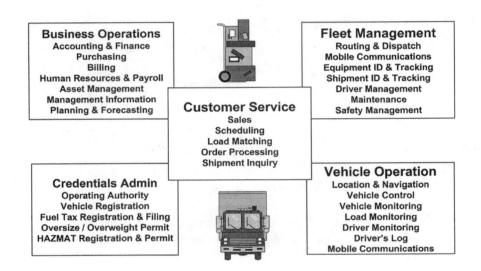

The business operations function is similar to comparable functions in other industries and a wide variety of COTS packages are available to support this area. However, these systems are not generally considered as part of ITS and are not discussed further herein. The credentials administration and vehicle operation functions are of such importance to ITS/CVO that they are addressed in their own separate sections in this chapter. This section focuses on the customer service and fleet management functions.

Problems in carrier operations

The motor carrier industry is a very competitive marketplace with small profit margins for the participants. Large carriers have a complex scheduling problem of matching vehicles and drivers to customer needs. Owner/operators with only one vehicle and one driver have to be able to identify customers and provide superior service with very constrained time and resources. Shippers and consignees are requiring JIT shipment, quick delivery and rapid response to shipping orders because of the pressures that they feel from their customers and competition. Nearly all motor carriers are faced with a requirement to provide better service with less resources. ITS offers potential help.

ITS objectives for carrier operations

Objectives for ITS in the customer service and fleet management aspects of carrier operations are to:

- Reduce costs
- Minimize transport time
- Improve reliability of shipping schedules
- Eliminate shipment errors
- Improve the ease of doing business for customers
- Improve flexibility in providing specialized service
- Improve driver work conditions and performance
- Improve safety

Key operational concepts for carrier operations

Key operational concepts guide the decision-making processes for the motor carrier industry as ITS/CVO are being implemented. In motor carrier operations, the concepts all reflect a need for improved customer service at minimal cost.

Total asset visibility

The term total asset visibility has its origins in the field of military logistics. It refers to the concept that a military commander and the personnel he commands must know what weaponry and supplies they have available at all times, and the status of that materiel. It applies equipment and load identification and tracking technologies so that information systems are aware of the location of items at all times. Military personnel have access to these systems via their command, control and communications systems. The concept of total asset visibility is now being applied to commercial logistics operations. For a carrier, it means that carrier personnel know where their tractors, trailers, containers and shipments are at all times. It also means that authorized personnel can access an electronic description of container, trailer, or shipment contents from any location where it is required.

Automated identification and tracking

Dedicated short-range communication (DSRC) transponders can be attached to tractors, trailers, containers and chassis for tracking purposes. DSRC technology is also referred to as automatic vehicle identification, automated equipment identification and vehicle-to-roadside communications. DSRC transponders use wireless communication to permit identifying a piece of equipment at a specific point such as a toll plaza, weigh station, or a terminal gate. Another technology, satellite tracking systems, can be used to provide wide-area (essentially anywhere) coverage on a query or continuous basis.

Automated scheduling, routing and dispatch

With JIT manufacturing and increasing demands for on-time delivery in all business sectors, motor carriers are turning to scheduling, routing and dispatch systems to help improve their ability to establish and meet exact shipping schedules. These systems can take as input a knowledge of the status of equipment, customers' shipment orders, maps, road and traffic conditions, driver availability and fuel and toll costs and use all of this to generate an optimized schedule for the carrier's vehicle operations.

Automated finding and bidding on loads

Several ISPs now offer services over the Internet for motor carriers to locate loads and bid on them. This is particularly useful for carriers trying to find backhaul loads.

Table 9–5
Key ITS/CVO Operational Concepts for Carrier Operations

- Total asset visibility
- Automated identification and tracking
- Automated routing and dispatch
- Maximizing equipment readiness and utilization
- Automated finding and bidding on loads
- Interoperability with customer systems
- Specialized load handling and logistics services

Interoperability with customer systems

Shippers and consignees increasingly want motor carrier systems to work closely with their information systems. Interoperability refers to the ability of two systems to work together to accomplish a common function. Interoperability is useful when a carrier wants to have its system work with a number of customer systems, all following a common set of interface standards.

Specialized logistics and load handling services

Shippers are increasingly looking to carriers to solve the shippers' logistics problems in ways that go beyond simple freight movement. They are looking for accurate and flexible scheduling to meet production and distribution demands that change dynamically. Hazardous materials loads require making information about the load and emergency handling procedures readily available (possibly over the Internet) to the emergency response team. High-value loads, such as electronics, may require special handling for in-transit shock and ambient environment control.

ITS technologies

Technologies used to support the customer service and fleet management aspects of carrier operations include:

- Identification and tracking
  - Bar codes
  - DSRC
  - Satellite tracking
  - Cellular tracking
- Information systems
  - Databases
  - Networks
  - EDI
  - EFT
  - Websites
- Communications
  - Wireless communications
  - Satellite communications
- COTS software (American Trucking Associations 1996)

—Cost and pricing
—Telemarketing
—Load advertising and finding
—Order acceptance
—Scheduling
—Load optimization planning and tracking
—Freight documentation
—Routing and dispatch
—Billing and payment
—Driver logs
—Driver performance, safety and accident analysis
—Drug testing records maintenance management
—Preventive maintenance scheduling
—Sales analysis
- Vehicle technologies (also see the "Vehicle Operation" section in this chapter)
—Automated diagnostics and maintenance

A representative operational scenario

An operational scenario will be used to illustrate how ITS technologies are being used to implement some of the operational concepts for carrier operations. Consider the example in figure 9–7.

Summary of ITS benefits

The benefits of applying ITS technologies to customer service and fleet management aspects of carrier operations are expected to include improved customer service at reduced costs. The service improvements will be in the areas of more reliable schedules, fewer delays and errors, improved ease of doing business and greater responsiveness to customers' specialized needs.

Vehicle operation

The vehicle operation function

The driver performs the vehicle operation function. He or she has the responsibility to arrive at a shipment's origin, pick up the shipment and take it to a specified destination in a safe, timely and efficient manner. This is the only function that actually moves freight! All the other functions in this chapter are in support of carrying out this core task.

Problems in the vehicle operation function

The problems faced by the commercial driver are:

- Tight schedules
- Traffic congestion and detours
- Road hazards
- Unsafe operations by other vehicles
- Drowsiness, inattention, or error
- Equipment failure
- Accidents
- Confusing road signage or routing directions
- Changing route requirements

Figure 9–7. Carrier operations scenario: dispatchers use real-time traffic, weather, equipment, driver and freight information to manage deliveries.

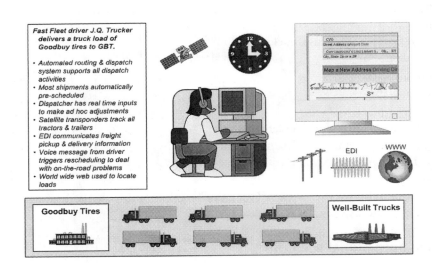

The Fast Fleet dispatcher, Diane, has an automated scheduling, routing and dispatch system that is used to support her daily activities. The system prepares weekly schedules for pre-scheduled periodic routes and allows for daily adjustments for ad hoc shipments and changes. The system is interfaced to a satellite monitoring system that tracks both tractors and trailers. It receives position updates several times a day or when triggered by an event, such as the driver dropping off a trailer. Receivers on tractors and trailers can also be queried on demand as required.

Much of Fast Fleet's freight volume is in support of customers who have standing contracts for transportation services and who have integrated their shipment ordering systems with the Fast Fleet order processing system via EDI. Many of these shipment orders are accepted, scheduled, dispatched, completed and billed without human intervention. But many situations still require the intervention and attention of the dispatcher.

The dispatcher has a screen that can be used to show the current position of all vehicles in a selected map area. Or it can show the map of a selected trip with current position and estimated time of arrival. The system schedules the work of the dispatcher by preparing lists of activities to do. These include drivers calling in late or sick, trips requiring a backhaul load, trouble calls from drivers on the road, shipment change orders and new shipment requests.

On the day of the scenario, Diane the dispatcher began by looking through the day's delivery schedule and scanning the activities list prepared for her by the routing and dispatch system. She also reviewed the traffic reports for the region. Fast Fleet subscribed to a traffic information service that packaged traffic and weather conditions and other travel information in a comprehensive package designed specifically for motor carriers and their drivers. Diane reviewed the notices and saw that road work on the route normally used to make deliveries of Goodbuy tires to Well-Built Truck manufacturing was causing delays of up to one hour. There was an alternate route available, so she used the routing and dispatch system to change the recommended route. The system

Figure 9–7, continued

automatically notified the driver of the change via e-mail and voice mail. Each of the drivers subsequently confirmed that they had gotten the message via his or her satellite communications link.

Later in the morning, one of the drivers delivering tires called in with a problem. The driver reported via his satellite communications phone link that his on-board monitor noted that his engine temperature was higher than normal. Diane checked with the maintenance people at the terminal. They reviewed the engine performance data via a satellite link and determined that it was a minor problem, did not affect safety and could be handled when the tractor returned to the terminal. Diane scheduled the vehicle for maintenance the next morning and notified the driver to continue.

Having dealt with one problem and ensuring that the Goodbuy tire flow would continue on-schedule to Well-Built, Diane began to tackle her other tasks of the day. She used a load matching service to find backhaul loads for several drivers. She ran schedules for the following week and reviewed them for any problems. She also scheduled a number of vehicles for periodic maintenance as recommended by the Fast Fleet vehicle maintenance system. She was able to accomplish all of this from her workstation because Fast Fleet had used a combination of COTS software application packages and some custom software to develop a comprehensive, integrated set of information systems to support essentially all their business processes.

ITS objectives for vehicle operation

Objectives for the vehicle operation function of ITS/CVO include:

- Improve safety
- Improve schedule performance
- Improve productivity
- Reduce shipment errors
- Improve driver working conditions
- Improve ability to respond to changing traffic and business conditions

Key operational concepts for vehicle operation

The key operational concepts in the vehicle operation area focus on collecting real-time data about the equipment and environment and presenting this information to the driver or using it for automated control.

On-board location and navigation

Several technologies exist that let the driver and vehicle know where they are located, within an accuracy of a few feet if necessary. These systems can also provide electronic maps and navigation aids. Use of these tools can eliminate problems of lost shipments or errors in shipment delivery location, can eliminate delays caused by driver navigation errors, and can help to avoid congestion delays.

Table 9–6
Key ITS/CVO Operational Concepts for Vehicle Operation

- On-board location and navigation
- Real-time monitoring of equipment, load and driver
- Communications between vehicle and dispatch
- Communications between vehicle and roadside

Real-time monitoring of equipment, load and driver

Automated sensors can now be obtained for virtually any equipment or load condition and even some driver conditions. These can give the driver immediate feedback on any unsafe equipment conditions or load problems (e.g., rising temperature on refrigerated cargo or excess shock on fragile items).

Communications between vehicle and dispatch

Communication systems can support voice communication between driver and dispatcher, message data between the driver and dispatcher (e.g., pagers, e-mail) and telemetry of vehicle monitoring data between the vehicle and computer systems at the carrier terminal.

Communications between vehicle and roadside

DSRC transponders and readers allow roadside systems to communicate with vehicles over a wireless link. This allows for conducting operational transactions with a vehicle at a particular point in a lane on a highway while it is moving, possibly at highway speeds. This has been used in three commercial vehicle-specific applications: electronic screening at weigh stations, electronic screening at international border crossing sites and terminal gate control. The most widely deployed DSRC application is for toll collection of passenger and commercial vehicles. DSRC is also used in traffic probe monitoring. DSRC is being considered for several other applications such as parking payment, in-vehicle signing and commercial electronic payment (e.g., for fast food).

ITS technologies

Present day heavy trucks can be equipped with a wide array of technologies to make the vehicle operation safer and more efficient (Johns Hopkins 1998c). Vehicles may have several dozen intelligent devices with embedded microprocessors. Technologies used to support the vehicle operation capability are listed in the table 9–7 and illustrated in figure 9–8. Several interesting examples of these are discussed below or illustrated in the subsequent scenario.

ATIS

Commercial vehicle drivers can benefit from ATIS services just as passenger car drivers do. Some ISPs are specializing in packaging traveler information for the trucking community (I-95 Corridor Coalition and the Northeast Transportation Institute 1998). These services include notices of congestion delays, incidents, roadwork, detours and adverse weather. The information is provided both via computer-to-computer links for dispatch systems and in e-mail and website format for human access.

Figure 9–8. On-board monitoring and control devices can improve safety and efficiency of vehicle operation.

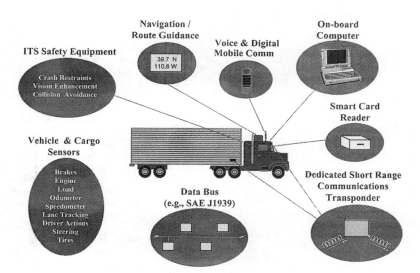

Advanced vehicle control systems

Commercial vehicles and their drivers can benefit from the same types of automated control systems that benefit passenger car drivers. These include intelligent cruise control systems that can help trucks maintain safe distances and operate at optimal speeds. Collision avoidance systems can warn a driver that another vehicle is in his blind spot. Lane tracking systems can detect a vehicle drifting out of its lane if a driver becomes inattentive or drowsy.

Networked monitoring and control devices

The SAE has developed several standards to guide networking of monitoring and control devices on commercial vehicles. This allows implementing new safety and vehicle control concepts by coordinating vehicle subsystems. For example, traction control systems have been implemented to prevent wheel spin. These systems will sense wheel speed and detect when a wheel on one side of an axle is spinning faster than a wheel on the other side. They then use the controls of the antilock brake system to brake the fast wheel. If all wheels on an axle are spinning too fast for the current engine speed, some systems automatically cut back on engine throttle (U.S. DOT 1998b).

Human interface engineering of driver controls

The dashboard of a modern commercial vehicle is looking more like an airplane cockpit and less like a passenger car dashboard. Vehicles may have several dozen electronic systems on-board. An easy-to-understand display and effective control panels are required to allow a driver to effectively monitor and use these systems. Poor human interface design will result in lack of use or even misuse of the new systems, and in an extreme case could even have a detrimental effect on safety.

Table 9–7
Vehicle Operation Technologies

ATIS	Computer-to-computer data exchange
	E-mail and websites
	Radio broadcast
Advanced vehicle control systems	Antilock braking systems
	Electronic braking systems
	Intelligent cruise control
	Side- and back-looking radar for proximity warning systems
	Lane tracking
Location and communications	Satellite location
	Satellite communications for telemetry or driver
	Cellular communications for telemetry or driver
	Cellular location
	DSRC for telemetry
	Paging and messaging services
	Networked mobile radio
	Navigation
Vehicle identification	DSRC toll transponders
	DSRC electronic screening transponders
	Bar coded equipment
	Optical character recognition
	Image recognition
On-board communications and networking	SAE J1587 Recommended Practice for Electronic Data Interchange between Microcomputer Systems in Heavy-duty Vehicle Applications
	SAE 1922 Powertrain Control Interface for Electronic Controls Used in Medium and Heavy-duty Diesel On-Highway Applications
	SAE J1939 A Series of Recommended Practices that Define Architecture and Protocol for a Serial Control and Communications Networks for Various Equipment Types
Vehicle systems monitoring	Brakes
	Tire pressure and wear
	Engine parameters
	Electrical system
	Transmission and drive train
	Fuel consumption
	Warning when maintenance is required
Driver monitoring	Smart cards
	Hours-of-service tracking
	Lane Tracking
	Steering wheel motion tracking
	Eye movement tracking
	Drowsy driver warning
Load monitoring	On-board scales
	Load security seals and monitors
	Load orientation monitors (e.g., tipping, overturn)
	Temperature monitors and controls
	Shock monitors
	Specialized container monitors: refrigeration, liquid tanks, gas tanks, hazardous materials
Load handling and business ops	Handheld and on-board computers
	Bar code scanners
	Computerized manifests, receipts and other business documentation
	Fuel purchases
	Scheduling and routing

Summary of ITS benefits

The benefits of applying ITS technologies to vehicle operation are expected to include improved safety, efficiency and flexibility, which all lead to improved productivity and service. They also improve driver working conditions, which leads to more satisfied drivers, less turnover and further cost savings.

A representative operational scenario

J.Q. Driver has worked for Fast Fleet for 10 years. He likes the work environment, especially the way Fast Fleet emphasizes safety and provides up-to-date, well-maintained equipment. He gets a weekly schedule that shows the trips he will make and includes adequate time for rest and scheduled days off. In general, he follows the weekly schedule as is. But occasionally, unanticipated changes cause last-minute rescheduling. For example, he was notified by e-mail (with an automated voice mail backup) that today's schedule was moved up an hour because of unusually heavy traffic along his planned route of I-75. Figure 9–9 illustrates the trip scenario.

Figure 9–9. Vehicle operation scenario: on-board sensors and computers linked via satellite to the dispatch office improve service, safety and productivity.

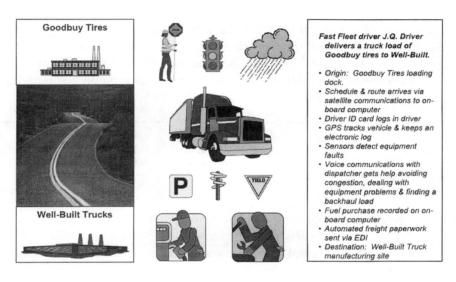

When J.Q. arrives at his truck, he downloads the most recent schedule and route information to his on-board computer. He swipes a plastic smart card through a reader to identify himself. The smart card is a credit card-sized device that contains memory, a microprocessor and close proximity communications to relay secure information, including driver identification and authentication information. The on-board computer only allows the driver designated in the itinerary to operate the vehicle. The computer is networked to various sensors on the engine, transmission, tires and brakes. It is also connected to a GPS receiver, a satellite communications link and a DSRC transponder. The computer maintains an hours-of-service log without any manual input from J.Q. Driver. This same information is used to support payroll processing. The computer also contains electronic copies of all shipment documentation and vehicle and carrier credentials. It is in fact a "paperless vehicle" for both business and regulatory purposes.

J.Q. proceeds on his way, guided by the on-board map and navigational instructions that are integrated into his dashboard. Voice directions are available, but he has turned these off because he is familiar with the route. About an hour into the trip his computer displays a traffic alert that was relayed from his dispatcher. There has been an accident at a roadwork site 70 miles ahead. He is advised to consider changing his route, just in case the accident is not cleared quickly. He accepts the recommended change and proceeds.

Figure 9–9, continued

Later during the trip, J.Q. notices that the antilock brake warning lamp has come on. He calls back to his dispatcher via his satellite communications link and asks for guidance. Since this is potentially a safety-related problem, the dispatcher directs J.Q. to a nearby truck stop. The dispatcher locates another driver with an empty trailer within a half-hour of the truck stop. She directs that driver to meet J.Q. at the truck stop and swap tractors. J.Q. drives directly to the truck stop and makes the switch. The necessary trip information is downloaded to the new tractor via satellite. While stopped, J.Q. refuels, pays for the fuel with his smart card and enters the volume of fuel purchased into the on-board computer via his smart card. Then J.Q. proceeds to make the delivery to Well-Built. Because his schedule had included one hour of slack time to allow for unexpected delays, he arrives within the scheduled time window.

When he arrives at Well-Built, he drops off his trailer. No paperwork is involved. His computer has logged the delivery and notified the dispatch computer of the delivery. The Well-Built receiving computer is aware of the location of the trailer (provided by GPS) and the contents (provided by an EDI notice of shipment). J.Q. enters the delivery-complete status on the computer and proceeds to pick up his backhaul load.

Safety assurance

What is safety assurance?

Safety assurance is concerned with improving safety in the operation of commercial vehicles. Safety assurance includes collecting information about safety performance; analyzing that information; and implementing regulations, training and procedures geared towards improving safety. A key element in safety assurance is the exchange of safety information.

Traditional approaches to improving safety have focused on the commercial driver and enforcement of roadway, compliance and credentialing statutes. There are federal motor carrier statutes intended to assure safe operations. In 1986, the U.S. DOT adopted the Commercial Motor Vehicle Safety Act. This act defined new national standards for commercial drivers, the equipment and maintenance of vehicles and the fitness of operating companies. The standards were incorporated in the Code of Federal Regulations, Title 49. The Office of Motor Carriers and Highway Safety[3] (OMCHS) is responsible for the issuance, administration and enforcement of the Federal Motor Carrier Safety Regulations.

As part of their strategic planning in 1997, the OMCHS set a goal to reduce the number of commercial vehicle accidents. To meet that goal, the OMCHS defined several objectives: reducing the risk of a crash occurring, reducing the risk of hazardous materials incidents and environmental damage, enhancing the safety of passenger carriers and improving the consistency and effectiveness of enforcement and compliance programs. Safety performance is monitored through a program of roadside inspections and carrier compliance reviews (U.S. DOT 1997).

Federal policy encourages states to enforce the regulations uniformly for both interstate and intrastate drivers and carriers. Federal regulations tend to focus on interstate transportation. Intrastate regulation is largely a state and local responsibility. To assure safe commercial vehicle operations, enforcement and inspection efforts must be consistently applied to both interstate and interstate operators (International Association of Chiefs of Police 1998).

Problems in safety assurance

- In 1997, 13 percent of the people who were killed in motor vehicle crashes died in crashes that involved a large truck (U.S. DOT 1999a).
- Inspections and compliance reviews are excellent tools to discover safety problems before they cause accidents, but resources to conduct inspections and compliance reviews are limited.
- Data from past inspections and compliance reviews are often not readily available to those who could benefit from reviewing the data.

ITS objectives for safety assurance

Objectives for the safety assurance aspects of ITS are:

- Collect, store and provide access to safety information
- Proactively identify unsafe operators
- Improve safety assurance program efficiency and effectiveness
- Provide safety compliance statistics to support policy decisions, rule making and program development
- Implement programs to encourage unsafe operators to improve their performance or to remove them from the highways

Key operational concepts for safety assurance

In safety assurance, the key operational concepts are focused on improving access to information and focusing resources on potential problem areas.

Table 9–8
Key ITS/CVO Operational Concepts for Safety Assurance

- Measures of effectiveness: accidents and fatalities
- Electronic safety records at roadside
- Base state for each carrier (safety record and credentials)
- Automated collection of inspection results
- Compliance reviews and electronic access to participating carrier's records
- Determining safety risk ratings
- Providing safety data to government and nongovernment stakeholders
- Comprehensive safety policy (deskside and roadside) implemented to improve safety

Measures of effectiveness: accidents and fatalities

Accidents (rates or numbers) and fatalities have been identified as the primary measures of effectiveness of the safety improvement initiatives for CVO. The ITS/CVO safety assurance processes collect data to measure these parameters and assess changes.

Electronic safety records at roadside

To aid inspectors and other enforcement personnel, infrastructure systems provide carrier and vehicle snapshots. The carrier snapshots provide details on the components of the carrier safety risk rating and credentials information. Vehicle snapshots contain information on vehicle safety records and credentials. (Driver snapshots that could provide details on driver safety performance and credentials have not been endorsed by the CVO community and are not planned for near-term implementation.) Vehicle snapshots will contain information equivalent to an electronic Commercial Vehicle Safety Alliance decal and electronic Out-of-Service status. From the vehicle itself, identifiers, a specially regulated load type flag (e.g., hazardous materials or agricultural), and the results of the last screening event will be provided. This basic information will allow roadside systems to link the vehicle to the snapshot and other infrastructure-provided data.

Base state for each carrier (safety record and credentials)

The base state processes credential applications for the carrier, using safety information to judge whether or not to grant the credential. The base state makes safety data available to other jurisdictions.

Automated collection of inspection results

Automated support for collecting and reporting inspection data increases the consistency in inspection reporting, removes the need to forward a paper copy for subsequent data entry and reduces inspection time. This may include collecting information from on-board safety monitoring systems, as well as using advanced technology such as automated brake testing equipment to support the inspection process.

Compliance reviews and electronic access to participating carrier's records

Electronic access to carrier records and automated support for collecting and reporting compliance review data increases consistency, removes the need for handling paper and speeds the auditing process.

Determining safety risk ratings

Safety risk ratings are determined uniformly for carriers. As part of the ongoing Performance and Registration Information Systems Management project, the Motor Carrier Safety Status (Safe Stat) algorithm was developed as a safety status indicator in the Motor Carrier Safety Improvement Program (U.S. DOT 1999b).

Providing safety data to government and nongovernment stakeholders

Providing safety data electronically to shippers, insurance companies, vehicle leasing companies and the general public allows them to use timely information in making their business decisions. Providing the information to carriers helps them analyze and improve their own safety performance.

Comprehensive safety policy (deskside and roadside) implemented to improve safety

In the long term, stakeholders should develop a comprehensive safety policy covering safety processes as well as supporting technology. Automation of part or all of the vehicle inspection process (e.g., electronic connection to brake testing systems) or driver inspection process (e.g., alertness testing) improves inspection accuracy, reduces inspection time and improves the inspector's work environment. The availability of on-board vehicle and driver safety monitoring systems will shift the focus from assessing the condition of the vehicle or driver via infrequent inspections to constant, real-time verification that the vehicle is functioning properly and the driver is alert and performing safely. Safety training programs, carrier safety practices and general business operations (e.g., trip scheduling) must be coordinated with technology improvements to achieve maximum benefit.

ITS technologies and representative systems

Figure 9–10 shows systems representative of the safety assurance components found in states today. Some states have all the components shown; others have only some of the components. As states move towards implementing ITS/CVO capabilities, it is expected that they will implement systems that perform functions equivalent to those depicted. For safety assurance, the systems include state and federal commercial vehicle credential and safety administration-related offices, roadside check stations (fixed and mobile) and information exchange systems.

Figure 9–10. Safety assurance: standardized interfaces and common identifiers make it possible to check safety performance roadside and deskside.

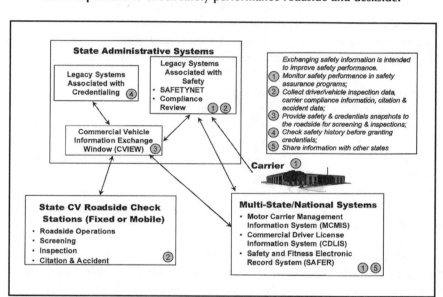

The primary state administrative offices include the designated lead Motor Carrier Safety Assistance Program agency and other enforcement agencies. Other state agencies also provide or have an interest in commercial vehicle safety information (e.g., vehicle registration, driver licensing, titling, permitting). These offices exist in each state or region, and they share information through various multistate and national systems. The state commercial vehicle (CV) Information Exchange Window (CVIEW) system supports the transfer of safety and credentials information (e.g., snapshots and reports) within the state and with the Safety and Fitness Electronic Records (SAFER) system. The state CVIEW handles information about all carriers and vehicles that operate in the state (both intrastate and interstate operators).

Multistate and national systems support the exchange of safety information between states and among other stakeholders. The primary safety-related information systems and networks include the SAFER system, the commercial driver license information system and the motor carrier management information system. SAFER manages and distributes snapshots for interstate carriers and vehicles.

Roadside check stations include those locations with a permanent structure or mobile facility (including police cruisers) that house elements of the information systems (e.g., computers and communication systems), inspection systems such as ASPEN, and the enforcement and safety inspection personnel. Brief descriptions of each of these systems can be found in the Commercial Vehicle Information Systems and Networks Glossary (John Hopkins 1998b).

The Commercial Vehicle Information Systems and Networks initiative supports the standardization of dataflows to carry summary (snapshot) and detailed (report) safety and credentials information. These dataflows provide a consistent basis for automating CVO information exchanges and processing, and to ensure interoperability among existing and developing CVO information systems. The American National Standards Institute Accredited Standards Committee EDI X12 transaction set 285 is used to carry snapshot information. EDI X12 transaction set 284 is used to carry CV safety report information.

The snapshots convey information about two major entities: carriers and vehicles. To minimize response time to requesters, snapshots will be stored nationally in the SAFER system, and within the state in the CVIEW system. SAFER and CVIEW snapshots are used for screening carriers and vehicles at mainline speeds at roadside check stations, for safety inspections, for limited credentials checking and insurance applications and for industry self-checks. Different subsets (called views) of the snapshot record available in SAFER and CVIEW for a carrier or vehicle will support different user systems.

Technologies used to support safety assurance include:

- Databases
- Networks
- Data analysis tools
- Portable computers
- Wireless communications
- Sensors
- Portable diagnostic devices

These technologies provide the capabilities for the collection, exchange and analysis of safety and credentials data among jurisdictions and between agencies (for example, an administrative center and the roadside check facilities) within a single jurisdiction. The technologies also support roadside operations by helping to automate the roadside safety inspection process, including the use of handheld devices to rapidly inspect the vehicle.

Summary of ITS benefits

Once implemented, the benefits of applying ITS/CVO technologies to safety assurance problems are expected to include improved safety performance and helping government enforcement resources be better focused on high-risk operators. Automated collection of information about safety performance and credentials status and improved access to that information are important enabling technologies.

Credentials administration

Operating a commercial vehicle in the United States requires many credentials. Vehicles must be titled and registered. In some instances, one set of credentials is required for carriers, vehicles, or drivers that will operate only within a single state (i.e., intrastate), and different credentials are required for those that will be operated in multiple states (i.e., interstate). Carriers must have adequate liability insurance and be authorized to carry certain types of "cargo" (e.g., hazardous materials, people and household goods). Special permits are required to operate vehicles that are over the standard legal weight or size. Drivers must be licensed to drive whatever size vehicles they intend to operate, and must meet medical standards. Carriers must pay fuel taxes for operating vehicles in each jurisdiction. Some states have additional credentialing requirements.

States have reached reciprocity agreements on vehicle registration and fuel tax payments for interstate operators. These are called base state agreements. According to the International Registration Plan (IRP), the states agree that a vehicle registrant can file with a base state, and receive one license plate and cab card. The base state will charge the registrant the sum of the fees due to all states in which the vehicle operates, based on miles driven in each state. The base state sends apportioned fees to other states. The International Fuel Tax Agreement (IFTA) is a similar arrangement in which a carrier files quarterly fuel tax returns with a base state on its operations in all states. The base state apportions the fuel taxes to the appropriate jurisdictions. All mainland states in the United States, as well as some Canadian jurisdictions, are part of the IRP and IFTA.

Credentials administration comprises:

- All aspects of applying for, reviewing and granting CVO credentials; and paying the associated fees
- Filing returns on fuel taxes; and paying the associated CVO taxes and fees
- Managing information about credentials and tax payment status; and providing information to users
- Supporting base state agreements and associated fee payment reconciliation

Problems in credentials administration

Paperwork, red tape and collecting and reporting the same information from and to different agencies have plagued credentials administration. Applicants experience delays when applying for credentials. Different customer groups have different support needs, and it has been difficult for government agencies to satisfy all of those customer groups. State government policies often encourage commercial vehicle operators to do business in their state, because of the revenues from CV credentials. At the same time, government agencies in those states are under pressure to reduce costs.

ITS objectives for credentials administration

Objectives for the credentials administration aspects of ITS include:

- Streamline credentials and tax administration
- Enable electronic credentialing and tax filing
- Enhance interagency and interstate data and funds exchange
- Provide credentials information to authorized officials

ITS/CVO solutions are being applied to credentials administration. Information systems, database and networks technologies are well suited to addressing these labor- and paper-intensive processes. Carriers, registrants and government agencies are motivated to participate in improvement initiatives, because they see opportunities for more efficient operations, more accurate records and reduced processing costs.

Key operational concepts for credentials administration

Key operational concepts for credentials administration focus on electronic credentialing and streamlining the support mechanisms for the base state credentials agreements.

Table 9–9
Key ITS/CVO Operational Concepts for
Credentials Administration

- Electronic credentials and paperless vehicle
- Ubiquitous (but secure) electronic data access
- Standard snapshots and reports for carrier and vehicle information
- Flexible implementation and deployment options

Electronic credentials and paperless vehicle

Using open standards, commercial vehicle operators apply for and receive credentials electronically. At some point in the future, by equipping the vehicle with a transponder and using the identifiers retrieved from the transponder as indices into infrastructure data, it will be possible to reduce or eliminate altogether the need to carry paper permits and other paperwork on the truck. Paper copies will become backup material rather than primary sources of credential information.

Ubiquitous (but secure) electronic data access

Information sharing within a single jurisdiction and across jurisdictions using electronic networks is a cornerstone of many ITS/CVO projects. Information systems are only as good as the quality of the data they use. Data must be accurate, current and safe from tampering or unauthorized disclosure. Authoritative sources are the official repositories for the data.

Standard snapshots and reports for carrier and vehicle information

Information exchange is enabled through the use of standards. Many elements of CVO require information about the credentials history for carriers and vehicles. Collecting the most-used information into standard messages simplifies systems since interfaces can be defined once, rather than negotiated between every pair of stakeholders. Credentialing actions may be based, in part, on a review of the safety information available from snapshots.

Flexible implementation/deployment options

The ITS/CVO architecture accommodates existing and near-term communications technologies. Both government and industry will choose from a broad range of options, open to competitive markets, in CVO technologies.

ITS technologies

Carriers use service providers, commercially available PC-based products, web-based products, or integrated fleet credentials and tax management and reporting systems. States have centralized or distributed credentialing facilities. Some states developed their own individual credential processing systems; others bought or will buy products from vendors. National or multistate systems facilitate the exchange of credentials-related information.

Technologies involved in credentials administration include:

- Computers
- Networks
- Information systems
- Databases
- EDI standards
- The Internet

As part of the CVISN architecture, ANSI EDI X12 transaction set 286 is used to carry credentials information. These technologies provide support for the exchange and evaluation of credentials data among jurisdictions and between agencies within a single jurisdiction.

A representative operational scenario

The scenario in figure 9–11 illustrates electronic credentialing. Electronic credentialing is an operational process that uses software under the applicant's control to send credentials applications and fuel tax returns to a state government agency, and to get electronic notification of credentials status in return. When feasible, the credential itself is returned electronically. Electronic payment is normally associated with electronic credentialing.

Several electronic credentialing options are being explored by CVISN prototype and pilot states. Many states are planning to try more than one option. Because the use of open standards is key to achieve interoperability, it is important that states provide some electronic credentialing option that supports the use of EDI X12 transactions or some other open standard.

Figure 9–11. One-stop/no-stop shopping scenario.

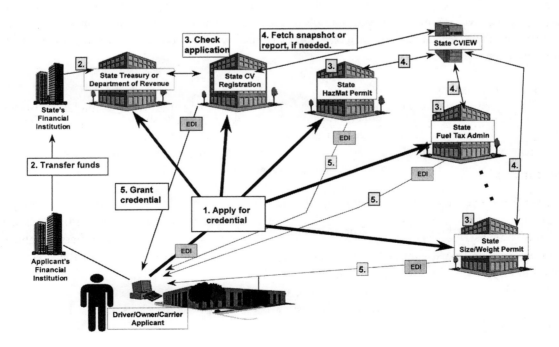

Summary of ITS benefits

The benefits of applying ITS/CVO technologies to credentials administration are expected to include improved service for commercial vehicle carriers and registrants, reduced costs and red tape for agencies and CVO customers and improved regulatory compliance.

Electronic screening

Screening is a selection mechanism to target high-risk operators and make efficient use of weigh station and inspection resources. Electronic screening is the application of technology to make more informed screening decisions. Properly implemented, electronic screening results in improved traffic flow, focused vehicle inspections and ultimately achieves the goals of increased safety and reduced operating costs. In electronic screening:

- DSRC may be used to identify the carrier or vehicle, store and transfer other screening data and signal the driver of the pull-in decision
- EDI may be used to transmit safety and credentials history (snapshot) data from the information infrastructure to the roadside systems to assist in the screening decision

DSRC involves a vehicle equipped with a transponder, and a roadside reader to receive messages from the transponder and to send messages to the transponder. EDI may be used to pass information to the roadside check station where the roadside reader is located.

As a vehicle equipped with a transponder approaches a roadside check station, the carrier and/or vehicle identifiers are read from the transponder, vehicle measurements are made, the identifiers are correlated with safety and credentials data, and a decision as to whether or not the vehicle should be pulled in is made and communicated to the driver at mainline speed. This screening process is performed electronically. Electronic screening comprises:

- Screening vehicles that pass a roadside check station based on identifiers read from the transponder, correlated with vehicle measurements and safety and credentials information from snapshots
- Determining whether or not further inspection or verification of credentials is required and then taking appropriate actions

Problems in screening

- It is difficult to identify which vehicles deserve closer scrutiny at the roadside.
- It is difficult to identify unsafe or illegal drivers or carriers at the roadside.
- At some roadside check facilities, traffic volume is very high. Pulling every commercial vehicle into the station to do even rudimentary checks is sometimes not practical or safe.

ITS objectives for electronic screening

Objectives for the electronic screening aspects of ITS include:

- Identify oversize, overweight and improperly credentialed vehicles
- Identify high-risk and improperly credentialed carriers
- Select higher-risk safety performers for closer scrutiny
- Provide safety and credentials compliance statistics to support policy decisions, rule making and program development

ITS/CVO solutions are being applied to screening. Safety and credentials information are being provided to the roadside, vehicle-to-roadside communications are supporting the identification of carrier and vehicle, and screening algorithms based on automated measurements and evaluation of safety history and credentials information are allowing enforcement officials to focus on higher-risk operators.

Key operational concepts for electronic screening

Key operational concepts for electronic screening focus on employing technology to improve the sorting process.

**Table 9–10
Key ITS/CVO Operational Concepts for
Electronic Screening**

- Interoperability among screening systems
- Widespread participation encouraged
- Up-to-date electronic information at the roadside
- Credential and safety checks at the roadside
- Use fixed and mobile roadside check stations
- Electronic screening is part of a comprehensive safety policy

Interoperability among screening systems

Multiple screening systems collectively service the continental United States. Interoperability of electronic screening systems is facilitated by agreements pertaining to:

- Sharing of CVO data
- Standards for EDI and common interfaces for DSRC (i.e., single transponder works with any electronic screening system)
- Common screening criteria

Widespread participation encouraged

Electronic screening programs encourage widespread carrier participation by providing clear benefits and openly disclosing how the screening process works and how screening data are used. Administrative processes facilitate the participation of individual carriers and vehicles.

Up-to-date electronic information at the roadside

Current information supports good decision-making. Proactively updating snapshot and other safety and credentials information for use at the roadside makes electronic screening processes effective, reliable, and trusted.

Credential and safety checks at the roadside

Being equipped with a transponder is not a guarantee of automatic bypass at roadside check stations. Both credentials and safety are checked during screening events.

Use fixed and mobile roadside check stations

States can deploy any combination of the following:

*   Fixed, attended sites on major routes for routine enforcement
*   Mobile, attended sites for surprise enforcement
*   Fixed, unattended sites on major routes to collect data on passing vehicles to more effectively plan when to deploy enforcement personnel
*   Mobile, unattended sites to collect data on passing vehicles to more effectively plan when and where to deploy enforcement personnel

Different stations may have different vehicle measurement capabilities, including devices such as static scales, weigh in motion and height detectors.

Electronic screening is part of a comprehensive safety policy

The general philosophy is to monitor most of the traffic with as few weigh stations as possible. This provides assurance that most vehicles are compliant and forces evaders to use less economically efficient routes, where there is still some risk of random inspections at mobile stations.

ITS Technologies

There are a variety of technologies that are used in electronic screening and a number of different ways in which they can be applied, for example:

*   DSRC for identification and signaling
*   Weigh in motion (WIM)
*   Automatic vehicle classification (AVC)
*   Automatic vehicle identification
*   Height detector
*   EDI
*   Vehicle tracking loops
*   Automatic signing
*   Computers
*   Screening and sorting algorithms
*   Networks

The application of electronic screening will depend on many constraints, including site limitations, availability of support staff and funding. Each roadside check station is likely to have a unique design.

A representative operational scenario

Figure 9–12 illustrates electronic screening. If a legal and safe commercial vehicle is equipped with a transponder, as it approaches a roadside check station equipped with a roadside reader, height and weight sensors, screening computer system and roadside operations computer system, the vehicle may be cleared to bypass the station. A vehicle that has no transponder is pulled in for further checks. Any illegal or unsafe vehicle is subject to further scrutiny, whether it has a transponder or not. Vehicles may also be pulled in randomly, regardless of safety, weight, size, or credentials status. For more detailed information on electronic screening, see the paper *CVISN Roadside Electronic Screening* (Johns Hopkins 1998a).

Figure 9–12 illustrates the real-time electronic screening process for a vehicle equipped with a transponder. Electronic screening also usually includes some daily preparatory activities. Before a roadside check station begins operations for the day, carrier and vehicle snapshots are transmitted from a central system (often the state CVIEW system) to each roadside check station. Data from the snapshots used for screening are summarized into quick-access tables and loaded into the screening system.

Figure 9–12. Electronic screening scenario.

**DSRC is used to identify the carrier and the vehicle.
Corresponding infrastructure data help with screening decisions.**

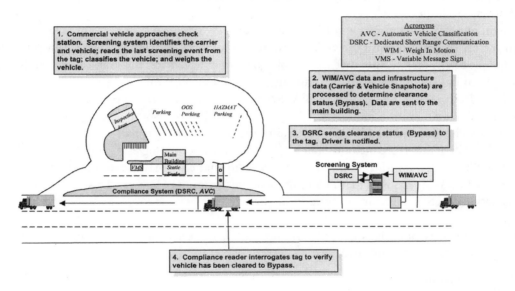

The roadside operations computer provides an operator interface to the roadside operations. The screening computer receives screening criteria from the roadside operations computer and collects inputs from all roadside sensors.

A screening algorithm implemented in the screening computer is used to make the screening decision based on sensor inputs and the screening criteria. There are five major components to the recommended automatic screening algorithm:

1. Transponder validation to authenticate the identifier(s)
2. Weight and size screening
3. Safety screening on the carrier and vehicle safety history derived from snapshots
4. Credentials screening, based on specific credential violations or history information contained in snapshots
5. A random selection factor to randomly pull in a selected percentage of vehicles

Selection for pull-in is made even if only one part of the algorithm suggests there is a problem, regardless of the status of the other conditions.

Summary of ITS benefits

The electronic screening ITS/CVO initiatives address identifying unsafe or illegal carriers or vehicles through the use of DSRC, sensors and evaluation of infrastructure-provided safety and credentials history data. The benefits of electronic screening are:

- Roadside resources can be better focused on high-risk operators
- Safe and legal operators can avoid unnecessary stops at multiple roadside check sites

CVISN

CVISN refers to the collection of information systems and communications networks that support CVO (Johns Hopkins University 1999). These include information systems owned and operated by governments, motor carriers and other stakeholders. The FHWA CVISN program is not trying to create a new information system, but rather to create a way for existing and newly designed systems to exchange information through the use of standards and the available communications infrastructure. The CVISN program provides a framework or architecture that will enable government agencies, the motor carrier industry and other parties engaged in CVO safety assurance and regulation to exchange information and conduct business transactions electronically. The goal of the CVISN program is to improve the safety and efficiency of CVO.

The CVISN architecture is the CVO information systems and networks part of the national ITS architecture. The CVISN architecture includes standards for interface technologies such as EDI and DSRC. These standards are being developed to promote interoperability and efficiency. Transportation Equity Act for the 21st Century (TEA-21) requires that ITS projects funded from the Highway Trust Fund must be consistent with the national ITS architecture and applicable standards.

Currently, the primary objective of the CVISN program is to develop and deploy information systems that will support new capabilities in three areas:

1. Safety information exchange
2. Credentials administration
3. Electronic screening

TEA-21 established the goal of deploying these capabilities to a majority of states by 2003. The CVISN program is using an approach based on an open architecture and standards so that these capabilities may be deployed in a manner that is interoperable from state-to-state from a motor carrier's perspective. The architecture will also enable the addition of further capabilities in the future. An overview of the vision for each of the current capability areas was presented in the preceding sections.

CVISN stakeholders—roles and relationships

The CVISN program is a voluntary effort. Its success is totally dependent on the cooperation of all stakeholders (Johns Hopkins 1997a). Stakeholders must have a willingness to honestly represent their point-of-view; to understand other stakeholders' requirements; and to collaborate to achieve mutually beneficial policies, plans and processes. There are three groups of CVO stakeholders making major ITS investments: carriers, states and the federal government.

Carriers
For a carrier to get the full benefit of ITS programs, it must at least make some level of investment in transponder and EDI technology. This allows participation in electronic credentialing and electronic screen-

ing programs. Further investments in fleet management software, on-board computers, mobile communications, office automation and other technologies will improve their internal processes and roadside operations.

States

Participating states must make an investment in information systems and other ITS technology. They must enhance their systems for licensing, credential and tax administration and safety assurance to be compatible with the national architecture. This primarily means supporting standard EDI transactions. They must establish an information infrastructure to provide data necessary for electronic screening at fixed and mobile sites. They must provide the data necessary to support electronic screening in other states. They must also provide electronic screening equipment at roadside sites.

Federal government

The federal government has expedited the deployment of ITS technology by providing technical, managerial and funding support. The CVISN architecture effort is a key element of technical support that provides a technical framework for states to implement their systems. Funding was provided for key research projects, operational tests and deployment efforts.

Other stakeholder groups include drivers, service providers, manufacturers, professional and trade associations, operational test participants and regional consortia.

Key CVISN operational concepts

The term operational concept refers to an idea for how a technology or system can be used to accomplish some function or process. Throughout this chapter, many operational concepts have been identified that were specific to a particular CVO function. The CVISN operational concepts incorporate all of these. But the CVISN architecture is more than the sum of its parts. The real purpose of the CVISN architecture is to emphasize some cross-functional integration concepts (Johns Hopkins 1996).

Table 9–11
Key Operational Concepts for CVISN

* Authoritative sources of data
* Information exchange across functional areas using open standards
* Standard identifiers for carriers, vehicles, drivers, trips and loads

Authoritative sources of data

The term authoritative source, also known as a system of record, is used to refer to the information system that can provide the correct answer to a question. The authoritative source is the final arbiter in case of conflicts about data validity. It is the legal source of the data. Data that have been authenticated by the authoritative source have been proven to be genuine. In some cases, data are stored immediately and authenticated later by authorized personnel or systems.

Information exchange across functional areas using open standards

If one concept had to be selected as the most important one for the CVISN program, it would be that open standards are used to exchange data among systems operated by different stakeholders. In particular, EDI is used for computer-to-computer exchanges between fixed computer sites; and DSRC standards are used for communication from vehicles to the roadside. The carrier and vehicle snapshots (discussed further in the "Safety Assurance" section presented earlier in this chapter) are specific types of EDI transactions that are particularly important to cross-functional integration.

Standard identifiers for carriers, vehicles, drivers, trips, and loads

Standard identifiers for key entities are essential to enable cross-referencing and standard look-ups in multiple information systems. A common scheme for identifying carriers, vehicles, drivers, cargo and trips must be adopted among all stakeholders that wish to exchange information.

What is the CVISN architecture?

The CVISN architecture is a subset of the ITS/CVO architecture. The ITS/CVO architecture is a subset of the national ITS architecture. The ITS/CVO architecture is a framework that serves as guidance for stakeholders in the CVO community to develop information systems, standards, interfaces, and subsystems to support identified user services. These user services are defined in this chapter's introduction. They were based on stakeholder needs and requirements, and they were an outgrowth of analyzing operational scenarios within the commercial motor vehicle environment.

The national ITS architecture is an organized approach to implementing, in a consistent manner across the United States, the various ITS user services envisioned for the next twenty years or more. It is a framework that lays out the boundaries, players and strategies for the process of information management. This framework provides guidance in developing standards and making deployment decisions that result in safety, efficiency, economies of scale and national interoperability. Figure 9–13 is a version of the national ITS architecture's sausage diagram that highlights the CVO-unique subsystems with thick borders and shading. CVO comprises four of these subsystems; and a more detailed architecture consistent with, and derived from, the national ITS architecture exists to support it. The CVISN architecture was developed from this subset of the national ITS architecture to provide a technical framework for the development of systems for implementing various ITS/CVO user services that use information systems and networks. The CVISN architecture is intended to guide implementations throughout all of North America to foster commercial motor vehicle safety and efficiency across United States borders into Mexico and Canada.

Figure 9–14 shows the CVISN architecture. The CVISN architecture is the ITS/CVO information systems and networks portion of the national ITS architecture. The CVISN architecture adds more detail in some areas (e.g., operational concepts and the EDI message requirements) to facilitate deployment.

The CVISN architecture defines:

- The functions associated with ITS/CVO user services
- The physical entities or subsystems within which such functions reside
- The data interfaces and information flows between physical subsystems
- The communications requirements associated with information flows

Key features of the CVISN architecture include:

- State systems are the authoritative sources for electronic CVO credential, tax and safety data.
- EDI standards provide common transaction formats for all CVO systems.
- State systems provide snapshot data proactively.

Figure 9–13. ITS/CVO architecture.

This version of the ITS National Architecture Subsystems Interconnect Diagram highlights the CVO subsystems.

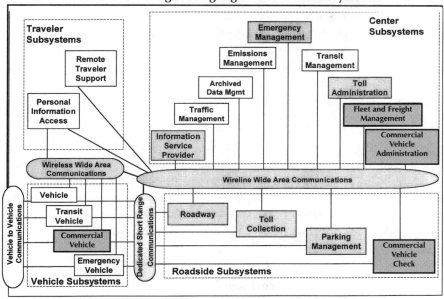

Figure 9–14. The CVISN architecture.

The CVO Architecture includes the information systems and networks in the ITS/CVO Architecture.

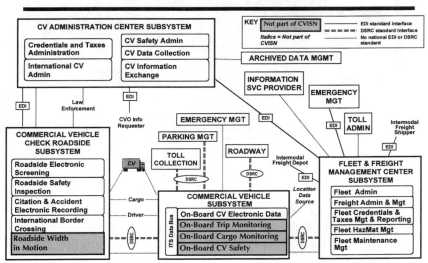

- The information exchange capability distributes commonly required snapshot data to the roadside and deskside.
- Commercial wireline and wireless wide area communications are used to provide data connectivity among all stakeholders.
- Vehicle-based and roadside-based equipment compliant with DSRC support screening, toll, traffic, fleet applications and border crossing processes throughout North America.
- Encryption and password technology ensure data privacy.
- The architecture supports customized and evolving capabilities.

The CVISN system design—stakeholders view

Figure 9–15 shows a high-level view of the CVISN system design. It groups systems by the three major stakeholder groups: carriers, states and multistate or federal systems. The carrier systems include systems located at the carrier headquarters or terminal that handle fleet and freight management activities. They also include the on-board vehicle ITS systems. The state systems fall into three groups, corresponding to the three functional areas of safety information exchange, credentials administration and electronic screening. The national systems include multistate credential clearinghouse systems as well as safety systems developed and operated by the FHWA. The CVISN System Design Description (Johns Hopkins 1997b) presents a more detailed version of this diagram and describes each of the components.

Figure 9–15. CVISN system design—simplified stakeholder view.

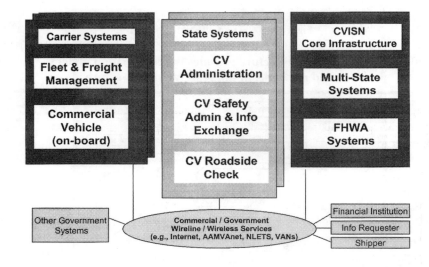

A simplified top-level design for a state's CVISN system

A state must develop or otherwise acquire new systems and modify some existing systems to implement the initial CVISN capabilities. There are many ways to do this and still be in conformance with the national ITS architecture and standards. A typical way that is modeled on the approaches taken by the CVISN prototype states, Maryland and Virginia, is shown in figure 9–16.

Figure 9–16. CVISN system design.

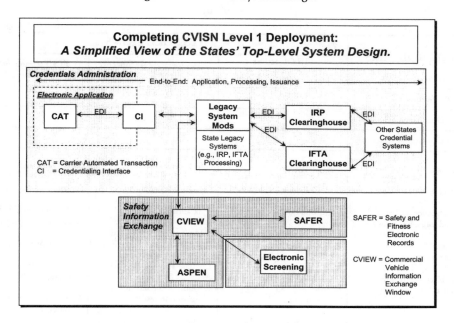

Figure 9–16 shows the three functional areas (safety information exchange, credentials administration and electronic screening) that are the focus of the CVISN program. Note that the interfaces among these three areas are relatively simple (at least when viewed at this high level). However, these cross-functional interfaces are at the core of the purpose of the CVISN program. Among other things, the CVISN architecture facilitates exchange of data over functional boundaries, enabling each area to improve the execution of its function. For example, the vehicle registration process can check a carrier's safety record to ensure that unsafe vehicles are not registered. Screening systems can check the credentials records to make sure that unregistered vehicles are not given a bypass. Safety systems can do real-time queries to check that drivers are licensed and vehicles are not known to be stolen.

Summary of ITS benefits

The CVISN architecture provides a common framework for the deployment of ITS/CVO functions across the nation. The CVISN architecture is more detailed than the national ITS architecture, focusing on issues and demonstrated solutions particular to CVO. The CVISN architecture recommends interface standards and operational agreements to promote a higher level of integration within functional areas and across functional areas.

Discussion questions

Question 1

How are the problems in CVO addressed by ITS objectives, operational concepts and technologies?

In this discussion, it might be effective to build a matrix that summarizes the problems and ITS solutions in each of the CVO functional areas covered in this chapter. The example below is partially completed. The numbers in the ITS solutions columns refer to the numbers of the problems in the CVO problems column.

Table 9–12
ITS Solutions

CVO PROBLEMS	ITS SOLUTIONS		
	ITS Objectives	Key Operational Concepts	ITS Technologies and Systems
Freight Movement			
Carrier Operations			
Vehicle Operations			
Safety Assurance 1. Too many fatalities involve large trucks 2. Inspections and compliance reviews are good tools, but resources to conduct them are limited 3. Data from past inspections and compliance reviews are often not readily available for review Summary of problems and ITS solutions: By automating the safety performance assessment processes, providing better access to safety performance data and analyzing past safety performance, the limited safety regulatory resources can help poor performers improve, and remove chronically unsafe performers from the road.	Safety Assurance 2., 3. Collect, store, and provide access to safety information 1., 3. Proactively identify unsafe operators 1., 2., 3. Improve safety assurance program efficiency and effectiveness. 3. Provide safety compliance statistics to support policy decisions, rule making, and program development 1., 2. Implement programs to encourage unsafe operators to improve their performance or to remove them from the highways	Safety Assurance 1., 2., 3. Measures of effectiveness: accidents and fatalities 3. Electronic safety records at roadside 1. Base state for each carrier 2. Automated collection of inspection results 2. Compliance reviews and electronic access to participating carrier's records 2. Determining safety risk ratings 3. Providing safety data to government and nongovernment stakeholders 1., 2., 3.Comprehensive safety policy	Safety Assurance *Systems:* 2., 3. State legacy systems associated with safety 3. State CVIEW 2. State CV roadside check stations 2., 3. Multistate/national systems *Technologies:* 2., 3. Databases 2., 3. Networks 1., 2., 3. Data analysis tools 2., 3. Portable computers 2., 3. Wireless communications 1., 2. Sensors 1., 2. Portable diagnostic devices
Credentials Administration			
Electronic Screening			

Question 2

What problems does the CVISN initiative address? What ITS solutions are part of CVISN? What benefits does the CVISN architecture provide?

Notes to instructors: In early deployments, the CVISN initiative is addressing CVO problems in the areas of safety information exchange, credentials administration and electronic screening.

Many ITS solutions are part of CVISN:

- The ITS objectives and operational concepts listed in the sections on safety assurance, credentials administration and electronic screening, together with most of the systems and technologies mentioned. The only objectives, concepts, systems, or technologies mentioned in those earlier sections that are not part of CVISN are those exclusively involving sensors.
- CVISN emphasizes the added benefits that can be realized by integrating the solutions across typical functional boundaries. For instance, safety can be improved by focusing enforcement on high-risk operators using electronic screening. Those who are at higher risk are identified through improved access to not only safety information but also credentials information. In turn, by evaluating safety performance during credentialing activities, high-risk operators can be identified and put into safety improvement programs.

The CVISN architecture provides a common framework that guides CVO stakeholders through implementation of ITS solutions to CVO problems. The open EDI and DSRC standards developed in association with the CVISN architecture are immediately accessible and useful to streamline individual system designs. The architecture incorporates lessons learned from early deployments.

References

American Trucking Associations Management Systems Council. 1996. *Motor Carrier MIS Directory.* ATA.

Bowersox, D. J., P. J. Daugherty, C. L. Droge, R. N. Germain, and D. S. Rogers. 1992. *Logistical Excellence.* Digital Press.

I-95 Corridor Coalition and the Northeast Transportation Institute. 1998. Fleet Forward Interactive CD and Brochure. I-95 Corridor Coalition and the ATA Foundation's Northeast Transportation Institute.

International Association of Chiefs of Police, Advisory Committee on Highway Safety. 1998. *The Highway Safety Desk Book.* Bureau of Traffic Safety, National Transportation Library, <http://www.bts.gov/NTL/DOCS/deskbk.html>.

ITS America. 1995. *National ITS Program Plan.* First Edition. Washington, D.C.: ITS America.

The Johns Hopkins University Applied Physics Laboratory. 1996. *Commercial Vehicle Information Systems and Networks (CVISN) Operational Concept Document.* JHU/APL, <http://www.jhuapl.edu/cvo/>.

The Johns Hopkins University Applied Physics Laboratory. 1997a. *Introduction to Commercial Vehicle Information Systems and Networks.* JHU/APL, <http://www.jhuapl.edu/cvo/>.

The Johns Hopkins University Applied Physics Laboratory. 1997b. Commercial Vehicle Information Systems and Networks (CVISN) System Design Description. JHU/APL, <http://www.jhuapl.edu/cvo/>.

The Johns Hopkins University Applied Physics Laboratory. 1998a. *CVISN Roadside Electronic Screening White Paper, Preliminary.* JHU/APL, <http://www.jhuapl.edu/cvo/>.

The Johns Hopkins University Applied Physics Laboratory. 1998b. *Commercial Vehicle Information Systems And Networks Glossary.* JHU/APL, <http://www.jhuapl.edu/cvo/>.

The Johns Hopkins University Applied Physics Laboratory. 1998c. *Survey of On-Board Technologies Applicable to Commercial Vehicle Operations.* JHU/APL, <http://www.jhuapl.edu/cvo/>.

The Johns Hopkins University Applied Physics Laboratory. 1999. *Introductory Guide to Commercial Vehicle Information Systems and Networks.* JHU/APL, <http://www.jhuapl.edu/cvo/>.

U.S. Department of Transportation, Federal Highway Administration, Office of Motor Carriers. 1997. *Strategic Plan, Fiscal Year 1997.* Washington, D.C.: U.S. DOT, FHWA, OMC, <http://www.fhwa.dot.gov/omc/strategi.html>.

U.S. Department of Transportation, Bureau of Transportation Statistics. 1998a. *National Transportation Statistics 1998.* Washington, D.C.: U.S. DOT, BTS, <http://www.bts.gov/btsprod/nts/>.

U.S. Department of Transportation, Federal Highway Administration. 1998b. *Technician Guidelines for Antilock Braking Systems.* Washington, D.C.: U.S. DOT, FHWA.

U.S. Department of Transportation, Federal Highway Administration, Office of Motor Carriers. 1998c. *Selected Office of Motor Carrier Statistics.* Washington, D.C.: U.S. DOT, FHWA, OMC.

U.S. Department of Transportation, Federal Highway Administration, Office of Motor Carriers. 1999a. *1997 Large Truck Crash Overview.* Washington, D.C.: U.S. DOT, FHWA, OMC, <http://www.fhwa.dot.gov/omc/Truck97.htm>.

U.S. Department of Transportation, Federal Highway Administration, Office of Motor Carriers. 1999b. *PRISM Overview.* Washington, D.C.: U.S. DOT, FHWA, OMC, <http://www.fhwa.dot.gov/omc/prism.htm>.

Endnotes

1. Mr. Kim E. Richeson is a member of the principal staff at the Johns Hopkins University Applied Physics Laboratory (APL) in Laurel, Maryland. Mr. Richeson is the manager for the APL Commercial Vehicle Information Systems and Networks (CVISN) Program. His email address is <kim.richeson@jhuapl.edu>.

2. Ms. Valerie B. Barnes is also a member of the principal staff at the Johns Hopkins University Applied Physics Laboratory in Laurel, Maryland. Ms. Barnes is the lead for APL's CVISN Architecture and Standards Project. Her e-mail address is <valerie.barnes@jhuapl.edu>.

3. As of January 2000, the Office of Motor Carriers was renamed the Federal Motor Carrier Safety Administration.

THE ROLE OF ITS TECHNOLOGIES IN TRAVEL DEMAND MANAGEMENT

BY C. Kenneth Orski • Past Chairman, TDM Council • Institute of Transportation Engineers

In recent years, transportation demand management (TDM) has assumed a significant role as an instrument of transportation policy. TDM is explicitly mandated in the Clean Air Act Amendments of 1990, in the Intermodal Surface Transportation Efficiency Act (ISTEA) and in the Transportation Equity Act for the 21st Century; and it is used in numerous local traffic reduction ordinances, development agreements, and transportation plans as a tool of congestion management, traffic calming and air quality control. This chapter provides a brief history of TDM and discusses the role that ITS technologies are beginning to play in enhancing TDM.

What is TDM?

TDM has been succinctly described as the art of influencing traveler behavior with the aim of reducing automobile travel demand, or redistributing this demand in space or in time. TDM seeks to promote these objectives by encouraging:

- Shifts from driving alone to traveling in high-occupancy modes of transportation (e.g., carpools, vanpools, public transit)
- Shifts from driving in peak periods, or on congested roads to driving in off-peak periods, or on less congested roads
- Reductions in total vehicle trips and vehicle miles of travel
- Limits on automobile use or changes in driving behavior in certain designated urban zones (e.g., central business districts, residential neighborhoods)

TDM measures include promotion of transit and ridesharing, flexible working arrangements (e.g., staggered work hours, flextime, telecommuting), traffic calming and driving restrictions and prohibitions. These measures may be implemented through laws and regulations, promotional programs, monetary and tax incentives, pricing policies, planning requirements, negotiated agreements with developers and employer trip reduction programs. Increasingly, ITS is being used to facilitate and enhance TDM.

A brief history of TDM

Although the acronym "TDM" has been used only since the mid-1980s, the concept of TDM first appeared during World War II when the public was urged to share automobiles for the trip to work in order to conserve gasoline. The concept was given additional impetus during the fuel crisis of the early 1970s, and in 1974 it was institutionalized as part of the transportation system management (TSM) requirement promulgated under the Federal Highway Administration-Urban Mass Transportation Administration joint planning regulations. In the original regulation, no distinction was made between supply and demand management;

both were seen as elements of TSM. Eventually, however, TDM came to be viewed as a separate policy tool, distinct from capacity (supply) management. Over a period of the last fifteen years, TDM has acquired professional legitimacy and political acceptability. TDM programs have been mainstreamed through local and regional transportation plans, local trip reduction ordinances, public ridesharing agencies, transportation management associations and employer trip reduction programs. In the course of its evolution, TDM has been invested with different purposes and objectives. Originally, the aim of TDM, as indeed of the entire TSM requirement, was to increase the efficiency and carrying capacity of existing transportation facilities, to conserve energy and to control the growth of local traffic congestion. In the 1980s, under the influence of the environmental movement, TDM began to acquire additional objectives: improving air quality, reducing solo commuting and promoting the use of public transportation. The ISTEA embraced TDM as a tool of regional congestion management, while the Clean Air Act Amendments of 1990 adopted TDM as an instrument of area-wide pollution control. Much of the debate surrounding TDM's effectiveness since then stems from the lack of a consensus on the objectives that TDM is supposed to serve.

The rise and fall of regulatory TDM requirements

The Employee Commute Options (ECO) mandate, promulgated in 1991 by the U.S. Environmental Protection Agency pursuant to the Clean Air Act Amendments of 1990, required all businesses employing more than 100 workers in ten "severe non-attainment areas" for ozone to implement trip-reduction programs designed to reduce the employees' average vehicle passenger occupancy by 25 percent.[1] The requirement was modeled after a similar Southern California regulation enacted in December 1987—Regulation XV, later re-named Rule 1501. Starting in the early 1990s, strong opposition to the California requirement developed on the part of the business community. Employers felt that the trip reduction requirement imposed a costly and unreasonable burden on them, because they could exercise little influence over their employees' travel behavior. Responding to strong pressures from business groups, public opposition and negative press, the California state legislature passed a law prohibiting any jurisdiction from requiring employers to implement trip reduction programs, unless required by federal law (Dill 1998).

The backlash against mandatory employer trip reduction also occurred at the national level. Strong opposition to the federal ECO requirement developed in several of the affected jurisdictions and culminated in the formation of a national coalition of employers, business organizations and transportation management associations, known as Mobility Coalition for Clean Air. With strong support from the Coalition, the U.S. Congress repealed the federal ECO mandate in December 1995. The repeal of the federal and California trip reduction regulations in 1995 to 1996 marked the end of attempts to force changes in driving behavior by mandates and government regulation. Today, travel demand is managed entirely through voluntary programs and market mechanisms.

TDM effectiveness— conclusions from U.S. experience

With more than 20 years of experience behind us, there is a solid foundation of data on which to base conclusions about TDM's impact and effectiveness:

1. *TDM has an important role in the growth management process.* TDM programs have been employed successfully in many jurisdictions to limit trip generation from new office development. Based on their demonstrated effectiveness, many local governments have made developer-sponsored TDM programs a condition of development approvals, while other jurisdictions have passed traffic reduction ordinances requiring major new projects to implement TDM measures (ITE 1996, U.S. DOT 1989). It is significant that, when the California legislature prohibited public agencies throughout California from requiring employer trip reduction programs, it specifically exempted local traffic reduction programs enacted for the purpose of mitigating traffic impact of new development.

2. *TDM programs have proved their worth as a tool of local congestion relief.* Employer-based TDM programs have helped to reduce spot congestion and lessen delays at intersections, freeway ramps and exits from parking facilities surrounding suburban office parks. There is also some evidence that TDM measures incorporated into local traffic management plans have helped to moderate the growth of congestion in suburban downtowns. TDM programs in the form of traffic calming measures have proved effective in reducing unwanted traffic, controlling aggressive driving behavior and increasing pedestrian safety in residential neighborhoods.

3. *TDM programs have not been successful in reducing the growth of vehicle miles of travel on an area-wide basis and thus are not an effective tool of controlling regional air pollution or managing congestion.* While some individual site-based TDM initiatives have achieved significant reductions in the drive-alone rate, on the whole TDM programs have failed to change commuter travel habits and have not met the trip reduction targets of state or federal air quality regulations. A study by Los Angeles's Commuter Transportation Services, Inc., which has been tracking commuter travel behavior in the Los Angeles region since 1990, reports that carpool, transit and drive-alone rates have remained remarkably constant during the 7 years of regulatory mandates that required employers to implement trip reduction programs. According to the report, a total of 78.5 percent of Los Angeles area commuters drove alone in 1996, compared to 78.2 percent in 1990; carpools and vanpools accounted for 14.5 percent in 1996, compared to 14.8 percent in 1990; and transit ridership rose fractionally, from 4.3 percent in 1990 to 4.7 percent in 1996 (Southern California Rideshare 1996, Young and Luo 1997).

Factors influencing solo commuting

As the 1995 Nationwide Personal Transportation Survey (NPTS) report observes, "the myth of Americans' love affair with their cars may actually be a marriage of convenience. Contemporary land use patterns require the use of private vehicles, whether or not we love those vehicles." Actually, the dispersed land use patterns are only one of several reasons for Americans' increasing reliance on their cars. Other reasons include changing travel patterns, increased presence of women in the labor force, the changing nature of employment and a lack of convenient transportation alternatives.

Travel-to-work patterns have changed dramatically during the decade of the 1980s. While some commuters still go from a suburban home to a downtown office and back at predictable times, just as their parents did 30 years ago, the great majority of contemporary workers have highly complex travel patterns. Working parents drop off and pick up children at day care centers on the way to and from work, they run errands, keep appointments during the day and shop after work. To working parents, nurseries and day care centers are daily destinations just as important as their offices. NPTS data show that approximately 30 percent of workers who leave work between 4 p.m. and 7 p.m. make incidental daily stops on the way home. Similarly, about 20 percent of all work trips between 6 a.m. and 9 a.m. include one or more daily stops on the way to work—these multiple function commutes (also known as "trip chaining") make an efficient use of time, and time has become a precious commodity to modern two-worker families. Unfortunately, multiple-stop commutes make mass transit and ridesharing alternatives inconvenient and often impossible to use. Without an automobile it is also difficult to leave work in a hurry in case of a family emergency. Having a car at work is a great anxiety reducer for workers with young children or elderly parents. Increased numbers of women in the workforce, especially mothers with young children, has been cited as another reason for the growth of solo commuting. Women are more likely to drive alone than men and the most pronounced auto dependency is among working women with young children (Pisarski 1996, Edmondson 1997).

Finally, the changing nature of employment may also have increased solo driving. Fewer factory workers must arrive at large factories to begin work all at the same time. Today's office workers and service personnel are more likely to arrive at staggered times, leave during the day to run errands, quit for the day at different times and perhaps even return to work in the evening at a second job.

All these trends impose severe constraints on the capacity to affect travel behavior and reduce automobile dependency. While the NPTS notes new demographic influences—such as the aging of the baby boom generation—that may influence the travel picture, there are no indications that the fundamental forces that are making American society ever more dependent on personal transportation will lessen or reverse direction in the foreseeable future.

Applying ITS technologies to TDM

As discussed above, attempts to implement TDM policies have met with less than complete success. However, ITS technologies offer the promise of realizing some of TDM's unfulfilled potential. While futuristic uses of communication technologies, such as in-vehicle navigation systems, have grabbed the headlines and captured attention of Sunday supplements, many ITS technologies are already quietly at work, making the job of transportation management more effective and efficient.

ITS technology is enhancing the management of travel demand in several ways. The following section describes specific applications of ITS in: (1) real-time traveler information, (2) interactive ridematching, (3) parking management, (4) dynamic pricing of highway capacity, (5) transit operations, and (6) telecommuting.

Real-time traveler information

Perhaps the best-known application of advanced communication technologies to TDM are electronic real-time traveler information systems. Traveler information systems provide commuters and other travelers with timely and accurate information about travel choices. This information can be received at home, at work, or en route via a range of communication media. Prior to departure, radio, television, telephone, pagers and computers can provide timely information about travel conditions, enabling travelers to choose the best travel mode, route and time of departure. Information about accidents, traffic speeds along given routes, weather and road conditions and special events that might disrupt traffic can be used by travelers to modify their travel plans. Information about transit routes, schedules and parking availability at rail stations can help travelers decide whether public transit is an effective option.

Once travel begins, car radios, visual displays, and other more advanced communication devices can provide travelers with updates about traffic conditions, transit service, incidents, and parking availability at destination. Roadside dynamic message signs (DMS), such as electronic signboards, and highway advisory radio (HAR) can alert motorists to current weather and road conditions. Visual displays at bus stops and rail stations can inform waiting passengers about arrival time and destination of the next train or transit bus. Vehicle-based route navigation systems containing map displays can guide motorists traveling in unfamiliar surroundings to their destinations. Real-time traffic flow data can alert motorists to traffic problems ahead and re-route them around accidents and congestion bottlenecks.

In the event of an accident or mechanical breakdown, emergency MAYDAY systems enable travelers and operators of transit vehicles to call for assistance. Global positioning systems can automatically provide car or bus location, even if the driver is disabled or cannot accurately describe the location. Consumer surveys indicate that MAYDAY systems are considered among the most valued features of traveler information systems.

Searching for destinations and roadside services can be aided by electronic yellow pages accessed through the Internet and kiosks located in airports, shopping malls, transit terminals, hotels and highway rest areas. Also available are in-vehicle traveler information services listing lodging, restaurants, roadside services, tourist attractions and weather or airline arrival and departure information.

The principal means of delivering traveler information are commercial radio and television broadcasts, which reach an estimated daily audience of 100 million people. Other information delivery channels include automated telephone inquiry systems, cable television, interactive television, electronic kiosks and the Internet. DMS and HAR are used to communicate to motorists information about driving conditions immediately ahead. More advanced information delivery systems include portable wireless communication devices (e.g., personal digital assistants), radio-data system (RDS) protocols, vehicle-based navigation and guidance units, and electronic message boards for transit passengers. The use of advanced traveler communication systems in the United States is still limited. In Europe and Japan, on the other hand, in-vehicle navigation devices, RDS, and electronic passenger information systems are already widely employed. It seems likely that the U.S. demand for advanced traveler communication devices will grow as the number of localities offering timely and accurate traffic information increases.

There are expectations that accurate up-to-the-minute traffic bulletins and travel advisories delivered over traveler information systems can influence people to change their route, time or mode of travel, and thus help to redistribute demand throughout the transportation system and reduce congestion and travel delays. Although traveler information systems have so far failed to produce observable changes in the overall traffic flow, traffic patterns, transit usage, or congestion levels, this does not mean that commuters do not act upon the information they receive. As the use of traveler information systems increases, the cumulative effect of travelers' response may become more noticeable.

Interactive on-line ridematching

Internal computer systems known as local area networks (LAN) or the Intranet are used in large workplaces to facilitate employee ridesharing. Intranets enable employees to do their own carpool matching using computer bulletin boards accessible through desktop computers or through touch-screen kiosks located in company cafeterias and public lobbies. Employees can enter their names, telephone numbers and carpool preferences into the database, confident that this personal information will only be shared with fellow employees. This overcomes one of the drawbacks of public regional ridematching systems—people's reluctance to provide personal data to public data banks and to enter into ridesharing arrangements with strangers.

Parking management

Parking information and guidance systems

Parking management is another aspect of TDM that has benefited from advances in communication technology. Electronic parking information and guidance systems provide motorists with accurate, continuously updated information about occupancy status of parking facilities. This allows motorists to select the most convenient parking location in advance and it spares them the frustration of a time-consuming search for a parking space. Typically, motorists approaching their destination encounter a tier of variable message signs showing a continuously updated inventory of available parking spaces at various parking facilities. Parking information and guidance systems can be used to facilitate access to parking garages in central business districts, surface parking lots on the periphery of downtown areas, park-and-ride lots serving suburban commuter rail stations, satellite parking lots at airports and parking areas surrounding sports and entertainment complexes. Still relatively little is known in the United States. Electronic parking information and guidance systems are used extensively in the cities of Western Europe, where severe congestion and shortage of space in city centers provide a strong incentive for their deployment. Overseas experience suggests that parking information systems can serve as an effective TDM tool. They can help to disperse parking demand, relieve downtown congestion, achieve more efficient use of existing parking facilities and guide tourists and visitors who are unfamiliar with the area. At special events, electronic parking information and guidance systems can guide patrons to remote parking lots and significantly reduce the time spent in a search for parking.

Controlled access to parking facilities

One of the most effective means of discouraging commuters from driving to work alone is to charge them market prices for parking in company parking facilities. This approach, however, often encounters challenges by employee unions because charging for previously free parking is viewed as an adverse change in conditions of employment. A creative way around this problem has been adopted by some companies faced with a Clean Air Act mandate to reduce employee trips. Each employee is issued a monthly debit parking card that gives its holder access to the company's barrier-controlled parking lot. This debit card is programmed to allow only a limited number of entries. For example, if a company wishes to reduce employee auto trips by 20 percent, it issues parking access cards good only for four entries per week. Having exhausted their monthly quota of parking privileges, employees are obliged to devise alternate commute arrangements, be it carpooling, taking transit to work, or purchasing a fellow employee's unused parking credits.

Dynamic pricing of highway capacity

ITS technology has also enhanced the feasibility of dynamic pricing of road facilities. While the concept of peak period pricing has been applied in many sectors of the private economy for many years, the use of variable pricing to control demand for road space in order to maintain a given level of service has been stymied by the complexity of collecting variable-rate tolls (i.e., tolls that vary by the time of day or with the level of congestion). Now, electronic toll collection technology allows variable-rate tolls to be deducted from the driver's pre-paid, stored-value tag while the vehicle is in motion. This cashless, remote toll collection capability has made it possible to control demand in real-time and maintain free-flowing traffic conditions on tolled facilities. This approach has found its first application on two highway facilities in California: the privately built and operated SR91 Express Lanes in Orange County, California; and the I-15 high-occupancy and toll lanes north of San Diego, California.

Transit service enhancements

Automatic vehicle location (AVL) systems (i.e., wireless technologies that track buses and report their position to a central control station in real-time) have been used by transit agencies to improve productivity and operating performance of their bus fleets for several years. Now, AVL systems are being applied to TDM by communicating bus schedule information to the public and allowing dynamic scheduling of transit services. Electronic displays at bus stops in numerous European cities inform waiting passengers when the next bus will be along, thus eliminating a common source of rider dissatisfaction with public transit.

Telecommuting

Advances in video conferencing, high-capacity voice-data links, wireless transmission and an ever growing array of portable communications equipment are allowing employees to work at home or at remote telework sites. This in turn contributes to reducing the vehicle miles of travel. Although further improvements in communications technology will no doubt make work at remote locations increasingly feasible, this form of travel management, according to informed observers, will depend largely on the acceptance of telecommuting by corporate management.

References

Dill, J. 1998. Mandatory Employer-Based Trip Reduction—What Happened? (January). Department of City and Regional Planning, University of California, Berkeley.

Edmondson, B. 1997. "Alone in the Car" (June). American Demographics Magazine.

Federal Highway Administration. 1997. Highway Information Update 2, no. 3 (November 24). Washington, D.C.: FHWA.

Institute of Transportation Engineers. 1996. A Toolbox for Alleviating Traffic Congestion (September). Washington, D.C.: ITE.

Pisarski, A. 1996. Commuting in America II. Eno Transportation Foundation.

Southern California Rideshare. 1996. State of the Commute Report (January). Southern California Rideshare.

U.S. Department of Transportation. 1989. Status of Traffic Mitigation Ordinances (August). Washington, D.C.: U.S. DOT.

Young, R. and R. Luo. 1997. Five-Year Results of Employee Commute Options in Southern California. Washington, D.C.: Transportation Research Board.

Endnote

1.   The "severe non-attainment areas" are: Los Angeles/San Diego, New York/ New Jersey/Connecticut, Philadelphia, Houston, Baltimore, and Chicago/Milwaukee.

BY John MacGowan • Director, Office of Bus and Truck Standards and Operations, Federal Motor Carrier Safety Administration • Federal Highway Administration

ADVANCED VEHICLE CONTROL SYSTEMS

Background

This chapter will provide the student with some background and understanding of the history and issues that have surrounded the development of advanced vehicle control systems (AVCS). This is not a new subject area, as the history will show. Moreover, it is steeped in science and engineering that today has amassed a considerable body of knowledge in the area of vehicle-highway automation.

The early concepts

Since people first harnessed the wheel for transporting themselves and goods, they have been looking for a way to automate that process. Hooking up animals to pull various devices on wheels was one of the first attempts at "automation." Then in 1887, along came the automobile in the United States (table 11–1). Since then an entire U.S. industry has developed around making automobiles and trucks more comfortable and convenient. More recently, as the results of some of the less desirable societal impacts of the automobile have been recognized, efforts have been directed towards making them safer and more environmentally efficient.

AVCS are not new. Visionaries have linked the fantasies of magic carpets and automobiles for decades. Attendees at the 1939 World's Fair in New York saw the General Motors (GM) exhibit on "driverless" cars. This was followed in the 1950s with GM concept cars that used radio and other mechanical systems to control the steering and speed of the vehicles. The aim was to provide the driver with a relaxing, hands-off, feet-off driving experience, taking full advantage of the new, high-design Interstate System that was beginning to connect all of the United States.

The 1960s continued the desires for more automated driving with the development of more advanced electronics such as transistors and better communications. More practical uses were being seen for this automation. With the increase in vehicle utilization growing (table 11–2), the need for considerations for driver assistance to provide safety and increase throughput on an increasingly more populated roadway, as well as giving the driver better information on navigation and route choice, began to become primary considerations for automating the driving function.

Modern concepts

In the late 1970s, spurred on by the availability of greater computing power, the Federal Highway Administration (FHWA) researchers sponsored a study by GM to develop concepts and system configurations for a fully automated highway system. Due to funding considerations, this study was terminated in 1980. However, this was not before the notion of fully automating a vehicle-highway system became rooted.

Table 11–1
U.S. Automotive Milestones

1887	Ransom E. Olds develops a steam-powered vehicle.
1894	Henry Ford's first car, a two-cylinder, four-horsepower carriage, goes forward but not in reverse.
1897	Ransom Olds starts a car company—the Olds Motor Vehicle Company in Lansing, Michigan.
1900	Delco invents the first electrical distributor for automobile engines.
1901	Speedometers used for the first time.
1903	Henry Ford forms his third auto company, the Ford Motor Company.
1903	David Dunbar Buick starts a Buick plant in Flint, Michigan and sells it to William Durant the next year.
1903	Glass windshields used on autos for the first time.
1908	Buick owner William C. Durant forms General Motors.
1908	Ford Model T goes on sale for $850.
1909	Automobile storage battery invented by Thomas A. Edison.
1911	First electrical self-starter developed by Charles Kettering.
1912	Standard Oil Company opens first gas station in Cincinnati, Ohio.
1914	First stoplight for traffic control appears in Detroit, along with the first STOP sign.
1914	Cadillac develops its first V8 engine.
1915	All-steel car body produced by The Budd Co. for Dodge.
1916	Stoplights, rear-view mirrors, and mechanical windshield wipers appear on some cars.
1916	Work begins on a nation-wide coordinated highway system.
1921	The automatic windshield wiper is invented by W.M. Folberth.
1922	George Frost invents the car radio.
1922	An affordable, completely closed car interior for year-round driving is featured on the 1922 Essex.
1923	Firestone introduces the automobile balloon tire.
1924	Vincent Bendix markets a four-wheel brake system.
1924	Walter Chrysler forms Chrysler Motor Corporation.
1925	Front and rear bumpers become standard equipment.
1925	The first interstate highway opens—the Lincoln Highway—between New York and San Francisco.
1929	Front-wheel drive is featured on the Cord L29 Roadster.
1930	Motorola introduces the first commercial car radio.
1934	Independent front suspension appears on Chevrolet.
1936	More than 50 percent of American families own automobiles, according to the Dept. of Commerce.
1937	Buick and Oldsmobile offer automatic transmissions.
1938	Air conditioning is offered by Nash-Kelvinator.
1938	Buick adds electric turn signals.
1949	Buick Riviera becomes the first modern hardtop convertible.
1949	Chrysler innovations include the first key-operated ignition and safety-cushioned dash.
1950	First use of production seat belts on two Nash models.
1950	Chrysler offers power windows, followed the next year with power steering.
1953	Chrysler's 12-volt electrical system becomes the industry standard.
1955	Motorola introduces the all-transistor car radio, the alternator and the electronic ignition system.
1955	Sealed-beam headlights and door safety latches become industry standards.
1956	The Federal U.S. Highway Act is passed, which calls for construction of 41,000 miles of interstate highways.
1958	Cadillac introduces cruise control.
1963	California's new Motor Vehicle Pollution Board requires the first emission controls (PCV valves) on automobiles sold in the state.
1965	The Federal Motor Vehicle Air Pollution Act is passed, heralding a new era of government regulation of the auto industry.

Table 11–2
Growth of Vehicle Utilization
Source: *Highway Statistics 1995, 1997,* FHWA.

Year	VMT (10^9)
1939	285.4
1950	458.2
1960	718.8
1970	1,109.7
1980	1,527.3
1990	2,144.4
1997	2,576.5

This same concept again took hold in 1992 with the advent of the Intermodal Surface Transportation Efficiency Act of 1991 (ISTEA), which included the mandate:

> The Secretary [of Transportation] shall develop an automated highway and vehicle prototype from which future fully automated intelligent vehicle-highway systems can be developed. Such development shall include research in human factors to ensure that success of man–machine relationship. The goal of the program is to have the first fully automated roadway or an automated test track in operation by 1997. This system shall accommodate installation of equipment in new and existing motor vehicles [§6054(b)].

In 1993, the FHWA researchers again sponsored a series of contracts under the automated highway system (AHS) program to address and assess 16 issues that experience had suggested must be overcome for a successful AHS. The result of this effort was that 15 teams of researchers examined various aspects of the issues, generating 90 final reports. The final conclusion of this activity was that there were no technical "show stoppers" that would prevent the definition of an AHS. Following this conclusion, a major cooperative agreement was reached with a consortium of state governments, industry and academia to work with the FHWA to work cooperatively with the future AHS stakeholders and users, to select the AHS configuration that may ultimately be deployed as the next major performance upgrade of the nation's vehicle-highway system.[1]

As a result of this agreement with the National AHS Consortium (NAHSC), the state-of-the-art in AVCS was advanced considerably. The NAHSC's work was brought to an early conclusion in 1998 due to a refocusing of federal priorities that resulted in the advent of the intelligent vehicle initiative (IVI). Both the AHS efforts and the IVI are part of the intelligent transportation system (ITS) program conducted by the U.S. Department of Transportation (U.S. DOT).

The IVI program brings together much of the AVCS work being undertaken within the U.S. DOT. It is its primary goal to jointly, with the motor vehicle and trucking industries, state and local DOTs and other stakeholders, accelerate the development, introduction and commercialization of driver assistance products to reduce motor vehicle crashes and incidents (U.S. DOT 1997). While safety is the principal motivation within the IVI, there are collateral objectives of increasing mobility, improving energy efficiency and environmental quality and improving the productivity of the national transportation system.

International interests

The United States has not been the only theater of interest in AVCS. In Europe, there has been ongoing interest in researching the benefits of this technology. The European Commission has funded research in programs that have focused on an electronic two-bar. This technology is most notably prevalent in the public–private project called Promote-Chauffeur, which is focusing on heavy trucks for automated convoying. In 1998, the Dutch Ministry of Transportation staged a demonstration of several scenarios of various technologies that raised a great deal of interest in automated vehicle control.

Japan has been aggressively pursuing automated control since 1995. In 1996, Japan staged a demonstration on a test track of automated control. Since then, the country has developed a program known as Smartway, which will implement a national infrastructure for enabling a wide range of ITS technologies and for information to be exchanged among drivers, cars and pedestrians. Among the technologies that will be supported will be a level of automated vehicle control.

The evolution of purpose

From this brief recitation of the history of AVCS, it is possible to see the shifts in objectives that have stirred the desires for automated driving. Beginning in the earliest days, the objective was for the convenience of the driver. The purpose was to make the transport of passengers as comfortable and as enjoyable as possible. This was the era of King Automobile. The image that fired the imagination of many researchers was a sleek, futuristic-looking vehicle, gliding down the nearly-empty highways while the driver read the newspaper, talked on the telephone, or conducted other business without concern for the vehicle control. Nothing was impossible in the postwar United States. The Interstate Highway System was the most sophisticated transportation system in the world, and why shouldn't there be equally sophisticated automobiles using it?

But comfort and convenience soon gave way to the realities of the need for efficiency. More and more vehicles on the roadway meant less and less capacity. Merely controlling signal devices was not sufficient to accommodate the numerous cars going from one place to another, satisfying the drivers' desires for mobility. It was considered possible to increase the throughput of vehicles by taking the driver out of the loop. Automation could much more efficiently control the automobiles with the greater degree of certainty of movement afforded by the wonders of automation. After all, drivers were unpredictable. Computers could control vehicle headways and even their path.

Eventually, the need for efficiency became coupled with the need for safety. The carnage on the highways was rising at an alarming rate. It was deemed necessary to stimulate the rate at which automation was being considered. It was decided by policymakers at the highest levels of the United States that it was necessary to develop a "blueprint" for building an automated vehicle highway system over the coming years. Having a system specification founded on a public and private partnership would give the transportation of the future a stake in the sand to move toward in a coordinated fashion, eliminating the losses due to incompatibilities and divergent goals. After all, this was the same thinking that lead to the development of the Interstate Highway System to begin with. Thus, there was a policy migration from achieving full automation from gradual development of vehicle-highway systems to developing a system concept that would be built towards in carefully researched steps.

The tremendous financial commitment required to sustain this line of research and development soon brought the program under closer scrutiny. The Transportation Research Board of the National Research Council was invited by the U.S. DOT to convene a blue-ribbon panel of experts from transportation, operations, communications, information systems, safety, human factors and vehicle design to review the FHWA's

AHS program. Their conclusion was that while the framework of the program was well intentioned, it was flawed to the extent that the program may not reach its desired goal (TRB, NRC 1998). This came at the same time as the U.S. DOT was seeking to consolidate its vehicle-related research and direct it more towards a safety goal while learning from the technical success generated from the AHS program.

Thus was born the IVI. This program was once again to be a public–private partnership, but in an arrangement of joint governance rather than a grant program. The program is devoted to improving safety in the vehicle-highway operations of passenger cars, large trucks, transit busses and specialty vehicles such as highway construction and maintenance vehicles and emergency vehicles. While the specific developments for each of these vehicle platforms will be achieved somewhat differently, the overarching goal remains consistent: to bring the life-saving potential of modern technology into reality more quickly.

In the case of the passenger vehicles, under the joint governance rules, vehicle manufacturers are participating in a research program that explores technologies in a noncompetitive manner. That is, fundamental research is being conducted that will allow each participating manufacturer to take the results of that fundamental research and then pursue its use in their own competitive, production-oriented way. Heavy trucks and transit bus research is being conducted in more of a developmental way. The bulk of the research here is of an applied nature with the intention of gaining real-world operational testing of the technology to assure its suitability for everyday use. Finally, the specialty vehicle research is being conducted under the direction of state governments as they strive to find safer, more efficient means of constructing and operating the highways and for providing safety and security to the traveling public. A typical example of their research is on snow plows that will be able to stay on the roadway during blinding snow storms without endangering the drivers and other vehicles or roadside obstacles.

From the foregoing, it is easier to see that the changing and growing demand for AVCS will eventually result in its deployment. In fact, some could argue that there is deployment now in the form of automatic brake systems and headway warning systems, to name two examples. Will the U.S. motorist ever see the magic-carpet ride envisioned decades ago? Only time will tell. For now, researchers and manufacturers are working together to assist drivers in safely operating their vehicle.

Lessons learned from the AHS program

This section is meant to convey some of the institutional and pseudo-technological findings that resulted from the AHS program. Why this program? Because it represents the culmination of much of the research that has been completed over the past years. Also, it is the antecedent of that which will follow in vehicle-highway automation.

The research that has transpired over the past several decades has remained surprisingly consistent in terms of objectives and characteristics. However, it was not until the U.S. DOT attempted to take the next quantum leap from research to reality that new concepts became more evident. These concepts dealt more with sociological and institutional realities than technological uncertainties.

Early analysis

During the period from the 1960s to the 1980s, many technical studies were completed to examine various trade-offs that would influence the AHS concept. From the beginning, AHS was seen as a system of vehicles and roadways that would improve safety and capacity. The fundamental question of how much intelligence to put in the vehicle and how much to put in the roadway has always been a central issue. The second fundamental issue has always been how to deploy the AHS.

During the twenty or so years of this early research, several system concepts were developed. These concepts typically focused on intra-urban trips by vehicles capable of automated (usually electronic) and manual control, where in the former case some form of managed guideway system would be needed, and in the later case conventional roadways would suffice. However, these were not the only concepts explored. In the automated mode, several concepts using automated pallets were explored. For example, pallets were envisioned with steel wheels, guided along by mechanical means and propulsion coming from cog-railway techniques. Other palletized automation examined tracked air cushion using linear induction motors for propulsion. There was even a dual-mode pallet where automobiles would be loaded on steel-wheeled pallets on elevated guideways with traction motors supplying the motive power. Notwithstanding the several concepts that were researched, the goals of an AHS centered about:

- Safety
- Throughput
- Energy conservation
- Comfort and convenience
- Environmental and community impacts

Typically, the research was structured by examining factors of system structure (i.e., division of intelligence between the vehicle and the infrastructure) and system operations (i.e., the method by which the vehicle and guideway are controlled). Naturally, a great deal of attention was given to the vehicle subsystems (i.e., body, propulsion, brakes and controls) and their respective contribution to the automated functions. Thus, the early literature contains a great deal of attention given to the vehicle itself.

Structural considerations typically focused on two major concepts. One approximately equalized the intelligence of the automated system between the vehicle and the infrastructure. The other placed the greatest amount of intelligence within the vehicle.

Operational considerations involved level of investment by stakeholders (e.g., drivers, system owners), relative risks that they assumed, deployment disruptions, and political feasibility. All of these factors were carefully weighed and their impacts addressed in designing a deployment and operations strategy.

Results of these early analyses concluded that, not surprisingly, systems where the greatest intelligence is vested in the vehicle are less costly per mile, and equally not surprisingly they had a lower capacity per lane to allow for the safety requirement of longer headways between vehicles due to equipment capabilities. Notwithstanding this, even the lower-capacity systems were expected to provide for 1.6 to 2.0 greater throughput over conventional vehicles and highways. Unfortunately, early analysis showed that the cost per lane mile of these systems, even though the intelligence investment was in the vehicle, was still on the order of 1.2 to 1.3 times that of conventional roadways. Combining the throughput gains with the construction losses resulted in a net system capacity costs of 20 to 40 percent. Other studies that looked several decades into the future and examined the costs where intelligence is more evenly distributed concluded that capacities could approach twice that of the equivalent conventional roadway.

These early pioneers of AHS concluded that AHS is technologically feasible. Moreover, AHS will be necessary as a cost-effective alternative to the growing safety and capacity problems that will plague our cities in the new millennium (Bender 1991).

Precursor systems analyses

The highway research community continued to consider AHS, spurred on by the early promising results. In the early 1990s, as a result of the growing political leadership toward investment in ITS, it was decided by U.S. DOT leaders that it was time to take what had been learned and apply the latest tools and technologies to the issues that loomed on the horizon towards making AHS a reality. Accordingly, 16 issues were identified for in-depth study by the nation's leading researchers in vehicle-highway technology. Most issues were examined by more than one research institute resulting in over 90 individual studies. The following is a brief listing of the issues and the findings from this research phase.

System-wide issues

The vision of AHS must be to move people and goods. This conveys several requirements of such a system. First, it must accommodate a variety of vehicle types. Second, it must be flexible in its adaptation to meeting user demands. That is "one size cannot fit all." It is very possible that a larger return on investment can be realized by the deployment of an AHS solely for transit purposes. Third, the benefits of an AHS must be readily discernable by the public.

The safety of the AHS must be placed above all else. It must be perceived and demonstrated as a safe system to use, and it must be perceived as a system that provides additional safety over conventional transport. Second to this, the system must be perceived as reliable. That is, it must have a high degree of availability and accessibility. Operational blockages must not prevent usage. Provisions must be made for emergency access and clearance of breakdowns due to vehicle malfunctions. Reliable operations requires that adequate backup systems are designed into the system.

Division of intelligence between the vehicle or the infrastructure is one of the most fundamental issues facing an AHS development. This basic system design issue will drive virtually all of the rest of the design issues. It will also affect operational considerations such as throughput and allocation of response between the system control and the driver control. The skills, responsibilities, and vigilance required of the driver are affected by this fundamental issue. One of the most difficult technological issues of an AHS design is the detection of obstacles in the roadway. How this is accomplished is a direct result of the division of intelligence.

Financially, there must be long-term support for deployment and operations. Many researchers believed that the responsibility for system operation and maintenance should remain with the present operational agencies, although several alternatives of private ownership and public–private shared responsibility offer promise. Also, AHS must be viewed as offering a strong rate of return for those who invest in vehicle and infrastructure development.

Regardless of system ownership, there must be operations and maintenance crews that are trained in the vagaries of theses new, sophisticated systems. Operators must quickly understand the ramifications of irregularities in system performance. Vehicle maintenance shops must have mechanics that are educated and trained in the new equipment.

Finally, there must be nationwide compatibility so that an operator from the northeast would feel comfortable using an AHS in the southwest. This implies that national standards are necessary to preserve safety and advance system development. This does not mean that flexibility in deployment cannot be practiced by different jurisdictions. It means that there is a common minimum level of functionality and that each level beyond that has robust system requirements that are common across the nation and that system and maintenance upgrades must be planned and designed into each system deployment. Another reason for nationwide standards is the realization that AHS must operate within an overall nationwide transportation system. The current system is a multimodal system. An ITS-enabling infrastructure is being deployed. It is this backdrop against which an AHS will be deployed, and it must take advantage of the context in which it is deployed.

Infrastructure issues

Research has shown that the roadway must have some degree of instrumentation. It is the balance of intelligence between the roadway and the vehicle that is critical. At a minimum, most techniques for vehicle control require a well-maintained roadway. This includes lane markings, communications beacons, barriers and any specialized sensors that may be required by ASH, such as magnetic "nails" buried in the lane for vehicle tracking.

Beyond this, it is commonly considered that AHS could operate with today's roadway designs for high-type functionality. However, new construction for AHS could be considerably cheaper in that most design concepts would permit narrower lanes due to greater lateral vehicle controls. Other concerns arise when AHS vehicles depart the AHS roadway, and what the demands on those other roadways will be is the subject of further research when a system concepts is converged upon. For this reason, it is not out of the question that AHS may require barriers between AHS-instrumented lanes and those adjacent lanes that may not be so equipped.

Vehicle issues

The robustness of today's vehicles is taken for granted by many. The level of sophistication in these vehicles that would be required of even the most infrastructure-intensive AHS is considerable. The stiff requirements placed on sensing, braking, engine, and transmission and ride performance controls will be staggering, although not insurmountable.

A great deal of attention has been given to lateral and longitudinal control with the result of several very promising technologies being developed. These issues have a heavy influence on the overall vehicle-highway system. For example, the determination of how to treat vehicles that are traveling in a noncoordinated fashion with other vehicles, versus those traveling in a platoon in which more information is available to each vehicle, affects the vehicle instrumentation as well as that of the roadway.

Another implication of the issues implied by vehicle-roadway integration is evident in vehicle check-in and check-out stations. If vehicles should have a high degree of self-reliance for on-board checking systems, then this will affect the roadway ramps and the rate at which vehicles can be processed into and out of AHS facilities. It also implies a greater responsibility on the part of the vehicle operator for vigilance and periodic off-site inspections. This can be countered with the responsibility being more vested in the infrastructure. How would the on-, off-, and slip ramps have to be configured for instrumentation and for redirecting nonvalidated vehicles? It is issues such as this that cause researchers to keep returning to the fundamental issue of division of intelligence between the vehicle and the infrastructure.

Deployment issues

Since the early days of AHS research, an "evolutionary" approach has been advocated. That is, transition to AHS must be planned, orderly and at a rate that is acceptable to the users and operators. For example, it is assumed that vehicle collision avoidance technology will precede AHS deployment and that user acclimatization to this technology is necessary for users to see the additional benefits achievable through AHS and as a result, AHS deployment will be demand-driven. The evolutionary approach also assumes that the early acceptors of the technology will cause a "build it and they will come" mentality, causing an exponential market penetration of AHS vehicles and roadways. In order for this to happen, several preconditions must be created.

Firstly, there must be a champion for AHS. There must be some influential government and industry representatives that are steadfastly behind the deployment and who carry sufficient influence to persuade transportation, financial and user nay-sayers to become accepting of the change. The difficulty with this is that it may be difficult to predict potentially significant societal changes that may result from AHS deployment. In addition there must be continuous communication with the community, and there must be public involvement at all phases of deployment so that the benefits of AHS are constant reminders of why it is important. It is also important that the community, users and other stakeholders be constantly apprized of accurate estimates of cost and time as well as of other potential markets and stakeholders who may share the cost and the benefits of the AHS.

Because the deployment of AHS will more than likely take place of a period of time ("evolutionary" versus "revolutionary") it is worthwhile to reiterate that a long-term funding stream must be identified. For this, it is absolutely essential that the public is accepting and anticipating AHS success.

Societal and institutional issues

There are many people who have been involved in AHS research who have commented that it is not the technological issues that present the challenges for AHS success. Rather, it is the societal and instructional issues that will cause the greatest obstacles to its deployment.

Environmental challenges are necessary to understand. There is the concern that improved mobility will induce more travel with the resulting increase in emissions and energy consumption. The concern is not only for a net increase in more vehicles taking to the AHS facilities, but also for the increased distances that drivers may travel as they alter the land use and development patterns of communities and metropolitan areas.

Another societal issue is that of equity of access. The same argument against AHS is often used in opposition to high-occupancy vehicle (HOV) lanes. That is that all of those who contribute tax funds to its construction are denied access to its use. Also, there is concern that all sectors of the demographic and economic mix will be denied access to AHS due to costly operating considerations. Lastly, accessibility to the elderly and physically impaired may pose questions of equity.

Liability is often cited as a potential show-stopper for AHS deployment. Research conducted suggests otherwise. It is true that when "the system" assumes control of the vehicle, then "the system" must assume some level of responsibility for consequences of any malfunction. The counter argument to this is that it is true that we live in a litigious society and that there will undoubtedly be legal challenges to AHS. However, there does not appear to be any reason to suggest that these challenges will have a greater rate of success than other well designed, deployed and operated public works system currently in operation.

Finally, the challenge of political opposition must be constantly countered with sound engineering and planning, stakeholder and champion demand and well reasoned financial plans for sustained operation. It is essential that potential political opponents begin to understand the benefits that can accrue to their constituents through market and other economic factors.

Summary of precursor systems analyses

The precursor systems analyses substantiated and extended the research that had been done to that point. Viewed most broadly, AHS is not the only large system intended for public use that has involved the use of new technology and has carried with it significant cultural and financial implications. There have been other comparable systems requiring that technological demands be met. The difference between innovation and invention is how well we apply the inventions to create a holistic innovation. Similarly, the way in which society addresses the issues of AHS will determine the success or failure of this promising systems application.

The NAHSC

By 1994, the time had arrived to bring about the reality of AHS. The U.S. DOT awarded a grant to NAHSC with the objective of:

> . . . to work cooperatively with the future AHS stakeholders and users, to provide leadership and focus to the nation's AHS efforts, and to select the AHS system configuration that may ultimately be deployed as the next major performance upgrade of the nation's vehicle-highway system. The stakeholders are the eventual designers, builders, deployers and operators of AHS. This program phase emphasizes identification and analyses of system alternatives, and selection, documentation and proof-of-feasibility of the preferred AHS approach.

The work plan of the NAHSC called for: identification of system goals and operational performance objectives; a proof of technical feasibility demonstration; identification and description of multiple, feasible AHS concepts; the selection of a preferred system, configuration; the prototype testing of the preferred system configuration; documentation of standards and specifications; and development and demonstration of partial control and control assist early deployment and transitional systems.[2] The work was to be done over a period of seven years. As it turned out, only the first two work elements were completed with considerable work devoted to the third before the U.S. DOT withdrew from the consortium to pursue other priority research agenda items.

Terms of the agreement

The terms of the agreement established six key target performance objectives of the AHS:

- *Safety*—significantly safety than today; collision free in the absence of malfunctions, and a malfunction management capability that minimizes the number and severity of collisions that occur as a result of AHS malfunctions.
- *Throughput*—significant increase in vehicles per hour per lane flow through increased density at free-flow speeds, stable traffic flow, and possible increase in speed.
- *Inclement weather operations*—the AHS must be able to operate at or exceed the performance levels of manual systems in the range of weather conditions that are typical in the continental United States.
- *Enhanced mobility*—substantially better trip time predictability and access and use by impaired, aged, or less experienced drivers.
- *Improved user comfort and convenience*—less strain on users, higher quality trip.
- *Reduced fuel consumption and emissions*—improved fuel economy and reduced emissions per vehicle mile traveled through smoother flow and compatibility with future vehicle propulsion and fuel designs.

It can be seen from these objectives that what had been learned heretofore served to guide what was to be considered the primary objectives of AHS. The completed research further allowed a going-in understanding of key target system characteristics:

- Affordability
- User desirability
- Continued efficient effect on surrounding non-AHS roadways
- Dual-mode vehicle instrumentation
- Reliable and modular system technology

- Noncontact electronics-based system control design
- Evolvability to build on current technologies
- Cars, buses and trucks must be supported
- AHS roadways were to be generally freeway types
- Convenient transfer between modes must be assured

It was seen from the very beginning of the agreement that if the consortium was to be successful, it must still address the critical issues that had been previously identified as critical issues. The development of an acceptable concept required solutions for eight major uncertainties:

- Vehicle check-in and check-out
- Lateral and longitudinal position detection and control
- Malfunction minimization and incident management
- Obstacle detection and avoidance
- Vehicle-to-vehicle and vehicle-to-infrastructure communication
- Intervehicle coordination
- Human factors and user acceptance
- Incremental deployment ability

Clearly, the lessons of the past research had been learned and the consortium was geared up to take on these challenges.

NAHSC composition
It was known from the outset that a carefully balanced array of expertise would be required to meet the objectives of the cost-sharing agreement. Such a team was assembled under the leadership of a vehicle industry representative, GM. Also representing the private industry sector was Bechtel and Parsons Brinkerhoff for their highway design experience, Delco Electronics for their expertise in vehicle electronics, and Hughes Aircraft and Martin Marietta (later to be renamed Lockheed Martin) for their systems engineering capabilities. The public sector was represented by the California Department of Transportation, in addition to the FHWA. Finally, academia was represented by the Carnegie-Mellon University Robotics Institute, which brought expertise in application of intelligence to vehicle sensing and control, and the University of California Partners for Advanced Transit and Highways (PATH) for their long-standing leadership in the field of AHS.

Because the NAHSC was to serve as a national focal point for AHS and build user acceptance, it was structured to accept other stakeholders whom were termed "Associate Participants." By the time the U.S. DOT withdrew from the NAHSC in 1997, the Associate Participants numbered 120 representing stakeholder categories of local and state government, transportation users, transit, environmental interests highway design industry, vehicle industry, electronics industry, commercial trucking interests, and insurance industry. The Associate Participants worked actively to provide information and feedback to the consortium's findings.

Revised objectives and characteristics
A principle accomplishment of the NAHSC was the publication of the AHS system objectives and characteristics. The NAHSC conducted careful reviews of past research and developed innovative decision-making tools of their own to ensure that the system objectives and characteristics were supportable and justified in the eyes of the stakeholders. As a result, they found that the original set of six objectives would remain essentially intact with the exception of all-weather operability, which was judged to be less of a system objective as it was a system design characteristic.

In order to carry this to the system characteristics level, they established fundamental guidelines and capabilities for the AHS concept. They had to deal with the issue of division of intelligence between the vehicle and the roadside. They chose to do this at a fairly high level—one that would allow them to continue to refine the concept as research and user acceptability dictated. The vehicle would contain the portion of the system that actually moves along an AHS including sensors, data processing, actuators, linkages, and communications equipment. The AHS would automate the driver functions of vehicle movement control including: AHS entry, AHS exit, obstacle detection and warning/avoidance, longitudinal and lateral vehicle control, navigation and vehicle position tracking, and maneuver coordination with other vehicles.

The concept recognized the imperatives of previous research to make the system flexible in application. As a result, the AHS concept would accept local tailored needs including highway networks in highly congested megalopolises; highway corridors in large, congested metropolitan areas; exclusive transit and HOV lanes; heavily traveled intercity highways; exclusive commercial vehicle lanes; sparse rural areas; long-distance interstate highways; and even the potential for roadway-powered electric vehicles.

The NAHSC conducted much work to properly identify what user objectives of an AHS would garner the necessary support for deployment. They found that seven objectives must be satisfied:

- Disengage the driver from driving for fully automatic control, with some degree of vigilance necessary in partial control
- Facilitate intermodal and multimodal transportation
- Enhance operations for freight carriers
- Support automated transit operations
- Apply to rural roadways
- Support travel demand management and travel system management policies
- Support sustainable transportation policies

Continued system definition activities of the NAHSC refined the original characteristics. As a result it was concluded that the system must include:

- Ease of use
- Inclement weather operations
- Affordable cost and economic feasibility
- Beneficial operation on conventional roadways
- Infrastructure compatibility even if some limited changes are required
- Operation of non-AHS and partial control vehicles
- Support for a wide range of vehicle types, but not all vehicle types (e.g., motorcycles and low-performance heavy trucks)
- Capability for progressive, planned deployment
- High availability
- Application flexibility
- Architectural modularity

In recognition of the adage of "that gets done what gets measured," the NAHSC identified potential measures of effectiveness for each of the performance objectives. It was not envisioned that all of these measures would be used. However, they were suggested as a means to see what appealed to potential users and what would be rigorous measures in the concept development and design work ahead. Table 11–3 presents those potential measures of system performance.

Demonstration 1997

As an element of the agreement requirements, the NAHSC was to conduct a demonstration of technical feasibility. This was conducted in San Diego, California in August 1997 following months of preparation for safety. Along with demonstration of several technologies, there was an exhibit of vendors and stakeholders that further showed the interest in AHS. The safety checks of the demonstrated technologies included certification procedures for controls, software, vehicle assembly, driver training, scenario script risks, vehicle trial performance, and fault tolerance. The result of this rigorous testing was a flawless demonstration that involved over 4,000 passengers experiencing some form of AHS.

The test track scenarios that were demonstrated were a number of platoon and autonomous vehicles using a variety of technologies, including:

- intelligent cruise control for passenger cars and heavy trucks;
- creep control (car-following in congested stop-and-go traffic);
- partial automation (lane-keeping and vehicle-following) for rural applications; and
- fully automated autonomous vehicles operating amongst nonautomated vehicles (i.e., capable of operating in today's traffic stream on today's freeways);
- fully automated vehicles operating in close-headway platoons for exclusive-lane operation, a mode that offers maximum throughput (at least 2 to 3 times today's average throughput);
- full automation of transit buses, to showcase automated transit operations; and
- collision warning system for heavy trucks (a commercially available product).

The utility of coupling a developmental effort with a demonstration is unquestionable. Staging a demonstration provides for harnessing interests of stakeholders while creating a venue for competitors to jointly "show-off" their products and enhance their visibility. It was learned that the demonstration event must be large and bold enough to attract sponsors and other ancillary meetings of associations and groups so that other influential leaders will attend, thus lending even greater exposure to the event. The extent of staff-years of preparation that went into the planning combined with the diversity of technologies and applications created a richness and added depth that accentuated the experience for the attending decision-makers. The value of experiencing the technology cannot be understated. Finally, as a direct result of preparing for the demonstration, it was found that the capabilities being developed were providing input to the concept teams as they examined the feasibility and robustness of various technologies.

Summary of other NAHSC findings

In addition to laying out the initial goals, objectives and measures, the NAHSC continued research in a number of other areas. The following is only a summary.

As can be seen above, much work to resolve the fundamental issues previously identified has been addressed. As a result it was concluded that fully automated AHS is feasible, but some partial automation will be needed in some jurisdictions to provide for evolutionary deployment. However, significant engineering, societal and institutional issues for full and partial deployment remain to be resolved. Nevertheless, the question is not whether there will be an AHS, but when will there be an AHS? AHS is a transportation system that must be and is capable of complementing other ground transportation systems.

In evaluating the AHS concepts it was reaffirmed that retaining diversity in system definition allowed for inclusion of unforeseen applications and inclusion of potential users that might otherwise have been bypassed. Also, this same diversity provides for evolutionary deployment. One of the issues of concern early on was the design trade-off decisions that emanated from the apparently competing objectives of safety as

Table 11–3
Potential Measures of System Performance
Source: AHS System Objectives and Characteristics, November 3, 1995.

PERFORMANCE OBJECTIVE	MEASURE OF EFFECTIVENESS	
Improved Safety	• Number of crashes • Number of annual fatalities due to crashes • Fatality rate • Number of injuries due to crashes • Injury rate • Severity of injuries on AHS vs. conventional highways • Accident rate per vehicle distance traveled • Total annual cost of all accident-related injuries • Number of HAZMAT crashes per distance traveled • Property loss	• Property loss per distance traveled • Travel security cost • AHS vs. non-AHS ration of occurrence of catastrophic crashes • Accident response time • Incident clearance time • Infrastructure damage by vehicles • Time to respond to malfunctions • Down time due to vandals • Probability of security violation due to a hacker
Increased Efficiency	• Vehicle per AHS lane per hour • Vehicles per right-of-way width per hour • Cargo per lane per hour • Check-in delay time • Entry rate—number of vehicles per hour • Exit rate—number of vehicles per hour • Check-out delay time • Reduction of throughput resulting from incidents/crashes	• Equivalent conventional lanes to carry traffic of one AHS lane • Incidents • Local delays due to blockages • Maximum safe speed • Vulnerability to system stopping single point failure • Average trip time • Standard deviation of trip time
Enhanced Mobility and Access	• Fixed route travel time • Fixed route travel time variation • Fixed route travel time distribution • Trip length distribution • Wait time at ingress • Wait time at egress	• Use by drives with disabilities • Equity—accessibility by all socio-economic groups • Transit coordination • Transit coverage • User perceptions • Training/licensing to qualify AHS drivers
Provide more Convenient and Comfortable Highway Traveling	• Driver involvement • Driver access • Interface complexity • Serviceability • Driver control usability • Driver attention load • Comprehension delay • User compatibility	• Learn ability • AHS driver population • Accessibility distribution • Distance accessibility • Stress reduction • User perception • Ride comfort • Vehicle certification frequency and cost
Reduce Environmental Impact	• Idle time • Speed variability • Acceleration/deceleration rates • Alternate propulsion compatibility • Emissions per distance traveled • Fuel efficiency	• Fuel consumption per distance traveled • Fuel consumption per time traveled • Acoustic noise level • Land use needed/reclaimed • Aesthetics • Electromagnetic field

represented by frequency of collisions and throughput. When this was considered, along with the trade-off between frequency and severity of collisions, it became clear that significant throughput increases can be gained without reduction in safety. Other analyses of AHS versus conventional roadway transport systems found several similarities between them. For example, they found that unit costs of civil infrastructure for dedicated AHS lanes are similar to current costs for HOV lanes, although the right-of-way required is less for AHS lanes. Other comparisons resulted in concluding that societal, institutional and liability issues are comparable. It was found that a fully automated AHS lane has the potential to provide significant savings in energy and emissions compared to conventional highway lanes. One overwhelming conclusion that was not expected at the outset but that proved to have a major effect on the direction of the research was the high level of interest of the stakeholders in the nontechnical issues surrounding AHS deployment.

One effect of this latter finding was the refocusing of the concept refinement work from a parallel analysis of three concepts to an analysis of a single-broad architecture. Another effect was that as the NAHSC was to be a national focal point it found itself at odds with the agreement tenant that specifically directed them to not look at the deployment steps, but to select, design and build a prototype of a fully automated AHS. This conflict in direction should not occur again in the future given the experience of the NAHSC. The immediate result was a close examination of technical issues that affect the concept deployment. Following are their conclusions.

- The automated operation in mixed traffic (i.e., a mix of vehicles with and without AHS instrumentation) would require the automated vehicle to possess sensing and cognitive abilities that match or exceed those of a human driver or else requires the human driver to participate in the driving tasks (partial control).
- Developers raised concerns for the need for a dedicated AHS infrastructure. This raised the "chicken or the egg" debate between vehicle providers and infrastructure providers. The coordination of these two groups is imperative due to their mutual dependency on one another.
- Benefits for partial and mixed AHS concepts appear to be substantially less than with full automation AHS; while this may be necessary for evolutionary deployment, it may not attract enough user support and investment interests at the outset.
- Finally, despite the challenges that have been given new light as a result of the NAHSC research, the conclusions for AHS are that it is an important investment in the future with the potential for significant safety, social and economic benefits with the result that it will be possible to garner the commitment of the necessary public and private sectors.

The future

Where does this line of research go from here? The IVI begins to lay the ground work to establish the environment for AVCS to develop. The focus of the research in IVI is safety, and specifically in collision avoidance. In order to conduct this research properly, attention is being given to both vehicle instrumentation and infrastructure instrumentation. New and innovative tools for conducting the analyses for system requirements are being developed that will be available for continued advanced research in AVCS. In addition, field tests are being planned that will not only demonstrate these technologies, but also will provide quantitative result of real-world application of the technologies. All of these actions will pave the way for future, renewed interest in fully automated vehicle control while providing for immediate benefits to the driving public today.

References

Bender, J.G. 1991. "An Overview of Systems Studies of AHS" (February). *IEEE Transactions on Vehicular Technology.*

Transportation Research Board, National Research Council. 1998. *National Automated Highway System Research Program, A Review.* Washington, D.C.: National Academy Press.

U.S. Department of Transportation ITS Joint Program Office. 1997. "Intelligent Vehicle Initiative Business Plan" (November).

Endnotes

1. U.S. Department of Transportation request for application to establish a national automated highway system consortium, DOT REA DTFH61-94-X-00001.

2. RFA DTFH61-94-X-00001.

BY Douglas L. Jonas • President • Matrix Management Group

Weather information for effective decisions

Weather impacts on transportation are pervasive. Tens of thousands of people are killed on highways in the United States every year and hundreds of thousands are injured. Property damage is great in every transportation mode. Weather is a contributing factor in many of the crashes and other incidents. Improving productivity through practices such as "just-in-time" manufacturing and shipping has created greater weather sensitivity. The exorbitant costs of delay and untimely trip completions negatively affect both individual results and the national economy.

Weather information tailored to the needs of decision-makers can be leveraged to maximize safety, efficiency, and the enjoyment of travel. "Weather" here is very broadly defined to include not only the dynamics of the atmosphere, but also effects such as electromagnetic radiation and the responses of ground, pavement, and rail to "weather." Too often, potential users and beneficiaries of weather information do not penetrate the generalization of "weather information" to identify the particular weather parameters, thresholds of intensity, and timing of events that particularly affect mission success. Similarly, providers of weather information may not be aware of the particular effects of weather on a transportation activity, and therefore the information provided is not tailored to the needs of operational decision thresholds.

There have been tremendous advances in the capabilities of the meteorological community in recent years. For example, a nationwide system of next generation weather radar (NEXRAD) with Doppler capability and sophisticated software to detect and diagnose severe weather has been fielded. The National Weather Service (NWS) is fielding the advanced weather interactive processing system (AWIPS) to enable local forecasters to integrate, process and transmit high-volume radar, satellite, upper air and surface observations. Computer facility upgrades accommodate advanced numerical weather prediction models. Mesoscale (local) forecasting techniques will greatly improve the timeliness and accuracy of small-scale, short-lived phenomena. Modernization and restructuring of the NWS has decentralized weather support so that full and equal capability to integrate weather information and provide locally focused products is available at all 119 weather forecast offices (WFO). A survey conducted for the Federal Highway Administration (FHWA) in 1995 identified 99 companies then providing or available to provide weather-related products and services to surface transportation. This number is believed to have increased. Fully automated observing systems are now commonplace at airports, and many other agencies employ sophisticated weather-observing platforms that measure a wide variety of atmospheric parameters.

Tailored weather support to transportation is available and widely used. Recognition of intelligent transportation system (ITS) requirements in the context of advancing meteorological capabilities bodes well for effectively leveraging weather information in a myriad of transportation decisions. The "Federal Plan for

Meteorological Services and Supporting Research," produced each fiscal year by the Office of the Federal Coordinator of Meteorology, provides a comprehensive articulation of the provision of meteorological services and supporting research by the federal government.

Effective weather information—targeted on the decision-maker

Many different activities operate within the same weather regime. The decisions that are made will determine whether costs are minimized, safety maximized, and efficiency and convenience optimized. By way of example, a supervisor of snow and ice control on a section of highway, a transportation management center, a long haul trucking dispatcher and a "soccer mom" may be destined to operate within the same weather; but their decision requirements are quite different. The snow and ice control supervisor will want to know whether the combined effects of preceding solar radiation, ground temperature, air temperature and so on, will result in the solution of precipitation on the pavement and residual magnesium chloride applied earlier will result in ice formation on the pavement. With this information, he or she can decide whether to call out off-duty personnel, select equipment configurations, and use chemical concentration or application rates—decisions of considerable cost and safety consequences. The transportation management center may want to know whether cross-winds at Exit 25 will exceed the rate at which the manufactured housing under tow is likely to capsize, or use the weather forecast as a proxy for a forecast of incidents and a basis for preparing response units. Pre-trip planning by a trucking dispatcher for a transcontinental trip will want to decide whether to take the shortest route (distance), or the longer, lower risk and lower unit operating cost route that avoids severe weather. The soccer mom may simply want to know whether the players need to bring warm coats—knowing the snow and ice control supervisor and transportation center manager will have made the right decisions to ensure the safety of her passengers.

Effective weather information is tailored to the decision-maker with responsibilities impacted by weather. Figure 12–1 displays the interrelationships among roles, types of weather information and the "money spot" (i.e., the decision-maker). Every relationship of weather information to transportation can be seen or inferred from this diagram. To leverage weather information to advantage, every element in this system must be working appropriately. The essence of planning and deploying transportation weather support effectively is to evaluate, arrange for and use each element of this system skillfully. Figure 12–1 is portrayed in terms of snow and ice control on highways, but it could be similarly restated for any weather-impacted activity. Note that the center of this system is the decision-maker. Action thresholds of the decision-maker drive the nature and timing of the weather information to be supplied, and the meteorology products and services needed are the inputs required to supply the information needed. Note that most arrows (interrelationships) go both ways. Ongoing interaction between those with the requirements and those providing the support is critical.

Climatology, a characterization of "typical" conditions at a time and place, supports planning. Creation and analysis of historical data centered on the parameter thresholds that matter will assist with such things as how much salt to stockpile, and whether and what types of snowplows to acquire.

Forecasts of weather and pavement conditions, what is expected to prevail at some point in the future for each particular element that impacts mission success, is at the heart of the system. Because the payoff of all decisions is always in the future, and forecast professional services are relatively inexpensive (compared to infrastructure), studies have shown this element to have the highest cost/benefit value.

Forecasts are derived from observations and analysis. Thus, weather and pavement condition data are critical to the forecaster. Observations from around the world combine to feed numerical weather prediction models. Providing for additional observations from data-sparse areas, such as along some highways, can enrich

Figure 12–1. Idealized Road Weather Information System-based snow and ice control information flow.
Source. Matrix Management Group

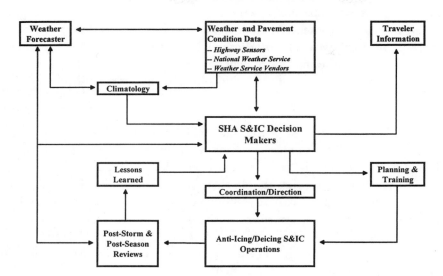

the information available to forecasters. One such example is highway agencies measuring pavement condition—temperature and chemical presence—and atmospheric information at numerous locations along roadways where no data source previously existed. The only sources are pavement sensors. Observations of current conditions feed both the analysis leading to forecasts, and directly to the decision-makers to support their review of the accuracy of the forecast and to take actions that respond directly to current conditions. Actions taken lead to actual operations in real time, but they also support planning and development of appropriate training. In an environment of continuous quality improvement, ongoing and mission-ending reviews identify the lessons to be learned, and these lessons in turn inform future tailoring of forecasts and decision-making. The diagram also takes note that the information provided to decision-makers, which is reinterpreted, supplemented and properly formatted, may have value to still other parties, such as for traveler information.

Characteristics of weather information

For weather information to be useful, and for it to be a factor in effective decisions, it must be differentiated. There are many types and segments of information that focus it where particular decision-makers need it. Weather data displayed for decision-makers are typically formatted and displayed differently for use by meteorological analysts and forecasters than for operational decision-makers. One person, perhaps, wants to know what the temperature will be tomorrow; another person wants to know the wind speed and direction right now; and yet another individual wants to know the derivatives of weather and heat-balance effects, such as pavement temperature, at a particular point in time. However, at a simple and fundamental level, the three aspects of weather information are (1) climatology, (2) observations, and (3) forecasts.

Climatology is an aggregation of historical data that taken together and analyzed can be used to characterize weather at a place and time. Many decisions are made based on knowledge of historic extremes; averages; seasonal and diurnal changes; and frequency of occurrence of temperatures, winds and weather elements (e.g., rain, snow, thunderstorms, freezing rain). Examples include how much chemical and abrasives to stockpile for winter maintenance, what type of maintenance equipment to select, what clothing and tools to provide, what safety equipment to load, where to place snow fences, operating ranges to build into temperature sensitive devices and so forth. Winter weather indexes are developed to characterize that which is "typical." That which is "actual" of a particular winter is then compared to the index to (1) explain and understand performance variations over time and between organizational units, (2) support supplemental budget requests and (3) develop training content. Another application is the use of downward-looking infra-red radiometers to create profiles of pavement temperature variation under varying sky conditions and sun angles, coordinated with "fish eye" camera documentation of associated roadside shade sources. This documentation supports interpolation between fixed points of pavement temperature observations and development of maintenance procedures.

National (U.S.) climatology is maintained by the National Climatic Data Center (NCDC) in Asheville, North Carolina; and it is accessible by a number of means, including via the Internet. Data is gathered from many sources determined to be soundly measured and reported, including NWS sites, Federal Aviation Administration (FAA) sites, worldwide sites coordinated through the World Meteorological Organization, military bases, Department of Interior's Remote Automatic Weather Stations, aircraft and ship reports, national cooperative weather observers, academic institutions and others. Many transportation organizations (and other weather-impacted groups) install sensors in data-sparse areas or in operationally significant locations, such as along highways or on bridges. The data generated are used to increase the accuracy and utility for local climatological applications, but they are often not included in the NCDC datasets for a variety of reasons.

Current observations of solar, atmospheric, and ground conditions provide data for analysis and preparation of forecasts by meteorologists, information to assist decision-makers in applying forecasts at the time of decision and real-time inputs to operational decisions. Also, observations are input to control systems and decision aids. For example, pavement temperature, air temperature and humidity may drive an algorithm that converts to a variable message sign text that advises of icy conditions. The primary sources of observations are as noted in the preceding paragraph as the sources of climatological data. However, technological advances in meteorology in recent years and ITS prospects, create an ever-richer base of observations.

The World Weather Watch is an integrated system that includes the Global Observing System, a coordinated system of methods, techniques, and facilities for collecting and exchanging weather observations on a worldwide scale and for dissemination of weather products from centralized locations (centers). The United States and Russia operate polar-orbiting meteorological satellites in sun synchronous orbits; and a number of countries operate geostationary earth satellites (GOES) over their region, the United States having GOES 8, 9, and 10 overhead as of 1999. The NWS operates NEXRAD with Doppler capability at 135 civilian locations in the United States. NEXRAD observes the movement of water droplets and allows precise identification of clouds and severe weather, and associated algorithms supports diagnosis and visualization of weather not previously possible. Highway agencies have installed weather sensors along highways and pavement temperature and condition (chemical and moisture presence) in pavements at over 1,000 (estimated) locations as components of road weather information systems. Handheld and vehicle-mounted, downward-looking radiometers to determine pavement temperature are now commonplace.

These and other observation mechanisms make the current state of the weather and its effects quite available to transportation decision-makers. Private sector, value-adding meteorological services (VAMS) package and display the current weather in response to decision needs. ITS holds the promise of even richer databases for analysis, modeling, and forecasting; and for observations of critical thresholds in the hands of decision-makers on the spot, at the time of decision, through instrumentation of mobile platforms—the very vehicles experiencing the weather.

Weather forecasts deal with the weather as it is going to be experienced in the future, whether it is just minutes from now, or next month. Because the outcomes of all decisions lie in the future, an accurate and timely forecast is the most valuable of weather inputs. Indeed, studies have shown that the rate of return on investment in forecasts is the highest of all elements in the system. To realize this value, however, and this is especially so in ITS, the forecast must be tailored to the decision-maker's particular requirements. The NWS analyzes worldwide data to produce numerous depictions of the atmosphere at standard observation times and forecast depictions in the United States. These include, for example, flows of temperature and moisture at standard pressure levels, location and intensity of jet streams, centers of low and high pressure and fronts at the surface, soundings of temperature and moisture at specific locations, and many more. These are typically produced twice per day and widely distributed. Numerical weather prediction models are a primary analytical and forecasting tool. Models use observations and extrapolations based on the energy equation to assign values to standard grids, and they then simulate dynamic changes based on natural energy exchange interactions. Computers perform this modeling process at several trillion calculations per second. The finer the grid resolution (i.e., the smaller the spacing between grid points), the more precise local area forecasts can be. This is because the finer resolution more closely reflects the atmosphere and terrain. At a 100-kilometer grid, for example, the effects of an entire mountain range and interactions with large bodies of water may be lost. Standard models have recently been on a 35-kilometer grid; but capability exists for 15-kilometer grid and even a 1-kilometer grid for a local area prediction system. The extent to which fine mesh models are applied depends on funding of computer systems. Larger-scale models are run once or twice daily, while some of the smaller-scale models are run as frequently as every 3 hours.

The NWS provides around-the-clock weather and flood warning and forecast services to the public for the protection of life and property and to meet the needs of all segments of the economy. Commercial VAMS build on NWS products to provide tailored support to specific user requirements. By way of just a few examples, these include: planning (6 to 24 hours) and operational (0 to 6 hours) forecasts of pavement temperature, snow accumulation, air temperature, and cross winds on particular highway routes for snow and ice control supervisors; extent of solar heating on rails, and therefore heat expansion and effects on operating speeds for railroad customers; and expert systems that combine local area terrain, weather, and operational procedures to supply decision aids. "Nowcasts," a combination of all that is known meteorologically and operationally at a time and place, collectively considered by the decision-maker and supporting meteorologists, establish the assumption of imminent conditions that is the basis for actions taken. Further outlooks predict weather conditions up to a week in advance.

Existing and potential ITS applications abound. Forecasts for the general traveler are available at kiosks for the next section of highway to be traveled. Highway conditions and current or forecast local weather are provided by highway advisory radio (HAR). Severe weather advisories can be provided over car radios by AM subcarrier. Visibility sensors in fog-prone locations provide a warning message by VMS when visibility falls below a predetermined level. Algorithms applied to NEXRAD data allow snowfall accumulation "nowcasts" at a scale as fine as an individual interchange. Applied climatology determines where to place snowfences so that snow is stored off the roadway at a cost of three cents per ton, rather than plowed at three dollars per ton.

Weather information is now or could be available via virtually any medium a decision-maker finds most useful. Data moves from a highway weather sensor remote-processing unit by long line, radio, microwave, cellular phone, or even microburst. Operating locations monitor both synoptic and local scale weather systems and general consumption weather forecasts over television. Weather radar summaries, data tabulations, and tailored weather forecasts are received by computer at the office and by laptop in the cab of a truck. Weather maps and forecasts for the route of a trip in progress can be overlaid on route finder technologies in the vehicle. Weather information is accessed on request from kiosks, by tuning into low-frequency HAR, or pushed into the user's presence via AM radio subcarrier frequencies.

The institutional framework

The government plays a large role in providing meteorological services and supporting research. The NWS, as mentioned earlier, provides around-the-clock weather, flood warning, and forecast services to the public for the protection of life and property and to meet the needs of all segments of the economy. NWS forecasters issue local warnings of severe weather such as tornadoes, severe thunderstorms, flash floods, and extreme winter weather; and the NWS operates the National Hurricane Center.

The Office of the Federal Coordinator for Meteorology (OFCM) ensures the effective use of federal meteorological resources by leading the systematic coordination of operational weather requirements and services, and supporting research, among the federal agencies. OFCM also prepares the annual "Federal Plan for Meteorological Services and Supporting Research"—an excellent reference.

The Department of Defense operates a military environmental service system to provide specialized meteorological, space environmental, and oceanographic analysis and prediction services in support of military forces. The military weather services also contribute to the national and international weather-observing capability by taking observations where there are no other conventional weather-observing capabilities. Observational data from these, and from specialized capabilities such as the Defense Meteorological Satellite, are also sent to civil facilities. The high-technology weather support environment may present opportunities for ITS to emulate. The National Aeronautics and Space Administration has a focus on detecting and forecasting mesoscale weather events for the demands of the space program. This requires exploitation of the latest technology, using such things as the Doppler Radar Wind Profiler and the Lightning Detection and Ranging systems. These capabilities are transferable to the ITS environment. Especially provocative for ITS are the visualization capabilities of the Goddard Space Flight Center, which can show weather features as seen from space, ranging from the "parade" of hurricanes over an entire season to an individual feature at the Golden Gate Bridge or the aftermath of flood damage.

The U.S. Department of Transportation is also both a provider and user of meteorological information. The FAA has the responsibility to provide leadership in the optimization of aviation weather systems and services. The U.S. Coast Guard collects and transmits marine and coastal weather observations and warnings, deploys and maintains offshore environmental monitoring buoys, and operates long-range radio navigation networks. The 1999 Federal Plan, for the first time, includes the FHWA as a "player," noting that safety, efficiency and mobility in the diverse programs of the FHWA require incorporation of timely weather and road condition information.

Commercial VAMS play a vital role in providing weather information focused on parameter thresholds at times and in media and formats critical to decision-makers. Meteorologists and decision-makers working together best work out the requirements and optimum weather information response interactively. Increasingly, public–private partnerships are used to establish open standards and protocols, and to deliver weather support services that draw on a spectrum of capabilities.

Academia plays several roles in the weather-ITS impacts interface. In addition to the obvious role of professional capacity building in meteorology and the multidisciplinary ITS arena, universities are actively advancing modeling, local area forecasting skills, visualizations of local weather systems, applied climatology, and other research of value to ITS. The University Corporation for Atmospheric Research, a consortium of 63 universities, and its National Center for Atmospheric Research (NCAR) have extensive capabilities for ITS-related research and development in the areas of (a) high-resolution detection and forecasting of hazardous or economically-significant weather conditions and (b) the design of state-of-the-art decision systems for ITS operations. NCAR is working with the ITS community, including the FHWA and the state DOTs, to implement this new science and technology. Some universities, such as the University of North Dakota, are even entering into public–private partnerships to provide weather observations and forecasts on demand from travelers for particular highway routes (e.g., Advanced Transportation Weather Information System for Rural Interstate Highways).

The American Meteorological Society (AMS) regularly features presentations addressing the weather-ITS interface at its annual meetings, typically attended by 4,000 people. The AMS leadership seeks to increase interaction between weather information users and providers.

The National Weather Association represents commercial weather information providers. Some VAMS have accumulated many years of experience—since long before ITS was conceived—assisting transportation agencies with weather products and services focused on transportation requirements. ITS America has established a Weather Information Applications Task Force to encourage interaction at the interface between meteorologists and intelligent transportation activities impacted by weather. The AMS has established a corresponding committee on ITS. These activities provide a "bridge" for the coordination of mutual interests.

Conclusion

It is clear that weather affects ITS technologies and the delivery of services. Weather observation, diagnosis, analysis, and forecasting capabilities are extensive and advancing rapidly. To leverage weather information to optimum advantage in intelligent transportation, it is critical that there be interaction in depth between those who understand ITS requirements and those who understand current and potential capabilities in the meteorological sector. Decision-makers who understand just which weather parameters and thresholds affect their activities, and know what weather to expect, can make decisions that will save lives, avoid injuries, save money and time, and protect property and other resources.

Bibliography

Perry, A. H., and L. J. Symons. 1991. *Highway Meteorology*. Department of Geography, University College, Swansea, Wales.

Matrix Management Group. 1993. *Road Weather Information Systems, Volume 1: Research Report, Volume 2: Implementation Guide*. Seattle, WA: Matrix Management Group.

BY Stephen Albert • Director • Western Transportation Institute •
Department of Civil Engineering • Montana State University

ADVANCED RURAL TRANSPORTATION SYSTEMS

Background

Rural areas contain over three-fourths of the nation's surface roads, or roughly four million miles of roadway. In addition, roads in rural and small urban areas possess unique features that can have an adverse effect on both traveler safety and economic issues. Transportation officials, therefore, are beginning to investigate the potential benefits of applying intelligent transportation systems (ITS) to the rural environment. Although advanced transportation technologies have evolved considerably since the conceptual planning associated with Mobility 2000 and Intelligent Vehicle-Highway Systems, little attention to date has been directed at rural needs or applications. The Intermodal Transportation Efficiency Act of 1991, which allocated $660 million to research and development, designated only $2 million (0.3 percent) of these funds for rural ITS use (excluding field operational tests).

The emphasis on ITS applications in urban areas focused on the following considerations: urban locations typically experience severe congestion, highway capacity is a critical issue and increased throughput of vehicles is desirable. It became apparent to many transportation professionals, however, that there are different yet significant rural transportation needs or problems that could be addressed using ITS technologies.

In recognition of the rural issues in need of attention, the U.S. Department of Transportation's (U.S. DOT's) Joint Program Office established the advanced rural transportation systems (ARTS) program in 1997. Because many of the ITS functional areas (e.g., ATIS, advanced public transportation systems) have been specifically addressed in previous chapters of this book, this chapter will focus on the unique issues, user needs and advanced technology applications that are associated with the rural environment. A discussion of the following topics is included:

*   Vision for rural ITS applications
*   Critical program areas (CPAs) for rural ITS programs
*   Rural needs and issues
*   Examples of existing rural ITS programs
*   Regional planning activities
*   Summary

Vision for rural ITS

The implementation of advanced technologies has the potential to change the way transportation engineers manage transportation systems and services in the rural environment. With ITS technologies, the transportation engineer will have an improved means of monitoring infrastructure and vehicle fleets, access to and sharing of regional data and a greater opportunity to disseminate information than in the past. It is envisioned that advanced technologies will affect operations, safety, mobility, tourism, trade and productivity, as well as provide virtually all transportation-related agencies an opportunity to work together to achieve common goals. The following sections provide an overview of how ITS may assist in these areas in the rural setting.

Operations

In the urban environment, the goal of ITS is to enable a transportation manager to collect, process and disseminate information through the use of advanced technologies to balance transportation system capacity. In the rural environment, where system capacity is not an overriding concern, the goal of ITS is to assist the transportation manager in monitoring the infrastructure and transportation operations to provide safer and more reliable transportation.

In relatively isolated regions, it is more costly to verify that problems exist because of the distances involved. Therefore, advanced technologies can be a particularly useful and cost-effective means to assist rural operators in managing the transportation system. Advanced technologies will provide the ability to remotely monitor and verify conditions, thereby reducing the costs of operations and maintenance activities, as well as improving the performance and efficiency of transportation staff in a rural setting.

The implementation of advanced technologies will enable traffic operations and maintenance staff to accurately detect and monitor factors such as dynamic weather conditions, pavement and bridge maintenance conditions, work zone locations and crews, or maintenance fleet activities. Through applications including pager activation systems, automated highway pavement management systems, permanent or mobile weather sensors, and excessive speed vehicle-warning systems, the operations staff may be able to provide a higher quality of service.

Moreover, the ability to collect pertinent information will enable transportation managers to make more informed decisions, and to disseminate pre-trip and en-route information to the traveling public to enhance traveler safety. Eventually, perhaps, many of the monitoring stations and fleet management systems will be automated to increase efficiency and reduce operating costs.

Safety

The primary objective of rural transportation is to improve safety. In contrast to a number of the safety measures that were developed over the years to lessen the consequences of motor vehicle crashes (e.g., crashworthiness of vehicles, breakaway barriers, removal of roadside obstacles), many ITS applications are designed to prevent the occurrence of crashes. In rural areas, ITS technologies may be particularly useful where single-vehicle, run-off-the-road accidents are over represented.

The application of ITS technologies to the existing transportation infrastructure has many potential benefits, particularly through the use of advance warning systems. It has been estimated that if a driver were warned of an impending collision one-half second earlier, 50 percent of rear-end and crossroad crashes and 30 percent of head-on crashes could be avoided. Furthermore, it was reported that 90 percent of all crashes could be avoided if an additional second could be provided (Diebold Institute 1995). Researchers have estimated that advanced transportation technologies could potentially save 11,500 lives; 44,200 injuries; and $22 billion in property damage nationally by the year 2010 (Diebold Institute 1995).

To enhance safety in the rural setting, a greater focus on ITS applications that provide for communicating potentially dangerous situations to the driver should be implemented. A study conducted in Montana,

Wyoming and Idaho concluded that approximately 85 percent of the crashes could be prevented through advanced vehicle control system countermeasures. The applications that appeared most promising included friction or ice detection and warning systems, intersection crossing detection, animal–vehicle collision avoidance and horizontal curve speed warning advisory (Gomke 1998).

Mobility

Providing traveler information for alternate routes or alternative modes of transportation can enhance mobility. Making potential users aware of transit services (e.g., routes, departure times, rates and stop locations) will help to increase the mobility of transportation-disadvantaged individuals. In the future, door-to-door transit service may be available upon request. Some transit agencies are starting to deploy pilot systems that provide customized services (FTA 1997). Personal vehicle users could benefit from ITS-enhanced information systems as well. Route information (e.g., on road closures or alternative routes in the event of closures or construction work) could reduce travel delays and inconvenience. Information could be provided to users in their home prior to their trip or directly to their vehicle through an in-vehicle system.

Tourism and trade

Effective deployment of ITS applications can also enhance tourism and trade. Regional servers could be used to consolidate tourism service information such as availability of lodging or scheduling of special events with transportation management information on the status of road construction projects, weather conditions and traffic congestion information. This information could be disseminated to the traveling public via highway advisory radio systems, kiosks, FM sideband for cable television, or variable message signs (VMS) in a more accurate, timely and coordinated manner than was previously available.

Productivity

ITS applications are thought to be very effective ways to increase the productivity of commercial vehicles operators. For example, goods could be routed so as to avoid areas of construction work or periods of heavy congestion, thereby saving both time and money. Also, the amount of paperwork and time spent at weigh stations could be reduced through the automation of inspection and clearance processes. Management systems using electronic clearance, vehicle tracking and electronic logs may prove successful at improving productivity levels.

CPAs

The CPAs listed below represent a general classification scheme for ARTS. Development of these categories evolved through rural outreach sessions and focus groups conducted in numerous rural communities (U.S. DOT 1997).

- *Traveler safety and security*—this CPA addresses the need for improving a driver's ability to operate his or her vehicle in a safe and responsible way and for improving driver notification of potentially hazardous driving conditions (e.g., poor road conditions, reduced visibility, obstructions, animals). Example projects in this CPA may include but not be limited to area-wide dissemination of information regarding weather and road conditions via radio, computers, or television.
- *Tourism and travel information services*—this program area includes methods to provide traveler information and mobility services to travelers unfamiliar with the rural area through which they are traveling. Example projects in this CPA may include dynamic speed warning message signs, intersection advance warning signing and animal–vehicle alert warning, among others.

- *Infrastructure operations and maintenance*—included in this CPA are measures to address the efficient and effective maintenance and operation of rural roadways and infrastructure to respond to changes in weather conditions, coordinate response activities, manage construction and work zones and automate maintenance activities. Example projects in this CPA may include road-weather information systems, weigh-in-motion sensors, closed circuit television cameras, and automated gate closure systems.
- *Emergency services*—this program area focuses on providing improved notification and emergency response when an incident occurs, including reducing the time to notify the appropriate emergency service provider(s), as well as providing additional crash details to enable appropriate, efficient responses. Example projects in this CPA may include mayday systems, hotline call-in programs and emergency fleet management tracking systems.
- *Public traveler services and public mobility services*—this CPA addresses the accessibility and coordination of public transportation services to rural residents or travelers. Operational improvements that would allow transit vehicles to be pre-cleared through congested areas or the use of electronic fare payment systems for easy boarding would fall within this program area as well. Other examples within this CPA may include automatic vehicle location systems, computer assisted scheduling and dispatching, automatic telephone information systems, enunciator systems, advanced fare collection systems and automatic vehicle identification systems.
- *Fleet management*—the fleet management CPA provides for the efficient scheduling, billing, routing, locating and maintaining of rural fleets. Also included in this area is the use of designated fleets or probes to collect, process and transfer field data to operations managers for response. Example projects in this CPA may include automatic vehicle location systems, vehicle and engine monitoring systems and others.
- *Commercial vehicle operations*—this CPA addresses the regulation, management and logistics of commercial fleet operations. Included in this program area would be projects designed to meet the needs of rural commercial vehicle operators, such as hazardous material identification, driver monitoring, rural addressing and enforcement and management efforts.

Rural transportation needs and issues

The rural environment, as described in this chapter, includes both rural areas and small urban centers (defined as having populations less than 50,000 people). The following is a partial list of characteristics that distinguish the rural traveler and rural setting from their urban counterparts (FHWA 1997):

- Trip lengths are greater than in urban areas and often include unfamiliar roadways.
- Alternative routes may not be available or are few in number.
- Tourists and other unfamiliar travelers represent a large proportion of rural road users.
- Many of the roadway miles are owned and operated by city and county governments.
- Rural roadways are more difficult to maintain, which means that severe and rapidly changing weather conditions are more problematic.
- Remote regions and rugged terrain present additional challenges.

Rural transportation needs and issues cover a wide range of topics, but this section will limit discussion to the following areas: traveler information needs, public transportation services, traffic management, tourism, emergency services and commercial vehicle operations. The potential ways in which ITS programs can affect each area will be described as well.

Traveler information needs

General travelers, for purposes of this discussion, are defined as private travelers who may be residents of either urban or rural areas. It is felt that these individuals may differ from commercial vehicle operators or service providers in terms of their perceived transportation needs and, therefore, are discussed separately.

In a national study conducted for the Federal Highway Administration (FHWA), JHK and Associates identified six categories for the classification of rural travelers' information needs (FHWA 1994a). Specifically, these included:

1. Trip planning and routing
2. Traveler advisory
3. Traveler services information
4. Safety and warning
5. Route guidance
6. Emergency services

Using focus groups, national telephone surveys and personal interviews, the researchers were able to analyze the perceived information needs of the general travelers in their sample. Results of the study revealed that the types of information or services most desired were those that provide hazard warnings, guidance in unfamiliar situations and emergency assistance. These categories include MAYDAY systems (to enable travelers to call for assistance in emergency situations), advance warning of hazardous conditions, information on road closures and delays and safe speed advisories. In contrast with urban areas, information on traveler services was viewed as least important to those in the study sample. There were no apparent differences in perceived traveler needs based on the respondents' place of residence. In other words, when traveling in rural areas, the urban and rural residents expressed similar information needs and preferences (FHWA 1994a).

This study also found that the stage of a trip (i.e., the timeframe in which the information was received) was believed to affect the immediacy of the information need, as well as the type of information sought. The authors divided traveler information needs into three trip stages: pre-trip, en-route (no problem) and en-route (problem). When responses were examined using this classification scheme, information needs encountered in the en-route (problem) stage were weighed as more important than information encountered in either the pre-trip or en-route (no problem) stage (FHWA 1994a). As noted in the preceding paragraph, emergency response and hazard warning information received during the en-route (problem) stage were considered of primary importance to the respondents.

In the pre-trip planning stage, travelers identified five types of information that they believed would be useful. In descending order of importance, these information needs included:

1. Trip routing
2. Road conditions
3. Weather conditions
4. Travel time
5. En-route facilities

Relative weightings indicated that information obtained in the en-route (no problem) stage on road conditions and weather was less important to the rural traveler than similar information obtained for pre-trip planning purposes (FHWA 1994a).

In a similar study, over five hundred telephone interviews were conducted to assess traveler needs in rural Minnesota (C.J. Olson Marketing Research 1994). Information on road conditions due to weather was found to be the most important kind of pre-trip information to the respondents, with weather-related road conditions also cited as the most serious safety concern. The vast majority of the respondents expressed interest in having emergency notification technology installed in their vehicle. As in the JHK study, emergency assistance was ranked as the highest priority in terms of information or service need (FHWA 1994a; C.J. Olson Marketing Research 1994).

The needs of rural travelers also were examined in two multistate studies conducted by the Western Transportation Institute, Montana State University-Bozeman. Surveys were administered to travelers in the Greater Yellowstone area (Carroll and Mounce 1997) and travelers in northern California and southern Oregon (Harry, Randy and Mounce 1998). In both surveys, respondents indicated that safety was their greatest concern. The particular concerns they noted were problems with passing trucks and other heavy vehicles and road conditions (e.g., rain, snow, ice, fog). Travelers also expressed concern about driving through construction zones and encountering debris, objects, or animals on the roadway. Similarly, information on road conditions was found to be the most important pre-trip planning information noted in both studies.

In general, it appears that safety represents the biggest concern for the rural traveler. Given the typical length of rural trips, and the relative isolation of many rural roadways, it is not surprising that emergency notification and response are important considerations for those traveling in rural areas. Warnings of hazardous situations, whether related to road conditions, weather, or obstacles in the roadway, were also of critical importance to rural travelers.

Public transportation

As with ITS programs, in general, public transportation issues and related ITS technologies have been thought of primarily in terms of large urban centers. It is becoming increasingly apparent, however, that greater emphasis should be focused on transit issues for residents of rural America. Unlike urban areas where public transportation service is implemented to provide transportation for employment purposes or as a means of reducing congestion, in rural areas the public transportation service affects the quality of life of many rural residents. In particular, rural populations and public transportation providers are faced with challenges in three areas.

Access
Data provided by the Federal Transit Administration (FTA) indicated that public transportation services are limited in rural America. Approximately 38 percent of the rural population has no access to public transportation and 28 percent has little access (FTA 1997). Their report also noted that one in nine rural households are without a private vehicle. When public transportation is available, little or no information is available about the services. Furthermore, service is sometimes restricted to weekends, evenings, or designated days of the week (FTA 1997).

Population density
The low population density in rural service areas makes it difficult to deliver public transit services. Where neighbors are miles apart, trip distances are long and travel to common origin and destinations are infrequent, public transportation providers may find feasible solutions to their problems difficult to identify and extremely costly to implement.

Fleet size, user needs and coordination

Rural transit agencies typically operate small fleets that provide service to sparsely settled areas. In fact, most Section 18 recipients (60 percent) serve areas with fewer than 100 persons per square mile using 8 to 15 passenger vans (James and Islam 1996). In addition to service limitations associated with the size of the fleets, rural transportation must also meet the diverse needs of a broad range of users including elderly, handicapped and financially disadvantaged individuals. The demands placed on the fleet staff by the service requirements, as well as the various vehicle equipment requirements, and the payment systems or subsides used to finance those services are also factors to be considered. Lastly, coordination may determine what types of transportation services can be provided to rural residents and whether or not providers could work together on meeting the needs of their rural residents.

In summary, the quality of life for many rural Americans is often directly related to their ability to travel, when needed. Whether that involves finding a ride to visit a friend or to accomplish necessary tasks, such as grocery shopping or trips to the doctor, individuals without transportation alternatives find their lives restricted in very real and consequential ways. However, the extent to which rural residents may be willing to use public transportation alternatives likely depends upon many factors, including convenience, cost and safety. In order for ITS to assist transit providers in meeting the transportation needs of rural Americans, those individuals in need of service and their specific mobility requirements must first be identified. Subsequently, efforts must be made to develop service that is both effective and efficient, which can best be accomplished by sharing information among agencies or service providers to optimize routing, coordinate trips and so forth. Effort to reduce fraud in claiming subsides for service providers are necessary, to insure that future funding is not jeopardized. The challenges facing those who seek to provide public transportation alternatives to rural residents are numerous, but the potential does exist for ITS applications to improve the quality of life for those faced with limited mobility.

Traffic management

Traffic management refers to all actions necessary to construct, operate and maintain the roadway. Needs identified by traffic management personnel can be classified into two categories: (1) highway operations and management and (2) construction and maintenance.

Highway operations and management

As compared to urban transportation providers, transportation providers in rural areas generally have fewer financial resources with which to operate, more lane-miles per capita to operate and maintain, smaller personnel base, wider variety of potential weather-related problems, limited communication coverage and fewer opportunities for institutional coordination.

Effective ITS solutions for rural highway operations and management should, ideally, enhance safety and be cost-effective, as well as provide for resource savings and efficiency, aid in institutional coordination and have limited maintenance requirements.

When transportation agency personnel were asked about information needs, the most important factors were the accuracy and timeliness of the information. As for the kind of information needed by service providers, safety and warning information was found to be the most essential to their operations (FHWA 1994a).

Construction and maintenance

The safe and efficient flow of traffic through construction and maintenance work zones is a major concern to transportation officials, the highway industry, law enforcement personnel and the traveling public. Work zone fatalities rose to an all-time high of 833 in 1993, with 55 percent of those fatalities occurring in rural areas (FHWA 1994b).

As described previously, many rural travelers are unfamiliar with their surroundings, and the lack of alternative routes make it difficult for drivers to avoid construction or maintenance work on rural roadways. These factors, coupled with the limited use of advanced warning or traveler information systems on many rural roads, suggest that rural areas might be prime candidates for ITS construction and maintenance applications. The passage of the Transportation Equity Act for the 21st Century increased the budgets in many rural DOTs, which could allow for the development and implementation of improved, more dynamic work zone construction warning and information systems.

Tourism

Tourism and economic sustainability are critical concerns to numerous rural communities. According to the Travel Industry Association of America, travel and tourism in the United States is the nation's largest export industry and second largest employer, accounting for over $430 billion in expenditures, with domestic travel (principally weekend automobile trips) accounting for $350 billion (Challenges and Opportunities for Global Transportation in the 21st Century, Conference Proceedings 1995).

An efficient transportation system is essential to rural communities who depend on tourism revenues. Outreach efforts to the travel and tourism community have identified concerns in the following areas: signing, timely and accurate information, coordination of traffic management alternatives, seasonal and special event traffic management, parking information, regional sharing of information and services and funding (Hill, Albert, and Foderberg 1995–1997; Western Transportation Institute and Montana State University 1997; Castle Rock Consultants 1996; McDade 1995; West Virginia Transportation Technology Transfer Center 1997).

Emergency services

As shown in figure 13–1, Rural environments have disproportionately higher traffic fatality rates than urban areas. Whereas 40 percent of the vehicle miles traveled occur on rural roads, these roadways sustain 61 percent of all motor vehicle fatalities (FHWA 1994b). Approximately 66 percent of the fatal crashes that occur in rural areas are single-vehicle, travel-lane departure incidents (National Safety Council 1994).

Low population densities, limited emergency response services between rural communities and the lack of communication coverage in many rural areas make it difficult to respond to crashes in rural areas. These factors have contributed to an emergency response time that is approximately twice that observed in urban environments (figure 13–2). A typical emergency response time in rural America is 58 minutes from the time of the crash to the victim's arrival at a medical center, versus 35 minutes in an urban setting (NHTSA 1994).

Commercial vehicle operation

The JHK and Associates study revealed that information on weather and road conditions was of primary importance to commercial vehicle operators. Other information potentially available through ITS applications was considered less critical to these other highway users (FHWA 1994a).

Figure 13–1. Motor vehicle accident data.
Source: U.S. Department of Transportation
(graphics by Montana State University).

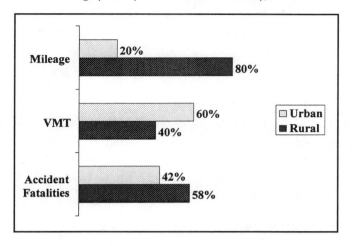

Figure 13–2. Emergency response times.
Source: Federal Highway Administration, *1994 Highway Statistics*
(graphics by Montana State University).

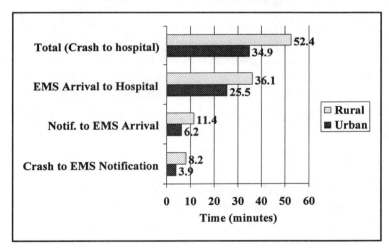

The movement of goods is critical to the economy of the United States, and the rural interstate system is an essential component in the process. Rural interstates are, in essence, the arteries that carry the flow of goods to be distributed to citizens throughout the country. Commercial vehicle operators have identified several transportation needs associated with rural travel such as the frequency with which they must stop at weigh stations for verification of permits, load limitation checks and safety inspections. Every time a commercial vehicle stops at a weigh station or a boarder crossing, it costs the carrier money. Therefore, measures to increase the operational efficiency of the system or reduce travel delays for commercial vehicle operators are considered of primary importance. For instance, vehicles traveling across the country often must pass through multiple tolling systems, whereas efficiency in terms of time savings could be realized through the use of electronic payment systems on toll roads.

Examples of existing ARTS programs

This section provides examples of existing ARTS applications within selected CPAs. A brief description of each project, including the objectives and intended benefits, are provided. It should be noted that some of these projects are in the early stages of implementation, so benefits attributable to the respective ITS application have yet to be determined

Traveler safety and security CPA

Idaho storm warning system (U.S. DOT 1998)
The goal of the Idaho storm warning system is to reduce multivehicle, visibility-related accidents in rural areas of the state. An operational test was administered to determine if the various sensor systems were effective at providing accurate and reliable weather data. The data are then used to provide general warnings, possible road closure information and speed advisories to travelers in the designated travel area. Information can be transmitted to the travelers using changeable message signs.

Tourism and travel information services CPA

Incident management using VMS (Deeter and Bland 1997)
The goal of this incident management project is to notify travelers of approaching hazards or incidents using VMS. Twenty-three of these VMS were installed on an interstate corridor. The signs are controlled by a central hub where the operator has an on-screen visualization of the network.

Infrastructure operations and maintenance CPA

Automated anti-icing and de-icing on underpasses (Deeter and Bland 1997)
The goal of this operation is to enable the remote application of anti-icing and de-icing chemicals to the roadway. The system uses atmospheric and pavement sensors to provide early warning of changing conditions. When weather conditions reach certain criteria, the application of chemicals is automatically performed. The system reports to maintenance personnel when the chemicals have been applied. The maintenance personnel also can call the system using a cellular phone to override the sensors and activate the chemical application.

Emergency services CPA

Rural coordinate addressing system (James and Islam 1996)
The rural coordinate addressing system is designed to improve emergency services through a low-cost addressing system. The state plane coordinates were collected for each rural residence using a portable global positioning system unit. These coordinates were put into a geographic information system (GIS) database and matched to each respective resident's phone number. This system lets the dispatcher or emergency service personnel identify the location of an incident on a digital map when a 911 call is received. The intended benefits of the rural coordinate addressing system include improved service for home deliveries or decreased response time in case of an emergency. The rural coordinate addressing system is a more cost-effective measure than the purchase of road signs to facilitate the location of residences.

Public traveler services and public mobility services CPA

Sweetwater Transit Authority Resources Computer-Assisted Dispatching (Advanced Rural Transportation Systems Compendium)
Three goals of this project were identified as (1) to significantly increase the number of riders served, (2) to accommodate same-day ride requests and (3) to reduce the cost per passenger trip. The Sweetwater Transit

Authority Resources developed a consolidated transit service in Sweetwater County, Wyoming. This service uses several ITS technologies, including mobile data terminals, automatic vehicle location and computerized dispatching. A digital, trunk-radio communications system may be used as well. A proposal exists to expand this service into all of southwest Wyoming. This service is being replicated nationwide.

To date, the Sweetwater bus system has doubled its monthly ridership. During the five years since the installation of the system, ridership has increased by a factor of five and the operating costs have decreased by 50 percent. This transit center is now serving approximately 20 agencies in the region.

Fleet management CPA

In-vehicle signing system for school buses at rail–highway grade crossings (ITS America 1996)

The goal of the in-vehicle signing system is to reduce accidents and fatalities associated with bus and train conflicts. The signing system includes a wireless communication antenna that is built into the railroad sign and an in-vehicle communication system that alerts the bus driver to the proximity of rail–highway grade crossings and the presence of oncoming trains. Interviews with the bus drivers suggest the in-vehicle signing system has been effective in warning bus drivers of the presence of a train at an at-grade rail crossing.

Consumer vehicle operation CPA

Dynamic truck speed warning for downgrade (Advanced Rural Transportation Systems Compendium)

The dynamic truck speed warning system is designed to enhance driver safety by warning the truck driver of potential collisions and rollovers. The speed warning system uses weigh-in-motion technology to determine the safe descent speed for trucks through a designated curve and downgrade. The safe speed is posted to the trucks using a VMS. The system also includes speed sensors downstream to evaluate the effectiveness of the system.

The truck speed warning system was installed on a narrow curve that has a design speed of 45 miles per hour (mph). The average truck speed around this curve has dropped from 66 mph to 48 mph since the installation of the warning system.

Regional management and coordination

Though it is not an official CPA, this area is becoming increasingly critical for regional cooperation. Following are examples of such projects.

California/Oregon advanced transportation system project

The goal of the California/Oregon advanced transportation system project is to plan, demonstrate, and deploy rural ITS to enhance safe, dependable, and convenient rural travel within the geographic area between Redding, California and Eugene, Oregon. The CALTRANS, the Oregon DOT, and various public and private partners are participating in the project. Specifically, a strategic plan for ITS will be developed and selected demonstration projects will be implemented to illustrate how ITS may be used as a tool in a rural environment. The study is intended to emphasize the need for multistate planning in order to meet rural traveler needs.

Arizona highway closure restriction system

The goal of this system is to increase coordination and data sharing between departments and agencies, enable the coordination and dissemination of real-time transportation information and provide a central location for response coordination. This system will build upon existing hardware, connections and software to develop an integrated method for sharing information and incident management responsibilities among the various agencies and departments involved. The highway closure information system in Arizona, for example, tracks each incident on the highway system in a user-friendly format using GIS. These incidents can include inclement weather, road closures, construction and maintenance activities and major events. The incidents are entered and updated by authorized persons from several agencies. The system improves the accuracy and timeliness of the information on road conditions that is available to both the decision-making agencies and the traveling public.

Regional planning

This section includes discussions of the following: (1) the rural ITS architecture, (2) the role that stakeholders can play in planning and implementing ITS applications, (3) the need for coordination and exchange of information among participating agencies or groups and (4) general recommendations or considerations to guide the planning process.

Rural ITS architecture

A rural ITS architecture was important to serve as a framework for the development of integrated transportation systems that would fully address the unique issues and needs of the rural transportation environment. A national ITS architecture had been previously established, but some felt that rural ITS should have its own architecture for the purpose of organizing rural functional requirements and systems interfaces (Hooper 1998).

Stakeholders representing urban, interurban and rural regions across the country provided input for the development of the national ITS architecture. It was evaluated during its development phase in terms of its ability to provide thirty different user services in three representative deployment scenarios (i.e., urban, interurban, rural) and found to successfully address the needs of all three regions. It was noted later that some rural user needs that were not contained in the original national ITS program plan may need to be reconsidered in light of newly identified rural requirements.

In that rural travel may easily involve regional or even multistate trips, an architecture that includes input from multiple rural stakeholder groups was felt to be important. A method that has been effective in developing a rural, multistate architecture project and that has used the national ITS architecture as a guide is illustrated in the figure 13–3 (Ulberg and Albert 1998). By following the process depicted in this figure, the rural needs to be addressed by specific projects can be mapped, while compatibility with the national ITS architecture is assured.

In summary, when developing an ITS application, it is important for it to fit into the overall transportation scheme for a region. In addition to conforming with the regional architecture, ITS applications must conform with the national architecture for ITS and the standards that are required by U.S. DOT in order to receive federal funding. Meeting these requirements should not be seen as a constraint, but rather as an opportunity to identify ways in which potential applications may be handled cooperatively, thereby reducing costs to individual agencies and avoiding unnecessary overlap of programs or responsibilities.

Figure 13–3. A method that is effective in developing a rural, multistate architecture project and that has used the national ITS architecture as a guide.
Source: Matthew Ulberg and Stephen Albert, *Greater Yellowstone Rural ITS Project: Regional Architecture Development* (Federal Highway Administration, July 1998).

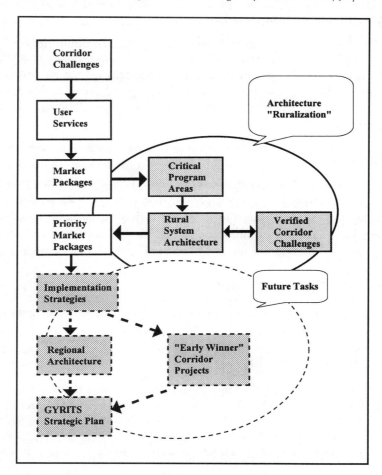

Stakeholders

In most rural areas, stakeholders may not recognize the importance of transportation in efforts to address community or regional challenges related to public safety, economic sustainability, or interagency cooperation and coordination. It is important to include representatives from various organizations in the planning and development of an ARTS program because the project actually may play a significant role in solving broader problems. The extent to which advanced technology applications in transportation could affect other issues in the community may not be immediately apparent to those outside the transportation field.

Rural ITS outreach workshops were conducted in Maine, New Hampshire, Vermont, West Virginia, Iowa, Nebraska, Kansas, Missouri, Utah, Arizona, Montana, California and Washington to identify potential stakeholders for future ARTS programs. Some of the workshops were sponsored by the FHWA with support from the ARTS committee of ITS America; others were part of ongoing research activities (Hill, Albert and Foderberg). With the cooperation of local technical assistance programs or technical transfer centers, a broad cross-section of stakeholders participated in the workshops. Attendees included representatives of law enforcement, tourism, chambers of commerce, agriculture, tribal nations, councils of governments, commercial vehicle operators, emergency managers and state and local transportation agencies.

Coordination and data exchange

The workshops revealed that the most common issues faced by rural communities are not technological, but institutional in nature. Similar to their urban counterparts, rural communities are challenged by the issues of communication, cooperation and coordination. The situation is, perhaps, more serious in rural areas because these locations typically do not have an MPO or a regional transit agency to facilitate or oversee cooperative efforts.

The most essential element of advanced transportation technology applications appears to be the ability to provide for regional data collection and information sharing. In rural areas, the development of large traffic management centers are unlikely. However, virtual regional transportation information centers can serve a similar purpose. A virtual center would consist of a regional server to consolidate data on transportation, safety, weather, transit services, tourism and so forth from a variety of sources and exchange information among institutions on a local, regional, or multistate basis. This data collection and dissemination process will increase awareness and coordination of responsibilities and activities across organizations and locations.

Considerations and recommendations

Several recommendations or considerations that will potentially affect the deployment of rural ITS systems are discussed below.

Tourism and economic sustainability

The economies of rural communities are changing from agricultural and natural resource-based to service and tourism-based economies. In the rural outreach workshops discussed in the preceding paragraphs, the issue of attracting tourists to rural communities was said to be critically important. Stakeholders felt this could best be accomplished by increasing the amount and quality of traveler information available to those visiting (or contemplating a visit to) the area. Workshop participants agreed that, if ITS applications are going to be successfully implemented in rural communities, tourism stakeholders should be involved in the development and implementation of the systems. Furthermore, the technologies selected for consideration should be ones that potentially can attract the tourist market or improve the quality of tourists' visits.

Target markets

In addressing transportation challenges and ITS applications, planners and engineers should look for target markets that provide an opportunity for local and regional agencies to work cooperatively. Examples of target markets at a local level may include tribal nations, national parks, tourist destinations and retirement communities. At a regional level, geographic areas (e.g., the Rocky Mountain region, Northern New England) that tend to attract travelers with similar interests and origin or destination preferences are thought to represent good target markets.

Operations and maintenance

Operations and maintenance issues, which frequently stem from budget and manpower constraints, are often key concerns among rural agencies that are considering the implementation of ITS technologies.

Limited funds often are used to keep roads in satisfactory condition, with the repair of potholes or the resurfacing of worn pavement taking precedence over other programs. Basically, there are two principals that should be followed when developing systems for possible implementation.

First, the less maintenance ITS applications require from the transportation agency, the better. It is highly unlikely that programs with excessive maintenance requirements will be given serious consideration in light of the budget and manpower limitations faced by most operations and maintenance departments. Obviously, if the agency cannot support the maintenance of the system, a different alternative or method should be developed.

Second, automated or semi-automated systems should be considered, if available, to minimize the amount of operational interaction required. This is especially important because operational personnel may not be available on a regular or full-time basis. Automating processes or combining applications using a common interface can reduce manpower requirements.

Partnerships

Partnerships can be a powerful tool for agencies to use in achieving their objectives. Basically, these partnerships can be characterized as either public–public or public–private, as described below.

An example of public–public partnerships would be multiple small towns or regions acting cooperatively in order to pool limited resources. By doing so, they may be able to acquire programs that would otherwise be too costly for any single jurisdiction to implement. Rural communities also can ask neighboring urban areas to form a partnership. The urban locations may represent the major traffic generators and, as such, they have a significant effect on the rural road system and a vested interest in the implementation of advanced transportation technologies.

In public–private partnerships, rural transportation agencies may be able to reach an agreement with private sector organizations to partner or pay for ITS programs in exchange for access to right-of-way or the opportunity for the private entity to make money.

Summary

This chapter illustrates some noteworthy differences that exist between urban and rural transportation environments and the corresponding problems encountered by travelers using roadways in these different locales.

The U.S. DOT has taken some steps toward the development of rural ITS applications, but much work still needs to be done. Current ARTS programs will serve as an example and as a starting point for future endeavors in advanced transportation technology applications. Demonstration projects will provide invaluable information to other rural transportation agencies in terms of both the benefits and any shortcomings in existing systems. Despite technological advances in recent years, it appears certain that rural transportation challenges will remain an issue. Thus, the opportunity exists for continued growth in the research and development of advanced rural transportation systems.

References

1995. *Challenges and Opportunities for Global Transportation in the 21st Century, Conference Proceedings, Travel and Tourism the Worlds Largest Industry: Transportation Challenges and Opportunities.*

Advanced Rural Transportation Systems Compendium. <http://169.135.1.58/arts/srvProjects.asp>.

Carroll, R., and J. Mounce. 1997. *Greater Yellowstone Rural ITS Priority Corridor Project, Rural Traveler Needs Survey* (September). Montana Department of Transportation and the Federal Highway Administration.

Castle Rock Consultants. 1996. Federal Highway Administration Region 7 Rural ITS Workshops (December). Washington, D.C.: FHWA.

C.J. Olson Marketing Research Inc. 1994. *Quantitative Market Research Regarding Travel/Transportation Needs in Rural Minnesota* (January). CastleRock Consultants and Minnesota Guidestar.

Deeter, D., and C.E. Bland. 1997. "Technology in Rural Transportation." *Simple Solutions* (October). Washington, D.C.: U.S. Department of Transportation, Federal Highway Administration.

The Diebold Institute of Policy Studies. 1995. *Transportation Infrastructure, the Development of Intelligent Transportation Systems.* The Diebold Institute of Policy Studies.

Hill, C., S. Albert, and D. Foderberg. 1995–1997. Federal Highway Administration Rural ITS Outreach Workshops. Washington, D.C.: U.S. Department of Transportation.

Federal Highway Administration. 1994a. *Draft Preliminary Assessment of Rural Applications of Advanced Traveler Information Systems* (April). Washington, D.C.: FHWA.

Federal Highway Administration. 1994b. *Highway Statistics.* Washington, D.C.: FHWA.

Federal Highway Administration. 1997. *Rural Applications of Advanced Traveler Information Systems: User Needs and Technology Assessment* (July). Washington, D.C.: FHWA.

Federal Transit Administration. 1997. *Briefings of the Advanced Rural Transportation Systems Committee, Rural ITS: The Transit Perspective* (February). FTA.

Gomke, R. 1998. *Rural Automated Highway System Case Study: Greater Yellowstone Rural ITS Corridor.* Western Transportation Institute and Montana State University.

Harry, S., R. Carroll, and J. Mounce. 1998. *California Oregon Advanced Transportation System, Traveler Needs Survey* (September). California Department of Transportation, Oregon Department of Transportation, and the Federal Highway Administration.

Hooper, R. 1998. *Rural ITS: the Role of Architecture, Standards, and Training* (Draft). Washington, D.C.: Federal Highway Administration.

ITS America. 1996. "Road Weather Information Systems in the United States" (June). *ITS America Fact Sheet,* no. 16. ITS America.

James, R. B., and T. Islam. 1996. Rural Transit: An Overview, Rural ITS Conference Proceedings (October). Center for Transportation Research, Virginia Tech.

McDade, J. 1995. *Rural ITS New England Workshops Summary* (August). Washington, D.C.: Federal Highway Administration.

National Highway Traffic Safety Administration. 1994. *Traffic Safety Facts.* Washington, D.C.: NHTSA.

National Safety Council. 1994. *Accident Facts.* Washington, D.C.: National Safety Council.

Ulberg, M., and S. Albert. 1998. *Greater Yellowstone Rural ITS Project: Regional Architecture Development* (July). Montana Department of Transportation and the Federal Highway Administration.

U.S. Department of Transportation. 1997. *Advanced Rural Transportation Systems Strategic Plan* (August). Washington, D.C.: U.S. DOT.

U.S. Department of Transportation. 1998. *Intelligent Transportation System Project Book.*

Western Transportation Institute, Montana State University. 1997. *Montana Rural ITS Outreach Workshop Report* (January). Washington, D.C.: Federal Highway Administration.

West Virginia Transportation Technology Transfer Center. 1997. West Virginia, Rural ITS Workshop (May). Washington, D.C.: Federal Highway Administration.

BY Donna Nelson, Ph.D. • Director • Maryland Transportation Technology Center, University of Maryland

ITS SUBSYSTEMS AND TECHNOLOGIES— MANAGING TRAFFIC, VEHICLES AND SYSTEMS

A variety of sensor technologies can provide the data that support traffic management and traveler information systems. Traffic management data and information are also supplied by cellular telephones, freeway service patrol reports, state police incident logs, call boxes/emergency telephones, closed-circuit television and environmental sensors.

This chapter describes some of the core technologies and subsystems that support the "roadway" subsystem as described by the National Intelligent Transportation System (ITS) Architecture and the centers that provide ITS services. These technologies are rarely used alone; rather they are combined to create the systems described elsewhere in this book.

Advanced traffic sensors and surveillance systems[1]

Surveillance systems monitor traffic flow and the environmental conditions that affect traffic management on highways and surface streets. The components of traffic surveillance systems generally consist of:

- Sensors and surveillance technology
- Data processing algorithms
- Communication networks

The sensors described in this section support integrated traffic management functions such as incident detection, information dissemination, traffic signal control and ramp metering. As used here, the term "sensor" includes the hardware and incorporated software that detects vehicles and converts the information into traffic flow data. The traffic flow parameters commonly used in ITS applications include volume, lane occupancy, demand, time and spatial headway, throughput, instantaneous and average vehicle speed, density, delay, stops, origin-destination data, turning movement and functional configuration (Klein and Kelley 1996, California Institute of Technology 1997).

Data processing algorithms can be located in the sensor hardware module, roadside cabinet, or at the traffic management center. Algorithms found in the sensor module usually extract raw data from the received signals, typically vehicle count and vehicle presence. The algorithms may also provide processed data such as headway, individual vehicle speed and time-averaged values of various traffic flow parameters. Algorithms found in roadside controllers also produce time-averaged data. Lane occupancies; 20-, 30-, or 60-second averaged vehicle counts; headway; stops; throughput and queue are typical parameters. Still other data processing occurs in the traffic management center, where roadside data are merged or fused with additional sources of information that support the traffic management function.

Traffic sensors and detectors

The sensors included here are inductive loop, magnetic, microwave radar, laser radar, passive infrared, ultrasonic, acoustic and video image processing. Although most of these technologies are relatively new applications to traffic management; inductive loop detectors are also included because they are in widespread use and, therefore, serve as a comparison for the performance of other sensor technologies. In-depth information on these sensors and their use can be found in the references listed at the end of this chapter (Klein and Kelley 1996, California Institute of Technology 1997, Carvel et al. 1997, Kranig et al. 1997, Gordon et al. 1996).

Inductive loop detectors

The inductive loop detector (ILD) is the most common sensor used in traffic management applications. The ILD consists of one or more turns of an insulated wire laid out in 6-foot diameter circles or 6-foot wide rectangles of variable length (Gordon et al. 1996). The loops are buried in a shallow sawcut in the roadway. A lead-in cable runs from a roadside pull box to the controller cabinet to an electronics unit located in the controller cabinet. The wire loop is excited with a 10 to 50 kilohertz (KHz) signal from the electronics unit, forming a local magnetic field above the roadway surface. When a metal vehicle stops on or passes over the loop, the inductance of the loop decreases, which in turn, increases the oscillation frequency. The electronics unit then sends a pulse to the controller, indicating the presence or passage of a vehicle. Newer versions of ILD use higher frequencies to identify specific metal portions on the vehicle, which can be used to classify vehicles.

Magnetic sensors

Magnetic sensors measure the disruption in the earth's magnetic field caused by the presence of a metal vehicle. Magnetic sensors are often used in place of loops on bridge decks where ILDs cannot be installed and in heavily reinforced pavement. Two types of magnetic field sensors are used for traffic flow parameter measurement. The first type, the two-axis fluxgate magnetometer, detects changes in the vertical and horizontal components of the earth's magnetic field. Fluxgate magnetometers operated in the pulse output mode sense the passage of a vehicle, yielding count data. When operated in the presence output mode, magnetometers give a continuous output as long as a vehicle occupies the detection zone and thus measures vehicle presence. The second type of magnetic field sensor detects perturbations in the earth's magnetic field produced when a moving vehicle passes over the detection zone. These magnetic sensors are induction magnetometers. Most cannot detect stopped vehicles nor provide presence measurements because motion is required for the sensor to produce an output signal (Klein 2001).

Microwave radar sensors

The types of traffic data received by a microwave radar sensor are dependent on the waveform used to transmit the microwave energy. The Doppler principle is used to calculate vehicle speed from a continuous wave (CW) microwave radar that transmits electromagnetic energy at a constant frequency, as shown in figure 14–1(a). Vehicle speed is proportional to the change in frequency between the received and transmitted signals and thus is determined by measuring the frequency change. The passage of a vehicle produces a frequency shift. Because only moving vehicles are detected by a CW Doppler radar, vehicle presence cannot be measured with this waveform.

Figure 14–1. Waveforms used with microwave traffic sensors.
Source: Lawrence A. Klein, *Sensor Technologies and Data Requirement for ITS,*
Courtesy of Artech House (Norwood, MA: 2001).

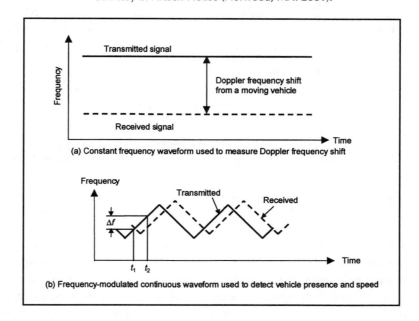

Both speed and presence can be measured using a frequency-modulated continuous waveform. As shown in figure 14–1(b), the presence of a vehicle is determined by measuring the change in range that occurs when a vehicle enters the field of view of the radar. Range is measured during the period where the transmitted frequency either increases or decreases with time. The range is proportional to the difference in frequency Δf that occurs at the transmitter between the time t_1 the signal is transmitted and the time t_2 it is received. Vehicle speed is measured using a range binning technique in which the field of view in the direction of vehicle travel is divided into range bins as shown in figure 14–2. A range bin allows the reflected signal to be partitioned and identified from smaller regions on the roadway. Vehicle speed is calculated from the time difference corresponding to the vehicle's arrival at the leading edges of two range bins a known distance apart.

Most commercially available microwave radar sensors used in roadside applications transmit electromagnetic energy at the X-band frequency of 10.525 gigahertz (GHz). Higher frequencies can be used to illuminate smaller ground areas with a given size antenna and thus gather higher resolution data. The size of the radar beam projected on the road surface (called a footprint) and mounting geometry are varied to monitor single or multiple lanes of traffic. Forward-looking wide beam radars permit more than one lane of traffic flowing in one direction to be monitored. Forward-looking narrow beam radars monitor a single lane of traffic flowing in one direction. Side-mounted radars project their footprint perpendicular to the traffic flow direction. Hence, they can provide data across several lanes of traffic, but generally not as accurately as can the same radar mounted in the forward-looking direction.

Infrared sensors

Infrared sensors can operate in active or passive modes. In the active mode, detection zones are illuminated with infrared energy transmitted from laser diodes operating in the near infrared spectrum. A portion of the

Figure 14–2. Range-binned footprints of forward-looking radar sensors.
Source: Lawrence A. Klein, *Sensor Technologies and Data Requirement for ITS,*
Courtesy of Artech House (Norwood, MA: 2001).

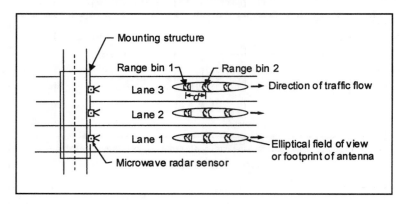

transmitted energy is reflected by vehicles traveling through the zones. The reflected energy is focused by an optical system onto an infrared-sensitive element mounted at the focal plane of the optics. The infrared-sensitive element converts the reflected energy into electrical signals that are analyzed in real time. The presence of a moving or stationary vehicle is determined by measuring the round-trip propagation time of the transmitted infrared pulse. The round-trip time will be shorter when a vehicle is present because the range between the sensor and vehicle is less than the range between the sensor and the roadway surface. Vehicle speed is measured by using two fixed beams, one pointed slightly ahead of the other. Speed is computed from the time difference during which the front of a vehicle passes through each beam and from the known ground intercept distance between the beams. Vehicle classification can be obtained by measuring the two-dimensional height profile of a vehicle (proportional to the distance from the sensor to the vehicle). The vehicle is classified by using an algorithm that compares the vehicle's profile against stored profiles for various vehicle classes.

Passive sensors do not transmit energy; rather they detect the energy that is emitted or reflected from vehicles, road surfaces and other objects in the field of view and from the atmosphere. The source of the emitted energy from the vehicles and road surface is gray-body radiation produced by the nonzero surface temperature of the emissive objects. As in the active infrared sensor, the received energy is focused onto a light-sensitive element located at the focal plane of the optics. When a vehicle enters the sensor's field of view, a signal is generated that is proportional to the product of an emissivity difference term and a temperature difference term, assuming the surface temperatures of the vehicle and road are equal. The emissivity term is equal to the difference between the road and the vehicle emissivities. The temperature term is equal to the difference between the absolute temperature of the road surface and the temperature contributed by atmospheric, cosmic and galactic emission. Thus, the change in emitted energy from the scene is used to detect the vehicle. Multizone passive infrared sensors measure speed and vehicle length as well as the more conventional vehicle count and lane occupancy (Klein 2001).

Ultrasonic sensors

Ultrasonic sensors transmit pressure waves of sound energy at frequencies between 25 and 50 KHz, which are above the human audible range. Most ultrasonic sensors operate with pulse waveforms such as those shown in figure 14–3; and they provide vehicle count, presence and occupancy information. Pulse waveforms are used to measure distances to the road surface and vehicle surface by detecting the portion of the transmitted energy that is reflected towards the sensor. When a distance other than that to the background road surface is measured, the sensor interprets that measurement as the presence of a vehicle. The received ultrasonic energy is converted into electrical energy that is analyzed by signal processing electronics. By transmitting pulse energy at two calibrated, closely-spaced incident angles, vehicular speed may be measured by recording the time at which the vehicle crosses each beam. This technique is similar to that used in laser radars. Constant frequency ultrasonic sensors that measure speed using the Doppler principle are more expensive than the pulse models. The Doppler model is designed to interface with the traffic management infrastructure in Japan.

Figure 14–3. Pulse-waveform as used in an ultrasonic traffic sensor.
Source: Lawrence A. Klein, *Sensor Technologies and Data Requirement for ITS,*
Courtesy of Artech House (Norwood, MA: 2001).

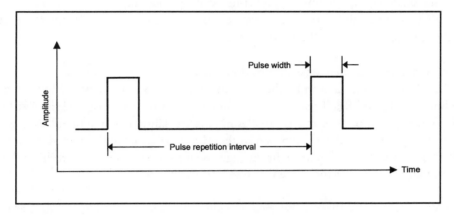

Acoustic sensors

Acoustic sensors measure vehicle flow rate, occupancy and speed by detecting acoustic energy in the form of audible sounds. The sounds are produced from a variety of sources within each vehicle and from the interaction of a vehicle's tires with the road. When a vehicle passes through the detection zone, a signal-processing algorithm recognizes an increase in sound energy and generates a vehicle presence signal. When the vehicle leaves the detection zone, the sound energy level drops below the detection threshold and the vehicle presence signal is terminated.

The sensors are configured with a two-dimensional array of microphones that receive the sounds produced by approaching vehicles. One model of acoustic sensor uses the time delay between the arrival of sound at the upper and lower microphones to detect vehicles in one lane. When the vehicle is inside the detection zone, the sound arrives almost instantaneously at the upper and lower microphones. When the vehicle is outside the detection zone, sound reception at the upper microphone is delayed by the intermicrophone distance. Preferred mounting is at a 10- to 30-degree angle from nadir. The detection range is between 20 and 35 feet. Sounds from locations outside the detection zone are attenuated. This model is not recommended where slow moving vehicles in stop-and-go traffic are present.

The second type of acoustic sensor uses a fully-populated microphone array and adaptive spatial processing to form multiple detection zones. This sensor can monitor as many as six to seven lanes when mounted over the center of the roadway. Five lanes are the practical limit when side mounted. Detection zones are equivalent to that of a 6-foot ILD in the traffic flow direction and are user selectable in the cross-lane direction. Mounting heights are between 20 and 40 feet.

Video image processors

Video image processors (VIP) detect vehicles by analyzing video images to determine changes between successive frames. A VIP system typically consists of one or more cameras, a microprocessor-based computer for digitizing and processing the video imagery and software for interpreting the images and converting them into traffic flow data. The image processing algorithms in the computer analyze the variation of gray levels in groups of pixels contained in the video image frames. By filtering out gray level variations resulting from weather conditions, shadows and daytime or nighttime artifacts, the image background can be removed and the objects identified as automobiles, trucks, motorcycles and bicycles retained. By analyzing successive video frames, the VIP is able to calculate traffic flow information.

VIP systems can be deployed to view upstream or downstream traffic. The primary advantage of upstream viewing is that incidents are not blocked by the resultant traffic queues. However, tall vehicles such as trucks may block the line of sight and headlights may cause blooming of the imagery at night. With upstream viewing, headlight beams can be detected as vehicles in adjacent lanes on curved road sections. Downstream viewing conceals cameras mounted on overpasses so that driver behavior is not altered. Downstream viewing also makes vehicle identification easier at night through the information available in the taillights and enhances track initiation because vehicles are first detected when close to the camera.

Three classes of VIP systems have been developed: tripline, closed-loop tracking and data association tracking. Tripline systems operate by allowing the user to define a limited number of detection zones in the field of view of the video camera. When a vehicle crosses one of these detection zones, it is identified by noting changes in the pixel imagery caused by the vehicle relative to the roadway in the absence of a vehicle. Closed-loop tracking systems permit vehicle detection along larger roadway sections. These tracking systems provide additional traffic flow information such as lane-to-lane vehicle movements. Data association tracking systems can identify and track a particular vehicle or groups of vehicles as they pass through the field of view of the camera. The computer identifies vehicles by searching for unique connected areas of pixels. These areas are then tracked from frame-to-frame to produce tracking data for the selected vehicle or vehicle groups. Future applications of data association tracking may allow vehicles to be identified and tracked as they pass from one camera's field of view to another's. This technique has the potential to provide link travel time and origin–destination pair information.

Summary

Sensors should be selected based on the particular requirements of the application and the maturity of the measurement technology at the time the system is specified and designed. Table 14–1 compares the strengths and weaknesses of the sensor technologies that have been discussed with respect to installation and performance in inclement weather and variable light. Most overhead sensors are compact and not roadway-invasive, making installation and maintenance relatively easy. All of these technologies are mature with respect to traffic management applications, although some may not provide the data required for a specific application

Table 14–1

Strengths and Weaknesses of Sensor Technologies

Source: Lawrence A. Klein, *Sensor Technologies and Data Requirement for ITS,*
Courtesy of Artech House (Norwood, MA: 2001).

Technology	Strengths	Weaknesses
Inductive Loop	• Flexible design to satisfy large variety of applications. • Mature, well understood technology. • Provides basic traffic parameters (e.g., flow rate, presence, occupancy, speed, headway, gap). • High frequency excitation models provide classification data.	• Installation requires pavement cut. • Decreases pavement life. • Installation and maintenance require lane closure. • Wire loops subject to stresses of traffic and temperature. • Multiple detectors usually required to monitor a location.
Magnetometer (Two-axis fluxgate magnetometer)	• Less susceptible than loops to stresses of traffic. • Some models transmit data over wireless RF link.	• Installation requires pavement cut. • Decreases pavement life. • Installation and maintenance require lane closure. • Some models have small detection zones.
Magnetic (Induction or search coil magnetometer)	• Can be used where loops are not feasible (e.g., bridge decks). • Some models installed under roadway without need for pavement cuts. • Less susceptible than loops to stresses of traffic.	• Installation requires pavement cut or tunneling under roadway. • **Cannot detect stopped vehicles unless special sensor layouts and signal processing software are used.**
Microwave Radar	• Generally insensitive to inclement weather. • Direct measurement of speed. • Multiple lane operation available.	• Antenna beamwidth and transmitted waveform must be suitable for the application. • Doppler sensors cannot detect stopped vehicles.
Infrared	• Active sensor transmits multiple beams for accurate measurement of vehicle position, speed and class. • Multizone passive sensors measure speed. • Multiple lane operation available.	• Operation of active sensor may be affected by fog when visibility is less than 20 ft or blowing snow is present. • Passive sensor may have reduced sensitivity to vehicles in its field-of-view in rain and fog.
Ultrasonic	• Multiple lane operation available.	• Some environmental conditions such as temperature change and extreme air turbulence can affect performance. Temperature compensation is built into some models. • Large pulse repetition periods may degrade occupancy measurement on freeways with vehicles traveling at moderate to high speeds.
Acoustic	• Passive detection. • Insensitive to precipitation. • Multiple lane operation available.	• Cold temperatures have been reported as affecting data accuracy. • Specific models are not recommended with slow moving vehicles in stop-and-go traffic.

Table 14–1, continued

Technology	Strengths	Weaknesses
Video Image Processor	• Monitors multiple lanes and multiple zones/lane. • Easy to add and modify detection zones. • Rich array of data available. • Provides wide-area detection when information gathered at one camera location can be linked to another.	• Inclement weather, shadows, vehicle projection into adjacent lanes, occlusion, day-to-night transition, vehicle/road contrast, and water, salt grime, icicles, and cobwebs on camera lens can affect performance. • Requires 50- to 60-ft camera mounting height (in a side-mounting configuration) for optimum presence detection and speed measurement. • Some models susceptible to camera motion caused by strong winds. • Generally cost-effective only if many detection zones are required within the field-of-view of the camera.

or may not be accurate enough. Others, such as VIP, are continuing to evolve, with new capabilities being added to measure additional traffic parameters, track vehicles or link data from one camera to that from another.

Weigh-in-motion sensors and systems

Weigh-in-motion (WIM) systems provide information on the dynamic weight of vehicles, as well as information on traffic volume and vehicle classification. WIM has been used in conjunction with static weighing systems in weight enforcement operations for nearly twenty years (Bergan 1999). More recently, WIM has been integrated into several ITS applications, including pre-clearance systems for commercial vehicles and hazard warning systems.[2]

Components of a WIM system

The components of a simple WIM, shown in figure 14–4, usually consist of one or two inductive loop sensors and the WIM sensor. Inductive loops are placed upstream and downstream from the WIM sensors. The upstream loop (loop 1) is used to detect vehicles and alert the system of an approaching vehicle.

The dynamic weight of a vehicle can be measured in several ways including: strain, change in capacitance, direct load measurement, change in electrical current (piezo-electric), resistive material sensors and light interruption (fiber optic sensors) Currently, the three most commonly used WIM technologies are: (1) Bending Plate WIM, (2) Piezo-Electric WIM and (3) Load Cell WIM (McCall and Vodrazka 1997). In addition, two emerging technologies, Quartz Crystal WIM and fiber optic technologies, promise to provide an accurate and cost-effective means for measuring dynamic vehicle speeds (Curnow 1998).

• *Bending Plate WIM* systems use plates with strain gauges bonded to the underside. As a vehicle passes over the bending plate, the system records the strain measured by the strain gauge and calculates the dynamic load. The static load is estimated using the measured dynamic load and calibration parameters. The calibration parameters account for the influences that factors such as vehicle speed and pavement/suspension dynamics have on estimating the static weight.

Figure 14–4. WIM layout.
Source: B. McCall and W. Vodrazka, *States' Successful Practices Weigh-in-Motion Handbook*
(Washington, D.C.: Federal Highway Administration, December 1997).

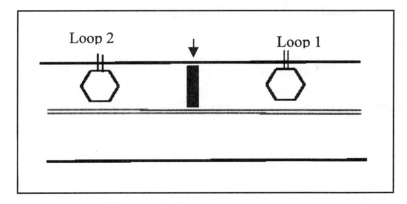

Figure 14–5. Components of a CCTV system.
Source: Donna Nelson.

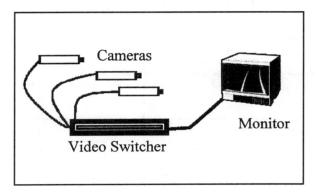

- *Piezo-Electric WIM* systems use "piezo" sensors to detect a change in voltage caused by pressure exerted on the sensor by an axle and measure the axle's weight. As a vehicle passes over the sensor, the system records the electrical charge created by the sensor and calculates the dynamic load. The static load is estimated using the measured dynamic load and calibration parameters.
- *Load Cell WIM* systems use a single load cell with two scales to detect an axle and weigh both the right and left side of the axle simultaneously. As a vehicle passes over the load cell, the system records the weights measured by each scale and sums them to obtain the axle weight.
- *Quartz WIM* uses a series of "pre-loaded" quartz sensors that are mounted in a high-strength aluminum element. The sensor is placed in a slot in the road surface and it is grouted with a compound designed to match the road surface properties. The sensitivity of this sensor is based on a "material" constant and therefore it does not change. These sensors can work at extreme temperatures and are accurate to +/_ 3%. The price of these sensors has dropped to just above the Piezo sensors and well below those of Bending Plate sensors.

- *Fiber optic technology* are being explored as part of the WAVE research program in Europe (Jacob 1999). Fiber-optic WIM have the potential to provide accurate systems at lower prices than existing technologies; and they are immune to many problems faced by other WIM technology, including electrical interference, humidity and resistance losses.

WIM applications

The *Weigh-in-Motion Handbook* (McCall and Vodrazka 1997) provides an in-depth treatment of the selection, installation and maintenance of Piezo-Electric, Bending Plate and Load Cell WIM systems (Chatters 1999). WIM sensor types, their application, accuracy and costs are summarized in table 14–2.

Table 14–2
WIM Sensor Characteristics
Sources: B. McCall and W. Vodrazka, *States' Successful Practices Weigh-in-Motion Handbook*
(Washington, D.C.: Federal Highway Administration, December 1997).

A. Curnow, "States of Weight: Developments in Weigh-in-Motion Applications,"
Traffic Technology International (April/May 1998, p. 104).

Sensor Type	Application	Accuracy highway speeds	Cost	Maintenance Costs
Bending Plate	Traffic data collection & weigh-station enforcement	+/- 5%	Moderate	Moderate
Load-Cell	Traffic-data collection & weigh station enforcement	+/- 3%	High	High
Piezo-electric	Traffic data collection	+/- 10%	Low	Low
Quartz crystal			Low-moderate	
Fiber Optic		+- 3%	Low to moderate?	

CCTV and VIP

CCTV and VIP technology forms an integral part of many traffic control applications, including roadway monitoring, incident verification and security. ITS applications rely on increasingly sophisticated video applications. These include automated incident detection, signal priority or access control, parking management, traffic surveys and data collection, traffic enforcement and video-based fire detection in tunnels.

CCTV

CCTV is a method of distributing video signals on a limited-access system. Access to the signals is confined to devices directly connected to a common circuit or system. By contrast, broadcast television signals are available to an unlimited number of receivers and access to such signals cannot easily be restricted or controlled.

CCTV system components

Components of a CCTV system include cameras at field locations, camera control accessories, monitors in the traffic operations center (TOC), videotape recorders (or other storage media), video switcher and a communications network that links central and field locations (figure 14–5).

Video cameras

A video camera produces a "video signal" by focusing an image onto a digitizing system called a charge couple device (CCD) array, which is essentially the same system used by computer scanners. The CCD sensor creates an analog signal from light. The signal output from the camera can be digital, analog or digitally processed analog. In a strictly *analog* camera, the signal remains in an analog format during the image production process. The signal might pass through mechanical components to adjust the image. In a *digital* output camera, the analog output from the sensor is converted to a digital format. Some image processing might occur within the camera. Outside of the camera, the signal is passed through an image capture tool to adjust the image and eventually to display it on an analog monitor. The third type of camera uses a technology called *digital signal processing* (DSP). The analog signal from the sensor is converted inside the camera to a digital format that can be digitally manipulated. For example, the functions of a DSP camera might include automatic backlight compensation, digital zoom and storage of preset camera parameters. After digital manipulation, the signal is converted back into an analog signal for transmission.

Both monochrome and color video cameras are used for transportation applications. Monochrome cameras, which produce high-sensitivity, high-resolution images in any type of illumination, are commonly used on freeways and interstates where most of the light is provided from passing vehicles and in rural areas with no lighting. Color cameras, which require full spectrum illumination and 10 times more light than monochrome cameras, perform well at most urban intersections where street lighting is available. High-pressure sodium and mercury vapor lighting provides a full spectrum of light, however low-pressure sodium light does not provide the proper light spectrum to provide a true color image. While monochrome cameras can provide a higher resolution, many people relate better to color images. Advances in color camera technology over the past five years have made the use of high-performance, high-sensitivity color cameras more common in more traffic applications.

Video cameras have a wide range of features and capabilities that include configuration, motion and lens control, alarms, inputs, outputs, labels, camera menu manipulation and the video switch. Video-camera capabilities are being addressed in the draft *National Transportation Communications Information Protocol Data Dictionary for CCTV* (Liddell 1998–1999).

Video switching

The video switcher is an essential component of any CCTV system for traffic surveillance and incident detection. A video switcher with "full matrix" switching allows any camera to be switched to any output, and it should also allow a single camera to be switched to multiple outputs, without degradation of the signal. Switching logic provides a set of rules that drive the matrix switcher. For example, the logic will prevent more than one camera from sending a signal to one output (Payne 1996).

Monitors

Video signals are created and recorded in several different "standard" formats around the world. The most common formats are the National Television Standards Committee (NTSC), PAL and SeCAM. In the United States, current ITS video surveillance and detection technologies are based on the NTSC standard. In early 1997, the Federal Communications Commission published a mandate intended to move the United States more rapidly to the use of digital television and the Advanced Television Standards Committee

(Abernethy 1998). Most of Europe (except France) uses the PAL format, as does Australia and some of South America. NTSC is used by North America, and a variation of NTSC is used in Japan. Secam, used almost exclusively by France, is functionally similar to PAL.

Communications

The transmission of video images requires more bandwidth (telecommunications capacity) than transmission of voice and data. The predominant means of transmitting video for traffic control applications has been by landline communications over coaxial cable or fiber optic cable. High capital or leasing costs are, however, making other communications options such as cellular networks, satellite transmission, packet radio and spread spectrum radio increasingly attractive. Chapter 17 discusses telecommunications technologies in more depth. The *Communications Handbook for Traffic Control Systems* provides a more extensive discussion focused on traffic control applications (Gordon et al. 1993).

Video surveillance systems[3]

The basic configuration of a video-surveillance application for advanced traffic management systems (ATMS) includes remote camera sites, hub sites and an operations center interconnected by communications systems.

Remote camera sites

The remote camera site is the area under surveillance. This may be an interchange, a rest stop, a congested ramp metering area, the display of a variable message sign (VMS) or various traffic signal intersections. Video and control signals are transmitted to a hub site, most commonly via multimode fiber optic cable.

Hub site

Video from multiple cameras is directed to a remote hub site for transmission to a TOC. At the hub site, the video signal is processed through a video switcher, and the base band video is directed to a single-mode fiber optic modulator. The single-mode fiber optic modulator transmits the video from the hub sites to the TOC.

A "satellite hub control panel" allows each hub to operate as an independent subsystem in the event that a break in the fiber optic single-mode cable or hardware problems cause a communications failure to the TOC. Video switching allows an operator to route a signal from one source to a destination. In traffic surveillance, video switching normally occurs at the hub site and is controlled from the TOC. Each hub usually serves at least three or four cameras. Hub sites and cameras can be added as the demand increases.

Advanced vehicle location and navigation technologies

Automatic vehicle location (AVL) describes a broad range of technologies that incorporate positioning technologies, mapping and communications. AVL technologies, rarely used as a standalone application, are an integral part of many ITS services such as route guidance, computer-aided dispatch, transit traveler information, commercial vehicle fleet management, mayday or motorist assist technologies, congestion detection and stolen vehicle recovery systems. The basic components of AVL and navigation technologies are:

- Location technologies and positioning systems
- Maps
- Map-matching and geographic information systems (GIS)
- Route guidance and path-finding technologies
- Route guidance

Positioning systems

Four types of position techniques are commonly used for ITS: dead reckoning, satellites, terrestrial radio frequency and map-matching. These technologies may be combined in a single system for more effective location technologies.

Satellite positioning systems

Satellite-based positioning systems are being used in every mode of transportation. An example of a global positioning system (GPS) is a satellite-based radio positioning and time transfer system designed, financed, deployed and operated by the U.S. Department of Defense. The satellites receive and store data transmitted by control stations, maintain accurate time using onboard atomic clocks, transmit information and signals to users and provide a stable platform and orbit for the transmitters. The control stations (ground facilities) are responsible for satellite tracking, orbit computations, telemetry and other activities needed to control the satellite. Table 14–3 describes a number of satellite-based positioning systems, including: GPS, geo-stationary earth orbit (GEO) satellites, low earth orbit (LEO) satellites, medium earth orbit (MEO) satellites and highly elliptical orbit (HEO) satellites.

Dead reckoning systems

With dead reckoning (DR) systems, the current position is calculated based on the last known position of the vehicle and the speed and direction the vehicle traveled to that point. Speed, distance and bearing (direction) are measured using a variety of sensors including odometers, altimeters, compasses, speedometers and inertial sensors such as accelerometers and gyroscopes. These data are then used to determine the location.

The main drawback of DR systems is that measurement errors accumulate. Even small errors in measuring the vehicle's bearing become quite large over time. DR systems are commonly integrated with GPS, overcoming many of the drawbacks of both systems. For example, GPS location coordinates are used to maintain the accuracy of DR location information, which is then used for navigation when GPS signals are interrupted.

Signpost systems

Signposts are infrared, microwave, or radio frequency (RF) devices mounted on the sides of the roadway. These signposts, or beacons, are capable of transmitting and receiving data from vehicles equipped with transceivers when these vehicles come in close proximity to the signpost. These systems can be either self-positioning or remote positioning. In the first case, a tag in the vehicle picks up a signal from the beacon. In the second case, the beacon senses a tag on the vehicle. The basic configuration includes antennas, transmitters electronics and receiver electronics.

Radio frequency identification (RFID) systems are becoming more common for applications such as parking systems and fuel management systems. For example, RFID is used in an automated fuel management system used in North Bay, Ontario, Canada (Veinot 1997–1998). As the driver pulls in, the vehicle is automatically identified using a radio signal between an in-ground antenna and the vehicle. A unique code is transmitted and once it correctly identifies and matches the vehicle with the information in the computer, the system authorizes the fuel pumps to turn on.

Table 14–3
Summary of Satellite Positioning Systems
Sources: E.J. Krakiwsky and Mohamed A. Abousalem, "An Overview of AVL
Positioning Technologies for ITS," Conference Proceedings: Third Annual World
Congress on Intelligent Transportation Systems (Orlando, FL: ITS America, October 1996).

E.J. Krakiwsky, "Navigation and Tracking Systems,"
ITS World Magazine (January/February 1996, vol. 1, no.1).

Global Positioning System (GPS)	The system comprises 24 positioning satellites enveloping the Earth at an altitude of approximately 20,000 kilometers. Standard GPS positioning service (with SA) provides horizontal positioning accuracy of 100 m and vertical positioning accuracy of 156 m 95% of the time. Inexpensive receivers make it feasible to receive data (location, heading and speed) as frequently as every second.
Differential Global Positioning System (DGPS)	DGPS is used improve the positioning accuracy of GPS to about 1 to 10 meters. A reference (or base) station is established over a point of known coordinates. The errors in the satellite measurements are continuously computed and are then transmitted, along with the satellite ID, to a remote user, who then uses them to correct their own ranges made at the remote site.
Global Navigation Satellite System (GNSS)	A European project intended to become the navigation tool for air, land and marine in the 21st Century. It will be developed and deployed in two stages. GNSS1, GPS augmented with GEO communication satellites, is planned for 1999. GNSS2, a new system, will replace GNSS1 in about 10 to 15 years, and will be backward-compatible with GPS.
Geo-stationary Earth Orbit (GEO)	GEO satellites orbit at altitudes of 36,000 kilometers in synchronization with the earth's rotation, and remain over approximately the same locations on the earth's surface near the equator. Due to their orbit, they require relatively large antennas at the earth mobile terminal to send and receive signals, making the equipment somewhat bulky. GEO is effective for applications that require wide-area coverage. The equipment and services are relatively costly.
Low Earth Orbit (LEO)	LEO constellations orbit at distances of less than 2,000 kilometers, provide global, low powered, low cost, handheld communications. Deployment is relatively recent.
Medium Earth Obit (MEO)	MEO satellites orbit at altitudes of roughly 8,000 km. A constellation (Odyssey) is in the design stage, with 12 satellites in space by the year 2000. MEOs require lower power than GEOs; require fewer satellites to provide global coverage than LEOs. Another constellation (Ellipso) is planned to incorporate MEO and HEO technology.

Cellular location technology

Researchers are exploring the use of cellular phone systems to determine location. This approach has several advantages (Drane and Rizo 1997). It makes use of an existing infrastructure, which significantly reduces the cost of establishing the service. Cellular phones already have a spectrum allocation and a large installed user base. Cell phones can potentially be used as "vehicle probes" in much the same way toll-tags are currently used.

Maps

While there are many different kinds of maps, the street maps used for vehicle navigation and location are usually either raster or vector maps. Raster maps are basically pictures, or "bit maps" of printed street maps. Raster maps are excellent for showing details such as city limits or altitude variations using contrasting colors or topography lines. Vector maps are essentially line drawings. Points, lines and polygons are stored in a database as x, y coordinates. Vector maps can show discrete geographic features (those with definite edges), but they show much less graphic detail than raster maps.

Raster maps have several drawbacks that outweigh their advantages for most AVL applications. Raster maps require much more storage space (in bytes) than do vector maps. They take longer to draw, and the orientation is essentially fixed, usually with north at the top of the screen. It is possible to rotate a raster map, however, so that the text on the map rotates with the picture. This means that the text would be upside down for a vehicle traveling south. These maps show the same level of detail regardless of their size, and increasing the size of the image changes the size of a map. The basic picture remains the same. Images that are enlarged or reduced may be difficult to read.

Vector maps are well suited to vehicle navigation because every element of a map is "unique." Street names can be drawn on the display after the map is rotated, allowing the text to remain right-side up. A vector map can be drawn to increase or decrease the amount of detail shown on the map. The scale determines what streets are shown and the size of the text.

Map-matching

GIS provide the link from a specific position information (location coordinates) to geographic information such as street names and addresses that may, in turn, be linked to a map. This process is called geo-coding or address-matching. While the GIS contains location information for specific coordinates within an area, often only major intersections are recorded with specific coordinates. Individual street numbers are interpolated using address-matching, which takes the nearest known street numbers and calculates where specific addresses are likely to be. Street numbers are not always evenly spaced however, and in most cases the AVL system should calculate a location within 15 meters of the actual location.

Map-matching techniques are used to determine the location of a vehicle relative to a map. For example, when a positioning system (like GPS) gives coordinates that do not correspond exactly to a road on the digital road map, a map-matching algorithm can be used to find the nearest road and locate the vehicle on that road. As a vehicle travels, the path it follows is obtained from sensor data and is correlated with the road network stored in a digital map. The coordinates of identifiable features such as intersections are used to position the vehicle. This information can then be used to correct for DR errors (Catling 1994). Map-matching requires accurate maps that reflect the real world. If a road traveled is not shown in the map, the map-matching algorithm will not consider the route valid.

Path-finding (or route-finding) and route guidance

Once the vehicle's position is known, some AVL systems plot a path from the current location to a desired location. In-vehicle navigation systems typically provide this information directly to the driver (route guidance). Fleet management systems often provide this information to a base station or dispatcher, where it may be used to develop routes and schedules in advance. The systems available to shipping and courier services can analyze different routes for fuel consumption and vehicle wear and tear. Dispatchers might also provide information to drivers via radio or cell phone as well.

Information dissemination and display technologies

Information dissemination is an essential component of ITS. Chapter 5 provides an in-depth discussion of traveler information systems. Other chapters discuss the display of information to support other ITS applications, including transit (chapter 8), rural ITS (chapter13), commercial vehicle operations (chapter 9), and advanced transportation management systems (chapter 4). The section below describes technologies common to a number of ITS applications. Chapters 17 ("Telecommunications Technologies") and 18 ("Information Technologies") provide additional information on the use of these devices.

A range of established and new technologies makes transportation information accessible to travelers in a variety of locations. Kiosks, television, radio, dynamic message signs (DMS) and telephone "hot-lines" have been used to disseminate information for a number of years. Access to information delivered using these technologies was limited to specific locations or times, and our ability to tailor the information provided to specific users was also limited. In recent years, the widespread use of pagers, cellular phones and the Internet are providing new, flexible alternatives. Cellular phones provide access to telephone-based information nearly anytime, anywhere. Internet access at home and in the office is also growing at a high rate. It is entirely possible to send predefined test messages using e-mail to some pagers and digital cellular phones.

DMS

DMS are a primary means of disseminating information to travelers prior to or during a trip. As the name suggests, DMS include those signs whose display is dynamic (or changeable), ranging from the somewhat outdated mechanical roller blind signs to the most modern highway VMS.

While ITS may use a wide variety of these devices, this section focuses on an overview of only one class of DMS: the VMS. VMS are available in a number of technologies. In all cases, individual pixels are addressable to form displays. The most common technologies used for ITS include reflective disk, bulb-matrix, light emitting diodes (LED), fiber optic shuttered (FOS), fiber-optic hybrid and LED hybrid.

Reflective disk

This technology, developed in the 1960s, has been widely used in many different fields, such as advertising, stock and commodity exchanges and transportation. A message is displayed by "flipping" disks or cubes that are matte-black on one side and coated with fluorescent or retro-reflective materials on the other side. The disks have a wide viewing angle but require illumination to be seen at night.

Bulb matrix

Bulb matrix VMS have been used in the commercial sign and transportation sign markets for many years. Messages are displayed using pixels formed with incandescent lamps. A simple bulb-matrix VMS might use a single bulb per pixel. More complex VMS may use multiple lamps per pixel with different colored lenses that fire at differing rates to produce color animations. The main drawbacks are that bulb-matrix VMS require frequent maintenance; power consumption is significantly higher then that of other available technologies; and they require frequent maintenance, including bulb replacement.

Light emitting diode

LED VMS use LED to create display pixels. Each pixel is comprised of one or more high-output LEDs, usually wired so that a pixel will function if a single LED fails. LEDs are almost always amber in color. LED VMS are sometimes described as "solid-state" signs. Even though the display itself contains no moving parts, an extensive fan and ventilation system is needed to cool the inside of the sign cabinet. The light output of LED VMS is somewhat less than that fiber optic VMS, however they are still highly visible.

FOS

The concept behind FOS technology is similar to that used for reflective-disk VMS. High-intensity lamps (typically quartz-halogen) illuminate the common ends of fiber optic harnesses. These harnesses are bundled and inserted into a shutter. The shutters are arranged into pixels to create the VMS display. Characters are formed using electromagnetic elements or shuttering devices to open or close the shutters. FOS, available in a variety of colors, provides a very visible display even in severe ambient conditions.

Fiber optic and LED hybrid VMS

These signs combine the characteristics of reflective-disk technology with the advantages of fiber optic or LED VMS. The reflective-disk portion of the VMS provides a wide viewing angle, good target value and good contrast when the sun is shining directly on the face of the sign. Fiber optic or LED technology provide high visibility at night or in ambient conditions where reflective-disk technology is not suitable.

Because the power consumption of reflective-disk technology is essentially zero except when the sign message is being changed, using the light-emitting portion of the signs only when needed significantly reduces the power consumption of the sign. For example, if a typical fiber hybrid DMS consumes 4,000 watts, the savings could accumulate to 48 kilowatt-hours per day on a single sign. It is easy to see how the savings can multiply on a traffic management system with fifty signs.

Technologies for delivering pretrip and en-route traveler information

Several methods of broadcasting traveler information have been around for some time. Highway advisory radio (HAR) and traffic broadcasts have been offered to commuters via television and radio, radio-data systems (RDS) for some time. More recently, cable television, the Internet, personal digital assistants (PDAs) and cellular phones have expanded the possibilities for providing traveler information before and during a trip.

HAR

HAR provides highway users with information in their vehicles using conventional AM or FM radio transmissions from the roadside with limited-range transmitters. HAR is used to provide notifications or warning of roadway incidents or congestion, warning of adverse environmental conditions (e.g., fog, ice), highway construction or maintenance, alternate route information, airport information, or tourist information.

Typical components of HAR systems are a broadcast antenna (vertically polarized monopole or buried radiating coaxial cable), grounding system, low-power roadside transmitter, communications link to a control center, recorder, message development facility and beacon-equipped static signs providing notification of traffic messages. HAR systems may be stationary or portable. Signs advise drivers to tune to a specific station. Messages are usually prerecorded; however, live broadcasts may also be used. HAR transmissions can be controlled from a remote location or on-site. Most HAR systems operate at the 530 or 1610 kHz frequency level; however, any available frequency can be used provided a low power level is used (FHWA 1997). While HAR can provide longer, more complex messages than DMS, drivers must take direct action to receive information. Automated HAR systems are similar to HAR, but they can automatically preempt programming to broadcast an advisory message.

RDS

A radio station actually uses only a very small portion of the radio spectrum assigned to it for broadcasting an audible program. RDS uses a small portion of this unused spectrum, called a subcarrier, to transmit information (Upchurch, Hansen and Ajah 1996). The RDS signal has the same range as its "host" radio station and the same level of reliability. Digital information transmitted on this subcarrier does not interfere with the audible program. An RDS receiver receives the signal and then decodes it or translates the digital information into text or audio information, which is then presented to the user.

The RDS-Traffic Message Channel is an ITS application that provides motorists with information. It is being widely deployed in Japan and in Europe (Dempsey and Nutttall 1998). U.S. interest in this technology is relatively recent. The European RDS-Traffic Message Channel uses a large dictionary of messages, which are then decoded and displayed by the receiver. A system now being tested in the United States provides only critical information in a very concise format (Orski 1998).

Computer (Internet)

Internet access is increasing rapidly, along with the variety of information and services available online. ITS-related applications are described in chapters 4 and 5 and in other locations throughout this book. A complete discussion of Internet and web technology is well beyond the scope of this book. In fact, the technology is changing so rapidly that any detailed discussion would be obsolete well before the book is published. The promise of this technology for a wide variety of applications, however, makes it difficult to leave out.

Internet in the vehicle

The Internet is also being extended into the vehicle. In 1998, Microsoft announced Auto PC, which links an in-car computer to mobile communications, entertainment systems, office software, and potentially, a variety of specialized applications for sales professionals, CVO operators and others (Scrase 1998). Speech technology allows drivers to control most functions of the on-board computer with simple voice commands, including the unit's digital radio and CD player. The computer can also give spoken instructions (such as navigation directions) or can read out e-mail messages on request.

Pagers, PDAs, and cellular phones

Alphanumeric pagers, PDAs and cellular phones are used to transmit traffic information (Starr and Wetherby 1996).

Electronic payment technologies: smart cards[4]

Smart cards are used for a variety of financial and nonfinancial applications. In recent years the use of these technologies has grown in the Far East and South America, and it is finally being adopted on larger and larger scales in the United States.

Transportation agencies are applying smart card technology to a wide range of transportation applications, particularly in transit, commercial vehicle operations and parking applications. The uses of smart cards in transportation goes well beyond electronic toll and fare collection. In China, smart driver licenses will help computerize drivers' information and traffic violation records and implement a network link to allow drivers to pay fines at banks.

Smart card technology is simple compared with earlier computer-based electronic payment systems. The basic components of a smart card implementation are: smart cards, smart card readers (including point of sale terminals), communications links and software.

Types of smart cards

There are two basic types of smart cards: memory cards and central processor unit (CPU) cards. Memory cards are data storage cards used primarily as cash-value (prepaid) cards to make pay phone calls and purchases. Their memory is typically 2 Kbytes (as compared with a magnetic stripe of 0.2 Kbytes), whereas the CPU card contains 1-32 Kbytes (typically 1-4 Kb) of memory operating at clock rates of 4-16 MHz (typically 4 MHz). CPU smart cards with 1-4 Kbytes of memory operating at 4 MHz is the de facto standard for electrical interoperability.

CPU cards, also called integrated circuit cards, may be contact, contactless or "combi" (both). Contact cards must come into physical contact with the reader. The contactless cards can be read from distances of under 1 inch (proximity cards), at distances of about 4 inches and at distances of up to several meters. Cards are made to conform with the International Standards Organization (ISO), PC/SC, Institute of Electronics and Electrical Engineers (IEEE) and other norms and standards. The world's largest smart card manufacturer is the French company Gemplus.

Smart card readers

Smart card readers differ depending on the capabilities of the cards. The size of a standalone reader may range from 4.5 x 4.5 x 2 inches to as small as 3 x 3 x .5 inch. Card readers for transit and rail fare payment and parking access are typically integrated into turnstiles or other equipment and are transparent (invisible) to the user. Standalone readers with screens, keyboards, or writing pads are used in restaurants and on vehicles or as PC-core (as in the PCMCIA Card) readers. They, too, are made to conform with ISO, PC/SC, IEEE and other norms and standards. Card makers and other companies such as SCM provide smart card readers.

Communications link

The system reader and the application host computer are typically linked by using an RS-232 link for distances of up to 50 feet or an RS-485 link for distances of up to 4,000 feet. The card and reader are linked using RF communications. The application-host computer may also be linked to a central computer system to allow data transfer records to be updated in real time.

Smart card software

Application software, card operating system software and reader software complete the smart card system. The applications software, usually the most critical software factor in day-to-day smart card system operations, include both "financial" or "nonfinancial" applications.

Electronic toll collection system

The toll-tag (transponder) of an electronic toll collection (ETC) system is typically mounted in the vehicle. Each toll lane is equipped with an RF antenna. Antennas are usually mounted in the center of the lane above the roadway; however, there are implementations where the antenna is embedded in the roadway. A reader connected to each antenna controls the communications between the transponder and the antenna. The reader sends a signal (via the antenna) to the tag to initiate communication. The tag then returns a unique identification number that identifies the vehicle (customer) to the ETC system. Depending on the type of RF tag used, the tag may transmit additional information (e.g., account balance, point of entry) and the reader may send back updated information to be encoded on the tag or smart card. The transponders or "tags" communicate with an antenna and reader in either an active or passive mode. An active RF tag transmits an RF signal to the antenna; a passive transponder modulates the signal it receives and reflects it back to the antenna.

RF transponder (tag) technologies for toll collection

Three primary RF technologies support electronic toll collection: RF tags, RF smart tags and smart cards with RF transponders. These tags can be classified into one of three types, depending on their communications capabilities:

- *Type 1 tags* contain read-only information about the vehicle and customer that is transmitted to the system. The information on the tag is fixed and the card has no data-processing capabilities.
- *Type 2 tags* contain a read and write area that allows information such as the date, time and point of entry to be recorded.
- *Type 3 tags* have communication ports that allow the tag to communicate with other devices in the vehicle.

Current RF tags use one of three frequency ranges: 900–928 MHz, 2.45 GHz or 5.8 GHz. Only the 900–928 MHz frequency range is currently used in the United States.

RF tags

RF tags may be either Type 1 or Type 2, and they may be used in either an active or passive mode. The maximum read and write range of the RF tag is just over 100 feet; however, in most applications the tag is within 20 or 30 feet of the antenna during communications. RF tags operate in half duplex mode; consequently they cannot send and receive data at the same time. RF tags have been used in toll applications around the world.

RF smart tags

RF smart tags contain a microprocessor that stores both fixed information such as vehicle and customer data and data that may be modified such as balance information. RF smart tags operate in full duplex mode, meaning that they are able to send and receive data at the same time. RF smart tags have not been used extensively either in the United States or around the world. Because RF smart tags operate in an active mode, their maximum read and write range is greater than RF tags (owing to their use of active transmission). As with RF tags, RF smart tags are usually 20 or 30 feet of the antenna during communications.

Smart cards with RF transponders

Toll collection systems that use smart cards consist of the smart card and a separate RF transponder (tag). The smart card is an integrated circuit device that contains a microprocessor and memory and stores account balance information. The RF transponder interfaces with the smart card and allows the smart card to communicate with the in-lane antenna and reader. Often, this RF transponder is actually a Type 3 RF tag. In addition, the RF transponder contains information about the vehicle that it transmits to the antenna and reader along with the smart card information. The transponders used employ either full or half duplex communications with either active or passive transmissions.

Smart cards with RF transponders are currently undergoing extensive trials in Europe. Automatic Debiting and Electronic Payment for Transport has designed and implemented field trials in automatic debiting technology, using advanced in-vehicle transponders that facilitate high-speed, multilane transactions between a roadside charging system and a smart card in the vehicle. This technology was demonstrated for urban pricing and parking applications, as well as for multilane toll collection in six sites across Europe.

References

Abernethy, B. 1998. "Digital Video: A Major Technology Change that is Being Overlooked." *Traffic Technology International* (August/September): 31–35.

Bergan, Art. 1999. "Preservation for the Nation: Integrated WIM and infrastructure management." *Traffic Technology International* (February/March): 90–92.

California Institute of Technology. 1997. *Traffic Surveillance and Detection Technology Development, Final Report* (March). Pasadena, CA: Jet Propulsion Laboratory, California Institute of Technology.

Carvell Jr., J.D., K. Balke, J. Ullman, K. Fitzpatrick, L. Nowlin and C. Brehmer. 1997. *Freeway Management Handbook* (August). Washington, D.C.: Federal Highway Administration, U.S. Department of Transportation.

Catling, I. (ed.). 1994. *Advanced Technology for Road Transport: IVHS and ATT.* Boston, MA: Artech House.

Chatters, K. 1999. "Perils of the Scales: Will WIM Ever Make the Grade." *Traffic Technology International* (February/March): 99–100.

Curnow, A. 1998. "States of Weight: Developments in Weigh-in-Motion Applications." *Traffic Technology International* (April/May): 104.

Dempsey, P. and I. Nuttall. 1998. "Marking a Market: First Steps to Driver Information Services." *Traffic Technology International* (April/May): 64.

Drane, C. and C. Rizo. 1997. *Positioning Systems in Intelligent Transportation Systems.* Boston, MA: ARTECH House.

Federal Highway Administration. 1997. *Freeway Management Handbook* (August). Washington, D.C.: FHWA, U.S. Department of Transportation.

Gordon, R.L., R.A. Reiss, H. Haenel, E.R. Case, R.L. French, A. Mohaddes and R. Wolcott. 1996. *Traffic Control Systems Handbook* (February). Washington, D.C.: Federal Highway Administration, U.S. Department of Transportation.

Gordon, R., R.A. Reiss, W.M. Dunn and D.R. Morehead. 1993. *Communications Handbook for Traffic Control Systems* (April). Washington, D.C.: Federal Highway Administration.

Jacob, B. 1999. "Wave Weighs in: Europe's WIM Research Project." *Traffic Technology International* (February/March): 84–88.

Klein, L.A. 2001. *Sensor Technologies and Data Requirements for ITS.* Norwood, MA: Artech House.

Klein, L.A. and M.R. Kelley. 1996. *Detection Technology for IVHS, Volume I: Final Report* (December). Washington, D.C.: Federal Highway Administration, U.S. Department of Transportation.

Kranig, J., E. Minge and C. Jones. 1997. *Field Test of Monitoring of Urban Vehicle Operations Using Non-intrusive Technologies* (May). Washington, D.C.: Federal Highway Administration, U.S. Department of Transportation.

Liddell, K. 1998–1999. "Coupled to Digital-Advanced Imaging Systems." *Traffic Technology International* (December/January): 97–99.

McCall, B. and W. Vodrazka. 1997. *States' Successful Practices Weigh-in-Motion Handbook* (December). Washington, D.C.: Federal Highway Administration.

Orski, K. 1998. "Rise of the Subcarrier: RDS in the USA." *Traffic Technology International* (October/November): 23.

Payne, R. 1996. "Specifying CCT Switching in ATMS." *Traffic Technology International:* 164–166.

Scrase, R. 1998. *ITS International* (January/February): 33–36, 38.

Starr, R. and B. Wetherby. 1996. "Traffic Information on Alphanumeric Pagers: An Evaluation of the Genesis Project" (October). *Proceedings: Third Annual World Congress on Intelligent Transportation Systems, ITS America, Orlando Florida.*

Upchurch, J., A. Hansen and M. Ajah. 1996. "Radio Broadcast Data Systems: The RAPID Field Operational Test" (October). *Proceedings: Third Annual World Congress on Intelligent Transportation Systems, ITS America, Orlando Florida.*

U.S. Department of Transportation. 1998. *Developing Traveler Information Systems Using the National ITS Architecture* (August). Washington, D.C.: U.S. DOT, F-7.

Veinot, F. 1997–1998. "Canada Goes Radio Gaga." *Traffic Technology International* (December/January): 87–89.

Endnotes

1. This section, "Advanced Traffic Sensors and Surveillance Systems," was authored by Lawrence A. Klein and Hualiang (Harry) Teng.

2. Source: Oregon's Operation Green-Light.

3. Prepared with the assistance of R. Roche, Mark IV Systems.

4. This section on smart card technology was prepared by Martha Harrell, CLI Corporation, Richmond Virginia.

BY Charles E. Thorpe • Principal Research Scientist •
Carnegie Mellon University

VEHICLE-BASED TECHNOLOGIES

This chapter describes technologies that are primarily on board the vehicle: the functions that need to be performed, the technologies that provide those functions and the infrastructure features that support those methods. Many of the functions that an intelligent vehicle provides are best supported with systems on board the vehicle, where there are no problems with communications delays and little reliance on other vehicles or the infrastructure. Besides technical advantages, vehicle-based technologies have an advantage in early deployment. As soon as a single vehicle is equipped with sensors, it will improve safety for that driver throughout the country, without waiting for the development and installation of a supporting infrastructure.

Many of these technologies, even though they are based on the vehicle, will perform best in conjunction with appropriate infrastructure. This may be as simple as maintaining lane markings to increase the reliability of a vehicle-based, run-off-road vision system, or installing radar retroreflectors on other vehicles to improve adaptive cruise control (ACC) systems. The ultimate in infrastructure assistance is the special lane, dedicated to properly equipped intelligent vehicles. At a more moderate level, the concept of a "sensor friendly highway" embodies modest infrastructure changes that enhance the operation of vehicle-based systems.

This chapter is arranged around a set of functions needed by intelligent vehicles and a discussion of potential technologies that may provide these functions. The genesis of this list comes from the work of the technology team of the National Automated Highway Systems Consortium. The Tech Team studied these problems both in the context of full automation and in partially automated steps suitable for incremental deployment. The list of functions, and many of the proposed solutions, are viable for the whole spectrum of intelligent transportation system (ITS) services. These functions include:

- Sensing other vehicles
- Sensing objects
- Sensing lane position
- Measuring absolute position and motion
- Predicting braking performance

In addition, this chapter includes discussions on crosscutting issues and future trends, such as reliability and emerging technologies.

Sensing other vehicles

An intelligent vehicle must know where other vehicles are. This is a crucial capability needed to support several services, including:

- *ACC*—where the vehicle automatically maintains a safe gap behind other vehicles
- *Forward collision warning*—in which the intelligent system watches the road ahead for stopped vehicles or other obstacles on the roadway

- *Lane change and merge collision warning*—to prevent collisions from the side
- *Rear collision warning*—to warn other drivers if they approach the intelligent vehicle too quickly
- *Automated highways*—the ultimate goal of hands-off, feet-off, fully automated driving

Geometry of vehicle sensing

The different services listed above require sensing in different directions, different ranges and different accuracies. Side looking sensors for lane-change and merge countermeasures are typically set up to cover the adjacent lane. These sensors have a range of approximately 5 meters, with as wide a field of view as possible. In typical configurations, two sensors are required to cover the front and rear sections of a car; up to five sensors may be needed on each side of a bus.

The range requirement for forward-looking sensors is set by their application and design speed. A passenger car travelling at U.S. highway speeds needs approximately 100 meters to enable the driver to react to an alarm and come to a stop on dry pavement. Heavier vehicles, vehicles with worn tires, or vehicles operating in snow or rain can require significantly longer distances. Thus an obstacle-detection sensor for forward collision warning needs a minimum range of at least 100 meters. ACC applications only deal with other vehicles moving at approximately the same speed, so their forward-looking sensors can have somewhat lower ranges.

Figure 15–1. Geometry of forward-looking sensors on a curved road. A sensor that looks straight ahead could miss an object in the travel lanes around a curve, or it could mistakenly generate a warning for an object off the road.
Source: Charles Thorpe.

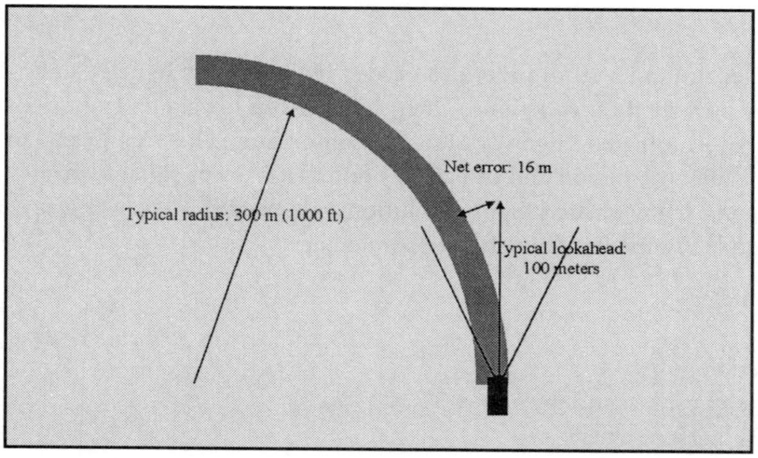

Rear-looking sensors are generally designed for lower relative speeds. Their main application is to warn of other vehicles approaching from the rear in adjacent lanes, and then to warn a driver who might start a lane change before checking for traffic. Because the relative speed is lower than for a forward-looking sensor, the required range is lower—approximately 50 meters.

Sensors designed to detect other vehicles need to handle the full range of vehicle types, from semitrailers to motorcycles. The latter, particularly when viewed from the rear, have a fairly small cross-section and do not have large metal surfaces to reflect radar. Sensors also must be designed to work in a wide variety of weather conditions, or at least to clearly indicate to the driver when the sensor has detected conditions too difficult for reliable operation and has shut itself down.

Separating targets from clutter

Measuring the position of objects in the scene is only the first step; the next step is deciding which of the objects are of interest. This is particularly a problem for forward-looking sensors. In order to handle curving roads, the sensors need to have a field of view of at least 12 degrees. But within a 12-degree swath in front of the vehicle, there may be many other radar reflectors—cars in other lanes, parked cars on the shoulder, road-side signs, and the like. The challenge is to separate the desired targets (i.e., objects in the vehicle's own lane) from the clutter (i.e., everything else that generates a radar return).

The simplest case is for an ACC system. These systems are designed and marketed as user convenience systems that handle other moving vehicles; they explicitly do not handle stopped traffic. The most basic ACC systems use a single spot sensor that covers the whole 12-degree swath in front of the vehicle. They throw out any returns that come from stationary objects, determined by comparing their own speed, from their speedometer, with the relative speed of the object, as measured by radar. They then select the closest moving object in their field of view and assume that is the lead vehicle that the system should follow.

Forward collision warning systems, in contrast, do need to be concerned with stationary objects, because a stopped object may well be a vehicle in their own travel lane. They need to know where a target is within the 12-degree field of view of the sensor. In order to know if an object is a collision threat, the sensor should be able to measure its lateral position with enough accuracy to place it in a particular lane. Roughly, at a range of 100 meters and a lane width of 4 meters, that creates a horizontal accuracy requirement of 4/100 or 0.04 radian. In addition, the system needs to know the geometry of the upcoming road. Road information can come from a variety of methods (descriptions are provided in this chapter's section on "Sensing Lane Position").

Vehicle motion prediction

In addition to sensing the current locations of other vehicles, it would be very useful to predict their intended path of travel. For fully automated vehicles, this can be accomplished by vehicle-to-vehicle communications. For any deployment scenario that involves human drivers, motion prediction requires driver modeling. Some unreliable hints may come from turn signals or brake lights, but more general predictions must take into account the current traffic situation surrounding each vehicle and whatever knowledge is available about that particular driver. Forward-looking sensors may provide the data for motion prediction, but generating useful information will require significant new research in human factors and driver behavior models.

Radar

The most common sensor is radar. In the United States, the 77GHz band has been set aside for automotive use. Radar works by bouncing a pulse of electromagnetic energy off of a target, measuring the time of flight, and dividing by 2c, where c is the speed of light and the factor of 2 accounts for the pulse travelling both from the radar to the target, and back again to the receiver accounts for the pulse going both to the target and back to the receiver. In practice, the time of flight is measured by frequency modulating the carrier wave, sweeping the frequency up or down or both. The frequency of the returned signal is compared with the frequency of the current outgoing signal. The difference in frequencies gives the time difference since the outgoing signal left, and therefore, the time of flight and the range. A difference in frequency can also be caused by the Doppler effect, which causes an approaching target to return a higher frequency and a retreating target a lower frequency. It is common in radars to sweep the frequency alternately up and down. Each sweep gives a measured frequency shift. The average of the two frequency shifts gives the target range; the difference between frequency shifts gives the Doppler shift, which in turn measures target relative velocity.

Some radars can also measure azimuth, or bearing, to a target. The most direct way to do this is to mechanically sweep a single narrow beam over the scene. The angle that gives the strongest return is reported as the bearing to the target. An alternative is bistatic radar, which has one transmit antenna and two receivers. The two receiving antennas are pointed in slightly different directions, typically one to the right of center and one to the left. The sensitivity of an antenna falls off for targets that are not located directly in front of the antenna; this is called the antenna pattern. A return that has exactly the same strength in each antenna must come from a direction half way between the antennas, directly in front of the car. A return that is stronger in one antenna than in the other comes from an angle toward the stronger return. The exact angle is given by the antenna patterns for that specific radar; see figure 15–2 for an explanation. Finally, bearing information can also come from phased arrays. In this case, a single antenna is used to transmit the radar signal, and a line of antennas receives the return. If the return comes from directly in front of the array, all receivers will see the echo at the same time, and the waveforms will be in phase. If the return comes from one side, the receiver on that side will see the waveform sooner, which will result in a phase shift between receivers. This kind of radar can cover the entire field of view with one measurement cycle, without any moving parts.

The significant advantage of radar is that it is usually capable of penetrating rain, snow and fog. Radar is also becoming affordable, and the advent of MMIC (millimeter-wave monolithic integrated circuits) will push costs down even further. The biggest disadvantage of radar is its limited resolution in azimuth. For radar antennas of a reasonable size for automotive applications, a typical beamwidth is 1 to 2 degrees. At a range of 120 meters, this gives a resolution across the road of 2 to 4 meters. While this is adequate for locating a vehicle in a lane, it is inadequate for any determination of vehicle shape.

A related problem is that many surfaces are highly specular (i.e., mirror-like) to radar. Radar does not usually reflect diffusely, as does light from a matte surface; instead, most surfaces act like a polished mirror. Thus, a small change in viewing angle can cause a large change in reflectance. A vehicle viewed from directly behind may have a strong reflection from the flat surfaces of the bumper, trunk, or license plate. That same vehicle viewed from a few degrees off center may have a much lower reflectance. Worse, the location of the peak reflectance may shift; from an off-center viewing angle, the strongest reflection may come from the external rear view mirror, which would give a different range and different bearing than a measurement to the rear bumper.

There are also concerns with the proliferation of radars on the road. The most obvious concern is blinding. If too many radar-equipped vehicles were on the road, particularly in oncoming traffic with no barrier separation, the transmitters from some vehicles would send a strong signal directly into the receivers of other vehicles. There are approaches to deal with this problem, such as spread spectrum techniques or pseudorandom coding, but each method comes with an increase in and cost of the radar system.

Finally, the long-term health effects of radars are not yet completely settled. Most proposed ACC systems disable the radar when the vehicle is stopped, to reduce the chance of short-distance exposure to pedestrians walking in front of the radar.

Ladar

Ladar, lidar, laser rangefinders and laser radar are all terms used to describe distance finding using a laser. The most typical ladars use technology similar to radars; a continuous laser beam is modulated, either in amplitude or through a swept frequency. The modulated beam is directed at a scene, and the returned beam is compared to the outgoing beam. The difference in phase (for an AM system) or frequency (for an FM system) between outgoing and incoming waves gives the time of flight, which in turn gives the range. Typical ladars use lasers operating at near-infrared wavelengths.

The first advantage of ladar is that the beam can be much narrower than that of typical radars. A laser can be focused by ordinary optical lenses. Typical ladar spot sizes range from 0.5 degrees down to 0.01 degrees. This gives very high acuity; while radar gives the general location of a target, ladar can give fine details of its shape and location.

A second advantage is that objects appear nearly the same in ladar as in ordinary light imaging. Because radar has a much longer wavelength, most objects appear specular (i.e., shiny). A small change in angle can cause a large change in radar reflectance. Ladar is much closer to visible light. Although there are shiny surfaces that will cause specularities, most common surfaces change appearance gradually with changing viewing angles. Furthermore, reflectors designed for headlights will also work for ladar, giving strong returns from vehicle reflectors and reflective road signs.

The main disadvantage of ladar is that it is sensitive to the same kinds of weather problems that block visible light. Snow, rain spray and fog all cause the ladar to be scattered or absorbed. There are two partial solutions for this. First, longer-wavelength ladars that operate in the far infrared bands are better able to penetrate many obscurants. Their use is being pioneered by the military for seeing through battlefield obscurants and by industry that needs to look inside furnaces. This technology is not yet mature or affordable for automotive applications. A second solution is to use direct time of flight ladars. In this design, a short (nanosecond duration) pulse is emitted, and a timer directly measures the time until the pulse returns. In dusty or foggy conditions, a pulsed ladar can be set to return the time of the last return, rather than the time of the average or peak return. Even if some or most of the ladar energy is backscattered by the fog, some small amount of light will make it through to the solid surface being imaged. The peak return may just give the range to the fog, but the last return will give the range to the solid surface behind the fog bank. Such sensors are still more expensive and lower resolution than continuous-wave sensors, because of the expense of sub-nanosecond timing circuits, but they are rapidly becoming practical.

Sonar

Sonar measures range in much the same way as ladar or radar. Typical sonars emit either a ping (single frequency pulse) or chirp (sliding frequency pulse), and wait for a returned signal that matches the outgoing signal. Sonar sensors have been popular in the robotics community for many years, beginning with the inexpensive sonars developed by Polaroid for their auto-focus cameras.

Sonars are limited in their effective range. First, sensing times are set by the speed of sound—about 343 meters per second. This means that sensing an object at a range of 100 meters would take 200–343 seconds, which would be a sizeable delay. Second, atmospheric attenuation is frequency-sensitive. High-frequency sounds do not travel as far as lower frequencies; but practical sonars need to operate above 20 kHz to avoid the range of human sensitivity.

Figure 15–2. Radar data from a phased array. The radar map shows the intensity of radar returns from each spot in the scene. Range increases to the right; bearing increases towards the top. The brightness of each point is the strength of return. The brightest spots correspond to the vehicles in the scene: A is a little to the right and close, B is a little farther and to the left, C is a car directly behind A, and D is the furthest car in the middle.
Source: Dirk Langer.

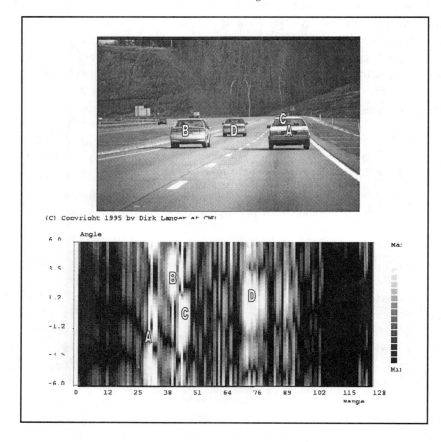

The result is that sonars are viable sensors for short-range systems, but not for long-range vehicle detection and tracking. Commercial sonar systems are beginning to be used for backup warning and side-looking object detection.

Communications

In an environment where every vehicle can be guaranteed to have a given level of ITS equipment, it is possible to determine the locations of other vehicles by communications. If each vehicle knows its own location (as described in this chapter's section on "Absolute Position and Motion Measurement") and is equipped with vehicle-to-vehicle communications (as described in this chapter's section on "Communications"), it is possible for every vehicle to be told the position of every nearby vehicle. In addition, it is desirable to transmit current velocity and control actions such as the onset of hard braking; or even, for a fully automated system, to communicate vehicle intentions. This level of information about future vehicle positions can be used to close up gaps, smooth traffic flow, and increase safety and throughput. Any system that depends on this information must either have a backup or must have system-level safeguards to ensure that every vehicle has reliable communications.

Driver modeling

In an environment where at least some vehicles are manually driven, it would be helpful to have a model of driver behavior for each vehicle. A model of other drivers would help in identifying over-aggressive behavior and providing cues for defensive driving.

Results are available in the research literature for headway keeping, lane keeping and other basic driver model parameters (Crossman and Szostak 1968; Godthelp, Milgram, and Blaauw 1984; Knipling and Wierwille 1994; McRuer, Allen, Weir, and Klein 1977). Most of these results come from careful instrumentation of the subject's car. There are many fewer results on watching the behavior of a car for a separate vehicle and inferring useful models of driver behavior.

Assistance and retroreflectors

There are several modest changes to other vehicles or to the infrastructure that can enhance the effectiveness of on-vehicle sensors for vehicle tracking. The more complex suggestions are covered in this chapter's section on "Sensor-Friendly Roadways" in the discussion of the "sensor-friendly highway."

A more modest proposal is to use reflectors on vehicles. If a particular type of sensor becomes standard, it would be possible to require all vehicles on the roadway to be equipped with a retroreflector. For laser sensors, the existing taillight reflectors would be adequate. For radar, a simple corner cube mounted on the rear of the vehicle would guarantee a strong return from a wide range of angles.

A slightly more sophisticated version of that idea is to make the retroreflectors semi-active. The Ohio State Frequency Selective Patch is a reflector that can change its polarization. It can be tied to the brake lamp, for instance, so that a trailing vehicle could use its radar to sense brake application and prepare to begin its own braking.

Comments

Vehicle sensing has drawn a large amount of attention and research resources. Several products are coming to market, for backup warning, for side collision warning for commercial vehicles, and for ACC. It will be important to track the reliability record for commercial systems and use that information to focus further developments.

Sensing obstacles

A second major technical problem for intelligent vehicles, related to vehicle detection, is obstacle detection. The goal is to sense any obstacle on the roadway that could damage the vehicle or cause it to bounce off course. The primary user services that obstacle sensing will support are forward collision avoidance and automated highways. Obstacle detection will also make important contributions to ACC and to run-off-road collision warnings. Obstacle sensing is similar to forward-looking vehicle detection, but much more difficult. While vehicles are large and mostly metallic, roadway obstacles can be much smaller and are made of a wide variety of materials that do not present a good target for some sensors.

There is no complete compendium of the kinds of obstacles encountered on highways. Accident databases, for instance, show only those obstacles that were hit. There may be other categories of objects that are on the road but are routinely avoided by drivers and therefore do not show up in accident reports. The following partial list of objects shows a large variety:

- State departments of transportation (DOTs) report cleaning up construction debris, fuel spills, car parts, tire carcasses and so forth.
- State highway patrols receive reports of washing machines, other home appliances, ladders, pallets, deer and other things.
- A survey commissioned by a company that builds litter-retrieval machines reports 185 million pieces of litter per week.
- Rural states report up to 35 percent of all rural crashes that involve animals, mostly deer but also including moose and elk as well as farm animals.
- A nonscientific survey of colleagues indicates that people have hit tire carcasses, mufflers, deer, dogs and even a toilet.

It is clear from this list that the kinds of objects that must be considered are very diverse. Some of the objects are metallic; others are wooden, concrete, rubber, ceramic, or organic. Some objects are stationary, and others are moving. Size ranges from small to large. Moreover, these objects occur on a wide variety of roads: hilly, curving, two-lane, congested urban and so forth. This gives a wide range of geometries and backgrounds in which obstacle sensing must work.

Many of the same general classes of sensors that are used for detecting vehicles will also work for detecting obstacles, but with much more sophisticated versions of the sensors and processing.

Ladar

Ladar with a narrow beam has the acuity to see small objects at long ranges. A typical ladar image is shown in figure 15–3. The bottom half of the image is the range image, coded so that darker points represent closer objects and brighter points more distant objects. The top half of the figure is reflectance, measuring the amount of energy returned for each pixel. The 3-D shape of individual objects is clearly visible in this data. There is a significant body of research results on using ladar to produce 3-D maps of terrain, which are in turn used for planning cross-country paths for off-road military vehicles.

For even smaller objects, ladar range images may not have enough resolution. Instead, the ladar reflectance channel may have better cues. In automotive applications, the ladar will hit the road surface at a very shallow grazing angle; and it will therefore have very little energy returned. Any obstacle that stands up from the surface will present a much less shallow angle to the laser, so even dark objects will reflect more energy than the road surface (Hancock 1999).

Polarimetric radar

Most radar configurations do not have the resolution to distinguish small objects from general roadway clutter. One technology that holds promise is polarimetric radar. A radar signal can be polarized, and a receiver can have a polarimetric filter built in to make it sensitive to a certain direction of polarization. In much the same way that polarized sunglasses filter out the glare caused by reflections from shallow angles, a polarized radar system can be tuned to selectively include or exclude returns from different surface types. Preliminary results from a study at the University of Michigan show some promise in reducing road clutter, which in turn will allow increased sensitivity in seeing small objects.

Stereo video

Two or more video cameras can be used to provide depth perception in much the same way that the human visual system works. If the same object can be located in two images taken from different positions, triangulation gives the range to that object. Stereo has many advantages: cameras are inexpensive; processing is becoming inexpensive; and the resulting depth map is automatically registered with the video image, which makes it easy to locate the road at the same time and in the same coordinate frame as the objects. Stereo, of course, has the disadvantages of any video system, notably with obscuration by fog and snow. Some of those problems can be ameliorated by using infrared sensors instead of video, but obscuration will still be a problem in really bad weather.

Figure 15–3. High-resolution ladar image. The bottom section shows range data, coded as brighter means farther; this gives 3-D shape information. The top section is reflectance, measuring the energy returned; this shows the appearance of objects.
Source: John Hancock.

Typical stereo vision systems do not have the range or acuity to see small objects at large distances on the road. The best systems achieve high resolution through a number of approaches:

- *Wide baseline*—putting the cameras on the extreme right and left of the car. The resolution in depth is directly proportional to the baseline.
- *Long focal length lenses*—depth acuity is directly proportional to focal length, so telephoto lenses help.
- *More than two cameras*—adding a third camera adds another source of signal to the system. If the third camera is mounted higher or lower than the first two, it provides additional information about range to horizontally textured surfaces that are hard to range with just two cameras.
- *Directly measuring object shape as well as range*—the system can be tuned to look for flat roads and tuned separately to look for vertical objects, by adjusting the slope of the expected surface and thus the shape of the search windows used in stereo correlation. If a window matches best when tuned to look for a vertical surface, then that location is probably an obstacle, not a part of the road. Output from one such stereo system (Williamson 1998) is shown in figure 15–4.

Exclusion

Finally, it may be necessary to consider ways to exclude as many obstacles as possible. For an automated highway, it would be possible to build fences along the side of the road to exclude animals. There still remains a problem with securing entrance ramps to allow vehicles in but not animals. There is some evidence that tall fences may be a bad idea: if a deer manages to get onto the road through an entrance ramp, and it cannot escape over a high fence, that deer will be even more of a problem.

Obstacle exclusion would also require making sure no objects fall off of vehicles. This would perhaps entail prohibition of any loose or uncovered load, and some means of ensuring that tire carcasses and other vehicle parts would not be dropped along the road.

Comments on obstacles

Of all the technical problems addressed in this chapter, obstacle detection is perhaps the most difficult. Many of the technologies have some promise; none are proven. The difficulty starts with problem formulation: it is not even easy to develop a catalogue of all obstacles that must be handled. This in turn makes it difficult to do comparisons of different approaches to detection and exclusion. For applications that require handling obstacles automatically, such as automated highways, much more work is needed.

Sensing lane position

Knowing a vehicle's position relative to the lane is important for many ITS user services. The obvious applications are run-off-road warning and automated highways. In addition, lane position information, and lane shape preview ahead of the vehicle, are also crucial for obstacle detection and helpful for ACC. A lane position sensor that works in extreme weather conditions would also be useful for snowplows. And new ITS services, such as lateral stability control assist for driving in crosswinds, would be enabled with good lane position sensing.

Magnetic markers

One of the most successful lateral position systems is based on magnetic nails, as developed by Wei-Bin Zhang at the University of California's Partners for Advanced Transit and Highways (PATH) program (Zhang 1997). In a typical installation, magnets are buried in the pavement in the center of a lane, at intervals of approximately 1.5 meters. The magnets are positioned vertically, either north pole up or south pole up. The intelligent vehicles are equipped with magnetometers under the front bumper. As the vehicle passes over the magnets, the magnetometers sense the direction and intensity of the magnetic field. This, in turn, provides both a measure of the lateral offset and a timing pulse when the vehicle passes over the magnetometer.

More sophisticated schemes add additional magnetometers. Additional sensors mounted across the front bumper increase the lateral range over which the sensors can detect the buried magnets. This is important, for instance, during lane changes, when the vehicle has to leave the magnetic markers in one lane and dead reckon until it can pick up the markers in the next lane. Additional sensors in the rear bumper give the lateral displacements at both the front and the rear of the vehicle, which are used to measure vehicle heading relative to the lane.

The pattern of the buried magnets, north pole up or south pole up, gives a binary code that is read as the vehicle passes over the magnets. This can be used to encode upcoming events, such as approximate curvature or locations of exits. Alternatively the magnets can be placed randomly, and the resulting pattern can be used as an index into a map. In the 1997 automated highway demonstration, buried magnets were used by two of the groups.

Figure 15–4. Stereo obstacle detection. Original image shown in the top section; detected obstacles highlighted in the lower section. The range to the sign post is approximately 100 meters. The system successfully detected the two 15-centimeter boards on the road, as well as the person and signpost next to the road and additional 10 obstacles off the road and in the distance.
Source: Todd Williamson.

Magnetic tape

Magnetic tape systems are similar to buried magnets. Instead of burying discrete magnets in the roadway, magnetic material is embedded in the tape used for lane markings and that tape is magnetically coded as it is installed. This requires a much more sophisticated sensing scheme, because the magnetometers on the vehicles are considerably further from the magnetic tape. The advantage of a tape-based system is that the infrastructure cost is potentially much lower. In environments that use tape for markers rather than paint, the additional costs of adding the magnetic material and encoding it may be much lower than the costs of drilling separate holes for magnets. There is also less damage to the pavement, and no concern with holes and freeze-thaw cycles. Magnetic tape systems have been shown in limited prototypes but not yet in demos at highway speeds.

Buried cable

The oldest and most tested system for lateral guidance is based on buried cables. Buried wire systems were used in the 1950s in the General Motors Firebird II prototype and in the 1960s in Ohio state's work. A buried wire system is currently in use in the Westrack system, a pavement test facility that has four automated semitractors pulling calibrated loads around a 2-mile oval track. Westrack has logged over 800,000 miles to date.

These systems place a wire in the pavement, buried in the center of the lane. The wire carries an AC current, typically voice frequency, which is sensed by coils in the vehicle. The direction of the electromagnetic field sensed by the pickup coils gives the lateral distance from the wire. While much of the system is similar to a magnetic nail system, the signal is continuous rather than discrete so there is no easy way to measure the distance along the track.

The big advantages of a buried wire system are its simplicity and reliability. In the Westrack system, all sensing and steering control are done with discrete analog components to eliminate any potential problems with computer software or hardware. Because the signal is active, it can be as strong as needed; and safety circuits can easily sense if the signal is interrupted. A secondary advantage of a buried wire is that different applications can use different frequencies of the AC signal; for instance, at an exit, the cable that goes down the main line can have the standard frequency, while the cable that follows the exit can carry a signal at a different frequency. Then the receiver on board the vehicle can switch frequencies to track one of the signals and follow the desired path.

The main disadvantage of the system is installation and maintenance of the cable. Because the signal on the cable is continuous, the cable must be smooth and continuous. Laying cable on a straight stretch of road is a matter of placing the cable straight before paving or making a straight saw cut for installing the cable after paving. But laying cable around a curve is more difficult. It is difficult to ensure that a cable stays properly curved with no kinks during paving or to maneuver a concrete saw to cut smooth curves in existing concrete. And if the cable ever becomes cut, the break needs to be found; and the cable is then dug up, spliced and re-buried.

Inductive loops

An inductive loop is similar in operation to buried magnets. Instead of a passive coil on the vehicle sensing permanent magnets, there is an active transmitting coil on the vehicle that energizes coils buried in the pavement. The buried coils in turn create an electromagnetic field that can be sensed by pickup coils on the vehicle. The vector direction of the field at the sensor is used to give the lateral offset to the coil, in much the same way that magnetic nail sensing works. These sensors are also discussed in chapter 14.

Frequency selective surface

The frequency selective surface (FSS), developed by Ohio state, uses the obstacle-detection radar as the lateral guidance sensor (Ozguner et al. 1997). The FSS is a strip of metal with patterns cut in it to reflect radar. The pattern consists of slots cut across the width of the strip. When a radar illuminates the strip, energy will reflect from the slots. If the slot spacing is an integer multiple of a half wavelength, the reflected waves from several slots will be in phase and will generate a strong return. In the FSS, the slot spacing is set to create this strong return when the strip is viewed at a shallow angle. For a flat road and a specified radar mounting height, this will give a strong return from a spot a known distance in front of the vehicle and little return from other locations. The radar measures the bearing to this spot, and it uses that as a signal for steering. In the simplest test installations, the FSS is laid down in the center of a lane and the vehicle steers to track the radar reflection directly. The FSS, unlike magnetic nails or inductive loops, gives preview information ahead of the vehicle, which simplifies controller design.

The big advantage of the FSS comes in a slightly more sophisticated design. The slots can be cut to give a return from a strip to the side, instead of directly in front of the vehicle. This allows the FSS to be embedded in lane marking tape, so there is no additional installation expense and no potentially confusing markings in the lane centers. Because there is no additional cost for a sensor (if an intelligent vehicle already has a radar), and little additional cost for lane marking, the FSS may prove to be the most cost-efficient solution. It is also possible to use more sophisticated sensing to examine the polarization of the returned signal, which is affected by water or snow cover, giving some cues as to the road condition immediately ahead of the vehicle.

Vision systems

Computer vision is perhaps the most difficult system to develop, but it is the easiest to integrate with existing infrastructure. A video camera is mounted in the vehicle, typically near the inside rearview mirror, and pointed at the road. A computer processes the video image stream and finds the road.

Vision for road following has been a major topic of research for at least the past 15 years (Turk, Morgenthaler, Gremban, and Marra 1988; Kickmanns 1997; Schaaser and Thomas 1990; Kenue 1989; Kluge and Thorpe 1995; Pomerleau 1990; Pomerleau 1996; Bishel, Coleman, Lorenz, and Mehring 1998). Many methods have been tried, including explicit following of painted lines, color-based image segmentation and neural nets. The early experiments used large vans filled with custom computers, and they moved only at slow speeds. Image processing demands significant computing power: a typical video image stream generates 7.5 million bytes per second. Until recently, real-time image processing was a laboratory curiosity. But in the past few years, the hardware has become much more practical. Video cameras have become small (less than 1-inch cube) and cheap (less than $10). The rise of computer power and the decrease in costs have been well-chronicled. The practical limits of applying video systems are no longer in cost or size, but in performance of the algorithms.

The most immediate application for these vision systems is run-off-road warning. A warning system is significantly easier to build than a full control system. First, the system does not have to be 100 percent available; if it encounters a situation that is too confusing, it can temporarily suspend warnings without dire consequences. Second, the lookahead required for warning is smaller than that required for control; so the range of the vision system can be reduced. This simplifies some of the algorithms, for instance: a perception system for warning may only need to calculate vehicle position and heading in the lane, while perception for control should also calculate road curvature. The shorter lookahead required also means that the vision system is looking closer to the vehicle, with less likelihood of occlusion by other vehicles, and fewer problems with looking through fog or other obscurants.

One of the most successful vision-based lane trackers is the AutoTrak system, developed by Pomerleau at Carnegie Mellon University and AssistWare as part of the National Highway Traffic Safety Administration's program, Run-Off-Road Crash Avoidance Using Intelligent Vehicle Highway System Countermeasures. AutoTrak now has over 60,000 miles of on-vehicle testing. As configured for warning applications, it looks for any high-contrast features that run parallel to the direction of the road. It tracks all the features to determine vehicle position and heading. In addition, it sorts through the features to try to detect solid or broken lane markers. AutoTrak suppresses warnings if the vehicle speed is slow, if the steering angle changes abruptly indicating an emergency maneuver, if the line disappears in a manner characteristic of an exit ramp, and so forth. In the most recent tests, AutoTrak has greater than 98-percent availability (time the system is working and ready to generate warnings) and less than one false alarm per five hours.

Even the best algorithms will still be limited by sensing. Typical CMOS and charge couple device video cameras are sensitive to wavelengths near the human vision spectrum, and they are thus, subject to the same problems drivers have with snow, rain and fog. Some work has been done on road following with other wavelengths. Thermal imaging has promise; some of the far IR wavelengths are used by the military for penetrating smoke and other battlefield obscurants. But in some conditions, such as several days of cloud cover and drizzle, the road, shoulders, and painted markings all settle to the same temperature; and there is little in a thermal image to provide cues for road recognition. At the other end of the spectrum, some work has been done in the ultraviolet (UV) band. One of the ideas is to use ultraviolet headlamps and lane mark ings that have fluorescent pigments. The UV illumination is invisible to the human eye, so backscatter from fog does not impede vision. The UV illumination that reaches the lane markings causes them to fluoresce in the visible spectrum. The effect is that the white lines appear to glow through the fog and are easier to see. The same kind of technique could also be applied to computer vision. Narrow-band illumination could be used, which would induce fluorescence from pigments in lane markers. Filters on the cameras could then be used to eliminate direct reflection but pass the fluorescence. This kind of technique will become more practi-cal in the near future as light emitting diode (LED) headlamps reach the market. The LEDs will inherently provide narrow-band illumination in three bands (i.e., red, green, blue); this will make fluorescent markings much more practical.

Comments

For all of the above systems, some sort of road preview is useful. Preview can come from sensing, maps, or both. Vision and FSS inherently provide some preview, but longer previews would also be useful. Magnetic sensors are inherently down-looking but can have some road shape information encoded. Additional infor-mation on the shape of upcoming curves can come from digital maps and a vehicle position sensor, as dis-cussed in the next section of this chapter.

Absolute position and motion measurement

Absolute positioning refers to knowing the location of the vehicle in world map coordinates, rather than rel-ative to the current lane. Position determination and motion measurement are not direct user services in themselves, but they play a role in many different advanced vehicle control and safety system services. At the most advanced level, highly accurate position information can be used directly in the control loop; at the coarsest levels, positioning is useful to cue other systems to likely events.

The most difficult challenges for positioning systems are in automated lateral control systems. Automated driving requires determining position within a lane to an accuracy of a few centimeters. Any lateral control scheme that relies solely on absolute positioning requires both highly accurate positioning and detailed maps. A less demanding scenario is to use less accurate information as an emergency control backup. If a primary sensor fails, a combination of positioning, map information and accurate motion measurement could be suf-ficient to bring the vehicle to a safe halt on the shoulder, out of the travel lanes.

Perhaps the most practical use of absolute positioning systems is as part of a larger system, incorporating sev-eral different kinds of sensing. As mentioned in this chapter's earlier sections on "Sensing Lane Position" and "Vehicle Control," steering control works best with a prediction of road location and curvature in front of the vehicle. It is possible to build systems that depend solely on on-vehicle sensing, but it may be easier to build a mixed-mode system that uses on-vehicle sensors for position relative to the road and map-based sys-tems for road preview. Beyond lateral control, such mixed-mode systems are also potentially useful for road shape prediction as part of systems that detect and track vehicles and obstacles.

Position and motion measurement are an important component of road friction detection, as discussed in this chapter's section on "Predicting Braking Performance." Comparing the actual motion of the vehicle, as sensed by inertial or other sensors, with the motion of the wheels, as sensed by wheel encoders, gives an important measurement of slip and therefore of road friction.

Global positioning system and pseudolites

The most popular source of position data is global positioning system (GPS). GPS works by having a constellation of satellites in known orbits. Each satellite broadcasts a timing signal. A receiver on the vehicle receives each timing signal with a delay proportional to the distance from the satellite to the receiver. Comparing the time delays from four satellites allows the receiver to solve for four unknowns, including three position variables (x, y and z) and one variable for absolute time. In practice, receivers attempt to lock on to the signal from as many satellites as possible in order to have redundant information.

The problem with this simple model of GPS is that signals do not travel in a straight line. Because of atmospheric disturbances, the signals are refracted, so the range measurements are corrupted. This can introduce position errors of tens of meters into raw GPS positioning.

The first solution is differential global positioning system (DGPS). DGPS uses a base station at a fixed location. The base station can compare its known position with the position calculated from GPS. The difference between those positions is the current error in GPS. That error can be broadcast over conventional radios to mobile GPS receivers. Each receiver can subtract out the current error and eliminate most of the positional error in the GPS calculations. In practice, rather than sending a total error, individual errors are calculated and broadcast for each satellite visible to the fixed base station. That way, if different mobile units see different sets of satellites, they can each apply the corrections that pertain to their own position solution. DGPS solutions improve the accuracy from tens of meters to a few meters. Various systems broadcast the position corrections via cell phone, radio link, or over a wide area via direct satellite broadcast. The best corrections come from a network of ground stations. A mobile receiver can then interpolate among the corrections for neighboring ground stations and calculate the best corrections for its current location.

DGPS is certainly accurate enough to notify a vehicle of an upcoming exit or the approximate location of a reported obstacle, but it is still too imprecise for lane keeping or headway maintenance. The next step in higher accuracy is carrier-phase GPS. Carrier-phase systems look not only at the coded time signal but also at the underlying waveforms of the carrier. Intuitively, a mobile unit and a base station could be initialized with their antennas co-located. Then, as the mobile unit moves, both units could count the number of waveforms they receive. If the mobile unit has received one more waveform than the base unit, it must be one wavelength closer to that particular satellite. Because the phase of a wave can be measured, the number of waveforms received can be resolved to a fraction of a wavelength; and the position can be solved to much smaller tolerance than a wavelength. Commercially available systems can provide position determination accurate to 2 centimeters in x, y and z.

In practice, operation of a carrier-phase system is a little more complex. Instead of starting with the antenna touching a base station antenna, the system can start up at any location; but it then takes tens of seconds or minutes to settle on its correct position. Once it has position lock, the receiver can move freely; and it maintains its position correctly. But if the line of sight to one of the satellites is broken, the system loses position lock and has to stop and resynchronize. This is not a problem for many applications, such as helicopters or agricultural machines, that operate in open spaces above obstructions. But a receiver on a car may lose lock every time it goes under a bridge or even an overhead sign.

For all types of GPS, operation in mountainous regions or urban canyons presents a problem. If only a small patch of sky is visible, it is unlikely that enough satellites will have direct lines of sight to enable solving for position. Worse, some of the signals may be received after reflecting from mountains or the sides of buildings. These reflected signals may be strong enough for the receivers to lock on, but they will generate incorrect position measurements. A solution is the deployment of pseudolites. These are fixed transmitters that operate like additional GPS satellites. A few pseudolites strategically placed in mountain passes, or a network of pseudolites in a city center, may provide nearly complete GPS coverage.

Inertial navigation

Inertial systems are referred to in the literature as inertial measurement units or inertial navigation systems (INSs). There are many techniques, both mechanical and electronic, for measuring acceleration. The acceleration signal is directly useful for some vehicle control applications. Integrating the acceleration over time gives velocity; integrating velocity over time gives distance. If an INS has three accelerometers, it can measure distance traveled in all three dimensions. Typically, an INS will also have gyros (mechanical or electronic) for measuring rotation rates. By including gyro information, the INS can determine both vehicle position and orientation.

The problem with an inertial system is that any small errors in measured acceleration are amplified by the integration process, which leads to linearly increasing errors in velocity and quadratically increasing errors in position. For applications such as submarine guidance, the solution is to use very expensive high-precision accelerometers and gyros. For automotive applications, the better answer is to use inertial systems in conjunction with other sensors.

It is very attractive, for instance, to combine inertial and GPS sensors. GPS provides absolute accuracy that does not drift over time, but it is subject to intermittent dropouts when the view of a satellite is occluded. INS provides accurate motion measurements, and it can be used to fill in GPS gaps over the short term. GPS and INS integration is a classic example in any basic textbook on Kalman filters.

Direct motion sensors

Optical correlators and Doppler radar provide direct measurements of vehicle motion by observing the ground. Optical correlators have been commercially developed for noncontact measurement of motion in industrial settings, such as measuring the velocity of steel sheets in the hot section of a rolling mill. The correlator uses a video sensor to watch small texture and other markings as they move through the sensor field of view. The rate of flow of the visual texture, and the height of the sensor, give the true motion of the object. Texture can be tracked in one dimension to give linear speed or in two dimensions to give a true velocity vector. In automotive applications, the correlator is mounted underneath the vehicle or behind the back bumper and then pointed down at the pavement. In a series of experiments at Carnegie Mellon, the velocity from an optical correlator was integrated over time to give a measurement of distance traveled accurate to 0.2 percent of the total distance (Kimoto and Thorpe 1997).

Doppler radar works by bouncing a radar signal off the ground. If the returned signal is at a different frequency than the outgoing signal, the frequency change is due to Doppler shift, which is proportional to speed over the ground. Doppler radars are commercially available for agricultural applications, where true ground speed is important information in evenly spreading chemicals. As with optical correlators, Doppler radars can be configured to measure speed in either one or two dimensions.

Comments

Absolute positioning and motion measurement are closely tied to lane tracking. Some lane tracking systems, such as magnetic nails, in effect consist of individual landmarks. If the location of each nail is carefully surveyed and recorded in an onboard map, nail tracking can give highly accurate measurements of absolute position. Going the other direction, accurate global position from GPS, coupled with road map data, provides strong predictions for vision or other lane tracking systems.

Current commercial maps are not accurate enough for lane tracking. The typical accuracies quoted are 14 meters. This is largely due to the origins of digital maps; the first generation is hand-digitized from paper maps that do not have the resolution to provide more accurate information. There has also not been a large market for highly-accurate maps. The 14-meter resolution is adequate for the in-vehicle map navigation systems and other large-scale commercial uses.

But maps are beginning to improve. The mapping companies are starting to verify and update their maps by driving their routes with accurate GPS receivers. As these techniques become more common, the accuracy of maps will certainly increase, which will make them increasingly useful for other ITS applications.

Predicting braking performance

The basic formulas for the time and distance required to bring a car to a stop are:

> Time = reaction time + speed / deceleration
> Distance = speed * reaction time + _ speed ^{2} / deceleration

Typical highway speeds are approximately 30 meters per second; typical reaction times range from 100 milliseconds for a fast computer-controlled sensor and brake actuator, to up to 2 seconds for a human driver. The dominant unknown factor is deceleration, or braking performance.

Braking performance is critical in setting several important parameters of intelligent vehicles. Safe spacing for automated control depends on the maximum achievable deceleration of both the current vehicle and the one in front. Spacing for ACC involves those factors plus driver reaction time, if the deceleration of the lead vehicle exceeds the authority of the ACC. The required sensor range to find stopped obstacles is set by the maximum stopping distance. A run-off-road warning system that tells a driver to slow down when entering a sharp corner needs to know how quickly the driver could scrub off excess speed. More generally, a system that could automatically assess braking capability would be useful for warning of worn tires or slippery road conditions.

Unfortunately, braking performance depends on many factors: vehicle design, vehicle loading, tire design, tire inflation, tire wear, brake condition, road surface type, road surface condition, road slope, road roughness and interaction with vehicle suspension, use of antilock brakes and so forth. Some of those parameters are easy to measure or to calculate. Automotive enthusiast magazines regularly publish the results of braking tests on new vehicles. Individual cars have widely varying results, from just over 1 g (1 times the acceleration due to gravity, 9.8 meters/second/second) to 0.5 g; heavy vehicles often have much lower performance. This gives a baseline under optimum conditions. Tire inflation and vehicle load are also possible to measure. But tire wear, and especially road surface condition, remain difficult to estimate.

Wheel speed measurement

The most obvious way to measure surface adhesion is to instrument all of the wheels with tachometers. Then the relative speeds of driven and nondriven wheels can be compared; or the speed of an individual wheel can be monitored for rapid changes due to slip, similar to the way in which antilock brakes or traction control work.

The problem with this approach is that the amount of slip under normal driving conditions does not vary significantly with road condition. When brakes are lightly applied, the wheels generate decelerating force and also begin to slip slightly. As the brakes are applied more heavily, both the force and the slip increase. At some point, depending on the surface, the friction will reach a maximum and then taper off, while the slip continues to increase. Eventually, the vehicle is sliding with the wheels locked at a 100-percent slip, as shown in figure 15–5.

Unfortunately, the shape of the force and slip curve for different surface conditions is almost identical for regions of low force. That is, if the brakes are only applied lightly, the vehicle will have approximately the same deceleration, and the same slip, regardless of the surface conditions. On a more slippery surface, the braking force will reach a lower peak. But the value of that peak cannot be predicted without applying significant brake force. This is not a problem for antilock braking systems, because they operate only under heavy braking. But for other ITS applications, it is not currently feasible to predict what the maximum available braking force will be just by observing the light braking or light accelerations encountered under normal driving.

Surface condition sensing

A second possibility is direct observation of the road surface from on-board sensors. It is certainly possible to detect snow and rain using video sensing and appropriate processing. It is much more difficult to estimate the depth of water cover, as anyone can attest who hit a much deeper puddle or pothole than was expected. It is also difficult to detect some kinds of ice.

Some work has been done with sonic sensors. A microphone located near the wheel wells can listen to the material being picked up by the tires and thrown against the car. For a particular car, with particular tires, on a particular kind of road, it is possible to tell by sound whether the road is dry, wet, or snow-covered.

More promising results come from active infrared sensors. Water, ice and snow all have different absorption bands in the IR. A sensor can illuminate the road surface at specific IR wavelengths, measure the amount of energy absorbed at each wavelength and make some determination of road condition. This kind of sensor has been proposed for aircraft icing detection.

The catch to IR sensing is that it is most effective looking straight down, in the shadow underneath the vehicle. If the sensor is aimed forward, it has to contend with ambient illumination; the beam spread is larger; and the angle of incidence becomes shallow, which will cause most of the energy to bounce away, especially on a wet surface. This means that it may be possible to determine the road condition where the vehicle is, but impossible to predict the road condition even a few meters ahead.

Infrastructure assistance

There are several automated weather stations currently available commercially. They typically measure surface temperature, air temperature, relative humidity and precipitation. In addition, they can be equipped with in-pavement sensors for salt content and effective freezing point of the saltwater mix on the roadway. Some systems also use IR sensors to directly measure ice and water depth. These systems are beginning to be deployed by transportation authorities to monitor locations that are subject to snow drifts or icing. See chapter 14.

It would certainly be feasible to have a network of automated stations and a low-bandwidth broadcast capability, so intelligent vehicles could take advantage of road condition measurements over the next stretch of road.

Figure 15–5 Slip curves for braking. As the brakes are applied, the slip increases. The force initially increases, and then it reaches a maximum and decreases. Note that the curves for wet and dry surfaces overlie each other for light braking.
Source: Charles Thorpe.

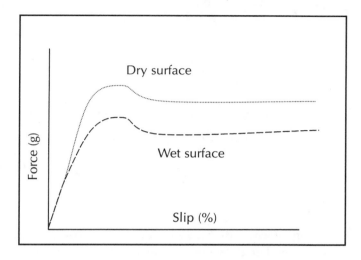

Discussion

This remains one of the most difficult problems in building intelligent vehicles. In the absence of good estimates of braking performance, ACC and other systems will have to maintain large gaps in order to maintain safety. Large gaps in turn could cause degradation in throughput, or they could encourage other drivers to cut in front of the automated vehicles.

Because none of the current on-vehicle systems provides a complete solution, mixed vehicle and infrastructure systems may be the best avenue for further development.

Reliability

Reliability of ITS systems, particularly advanced electronics, is a key crosscutting concern. Intelligent vehicles will expose more of the public to more complex safety-critical electronics than ever before. While there is a significant body of engineering on reliable computing and electronics, much of the practical experience is in high-tech, high-dollar value environments such as aircraft or nuclear power plants. The automotive environment is different in many aspects:

- *Cost sensitivity*—usual practices that involve triplex redundancy of critical components may not be affordable in automobiles.
- *Equipment used until end-of-life*—in most safety-critical tasks, preventive maintenance schedules call for replacing electronics before the end of their design life. Most analyses assume a constant low failure rate, typical of well-maintained components. In contrast, in the automotive environment, many components are never replaced until they fail.
- *Operation in uncontrolled environment*—vehicles operate in a much harsher environment than computer machine rooms. Moreover, many vehicle operators are relatively unskilled and untrained compared with professional computer operators.

- *Very large scale of deployment*—an extremely improbable event, one that occurs once in 109 hours, would cause one failure in 73 years in the U.S. commercial air fleet. That same probability would cause a failure once every 4.5 days in the U.S. ground vehicle fleet, because of the much higher number of vehicles. Even though the risk to a passenger might be the same in both cases, the public perception of risk could be much higher for ground vehicles.

All reliability experts agree on at least one conclusion: reliability has to be a major theme of the complete design, not an add-on or an afterthought.

Redundancy

The most straightforward way to achieve reliability is to have redundant components in the critical path. The number needed depends on the kind of fault that might occur.

Duplex reliability is adequate for many cases where a failed component is easy to detect, and it can be quickly switched out. In computing, highly available systems such as airline reservations systems often have two copies of every processor, disk, and the like.

In other situations, when two components disagree it is not obvious which one is correct. Here the usual design practice is triplex redundancy. Three systems run in parallel, with a voter comparing the three outputs. If two components agree and the third disagrees, the two that agree are assumed to be correct and the third one generates an error. This is the common design in real-time control applications. The weak link in the design is the voter: unless it is carefully designed, it can become the weak link, subjecting the entire system to a single-point failure.

A less-costly alternative is to use heterogeneous redundancy. Instead of replicating a safety-critical component, a different method can be found to provide the same functionality, using components that already exist for a different purpose. An example for intelligent vehicles is to use differential braking for steering backup. If the main steering system fails, the vehicle can be steered to a safe stop clear of the travel lanes by applying different braking forces to the two rear brakes, inducing a yaw and slowing the vehicle at the same time.

System-level safety and reliability

Another complementary approach to safety is to build safety in at a system level rather than with redundant components. A radical example of this is the platoon concept developed by PATH for automated highways. Most systems achieve safety by separating vehicles. A platoon bunches vehicles tightly together, with spacings of a few meters or less. In the unlikely event of a serious system malfunction that causes a collision, the vehicles will be so tightly packed that they will not have space to build up large differences in speed. Any collision will be at a low relative velocity, and it will therefore be much more likely to be minor and survivable.

Emerging technologies

Many other technologies will appear on intelligent vehicles of the future. The current intelligent vehicle initiative program is mostly focused on driver assist features. Future generations of vehicles, with added functions, will have to add models of vehicle dynamics for control; actuators to control the throttle, brake, and steering; methods to assess the driver's alertness; and communications systems. In addition, as intelligent vehicles become more common, it will be important to consider modest changes to the roadway infrastructure to enhance the reliability and effectiveness of the vehicles' sensing.

Vehicle control

Many of the more sophisticated ITS services will require some element of automated control. The simplest example is ACC, with control of only the throttle. Other services will add control of brakes, steering, and combinations. The ultimate extreme is the closely spaced vehicles in the platoon option for an automated highway. At those close spacings, vehicles can be safely operated only by computer control; human drivers have neither the fast reflexes nor the acute perception required to maintain the precise control needed.

Vehicles are designed for human control; automating steering, throttle, and brake is not always a straightforward task. Full modeling of engine dynamics or suspension dynamics is complex, and it fills many standard automotive textbooks. For automated control, the models can be carefully built by hand; or they can be learned and adapted on the fly. Some measure of adaptation is probably necessary, to account for variations in load, atmospheric conditions that affect engine performance and wear on components.

Automated control becomes particularly challenging in a number of circumstances:

- *Emergency maneuvers*—control systems optimized for smooth performance at cruise will not work for abrupt maneuvers in emergency situations.
- *Equipment failure*—special controllers need to be designed to cope with tire blowout or loss of power brakes or power steering.
- *Heavy vehicles*—the load, and the distribution of the load, vary much more for a heavy truck than for a passenger car. Truck controllers need to be much more adaptable than light vehicle controllers.
- *Low speeds*—engine and transmission dynamics are hardest to model at slow speeds. Applications such as automated snow plows or semi-automated busses will require careful throttle control design.
- *Low-friction surfaces*—as addressed earlier in this chapter's section on "Predicting Braking Performance," it is difficult to predict the effective coefficient of friction on a particular road surface. This affects not only braking performance but also the design of throttle and steering controllers.

Actuators

In the past, adding controls to a vehicle has been difficult. There is no straightforward way to add computer controls to existing hydraulic brakes, hydraulic power steering, or an analog cruise control. But the situation is changing rapidly. Electronic steering, brake and throttle are already becoming commercially available, driven by non-ITS concerns. Once electronic actuators are already installed, it becomes much easier to add computer control, without having to add bulky motors or hydraulic systems. For many intelligent vehicle applications, the new electronic actuators will be immediately useful. For specific high-performance applications, special-purpose actuators may still need to be designed. For instance, in closely spaced platoons the longitudinal reaction times need to be very quick, because the distance to the next vehicle is very short. This requires custom designs of fast and precise brake and throttle actuators.

Driver condition

One of the most important human factors issues is assessing the state of alertness of a driver. In most ITS scenarios, drowsiness is a direct safety hazard. In an automated highway, the driver is out of the loop; and the systems will have to assume that the driver may fall asleep. Here, the issue is determining driver state before returning control from the automated system to the manual driver.

Several systems have been proposed or developed. The most direct measures of drowsiness come from video-based systems watching the driver's eyes. The percentage of time the eyes are closed is strongly correlated with physiological measures of drowsiness. One perclose monitor works by illuminating the eye with two frequencies of infrared illumination and viewing the eye with a camera. When the eye is illuminated with one frequency, a normal baseline image results. When the second frequency is used, it produces an image with a strong reflection from the retina (similar to the "red-eye" effect in flash photography). Subtracting the two images gives a bright spot if the retina is visible. If there is no bright spot, the eye is assumed to be closed. These systems work well in the lab, but they still require some development to deal with bright external illumination and with drivers wearing sunglasses.

A different approach is to measure driver performance. A run-off-road system can measure a driver's lane-keeping performance. If the driver begins to weave more than usual, the system can sound an alarm and suggest that the driver pull over. Even without a vision system, it is possible to make some inferences of driver state from steering wheel motion. A steering pattern of many small corrections is typical of an alert driver. A driver falling asleep may make no correction for a longer time, and then suddenly jerk the steering wheel to correct the large lane position error.

Communications

Intelligent vehicles need communications for a number of purposes. Infrastructure-to-vehicle communication is useful for traffic reports and other large-scale broadcasts, as well as local area warnings of congestion or isolated road conditions. Vehicle-to-vehicle communication is an important part of some automated highways schemes. Vehicles that communicate the onset of braking or the locations of obstacles can give better system performance for cooperative ACC systems.

The technologies being considered for these different uses include active radio transmission, infrared wireless links and beacon and tag systems. In situations that involve many communicating vehicles, there are many issues involving forming and managing temporary local area networks, bandwidth and frequency allocation, guarantees about delivery time, and interference from roadside transmitters.

Sensor-friendly roadways

Sensors and systems will work best in a properly designed environment. Current roads have signs and overpasses that reflect radar, lane markings that may be painted or applied stripes or Bott's dots, and many other artifacts and variations that create a challenging environment for sensing. A sensor-friendly roadway would address many of those problems. For instance, for the specific problem of radar-based systems, roadside clutter could be handled in several ways:

- *Moved*—sign posts could be placed farther from the travel lanes.
- *Masked*—radar-absorbing material could be inexpensively applied to objects, such as bridge abutments, to reduce the amount of energy reflected.
- *Marked*—polarizing reflectors, or filters that absorb only a narrow frequency band, could be applied to large objects. They would then still appear in a radar return, but they would be marked in the radar signal as known fixed objects that are safely off to the side of the road.
- *Mapped*—the locations and signatures of fixed objects could be stored in a map and provided to individual vehicles. If an object with a matching signature appears where predicted, it can be recognized as safely off the travel lanes.

Comments

It is apparent that few of the technical solutions in this chapter are either fully vehicle-based or fully infrastructure-based. For lane following, for instance, all of the solutions have some sensor on the vehicle, either relatively sophisticated such as vision or much simpler such as magnetometers. All of the solutions are also sensing something in the infrastructure, either something already there for other purposes (road edges and lane markings) or something specially added (magnetic nails). So every system is a mixed system, with varying emphases on infrastructure complexity versus vehicle complexity.

The decision on which of the solutions is most effective is really a cost–benefit decision. Again, using lane tracking as an example, for snow plow guidance in a particular mountain pass, the length of the affected roadway is short, so infrastructure costs are low and the benefit from having a nonvision sensor is high. For run-off-road warning, where the system should work on all U.S. roadways, the infrastructure cost would be high, pointing toward a vision-based solution.

A number of nontechnical factors enter into these cost/benefit discussions. Who pays for installation? How much maintenance is required? Is there a potential problem with security and vandalism? If there is a public infrastructure cost, are there issues of social equity?
Answering these questions will take careful analysis of particular operating scenarios and environments. It will also continue to take involvement from all the participants: public stakeholders, technology providers and private equipment suppliers.

References

Bishel, R., J. Coleman, R. Lorenz, and S. Mehring. 1998. "Lane Departure Warning for CVO in the USA." Proceedings of International Truck and Bus Meeting and Exposition, Indianapolis, Indianapolis (November). SAE International.

Crisman, J., and C. Thorpe. 1993. "SCARF: A Color Vision System that Tracks Roads and Intersections." *IEEE Trans. on Robotics and Automation* 9, no. 1 (February).

Crossman, E. R., and H. Szostak. 1968. "Man-machine models for car steering." Proceedings on Fourth Annual NASA-University Conference on Manual Control (March).

Dickmanns E. D. 1997. "Vehicles Capable of Dynamic Vision." Proceedings on 15th International Conference on Artificial Intelligence, Nagoya, Japan (August).

Godthelp, H., P. Milgram, and G. Blaauw. 1984. "The development of a time-related method to describe driver strategy." *Human Factors* 26, no. 3.

Hancock, J. 1999. "Laser Intensity-Based Obstacle Detection and Tracking" (February). Ph.D. thesis. Carnegie Mellon University.

Kenue, S. K. 1989. "Lanelok: Detection of Lane Boudnaries and Vehicle Tracking Using Image-Processing Techniques" (November). *SPIE Mobile Robots IV.*

Kimoto, K., and C. Thorpe. 1997. "Map Building with Radar and Motion Sensors for Automated Highway Vehicle Navigation." Proceedings of IROS 97, Grenoble, France (September).

Kluge, K., and C. Thorpe. 1995. "The YARF System for Vision-Based Road Following." *Mathematical and Computer Modelling* 22, no. 4–7 (August-October): 213–233.

Knipling, R., and W. W. Wierwille. 1994. "Vehicle-Based Drowsy Driver Detection: Current Status and Future Prospects." Proceedings of IVHS America (April).

Langer, D. 1997. "An Integrated MMW Radar System for Outdoor Navigation" (January). Ph.D. thesis. Carnegie Mellon University.

McRuer, D., R. W. Allen, D. Weir, and R. Klein. 1977. "New Results in Driver Steering Control Models." *Human Factors* 19, no. 4.

Ozguner, Umit et al. 1997. "The OSU Demo '97 Vehicle." Proceedings of IEEE Conference on Intelligent Transportation Systems, Boston, Massachusetts (November).

Pomerleau, D. 1990. "Neural Network Based Autonomous Navigation." Vision and Navigation: The Carnegie Mellon Navlab. Ed. C. Thorpe. Kluwer Academic Publishers.

Pomerleau, D., and T. Jochem. 1996. "Rapidly Adapting Machine Vision for Automated Vehicle Steering." *IEEE Expert* 11, no. 2.

Schaaser, L, and B. Thomas. 1990. "Finding Road Lane Boundaries for Vision Guided Vehicle Navigation." Proceedings of IROS 90 (July).

Turk, M., D. Morgenthaler, K. Gremban, and M. Marra. 1988. "VITS-A Vision System for Autonomous Land Vehicle Navigation." IEEE PAMI (May).

Williamson, T. 1998. "A High-Performance Stereo Vision System for Obstacle Detection" (October). Ph.D. thesis. Carnegie Mellon University.

Zhang, Wei-Bin. 1997. "National Automated Highway System Demonstration: A Platoon System." Proceedings of IEEE Conference on Intelligent Transportation Systems, Boston, Massachusetts (November).

BY Michael Kushner • Consultant

Purpose of intelligent transportation systems

In the United States, it is estimated that approximately six million people per day use public transportation.[1] However, more than three quarter of a million American workers commute to work daily, using single-occupancy vehicles. This amount of traffic on our roads and highways causes traffic congestion, environmental pollution and wasted time. For many years, we have sought to solve the problems of traffic congestion, inefficiency, danger and pollution by building more and wider highways. This approach is no longer adequate. The pouring of additional asphalt and concrete added capacity, but it cannot keep pace with the increased demands of our transportation system. In response, Congress passed the Intermodal Surface Transportation Efficiency Act of 1991 (ISTEA). ISTEA called for the creation of an economically efficient and environmentally sound transportation system that will move people and goods in an energy-efficient manner and will provide the foundation for a competitive American transportation industry. That new paradigm was reinforced in 1998 with the enactment of the Transportation Equity Act for the 21st Century (TEA-21).

A broad range of diverse technologies, known collectively as intelligent transportation systems (ITS), holds the answer to many of our transportation problems. ITS comprises an array of technologies, including information systems, communications, information processing, management control systems and electronic subsystems. Infusing these technologies into our transportation system will save lives, time and money.

How ITS can improve transit

Before describing how ITS can enhance transit operations, we need to describe how a transit agency operates. The following section in this chapter begins with such a description and then moves on to address the issues that ITS can address for transit systems.

Transit management basics

Following is a brief summary of transit agency operations. The purpose is to lay a foundation for explaining transit applications of ITS and where benefits may be realized. It is not intended as instructions to transit operators on how to manage operations, but rather information on how transit operations can be improved.

In the last several decades, transit agencies in the United States have struggled financially. Many fleets and facilities are aging and in need of replacement. While it is true that some transit agencies have for a long time regarded technology as a way to improve operations, many transit system managers have been more concerned with major equipment acquisition and maintenance than with technological advancement.

Generally, transit fleet management is the responsibility of the dispatch center, with assistance provided by field supervisors. The dispatch center is the hub of the operation. In agencies where ITS technologies have not been employed, dispatchers keep track of each vehicle through a voice radio link and respond to a vehicle operator as problems are reported. Operations are carried out as simply and logically as possible. If a bus operator cannot be located and there is reason for concern, the field supervisor will go out and search for the vehicle. Before leaving the garage, bus operators are given instructions regarding their assigned routes and schedules. It is the driver's responsibility to watch the clock and compare arrival and departure times at specific points along these routes, called time points. It is also the driver's responsibility to comply with legal requirements of the Americans with Disabilities Act (ADA) such as assisting passengers who are visually impaired by announcing bus stops or assisting them to board a vehicle if necessary.

To ensure that schedules and public time tables accurately reflect what is occurring in the field, there must be some kind of feedback and reporting system to the scheduling department. The actual routing of the bus is usually reflective of demand. The transit agency tries to run buses in areas of potentially high ridership, always balancing the need to traverse as many streets as possible with the need to provide the quickest route for the riders. The planning and updating of bus routes is heavily dependent on ridership information. To determine whether a segment of a route is productive and should be continued, the planner must know exactly when and where riders get on and get off the bus. In most transit systems without ITS technologies, this information is collected by employees called "ride checkers" who sit on the bus and record by hand (or on a handheld device) the time and location of each stop as passengers enter and exit the bus. The number of passengers is determined and recorded by the ride checker along with the time and location information. This information is typically gathered no more than a few days each year for each route. In many systems it is gathered less often. It is a requirement of the transit agency to periodically report this data to the Federal Transit Administration (FTA). This data, along with other demographics, determines the amount of federal subsidy each transit agency will receive.

Problems addressed by transit ITS

Now that we have a working description of transit operations, we can focus on the problems that these operations face. These problems are articulated by customer complaints such as the following:

- "The bus doesn't go where we want to go."
- "I never know when the bus will arrive."
- "I have to waste too much time when I transfer."
- "I don't feel safe."
- "It costs too much."

Although not every system experiences every complaint, this list should look familiar to many transit agencies.

Inconvenient bus routes

Let's discuss how the advanced public transportation system (APTS) addresses the first complaint: "The bus doesn't go where I want to go." Transit planners armed with more accurate and up-to-date ridership information can plan routes that serve the public better. A geographic information system (GIS) with demographic data tells a planner where potential customers live and work. Automatic passenger counters (APC) provide agencies with more and better ridership data at a lower cost, and they are more effective than using "ride checkers." Better data are the foundation for better planning. In some cases route deviation will help provide better service. With automatic vehicle location (AVL) and in-vehicle electronic guidance, route deviation is easier to monitor and control and passenger service can be improved. The bus may actually go where the potential rider wants to go, and the rider can request a specific itinerary. Electronic kiosks, desktop and handheld computers and interactive television are a few of the devices that can bring bus route information and trip itinerary planning quickly and directly to a wider market of potential customers. These electronic systems can help implement on-demand public transit service, "the goal of all public transit agencies."

Anxiety waiting for the bus

The second complaint—"I never know when the bus will arrive"—is often cited in market research. If we do not know when the bus will arrive, the perceived waiting time can be much greater than the actual waiting period. With AVL and passenger information devices located at bus stops, the customer is informed whether he or she has missed the bus and when the next one will arrive. With this information, the customer can decide if there is time for a phone call or a cup of coffee. Most importantly, anxiety is greatly reduced. Electronic data systems and public data networks make it easy and cost effective for transit agencies to "predict next bus" arrival and communicate this information to riders through a number of communications devices.

Long transfer times

In many transit systems, particularly large systems, timed transfers are difficult to execute. Customers may be stranded at transfer points for long periods of time if the bus they are on is late and the next bus has departed. With AVL, dispatchers are aware of impending delays and can advise the waiting bus of the estimated arrival time of passengers wishing to make a connection. This "connection protection" can reduce waiting time significantly in case of infrequent service. Along with next predicted bus arrival, dispatchers can be armed with productivity tools to enhance transit operations.

Electronic fare payment

One feature of an electronic fare payment system is that, like credit cards or automatic teller machine cards, it allows quick transactions that do not require the handling of cash. Rather than paying for each and every transit trip, the smart card user pays for a number of trips at one time, just as the auto user pays for a number of trips by periodically paying for vehicle maintenance or monthly loan payments. In addition, the smart card's convenience can attract more people to purchase bulk fares such as unlimited monthly passes. Once you have paid for your monthly pass, you perceive that each additional transit trip is free. Just as after paying for your car insurance, each additional auto trip does not incur any additional insurance charges. The electronic "smart card" improves transit agency efficiency, reduces theft and reduces the cost of operations.

Table 16–1
FTA's Vision Strategies
Source: Federal Transit Administration, *Transit Planning and Research Programs Fiscal Year 1994*, Report# FTA-TTS-5-95-1.

1. Maximize security and safety on transit systems for service users (safety)
2. Foster customer-oriented public transportation (customer-oriented)
3. Foster industry adaptability to enable the industry to respond to changes in transportation patterns, technologies and needs (adapt to change)
4. Maximize a multimodal approach to transportation (multimodal)
5. Ensure a quality organization that emphasizes mutual respect (quality organization)
6. Ensure the highest level of transit service assistance delivery (highest level)
7. Promote linkages between transit needs and community needs (links to community)
8. Foster a positive image for public transportation and FTA (positive image)

Technologies and applications

How can ITS help the transit industry meet these high standards? Table 16–2 shows which vision strategies are addressed by each of the ten technologies.

Table 16–2
ITS Implementation of Eight Vision Strategies
Source: Federal Transit Administration,
Transit Planning and Research Programs
Fiscal Year 1994, Report# FTA-TTS-5-95-1.

Technologies	Safety & Security	Customer-Oriented	Adaptability	Multimodal	Quality Organization	Highest Level of Service	Community Needs	Positive Image
AVL	X	X	X	X	X	X	X	X
ATMS Integration		X	X	X		X		X
GIS	X	X				X	X	
In-Vehicle Annunciators		X				X		X
APC		X	X			X	X	
Automated Itineraries		X		X		X		X
Variable Message Sign and Monitors		X				X		X
Interactive Kiosks		X				X		X
Signal Priority		X	X	X		X		
Electronic Fare Collection		X		X		X		X

Fleet operation and management

The following explanations of APTS technologies provide information to help transit agencies plan for more efficient and cost-effective operations. Implementation of these technologies will also allow for better planning of services, better fleet management and improved customer service. The result will be a more efficient use of resources and more consistent service for transit riders.

AVL

AVL for transit is a system that allows dispatchers to know the location of each of their buses all of the time. There is a global positioning system (GPS) receiver and tracking device on each bus. A graphic display located in the dispatch center allows the dispatcher to see and read the location of each bus on a geo-coded map display. Most transit AVL systems take advantage of GPS to determine the locations of all the buses in the fleet. Some systems use a technology called "signpost." AVL can be used to determine if the buses are running on time and on route. The AVL system will also indicate if an operator is in an emergency situation or needs to be routed around problem locations such as traffic accidents. This bus location information can also be shared with the customer information center to provide patrons with more accurate trip itineraries and vehicle arrival times. This same information can also be communicated directly to customers via personal communications devices, and it will let them know the location of their bus.

Figure 16–1. AVL systems overview.
Source: NextBus Information Systems, Inc.

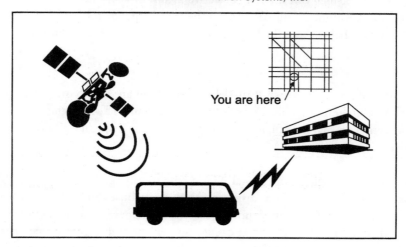

You are here

The AVL system generates reports that can be used to plan schedules and routes and to verify what actually occurs on the roadways. The *Benefits Assessment of Advanced Public Transportation Systems* reports that transit agencies with AVL most often cited the following primary benefits:

- Increased transit safety and security for drivers and transit users
- Improved operating efficiency with potential reductions in fleet requirements and nonrevenue vehicle miles (nonrevenue vehicle hours)
- More uniform and reliable transit service that promotes increased ridership
- Improved response to transit service disruptions (i.e., route, traffic and vehicle breakdown disruptions)
- Increased control of fleet and driver operations and fleet dispatch functions
- Improved information for transit route planning and vehicle/driver scheduling systems
- Increased information for integration with other transit APTS technologies (e.g., transit information systems, route/stop annunciators, APC)
- Increased information for integration into other ITS technologies (e.g., traffic signal pre-emption or priority systems, traffic flow metering)[2]

Security and safety are enhanced when the location of the bus is known. Combining AVL with a silent alarm allows the bus operator to send an instantaneous distress signal to the dispatch center. The dispatcher knows the location of the bus with an emergency and can call for immediate assistance without further action on the part of the driver. AVL fosters customer-oriented transit by helping transit agencies provide consistent and reliable service. The driver and the dispatcher are aware of deviations from route or schedule and can take corrective action without delay. Service is more responsive to change because the dispatcher has more information, can see where all buses are located at any time and can communicate the need for corrective action.

AVL can assist a transit agency in becoming a quality organization that emphasizes mutual respect by allowing data from AVL to resolve discrepancies about driver performance between management and bus operators. AVL data and reports, which track on-time performance and provide playback monitoring, furnish evidence that eliminates arguments based on opinion. This same information can be used in evaluating customer complaints. AVL helps ensure the highest level of service delivery and fosters a positive image because it allows the opportunity for a carefully monitored transit system. If dispatchers have enough information to carefully monitor the system, they can suggest corrective action to keep buses on schedule and prevent bunching of buses. AVL (combined with APC) gives the transit agency the location of passenger boardings and exits. This information helps the transit agency know the needs of the community.

ATMS integration

If the operations center of a transit agency is tied electronically to an ATMS outside of the transit agency, we say that we have ATMS integration. This integration and electronic data exchange allows controllers in the transit management center to share traffic information data, and it helps make both operations more efficient and productive.

If a transit system is integrated with the regional ATMS, the transit agency has access to real-time traffic information. Armed with this information, dispatchers can route buses around congestion and move them through traffic more efficiently. They can respond quickly to changes in the traffic pattern and adapt as necessary to current conditions. Through on-street camera surveillance, emergencies may be spotted more quickly and intervention by controllers can be accomplished more efficiently. Bus operators, who are generally present on most arterials and numerous local streets, can provide firsthand information to the ATMS about incidents and congestion that is out of camera range. This in turn provides a source of "probe" information, which is more dynamic and more nearly represents current traffic conditions.

ATMS integration helps create a multimodal system because dynamic data information can be provided to variable message signs (VMS) on the highways and it can direct traffic to transit stations and/or park-ride lots as conditions warrant. This data integration promotes the highest level of service by moving transit through and around traffic congestion more quickly. An integrated approach to transportation systems is expected by the customer and therefore creates a positive image for transportation providers.

Signal priority

Signal priority is a system that extends a traffic light's green time in favor of buses and streetcars. In signal priority, the traffic signal system is designed to receive information from a transit vehicle or central control system indicating that the transit vehicle is approaching the intersection. The traffic signal it is approaching should maintain a few more seconds of green time to allow an approaching transit vehicle to clear the intersection. If the signal is red when the transit vehicle approaches, the system may "steal" a few seconds of green time from the cross-street and turn green for the transit vehicle a few seconds earlier than it would have without priority.

The advantage of signal priority for transit is that it helps keep transit vehicles on schedule. It can produce a faster run-time, which in turn reduces the number of vehicles needed on a particular route. This can amount to large savings for the transit system. Better on-time performance translates into more riders, which is nearly always the goal for transit.

Traffic signal priority devices may be tied in with an ATMS so that buses running behind schedule will receive a few seconds of extra green time, allowing them to clear intersections. This technology helps keep buses on schedule and helps traffic along the bus route move more smoothly. Tight integration with an ATMS allows traffic engineers to give priority to buses while maximizing traffic flow. This results in customer-oriented service, an ability to adapt to change and provides a high level of service. Traffic signal priority represents a multimodal approach to resolving transportation problems.

APC

The foundation of good transit planning is accurate ridership data. To determine whether a segment of a route is productive and should be continued, the transit planner must know exactly when and where riders get on and get off the bus (origin/destination data). In most transit systems this information is collected by employees called "ride checkers" who sit on the bus and record by hand (or on a handheld device) the time, location and passenger count at each stop as passengers enter and exit the bus. APCs can record all of this information automatically and create reports useful to the planner. The most prevalent APC technology uses infrared beams at the doors or pressure-sensitive mats on the steps to automatically count passengers getting on and off the bus. Errors in counting are reduced because of the use of APCs. The APC uses the geo-coded location obtained from the GPS receiver to create a record of location and time and stores this data in the vehicle logic unit (VLU). The VLU then downloads this data on a daily basis to the planning department. A properly designed APC system will yield accurate data in a timely and economical manner. Data gathering for passenger counts becomes more accurate and timely, and planning functions are more effective.

APCs and the associated data provide transit planners with information to tailor bus routes to the needs of the community. This yields a more customer-oriented transit service plan and increased ridership with corresponding increases in revenue. For the same reasons, dynamic data provided by APCs allow planners to respond to changes in transportation patterns by modifying route structures. This assures a continued high level of service and improved customer satisfaction. This data, integrated into the transit database, becomes a valuable planning and management tool.

GIS

GIS allows a transit agency to collect, store, analyze and display data by geo-coded location. The information is presented on a geo-coded map display in the dispatch center. Other data such as landmarks, bus stops, street locations, emergency services and so forth are linked to the map database. Nearly every aspect of public transportation is related to moving people and vehicles from place to place over time. So GIS and transit are natural partners. For example, real-time bus information combined with GIS gives a transit agency the ability to inform customers of the exact location of a transit vehicle. In addition, with other electronics on the bus such as APC, the bus stop and the bus rider can be informed of predicted bus arrival, as well as available seating capacity. Other information can also include whether the bus stop has a shelter or sidewalk and whether it is handicap accessible. With this wealth of information, geo-coded and part of the transit database, the transit operator can now develop a schedule for daily maintenance and when the bus shelter was cleaned or painted. In other words, a comprehensive bus stop database and maintenance plan can be implemented. This used to be something transit operators could only dream about. GIS has given the transit operator a powerful real-time and data dynamic working tool. Until software providers built these tools, using GIS technologies, operators were overwhelmed with the tasks necessary to maintain this critical database. For planners and schedulers the information can include land use, population, employment, street geometry, turning radii, street restrictions and more. All of this data, related to a geo-coded map, helps planners establish routing plans, route shapes and bus headways.

The information is stored in a database and can be displayed as a computer map. To read the information about a bus stop, a planner can click on the bus stop and the map and a list of information about the bus stop will appear on the computer display. The planner can analyze the information, determine a course of action and implement a plan or schedule with relative ease. For example, a planner can determine how many bus stops have shelters or which bus stops have not been painted within the last three years.

A GIS and its associated database creates an environment in which transit may be more customer-focused. Without GIS, planners typically use street maps, tabular demographic information, city directories and various other disparate pieces of information. This needed information can be purchased in electronic form and loaded into a GIS, allowing a planner to access fairly up-to-date information in a useable format. The safety benefits are realized when the GIS is shared with emergency operations fostering faster response times.

With GIS we can provide the highest level of service because we can track where our customers live and work. We have a powerful link with the community needs because we can store, analyze and retrieve a great deal of information about the community.

Fare collection

Electronic fare collection is a system in which customers use media (cards) instead of coins or tokens to pay for transit rides. The goal of electronic fare collection is to reduce the need for a transit agency to count, collect and distribute or handle coins, bills or tokens. The reason for wanting to eliminate the handling of currency is that this task is very expensive for transit agencies because of the weight, size and value of coins. Large sums of money tend to invite crime and require expensive security. The desire for a cash-less system has given rise to several different approaches. Some systems are using a medium that can be used in a number of applications such as transit, retail purchases and banking. Some transit systems are using media that can be used to pay transit fares as well as to pay for parking or tolls.

All of these techniques involve some kind of card with an integrated circuit or magnetic strip. The card replaces coins, bills and tokens. Quoting from Benefits Assessment of Advanced Public Transportation Systems, transit systems with APTS electronic fare payment systems cited the following primary benefits:

- *Improved security of transit revenues.* This benefit comes from reduced fare evasion. New York City Transit, which in 1993 installed a magnetic stripe system, received an additional revenue capture of $43 million and in 1994 an additional $54 million, as a result of tightened revenue security measures and savings from reduced fare evasions.[3]
- *Customer convenience.* Electronic fare payment makes it easier for a customer to move across regional transportation services through a single payment medium. The need for tokens, exact fare and transfer slips is reduced.
- *Expanded base for transit revenue* through increased market opportunities, interest earned on prepaid fares, transaction fees and unused value on prepaid, stored value cards.
- *Reduced fare collection and processing costs.* Applications of electronic fare payment systems reduce agency costs in the counting and handling of cash, tokens and transfers. In some cases, these functions are borne by banks, credit card companies or other financial management institutions. New Jersey Transit estimates cost savings of up to $2.7 million in reduced labor costs of handling cash and tokens.[4] Ventura County estimates that their smart card system will save the agency $9.5 million in reduced fare evasion, $5 million in reduced data collection costs and $990,000 in reduced costs of handling fares and transfer slips.[5]

Electronic fare collection can provide a seamless payment system for various modes of transportation encompassing a number of jurisdictions and agencies. Smart cards have been developed that can be used for purchases at fastfood restaurants, theaters and the like as well as on transit. These advanced payment systems greatly reduce the burden of handling cash for the transit agency and provide the convenience of high-quality service for the customer. The application of smart cards to transit demonstrates cooperation with financial institutions, which fosters a positive image for transit.

Automated trip itineraries and telephone information centers

In many transit systems there are customer information operators who manually help customers plan their transit trips. These operators, in a telephone information center, use street maps, printed schedules and their own experience to inform customers of how to get to their destinations. With automated trip itineraries, a customer information operator may enter the starting point of the trip and the ending point of the trip. The trip itinerary planning system will create a plan for the customer based on the origin and destination data and any special conditions that need to be considered. Several software vendors have built automated systems and currently provide them to the market. These same software providers can provide a cost/benefit analysis to justify the investment for a system. Automated trip itineraries that are integrated with AVL can calculate the best trip for a customer based on which buses are on schedule and the physical location of the passenger.

Many automated trip itineraries begin with walking instructions to the bus or train stop, state which bus or train to catch, what transfers to make, how long the trip will take and what the cost will be. The advantage of automated trip itineraries is that they are fast and repeatable. The customer does not have to make repeat calls to find the "best" operator because all of the operators are using the same information. Customers do not have to wait "on hold" to get information, and there are fewer dropped calls. With good information there is a better chance of attracting new riders unfamiliar with the service. Because automated trip itineraries are electronic, they may be accessed from sources such as home or work computers, kiosks and interactive television. Most transit systems with automated trip itinerary planning also provide schedules, fares and general information through electronic means. The provision of electronic information to a variety of devices and locations helps the transit agency get information into the hands of the customers and potential customers.

Transit information can become an effective part of a regional integrated traveler information system. Trip itineraries, traffic information and tourist information can be made available on the Internet, with handheld devices, telephones, interactive kiosks and other devices.

In-vehicle annunciators

In-vehicle annunciators are generally audio and visual presentations of next-stop information. A sign posted at the front of the bus, and perhaps another in the middle of the bus, will flash or scroll a sign giving the name of the next bus stop, cross-street, or landmark. At the same time, a pre-recorded message will play with the same information. This helps passengers who are visually- or hearing-impaired to recognize their location. The information is helpful to all customers—particularly if they are new to the route or are not paying attention to their location. In-vehicle annunciators help transit agencies meet requirements to make bus stop announcements as specified in the ADA.

Because they are consistent and clear, in-vehicle annunciators are customer-oriented and ensure a higher level of service by advising the customer of an approaching stop and of the present location. They foster a positive image because they visibly demonstrate an effort to communicate to the customer. Triggering of the annunciator is done using the VLU. The VLU is integrated with the GPS receiver so that accurate, automatic activation of the annunciator can take place. In other words "the right announcement, at the right time, in the right location" is all done automatically. This relieves the bus operator of a work load, while at the same time providing clear, accurate and timely announcements for the rider. This is a tremendous improvement to customer service. In addition, transit agencies can use these annunciators for advertising messages, thereby developing a source of revenue.

Next bus arrival and predicted arrival

Customer information systems have evolved into robust customer service systems. Technologies in computing, algorithms and displays have made it possible to notify transit riders, in advance, of the predicted arrival of a transit vehicle at a unique transit stop. These predictions are conveyed to passengers via a multitude of display devices. These display devices include:

- VMS and monitors
- Interactive kiosks
- Handheld personal communications devices
- Shelter displays
- In-home and in-office light emitting diode (LED) and liquid crystal displays (LCD)

VMS and monitors

We are all familiar with monitors that are used in airports to tell customers the gate number and arrival time of their flight. Transit agencies, with AVL, can determine whether their buses are running on time and can post that information on a monitor or VMS at a bus stop. Customers may glance at the signs and tell immediately how long they will have to wait for the next bus. They can then decide whether they want to run an errand and return to the stop or remain at the stop. Knowing when the bus will arrive can greatly reduce the customer's anxiety level, especially if the bus has not arrived by its scheduled time. Monitors are typically used in areas where several buses will arrive and depart while smaller message signs are used at stops that serve only one or two bus routes.

Interactive kiosks

Interactive kiosks are computers that are housed in a container that deters theft and vandalism. Customers may approach the kiosk and through a keyboard, mouse, or touch screen request information. Many kiosks carry a variety of information, ranging from weather to traffic. Kiosks with APTS information may have route and schedule information, automated trip itineraries and on-time status of buses. There are several benefits obtained from these systems:

- *Increased transit ridership and revenues.* Customer information systems have been found to be effective in promoting transit services to current and potential transit patrons. The availability and ease of access to this information enhances the potential for keeping existing transit riders and attracting new users and transit revenues.
- *Improved transit service and visibility within the community.* The applications of customer information technologies are often used to demonstrate the full range of services and area coverage offered by public transportation in the community. This is especially true in larger metropolitan areas where extensive and more complex routes, fare structures and multimodal choices of transportation services often exist.
- *Increased customer convenience.* The applications of customer information technologies provide a more convenient and potentially lower cost alternative for disseminating traveler information to transit riders, as compared to published transit schedules and telephone information systems. The application of these systems, especially in high-density travel areas of cities (e.g., transportation centers, major city attractions, malls) have proved to be very effective and convenient to transit riders.
- *Enhanced compliance with ADA requirements.* Customer information systems, including electronic displays, annunciators and terminal/information kiosks, are effective technologies to enhance transit services to patrons who are visually or hearing-impaired and to promote an agency's compliance with ADA requirements.[6]

Handheld personal communications devices
The handheld bus tracker is a wireless communications device that provides next bus arrival information along with standard paging services. Normally, the user can select a combination of routes and stops and will receive messages with next bus arrival information.

Shelter displays
A shelter display is a specially designed LED sign integrated with a paging receiver or some other type of data communications system. Shelter equipment is typically designed to be vandal-resistant and is usually powered by shelter power.

In-home and in-office LED and LCD displays
These displays are similar to shelter and handheld displays relative to their operation. The displays, however, are designed to be aesthetically pleasing and to match appropriate decor.

Architecture and standards

Why do we need an architecture and standards?

A transit agency must ensure that the APTS it creates is functional, useful, affordable and able to "grow" in the future. Many pitfalls, however, could threaten a system's value. By selecting a particular technology, will the agency be forced to choose between buying all future additions from the same vendor (at any price the vendor names) or having to scrap the system and begin again? Will the chosen technology communicate with the technology of the other transit systems in the region? Is the technology compatible with the technology used by the highway department, so that a communication link can coordinate operations between the two agencies? Will the technology support enhancements to the system? For example, will the AVLs that are being installed now communicate with the in-vehicle annunciators, APCs and electronic fare box that will be installed in the future? Clearly, the industry needs a common set of rules so that our information can be shared between agencies and departments, regardless of the technology used.

Architecture

In response to these and other concerns, a national ITS architecture has been created. The architecture does not specify what systems should exist in various locations, but it does paint a picture of how systems relate to each other. It explains what data elements should be communicated and the physical interface required. Protocol for communications are covered in those documents that relate to the National Transportation Communications for ITS Protocol (NTCIP). In the transit market a body of standards relating to communications protocols are being developed as part of the Transit Standards Consortium (TSC). For those who are beginning the process of thinking through what they want for their own agency, the architecture provides a top-level design that can be used almost as a check list. The system designer can take advantage of a reserve of information and does not have to reinvent the wheel. The following figures illustrate the various systems and their relationships for both the entire architecture and the portion pertaining to APTS.

Benefits of using the national ITS architecture

The existence of a common, national architecture for ITS has numerous benefits:[7]

- *National compatibility.* As travelers and commercial vehicles move within the United States, the equipment on their vehicles continues to support them at all locations.
- *Multiple suppliers.* More vendors will be supplying compatible equipment, leading to competition and less expensive equipment.

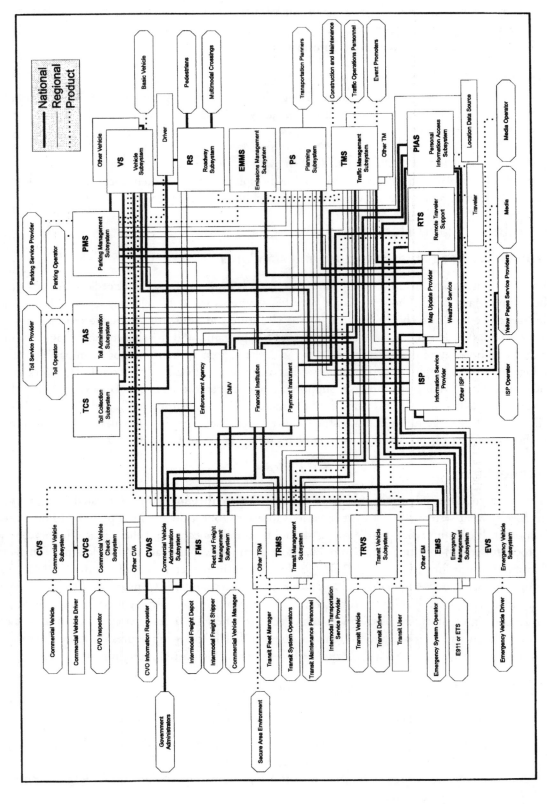

Figure 16–2. Physical architecture interface diagram.
Source: Federal Highway Administration, National ITS Architecture
Transit Guidelines—Joint Program Office, Publication# FHWA-JPO-97-0017.

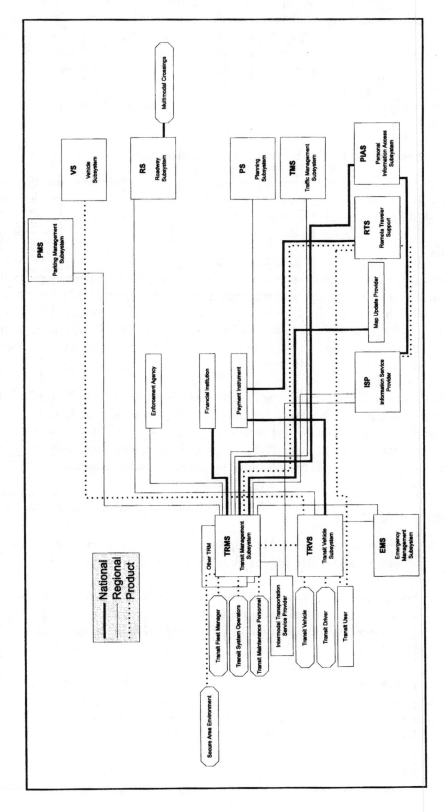

Figure 16–3. APTS interface diagram.
Source: Federal Highway Administration, *National ITS Architecture*
Transit Guidelines—Joint Program Office, Publication# FHWA-JPO-97-0017.

- *Future growth.* By following an "open systems" approach, the architecture provides the agency with the flexibility to update or expand the system without being tied to a particular vendor's technology.
- *Support for ranges of functionality.* The architecture supports high-end and low-end features. Basic services can be provided free, while value-added services can be provided on a fee basis.
- *Synergy.* The architecture considers the requirements for multiple functions and allocates systems to optimally support those functions.
- *Risk reduction.* The architecture's common framework reduces risk for implementers, manufacturers and consumers alike.

Additional resources on the national ITS architecture

The document describing the national ITS architecture is over 5,000 pages long, far too cumbersome for most people to read from start to finish. However, a number of other documents have been written to guide users through the architecture.[8] See table 16–3 for more information.

Standards

The architecture describes a framework, but not how the pieces should relate to each other in the excruciating detail necessary in today's digital world. That is the function of standards. Most of the standards activity concerning APTS began with the Transit Communications Interface Profiles (TCIP) and will be continued by the TSC. TCIP is a family of standards under development that will focus on data interfaces.[9] It will enable electronic data exchange among transit agency departments, traffic and transportation management entities and information service providers.

TCIP will be a subset of the NTCIP. The NTCIP was created in 1992 by the National Electrical Manufacturers Association to develop a common interface for traffic field devices. In 1995, the Federal Highway Administration recommended broadening the scope to include the systems supported by the national ITS architecture. In particular, NTCIP's scope was expanded to ensure that different devices were interoperable and similar devices manufactured by different vendors were interchangeable on the same communication infrastructure.[10]

What will the TCIP do?

What will be the function of TCIP? It will help various agencies share information, as described in the following excerpts from the TCIP web page at <http://www.tcip.org>.

Transit operators face problems in today's information age. The challenges are the same whether operators are designing a trip itinerary for a customer using real-time information, making service changes based on APCs and AVL-collected travel times or modifying fare structures based on actual passenger travel distance and transfer data.

Chances are, once operators overcome institutional and budget obstacles, they come up against data problems: data kept by the planning department is in one format, maintained in a different format by the maintenance department and in yet another format by the dispatch and transit information centers. Data incompatibility has been the stumbling block for many APTS projects.

The TCIP effort will define data interfaces that will allow data to flow among departments, and between and among applications and other external entities such as traffic management centers (TMC) and emergency

Table 16–3
National ITS Architecture Information Sources
Source: ITSA, *Improving Transit with Intelligent Transportation Systems* (December 1998, page 12).

The following documents are available from the ITS Joint Program Office at the address below.

- *National ITS Architecture Transit Guidelines: Executive Summary*
  (publication no. FHWA-JPO-97-0016)

- *National ITS Architecture Transit Guidelines: Technical Edition*
  (publication no. FHWA-JPO-97-0017).

- *The National Architecture for ITS: A Framework for Integrated Transportation into the 21st Century*

- *Building the ITI: Putting the National Architecture into Action*

This office also has 16 national ITS architecture documents available for a fee. They may be purchased as a set or individually \from the ITS Joint Program Office or from the ITS America bookstore at the address below. The latest architecture documentation is also available online at <http://www.itsa.org/public/archdocs/national.html> and <http://www.odentics.com/itsarch>.

Additional information may be obtained from:

ITS Joint Program Office (HVH-1)
Federal Highway Administration
U.S. Department of Transportation
400 Seventh Street, S.W.
Washington, D.C. 20590
Website: <http://www.its.dot.gov>

ITS America
400 Virginia Avenue, S.W., Suite 800
Washington, D.C. 20024
Telephone: (202) 484-4847
Website: <http://www.itsa.org>

Office of Mobility Innovation (TRI-10)
Federal Transit Administration
U.S. Department of Transportation
400 Seventh Street, S.W.
Washington, D.C. 20590
Telephone: (202) 366-4995
Website: <http://www.fta.dot.gov>

PB Farradyne Inc.
Attn.: ITS Planning
3200 Tower Oaks Boulevard
Rockville, MD 20852
Telephone: (301) 816-2760
E-mail: <transitguide@farradyne.com>

management centers. The TCIP was initiated in November 1996. Funded by the U.S. Department of Transportation's (U.S. DOT) Joint Program Office for ITS, and developed by the Institute for Transportation Engineers (ITE), the TCIP effort is a one-year standards development effort designed to provide the interface structures that will allow disparate transit components and organizations to exchange data. Additional descriptions of what the TCIP will do are provided by the following excerpts from the Project Plan:

> The project will define the information and information transfer requirements among public transportation vehicles, the TMC, other transit facilities and other ITS centers; develop physical and data link requirements; develop required message sets and establish liaison and coordinate between ITE and other standard development organizations on the development of related standards.

The project will provide the leadership to coordinate, develop and deploy a comprehensive set of TCIPs that allow effective and efficient exchange of data used for ITS user services and transit operations, maintenance, customer information and planning and management functions. The scope provides for interfaces among transit applications to communicate data among transit departments, other operating entities such as emergency response services and regional TMCs. The results of this effort will be a set of provisional standards for TCIP.[11]

TSC

The TSC will build on the work begun by the TCIP. The TSC (a public–private, nonprofit organization) will facilitate the development of all transit standards and will follow up development with standards testing, maintenance, education and training. Like the TCIP, the organization will include transit agencies, standards bodies, vendors and other interested parties.

The TSC will not be another standards organization. It will help set the agenda for the transit industry's standards efforts and work with existing standards organizations to achieve the industry's goals. For further information on TCIP and TSC, please see <http://www.tcip.org> and <http://www.tsconsortium.org>.

Transit control center

The transit control center (TCC) is the hub of transit ITS operations. Host processors in the TCC contain a large centralized relational database that warehouses all the transit information about fleet operations, equipment inventory, employee job assignments, incidents regarding transit operations and archived historical operating data. These relational databases are typically an Oracle or Informix database with SQL capability. In an attempt to standardize the data elements of a TCC database, the TCIP is in the process of developing a set of data element conventions and standard nomenclature to assure the ability to integrate a TCC with the ATMS control center. The benefits of this integration include the transfer of information between centers to effect an improved level of management of transit fleet operations. The interchange of traffic conditions, for example, gives transit dispatchers an opportunity to divert transit vehicles around traffic bottlenecks, accidents or other unusual conditions; and it maintains a high level of service for the transit rider. Likewise, transit vehicles working as probes in a traffic network can provide real-time dynamic traffic information to a TMC, thereby making the TMC more effective.

Overview of computer-aided dispatch and AVL system

To understand the role of the TCC it is necessary to show how and why the center is the hub of transit operations. Figure 16–4 provides an overview of a typical computer-aided dispatch and AVL system. Real-time location and incident data are collected on the intelligent vehicle, sometimes referred to as the "smart bus." The electronics package on the smart bus gathers data on location by receiving satellite location data from the constellation of GPS satellites deployed by the Department of Defense. The data are then corrected to reflect exact vehicle position within 15 meters, and they are merged with others on vehicle-monitored data, such as engine operating conditions, passenger counts, performance to schedule and other characteristics defined by the transit property. Most VLUs can accept a series of data inputs from interconnected electronic subsystems on the vehicle when they are integrated with a J1708 vehicle area network (VAN). The data are then communicated to the TCC through wireless private mobile radio or public radio networks, where they are gathered, processed, analyzed, catalogued and filed as necessary. These communication networks provide both a voice and data link to the TCC. The process of collecting and processing gather dynamic data from the smart bus and puts the TCC in the position of converting dynamic real-time data to information. The operations of the TCC puts the control center at the hub of converting data into knowledge. It is the use of this knowledge database that allows the transit property to improve transit operations, reduce the cost of operations, insure a higher level of security for bus operators and passengers and improve customer service with better on-time performance. For example, using a voice or data link to the vehicle operator, a TCC controller can issue instructions to divert a vehicle around a traffic incident, thereby maintaining on-time performance.

Figure 16–4. Computer-aided dispatch and AVL system.
Source: Orbital-TMS.

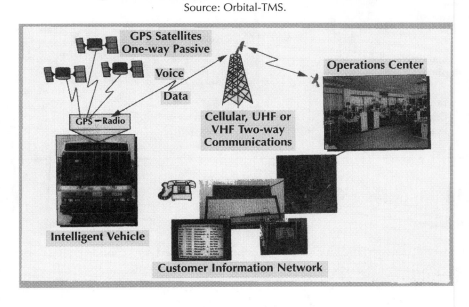

Typical TCC

At the TCC, controllers, sometimes referred to as dispatchers, monitor the data being transmitted to the center. Data are received by the host processor, and incidents are identified and displayed on computer workstations. Incidents are identified by the host processor based on parameters established by the transit property. Typically, incidents include vehicle schedule performance, location of the vehicle on a route map, emergency incidents reported by the vehicle operator, maintenance status of the transit vehicle and other data specified by the transit agency. Several suppliers provide turnkey software packages to perform this function. Many of these software packages permit user-identified parameters to be adapted for an individual transit agency. Core tasks performed by these software programs include:

- Maintain the central database
- Produce incident reports
- Manage fleet voice and data communications
- Store and forward information for distribution
- Archive data for retrieval
- Interface to the agency MIS through wide area networks or local area networks

Figure 16–5. Transit control center.
Source: Orbital-TMS.

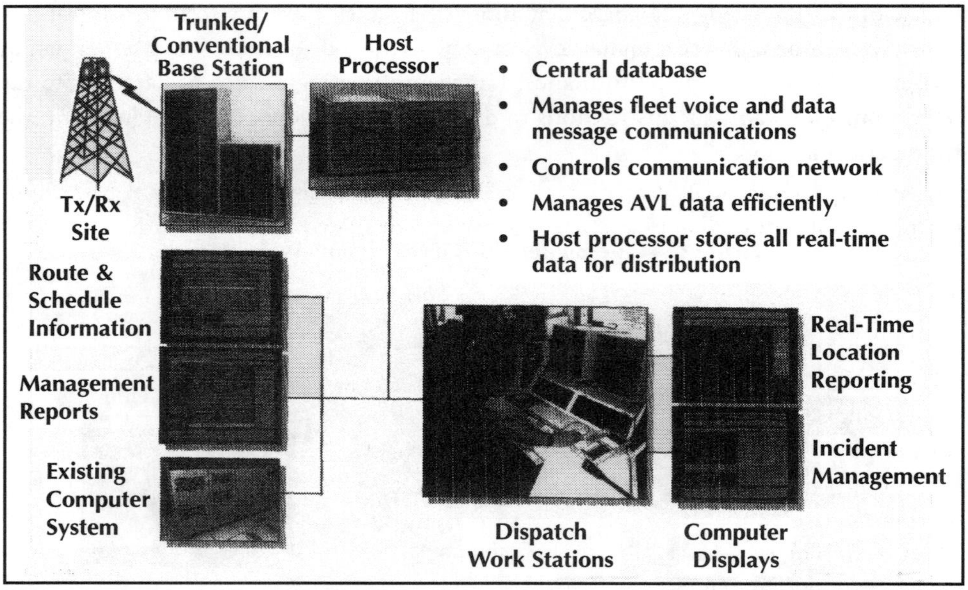

Transit vehicle subsystems

Systems overview

Transit vehicles of the nineties and their authorities have progressed far beyond the needs of a basic vehicle with a coin box. The costs of vehicles, operations personnel, maintenance and federal requirements have necessitated a number of electronic vehicle enhancements to efficiently and effectively manage and conduct business. Regardless of fleet size, integrated electronic data communications systems will require implementation. As agencies continue to move forward in their desire to implement ITS, additional vehicle requirements are identified.

These additional vehicle requirements caused a rapid advancement in the development of electronic systems and devices to satisfy transit applications. Often, these systems and devices were developed using a proprietary protocol. Although the initial contracts that led to the development of these devices was awarded on a competitive basis, the use of proprietary designs has restricted a transit authority's ability to seek future competitive procurements. The strategy of using proprietary designs was an attempt by suppliers to control future procurements. These proprietary designs often included a proprietary software protocol or a unique mechanical or electronic interconnection. This precluded the ability to integrate the various electronic devices into a compatible, functional, integrated data information and management system, as well as forcing the transit authority into a sole-source procurement process.

In response to these challenges, the U.S. Department of Transportation's FTA, with cooperation of the Intelligent Transportation Society of America (ITSA), created a VAN subcommittee to study and recommend a solution to the problem of integrating on-vehicle electronic components, data functions and communication interfaces. The VAN subcommittee is a component of the APTS Technical Standards Task Force and consists of representatives from agencies, academia, integrators, manufacturers, industry consultants and the Canadian Ministry of Transportation.

VAN integration objective

The VAN was born with these guidelines:

- Minimize hardware cost and overhead
- Provide interchangeable components and open standards on vehicles while permitting proprietary considerations
- Provide flexibility for expansion and technology advancements with minimum hardware and software impact on in-place assemblies
- Provide original equipment manufacturers, suppliers and after-market suppliers the flexibility to customize for product individuality and for proprietary considerations

The electronic functions and devices addressed include (figure 16–6):

- Automatic annunciators
- Bus priority (traffic)
- Collision avoidance
- Door status units
- Drive train monitoring
- Fare collection
- Future ITSA technologies
- Maintenance port and printer
- Mobile data terminals
- Passenger counters
- Silent alarms and remote silent alarms
- Smart card unit
- Trip and event recorders
- Unit inventory
- Vehicle control head
- Vehicle identification
- Vehicle location units
- VLU
- Vehicle signage
- Vehicle status point monitors
- Vehicle turntable
- Wayside communication

The VAN committee considered existing, proposed and even proprietary standards in its effort to identify the most sufficient, reliable and cost-effective solution, with the ability to be transportable across all types of transit vehicles (figure 16–7). Ultimately, an existing standard was agreed upon as having identified itself as meeting all of the defined criteria:

- Associated environmental standards
- Cost effective
- Efficient
- Field experience in environment
- Modular and scaleable
- Open architecture
- Product infrastructure
- Reliable in environment
- Simple
- Sufficient

Figure 16–6. ITSA, TCIP and International Standard Organization VAN standard.
Source: Institute of Transportation Engineers, ITE-J1708 Specification.

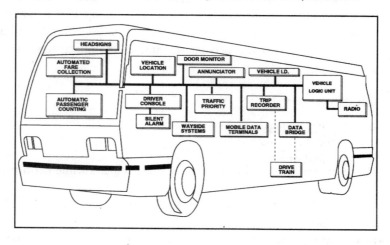

Figure 16–7. Transportable solution.
Source: Institute of Transportation Engineers, ITE-J1708 Specification.

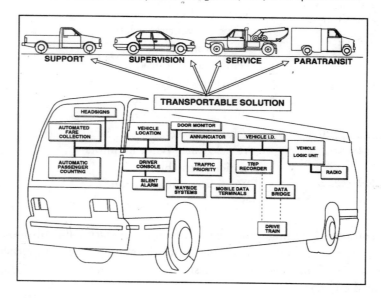

Final VAN standard

The resulting standard is addressed by three related Society of Automotive Engineers (SAE) standards: the hardware and communications format by SAE-J-1708, the protocol by SAE-J-1587 and the environment requirements by SAE-J-1455. Work is underway to convert a "de facto" standard cable and connector to a SAE-J-XXX standard with a release by the SAE expected in 1999 (figure 16–8).

Figure 16–8. J1708 Van standards family.
Source: Institute of Transportation Engineers, ITE-J1708 Specification.

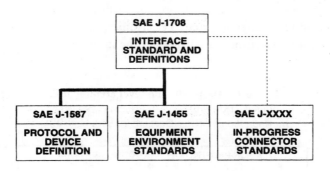

Acceptance of the modular nonproprietary concept has been widespread. After it was released as an official standard by the SAE in 1994, it became the first standard ever adopted by ITS America. In 1996, VAN became a fundamental component in the TCIP effort. In 1997, the countries of Australia, Canada, Denmark, France, Germany, Japan, Korea, Netherlands, New Zealand, Sweden and the United Kingdom voted to accept VAN as an official work item in the International Standards Organization (ISO) at the TC204/WG8 meetings in Berlin, Germany. VAN requirements in transit procurements started in 1994 and continue today (figure 16–9).

Figure 16–9. Standards and developmental timelines.
Source: ITSA, *Improving Transit with Intelligent Transportation Systems* (December 1998, page 121).

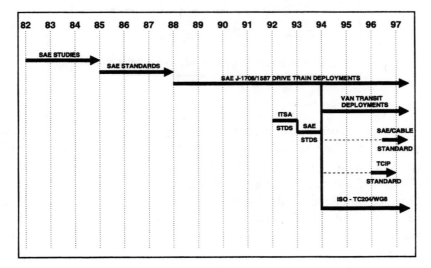

Simply put, it means that a transit agency can now specify and procure a given electronic device from multiple sources with the resulting devices able to interchangeably communicate with the rest of the vehicle's devices (figure 16–10) just by specifying SAE J-1708 standards in the procurement document. While two devices may look different and have different internal electronics, they are interchangeable because they understand and speak an identical electronic language; but the implications go much further.

Figure 16–10. J-1708 top-level architecture.
Source: ITSA, *Improving Transit with Intelligent Transportation Systems* (December 1998, page 121).

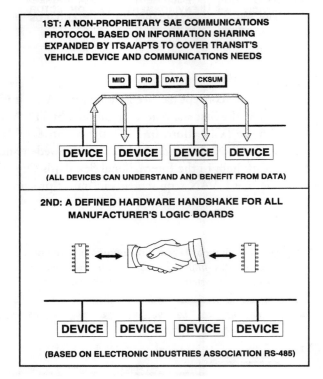

Manufacturers now have the opportunity to market commodity building block devices while competing on pure performance issues (e.g., speed, accuracy, power demands). They no longer have to build, stock and support a stable of custom products uniquely developed and paid for by various agencies. Agencies now have the opportunity to "assemble" a system meeting their special needs and budgetary limits, by selecting the functions and performance requirements afforded by an open-architecture marketplace. Because of the modular nature of the device standards, additional device and functional expansions could occur without discarding previous investments.

Through the standardization of communications and hardware interfaces, the entire on-vehicle system becomes transparent to the vehicle on which it is installed. This enables a single implementation solution to be transportable to a bus, minibus, trolley, streetcar, para-transit van, truck and sedan types of vehicles without regard to the type of power train being used by the vehicle.

Under the ITS initiative, transit has the excellent position of benefiting from many industries and technologies that traditionally have not served the transit industry. Some of these "new-found" suppliers could resolve problems that have challenged transit for years. But the first question often confronting a new supplier is "Has your product ever been on, and survived in, a transit vehicle?" This prevents these suppliers from entering the transit market, and it represents a significant hurdle to overcome. The adoption of industry standards and communications protocols can eliminate this barrier to entry and result in more cost-effective systems being offered to the transit industry. While there are numerous military standards that could be imposed in an attempt to qualify these suppliers, many of these standards require considerable testing and an expensive nonrecurring engineering effort. Smaller agencies cannot afford these costs, and suppliers are not in a position to "customize" a solution for all transit agencies. As a result their new solutions may never see transit service. This could be transit's loss, and it could discourage potential new suppliers and their solutions from entering the transit market. The goal of the national standards and protocol effort is to eliminate these barriers and open up the field to more suppliers.

Relationship with TCIP and NTCIP

Nonproprietary information made available on the vehicle is significantly enhanced when it is also available in a nonproprietary database format at the fixed end transit management system (figure 16–11). TCIP has mapped the data from the vehicle into a target database schema that allows multiple vendors to access the data in a nonproprietary and standardized manner. Over time, the savings to an agency will be significant because each new contractor will not have to reverse engineer the organization and content of an unknown proprietary database. Nor will data users within an agency be confounded in their attempt to locate and use data.

Figure 16–11. Transit communications interface profiles.
Sources: NTCIP Steering Group.

Institute of Transportation Engineers, "The National Transportation
Communications/ITS Protocol: An Introduction," *ITE Journal* (December 1995).

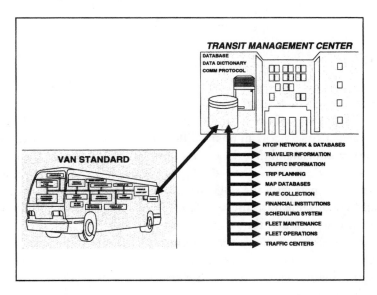

Since the TCIP is a component part of the NTCIP, interfacing between transit and transportation Centers will be greatly expedited and simplified as the management of all transportation becomes seamless.

Relationship with ISO

As mentioned earlier, the VAN standard has been accepted by the ISO as a formal work item, leading to an international standard through the efforts of the U.S. Technical Committee 204, Work Group 8. This effort has the support of the SAE, who currently is the holder of the standard. The result of this effort would be to open up world class markets, increase product volumes and decrease costs (figure 16–12).

Figure 16–12. International Standards Organization.
Sources: NTCIP Steering Group.

Institute of Transportation Engineers, "The National Transportation Communications/ITS Protocol: An Introduction," *ITE Journal* (December 1995).

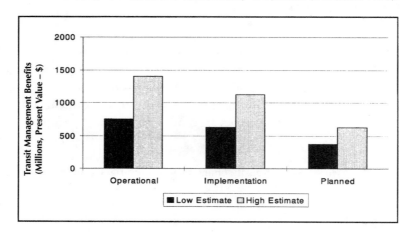

Transit without ITS

Where will transit be without the implementation of ITS? Disadvantaged. Manual systems are labor-intensive and often lack important data needed to make spontaneous changes. It is impossible for a bus supervisor to know the location of all buses at all times. In the rare occurrence of crime, knowing the exact location of a bus for dispatching emergency services can be the difference between life and death. Passengers and drivers feel more secure when they understand that the bus location is always known.

It is difficult for transit to compete with the single-occupant vehicle (SOV) because the SOV offers door-to-door service on demand. A convenient, secure and dependable transit system offers amenities that the SOV cannot. Transit customers can use travel time to read, do paperwork, knit or just relax while a professional driver copes with traffic. Research has shown that transit customers can save thousands of dollars each year on vehicle maintenance and operating and parking fees. Transit customers often state a sense of community and well-being as reasons why they choose transit. But transit must maintain and increase its convenience, security and dependability to attract and keep customers. ITS provides tools that can do so.

As highway systems and vehicles become more efficient and convenient with monitoring and surveillance, in-vehicle route guidance that is updated with real-time information, electronic toll collection, improved incident management and collision avoidance systems, the automobile becomes even more attractive and desirable. The relative desirability of transit will decrease unless the transit industry embraces existing technology and risks the development of improved technology.

Benefits of transit ITS

Figures 16–13 and 16–14 illustrate ranges of benefits for transit ITS. These benefits are from *Benefits Assessment of Advanced Public Transportation Systems.*[12] This study identified 265 APTS deployments that are currently operational, under implementation or planned for implementation over the next 10 years. The projected total benefits of these deployments are estimated to range from $3.8 billion to as high as $7.8 billion. Of these deployments approximately 44 percent of the total benefits are accrued from transit management system deployments, 34 percent from electronic fare payment system applications, 21 percent from automated traveler information system deployments and with the remaining 1 percent from demand-responsive transit and computer-aided dispatching system operations.[13] For more information on these benefits and details on all assumptions used in calculations you are encouraged to obtain a copy of the study (publication number FHWA-JPO-96-0031) from the National Technical Information Service in Springfield, Virginia 22161. Also, the FTA intends to place the document on their website: <http://www.fta.dot.gov>.

Transit management systems

The projected management system benefits are depicted in figure 16–15. These benefits are based on surveys and analyses conducted by the Volpe National Transportation Research Center. They include current operations, future deployments and planned projects. Because there is uncertainty in future applications, a range (from low to high) is depicted.

Figure 16–13. Transit management benefits.
Source: Volpe National Transportation Systems Center,
Benefit Assessment of Advanced Public Transportation Systems.

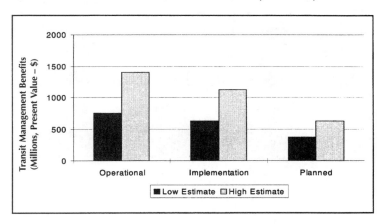

Figure 16–14. Traveler information benefits.
Source: Volpe National Transportation Systems Center,
Benefit Assessment of Advanced Public Transportation Systems.

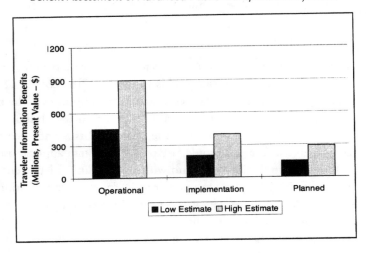

Figure 16–15. Total APTS benefits.
Source: Volpe National Transportation Systems Center,
Benefit Assessment of Advanced Public Transportation Systems.

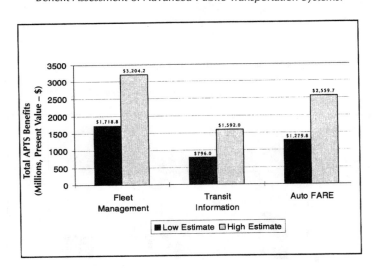

Summary of benefits

All of these benefits translate into revenue for transit. Because the technologies are new, transit systems are discovering more benefits as APTS projects progress. As more information is available, agencies find more uses for the information.

Bibliography

Electronics Industries Association. 1983. "Standard for Electrical Characteristics of Generators and Receivers for Use in Balanced Digital Multipoint Systems" (April). Standard RS-485 (EIA RS-485).

Kushner, M. P. 1992. Feature Shock, Data Fusion and Systems Integration for Advanced Public Transit Systems (May). Second Annual IVHS America Meeting, Newport Beach, California.

Society of Automotive Engineers. Joint SAE/TMC Recommended Practice for Electronic Data Interchange Between Microcomputer Systems in Heavy Duty Vehicle Applications (SAE-J-1587).

Society of Automotive Engineers. Joint SAE/TMC Recommended Environmental Practices for Electronic Equipment Design (SAE-J-1455).

Society of Automotive Engineers. Serial Data Communications Between Microcomputer Systems in Heavy-Duty Vehicle Applications (SAE-J-1708).

Society of Automotive Engineers. Powertrain Control Interface for Electronic Controls Used in Medium and Heavy Duty Diesel on Highway Vehicle Applications (SAE-J-1922).

Smith, H. H. 1998. *Improving Transit with Intelligent Transportation Systems* (December). ITS America.

Endnotes

1. *APTA Fact Book.*

2. Drancsak, M. 1995. *Transit Planning and Research Programs Fiscal Year 1994 Project Directory* (March): page 8. Available from Federal Transit Administration, Office of Technical Assistance and Safety, 400 7th Street, SW, Room 6100, Washington, DC 20590, Fax: (202) 366-3765.

3. "Time to Get Smart." *Mass Transit* (November/December 1995).

4. ITS America. 1995. *ITS Technologies in Public Transit: Deployment and Benefits* (February).

5. Federal Transit Administration. 1996. *Advanced Public Transportation System Benefits* (January). FTA.

6. Federal Transit Administration. 1996. *Advanced Public Transportation System Benefits* (January): pages 14–15. FTA.

7. U.S. Department of Transportation. *Intelligent Transportation Systems Building the ITI: Putting the National Architecture into Action:* page 19. U.S. DOT.

8. U.S. Department of Transportation. 1997. *National ITS Architecture Transit Guidelines: Executive Summary* (January): pages 11–12. U.S. DOT.

9. *TCIP Fact Sheet.* Version 1.1 (January 1997). Palisades Consulting Group, Inc.

10. NTCIP Steering Group. 1995. "The National Transportation Communications/ITS Protocol: An Introduction." *ITE Journal* (December): pages 36–40.

11. *TCIP Project Plan* (August 29, 1997): page 1.

12. Federal Transit Administration. 1996. *Advanced Public Transportation System Benefits* (January). FTA.

13. Federal Transit Administration. 1996. *Advanced Public Transportation System Benefits* (January): page v. FTA.

BY Ben Gianni • Vice President, Advanced Network Systems Center • Computer Sciences Corporation

TELECOMMUNICATIONS
TECHNOLOGIES

The role of telecommunications in intelligent transportation systems

A means to an end. This simple cliché aptly describes the role that movement of data and information should play in intelligent transportation systems (ITS). Although not directly apparent to the users of ITS capabilities and not always thought of as a critical portion of the deployment, the entire spectrum of ITS program delivery depends on telecommunications to make it work. From providing data to users of in-vehicle systems or vehicle-to-vehicle communications, communicating from roadside-to-vehicle, from roadside-to-centers, centers-to-centers, within centers and to-and-from the public, telecommunications is a sometimes hidden but key enabler to all other forms and functions of ITS.

Figure 17–1 shows various ITS functions described in the U.S. national ITS architecture. The connecting lines indicate how transporting data and information supports ITS. Note that the national architecture does not define or describe individual methods of information movement; it only defines the need for interaction. Thus, it is necessary to first define the telecommunications capabilities needed to support an ITS and then to identify and describe the telecommunications technologies that can meet those ITS system needs.

Figure 17–1. The supporting role of telecommunications.
Source: Adapted from the U.S. National ITS Architecture,
available from work sponsored by the U.S. DOT, ITS Joint Program Office.

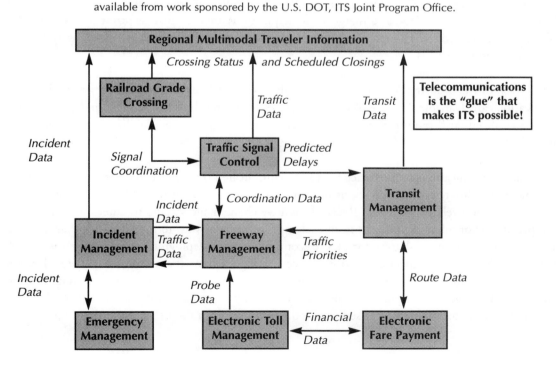

Multimedia networking

Telecommunications in its simplest form entails the communication of voice and data between remote sites; this was once the exclusive domain of the telephone providers, however, things have changed substantially in the last decade. The growing need to transmit still and now moving pictures (i.e., video) and the voracious appetite for telecommunications capabilities by business and Internet users worldwide have transformed it into a $20-billion-plus multimedia networking industry that, according to the Federal Communications Commission (FCC), represents one-seventh of the U.S. economy. Furthermore, the demand for information technology and telecommunications services is growing at twice the rate as the trade in goods worldwide.

The telecommunications industry includes hardware vendors, software companies, traditional telecommunications services providers, cable companies, systems integrators and consultants, as well as government jurisdictions themselves or in combination with private sector partners of all types.

A great number of telecommunications and networking technologies can be used to satisfy ITS needs, and the list is growing. The ITS practitioner has many choices, from basic analog phone lines to advanced technologies like global positioning satellites (GPS), asynchronous transfer mode (ATM), synchronous optical networking (SONET), cable television, and digital subscriber lines (DSLs), all of which continue to emerge and evolve in performance, availability and price. The goal of multimedia networking for ITS is to transport ITS information, whatever its type, from the source(s) to the consumer(s) with a level of quality consistent with the type and use of that information.

The telecommunications industry in the United States

Few industries have undergone more change in less time than the telecommunications industry. Pushed by the federal government's need for robust and secure technologies and pulled by the burgeoning growth of the Internet, the industry growth can be measured in terms of billions of dollars and thousands of providers over the last decade. In September 1998, the FCC identified more than two thousand telecommunications service providers operating in the United States. New companies emerge, mature ones enter new markets with new products and services, and mergers and acquisitions are the norm as profit/loss is realized and market share thus concentrates. The regulated telecommunications industry is now defined by eighteen different sectors, shown in table 17–1.

Keeping track of the industry becomes more difficult, specialized and time-consuming each day. Hundreds of publications are available, from bookstore magazines reviewing the latest modem and error correcting protocol to specialized tariff monitoring reports that compare the cost and availability of public telecommunications services.

Today's telecommunications marketplace for ITS is complicated by the fact that a number of jurisdictions have deployed private telecommunications networks in their rights-of-way and facilities (traffic centers and other transportation-related facilities). Recent legislative changes allow states to enter into agreements to obtain private-sector telecommunications in exchange for right-of-way, termed resource sharing. The practical issues related to resource sharing for ITS telecommunications deployment are addressed in this chapter's section on "ITS Telecommunications and Resource Sharing." Potential access to up-to-date telecommunications infrastructure quickly through resource sharing has heightened the need of transportation agencies to better understand and then to plan, develop, integrate, operate, manage and maintain multiple sources and types of networking technologies and services to the best benefit of the ITS program.

Table 17–1
Telecommunication Industry Sectors
Source: Federal Communications Commission.

1. Competitive Access Provider or Competitive Local Exchange Carrier
2. Cellular, Personal Communications Service (PCS) and Specialized Mobile Radio Wireless Telephony Service Provider
3. Incumbent Local Exchange Carrier
4. Interexchange Carrier
5. Local Reseller
6. Operator Service Provider
7. Other Local
8. Other Mobile Service Carrier
9. Other Toll Service Provider
10. Paging and Messaging
11. Pay Telephone Provider
12. Private Service Provider
13. Pre-paid Calling Card Provider
14. Satellite Service Provider
15. Shared Tenant Service Provider
16. Special Mobile Radio-Dispatch
17. Toll Reseller
18. Wireless Data Service Provider

The following example illustrates the growing complexity of the changing telecommunications landscape. A local government and a cable franchise operator agree to share coaxial cable media for the purpose of transporting traffic video from the field to a metropolitan traffic center. The local government's transportation entity uses analog voice lines and traditional circuit-switched leased lines provided by a local exchange carrier (LEC) to cover geographic areas of its road system not served by cable, and to allow local media to access their system. Competitive pressures and the need to improve service led the cable franchise operator to upgrade its system to use digital transmission equipment as part of a fiber optic upgrade plan. As a result, the transportation entity was required to upgrade equipment in the field and centers. When the local government pursues an enterprise fiber optic network project to link many of the jurisdiction's facilities with ATM and SONET, it must merge three completely different technologies from four sources into a viable, seamless network to continue to meet their growing demands for voice, data and video transmission to support their ITS program.

Adopting a life cycle engineering methodology, such as the one described in this chapter's section on "Telecommunications: A Total Life Cycle Methodology," to manage telecommunications becomes critical in an environment of technological change and evolution. The next section covers the current state of the public telecommunications industry, where it is evolving from, and where it appears to be heading.

Telecommunications providers

Hardware vendors and the Regional Bell Operating Companies (RBOCs), now known as the Incumbent Local Exchange Carrier (ILECs), have traditionally provided telecommunications services to transportation entities. Currently seven major ILECs cover most of the United States. Since the 1996 Telecommunications Act was enacted to increase competition (and lower prices to the consumer), approximately 500 competitive LECs (like Competitive Local Exchange Carriers [CLECs]) have formed to challenge the ILECS and offer alternatives to the industry. Currently they make up approximately five percent of the local exchange marketplace. Of these 500, approximately 15 offer services other than residential telephone service that apply to the ITS requirements set discussed earlier (1998a).

Long-distance providers, now known as Interexchange Carriers (IXCs) have also been traditional providers to transportation entities for Inter-LATA (local access transport area) requirements. Based on FCC-defined territories for and between metropolitan population centers served by RBOCs, IXCs provide connectivity from one population center to the next. Typically, states are divided into at least one LATA, making this a necessity. The numbers of ILECs and IXCs are shrinking because of high-profile mergers, undertaken by telecommunications companies to protect and grow market share and to limit the financial effect of telecom reform and competition. Figure 17–2 provides some insight into the rapid consolidation that began occurring in the industry immediately after the 1996 telecom reform act.

Table 17–2 provides a current snapshot of the ILECs, CLECs and IXCs. The geographic areas they operate in are provided for the LECs. For a comparison of ILEC coverage, the total sheath miles of fiber as reported to the FCC Common Carrier Division is given; and for a comparison of IXCs, the total fiber route miles as reported to the FCC Common Carrier Division is given. All fiber mile figures are for 1997.

Perhaps the most rapid growth in the industry has been in the number of Internet-related service providers. The Internet provider community is tiered, starting with access to consumers in terms of browser software and portals (i.e., initial web screens and the servers that host them); and followed by providers of the physical Point of Presence (POP), the carrier Central Office (CO), and finally the physical infrastructure and media (i.e., fiber, copper, wireless receivers/transmitters) that carry the traffic. A query from a web browser or web search engine on the words Internet Service Provider will yield an astonishing number of sellers of Internet access to the home and business marketplace. They range from the familiar ILEC companies to cable companies to IXCs and small boutique companies who own only a web server, a T1 to the Internet, and a credit card reader.

Underlying telecommunications carrier infrastructure

The telecommunications network consists of public and private networks. Private networks are owned, managed and exclusively used by an entity. The telecommunications networks developed by state transportation agencies are an example. A public network may be owned and maintained by one entity and may be leased to a variety of entities. These networks use essentially the same building blocks, whether the network is private, public, or some hybrid combination of the two. Figure 17–3 shows a simplified representation of the legacy public telecommunications infrastructure in place since the 1970s.

Traditional leased lines based on 1960s and 1970s technology were designed to carry voice traffic. Twisted pair copper wires carrying 64 kilobit per second (kbps) of digital bits connect customers to a carrier CO. These 64 kbps channels or DS0s, are merged into larger streams, 24 at a time, by time-division multiplexing equipment to create a 1.544 Megabit per second (Mbps) T-1 line. At the CO, the T-1 lines are merged to

Figure 17–2. Telecom reform.
Source: "The New Public Network," *Data Communications* (October 1998, 86, figure 1).

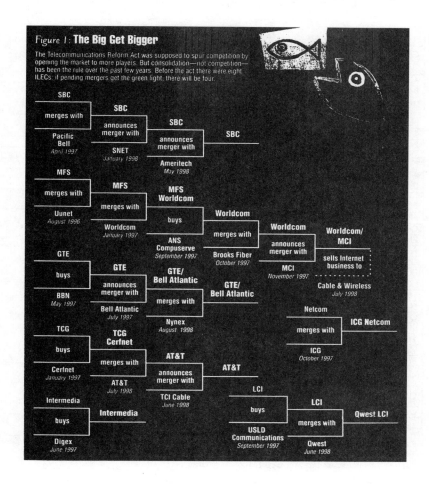

form DS-3 pipes, carrying 45 Mbps. Digital access cross-connect switches (DACS) switch T-1 traffic to and from multiple CO locations, providing flexibility and, to some degree, rerouting (i.e., it takes time because a human is required to reprogram a traditional DACS). CO-to-CO links consist of one or more DS-3s. Originally, the DS-3s are conditioned bundles of copper wire. These connections are now over fiber. The COs are linked together into redundant, meshed networks thereby creating high availability in the core of the network.

In the 1980s and early 1990s, the need for more bandwidth, higher reliability and faster recovery from physical line cuts brought massive investment from telecommunications vendors in fiber optics and SONET equipment. SONET allows multiple DS-3s to be aggregated onto several topologies of fiber optic connections, including the popular ring topology. Multiple access lines into multiple CO physical locations via aerial cables or buried cables created a fault-tolerant telecommunications network outside of the consumer's facility. Devices that adapt local customer premise equipment (CPE) to the DS0 and T-1 signaling and frame input/output characteristics facilitated the move from voice to data.

Table 17–2
Current Providers of Telecommunications Services
Source: "Alternate Service Providers," *Data Communications* (September 1998, 52 and 54).

Incumbent Local Exchange Carriers		
Company	States in Territory	Number of Fiber Sheath Miles
Ameritech (Hoffman Estates, Illinois)	5	326,000
Bell Atlantic Corp. (Philadelphia, PA)	13 (includes NYNEX)	739,000 (does not include NYNEX)
Bellsouth Corp. (Atlanta, GA)	9	602,000
GTE Corp. (Irving, TX)	27	492,000
Pacific Bell (San Francisco, CA)	1	146,000
SBC Communications Inc. (San Antonio, TX)	5	369,000
US West Co. (Denver, CO)	14	396,000

Inter-Exchange Carriers	
Company	Fiber Route Miles
AT&T (Basking Ridge, NJ)	38,704
Consolidated	621
Electric Lightwave	1,054
Frontier (RCI)	3,341
GST Telecom	769
IXC	4,647
LCI (San Antonio, TX)	2,743
MCI (Washington, D.C.)	25,234
Norlight (was MRC)	1,100
Qwest	4,358
Sprint	23,574
TCG	NA
Valley Net	NA
WorldCom (Omaha, NE)	19,619

Competitive Local Exchange Carriers	
Company	Coverage
Covad Communications Co. (Santa Clara, CA)	San Francisco Bay area, CA
Cox Communications (Atlanta, GA)	Chesapeake Bay area, MD; New Orleans, LA; Norfolk, VA; Oklahoma City, OK
Electric Lightwave, Inc. (Vancouver, WA)	Boise, ID; Phoenix, AZ; Portland, OR; Sacramento, CA; Salt Lake City, UT; Seattle, WA
E.spire Communications Inc. (Annapolis, MD)	37 cities
Focal Communications Corp. (Chicago, IL)	Chicago, IL; New York, NY
Harvardnet (Boston, MA)	Boston area, MA; Portland, ME
ICG Communications Inc. (Englewood, CO)	Alabama, California, Colorado, Kentucky, North Carolina, Tennessee
Intermedia Communications Inc. (Tampa, FL)	Local service in 20 states; long distance in 50 states
Nextlink Communications Inc. (Bellevue, WA)	California, Georgia, Illinois, Nevada, New Jersey, New York, Ohio, Pennsylvania, Tennessee, Utah, Washington
Northpoint Communications Inc. (San Francisco, CA)	Boston, MA; Los Angeles, CA; San Francisco Bay area, CA
Rhythms Netconnections Inc. (Englewood, CO)	San Diego, CA; San Francisco Bay area, CA
TCG Cerfnet (San Diego, CA) (now AT&T)	60 U.S. cities
Teligent Inc. (Vienna, VA)	28 states and Washington, D.C.
Vitts Networks Inc. (Manchester, NH)	Boston, MA; Connecticut; New Hampshire; New York

The U.S. cable television system has developed a similar, yet simpler physical infrastructure. Local subscribers are served by set-top boxes via copper coaxial cable or fiber optic cable drops, which are fed by a fiber optic trunk from a cable television head end where programming originates or is obtained via satellite or other high-speed source. More recently, as digital cable and video-on-demand (movies at home through cable) became a service offering, service access gateways (large PCs or workstations) were added to the cable head end and connected to a programming source via a wide area network (WAN). Figure 17–4 shows a typical cable television network.

Figure 17–3. The underlying legacy telecommunications network infrastructure.

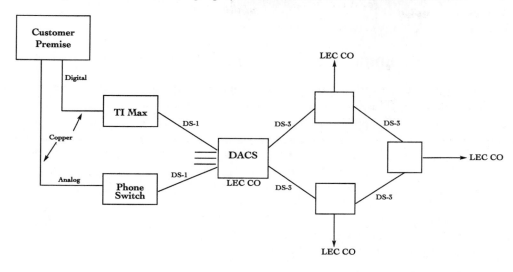

Figure 17–4. The underlying legacy analog cable TV network infrastructure.

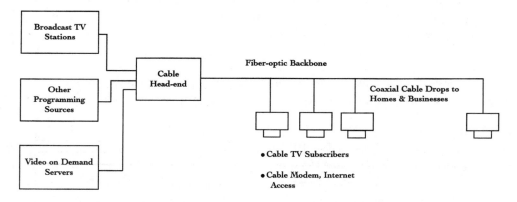

By some estimates, the installed base of public circuits serving business and residential users just described numbers in the millions. Data Communications magazine estimates there are 13.3 million fiber lines and 123 million copper lines in North America today (Cray and Makris 1998a). In addition, transportation entities, whether deploying or leasing the same technology, have spent hundreds of millions of dollars in meeting their ITS telecommunications.

These network foundations have served multimedia-networking needs well for the better part of a decade, but with a severe limitation—they are physically separate networks! The fact that they are isolated creates a number of less than desirable circumstances for network users. Although there are many ways to work around these limitations, the underlying digital, synchronous infrastructure may still be inefficient for applications that integrate voice and data with video. Adding a digital data application to a legacy analog network can also require the addition of expensive, leading-edge equipment and software; and new ways of controlling and managing the network and its users. At the current time, both networks are evolving and converging. Carriers and technology vendors are also making massive investments in new fiber optic infrastructure, to include Dense Wave Division Multiplexing (DWDM), ATM and DSL technologies. Because no other technologies appear imminent at this time, much attention is being paid to these technologies as the cure for many future telecommunications networking solutions, including ITS.

An overview of telecommunications technologies for ITS

Many excellent texts provide in-depth information about telecommunications technologies and fundamentals of networking technology. This section briefly introduces some of the communications techniques and technologies used to support ITS applications for local area networks (LANs) used to network traffic management computers, as well as the networks needed to connect centers to other centers or to ITS devices in the field.

Plain old telephone service

Plain old telephone service (POTS) is the telephone service currently used by most households for voice and sometimes data communication. The service is analog, switched (not dedicated), usually low speed, and inexpensive. POTS is transported via unconditioned copper-wire pairs.

Digital data service

Data rates range from 2,400 bps through 64 Kbps, and T1 rates at 1.54 Mbps to DS3 rates at 45 Mbps. T1, DS3 (T3) and digital data services (DDSs) are considered dedicated private line services where the links are permanent and open pipes. Most DDS services are provisioned via conditioned copper twisted pair wires with higher speed service optionally provisioned over fiber optic media.

Multiplexing

Multiplexers accept lower-speed voice or data signals from user applications and combine them into one high-speed stream for transmission. At the receiving end, the multiplexer demultiplexes these signals.

Time division multiplexing

Time division multiplexing was developed in 1955 to replace frequency division multiplexing (FDM) in the public networks to eliminate noise problems and increase the quality of the public networks. It uses digital time separation rather than frequency. A dedicated time slot is allocated to each device connected to the low-speed side of the multiplexer. Time division multiplexing uses one common high-speed bit stream; its aggregate bit rate is limited only by the speed of the attached device. Both copper and fiber optic cabling can be used as media. Each input device is assigned its own time slot or channel into which data or digitized voice is placed for transport over the link (for example, a T1 line). The link carries the channels from the transmitting multiplexer to the receiving multiplexer where they are separated out (or demulitplexed) and sent on to assigned output devices. If an input device has nothing to send, the assigned channel goes unused. Time division multiplexing is best suited for data rates above 19.2 Kbps, and it can accommodate larger numbers of subchannels than FDM. It can also support a digital high-speed link used primarily for transmitting large volumes of data across a WAN. Figure 17–5 shows the concept of time division multiplexing.

Frequency division multiplexing

Frequency division multiplexing (FDM) was the original technology developed for the public networks. FDMs require an analog channel for transmission but can take as input either analog or digital sources. Each FDM input channel is allocated a spectrum of the high-speed link that is equal to the capacity of the end device. For example, in cable television separate frequencies for the base video, color and audio are modulated onto separate frequencies. The composite signal fits into 6 MHz bandwidth. FDMs do not require

Figure 17–5. Time division multiplexing.
Source: Ben Gianni.

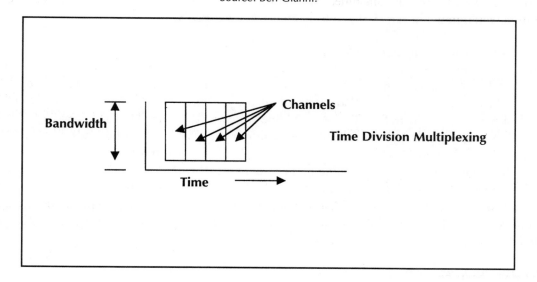

modems because they generally perform modulation and demodulation themselves. The earliest FDM multi-plexers used frequency division to allocate resource capacity. One frequency identifies a mark and a second frequency identifies a space. FDMs require the use of an analog channel. Analog transmission facilities have been replaced by digital facilities by major service providers. FDMs can be employed when bandwidth on the transmission medium exceeds what is to be transmitted. Any number of input signals can be transmitted simultaneously if modulated onto and around different carrier frequencies and separated by a guard band. This is done to avoid problems inherent to FDM from cross-talk and intermodulation noise. FDM is typi-cally used to send signals in one direction only. Familiar examples of its applications are cable television and its 6-MHz bandwidth for each channel and broadcast television. Coaxial cable is an often-used media for FDM. Wavelength-division multiplexing (WDM) on optical fiber is the same as FDM over coaxial cable. Commercial implementations of wideband WDM uses two wavelengths per fiber strand in the 1300 and 1550 nanometer wavelengths. Research of narrowband WDM has increased the number of carrier wave-lengths beyond two as WDM is being deployed in many SONET networks at this time.

SONET

SONET is expected to provide much of the transport infrastructure for very large voice and data networks for the next three to four decades, in much the same way that T1 and its extension, T3, have provided the transmission infrastructure of the past two decades.

SONET is an industry standard for high-speed transmission over optical fiber. SONET networks offer great amounts of bandwidth, integral fault recovery and network management, and multivendor equipment inter-operability. It is designed to be as independent as possible of the specific services and applications it is intended to support.

The base signal rate of SONET is the synchronous transport signal level 1 (STS-1), which provides a transmission rate of 51.84 Mbps. The optical equivalent of STS-1 is called optical carrier level 1 (OC-1). These signals can be multiplexed hierarchically to form higher rate signals.

SONET connectivity and services

SONET provides multiple ways to recover from network failures, including automatic protection switching, bi-directional line switching, unidirectional path switching, and universal connectivity. Automatic protection switching is the capability of a transmission system to detect a failure on a working facility and switch to a standby facility to recover the traffic. Bi-directional line switching uses two fiber pairs between each recoverable node to support a signal transmitted across one pair of fibers. When a fiber link fails, the node preceding the break loops the signal back toward the originating node, where it travels different fiber pairs back to its destination. Unidirectional path switching uses one fiber pair between each recoverable node to support a signal transmitted on two different paths around the ring. At the receiving end, the network decides and uses the best one. When a fiber link fails, the destination switches to the alternate receive path. Of course, proper physical placement and alignment of fibers that consider geographic separation of pairs is critical to this capability.

SONET transmission speed

The SONET transmission speed standard ranges from 51.84 Mbps to 2.488 Gbps. Table 17–3 shows the standard SONET transmission rates. The basic building blocks used in the SONET signaling hierarchy are STS-1/OC-1 (51.84 Mbps) groups that are multiplexed to higher-rate signals. The OC-1 frame (used to construct all larger frames) has a 9 x 90-byte format that allows for efficient packing of data rates in a payload of 783 bytes. Among other types of information, SONET overhead contains framing information, error monitoring channels and format identification information. The SONET frame format supports such large payloads along with overhead channels to allow for complex self-diagnostics and fault analysis to be performed in real-time.

Table 17–3
SONET Rates

STS Level	OC Level	Line Rate (bps)
STS-1	OC-1	51.84 M
STS-3	OC-3	155.520 M
	OC-9	466.560 M
	OC-12	622.080 M
	OC-18	933.120 M
	OC-24	1.244 G
	OC-36	1.866 G
	OC-48	2.488 G
	OC-192	9.952 G
	OC-256	13.271 G

SONET protocol layers

The SONET transmission protocol consists of four layers:

1. *Photonic layer*—the electrical and optical physical interface for the transport of information bits across the physical medium. This layer converts the synchronous transport signal (STS-N) electrical signals into optical carrier (OC-N) optical signals and performs functions associated with the bit rate, optical pulse shape, power and wavelength without the use of overhead.

2. *Section layer*—deals with the transport of the STS-N frame across the optical cable similar to that of the data link layer (layer 2) in bit-oriented protocols. This layer establishes frame synchronicity and the maintenance signal. Functions performed in the section layer include framing, scrambling, error monitoring and order wire communications.

3. *Line layer*—provides the synchronization, multiplexing and automatic protection switching (APS) for the path layer. It is primarily concerned with the reliable transport of the path layer payload (i.e., voice, data, video) and overhead, and allows (via APS) automatic switching to another circuit if the quality of the primary circuit drops below a specified threshold.

4. *Path layer*—maps services (e.g., ATM) into the SONET payload format. This layer provides end-to-end communications, signal labeling, path maintenance and control, and it is accessible only by equipment that terminates this layer.

SONET virtual tributaries

SONET framing can accommodate both synchronous and asynchronous signal formats where the payload can be subdivided into smaller virtual tributaries (VTs) to transport signals using less than DS3 capacity. Because VTs can be placed anywhere on higher-speed SONET payloads, they provide effective transport for existing North American and international formats. Each VT has its own overhead bits and functions within the STS-1 or OC-1 signal. SONET defines VT mappings for the most common North American tributary (DS1 at 1.544 Mbps). The SONET standard also provides for tributaries that have not yet been defined: 10 Mbps for Ethernet and 16 Mbps for token-ring LANs. Table 17–4 lists standard SONET VT support options.

Table 17–4
VT Support Standards

VT Level	Line Rate (bps)	Standard
VT1.5	1.728 M	DS1
VT-2	2.304 M	E1
VT3	3.456 M	DS1C
VT-6	6.912 M	DS2
VT6-N	N x 6.9 M	future
Async DS3	44.736 M	DS3

SONET network components

SONET-compliant network components or elements include add-drop multiplexers (ADMs), Broadband Digital Cross-Connect (BDCS), Wideband Digital Cross-Connect (WDCC), Digital Loop Carrier (DLC), regenerators, and SONET CPE. The ADM provides interfaces between the network signals and SONET signals. The BDCS interfaces SONET signals with DS3s. The WDCS is a digital cross-connect that terminates SONET and DS3 signals, and provides the basic functionality of VT and/or DS1-level cross-connections. The DLC is similar to the DS1 digital loop carrier and can accept and distribute SONET optical-level signals. The regenerator is similar to a data repeater and drives transmitter with the output from a receiver, lengthening transmission distances. SONET CPE is installed on the customer site or premise and provides an interface to carrier-provided SONET services.

Integrated services digital network

Integrated services digital network (ISDN) allows a digital, dial-up connection to be made over existing copper, twisted-pair wires from a limited distance. A major benefit of dial-up ISDN is that customers only pay for what is used to establish remote connections. ISDN can meet or exceed dedicated line speeds (e.g., T1). Most equipment vendors currently support data transfer at 56/64 Kbps. A circuit-switched or digital dial-up network enables links to form on demand for the duration of a dial-up session. The links act as open pipes. Within a region of service, the cloud includes the end points. A link can be established within seconds. Redundant paths exist between the end points.

ISDN is offered by most RBOCs in two basic forms: ISDN basic rate interface (BRI) and ISDN primary rate interface (PRI). ISDN BRI is a digital dial-up service that provides two 64-Kbps bearers, or B channels, and one 16-Kbps D channel used for signaling. The B channels can be configured to handle voice or data, usually in data-intensive applications. A 128-Kbps data stream is split between two B channels and reassembled at the other end using inverse multiplexers. One of the B channels may also be used for voice, while the other is used for data. PRI provides twenty-three 64-Kbps B channels and one 64-Kbps channel for signaling. The following equipment is required when ISDN service is used:

- NT1 (network termination and supply module)
- ISDN terminal adapter (when used directly from an end computer)
- ISDN telephones
- ISDN bridges or routers (when shared via a LAN)

The NT1 converts the two wire cables from the telephone company central office (RJ-11 phone jack) to four wire cables used by other ISDN equipment. The NT1 provides required echo canceling and multiplexing. The four-wire side of the NT1 is connected to an ISDN terminal adapter.

The ISDN terminal adapter converts the ISDN signal to one suitable for a serial line, an ISDN phone, an ISDN bridge or router, or an ISDN-ready workstation. More expensive terminal adapters provide automatic connect and disconnect in response to service requests and inactivity and dialing of multiple numbers simultaneously for conference calls. Bridges and routers can also be used to support an ISDN network. An ISDN interface (typically a serial interface for the router) is provided on one side, and an Ethernet or other network protocol interface is located on the other side. Many of the bridges and routers provide a means of automatically connecting or disconnecting from the service (the same features found on the more expensive terminal adapters). These products can also work with third-party inverse multiplexers that can group two B channels (64 Kbps) together to create a single 124-Kbps channel.

Frame relay

Frame relay service (FRS) is a data communications service that provides connectivity between widely distributed locations. This connectivity is provided via permanent virtual channel (PVC) connections implemented across facilities using a switch dedicated to high-speed data services. FRS is used for high-speed, inter-premise connections to multiple locations within a LATA, via a subscriber network access line (NAL).

A NAL is a dedicated digital line that uses the FRS user network interface (UNI) standards. This line provides the connection from a customer's site to the telephone company hub or service-wiring center. The effective data rate of this line is 56/64 Kbps for narrow-band access and 1.538 Mbps for wide-band access (T1). Each NAL is assigned at least one PVC, but the customer can subscribe to multiple PVCs. Multiple PVCs are implemented using address mapping, which enables the customer to have multiple virtual connections to various locations. A PVC is an FRS virtual connection between two customer locations. The call is set up by a service order rather than by dial-up signaling. FRS consists of the following:

- One FRS subscriber NAL from any site to the central office equipped with a FRS switch
- One FRS PVC connection assigned to the FRS NAL
- Formation of the initial address map
- Unlimited usage

The service transports FRS data units within a LATA, from one subscriber NAL to one or more different subscriber NAL(s). Each FRS data unit is delivered unchanged from the source to the destination. Some optional features available with the service include the following:

- *Additional PVCs for each subscriber NAL*—provides the assignment of additional PVCs to the Subscriber NAL. The Telephone Company may limit the number of additional PVCs to be assigned.
- *Group address*—allows customers to send a single data unit to several intended recipients. The recipients are identified by the assignment of a group PVC used as the destination for the Frame Relay unit.
- *Committed information rate (CIR)*—the CIR provides a mechanism for sites to prioritize critical data on a PVC basis across a selected NAL. A customer would have to elect to reserve bandwidth for high-priority applications on a per PVC basis. The CIR is limited by the bandwidth of the subscriber NAL. This feature allows all users to maintain the capability to transfer data within their CIR without potential packet data discard due to network congestion.

The customer is responsible for providing any required routers, data service units, channel service units and the cable connection from the LAN to the FRS interface. FRS can be combined with ISDN supplemental services and ISDN back-up services.

Asynchronous transfer mode

Asynchronous transfer mode is a standards-based technology that can operate at speeds ranging from T1 to 622 Mbps and beyond (Computer Sciences Corporation 1994). ATM is most often implemented in a WAN. ATM allows multiservice network architectures to be created that can transport a wide range of information (e.g., voice, video, data) over a local network or one covering an entire state. This capability makes the technology unique.

ATM was created to handle high-speed, carrier-to-carrier switching. Packet switching offers greater bandwidth efficiency, but its high delay characteristics make it suboptimal for voice and video use. Circuit-switching as defined in the legacy voice network, with its very low delay, is appropriate for voice; but it cannot provide sufficient bandwidth for data cost-effectively. Cell switching, which is used in ATM, is better suited than packet switching for real-time communications such as voice and video.

The ATM protocol uses a fixed-length, 53-byte cell (a 5-byte header followed by 48 bytes of data). The cell contains packet and address information. The small cell size and the fixed cell length allow most switching tasks to occur in hardware. Cells that are switched quickly create less delay. This makes cell switching better than packet switching for voice and video. The ATM switch reduces all digital traffic—voice, video, data, fax or graphics—into cells. The ATM switch brings together a fixed length cell that provides a common ground for data packet transmission and time division multiplexing.

Network data is bursty in nature, creating bandwidth requirements that can differ greatly over time. Time division multiplexing can dedicate channels of bandwidth to data transmission and therefore do not provide bandwidth efficiently. ATM cells support both methods by allocating bandwidth only when traffic is sent; or by providing time slots for continuous, fixed-bandwidth traffic. ATM provides the creation of logical networks instead of networks based on geographic proximity; guaranteed full bandwidth between end nodes; and the ability to move voice, data, graphics and video at Gigabit speeds.

ATM cell formats

ATM uses cell relay to support different traffic types such as voice, video and data. An ATM customer's traffic that is usually made up of variable-length units is segmented into small, fixed-length units called cells after it passes the CPE. The cells are fixed at 53 octets with a 5-octet header (overhead) and 48-octet payload. Unlike many systems today, cell relay uses no shared medium. Instead, cell relay uses point-to-point links between end nodes and a high-speed switching system. The use of cell technology is growing rapidly, partially because it uses fixed-length cells. Fixed-length cells offer more predictable performance in the network than variable-length frames. Transmission delay and queuing delay are also more predictable. Fixed-length buffers used with cell relay technology are easier to manage than buffer allocation for variable-length frames.

ATM quality of service

Quality of service (QOS) guarantees are used with ATM networks to define the loss, delay and variation in delay associated with the transmission of data, voice, or video traffic. Table 17–5 shows the classes and characteristics of ATM services. The table includes a description of the traffic type and the associated guarantees in QOS.

The ATM topology is a star-wired, point-to-point configuration. Nothing precludes this topology from being a multipoint or shared medium arrangement. ATM supports multimedia services with the switching of voice, video and data traffic through the same switch fabric. The interconnection of LANs is also supported through convergence and segmentation reassembly operations for connectionless data transfer. Convergence services are provided for fixed-bit rate video, variable-bit rate video and voice operations.

Table 17–5
Classes and Characteristics of ATM Services
Source: Computer Sciences Corp., 1994.

Service	Description	Guarantees			
		Loss	Delay	Feed-back	Band-width
Continuous bit rate—constant bit rate pipe for voice, circuit emulation, or continuous bit rate video.	Peak cell rate, contracted cell delay variation (CCDV)	Yes	Yes	Yes	No
Variable bit rate—real-time—used for the transport of variable rate information, supports voice using silence removal, provides tight bounds on delay, uses compressed packet video.	Peak cell rate, CCDV, sustained cell rate, burst tolerance	Yes	Yes	Yes	No
Variable Bit Rate—nonreal-time—used for transaction processing applications.	Peak cell rate, CCDV, sustained cell rate, burst tolerance	Yes	Yes	Yes	No
Unspecified bit rate—uses best effort deliveries with no QOS guarantees.	Unspecified	No	No	No	No
Available bit rate—fair and rapid access to spare network capacity	Peak cell rate, CCDV, sustained cell rate	Yes	No	Yes	Yes

ATM layers

PHYSICAL LAYER

The physical layer defines transport systems for SONET, T3, optical fiber and twisted pair. SONET is the recommended infrastructure for implementing public ATM networks. SONET facilities and availability are limited, however, so the UNI recommends the use of DS3 and a physical layer definition similar to fiber distributed data interface to provide a 100 Mbps private ATM network interface. OC-3 rates over single and multimode fiber along with low-speed (T1) is quickly becoming the defacto implementation for ATM.

The SONET physical layer functions are further subdivided into the physical medium dependent (PMD) sublayer and transmission convergence (TC) sublayer. The PMD is the physical medium and transmission characteristics of the SONET OC-3 (155.52 Mbps), using single-mode fiber or multimode fiber. As bandwidth needs grow, additional SONET physical medium specifications are added to the PMD. The TC sublayer describes attributes that are independent of the physical medium. The TC sublayer generates and processes the overhead of the SONET frame structure and specific broadband ISDN integrated services digital network functions, such as error checking a cell header, and inserting cell delineation information in the STS-3C frame.

Transporting ATM cells over existing DS3 facilities requires using a physical layer convergence protocol (PLCP), a subset of the PLCP defined for Institute of Electrical and Electronics Engineers (IEEE) 802.6, and Bellcore TR-TSV-000773. ATM cells are mapped into a DS3 PLCP that is in turn mapped into the payload of a DS3 frame. DS3 PLCP mapping can begin anywhere in the DS3 frame. Twelve ATM frames, each preceded by four octets of overhead, are mapped into the DS3 PLCP frame. The overhead provides alignment and error control. The ATM cell header contains the routing and control information used to transfer the information field through an ATM network as well as control information intended for the peer.

ATM LAYER

The ATM layer is primarily used for connection identifiers. The 48-octet information field contains one ATM adaption layer (AAL) service data unit. The cell header contains the generic flow control (GFC), routing field, payload type (PT), cell loss priority (CLP), and header error check (HEC) fields. The GFC is a 4-bit field that provides standardized local functions such as quality-of-service and flow control. The routing field has a virtual path identifier (VPI)/virtual channel identifier (VCI) that is used to route the cell through the network. The total number of bits available for VPI and VCI subfields is negotiated prior to subscribing to the network. The PT is a 3-bit field used to show whether the cell contains user, connection management, or network congestion notification information. The CLP field is 1 bit. When set to 1, the field may be discarded in the event of network congestion. The HEC is an 8-bit field used by the physical layer for finding and correcting errors in the cell header. The header validates the VPIs and VCIs and prevents cells from going to the wrong UNI. Cells received with header errors are discarded. Higher-layer protocols handle initiating lost cell recovery tasks.

ATM AAL

The ATM AAL is located between the ATM layer and the higher-layer protocols. The AAL services are completely dependent on the user. AAL is further subdivided into two sublayers: the segmentation and reassembly (SAR) sublayer and the convergence sublayer (CS). Several emerging technologies, such as IEEE 802.6 Metropolitan Area Network and switched multimegabit data service (discussed later in this book), use convergence and SAR functions similar to ATM. While each technology uses this technique in a slightly different way, both create a 53-octet cell. The CS provides services to higher layers across the AAL service access point. CS fields detect the loss of data and perform other functions as needed by the higher-layer protocol. The convergence function accepts user traffic and appends a header and trailer to the information unit. The length of the header and trailer varies.

ATM uses convergence functions for connection-oriented and connectionless variable bit rate (VBR) applications. Isochronous services, such as voice, video and high-fidelity audio are also supported. The convergence functions are used for designated constant bit rate (CBR) services. SAR are provided for data services that use protocol data units that differ from an ATM cell. Convergence services give the ATM layer standardized interfaces. This layer then relays, routes and multiplexes the traffic through an ATM network.

The AAL can support different types of applications where timing is required between source and destination, bit rates are variable or constant and the session is connection-oriented or has connectionless service requirements. VBR applications use services that are data delimiting, provide bit error detection and correction, and provide cell loss detection. CBR applications use source clock recovery and provide detection and replacement of lost cells.

To minimize the number of AAL protocols, four classes of service are defined to support either VBR or CBR applications. Class A uses a CBR connection-oriented mode, where the timing between the source and destination are required. Class A service is used for circuit emulation or CBR video. Class B is a VBR service using a connection-oriented mode, where the timing between the source and destination are required. Class B service is used for VBR video and audio. Class C is a VBR service using a connectionless mode, where the timing between the source and destination are not required. Class C service is used for connection-oriented data transfer. Class D is also a VBR service using a connectionless mode, where timing between the source and destination are not needed. Class D service is used for connectionless data transfer (e.g., LANs).

ATM PVCs

ATM is a connection-oriented service. It requires the establishment of a connection between an origin and destination before data can be transferred. PVCs are the connections between logical or physical communications interfaces that are established by network management software or provisioning actions. Once made, they are left to continue indefinitely; hence, the term permanent (i.e., permanent virtual circuits). The physical connection is by wire or fiber (or wireless) and can take from minutes to days to establish depending on the nature of the underlying infrastructure. They are common to ATM as well as X.25 (a standard for public, packet data switched networks) and FRS.

Connections are usually pre-mapped through the network using basic procedures for PVC call setup. Links from end points are directed into a network made up of switches represented here by the cloud. The arrows are open pipes. Connections among end points are PVCs. Configuring new PVCs requires no changes in equipment. Redundancy can exist between end points.

Switched virtual circuits

Like PVCs, switched virtual circuits (SVCs) are connections established between interfaces to transfer data. If control and signaling software or operator action is used to bring the connection up and down dynamically, it is known as a virtual circuit. SVCs are used in ATM, ISDN, X.25 and FRS. The sequence of steps in establishing and tearing down an SVC is similar to how people make a simple phone call. The advantages are the same as well, specifically allowing fixed resources to be shared in time by many users or devices. It is especially appropriate for data and video that is used intermittently across the network from many different sources and destinations.

Currently the Maryland State Highway Administration is deploying a statewide ATM network in support of its advanced transportation management system and is using the technology directly to provide a sophisticated closed circuit television camera management system. A key reason why ATM technology was chosen for this function was that the video, the computer, and LAN data needed to manage and control the cameras and the organization's administrative data could operate over a single telecommunications network, thus avoiding costs of additional, dedicated telecommunications networks.

DSL

The family of DSL technologies allows high-speed multimedia communications over existing copper twisted pair infrastructure. This makes the technology attractive for video because multimegabit throughput is possible at voice line costs. There are various gradations of performance that depend on the gauge and condition of the copper wires, length of the wires and equipment at either end. These include asymmetrical digital subscriber line (ADSL), high data rate digital subscriber line, single line digital subscriber line and very high data rate digital subscriber line.

ADSL, earliest in its commercial deployment, is perhaps the most promising. ADSL operates from 1.544 to 8 Mbps for downstream transmissions and up to 800 Kbps for upstream transmission. Hence the name ADSL and its attractiveness for traffic video applications. ADSL modems are required on either end of the copper wires, and they are typically obtained from the LEC as a service at the central office. ADSL can operate up to 18,000 feet between modems on common wire gauges used in the POTS network. Early use has brought attention to the state of the existing local loop copper infrastructure where the existence of bridge taps and other factors can work to reduce the actual distance and performance tradeoffs available for ADSL. Notwithstanding, it has proven successful for video and web applications at a much lower cost than traditional video solutions. Ultimate usefulness of DSL technologies will depend to a great extent on the carriers' willingness to deploy it.

Ethernet, 10-baseT, switched ethernet, fast ethernet and gigabit ethernet

Ethernet network technologies and equipment have provided network managers with cost-effective resources in-building LANs for the last two decades. First implemented as a shared, 10 Mbps LAN over thicknet cabling; improved in packaging to centralize electronics within wiring closets (10Base-T Hubs); enhanced to mitigate growing congestion on these LANs by allocating 10 Mbps to each station (switched ethernet); and later reengineered to provide 100 Mbps and then 1 Gbps to keep its standard computer access technology alive for multimedia applications, no set of technologies have proven more successful and useful than these.

Wireless technologies

Analog cellular

Cellular telephony is based on a growing system of geographic cells that provide transmission and reception via a set of radio frequency channels between mobile units and tower infrastructure. Currently, the FCC has allocated 832 full-duplex channels to each market. Each market has two licenses allowing for 416 channels per operator. The diameter of an individual cell can be as large as 20 miles. The cells are interconnected (i.e., roaming) to each other, to the local exchange provider in the area and to the interexchange provider. The strength of the cellular system is its flexibility to add an unlimited number of users by reusing frequencies in adjacent cells and changing cell size dynamically (CRC Press 1999).

Cellular digital packet data

Cellular digital packet data (CDPD) provides digital transport over the cellular channels. The information to be transmitted is decomposed into packets and transported during voice silence periods (up to 30 percent of a voice call or more). Channel-hopping techniques allow several channels to be used for a digital data transmission. The advantages of CDPD include quick call setup time, 9.6 kbps throughput, forward error-correcting protocols, availability, and use of the underlying cellular technology infrastructure.

Broadband PCS

Broadband PCS is broadly defined by the FCC as "radio communications that encompass mobile and ancillary fixed communication services that provide services to individuals and businesses and can be integrated with a variety of competing networks." Broadband PCS could also be used in the development of more advanced wireless phone services capable of pinpointing the subscriber's location. Broadband PCS will most likely be used to provide a variety of mobile services including an entire family of new communications devices using very small, lightweight, multifunction portable phones, portable facsimile, and other imaging devices; new types of multifunction cordless phones; and advanced devices with two-way data capabilities. Broadband PCS systems will be able to communicate with other telephone networks as well as with personal digital assistants, allowing subscribers to send and receive data and video messages without connection to a wire.

Broadband PCS is in the 2 GHz band of the electromagnetic spectrum, from 1850 to 1990 MHz. The spectrum allocated for Broadband PCS totals 140 MHz; 20 MHz in that block is reserved for unlicensed applications that could include both data and voice services (see <www.fcc.gov> for more information).

Dedicated short-range communications

Dedicated short-range communication (DSRC) has generated much debate and confusion within the ITS community. The technology is intended to meet the requirements for many of the applications defined by the national ITS architecture. DSRC uses nonvoice radio techniques and frequencies to transfer data over short distances between fixed roadside assets and mobile radio units, between mobile units and between portable and mobile units. DSRC systems also transmit status and instructional messages related to the units involved. DSRC equipment is composed of two principal components: (1) a beacon or roadside unit and (2) a transponder or on-board unit. The beacon controls the protocol, schedules the activation of the transponder, reads from or writes to the transponder and assures message delivery and validity (FCC Part 90).

Currently two standards development organizations, the IEEE and the American Society of Testing and Materials (ASTM) are involved the creation of standards for the manufacture and use of DSRC systems. The objective is to foster interoperability between different manufacturer's systems—a state that currently does not exist. The IEEE's activity is geared toward standard message sets, and the ASTM's activities are geared toward defining physical and data link layer standards per the open systems interconnection seven-layer model.

For physical mediums, the draft standards describe the following frequency ranges: 902–904, 909.75–919.75, 919.75–921.75 MHz, of the 902–928 location and monitoring service frequency band allocated by the FCC but unlicensed on an individual basis. Additional bands (2450 MHz or 5.8 GHz) may be allocated on a national basis for ITS DSRC applications. Some contest the safety of using the 5.8 GHz band because of possible interference with, in one case, electrically-sensitive individuals. Others contest use of this band because it may interfere with amateur wideband operators.

For the data link control layer (layer 2), a time division multiple access messaging protocol is defined in which both the downlink and uplink are completely controlled by the roadside beacon equipment. The protocol provides a mechanism to assure reliable completion of each transaction in the communication zone. The application layer (layer 7) defines specific functions and message formats to support ITS and other services. Implicit or preset message formats may be used. Data encryption, data certification and mutual transponder and beacon authentication may be performed. The network layer (layer 3), transport layer (layer 4), session layer (layer 5) and presentation layer (layer 6) are not considered in relationship to current standards because of the short range, short duration nature of the DSRC system (ASTM Subcommittee E17.51).

FM subcarrier

A radio station actually uses only a very small portion of the radio spectrum assigned to it for broadcasting its audible program. Radio-data systems (RDS) use a small portion of the unused spectrum, called a subcarrier, to transmit information. Digital information transmitted on this subcarrier does not interfere with the audible program. The RDS signal has the same range as its host radio station and the same level of reliability. An RDS receiver receives the signal and then decodes it, or translates the digital information to text or audio information, which is then presented to the user. Either fixed or mobile (i.e., portable) receivers, similar to the existing paging network, can be used depending on the broadcasting technique used and how power is used and conserved. Domestic implementations have used the 76 KHz frequencies consistent with the International Telecommunications Union-Radio Communications Sector Recommendation 412 (see <www.info-telecom.com> for more information).

The RDS was developed as a European standard (i.e., ETS 300 751) for the transmission of digital data using subcarrier modulation on broadcast FM radio stations. The system was initially conceived to provide services to broadcasters that would support a new generation of intelligent radio receivers. Included in the capabilities are various traffic alert and traffic congestion information types. Data is transmitted synchronously at 1187.5 bps (the 19 kHz stereo pilot tone divided by 16) as double sideband, suppressed carrier AM, centered at 57 kHz (3 times the 19 kHz pilot tone) in the baseband. On average, 11.4 data groups are transmitted per second with each group consisting of 4 blocks of 16 data bits and 10 error-correcting bits each. Typically, 7 or 8 groups are available each second beyond the basic broadcast services requirement with each group yielding 35 to 37 discretionary bits. This suggests an available throughput of almost 300 bps for other services (see <www.dgps.com> for more information).

RDS has been widely embraced in Europe. Currently, 70 percent of European FM broadcast stations provide RDS services, and almost half of the new cars delivered are equipped with RDS-capable radios. Radio broadcast data standard (RBDS) radios are becoming available in the domestic after-market as well as directly from automobile manufacturers, and there are now reportedly over 50 stations in the United States broadcasting RBDS on their 57 kHz frequency (see <www.dgps.com> for more information).

Microwave

Microwaves are very short waves in the upper range of the radio spectrum used mostly for point-to-point communications systems. Much of the technology was derived from radar developed during World War II. Initially, these systems carried multiplexed speech signals over common carrier and military communications networks; but today they can handle all types of information (e.g., voice, data, facsimiles, video) in either an analog or digital format. Over the years, these systems have matured to the point that they have become major components of the nation's public switched network and essential mechanisms that private organizations use to satisfy internal communications requirements and to monitor their primary infrastructure. As the nation's cellular and personal communications systems grow, point-to-point microwave facilities, serving as backhaul and backbone links, enable these wireless systems to serve the country's less populated areas or rugged terrain on an economical basis.

Early technology limited the operations of these microwaves to radio spectrum in the 1 GHz range; but because of improvements in solid state technology, commercial systems are transmitting in the 40 GHz region. In recognition of these changes, the FCC recently adopted rules allowing the use of spectrum above 40 GHz. Before considering use of microwave, a frequency search by a credited frequency coordinator must be performed. Organizations recognized for this purpose are listed by the FCC (see <www.fcc.gov> for more information).

Satellite communications

The current space-based telecommunications environment is characterized by satellites orbiting the earth at various distances and at different spatial relationships with respect to the earth. Geo-stationary satellites orbit the earth at a constant altitude of 22,300 miles and provide a very wide coverage area. These are known as geostationary orbit satellites. Low earth and middle earth or nongeostationary orbiting (NGSO) satellites orbit the earth at between 500 to 7,000 miles and are arrayed in a constellation of satellites because of smaller coverage areas. The popular GPS uses 24 NGSOs to provide position location services (i.e., three-dimensional positioning, velocity, time) for fixed or vehicle-mounted devices. Each of the satellites transmits on L-band frequencies (1575.42 MHz). There are two types of GPS services defined by accuracy. Standard positioning service (SPS) provides civil users predictable accuracy to 100 meters horizontal and 156 meters vertical. To overcome measurement error in SPS, a differential correction signal can be provided to a GPS receiver known as DGPS. Accuracy can be improved to between 1 and 8 meters in this case. There has been an initiative underway since 1994 to develop a nationwide DGPS service that could be used by transportation entities for ITS and other public safety and transportation functions that is modeled after a Coast Guard service. See the Nationwide DGPS Report (1998) for more information on the background and a cost/benefit analysis for this effort.

To complete a satellite communications network, earth stations and control centers that provide gateways to the terrestrial network and earth–space segment management and operations respectively are needed. Satellite networks typically provide relay services between terrestrial devices and networks for highly mobile or remote devices that cannot be serviced by terrestrial networks or other wireless networks. Recent developments in satellite network systems have made mobile-to-mobile services closer to reality as well as providing advanced protocol services, such as ATM transport via satellite. The Telecommunications Industry Associations has recently formed a Satellite ATM group to study various technical issues involved (IEEE Network 1998).

Telecommunications: A total life cycle methodology

Any methodology used to assist in the development and deployment of telecommunications technology for ITS should begin with an examination of the basic concepts and needs of the ITS program. It should use a system engineering process that: (1) develops ITS telecommunications goals, objectives and requirements; (2) assesses available technologies that can meet the requirements; and (3) provides for technical trade-off studies and produces viable alternatives. A starting assumption for the use of such a methodology is that the ITS functions, programs, or capabilities that require telecommunications exist either by mandate or public policy decision. Further, the methods discussed in the following section assume that the overall benefit to the public for any approach to providing telecommunications for the ITS program is essentially the same.

The systems engineering methodology

The most reliable way to select one or more telecommunications technology solutions is to consider multiple technical alternatives that accomplish similar objectives, and then evaluate each alternative using the same set of technical requirements. Figure 17–6 illustrates a five-step requirements analysis methodology.

Once technical requirements have been generated, they should be validated to insure some degree of consensus by the relevant ITS stakeholders. The requirements should also remain as constant as practical throughout the analysis to avoid developing the wrong solution or solutions for a moving target. This implies that the requirements must be documented and managed over time. And finally, the requirements must eventually provide enough technical detail to allow the telecommunications engineer to develop reasonably detailed technical alternatives.

In order to identify a successful telecommunications technology solution at the lowest possible cost, it is critical to consider multiple alternatives. The appropriate number of alternatives depends on specific issues and constraints for the project; such as size of the project, time, funds, availability of technology and other external stimulus that affect the project. A minimum of three to four alternatives with substantial technical differences will increase the chances of finding the best alternative. Consideration of technology solutions that: (1) make best use of the commercial services infrastructure in place, (2) consider the transportation entity's ability and wherewithal to build telecommunications capacity and (3) provide combinations of the two, will increase the chances of finding a technically acceptable and cost-effective alternative.

Figure 17–6. Requirements analysis methodology.
Source: Ben Gianni.

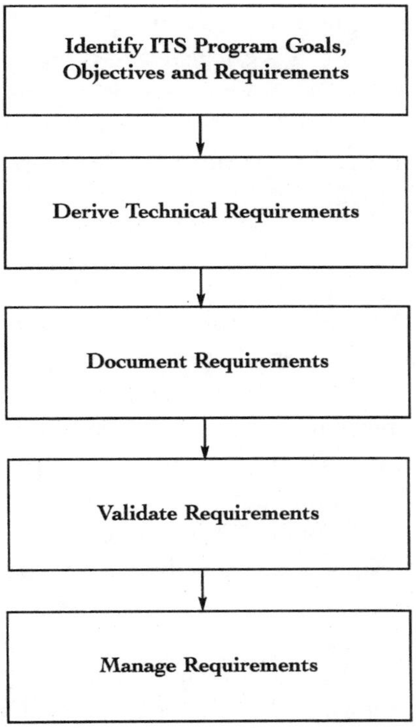

A well-practiced approach to developing telecommunications technology solution alternatives is based on the concept of technical architecture. Each alternative technical architecture should describe: (1) the selection of prevailing technical standards that are considered and how the technology that addresses them are assembled in a telecommunications network; (2) the physical topology of the network that represents how network components are connected to satisfy transfer of information between endpoints; and (3) the technology implementation strategy that is addressed when technology is deployed, how it is controlled, managed, and interfaced to all other ITS program components.

A technical architecture includes enough technical detail to allow life cycle costs to be accurately predicted while still allowing design flexibility in choosing specific products and services for implementation. The level of technical detail included is a compromise between the time spent and the risk of severely under estimating or overestimating costs. For a complex statewide telecommunications network to support ITS functions, devices, and systems, a period of four to six months should be sufficient for developing several technical architecture alternatives.

Formal selection criteria should be used when considering multiple technology solutions. These may include: age of the technology, complexity, schedule risk that will be incurred as a result of implementing each alternative, relative ease of implementation, ease of use and maintenance, security, overall capacity considerations and technical maturity and obsolescence factors as well as other subjective engineering criteria.

Telecommunication costs analysis

A strategy exists for analyzing the costs of obtaining telecommunications capacity to meet the requirements of jurisdictional ITS programs. It is a structured methodology that uses generally accepted engineering methods and follows federal guidelines for performing cost-effectiveness analyses as defined in the "Office of Management and Budget Circular A-94" (revised October 29, 1992). A special focus has been placed on analysis of costs of owning versus leasing telecommunications for the ITS. This strategy is a formal three-step methodology. The steps are: (1) define costs; (2) calculate and compare alternative life cycle costs; and (3) perform sensitivity analyses on life cycle costs. For a substantial treatment of the subject of cost tradeoff methodology, including lease versus buy for ITS telecommunications, refer to publication number ITS Telecommunications: Public or Private? A Cost Tradeoff Methodology Guide (publication number FHWA-JPO-97-0014, HVH-1/5-97 [5M] QE).

Lease versus buy

The consideration of options to lease or buy (i.e., build) ITS telecommunications is an integral part of the cost analysis for a transportation entity. The term lease refers to the payment of monthly recurring costs in exchange for telecommunications services provided by the carrier(s). The term buy refers to the construction of wireless or wire line components, possibly in the right-of-way, to obtain telecommunications capacity. Because total life cycle telecommunications costs can easily be one-half of total program costs, it is important to consider the balance of telecommunications and other critical ITS resources in terms of overall budgetary constraints. Depending on the scale of the project, from corridor to statewide projects and available funding, leasing telecommunications capacity can be a cost-effective enabler and not a barrier to program deployment.

When considering alternative solutions over a multiyear life cycle, the point in time when cumulative costs of two different options converge is known as the break-even point. The associated elapsed time from the beginning of the life cycle is called the payback period. The number of life cycle years to be analyzed should be large enough to determine if a break-even point exists for lease versus buy, but not so large that key assumptions regarding costs trends and the availability of technology are invalidated.

The rate of technological change

Although the lease versus buy issue is an important one, other critical factors can affect ITS communications and thereby the success or failure of an ITS program. In too many cases, telecommunications capacity is obtained that does not meet the organization's operational needs or that exposes the agency to unnecessary risk. These cases usually arise from a lack of understanding or consideration of the risk factor of certain technologies or the technology's maturity. Gauging the rate of technological change and how it may affect the successful integration and use of telecommunications technologies has been one of the most difficult issues facing ITS deployment. Using a technology too early risks higher prices and problems with dependability or reliability, while waiting too late in its life cycle risks early obsolescence and the possibility of higher replacement costs. The key to mitigating these risks, as in mitigating any risk, is seeking the proper information about the technology or service. Asking the pertinent questions of the carrier or vendor, of the carrier's or vendor's users, of the regulators if appropriate and most importantly of their technology suppliers will typically yield this information.

ITS telecommunications and resource sharing

Since the enactment of a Telecommunications Act in 1934, which established the Bell network, perhaps no other action has had more of an effect on ITS telecommunications and also on telecommunications in general than a single, recent act of the Congress of the United States. The Telecommunications Act of 1996 was "An Act to promote competition and reduce regulation in order to secure lower prices and higher quality services for American telecommunications consumers and encourage the rapid deployment of new telecommunications technologies." A major portion of the act was dedicated to language that provided for competition in the local exchange market (hence the emergence of competitive local exchange carriers). A complimentary portion of the act provides an incentive for that competition and language that allows LECs to participate in the long-distance market, but only after ensuring competition in their local domains.

The act also addressed the state government's use of rights-of-way for telecommunications. Table 17–6 shows section 253 of the 1996 Telecommunications Act. In addition to preserving the rights of states to manage their rights-of-way, it also allows states to use of those rights-of-way in agreements with telecommunications companies, commonly known as resource sharing. Shared Resources: Sharing Right-of-Way for Telecommunications, Identification, Review and Analysis of Legal and Institutional Issues, an FHWA report, provides a comprehensive discussion of resource sharing.

A practical perspective on resource sharing

Private telecommunications providers and public governmental transportation entities now have the legislative enabler to partner. This is, however, a long way from safe, productive and operationally viable telecommunications capacity with which to base plans for deploying ITS capabilities. Some practical matters must be dealt with. First, the public entity must develop and use a strategy, perhaps through public policy or solicitation, for dealing with prospective telecommunications partners who have interest in the right-of-way. Once this is in place, the public entity can ensure safety and determine those interested in partnering in a mutually beneficial, nonexclusive and nondiscriminatory way. Second, the public entity must then have available technical expertise in place to evaluate how or in what way the capacity of the private partner can and should be used, so that a win–win scenario is achieved and, in terms of the ITS program, usable capacity is integrated.

Table 17–6
Section 253 of the 1996 Telecommunications Act
Source: <www.fcc.gov>

Sec. 253. Removal of Barriers to Entry

(a) **In General**—No State or local statute or regulation, or other State or local legal requirement, may prohibit or have the effect of prohibiting the ability of any entity to provide any interstate or intrastate telecommunications service.

(b) **State Regulatory Authority**—Nothing in this section shall affect the ability of a State to impose, on a competitively neutral basis and consistent with section 254, requirements necessary to preserve and advance universal service, protect the public safety and welfare, ensure the continued quality of telecommunications services, and safeguard the rights of consumers.

(c) **State and Local Government Authority**—Nothing in this section affects the authority of a State or local government to manage the public rights-of-way or to require fair and reasonable compensation from telecommunications providers, on a competitively neutral and nondiscriminatory basis, for use of public rights-of-way on a nondiscriminatory basis, if the compensation required is publicly disclosed by such government.

Both wireline and wireless capacity can only be viewed as a productive operational asset if it is accessible to the ITS devices, computers, centers, or networks that make up the ITS operational assets. Whether it is a wireless tower or airtime, strands of dark fiber optic cabling or an interface to network bandwidth, planning access to the shared resource is a critical element of a successful partnership. Beyond initial access, several issues are critical. An agreement that covers operating procedures such as access to resources for routine preventative and emergency maintenance should be covered. Documentation of the initial configuration of resources, as well as a plan for ongoing management of the configuration through planned or unplanned changes to it, and plans for eventual upgrade or insertion of new technology for additional capacity must be considered.

References

1998. "Rationale for the Development of a DGPS Policy and Implementation Plan for a Nationwide DGPS Service." *Nationwide DGPS Report* (March 24).

American Society for Testing Materials. 1998. ASTM subcommittee E17.51, standards draft on DSRC.

Computer Sciences Corporation. 1994. *Telecommunications Network Compatibility Study* (May). U.S. Agency for International Development.

Cray, A., and J. Makris. 1998a. "The New Public Network." *Data Communications* (October): 86, figure 1.

Cray, A., and J. Makris. 1998b. "The New Public Network." *Data Communications* (October): 46.
CRC Press. 1999. *Multimedia Networking Handbook 1999.* CRC Press LLC: 20–1 and 20–2.

FCC, Part 90—Private Land Mobile Services of title 47 of the Code of Federal Regulations

Federal Highway Administration. 1998. *Shared Resources: Sharing Right-of-Way for Telecommunications, Identification, Review and Analysis of Legal and Institutional Issues.* Washington, D.C.: FHWA.

Institute of Electronics and Electrical Engineers. 1998. *IEEE Network* (September/October): 61.

Makris, J. 1998a. "Alternate Service Providers." *Data Communications* (September): 52. CMP Media Inc.

Makris, J. 1998b. "Alternate Service Providers." *Data Communications* (September): 52 and 54. CMP Media Inc.

BY Alisoun Moore • Chief Information Officer •
Maryland Department of Transportation

**INFORMATION
TECHNOLOGIES**

The purpose of this chapter is to provide a basic understanding of information system development. The chapter introduces basic information system concepts, describes the benefits and risks of information system development and makes the case for a formal, methodological approach to system development. It also delineates the elements of successful system development and describes several of the most notable methodologies for developing information systems. Finally, the chapter provides a technique for objectively assessing an organization's ability to undertake complex system development projects.

Only a few general references are made to intelligent transportation systems (ITS). ITS is a relatively new phenomenon relating to the building of information systems to better manage transportation systems. ITS represents the integration of two major disciplines: information systems, comprised of hardware, software and communications networks; and transportation systems, comprised of the transportation infrastructure (e.g., roads, bridges, transit), vehicles and devices (e.g., radar detectors, traffic lights). Because specific transportation components relative to ITS are presented elsewhere in this volume, this chapter provides a general overview of information system development practices without specific reference to ITS.

Information systems and our changing world

Information systems have become a ubiquitous part of our lives. We are clearly in the midst of an information revolution that has forever altered the ways we conduct business, communicate with each other at work and at home and engage in commerce. The impact of information systems on business has been particularly dramatic. Once relegated to finance or payroll units, information systems are now integral to nearly all business operations. Modern information systems have made possible automated production lines and just-in-time inventory systems that have been responsible for dramatic productivity gains in recent years.

The need for a formal approach to system development

Given the obvious benefits of information systems, most organizations have embarked on often very expensive programs to automate core business functions, sometimes with disastrous results. System development is a high-risk venture. Studies indicate that as many as 75 percent of all systems can be considered failures. A 1994 study by Standish Group International indicated that 31 percent of all systems are terminated before completion and that 52 percent cost in excess of twice the budgeted amount and take three times longer to complete than scheduled (Bullekey 1996). Why is the failure rate so high? Systems fail for many reasons, often as a result of the technical complexity of the system or the delicate interaction between a system and the organization. Capers Jones traces the failure of system development to the process used to develop the system, the competency of the organization in developing systems, or the lack of management and user support for a new system.

To mitigate failures stemming from the inherent complexity of building a system and to improve the quality of the system produced, developers have learned to use formal, disciplined methods to build systems. A development methodology provides a method or processes for each phase of the project. Organizations select or develop the method they are comfortable with and use it to develop the system.

Table 18–1
A System Development Failure
Sources: R. L. Glass, "Software Runaways: Lessons Learned from Massive Software Project Failures" (Upper Saddle River, N.J.: Prentice Hall PTR, 1998).

State Auditor of California, "The Department of Motor Vehicles of Information Technology Did Not Minimize the State's Financial Risk in the Database Development Project" (August 1994).

Capers Jones separates software systems failure into two categories: those systems that experience relative failure and systems that experience absolute failure. Generally, relative failure is defined as a system that exceeds cost and schedule by 50 percent or more, or a system that was so poorly developed that it failed to provide full client functionality for at least six months after it was delivered. Absolute failure refers to systems that were terminated before completion. The following case is an example of an absolute failure (Glass 1998).

In the late 1980s, the California Department of Motor Vehicles (DMV) undertook a system development effort to migrate its existing driver licensing and vehicle registration systems from an IBM ES/9000 mainframe platform to 24 Tandem Computers Cyclone machines running their proprietary database, the Non-Stop Cyclone SQL relational database. The existing system did not use relational database technology and therefore the DMV had little experience with the new technology. The new system would have to accommodate the state's 31 million drivers and 38 million vehicles and handle transaction demands from more than 40,000 users with peaks of 30 transactions per second and 1 million per day. The existing mainframe system was struggling under the volume having been originally based on 1960s technology. It was time for a new system.

Software problems stalled the development effort. The technology was untried, and it was difficult to write software for the new database because the developers had little experience with it. Once developed, system response times on the transaction load were extremely slow. The system could not handle full production transaction demands.

Project management was poor. The DMV had difficulty in adequately managing the development effort. They did not track the project milestones, expenditures, or software development efforts. They did not fully outline the objectives of the new system. The DMV had not only failed to manage the project properly, but also it had made a bad decision by adopting an untested technology that they and their software developer had little experience with and that could not handle the transaction demand. After much delay and $44 million dollars in expenditures, the project was canceled. As a result, the state had to continue to rely on the already stressed existing system and taxpayers were out $44 million dollars.

Information system concepts

As the case study suggests, the key to successful system development is an understanding of how a proposed information system will interact with the environment (i.e., the organization) within which it will function (i.e., high-volume transaction demand, fast response times). Information systems rely on feedback to adjust to their environment, much like a heating system uses a thermostat to adjust room temperature in response to temperature fluctuations. Information systems and organizations interact in complex and often unpredictable ways. Systems developers must bring to bear not only a thorough grasp of information technology (IT), but they must also acquire an equally comprehensive understanding of the organization whose processes they wish to automate. At this point, it would be useful to further define these key terms and how they are used in the context of system development.

Information systems

A "system" is a set of interrelated components working together for a purpose. An "information system" is a system that processes, stores and distributes information. Typically, information systems accept inputs from its environment, process the inputs and then output new or augmented information back into its environment. "Information" is data (raw facts) that have been processed into a form that is meaningful to humans. While information systems can be, and often are, manual (such as a library card catalogue), this chapter focuses on digital (or computer-based) information systems.

The organization

An "organization" is a collection of people in a defined structure with a defined purpose. An organization takes resources from its environment and turns the resources into an output. For example, a factory converts raw material into finished goods, a bank provides banking services, or a transportation department builds a transportation system to move people and goods. Organizations are organic in that they must react to their environment in order to survive. In other words, an organization's ability to change in response to environment changes is crucial to its survival. The Swiss watchmakers who prided themselves on their superior watches witnessed their commanding market share of watch sales precipitously erode when Japanese and American manufacturers adopted new quartz crystal technology that offered consumers unparalleled accuracy. Transportation departments faced with an unrelenting increase in vehicle trips and congestion must look to other solutions besides traditional and expensive capacity builds. Organizations may be composed of many subsystems and may themselves interact with larger organizational systems.

The interaction between information systems and the organization

Every information system operates in a larger organizational context that includes the policy, legal and economic environment. These include program rules, business processes, management techniques, as well as human and organizational limitations. An information system can be considered a manifestation of the conceptualization of an organizational process. It requires that a particular business need, process, product, or set of processes be automated in some way. In order to function properly, the information system must be integrated as closely as possible with the business purpose, processes, people and policies.

Unfortunately, the components of information systems (i.e., software, hardware, telecommunications networks) require detailed instructions that translate the objectives of the system into discreet instructions and data sets that can be manipulated by computers. Translating into software what an organization wants or needs is extremely difficult because a developer must conceptualize and translate loosely defined and dynamic organizational goals and processes into a software system that is inherently complex and precise. According to Frederick Brooks, author of the classic The Mythical Man-Month (1995):

> The essence of a software entity is a construct of interlocking concepts: datasets, relationships among data items, algorithms and invocations of functions. This essence is abstract, in that the conceptual construct is the same under many different representations. It is nonetheless highly precise and richly detailed.

Brooks also states: "The hardest part of building a software system is deciding precisely what to build. No other part of the work so cripples the resulting system if done wrong. No other part is more difficult to rectify later."

Figure 18–1. Organizational and system environment.

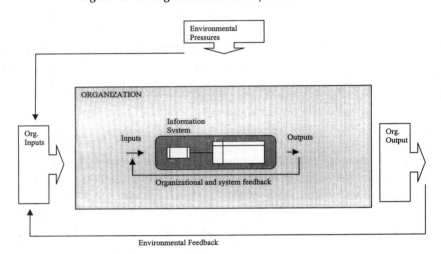

Overview of the system development cycle

Every system project has a life cycle that takes it from a conceptualization stage through development and ultimately implementation. In order to build an effective information system for an organization, developers employ a variety of methods to ensure that quality systems are built to meet an organization's business objectives. A system development methodology can refer to one of two things: either to a defined set of processes used to develop a system, or to a technique or set of techniques that is used to carry out a particular process or set of processes. Because there are many different methodologies to use, developers or project managers must choose the methodology that best meets the needs of the project and one in which they have expertise.

The implementation of a system usually requires that the system be integrated with an organization's existing work process or that the process be re-engineered as a part of the system development effort. Therefore the methodologies employed cannot simply address the technical components of systems design, software coding and systems integration, but must precisely specify what it is the organization is trying to achieve and to identify and manage the effect of the system on the organization's culture, people and business processes. Often system developers must act as change agents because a new system will likely change an organization's business processes or even how it conducts business. Developers must consider methodologies that actively engage the organization throughout the process in order to extract from the organization its requirements and to ensure the organization accepts and integrates the new system within its structure.

There are many different methods and techniques used, but most systems go through a generic life cycle that include the following activities:

- System conceptualization and feasibility analysis
- System requirements and needs analysis, operational conceptualization
- System design
- Construction and implementation
- Maintenance

Feasibility analysis

One of the most important and often overlooked components of any methodology is the feasibility analysis. The organization needs to fully understand why the system is needed and analyze its chances for success. A system should be analyzed for three elements of feasibility: technical, economic and operational (figure 18–2).

The first questions that an organization should ask when considering a system development project are whether technology is appropriate for the application and, if so, is the technology available and mature enough to be used? If the answer to either question suggests that the project is not technically feasible, then it cannot possibly be economically or operationally feasible because it simply will not work.

Assuming the project is technically feasible, it should be analyzed regarding its operational impacts. Will the existing organization accept the system once built? Will it improve an existing process? Will it prove to be too onerous for the users in terms of technical complexity? Do the users want it to begin with? For example, an insurance company developed a system to automate filing of claims only to discover that once implemented it took four times as long to file claims.

The users never used the system and it was therefore operationally infeasible. As with technical feasibility, if a system is operationally infeasible, it cannot be economically feasible because it will ultimately fail and the organization will lose any investment it has made and not reap any economic benefits the system was intended to provide.

The last element is economic. A system is economically feasible if the benefits outweigh the costs. A system is economically infeasible if it adds no business value either presently or in the future. While this may seem like a simple proposition, it is in fact quite complex because the organization must calculate business value in terms other than just monetary benefits. For instance, a new system like an automated teller machine (ATM) service may be costly to purchase for a bank and economic returns negligible because of high maintenance costs. However, the bank must also take into account the potential cost of loss of customers who desire the ATM service if the bank does not offer it. The value of this information system includes such concepts as competitive advantage and organizational survival. Similarly, a transportation department that finds it increasingly difficult to build additional capacity in highly congested areas because of the lack of land, environmental impacts and interest group opposition, may want to consider ITS systems to more efficiently manage their existing transportation networks even though the system development and implementation cost is high. The calculation of the economic feasibility of such a system must factor in the impact of the failure to build it—the organization cannot perform its basic mission in light of a changing environment (i.e., increasing vehicle trips leading to increased congestion). The point of the two examples is to illustrate the complexity of economic value and feasibility decisions in building new systems.

Figure 18–2. Feasibility analysis.
Source: L. Kozar.

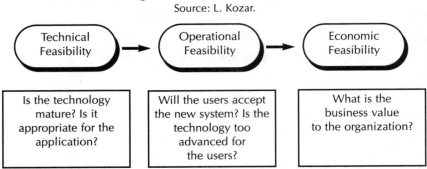

In summary, the benefit of a feasibility analysis is to ask the basic questions of why the system is needed and what problem it is trying to solve, and to analyze whether it has good chance to succeed. Once it has been determined that a system is needed and is feasible, the next phase is to analyze the requirements of the system in enough detail to create technical alternatives to developing and designing the system.

System analysis

System analysis is the process of understanding what the organizational objectives and requirements are for the new system. This requires a thorough understanding of the problem and benefit the organization is trying to address and determining the best system solution. The analysis must develop a set of detailed information requirements to ensure the system can provide a useful solution. This generally means that the analyst must identify the business purpose of the system; who needs what information; as well as where, when and how it will be used. During the analysis phase, the analyst must define what the organization is trying to accomplish with the new system by carefully analyzing existing processes and the business environment in order to determine the best solution. Perhaps equally important, the analyst must determine how the organization is going to adopt the solution.

System analysis requires extensive interaction with the organization. It can be a difficult process because oftentimes existing business processes are not clearly defined with respect to purpose, and users can disagree on what should be done to solve the problem. The development of a new system represents an opportunity for an organization to redefine how it conducts business.

The information requirements must be defined in sufficient detail to be measurable in order to determine if the system once built has satisfied the requirement. In other words, a requirement that states "the system must be up all the time" has to be quantitatively defined in order to engineer and test. A more suitable requirement would be that the "system must be available 99.9 percent of the time." It is this requirement that will be engineered in the design and can be tested with little ambiguity. Without well-defined and measurable requirements, users and developers may disagree on whether the system has satisfied the requirements. It is extremely costly to change a system to meet redefined requirements after it has already been designed, coded and implemented. For this reason, defining system requirements is the most important and difficult step in a development life cycle.

System design

The step in the development cycle is to determine how the system will meet the requirements defined in the analysis phase. The design process has three components: (1) system alternatives analysis and selection, (2) detailing of the selected solution and (3) creation of the detailed physical design. It is in the design phase that the design specifications are developed for all components of the system to be delivered. The developer drafts a blueprint for constructing the system. The design specification addresses all elements of the system, detailing such items as inputs and outputs, the user interface, the database model, hardware requirements, program modules and reports and security controls. The design also creates the blueprint for organizational change, including new procedures, training, process redesign and a cutover plan to the new system.

Once the information requirements are gathered in sufficient detail, the development team then puts together several alternative solutions. Each one of the solutions meets the requirements of the system but will have varying costs, technical complexity and operational impacts. The alternatives provide a list of possible solutions with functions covering costs and the advantages and disadvantages of each proposed solution. The costs and functional components define the boundary of the system for the organization. An organization and developer together select the best solution and then proceed with a more detailed logical design of the system.

The "logical design" lays out what the system components are in a conceptual form that users can understand. It describes the process flows, information flows and functional capability, data models and controls of the system in schematic form for the user. This allows the user and developer to understand the system and make any changes before creating the physical design and, more importantly, before implementing the system. It is much easier and less expensive and time-consuming to make changes to a logical design than a physical design or after the system has been implemented.

Construction and implementation

When the logical design is completed and agreed on it is translated into a detailed "physical design." The physical design lays out the specific technical design for the new system. Detailed specifications are created for the hardware, software, physical databases, controls and organizational procedures for using the new system. The physical design provides the detailed blueprint for building the system. During the implementation phase, the system is actually built, tested and fielded. Implementation includes programming, component integration, testing, training and transition.

Most information systems usually require programs to be written and tested. In some cases the system will use commercial-off-the-shelf software (COTS), which must be integrated and customized to conform to the system specification. Systems may also use a combination of COTS and developed code, in which case each component must be tested individually and then together to ensure that the full system works as intended in a production environment. A common example of the use of COTS software is the use of a commercially available database system like Oracle or IBM's DB2. The COTS database provides for storage and retrieval of data elements without having to create and code basic database functions from scratch. Programs are then written to interact with the database product.

Testing is an integral part of the implementation phase. Testing must be done at three levels. First, the individual components of a system such as software programs, hardware components and new procedures are tested. Next all the components need to be tested in a system test to see if the system as a whole operates properly. The performance of the system is tested for adequate response times, peak load performance, security and procedural integrity. The final test is the acceptance test whereby the organization formerly accepts the system after it has been tested and users agree that it is ready for a production environment. This is where the measurable criteria laid out in the requirements definition phase become critical. If criteria for what the system is suppose to do are not defined and measurable, then users and developers may never agree on what is being accepted.

Testing is a very labor-intensive process due to its iterative nature. Software must be debugged and retested; and the system test must discover where errors have occurred, remedy the errors and perform the test again. Oftentimes organizations and developers fail to provide for the necessary time to properly test a system, wanting instead to rush the system into production. This practice only leads to the tasks of debugging and fixing system errors performed in the production environment where management must now contend with the added burden of intensified user dissatisfaction. Simply put, errors have to be corrected and it is best to have them corrected in a test environment before the system goes into production.

Once the system has been put into production, the last component of a system life cycle is "maintenance." Maintenance covers any system enhancements, upgrades (hardware and software) and corrections made to the system after it is in production. Maintenance enhancements can be significant and may introduce new errors to a production system. New enhancements should be thoroughly tested because errors to a production system can be detrimental to an organization that relies on the system to perform critical business functions.

Traditional system development life cycle methodology

The system development life cycle or waterfall model is one of the oldest methods for developing systems. It follows a set of progressive stages in which each stage has a defined output or deliverable that is used as an input into the next stage (figure 18–3). Each phase of the system life cycle is carried out in sequential fashion. Although the waterfall approach has been used extensively over the years in the production of successful systems (and in some failures as well), it has several shortcomings. The model has been criticized for its rigid design and inflexible procedures. Critics point to the following flaws in this approach:

- Assumes one system cycle, when in fact systems are naturally iterative.
- User involvement occurs in the beginning of the project during system analysis and then only at the end of the project in the implementation phase. This assumes that the users know exactly what they want up front and their requirements do not change during the life cycle. Unfortunately, users are often uncertain about their requirements, and environmental pressures on the organization can change requirements for the system. The waterfall model is inflexible in dealing with changing or uncertain requirements.
- The process can be long and very resource-intensive, yet it does not yield results until the end of the cycle when user requirements may have changed. Therefore the delivered system may be obsolete, negating the investment the organization has made.

The problems with the waterfall model created demand for better methods that would yield faster results, be more flexible with respect to refining user requirements and accommodating new requirements. One such approach is the incremental or iterative approach (Brookes 1995). This approach divides the project into small parts or modules, each based on a specified function. Each function is developed and tested for feedback from the users before the next module is developed. At each iteration, a software product is developed as an incremental and early release. The system is incrementally grown after each functional release. Users can offer feedback early in the process and, because the process allows for functional releases of software, an organization can build to budget based on functional components. This provides for some functionality early in the process and improves the morale of the development team and user community. The process allows for managed growth once the system is built by continuing the functional incremental development in versioned releases of the software.

Figure 18–3. Systems development life cycle.
Source: Kozar and Laudon.

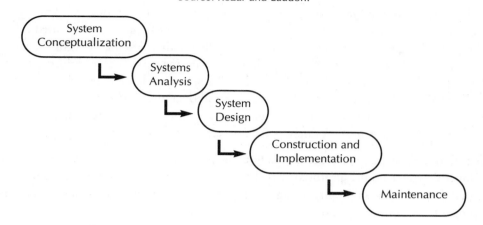

The incremental approach does not come without some costs. The user community needs to be actively engaged in each iteration and release to provide feedback and testing on the modules. This requires a time commitment from the users who normally perform other jobs. The interactive nature of the process can also delay the project because of increased communications. The process needs to be well managed to control increased avenues of communication between user and developer. Informal requests for changes must be managed in a structured way to prevent resources from being used for low-priority or even fruitless requests. The scope of the project can quickly get out of hand because user feedback may lead to increased customer demands that may exceed the intended budget and elongate the total project schedule.

Object-oriented development methodologies

Object-oriented technologies offer developers a different and, some would argue, faster approach to develop systems. Object-oriented software development differs from traditional development in the way it handles the issue of business procedures and data models. In traditional development, the analysis phase first defines business procedures and then the data elements necessary to carry out the procedures; this process fundamentally separates the procedure from the data. In object-oriented development this distinction is done away with. Instead the business is viewed as a set of objects. An object according to Yourdon (1996) is "an independent, asynchronous, concurrent entity which 'knows things' (i.e., stores data), 'does work' (i.e., encapsulates services) and 'collaborates with other objects' (by exchanging messages) to perform the overall functions of the system being modeled." An object combines the data and procedure of a business concept and therefore is attractive because it is a self-contained bundle of information and functionality that can be invoked via messages. Because the objects are self-contained in terms of having the data and procedures together, developers can reuse objects.

Object-oriented development offers the promise of combining design and programming because developers can draw upon object libraries composed of already written and reusable objects. The advantage is that systems will be developed faster with already tested and debugged object code. Unfortunately, the use of object-oriented technology is still in its infancy. The primary roadblock to its widespread use is that it requires a different conceptual approach to programming and system development. Object-oriented analysis techniques are still relatively new and not widely practiced, though this will change as the benefits of the technology outweigh the steep learning and relearning curves.

Prototyping

The prototyping model was developed based on the assumption that the user does not know or cannot communicate all of their requirements at the outset of a project. The prototyping model is used as a way of (1) rapidly building a working system and (2) to allow users to define their requirements by reacting to prototypes of the system to be built. A prototype is a preliminary working version of an information system for demonstration and evaluation purposes (Laudon 1998). The idea is to develop a working or "mock-up" prototype of an intended system and to present it to the user and document their reactions to it. This process provides a method for users to determine their requirements for the system because they are allowed to "drive" the system before it goes into production. The process is iterative with four basic steps:

1. Users identify their basic requirements to the developer.
2. The developer develops a quick prototype based on those requirements using either screen displays or a fourth-generation language (a programming language with English-like commands that is easy to develop programs with, thereby cutting down on development time).
3. The user is then required to use the prototype. The user identifies to the developer what he or she does and does not like, and another iterative cycle is performed.
4. The developer revises the prototype based on the user's input.

The iterations continue until the user is satisfied with the prototype (Jenkins 1985). The entire process can be done in just a few weeks and should have a defined end point. Upon completion the prototype can be used "as is," can be thrown away because it is only needed for a short time, can provide a basis for requirements definition in a larger iterative or traditional system development life cycle, or it can be used as a demonstration prototype for the final system.

A variation on prototyping is rapid application development (RAD). RAD introduces strict time limits on each development phase and relies heavily on rapid applications tools that allow for quick development (e.g., fourth generation languages). This process requires that users commit almost full-time to engage in application development workshops. Prototypes are developed as part of the intensive workshops.

The disadvantages of prototyping are that the method can lead to user dissatisfaction because the user thinks the system is completed when it is not. The prototype is a simple simulated system that lacks the "behind-the-scenes" work of database design, documentation, testing, and full functionality. The necessary detailed components of a robust system are not there and users must wait for the full system to be developed. Conversely, management may decide to use the hastily developed prototype only to discover that it cannot scale to a larger implementation or that it is difficult to maintain again because it was not tested or designed in a more thorough manner.

Prototyping is not suited for all system projects. While the method is good for small decision-support systems or for requirement analysis and user interfere design for large systems, the method is not suited for large complex systems.

Organizational readiness and experience

Developing and maintaining new systems requires a technical workforce that is expert in development methodologies, programming and tools necessary to build them. Alongside of having a technically proficient workforce, organizations must have procedures and quality assurance processes in place to assure the technical workforce works within an environment that mitigates risks of unbridled practices. This generally separates poorly developed systems from well-designed and developed systems. System development is a high-risk venture requiring proficiency in technologies and well-defined and practiced processes. Management must assess the capability of the organization to develop a system based on their staff's proficiency as well as the experience the organization has had in successfully developing systems of similar size and complexity. This assessment should be as objective as possible by internal management because of the high-risk nature of system development work. The assessment can be aided by the software Capability Maturity Model (CMM), which provides a descriptive approach to analyzing an organization's maturity in developing software systems.

Fundamentally, an organization must determine if an outside provider can develop a system more cost-effectively than it can do itself using internal resources. This is a seemingly simple binary decision; but to make it requires that the organization, particularly top management, first understand the complexity of system development, its own internal capabilities for developing software and its ability to manage contractors if it does decide to award work to an external provider.

Traditionally, non-IT organizations view their internal information systems group as a utility or expense function necessary to maintain systems, but essentially as a service to other internal business units that perform the core work of the organization. For example, a transportation department builds and maintains roads and bridges; it only provides IT services as support to the core mission of providing a transportation system. This introduces the concept of "core competency." A core competency is defined as an activity in which the organization does the best or is a world class leader (Laudon 1998). A transportation department may be a leader in its field for its mass transit system, or a software company may be a leader for its web browser software package; in each case the core competency is the activity in which the organization does best and is a leader. Core competency is usually gained by having a knowledge base of how to perform the activity. This can be gained by having many years of experience in performing an activity (a transportation department), or having people with the knowledge necessary to perform the activity (a software firm or research group). Organizations may look to outsource IT activities to IT firms that have a core competency in providing those services. "Outsourcing" is the turning over of a function in part or in full to a third-party contractor (Minoli 1995). There are several reasons to outsource technology functions:

- *Cost savings.* A technology firm may offer cost savings because they have developed more efficient processes for providing the services. Because the firm specializes in technology, they can create economies of scale by leveraging the cost of services across many clients.
- *Technical excellence.* Technology firms have a core competency in developing systems from the experience they have gained over the years. Because the firms specialize in technology, it is in their best interests to attract and retain highly skilled staff by offering career growth and continuous technology training.
- *Service quality.* A technology firm under contract may be more responsive to service issues than internal employees because the technology firm would lose business if service levels are not met. It may be easier and quicker to improve service quality by outsourcing than by changing internal culture and business processes.
- *Skills unavailable or scarce.* An organization can free up scarce internal personnel resources for other activities by outsourcing technology activities. An organization may be able to access skilled labor resources that it does not have and cannot attract because of a competitive labor market.
- *Flexibility.* An organization may be able to handle more technology projects without increasing its staff by outsourcing. This is a way to handle fluctuations in project workload when the workload becomes more than the internal staff can reasonably accommodate.

If an organization determines that it needs to outsource, it must also recognize the potential disadvantages of outsourcing. Outsourcing also requires the organization to have another key competency—managing contractor relationships. Understanding the disadvantages of outsourcing is important to managing the contractor relationship, in order to mitigate the adverse consequences of an outsourcing relationship. Generally, forming a strong trust relationship with the contractor becomes critical to the success of the relationship because both parties are dependent on the success of each other. An organization reaps the benefits of a competent contractor while the contractor is rewarded with continued business. The potential disadvantages of outsourcing are (Laudon 1998; Minoli 1995):

- *A loss of control.* An organization cedes control of a function to an outside firm. This loss of control, if not managed, can carry a risk of opportunistic practices (higher pricing or inflexible services) by the contractor because they fully control the function. The organization becomes captive to the contractor.
- *Inflexibility.* Contractors are bound by the contract they sign. If an organization's business requirements change, it may not be able to get the contractor to adapt to the new business requirements because of the original contract limitations. Often, contracts must be renegotiated in response to changing business requirements.
- *Dependency.* An organization is dependent on the contractor's business success. The organization may be at risk if the contractor becomes unprofitable or goes out of business, because service will likely deteriorate as a firm struggles to survive.
- *Strategic loss.* The potential of loss of strategic information is increased because contractors can leak such information to competitors or use it themselves for their own gain.

In order to mitigate the disadvantages, it is important to select a competent and trustful partner. Generally, a contractor should be selected that has:

- Knowledge of the organization's business
- A proven track record of successful engagements
- Flexibility in working with the organization as it changes in response to business changes
- Technical competence in the technology areas to be outsourced
- Financial stability
- Competitive prices

In conclusion, it may be necessary to contract out system development work to a firm specialized in the field when an organization does not have ability to perform the function internally or a contractor can simply do it better. An organization must be willing to work with and manage the contract relationship to realize the full benefits of the engagement and mitigate the disadvantages. A contract relationship is a complex one to develop and manage, and it should be emphasized that it takes both parties to make it succeed.

Quality software development

The development of quality software systems entails more than just programming excellence. One of the most important criteria for developing quality software systems is the use of well-defined system development methodologies such as those just described. It takes organizations years to learn and consistently employ such methodologies. Increasingly, organizations instituting quality procedures for internal development staff or requiring such procedures of their external contractors to ensure robust systems are developed. One of the best-known quality software development models is the Software Engineering Institute's (SEI) CMM. Adopting the processes of the CMM does not, however, guarantee that an organization will develop a successful software system. According to Jones (1996), the most important predictor of an organization's ability to develop successful and robust software systems is the familiarity of management, staff and users with the technologies. The more experienced the organization is the higher the likelihood of successful system development.

SEI's CMM

While the concepts of programming can be learned relatively quickly and the use of computers has become ubiquitous in today's organizations, there is ample evidence to suggest that most software disasters are caused by an organization's inability to adequately manage the software development process. In 1986, the federal government requested that the SEI of the Carnegie Mellon University develop a method by which it could better assess the performance of its software development contractors. In 1991, SEI published version 1.0 of the CMM.

The CMM defined a process maturity framework for assessing an organization's ability to develop software. The CMM describes the level of system development maturity by examining the organization's established software processes. A software processes defines a set of activities (e.g., coding, testing, documentation) an organization employs to develop and maintain software. According to the CMM, a set of software processes in turn describes an organization's software process capability. According to CMM, "A software process capability describes the range of expected results that can be achieved by following software processes." The software process capability determines the level of an organization's maturity. The CMM defines an organization's maturity in terms of its practiced key process areas (KPAs) in developing software. An organization's software capability is measured against the yardstick of these KPAs, which can be used to improve internal processes or to adopt new ones in order to raise an organization's maturity and process capability. The CMM is a descriptive model in that it does not prescribe those KPAs that are necessary to raise an organization's maturity level.

Generally, an immature organization lacks clearly defined or repeatable software development processes; software development is chaotic and development is often on the fly. Success of software development rests with the efforts of individual programmers or "heroics." Such organizations have no estimating procedures, no defined testing plans and no consistent approach from project to project. Risk of failure is high, and even if projects are completed they are often of low quality. The organization does not have a core-competency in software development and will have to adopt and institutionalize several processes to become mature.

Conversely, a mature organization has well-defined processes that ensure product quality consistently from project to project. This is done through institutionalized processes that objectively measure the development and quality of the product and can adjust the process to improve the product. Realistic estimates in terms of cost, manpower and time are made based on historical data and experience. Risk of project failure is mitigated through the well-defined software process capability. The mature organization has developed a core-competency in software development and can consistently produce quality software.

The CMM defined five levels of software process maturity. Each level defines a set of software process goals and marks an improvement in the organization's software process capability.

- *The initial level.* This level is characterized by having virtually no defined software development processes or management practices around software development. There are little planning, budgeting, scheduling, or other organizational procedures to guide the project. When the project begins to falter the solution is often to resort to talented individuals, or "heroics," to complete the project. Without sound management practices and processes, the software process capability is unpredictable.

- *The repeatable level.* At this level the organization has employed management practices and policies around the software development process. Project management controls have been implemented, resulting in a repeatable and stabilized process for the organization. Projects are realistically scheduled, monitored and tracked. Software requirements are defined and project controls are followed. The organization has experience in software development from previous projects and has learned to control the process to desired outcomes. The software process capability is disciplined and repeatable.
- *The defined level.* The organization at this level has achieved all the processes of the repeatable level, but the software development process is now well defined, integrated and documented; it has been standardized for the entire organization. Management and technical staff has been trained in the process and uses it on all projects. The software process capability is standard and repeatable and based on a well-defined and documented organizational standard.
- *The managed level.* At this level the organization has incorporated measurable quality goals and can benchmark software process metrics against data from previous projects. The organization has a rich history of data from which it has established boundaries of expected results for productivity and quality for software projects. The software process capability is measurable and, therefore, predictable. With the capability to detect trends in the software process in a quantitative way, an organization can detect problems as soon as they occur.
- *The optimizing level.* The organization has not only mastered all the preceding levels but now systematically focuses on continually improving the software process. The organization can recognize defects and weaknesses, analyze their cause, and improve the software process to overcome them. The software process capability is characterized as continuously improving.

It is important to note that the above-listed CMM model, even if adopted by an organization, cannot guarantee successful system development efforts. While the CMM cannot guarantee success, organizations that have incorporated well-defined system development and quality practices can reduce the risk of failure. Moreover, based on the work of Capers Jones (1996), it is indicated that organizational experience and core-competency in software and system development is a key determinant of software project success.

Project management

Overlaying the entire development process is the critical and important job of managing the project. Project management is essential to any system development effort. The system development methods described above explain how systems are developed, but they do not address the "what to do" process of managing the project.

According to Hallows (1998), "A project is a set of activities that has a clearly defined start and end and that produces a tangible result." A project has three distinct phases:

- Defining the project
- Planning the project
- Doing the project

Defining the project

Many projects take the "ready, fire, aim" approach, thus failing to identify first exactly what it is the project is suppose to do for the organization or client. Unfortunately, bravado can overtake the most serious developer or clients, causing them to forgo the elementary task of defining a project scope so that they mutually understand its purpose. Defining the project means describing exactly what has to be done in such a way that all stakeholders understand it. This phase of the project is critical to clearly define the scope of the project, roles of stakeholders and how work will be reviewed and approved.

Table 18–2
Five Maturity Levels and their KPAs
Source: M.C. Paulk et al., "Capability Maturity Model for Software, Version 1.1"
(Pittsburgh, PA: Software Engineering Institute, 1993).

Level	Software Process Capability	Key Process Areas
5 Optimizing	Continuous process improvement	• Defect prevention • Technology innovation
4 Managed	Predictable; focus is on the quality of the software using metrics to maintain performance within expected boundaries	• Measurement and analysis • Software quality management
3 Defined	Standard and consistent; common organization—wide understanding of defined software process	• Peer reviews • Intergroup coordination • Software product engineering • Integrated software management • Training program • Organizational process definition • Organization process focus
2 Repeatable	Disciplined; stable; and processes can be repeated	• Configuration management • Quality assurance • Subcontractor management • Project management (planning, tracking, monitoring) • Requirements definition and adherence
1 Initial	Unpredictable; success dependant on "heroics"	None

Activities in this phase include: determine the scope of the project, get commitment of the sponsor, define key objectives or deliverables of the project and create the project team. Also, it is important to decide how work is to be reviewed and approved by the development team and client. Defining who is to do the work, and assigning project teams for both the developers and users, is a critical part of defining the project.

PLAN THE PROJECT

Planning the project lays out in sufficient detail (a close approximation) of what it will take to do the project. Poor planning can be disastrous to a project because there may be little indication of what the project really requires in order to complete it. This can lead to unreasonable expectations in terms of cost and schedule, resulting in cost overruns, short cuts in the development cycle (i.e., shortened testing phase), and a poor quality product. Capers Jones (1996) describes this phenomenon as:

> ...a capacity for almost infinite self-delusion. Managers and clients often establish a totally unrealistic schedule for delivering a major system in half the time ever required for similar projects, without even bothering to check or validate the date. Then they move into full development with such amateurish planning and tracking that they don't realize until a few weeks before disaster strikes that the whole schedule was essentially an impossible fantasy.

Planning is a crucial phase in managing the project and includes the following activities:

- Define risks and strategies to mitigate them.
- Define and document the structure and organization of the project.
- Develop a realistic and detailed list of project work activities and relationships between activities (i.e., defining system requirements must precede system design). This is commonly referred to as the "work breakdown structure."
- Develop a realistic estimate of time and resources the work will require.
- Develop a list and schedule of milestones—quantifiable and measurable states of completion or deliverables (Kozar 1989).
- Assign resources to perform the work.
- Define the project budget and estimate costs.
- Create the project management plan.

Several software packages are available to help the project manager create the project management plan. These packages aid project managers in defining, assigning, tracking and revising project plans. The packages can allow managers to input estimates and work breakdown structures into an easy-to-read form such as a Gantt Chart. A Gantt chart is a chart that allows a project to be viewed by task, time and dependencies between tasks.

The most critical component of the project plan is the work breakdown structure, which is a list of activities, costs, and time required for each. Accurate estimating of work tasks is critical to the project plan. Estimates are best made by those who will do the work. These estimates should be made based on the informed knowledge of those who will perform the work, not on a project deadline. The estimates should be reviewed for accuracy by knowledgeable peers (Hallows 1998).

DOING THE PROJECT

Once the project plan has been established, it is now time to begin and run the project. Like choreographing a dance, the project manager must assemble a team, direct their activities, monitor their performance and complete the project objectives to their client's satisfaction. As with a dance master, project management requires an ability to work with people, develop their talents, understand all phases of the project and its objectives and understand quality systems and what it takes to achieve them.

Running a project requires several activities to be performed. The project manager is the leader who must build a successful development team as well as a strong partnering, trust relationship between the team and the client. This relationship management must be in place throughout the project. The project manager must track the progress of the project, diagnose problems, create solutions and re-estimate work all with the eye of meeting the project objectives. The project manager must also referee scope changes. There should be a clearly defined process for requesting and approving project changes. Changes carry with them additional costs and schedule impacts that the client and development team need to fully understand. The project manager orchestrates the project activities together to deliver a quality product and one that meets the client's objectives.

Building information systems requires a broad array of skills and knowledge. It requires organizational procedures and experience in addition to individual talent. It requires the understanding of the system development process(es) and an understanding of the subject matter of the particular organization that the system is being built for (i.e., transportation engineering for ITS). It requires an understanding of organizational theory, cultures, change management and business processes in addition to software programming and hardware specifications.

Technology future

Technology will continue its fast pace of change. This is evident by looking at one of the most important technologies of our day, the Internet. The Internet has changed and is continuing to change the way we live and do business since its birth. Other technologies such as advanced speech recognition, multimedia networks and real-time applications will evolve and create, as yet, unforeseen applications particularly in the way we communicate with each other and with machines. Organizations will continue to use technology to create new ways of doing business or in enhancing productivity and service delivery.

There will be a natural evolution and growth of software and system integration firms that have mastered the art of systems and software development. These firms will provide core competencies in technology that nontechnology firms will find difficult to match in either cost or quality. Evidence of this can be seen in the proliferation of package software products produced by high-technology firms and their rapid adoption by organizations and also of the outsourcing trend. Organizations, however, must be cognizant of the system development methods and techniques and how systems become integrated within an organization in order to assess their benefit and risks. Perhaps most importantly, organizations should understand the high risks of system development and the success factors for system development in order to assess their ability or an external provider's ability to successfully develop and implement systems.

No matter how rapidly technology changes, the concepts presented in this chapter can help those making technology decisions for their organizations. While technology is exciting and may seem deceptively easy in the way we use it, it is not easy in its development and introduction into an organization.

References

Brooks Jr., F. P. 1995. "The Mythical Man-Month: Essays on Software Engineering—Anniversary Edition." Reading, MA: Addison Wesley Longman.

Bullekey, W. 1996. "When Things Go Wrong" (November 18). Wall Street Journal.

Glass, R. L. 1998. "Software Runaways: Lessons Learned From Massive Software Project Failures." Upper Saddle River, NJ: Prentice Hall PTR.

Hallows, J. 1998. "Information Systems Project Management: How to Deliver Function and Value in Information Technology Projects." New York, NY: American Management Association.

Ince, D. 1994. "ISO 9001 and Software Quality Assurance." London: McGraw-Hill.

Jenkins, M. A. 1985. "Prototyping: A Methodology for the Design and Development of Applications Systems" (April). SIM Spectrum 2, no. 2 (April).

Jones, C. 1996. "Patterns of Software Systems Failure and Success." New York, NY: International Thomson Computer Press.

Kozar, K. A. 1989. "Humanized Information Systems Analysis and Design: People Building Systems for People." New York, NY: McGraw-Hill.

Laudon, K. C., and J. P. Laudon. 1998. "Management Information Systems." Fifth Edition. NJ: Prentice Hall.

Martin, J., and J. J. James. 1995. "Object Oriented Methods: A Foundation." Englewood Cliffs, NJ: Prentice Hall PTR.

Minoli, D. 1995. "Analyzing Outsourcing." NY: McGraw-Hill.

Paulk, M. C., et al. 1993. "Capability Maturity Model for Software, Version 1.1." Pittsburgh, PA: Software Engineering Institute.

Yourdon, E., and C. Argilia. 1996. "Case Studies In Object Oriented Analysis and Design." Upper Saddle River, NJ: Prentice Hall.

BY Robert Parsons, PE[1] • Principal •
Parsons Transportation Associates

CHAPTER 19

ISSUES IN DEVELOPING AND IMPLEMENTING THE NATIONAL ITS ARCHITECTURE

Background

The concept underlying intelligent transportation systems (ITS) is the integration of various ground transportation systems (i.e., transit, freeways) into a system of systems. The basic philosophy is to share facilities and data to provide an almost seamless ground transportation network. ITS is mostly about the collection, analysis and distribution of transportation information. To promote a free access to this information there must be a basic framework from which ITS stakeholders[2] all operate. We call that framework the system architecture.

What is an architecture? The *American Heritage Dictionary (Microsoft Bookshelf '95)* defines a system as "A group of interacting, interrelated, or interdependent elements forming a complex whole. A functionally related group of elements, especially: … A group of interacting mechanical or electrical components." A system architecture is a framework that describes how system components interact and work together to achieve the system goals. It describes the system operation, what each component does and what information is exchanged among the components. All systems have an architecture, whether it is specifically developed or happens by default.

This chapter describes the systems engineering movement within the ITS community and presents the ITS national architecture through use of everyday examples that users (travelers and shippers) can envision. Lastly, it discusses the major issues faced in developing the architecture, and the issues that must still be addressed in developing standards and implementing the elements and operating the ITS systems in regions, counties and cities around the country.

The system architecture concept

The concept of a system architecture emerged after World War II, with the development of complex airborne weapon systems. Large system program management procedures were initiated following the explosion of an Atlas Intercontinental Ballistic Missile in one of its underground silos. No formal configuration management[3] systems were in place before that accident, therefore the specific design details of that missile were not readily known. As a result of this and other incidents, the Department of Defense initiated a new series of procedures and processes to assure that new weapon systems were system engineered throughout the life cycle of the systems.

The process of defining large, complex systems has been refined during the last several decades. This system engineering process uses the system architecture concept. It is commonplace in the aerospace, telecommunication and computer fields today. One can obtain degrees in system engineering from major U.S. universities.[4]

The long historical trend toward increasingly complex systems is accelerating, driven by world-wide communications, surveillance, air transportation and finance. What were once local markets became national ones, then regional ones and now global ones. National boundaries to research, engineering, development, manufacturing, distribution and servicing have all but disappeared: attempted protectionist measures instead usually have led to higher costs and measurable economic decline (Rechtin 1991).

In his book *Systems Architecting: Creating and Building Complex Systems,* Rechtin continues to forecast future major systems that will require much global attention in the future. His list includes the following:

- Shuttle C Hypersonic Transport
- Lunar surface base
- National research and education network
- Controlled access highway networks
- Electrical automobile complexes
- Low observable close air support
- Underseas habitations
- Image motion-detection radars/infrared sensors

Current and expected ITS activities and technologies can be inferred from some of Rechtin's projections above.

The traditional approach to surface transportation

Ground transportation facilities in the United States have been planned on a project-by-project basis, and the elements of these systems have been developed independently. The notable exception was the Interstate Highway System. Although it was envisioned and designed as a single system, it too was funded and built in project-size pieces by various states.

Why did this happen?

The factors that lead to this include:

- *Funding guidelines*—projects were encouraged with little guidance on the creation of a system of projects. Most projects seemed to be isolated rather than integrated with other projects. For example, a transit line might evolve but its operation was not to be integrated with the management of freeways or city streets.

- *Proprietary designs*—many existing transportation elements based on proprietary designs are not compatible with other similar systems in an adjacent jurisdiction. These legacy projects lock agencies into a single source of support, making them captive of a sole vendor for upgrade and parts supply.

- *Procurement practices*—project-oriented procurement contributed to this balkanization of projects. Striving for low-cost projects rather than lower cost transportation systems tended to attract system designers who relied on their own priority designs or hardware. But, unfortunately, these were shortsighted savings since these closed systems would not integrate together easily. Thus many autonomous pieces of systems have been deployed around the country. Today these have been called stovepipe projects.

- *Operator focus*—part of this problem was due to a lack of system engineering practice in ground transportation. Leaders were simply not systems-oriented. Focus was by operator experts who knew little, if anything, about other ground transportation concepts, let alone the commonalties of these sub systems and the synergism that could be gained via effective integration. These modal experts sought little input from related stakeholders, and the projects tended to remain isolated from other local deployments.

- *Isolated projects*—there was little or no interaction among projects, even in areas where these systems must coexist. For example, at railroad grade crossing intersections, the management systems of the highway and railroads were not integrated. In some cases there was not even communication between the two systems.

But why consider a systems approach for ITS?

Prior to the Intermodal Surface Transportation Efficiency Act (ISTEA) and ITS, federal ground transportation funds were generally distributed using a formula, which in turn were based upon miles of roads, population, or some other criterion that was beyond the control of those responsible to operate, or more progressively, integrate these systems. Projects were reviewed for individual merit (or political appeal) rather than as a part of an integrated transportation system. Individual projects were funded on a project priority basis. This project-by-project orientation tended to further balkanize the process politically. Transportation plans were mostly a collection of bottoms-up projects, rather than a top-down integrated system of transportation subsystems. ISTEA by name implied integration. It called for coordination between the modes and a national ITS strategic plan. It also required a national ITS architecture.

The Transportation Equity Act for the 21st Century (TEA-21) defined the actions required by the U.S. Department of Transportation (U.S. DOT) to implement ITS in a timely manner. It set a standards timeframe and gave the secretary the authority to set such standards if the private voluntary societies failed to make effective progress. It also defined ITS interoperability to protect mobile users so that their purchased equipment would operate from locale-to-locale. While this is no trivial matter, the guidelines were established and U.S. DOT was required to define those standards that were deemed critical to the provision of national interoperability of key ITS services. Congress decided that ITS was to be addressed as an integrated system, employing system engineering disciplines.

The idea of system analysis as it emerged in aerospace, electronics and telecommunications complex systems is still new to most engaged in transportation planning, engineering, operations, or maintenance. Few transportation professionals have formal training or practical experience with systems engineering. Transportation planners and engineers must be trained in systems concepts and methodology, and a new breed of transportation professionals must be developed for the future.

That reorientation towards systems concepts began as the architecture was being developed. The architecture development process selected purposely relied heavily on user–builder–operator input. This forced the current stakeholders to understand the basic systems approach to develop large-scale integrated activities.

This sharing of common resources—sensors, communications, computation capability—can provide a great improvement in service at a fraction of the cost of trying to perform all the transportation functions separately within each dedicated subsystem facility. This idea of sharing could also prove the key to solving the illusive intermodal problem. As the various modes get accustomed to using a shared database, they will see the mutual advantages of providing better intermodal linkages.

However, it is this sharing of resources that may doom ITS, unless a large-scale education effort can convince subsystem managers that real benefits can flow to all via the sharing philosophy. While the U.S. DOT has provided extensive special courses on the architecture for practitioners, the transportation schools in universities are not significantly changing their transportation courses to reflect this systems aspect of ITS. Those in charge of the system elements, such as traffic management, tend to overly possess these resources and do not think or want to share information. The reasons vary, but prior to ITS little status data was shared among sister agencies, let alone private-sector providers operating in the same area.

There is much interest on possible use of advanced sensing; data analysis and fusion; and distribution of information to those that build, operate and use these systems. There is less regard to assure that the many diverse aspects of ITS are integrated, even though the U.S. DOT has stressed this aspect, so that they effectively co-exist and share common information to enhance overall system performance and lower infrastructure, operating and user costs. Many ITS benefits will be possible because users and operators of the diverse and independent elements of our transportation systems can gain real time information about scheduling, pricing and availability of these system elements so that intermodal and multimodal trips become commonplace and convenient. However, in order to accomplish these total system benefits, certain commonalties are needed. Key standards are needed to enable joint use of common information and the sharing of data banks. Congress has decreed and the U.S. DOT identified these key standards in 1999.

The national architecture program

The evolution of the architecture for the national ITS is unprecedented in civil transportation history. System-related ITS activities started in the late 1980s at the Partners for Advanced Transit and Highways (PATH) program at the University of California at Berkeley. There was concern that the early advanced traffic management work by PATH and the California Department of Transportation might prevent system expansions to eventually include vehicle control concepts. Consequently, discussions and some mutual work was initiated between researchers at PATH, AT&T and Rockwell International to explore the use of architecture concepts previously employed in large-scale systems. In 1991, PATH researchers presented the first preliminary architecture concept (Varaiya and Shladover 1991).

Many of those who pioneered Mobility 2000, and later ITS America, understood the value of a systems approach and were instrumental in the integration of the different transportation elements. Parsons was named chairman[5] of the system architecture committee at the first ITS America annual ITS meeting in 1991.

The first assignment of the committee was to complete the definition of ITS goals and objectives that could then be used to state system requirements. The committee also considered alternative approaches and methodologies to the development of a national architecture and, in early 1992, forwarded draft recommendations to the ITS America coordinating council and board of directors for their review.

In March 1992, ITS America forwarded the recommendation to Secretary of Transportation Andrew H. Card, Jr. that the department undertake an ITS national architecture development effort. The program recommendation in part stated:

> No one organization has a monopoly on the best ideas or approaches. We are proposing a variant of an approach used often by the Department of Defense during system concept formulation: the selection, through competitive procurement, of multiple teams made up from industry, academia, and the public sector to carry out in parallel and cooperative architecture synthesis and definition studies.

The recommendation concluded by stating:

> These studies are launching a very large and important endeavor, a total sea change for transportation. It is worth investing the time and resources to ensure that the R&D is efficiently carried out and that the much larger deployment investment yet to come is intelligently based on sound architecture and design concepts.

The national ITS architecture program

Four teams selected by the U.S. DOT in September 1993 to develop the architecture worked independently to develop an alternative architecture based upon a twenty-year planning horizon. The program consisted of two phases with a down-select from four to two teams at midpoint. The architecture was designed to provide functions to support ITS user services and, more importantly, to define the requirements for ITS standards.

When Congress authorized the development of the national ITS architecture by the U.S. DOT, it also gave ITS America a charge in the architecture process—to work with the U.S. DOT and engage the other non-federal stakeholders in a consensus process. After three years of development,[6] the national ITS architecture was approved by the U.S. DOT and ITS America in 1996. Two additional user services have been added—Highway Railroad Interface and Archived Data for planning use. Thus, it is true that the national ITS architecture is a living tool that is and will continue to be expanded when needed to provide coverage for new user services.

Consensus-building process

Consensus-building was done in parallel to and interacting with the team's architecture definition. ITS America formed a large consensus task force with representation from national organizations interested in or affected by the ITS movement. A listing of the organizations represented is shown in figure 19–1. Some members were proponents of ITS, some were critics, and others were unfamiliar with ITS.

There were three major activities of the consensus task force:

1. To review and comment on the user services being refined by the Federal Highway Administration (FHWA) and ITS America
2. To help identify the ITS implications or policy issues the architecture team should address
3. To participate in the formal down-select process for the architecture teams, along with the government evaluators

The task force did not vote on issues. Rather, consensus was achieved by give-and-take and when all members could live with a position even though some did not like the compromise. The task force considered the implications of each concept and provided a real world review of the architecture. As some of these implication are at odds with others, one can see why the phrase was coined "the best architecture is one that can be implemented." Technical excellence in the architecture was not the overriding goal. A desirable architecture was one that most stakeholders can and would support and work to implement.

The architecture organization

The FHWA managed architectural teams and U.S. DOT formed a policy group to exercise program oversight. The U.S. DOT policy group, chaired by the deputy secretary, included executive members of the FHWA, Federal Transit Administration, National Highway Traffic Safety Administration, the Research and Special Program Administration and the Federal Railroad Administration, as well as the newly created ITS

Figure 19–1. ITS architecture consensus task force.
Source: U.S. Department of Transportation.

American Association of Motor Vehicle Administrators	International Taxicab and Livery Association
American Association of State Highway and Transportation Officials	IVHS Canada
American Association of Port Authorities	National Association of Counties
American Association of Retired Persons	National Association of Governors' Highway Safety Representatives
American Automobile Association	National Association of Regional Councils
American Automobile Manufacturers Association	National Conference of State Legislatures
American Bus Association	National Emergency Numbers Association
American Consulting Engineers Council	National Governors' Association
American Electronics Association	National Industrial Transportation League
American Portland Cement Alliance	National League of Cities
American Public Transit Association	National Private Truck Council
American Public Works Association	National Safety Council
American Road and Transportation Builders Association	Public Technology, Incorporated
American Trucking Associations	State and Territorial Air Pollution Program Administrators/Association
Association of American Railroads	of Local Air Pollution Control Officials
Council of Standards Organization	Surface Transportation Policy Project
Council of University Transportation Centers	Telecommunications Industry Association
Electronic Industries Association	TRANSCOM
Environmental Defense Fund	United Bus Owners of America
Human Factors and Ergonomics Society	United States Chamber of Commerce
Institute of Transportation Engineers	
International Bridge, Tunnel and Turnpike Association	

Joint Program Office (JPO). U.S. DOT also established a management committee to coordinate the interdepartment aspects of the architecture. ITS America continued management attention to the process with both the coordinating council and board of directors reviewing the architecture development.

Mitretek and Jet Propulsion Laboratory provided assistance to the ITS JPO. The organization chart for this unique effort is presented in figure 19–2.

Figure 19–2. The architecture organization.
Source: U.S. Department of Transportation.

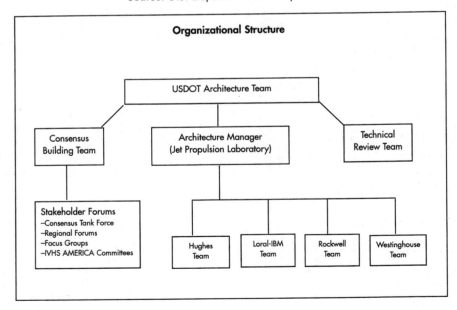

In September 1993, the FHWA selected four teams from approximately a dozen proposals. The successful teams were lead by Hughes Aircraft, Loral Federal Systems, Rockwell International and Westinghouse. During phase I, the teams worked to create a vision and approach. At the end of phase I, two teams were selected to work cooperatively during phase II. These teams are listed in table 19–1.

Table 19–1
Phase 1 Architecture Teams [7]
Source: Summary Report of ITS Architecture Development Program, Phase I,
November 1994—an ITS America/DOT-ITSJPO document given out during
public forums held throughout the country during late 1994.

Hughes Aircraft	Loral Federal Systems	Rockwell International	Westinghouse Electric
• Delco Electronics • Electronic Data Systems • General Motors • Hickling • JHK & Associates • Michigan DOT • Minnesota DOT • Sprint • University of Minnesota	• Ameritech • Louis Berger & Associates • New Jersey Highway Authority • Oakland County Michigan Road Commission • Siemens • University of Michigan	• Apogee Research • California PATH • California DOT • George Mason University • GTE Laboratories • Honeywell • Iowa State University • New York State DOT • Texas DOT • Texas Transportation Institute	• Bell Atlantic Mobile Systems • Calspan • Florida DOT • Frederic R. Harris • Harris Corporation • Maryland DOT • University of Florida • Washington State DOT

This process also provided a mechanism to assure that the technical details were accurate. A special technical review team[8] of experts in critical fields were charged to review the team contractual material and perform technical assessments of those reports. This team of honest brokers saved others following the architecture process the drudgery of examining all the technical details.

During phase II the two remaining teams, including Loral Federal Systems and Rockwell International, worked collaboratively. This was better for the stakeholders and it was as if there were one team sharing assignments and preparing only one set of documentation. It was no longer a race[9] to see who wins, but rather an evolutionary process to assure that all legitimate concerns were considered in trade studies supporting the balanced final concept.

The national architecture

An architecture is an abstract thing. In the case of ITS, the architecture mainly focuses on interfaces that tie the many ITS pieces into the new system. But it is more than a definition of interfaces, identification of the communication necessary to realize the interfaces is a key component of the infrastructure. As shown in figure 19–3, there is a vision, a logical architecture, a physical architecture, an implementation strategy and a definition of the standards requirements all contained within the idea of an ITS architecture. Thus the architecture defines the ITS information exchanges necessary to integrate the many ITS functions. It also defines the standards that, when developed, would enable widespread ITS implementation.

Figure 19–3. ITS architecture documents.
Source: U.S. Department of Transportation.

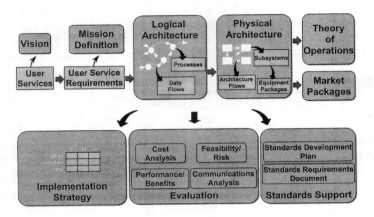

Vision

The ITS architecture is presented in terms of a logical architecture, physical architecture, implementation strategy and standards requirements. The development of the architecture was based on a vision statement that sketches several possible scenarios of ITS development over the next twenty years. It describes how travelers and system operators may be able to use and benefit from ITS technologies in their day.

To better relate ITS to end users, a concept of user services was devised. It replaced the rather vague goals and objectives that had been employed to envision where ITS was aimed. The consensus task force complained that they could not grasp the ideal goals and objectives—they suggested "tell us what services ITS might provide." Thus user services played that role and served as the basic requirements for the ITS architecture development.

A logical architecture defines the processes (i.e., functions) and data flows needed to meet the user service requirements. These processes and data flows are then grouped to form transportation management functions (e.g., manage traffic) A logical architecture is essentially a tool to help identify the system functions and information flows and to guide development of functional requirements. Logical architectures should be independent of institutions and technology; they do not define where or by whom functions are performed in the system, nor how functions are to be implemented.

The physical architecture is a high-level framework that depicts how components or subsystems link together to form an ITS. It describes the interfaces between these subelements and explains the data flows among these elements. Thus the architecture lays out the communication layer that enables all necessary ITS subsystems that collect, process and distribute ITS information to work together. Further, it illustrates how these internal ITS elements communicate with external components and with the people and bodies outside the ITS system who use this information when they participate in ITS activities. These external components (over 55 have been defined) are referred to as terminators by the architecture development team. These terminators are shown in figures 19–4 and 19–5.

Figure 19–4. Terminators establish the architecture boundary in the real world.
Source: U.S. Department of Transportation.

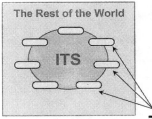

Users
19 Terminators:
•Driver
•ISP Operator
•Transit User
•Etc.

Terminators

Environment
7 Terminators:
•Environment
•Roadway
•Etc.

Related Systems
34 Terminators:
•DMV
•Financial Inst.
•Other Vehicle
•Etc.

Figure 19–5. Architecture terminators.
Source: U.S. Department of Transportation.

RELATED SYSTEMS
- ☐ Archived Data User Systems
- ☐ Basic Vehicle
- ☐ Commercial Vehicle
- ☐ Construction and Maintenance
- ☐ CVO Information Requestor
- ☐ DMV
- ☐ Emergency Telecommunications System
- ☐ Enforcement Agency
- ☐ Event Promoters
- ☐ Financial Institution
- ☐ Government Administrators
- ☐ Government Reporting Systems
- ☐ Intermodal Freight Depot
- ☐ Intermodal Freight Shipper
- ☐ Location Data Source
- ☐ Map Update Provider
- ☐ Media
- ☐ Multimodal Crossings
- ☐ Multimodal Transportation Service Provider
- ☐ Other Archives
- ☐ Other CVAS
- ☐ Other Data Sources

RELATED SYSTEMS (Cont.)
- ☐ Other EM
- ☐ Other ISP
- ☐ Other Parking
- ☐ Other TM
- ☐ Other TRM
- ☐ Other Vehicle
- ☐ Payment Instrument
- ☐ Rail Operations
- ☐ Transit Vehicle
- ☐ Wayside Equipment
- ☐ Weather Service
- ☐ Yellow Pages Service Providers

ENVIRONMENT
- ☐ Environment
- ☐ Potential Obstacles
- ☐ Roadway
- ☐ Roadway Environment
- ☐ Secure Area Environment
- ☐ Traffic
- ☐ Vehicle Characteristics

USERS
- ☐ Archived Data Administrator
- ☐ Commercial Vehicle Driver
- ☐ Commercial Vehicle Manager
- ☐ CVO Inspector
- ☐ Driver
- ☐ Emergency Personnel
- ☐ Emergency System Operator
- ☐ ISP Operator
- ☐ Parking Operator
- ☐ Pedestrians
- ☐ Toll Administrator
- ☐ Toll Operator
- ☐ Traffic Operations Personnel
- ☐ Transit Driver
- ☐ Transit Fleet Manager
- ☐ Transit Maintenance Personnel
- ☐ Transit System Operators
- ☐ Transit User
- ☐ Traveler

Figure 19–6. Architecture subsystems.
Source: U.S. Department of Transportation.

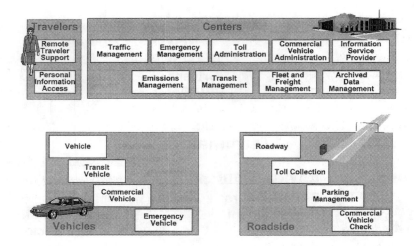

The physical architecture is presented in three layers—the institutional layer, the transportation layer and the communication layer.

1. Layer 1 describes the institutions and the relationships (barriers) between them. These include federal, state and local governments; consumers; producer interests; and special advocacy groups.

2. Layer 2 describes the transportation elements and their integration necessary to provide the array of user services. This has further been defined in four systems: travelers, centers, vehicles and roadside equipment that share functional, deployment and institutional characteristics. In all there are 18 subsystems, as shown in figure 19–6. It also defines the standard requirements that, when developed, would enable widespread ITS implementation.

3. Layer 3, the communication layer, is critical to the success of ITS. It overlays the transportation layer and provides the means to transmit the right information in a timely and secure manner. Four communication channels are defined: wide-area broadcast, roadside-to-vehicle, vehicle-to-vehicle, and wireline. These channels reflect investment decisions and will drive the early standards work. Market penetration and data flow will depend upon the cost of communication. The cost will vary by who builds, operates and maintains these systems.

It is easier to explain what the architecture is not. It is not a design, nor is it even a design concept; nor does it provide information on how to build the system. It does not have a cost or definable benefit until a specific system is designed that is based upon the framework. There are many designs that will evolve from this architecture. Thus the architecture is dimensionless and measureless.

Policy

The architecture was purposely developed as policy-neutral. Thus, the architecture is a toolbox that local governments can use to address local concerns and to enable or enforce specific policies. It does not recommend approaches to local or national (like clean air) concerns; however, it is capable of addressing such implications. For example, if some communities wished to use road pricing as a means to limit congestion (i.e., stop-and-go traffic) that significantly increases pollution, then the architecture can accommodate this. Features such as metering, tag reading and the means to bill customers for road use by time of day are also addressed in the architecture.

These attributes became so important to the stakeholders that the FHWA required the teams to report progress in each implication area at key program reviews. A short summary of the attributes is shown on figure 19–7. Local transportation and policy options are left to local decision-makers and politicians. For example, the architecture does not choose between alternatives, like central verses distributed information processing; the architecture can accommodate either, as it can be tailored to support specific local policy choice such as road or congestion pricing. These choices will be reflected in detail designs of specific ITS implementations.

Thus the national architecture will support a family of designs that can range from a bare-bones element with minimum cost and few benefits, other than national compatibility, to richer designs that provide a near full array of ITS services. These full-fledged designs will emerge in larger urban areas that will have public and private service providers that can aggregate sufficient market to pay for the sensing, processing and distribution of real-time information to a variety of clients.

Figure 19–7. ITS architecture implication areas.
Source: U.S. Department of Transportation.

Deployment	Effect on the rate of ITS deployment
Equity	Effect on the distribution of benefits and costs
Financing	Effect on financing deployment, operations and maintenance
Institutions	Effect on institutions and organizations
Market	Effect on the development of the market
Operation & maintenance	Effect on operating and maintaining ITS
Policy & regulation	Effect on implementing current and setting future policies and regulations
Privacy	Effect on the privacy of individuals and organizations
Safety	Effect on transportation system safety
Standards	Effect on current and future standardization efforts

The architecture is oriented to take advantage of existing and emerging general purpose communication infrastructure to reduce costs and mitigate risk. The private sector has built and is operating an expansive telecommunications network that can be leveraged to support a significant number of ITS user services. This layer includes those who deploy, manage and maintain these communication networks; those who run the billing and clearinghouse functions associated with electronic payment services; communication equipment manufactures; and individual commercial users who employ the basic communication service to provide value services.

The following figures illustrate how these communication services will support ITS. Figure 19–8 illustrates wireless type of information that can be distributed to drivers via cellular and wide-area broadcasts. Figure 19–9 shows vehicle-to-vehicle communication that will enable the family of safety warning devices[10] and, eventually, automated traffic lanes.

Figure 19–9 shows the vehicle-to-roadside communications, which is commonly called dedicated short-range communication (DSRC); and there is much ado in this area. The hot applications are tolling and truck clearance applications. Some installations (such as seen in Houston, Texas) use DSRC to track vehicles and then apply that information to the central traffic management system. Some argue this may be a less expensive method to obtain system surveillance than the installation of typical loop inductive sensors. The current issue is how to develop the near-term standards without harm to one of the suppliers. An ITS America task force has been established to work out a solution, while at the same time developing standards so that more ITS implementation can proceed. As ITS applications grow, this DSRC channel is expected to carry more messages, as is depicted in figure 19–10.

Figure 19–11 is used to illustrate the application of extensive wire-line communications. Traffic management is probably the most demanding of the ITS services, and one can envision from this figure the many forms of wire services that may be employed. The other ITS center applications parallel traffic control in the use of wire-line communication.

Figure 19–12, which spans the transportation and communication layers, depicts how the 18 transportation subsystems communicate with one another. While complex, it gives the reader an overview of how communication interconnects to provide information needed by the user services. The oblong-shaped areas represent the four aforementioned communication channels required to support the architecture, and the solid lines between the various subsystems depict how data will flow.

Major policy concerns or issues

The architecture teams were careful not to embed policy into the architecture. One option that was closed out was beacon-based systems. It was felt that the complexities and costs of beacon-based route guidance did not warrant its inclusion. Although modest beacon systems (similar to the Houston beacon) can be supported, those requiring massive data flows cannot. Other policy issues include:

- *Omission*—intermodal freight. This is now being considered as an update to the user services. Transportation planning data recently was added as a new user service.
- *Technical*—regarding the communication links, especially the vehicle-to-roadside. This involves trucking regulation interests wishing to electronically transmit essential credential data via a robust tag and the less demanding needs of toll tags. In addition, the vendors will probably fight a unified approach so this may become a make-or-break issue and set the limits on early ITS penetration into the market.
- *Implementation.* Some implementation issues closely depend on the ability of the architecture to accommodate software or hardware elements needed to enable or support implementation. A few are highlighted here:
  — Privacy algorithms can either protect individual or provide such data to law enforcement agencies for police action if that is the local preference.
  — Central versus distributed route guidance information is also a local choice as it drives the cost of ground-based equipment and operating costs to provide these services.
  — Pricing is a mechanism to balance traffic flows at selected times of congestion, and this has been introduced in some areas with good public acceptance and overall results.

Figure 19–8. "Wide-area wireless" mobile data communications.
Source: U.S. Department of Transportation.

Examples:
- **Cell phone**
- **Pager**
- **2-way radio**
- **Broadcast**

Figure 19–9. Vehicle-to-vehicle communications.
Source: U.S. Department of Transportation.

Examples:
- **Collision avoidance systems**
- **Automated Highway System**

Applying the architecture

One goal of the architectural effort was to set the requirements for standards that in turn would enable inter-operability of mobile ITS equipment so ITS users could use their equipment in various locations. This feature will significantly enlarge the market for on-board equipment and assure a strong national supplier base.

While the national architecture defines functions and message sets necessary to support all user services, it was never intended that most locales would need or desire all these services. Therefore, as ITS is implemented locally, there is a need to select which user services will be implemented in that locale.

Figure 19–10. Dedicated short-range communications.
Source: U.S. Department of Transportation.

Examples:

- ## Electronic Toll Collection
- ## Emergency-Vehicle Signal Preemption
- ## Electronic commercial vehicle check

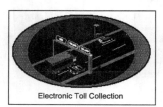

Figure 19–11. Wireline communications (fixed point to fixed point).
Source: U.S. Department of Transportation.

Examples:

- ## Telephone wires
- ## Fiber-optics cable
- ## Microwave towers

Applications:

- ## Center to Center
- ## Center to Roadside
- ## Kiosks
- ## Home/Office users

The teams have accumulated rich resource data that should save much labor for those charged to implement. For example, it defines the data flows and data to make message sets. The logic and hard dog work has been done, and one needs to prepare specific messages within a specific design application.

This resource is a valuable national tool that is being updated as needed by the U.S. DOT and a residual team of architects. It should greatly simplify the job of implementing ITS to provide locally desired ITS services throughout the country. The national architecture is available on CD-ROM from the U.S. DOT's ITS JPO[11] or ITS America, or documents may be electronically downloaded on the Internet from <www.itsa.org>.

Figure 19–12. ITS Communications Systems
Source: U.S. Department of Transportation.

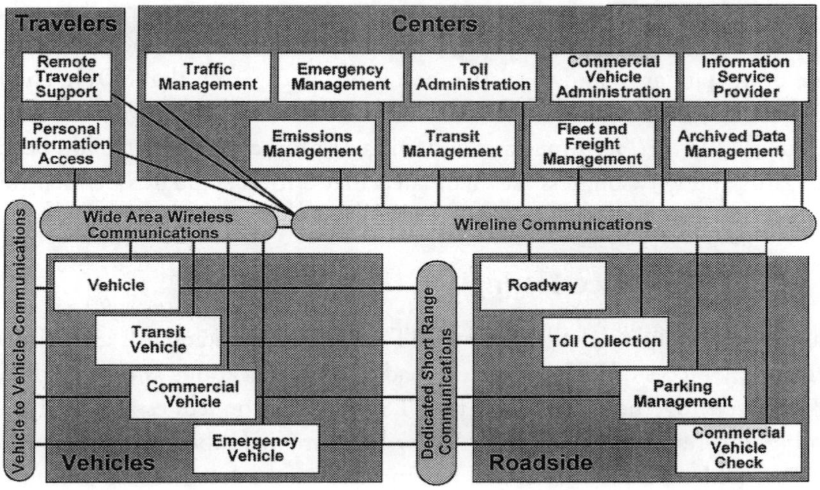

At first the U.S. DOT had indicated that there will be regional architectures, and this confused many planning early implementation. Later, "architecture" was defined as a high-level framework whose goal is to get stakeholders to work together on regional transportation problems. The term seems to have been accepted by transportation professionals.

Post-architecture actions

Education and training

Education, both of practicing professionals and old and new transportation engineers and planners, continues to be the number one obstacle blocking large-scale ITS implementation. The decades of stove piping ITS elements is not going to cease easily. It has been a decade since the writer started discussions with the large industry regarding how they developed systems in other sectors. We have had six years of organized architecture development and standards activities with a heavy emphasis on stakeholder participation, and few still really understand system integration. Yet with all this background, there are not many active in ground transportation today that are systems-oriented.

The ITS architecture is described using system engineering terminology that is not familiar to most transportation engineers or practitioners. Therefore, transportation practitioners do not easily understand the architecture documentation. However, there has been and will continue to be training classes offered by the U.S. DOT to acquaint practitioners with how to use the vast amount of documentation to aid in implementing ITS.

Universities must change their curriculums to place more emphasis on systems engineering and the integration of the transportation elements. The how to of transportation systems development and the acquisition of information collection, processing and distribution resources that can be shared is needed. Because education is a time-dependent process, ITS implementation will continue to lag.

Standards

Both public and private sectors need standards to enable implementation. While the architecture teams anticipated this need and laid out standards requirements and a process to evolve these, the actual issuance of the standards is by nature a very slow process. Volunteers are needed to staff the SDO and the many committees that prepare draft standards, and then each one is balloted within that SDO. There are three positive steps: (1) U.S. DOT made funds available to help SDOs defer the costs of travel and administration to try and speed up the process, (2) the ITS America standards and protocol committee has been aggressive in its pursuit of new standards and (3) Congress has mandated that critical standards be identified by mid-1999 and implemented as quickly as possible.

Interoperability and compliance testing

There are significant interoperability challenges with ITS, because the standards are being developed by organizations that address only pieces of ITS—vehicles, roads, communications and so forth. Will these separate standards function properly together and deliver the ITS services as hoped, especially if interoperability is required? That is a big uncertainty and concern. A new ITS America subcommittee on interoperability was created in June 1997 to address this concern and recommend methodologies and procedures to enable one to define test suites to provide consumer assurance regarding interoperability performance. ITS is not the only sector that is concerned with the interoperability of information technologies. The National Institute of Technology and Standards has identified this problem and held a special workshop in October 1998 (Parsons) to identify issues and potential solutions to these problems.

Conforming ITS designs

One of the hottest ITS issues is what constitutes conformance to the architecture. Congress elevated this issue when it required, as a part of the TEA-21 legislation, that use of federal funds must be restricted to those systems conforming to the national ITS architecture and standards. The prime difficulty with this requirement is that it will be years before sufficient ITS standards are available to guide conformance decisions. Thus in the interim one must conform to an architecture that was purposely kept at a high level and left flexible to serve many local needs. The result is that states are accusing the FHWA of too much oversight into their planning and design process. This will continue until some organization (e.g., U.S. DOT, ITS America) defines what designs will conform. This could take the form of an approved ITS project listing wherein sample designs having different performance levels of service, such as tolling. Such a guide must also give implementers cost and other key implications, as well as an idea of the benefits, related to each sample design that conforms to the architecture.

Architecture and standard change control

The architecture is a living documentation, one that will be updated as needs or technologies change. Changes in the architecture, standards and conforming ITS designs must be approved. The U.S. DOT has set up the process to make architecture changes. A new railroad grade crossing user service has been added, and two others are in process. At publication date, it had not been decided if DOT will continue the maintenance or contract with ITS America for that service.

Architecture documentation

The reports on the national architecture include the following: equipment, infrastructure and the cost of operating the transmission services. Major volumes are:

- *Vision*—an overview of the nation's transportation system in 5, 10 and 20 years.
- *Mission definition*—the national architecture's goals and objectives, how ITS will accomplish these, description of user services and how users relate to these.
- *Theory of operations*—an overview of the technical description of the architecture in operation to illustrate how it would function.
- *Logical architecture*—a representation of the functional flow of data that depicts the input and output of information to support user services and strategic requirements to process data.
- *Physical architecture*—a description of the physical subsystems, service packages and data flow between the two. It also identifies inputs and outputs within the transportation layer of the architecture.
- *Traceability matrix*—a set of links tying user services to the logical and physical architecture demonstrating the tie between services and elements of the architecture.
- *Evolutionary deployment strategy*—an assumed design to give the reader a vision of ITS implementation and the issues expected in the short-, near- and long-term. It also provides insight on maintaining open systems within the architecture.
- *Evaluation plan*—the team's plan and methodology to evaluate the architecture.
- *Evaluation results*—a presentation of the technical, operational, feasibility, risk and human factors; costs; and computer modeling results from the team's evaluation of the architecture.
- *Implementation plan*—a presentation of how the team envisioned an evolutionary implementation of the architecture. It shows what public- and private-sector actions are needed to support such an assumed implementation.
- *Standards requirements*—a temporal plan (architecture team's opinion) of what standards would be needed to support implementation.
- *Standard development plan*—a plan (again the team's opinion) of how these standards could be developed.
- *Executive summary*—a top-level review of the architecture and its implications to those who implement hardware, software, or special facilities.

Useful documentation and tools developed by the U.S. DOT include an interactive CD that contains all pertinent architecture data. This is updated as changes are released (about every year). In addition, there is a U.S. DOT website where one can obtain the latest architecture information.

Acknowledgment

The author wishes to thank the U.S. DOT architecture team for providing him with the figures in this chapter.

References

Parsons, R. E. 1998. Paper presented at the National Institute of Standards and Technology. "Advancing Information Technology Measurements and Testing" Workshop, held October 26–27, Gaithersburg, MD.

Rechtin, Eberhardt. 1991. *System Architecting—Creating and Building Complex Systems.* Englewood Cliffs, N.J.: Prentice Hall, 305.

Varaiya, P.P. and Steven E. Shladover. 1991. "Sketch of an IVHS System Architecture." Vehicle Navigation and Information Systems Conference Proceedings 1: 909–922. Society of Automotive Engineers.

Endnotes

1. Parsons is a consulting ITS engineer from Midlothian, Virginia. He founded the PATH program at University of California at Berkeley (director from 1986 through 1993) and was the chairman of the ITS America system architecture committee from 1992 through 1998. He also founded the ITS America inter-operability subcommittee, which is striving to develop procedures and methodology to ascertain interoperability of key ITS services.

2. Stakeholders are those directly affected or influenced by introduction of the IVHS (now ITS) decision-making process.

3. Configuration management tracks design status (hardware and software) and changes that have been approved and installed in field deployments. It further establishes dates that system changes become effective in the field, so that users are informed of when they must upgrade their equipment.

4. Major U.S. universities that offer degrees in system engineering include the University of Southern California, George Mason University, and others.

5. Jack Kay, president of JHK, was the initial chair of the system architecture committee that started work on ITS goals and objectives.

6. The system engineering committee of ITS America had studied the need for a national architecture and options for its development for three years prior to this development effort by the U.S. DOT-sponsored teams.

7. The four teams in Phase I of the National ITS Architecture Development Program were: IBM (later changed to Loral), Rockwell International, Hughes and Westinghouse. In Phase II, Loral (later changed to Odetics, ITS and now prospectively changing to Iteris and Loral [changed to Lockheed Martin]) were under contract to FHWA, DOT. Also making up the "Team" is FHWA, JPL and Mitretek. Phase II was completed in January 1997. The U.S. DOT is now in the process of maintaining the National ITS Architecture and supporting ITS Deployment and National ITS Architecture Training. The National ITS Architecture is also in the process of its fourth update. Lockheed Martin and Odetics (Iteris) is under contract to FHWA, DOT to provide work in support of this effort.

8. Professor Emeritus Kan Chen, University of Michigan, was chair of this team.

9. This competition restricted some information from the stakeholders during phase I.

10. Safety warning devices include collision warning, collision avoidance, adaptive cruise control and the like.

11. The National Architecture and supporting documents are available from the U.S. DOT's Joint Program Office (JPO) for ITS. They can also be downloaded in PDF format from JPO's National ITS Architecture home page <www.its.dot.gov/arch/arch.htm>.

BY Richard J. Weiland • President • Weiland Consulting Co.

AN INTRODUCTION TO STANDARDS FOR ITS

Background—an introduction to standards

This section provides a brief introduction to standards and the reasons that we pursue them; and to the characteristics of the three notable types of standards: de facto, regulatory and consensus. We will discuss the challenges involved in developing standards and the particular challenges of developing intelligent transportation system (ITS) standards.

Why standards are important

Imagine a world where technical anarchy reigns. Every electrical appliance has its own peculiar needs for voltage and cycles per second and, to make sure it is connected only with the right kind of electricity, has a plug different from all other appliances. Every CD or tape cassette requires a specially tailored device to play it, because sizes, speeds and media formats are all different. A different radio is needed to receive the programs broadcast by each station. Clothing manufacturers each use their own scheme for stating the sizes of slacks and dresses. Each car and truck requires custom-blended fuel, and the pedals and dials in one vehicle bear no particular resemblance to those in another. For every software program, a special computer has to be designed to run it. Nuts and bolts are produced from scratch for every assembly job—new projects and machines do not use the bolts designed for a previous application.

Wasteful? Duplicative? Expensive? Inconvenient? Confusing? That is what a world without standards would be like! Standards are agreements, by industries and governments, to do things consistently—to select a single way (or at least only a few ways) to address a particular problem, so that waste can be avoided, wheels do not have to be continuously reinvented, costs can be contained and confusion is minimized. In the United States, 60 Hz, 110-volt electricity is all but universal in homes and businesses; and the plugs on our appliances fit consistently into the sockets in our walls. A CD player plays any CD. FM radios are well-equipped to receive all the FM stations in town (and they will work unaltered in other towns, too). A 16.5–33 shirt from any store fits me pretty well, and my car runs cheerfully on regular unleaded gasoline of any brand. Lots of different computer programs—from games to word processors to spreadsheets to automated art studios—all run on the same PC. There are lots of kinds of nuts and bolts, but not very many kinds relative to the quantities used or to the number of genuinely different kinds of assembly jobs; and any particular kind of bolt is available, interchangeably, from many manufacturers. So, what do standards do? They:

- Lead to compatibility and interoperability
- Help build marketplace confidence
- Encourage producer investment and involvement
- Promote the growth of industry

Standards lead to compatibility and interoperability

The primary by-product of standards is consistency—in the way products work and in the way they interact with other products and systems. This has two essential components: compatibility and interoperability.

Compatibility means that adjoining devices or systems can work together cooperatively (or at least without interfering with one another), and that a variety of similar (if not identical) components can be substituted for one another. Compatibility also means that devices can be connected to one another without the need for special interfaces. We expect, for example, that pretty much any set of speakers can be substituted for any other set of speakers connected to a stereo system, and that disconnecting one set and connecting up another is straightforward. This is because certain assumptions have been agreed upon regarding the form and strength of the signal that is delivered to the speakers by the amplifier; and regarding the wires, plugs and jacks that join them. Similarly, we expect that a pocket calculator designed to run on AA batteries will not care whether the batteries are carbon-zinc, alkaline, or lithium based, provided appropriate conventions have been observed about shape, size and delivered voltage—the characteristics that define a particular kind of battery. Computers that are IBM PC-compatible are all expected (within limits) to run the same software and behave fairly consistently when the software is loaded.

Interoperability means that the same product will operate correctly and consistently in multiple environments. We not only expect that two different radios will operate similarly in a particular area (compatibility), we also expect that the same radio (television, cellular telephone, electrical appliance) will operate correctly in any part of the country (interoperability). We not only expect that one box car can be substituted for another in a freight train (compatibility), but that a particular railroad car can be operated on tracks across the nation. Note that in many cases interoperability depends on the consistency of infrastructure, not just product design, in multiple places (e.g., train tracks).

Standards help build marketplace confidence

Especially when a field of technology is just emerging, standards help to convince a bashfully toe-dipping buying public that the technology is here to stay, and that investments in the products of the technology will not suddenly become obsolete.

Both for consumers and for business, one of the riskiest technology investments is in products available only from a single supplier, regardless of how brilliant or innovative the product may be. If the product technology has a single point of supply, the failure of that single supplier means the demise of the product; there is no ongoing support, no updated versions, and potentially no way to repair products that break. As further discussed below, standards help encourage multiple suppliers to get into the same market—in competition with one another, but all producing reasonably interchangeable products. The failure of one such producer does not imply the simultaneous demise of the product concept.

Good standards do not unduly constrain innovation, but they do help promote long-term consistency. Standards help persuade buyers that their current purchase will not become obsolete too quickly, even when innovation occurs. Standards help foster forward and backward compatibility to increase the product life. Plain monaural FM radios are able to receive and play programs broadcast in stereo. Two-prong plugs still fit into three-prong outlets (though admittedly not vice versa). You do not generally need the latest and most capable PC to run most software programs, new or old.

In addition, standards that are debated, developed, and adopted in respectable forums, like the kinds described later in this chapter, are a prescription for quality. We can reasonably expect that a product built to recognized standards will be responsive to the quality requirements of a wide target audience.

Standards help encourage producer investment and involvement

The same factors that encourage buyers to step forward also encourage producers to enter the industry. The existence of standards means that a new producer can enter the market with the assurance that its products will be acceptable to an existing and growing market. There will typically still be a lot of room for differentiation based on quality, appearance, price, and service, but most of the battle of product introduction will have already been fought and won. New manufacturers of radios and CD players do not have to start from scratch. Manufacturers of genuinely fungible products (e.g., nuts and bolts) need only respond to an unmet demand, even if they do not particularly distinguish their products from their competitors'. The larger market that standards promote also offers the promise of economies of scale: profits can be greater, even when prices to consumers are lower, by being able to make larger numbers of similar products, rather than tailoring each copy to a different set of specifications.

In addition, especially in new technology areas, standards encourage the market by helping to reduce exposure to product liability suits. Many people believe that, especially in the United States, product liability suits significantly delay the introduction of technology. The concern is that the consequences of new technology are not always well understood, and that people are not yet familiar with how to use new products safely. Suits claiming negligence or foreseeable misuse can result in judgments for many millions of dollars. Standards help to minimize the risks, both of adverse effects on users and liability exposure to producers. First, the existence of standards means that manufacturers know the minimum quality and performance levels they have to achieve to be responsible producers. Such quality and performance standards will have been the result of extended, industry-wide consideration and exploration; and they can generally be counted on to be satisfactory to a broad range of interested parties. Producer adherence to these standards provides end users with considerable assurance of safety and reliability. Second, because of the way standards are arrived at through industry consensus, when liability suits do occur, producer conformance to widely-accepted industry standards is considered to be an important and compelling demonstration in court that the producer has not been negligent.

Standards help promote industry growth

Taken together, both sides of the standards equation—enhanced marketplace confidence and greater, quicker producer investment—mean a more rapidly growing industry. Compare the videotape industry (which struggled for years with multiple incompatible recording formats) with the CD industry (in which the CD format was widely agreed upon before going to market). The CD industry grew rapidly almost from its inception, while videotapes did not really take off until the Beta versus VHS dispute was resolved.

In the transportation arena, standards are recognized as major enablers of technology, and the absence of standards as a technology inhibitor. For example, multiple incompatible technologies for electronic toll collection arose in the early 1990s. Truckers were dismayed at the notion of having to carry a different electronic transponder for every toll system they traversed. Toll operating authorities were often daunted by the prospect of contracting for expensive, unstandardized equipment from single suppliers. At this writing, efforts are underway to develop standards for electronic toll collection that will foster national interoperability, providing comfort to toll authorities, simplicity to toll payers, and the prospect of streamlined production and enhanced profitability to system producers.

Risks of under-standardizing

The bottom line is that nonexistent or inadequate standards add to the risk, cost and uncertainty of industrial deployment. Markets are inhibited, delayed, or stunted. The cost of technology development is increased; and prolonged technical wrangling over which of multiple, slightly different technical avenues to pursue delays product introduction and acceptance. The absence of standards can lead to local or regional solutions, especially where infrastructure is involved, sometimes with unfortunate long-term consequences. Australia, for example, is still trying to work its way out of the bind resulting from the 19th-century adoption of different rail gauges in each of its states that made interstate rail traffic essentially impossible. The European and U.S. rail communities are still confronted by multiple technologies for delivering electricity to locomotives, including elaborate and expensive mechanisms to switch a moving train from overhead to third-rail power at critical junctions.

On the other hand, it is possible to standardize too soon, before technology has sufficiently matured or is fully understood. Users of personal computers labored for years under the constraint that limited program sizes to 640 kilobytes, even when computers had millions of bytes of available memory. Europe is struggling with upgrading a standardized but primitive radio data system that was innovative and pioneering in its day, but which was built around the very low data rates and other technical constraints that were then the state-of-the-art.

Determining whether the time is ripe for standardization is a constant debate in industrial technology. Standardization too soon means unnecessary constraints and the inability to take full advantage of innovation. Standardization too late risks obsoleting a large installed technology base, with all the attendant political and economic tangles that such obsolescence entails. With no crystal ball, but plenty of competing vested interests, this debate is unlikely to go away.

Kinds of standards

There are actually three different kinds of standards, distinguished by who the developers are and how, if at all, the standards are enforced. These are:

- De facto standards that arise mainly through marketplace forces, rather than organized industry-wide efforts
- Regulatory standards that are created by government agencies, essentially with the effect of law
- Industry consensus standards that are constructed through formalized but voluntary participation of multiple interested parties

After the discussion immediately below, industry consensus standards will be the focus of most of the remainder of this chapter.

De facto standards

De facto standards are determined by the marketplace, sometimes through the predominance of a particular supplier (e.g., MS Windows®), sometimes through prolonged market struggle in which one party ultimately emerges victorious (e.g., the VHS® videotape format), and sometimes through a cooperation of several producers (e.g., compact discs).

Such a cooperative standard, recently emerged, is the DVD format for putting a complete motion picture on a single 5-inch optical disc. Two different manufacturing consortia had proposed quite different formats and, as can be expected in such cases, the industry was at a standstill waiting for a resolution—neither movie discs nor players for these discs were being produced, except in prototype. The compromise resolution of these consortia was hailed in the press as an industry-enabling event: a single-video format that everyone could use.

Open versus proprietary standards

De facto standards are most common in industries with just a few dominant participants who can, within limits, dictate the standards. It can be argued that such standards favor these dominant participants, at least initially. However, such standards can also help to speed the entry of smaller competing producers, especially when these de facto standards are made open rather than proprietary. Open means that other industry entrants are invited and encouraged to build products in accordance with the standards. This can happen through the originator's licensing others to use the standard technology or by its putting the technology and standard into the public domain. Proprietary means the opposite—the developer does not allow anyone else to build to the standard.

A notable example of the value of open standards is the personal computer. IBM essentially dictated the hardware and software architecture (Intel chips and, initially, Microsoft's MS-DOS® operating system), but it opened this architecture to other vendors. IBM remains a major producer of PCs, but alongside a large number of other hardware producers, some of which have also been highly successful.

But why would a manufacturer open up its de facto standards for use by others? As PCs have demonstrated, such an action strongly encourages industry growth. IBM arguably sells more PCs in competition with other vendors than it would have by keeping the architecture proprietary. In addition, larger volume hardware sales also promote the sale of compatible software whose dollar volume may well exceed the hardware's. At the same time, the availability of a wide range of software products encourages more purchases of the hardware—a mutually beneficial positive feedback loop.

Contrast this with the Apple Macintosh, whose architecture was kept proprietary for most of its life. Although some would argue that Macintosh hardware and operating software are technologically superior to the PCs, the vast majority of the marketplace belongs to PCs. A far narrower array of software is available for the Mac, and peripheral hardware (e.g., printers) is typically more expensive for Macs than PCs. Many people believe that this was largely a result of the PC's architecture and standards being open while the Mac's were not.

The recording industry provides an equally good example. Open de facto standards for the CD format facilitated hardware (player) sales; but, more importantly, they facilitated sales of the discs themselves, for which both the margins and the total dollar volume are much larger than for players.

Regulatory standards

Regulatory standards are created and enforced by government agencies at all levels. Such standards include regulations relating to food handling; safe working environments; air quality; and, of course, a large number of standards related to transportation. These include infrastructure-related standards dealing with such subjects as the uniform appearance of roadside signs and the curvature and banking of pavement. They also include vehicle-related standards such as fuel economy, crash worthiness and so forth.

Some regulatory standards coordinate and allocate scarce public resources. A notable example is the allocation of radio frequency bands for particular purposes: two-way commercial radio, FM broadcast, television channels and so forth.

Regulatory standards are at their best when they deal carefully with issues of public health and safety, areas in which marketplace forces left to themselves might unduly sacrifice such considerations for apparent economy. Enhancing air quality by reducing emissions, for example, may require both more expensive fuel and more expensive vehicles. Such tradeoffs are difficult to implement on an individual basis. Even with general agreement that air quality is a public good, individual vehicle owners are unlikely to make individual sacrifices in favor of air quality in large numbers unless others do the same, and vehicle manufacturers and motor fuel companies are unlikely to make air-friendly (but more expensive) choices available without a sizeable population willing (or constrained) to make such a choice. In these cases, the delegated decision-making represented by a regulatory standard helps make the decision economically viable.

In some cases, the marketplace overtakes regulation and makes it less obviously necessary. Safety in automobiles has become a major selling consideration, and safety-oriented devices like antilock brake systems and airbags essentially became standard equipment ahead of regulatory mandates.

Industry consensus standards

Industry consensus standards are voluntary standards agreements, worked out through the cooperation of interested parties. Interested parties include technology vendors, technology users, government agencies at all levels, advocacy groups, industry consultants and others.

In many cases, such standards are developed under the aegis of a nationally recognized standards development organization (SDO), accredited in the United States by the American National Standards Institute (ANSI). Quoting the description on its web page, ANSI is "a private, not-for-profit membership organization that coordinates the U.S. voluntary consensus standards system and approves American National Standards. ANSI consists of approximately 1,300 national and international companies; 30 government agencies; 20 institutional members; and 250 professional, technical, trade, labor and consumer organizations." Accreditation by ANSI (or by corresponding national standards bodies in other countries) helps to assure that the standards development process is:

- *Open*—that standards are developed via a process that is visible and open (no hidden, smoke-filled rooms).
- *Inclusive*—that all interested parties are given the opportunity to participate.
- *Conducted in accordance with due process*—that standards development proceeds through a number of well-defined stages, including checkpoints at which the process itself is carefully examined for fairness.
- *Consensus-based*—that approving a standard requires general agreement, typically arrived at through cooperation and compromise. Consensus does not mean unanimity, nor does it mean rule by simple majority. It means that dissenting voices have been listened to and adequately accommodated, and that the result is reasonably agreeable to a large majority of participants.

Why consensus standards are hard

It is widely recognized that the development of consensus standards is a long, slow, tortuous process. There are a number of reasons why this is the case.

- *Work is mainly political, not technical.* The development of consensus standards obviously includes a lot of technical content and some amount of technical wrangling. However, reconciling technology is not what makes standards development hard and slow. The difficulty comes from the fact that standards development is mainly a job of reconciling and harmonizing conflicting vested interests. A particular approach is proposed as a standard not only because it has technical merit, but also because there is an investment—of time, of energy, of money—in that approach.

If our approach becomes the standard, then we are that much further ahead of the competition in being able to exploit the market. If their approach becomes the standard, then our investment may get discarded, requiring us to play catch-up in the market. On the other hand, if we cannot arrive at a compromise (at a consensus approach that everyone can buy into), then the whole market may be delayed, and everyone will lose.

A lot of the time and effort involved in developing standards is spent—though not too much, we hope—in jockeying for position: each party preserving as much of its technical advantage as it can without hamstringing the whole process. While the language will generally be technical, the activities relate intensely to politics and economics.

- *Work depends on volunteer effort.* In the United States particularly, despite its recognized importance, standards-making is typically a part-time, additional responsibility, not a primary job. Indeed, the best advocates for a particular approach are typically the engineers, scientists and technologists who develop and exploit these approaches. The time they spend on standards is time away from the work station and laboratory.

Standards committees typically meet at intervals ranging from every other month to twice a year, and it is well-recognized that the primary function of a meeting is to provide a deadline for accomplishing the tasks laid out at the previous meeting. In some cases, participants will be assigned full-time to standards work, or consultants will be engaged to do standards-related research or write drafts. However, in most cases, standards development depends on the part-time resources of multiple, scattered participants.

Then why develop standards this way?

Why make standards this slow, complicated, political way? The answer is that in most cases, this process produces the best, most durable, most widely accepted standards. Keep in mind that industry standards, whether de facto or consensus, are adopted and used voluntarily, as well as developed voluntarily. Anyone can put a standard forward; but, in most cases, no one is under any obligation to follow it, beyond the exercise of their best judgment.

De facto standards work when a small number of players representing a large fraction of the producer community can dictate them. When major participants cannot agree, or when the market is divided among many participants, de facto standards can take a very long time to emerge. A classic example, already mentioned, was the prolonged dispute between the Beta and VHS formats for home videotape. Neither Sony Corporation (Beta format) nor JVC Corporation (VHS format) was prepared to cooperate and compromise before going to market, and the marketplace took many years to make VHS its ultimate choice. Sony has been more successful in getting an industry consensus on its 8-millimeter videotape format for compact camcorders.

Why ITS standards are particularly hard

Developing ITS standards presents challenges even beyond those of typical consensus standard-making. These include:

- *The newness of the ITS field.* As a recognized field of professional activity, ITS is only about ten years old at this writing. As such, it has had only minimal opportunity to define itself. In addition, because ITS makes heavy use of computers and telecommunications, it finds itself working with and dependent on very rapidly evolving technology.

- *ITS is interdisciplinary.* By its nature, ITS draws on multiple engineering and technical disciplines, including automotive engineering, civil engineering, computer science, electrical engineering, telecommunications and transportation engineering. Although it draws on each of these disciplines, ITS does not include the entire scope of any one of them. As a result, while many of the practitioners of each discipline have interests in ITS, they have other, nonoverlapping interests as well; and no single group of discipline-oriented practitioners covers all of ITS. This means that ITS standards work needs to draw on the services of multiple experts from many fields; and the success of this work depends on their working cooperatively and constructively together, despite their diverse backgrounds and competing interests.

- *Partnership issues.* In addition to being interdisciplinary, ITS also draws on multiple sectors of the economy, including:
  — *The private sector*, which builds and delivers ITS products and services to both public and private consumers
  — *Academia*, which provides initial training to ITS practitioners and performs an important portion of basic ITS research
  — *Public agencies at all levels of government*, which, among other things, are the primary deployers of transportation infrastructure, and their consultants

  One of ITS' innovations is in bringing these very disparate sectors together. However, the divergence of these sectors' backgrounds, goals and motivations, and the relatively brief time that participants have had to build mutual trust and productive working relationships, sometimes makes effective cooperation difficult. Although this challenge is not unique to standards-making, it is particularly vivid in this area, because of the broad range of interests on which standards impinge.

- *Architecture.* For most of its short life, ITS was without an overall organizing framework under which standards could be consistently and compatibly developed. In the early 1990s, recognizing this vacuum, ITS America[1] recommended that the U.S. Department of Transportation (U.S. DOT) conduct an aggressive program to formulate an overarching national system architecture for ITS. In 1996, the national ITS architecture program began delivering its recommendations, including a framework for interface standards that are particularly important for fostering national ITS interoperability. The architecture has been generally well-received by the ITS community. The most recent transportation bill, Transportation Equity Act for the 21st Century (TEA-21), provides strong encouragement for new ITS systems, particularly infrastructure-oriented systems, to conform to the architecture. More germanely for this chapter, the architecture has finally provided an organizing framework within which to advance ITS standards development.

Nonetheless, for all the challenges of standards-making in general and of ITS standards-making in particular, the ITS world has made significant progress in creating a reasonable process for standards creation and in developing important ITS standards. The remainder of this chapter will focus on the roles and activities in this process; and it will provide pointers to where information can be found on completed, in-process and needed ITS standards.

ITS standards-making

In this section, we will identify the participants in ITS standards-making and the roles they play, and the standards development process as it works in North America.

Roles and participants

It should first be understood that standards-making is generally open to all interested individuals, and that participants, as individuals, are all on the same footing. From the viewpoint of the process, each has an equal opportunity to participate and each has an equal voice. In practice, of course, opportunities to participate will be constrained by the time and funding available to a potential participant, and influence, at least in part, will be proportional to the energy, motivation, skill and commitment of the people who actually participate. Ultimately, however, even the loudest and best-funded individual voice cannot prevail unless it can assemble a consensus, both to pass a particular standard and to promote its acceptance by the community at large. In addition to these individual roles, however, there are a number of important institutional roles in the development of ITS standards, including those of:

- The federal government (notably the U.S. DOT)
- State, regional, metropolitan and local governments
- ITS America and its technical committees, including the Committee on Standards and Protocols
- The SDOs

Federal role

Among many other provisions, TEA-21 (and before that the Intermodal Surface Transportation Efficiency Act) prescribes a strong federal presence through the U.S. DOT in the development and promotion of ITS standards. TEA-21 directs the U.S. DOT to identify critical ITS standards needs and to make sure that these critical standards are in place by 2001, if necessary by promulgating provisional standards itself. The U.S. DOT's focal point for ITS standards is the ITS Joint Program Office, which provides a multimodal and intermodal perspective on ITS.

DOT's own vision for the deployment of ITS—making the transition from an emphasis on physical infrastructure to an emphasis on systems—depends significantly on the prompt development and widespread acceptance of a variety of standards in the context of the evolving national ITS architecture. The U.S. DOT has accepted the responsibility to encourage, facilitate and catalyze the creation of ITS standards. As the contracting agency for the national ITS architecture program, the U.S. DOT was a major influence in supporting the development of an ITS standards framework and the identification of standards important for fostering national ITS interoperability. In addition, the U.S. DOT has direct responsibilities for standards relating to safety and the public welfare, notably through the regulatory activities of the National Highway Traffic Safety Administration.

There is a risk that a too-strong federal role could jeopardize the ITS standards development process, rather than facilitate it. Consensus standards-making is a sturdily and stubbornly independent process, a fact that is generally to the industry's benefit. If the U.S. DOT's participation were to create the impression of trying to dominate the development of ITS standards, the result could be counterproductive. Achieving consensus would be extremely difficult; and short of compulsion, the community might well decline to adopt such standards. The U.S. DOT had to execute a very careful balancing act in identifying and following through on the critical standards described in TEA-21. Identifying too few standards as critical could have resulted in too little ITS consistency and interoperability, while too many critical standards could have overburdened the standards development system or discouraged it altogether through the prospect of U.S. DOT-imposed provisional standards.

However, it is clear that the judicious application of the U.S. DOT's ideas, energies and funds has been and can continues to be enormously useful in advancing the ITS standards program. The U.S. DOT provides individual experts from its ranks to participate with others in standards development. In addition, the U.S. DOT is working to help fund the activities of SDOs, facilitate participation by experts who might not otherwise be able to do so and encourage the use of contractors to research technology issues and options and to prepare drafts for committee consideration.

State, regional, metropolitan and local government role

Nonfederal agencies constitute an important collection of users and deployers of ITS technology, particularly with regard to the infrastructure for gathering and disseminating travel information and managing the overall transportation system. Unfortunately, such agencies often do not have the funding or the legislative encouragement to participate in national standards efforts. This situation presents the risk both of having systems and standards developed that are not adequately responsive to the needs of these users, and of developing solutions that are local or regional in scope rather than national. Efforts are being made to avoid these risks, through federal support of state and local standards participation and by nationally coordinating the local input and involvement of these agencies via ITS America's state and regional chapters.

ITS America

As the embodiment of the nationwide public–private ITS partnership, ITS America is a natural point of focus for the diverse interests and constituencies that make up the ITS community. Although its charter permits it to develop standards directly if necessary, ITS America has chosen to direct its efforts toward facilitating coordination and communication among the other participants. In particular, ITS America serves as a multidisciplinary forum for the articulation, coordination and documentation of the community's requirements for ITS standards, rather than for the writing of the standards themselves.

The primary home for this requirements development is ITS America's technical committees, with coordination from the Committee on Standards and Protocols. ITS America's Architecture and Standards Department provides staff support for standards-related activities (as well as for architecture activities). The Advanced Public Transportation Systems Committee drafted the first ITS-specific standard, for a smart electronic data bus for ITS-enhanced public transit vehicles (the "Smart Bus for Smart Buses"). Several ITS America technical committees have formed subcommittees specifically for the exploration of standards in their respective core areas.

SDOs

The SDOs, which actually write and approve standards, are often ANSI-accredited professional societies, like the Society of Automotive Engineers (SAE) or the Institute of Electronics and Electrical Engineers (IEEE). Such societies are a natural focal point for the practitioners of particular technical disciplines germane to ITS. SDOs can also be industry associations such as the Telecommunications Industry Association (TIA), which is also accredited as an SDO by ANSI; or other professional organizations with more limited memberships such as American Association of State Highway and Transportation Officials (AASHTO). AASHTO is an example of a respected and influential SDO (focusing primarily on highway infrastructure standards) that has not sought ANSI accreditation, because its standards-making process is not designed for open participation by the industry at large. Some SDOs are specifically established for the purpose of setting standards. The American Society of Testing and Materials (ASTM) is a notable example. Table 20–1 lists several prominent SDOs involved in ITS, including addresses, fax and phone numbers, and Internet home pages, where available.

About a dozen SDOs are members of the ITS America Council of Standards Organizations (CSO), a special subcommittee of ITS America's Standards and Protocols Committee. The function of the CSO is to foster communications among ITS-related SDOs, assure that the ITS community's standards needs are communicated to the SDOs, help minimize duplication of effort and generally serve as a focal point for interactions between the SDOs and the rest of the ITS community.

Table 20–1
Selected U.S., International and European Multinational Standards Organizations

Name	Address	Phone/Fax/Web Page
American Association of State Highway and Transportation Officials	444 North Capitol Street, N.W. Suite 249 Washington, DC 20001 USA	T: 1-202-624-5800 F: 1-202-624-5806 http://www.aashto.org
American National Standards Institute	11 West 42nd Street New York, NY 10036 USA	T: 1-212-642-4900 F: 1-212-398-0023 http://www.ansi.org
American Society for Testing and Materials	100 Barr Harbor Drive West Conshohocken, PA 19428 USA	T: 1-610-832-9500 F: 1-610-832-9555 http://www.astm.org
Consumer Electronics Association	2500 Wilson Boulevard Arlington, VA 22201 USA	T: 1-703-907-7600 F: 1-703-907-7675 http://www.ce.org
Comité Européen de Normalisation	36 Rue de Stassart B-1050 Brussels, Belgium	T: 32-2-550-08-11 F: 32-2-550-08-09 http://www.cenorm.be
Comité Européen de Normalisation Electrotechnique	35 Rue de Stassart B-1050 Brussels, Belgium	T: 32-2-519-68-71 F: 32-2-519-69-19 http://www.cenelec.be
Electronics Industry Alliance	2500 Wilson Boulevard Arlington, VA 22201 USA	T: 1-703-907-7500 F: 1-703-907-7501 http://www.eia.org
European Telecommunications Standards Institute	06921 Sophia Antipolis Cedex France	T: 33-92-94-42-00 F: 33-93-65-47-16 http://www.etsi.org
International Bridge, Tunnel, and Turnpike Association	2120 L Street, N.W., Suite 305 Washington, DC 20037 USA	T: 1-202-659-4620 F: 1-202-659-0500 http://www.ibtta.org
International Electrotechnical Commission	3 rue de Varembe P.O. Box 131 CH-1211 Geneva 20 Switzerland	T: 41-22-919-0211 F: 41-22-919-0300 http://www.iec.ch
Institute of Electrical and Electronics Engineers	445 Hoes Lane P.O. Box 1331 Piscataway, NJ 08855 USA	T: 1-732-981-0600 F: 1-732-981-0027 http://www.ieee.org
International Standards Organization	1 rue de Varembe P.O. Box 56 CH-1211 Geneva 20 Switzerland	T: 41-22-749-91-11 F: 41-22-733-34-30 http://www.iso.ch
Institute of Transportation Engineers	525 School Street, S.W., Suite 410 Washington, DC 20024 USA	T: 1-202-554-8050 F: 1-202-863-5486 http://www.ite.org
International Telecommunications Union	Place des Nations CH-1211 Geneva 20 Switzerland	T: 41-22-730-5111 F: 41-22-730-7256 http://www.itu.ch
Society of Automotive Engineers	400 Commonwealth Drive Warrendale, PA 15096 USA	T: 1-724-776-4841 F: 1-724-776-5760 http://www.sae.org
Telecommunications Industry Association	2500 Wilson boulevard Arlington, VA 22201 USA	T: 1-703-907-7700 F: 1-703-907-7727 http://www.tiaonline.org

The ITS standards development process

Like other nontrivial technical products (including the standards created for other industries), the development of ITS standards proceeds through several life-cycle stages, most notably:

- Identification of need
- Requirements analysis
- Development and approval
- Acceptance and use
- Maintenance and retirement

Identification of need

The need for an ITS standard can be identified in several ways. In some cases, technology vendors will do the identification, perceiving that the time is ripe for standardizing a product, process, or interface to help advance the industry and their business. In some cases, user groups will take the initiative to harmonize multiple overlapping technologies that are impeding their ability to do low-risk, cost-contained procurement. In some cases, government agencies will identify the need for a standard to protect health and safety or otherwise advance the public interest. In the ITS world, the work of the national ITS architecture program included identifying particularly crucial standards. An important role of the ITS America Standards and Protocols Committee and the CSO is to stay abreast of newly identified needs for standards, so that the process of transforming a need into a standard moves forward systematically and promptly.

Requirements analysis

Requirements analysis is the job of determining what the standard has to accomplish: defining the problem that the standard is expected to solve. It helps to define the scope of the standard and the subject areas that the standard needs to address. The requirements justify and document the identified need. In some cases, the players who identify the need for a standard will also define the requirements. In ITS, this is particularly true for standards needs identified by the national ITS architecture program. The program's purview included high-level requirements analysis for the standards needs that it identified. In some cases, requirements analysis will be the initial step pursued by an SDO, in preparation for writing a standard, especially when the need for a standard arises directly from industry.

In many cases, the determination of requirements for an ITS standard is the work of ITS America's technical committees. ITS America has established a general procedure for the definition of standards requirements and for their transmission to one or more SDOs. This process seeks to involve interested user and technology vendor groups in establishing their needs in a particular standards area. It also begins the process of engaging the attention of one or more appropriate SDOs, to whom the requirements will be handed off upon completion.

In addition, as requirements unfold, some standards issues will arise that are of particular interest to the ITS community in general or that have policy implications for ITS America or the U.S. DOT. In these cases, the Standards and Protocols Committee is responsible for assuring that information about these standards issues flows in appropriate directions.

Development and approval

The work of actually constructing a consensus ITS standard invariably takes place within an SDO, based on identified needs and requirements. In most cases, an ITS standards topic will fall clearly within the scope of a particular SDO (e.g., SAE for automotive construction issues, IEEE for electronics and telecommunications, the Institute of Transportation Engineers [ITE] for transportation engineering, AASHTO for roadway infrastructure, ASTM for materials). The request to an SDO to undertake a particular ITS standards effort will often be made through ITS America's CSO, which also serves to resolve situations in which portions of a standard need to be divided among multiple SDOs or where the allocation of work is not obvious. A subgroup within an SDO will often exist for handling ITS-related matters. SAE has an ITS Division. IEEE has an ITS Standards Coordinating Committee. ITE has an ITS Council.

The SDO will form a standards writing committee, typically by seeking appropriate subject matter experts from within its membership (although once the committee is formed, any interested party is welcome to participate). Membership usually includes both vendors and users of the relevant technology. A chairperson and a recording secretary are appointed. The committee meets periodically (typically two to six times a year) to scope out the needed standard, explore existing standards work that may be relevant, commission and review relevant research and construct a draft in accordance with the drafting and formatting guidelines of the SDO. As previously observed, much of the actual work of a committee is done between meetings. At meetings, this work is reviewed, conflicts are resolved and new assignments are made. Comments may also be received from elsewhere in the community, which are invariably seriously and conscientiously considered in proceeding toward the draft standard. Progress is reported to the SDO and other interested parties.

This brief overview does not adequately capture the volume of work performed, or the energy and creativity involved in harmonizing diverse technical and business interests into a single consensus standard. The effort is often intense and feelings are often high. The fact that consensus is in fact generally arrived at is a tribute to the dedication and hard work of the thousands of professionals involved in the process.

When the committee arrives at a solid draft that appears to adequately accommodate the divergent interests of the committee members, the draft is sent out for a written committee ballot. The rules for draft acceptance vary somewhat among SDOs, but in general, approval requires a significant fraction of the membership to vote (typically at least 50 percent) and for there to be a significant approving supermajority (like 70 percent in favor). Regardless of the vote, any important areas of disagreement must be addressed and resolved. Multiple ballots on an evolving draft standard are often required before consensus occurs.

Once the committee has passed the draft, it is subjected to review by the SDO, often in multiple stages. Such a review generally does not second guess the technical content of the standard. Rather, the primary function of the review is to assure that the rules for standard development were followed, including openness, due process and arrival at consensus. If defects in the process are discovered, the draft standard is returned to the committee for further work that repairs the defects. Once all approvals have been secured, the standard is official. It is published and publicized by the SDO and made readily available to the industry.

Acceptance and use

In general, the use of industry consensus standards is voluntary; no one is forced to use them. However, it can reasonably be expected that the industry participants who worked to develop the standard will be inclined to adopt it, for all of the good reasons indicated at the beginning of this chapter, and other industry participants will often follow suit. When the people write specifications for the products and systems their companies or agencies want to acquire, they will frequently include relevant standards as part of the specification. The inclusion of such standards in these specifications will in some cases be a precondition for certain kinds of government funding.

Natural selection often applies to standards: good ones are adopted and widely used, while poor ones are used briefly and either discarded or ignored altogether.

Maintenance and retirement

Although standards are intended to be a stabilizing force, it is important that they not cause technical stagnation or force practice to trail very far behind the state-of-the-art. Recognizing that the state-of-the-art is often very fluid, most SDOs require that standards be periodically reviewed. On a regular schedule (on the order of every five years), committees are formed to revisit each of its standards then in force. The two simpler outcomes of this review are at opposite extremes: the committee can determine that the standard is still serviceable without modification, or it can determine that the standard is no longer relevant and should be withdrawn. Renewing a standard still requires a vote of a relevant expert group within the SDO followed by SDO approval. Withdrawal is usually simpler, unless there is strong industry difference of opinion on such an action. If interest in the standard is so low that it is not even possible to assemble a review committee, there are usually SDO provisions to retire it automatically. The more complicated case is a determination that the standard is relevant but outdated and needs to be revised. In this case, a process is followed that is very similar to the one used for creating a standard; it merely does not need to start entirely from scratch.

International ITS standards

In this section we will explore ITS standards-making on the international level and the new set of challenges involved in harmonizing standards across national boundaries.

Background

In the introduction to this chapter, we identified a number of things that are widely standardized: electrical current and plugs, clothing sizes, nut and bolts and so forth. It may have occurred to you at the time that there are some very important ways in which these things are not standardized, most notably across oceans and often across national borders on the same continent. Outside of North America, much of the world uses 220 volt, 50 Hz electricity (although Japan uses 100 volt, 50 Hz). Wall plugs vary widely from country to country. (Indeed, I am typing this paragraph on a trans-Pacific flight for which my baggage includes an entire kit of plug adapters.) In Europe, telephone jacks vary from country to country and sometimes within a country. Outside of the United States, clothing sizes, nuts and bolts are measured using millimeters and centimeters rather than inches. Driving rules and car safety regulations change with each border. Videotapes that work in the United States and Japan do not work in European VCRs and vice versa. On the other hand, pocket radios and compact discs are generally interchangeable around the world, and you can reliably send a fax from a fax machine or PC just about anywhere and have it correctly received just about anywhere else. What is going on here?

In brief, the standardization of much technology traditionally stopped at national borders or at sea shores. Although international SDOs have been in place for many years, the standards they worked on tended to be highly specialized, focusing on products and technology that were clearly international in scope; or which had to do with radio transmissions, which are hard to keep strictly within national borders. Why make a global standard, say, for electronic toll collection transponders, when a truck is unlikely to pay tolls on both sides of an ocean?

This misses the point, of course, that global technology standards create global marketplaces; economies of scale for producers; and cheaper, more robust products for purchasers. It sometimes misses other points as well. Cellular telephones are standardized in North America and separately standardized in Europe, but these standards are not compatible with one another. One reason for this was that when the standards were originally being created, cellular meant car phones. Too few people visualized the proliferation of portable cellular phones and the desirability of having these pocket phones interoperable around the world. With the amount of cellular infrastructure already in place, this is going to be a difficult area to reconcile. Some international standards discovered their scope just in the nick of time: until Australia spoke up, the standards for transoceanic cables were about to be set only to handle the distance from North America to Europe.

In recent years, there has been a growing recognition that most technology and products are potentially international in scope and a consequent growing interest in developing global standards from firms who want to sell to a global marketplace.

This recognition has been particularly acute in Europe, where the transition from national markets toward a European Union (EU) has sharply increased the necessity for international standardization within Europe.

However, this recognition also exists in North America and the Pacific Rim, who are joining forces with Europe to create genuinely global standards. International standards development has fallen into three general categories: telecommunications, electronics and everything else. There are both European multinational standards organizations and global standards organizations for each of these three categories (table 20–2).

Table 20–2
International and European Multinational Standards Organizations

	Telecommunications	Electronics	Everything Else
International	International Telecommunications Union	International Electrotechnical Commission	International Standards Organization
European Multinational	European Telecommunications Standards Institute	Comité Européen de Normalisation Electrotechnique ("European Electrotechnical Standards Committee—CENELEC)	Comité Européen de Normalisation ("European Standards Committee"—CEN)

On a global level, the largest international standards organization, and the one most generally relevant to transportation, is the International Standards Organization (ISO), headquartered in Geneva, Switzerland. The ISO acronym is particularly pleasing, since the prefix iso- means the same. Over 100 countries are members of ISO, through their respective national standards bodies. ANSI is the ISO member body for the United States, Standards Canada for Canada, Deutsches Institut für Normung for Germany, and others. ISO's work is conducted through a series of technical committees (TCs), now numbering into the hundreds, including the venerable TC 22 (road vehicles) and the rather new TC 211 (geomatics), both of which impinge on ITS. You may have heard of ISO through the attention given to the ISO 9000 series of quality standards, or by looking on the side of a box of film, whose speed is ISO-standardized.

When ISO sets up a technical committee, each country decides whether to be an active and voting participant in its work (a P-Member), an observer on the TC's mailing list (an O-member), or a nonparticipant. At minimum, P-Member countries are expected to review and vote on TC-developed draft standards. More typically, P-Members provide experts to serve on the TC's standards writing subcommittees and working groups. Each P-Member, regardless of country size or the number of experts it supplies, has one vote at the TC level. To formulate national positions on TC issues and appoint experts to a TC, P-member countries often form a domestic advisory group related to the TC. In the United States, these are called technical advisory groups (TAGs). The International Electrotechnical Commission (IEC) and the International Telecommunications Union (ITU) operate under a similar structure. IEC specializes in standards relating to electronics. ITU specializes in telecommunications. ITU is a treaty organization, not a formal standards body, but the effect of its work is much the same. All three organizations maintain close liaison with one another and work cooperatively in areas that overlap multiple fields of expertise.

It is fair to say that developing international standards is even more difficult than developing national standards. This results from the broadened range of diverse vested interests, sometimes conflicting national policy and regulations from one country to another, and the added complication and expense of international travel to conduct standards activities. Language barriers complicate things further to an extent; but in general, English has emerged as the language in which international standardization is conducted.

International ITS standardization

In 1991, through the urging of SAE, ANSI proposed that ISO form a new TC on ITS-related matters. In 1992, a vote of ISO members approved the proposal, and ISO formed TC 204. At its first meeting, in Washington, D.C. in April 1993, TC 204 chose a name for itself: Transport Information and Control Systems (although there is now a movement underway to change the name to Intelligent Transport Systems). It also created a scope statement and defined its working group structure (table 20–3). Because the United States made the initial proposal to form TC 204, ISO named the United States to be TC 204 secretariat, with responsibility for administering the TC. ANSI designated SAE to handle this responsibility.

Table 20–3
TC 204 Scope and Structure

TC 204 Scope:

Standardization of information, communication, and control systems in the field of urban and rural surface transportation, including intermodal and multimodal aspects thereof, traveler information, traffic management, public transport, commercial transport, emergency services and commercial services in the transport information and control systems field.

TC 204 Structure:

Working Group	Name	Convenor	US Working Advisory Group Administrator
1	System Architecture	United Kingdom	ITS America
2	Quality and Reliability Requirements*	United States	IEEE
3	Database Technology	Japan	SAE
4	Automatic Vehicle Identification		
5	Fee and Toll Collection	Netherlands	IBTTA
6	General Fleet Management*	United States	
7	Commercial Fleet and Freight Management	Canada	American Trucking Association
8	Public Transport/Emergency Fleet Management	United States	Volpe Transportation Research Laboratory
9	Transport Information Management and Control	Australia	ITE
10	Traveler Information	United Kingdom	SAE
11	Route Guidance and Navigation	Germany	SAE
12	Parking Management*		
13	Man-Machine Interfaces**	United States	SAE
14	Vehicle Road Warning and Control	Japan	ITS America
15	Dedicated Short-Range Communication	Germany	ASTM
16	Wide Area Communications	United States	TIA

* Dormant
** Most activities now being performed by ISO TC22 (Road Vehicles), Subcommittee 13

ITS America took on the job of administering the U.S. TAG for TC 204. The U.S. TAG meets periodically to elect officers, appoint the U.S. delegation to TC 204 plenary meetings, confirm working advisory group nomination of experts to the working groups (WGs), identify and confirm convenors and rapporteurs (secretaries) for U.S.-convened WGs and establish U.S. positions on issues that the TC will address. Each delegate is appointed with the understanding that he or she represents the United States and the positions formulated by the TAG, not the delegate's personal or corporate viewpoint.

An analogous European technical committee had already been formed by the Comité Europeèn de Normalisation (CEN): TC 278, entitled Road Transport and Traffic Telematics. To minimize duplication of effort and the likelihood of pursuing different standards directions on the same subject, ISO TC 204 and CEN TC 278 joined forces under an existing agreement between ISO and CEN called the Vienna Agreement. Where the same subjects were going to be pursued by the two TCs, a single joint working group was formed, encompassing the experts from both organizations. In the cases where TC 278 had already made significant progress on the work item, leadership for the work item was delegated to CEN TC 278. In other cases, leadership was assigned to ISO TC 204. Draft standards developed by these joint efforts are voted on, in parallel, by both ISO and CEN. TC 204 also established liaison with ISO TC 22 (road vehicles), ISO TC 211 (geomatics), IEC and ITU.

Since its inception, TC 204 has been meeting in plenary session twice a year. Plenary sessions are for the purpose of reviewing and approving proposed work items (that is, proposals for writing particular standards), exchanging information, updating administrative structures, and reviewing the draft standards developed by its working groups and releasing them for full written ballot by P-Member countries. Plenaries are held in the second half of each year in conjunction with the annual ITS World Congress, which rotates among North America, Europe and the Pacific. On the first half of each year, TC 204 meets in another location chosen to provide variety and balance to the World Congress locations. TC 204's working groups often meet in conjunction with the semiannual plenary, as well as at other times and places, depending in part on which countries send experts to the particular working group, on the other professional activities going on and, of course, on the level of activity within that particular WG.

Challenges for the future

In this section, we will try to look ahead to the challenges that the ITS standards community will face as the industry continues to grow and mature. In particular, we will discuss the need to keep ITS standards up with emerging technology; how the process can be accelerated; the harmonization of domestic and international standards efforts; and issues related to getting standards, once written and approved, to be adopted and used by the ITS community. For the most part, these challenges do not have quick or easy solutions; but their continuing consideration is important to making progress on these important fronts.

Challenge: keeping up with technology

ITS represents a particularly vivid example of the difficulty of developing and maintaining standards in an arena of rapidly evolving technology. The world of surface transportation is going through a major upheaval as government priorities and popular sensibilities trend away from the construction of more roads and rails and toward the better use of existing infrastructure through the use of computer and communications technologies. This is further complicated by the fact that computer and communications technologies themselves are going through a rapid and apparently unending technical evolution themselves.

In such an environment, ITS standards-making must be particularly sensitive and astute if the standards under development are to avoid becoming obsolete and irrelevant before they can even be approved. There are a number of ways to facilitate this, including:

- Carefully modularizing the topics that standards address
- Focusing standards primarily on interfaces rather than devices
- Addressing performance requirements rather than designs

Modularize standards topics

Good system design in general requires that complex systems be built from small, independent, self-contained components. This is no less true for standards than for computer software or electronics design.

Keeping the pieces small means that each can be developed in a relatively short time by relatively few people who are focused on the task. Keeping the pieces independent allows a particular standards development activity to operate without intimate interaction with large numbers of other standards activities. Among other things, this means that the action of one standards activity will not produce changes to the work plans of another standards activity. Keeping the pieces self-contained means that a standards effort produces a complete useful result in and of itself, without dangling loose ends.

In the world of fax machines, for example, it made sense separately to standardize (1) the cord and plug that connected the fax machine to the telephone system, (2) the protocols through which fax machines connect to one another and (3) the compact encoding of the fax image itself. Among other things, modularization allows significant innovation to take place in one part of technology, even to the extent of requiring some new standards in that area; but it leaves surrounding portions of technology (and their related standards) undisturbed.

Focus on interfaces

Interfaces are the connections that join one part of a system to another. Especially in an environment where devices and applications are rapidly evolving, it makes sense to focus standards work primarily on how these devices and applications will connect and communicate with one another. For example, in audio systems, the interface between the amplifier and sound sources is well-standardized, allowing a variety of different sound sources (e.g., FM tuners, CD players, televisions) to be plugged into the amplifier. Some of these sound sources were not even conceived of when the interface was standardized, but the existence of this standard made it easy to introduce new sound sources into the audio environment. Similarly, although the interfaces between the amplifier and speakers and between the amplifier and sound sources are standardized, this does not require the standardization of amplifier technology. Amplifier technology can be based on vacuum-tube technology or solid-state components, for example, without requiring any changes to tape deck or speaker design.

In the same way, much ITS standardization, both domestic and international, is focusing on the interfaces between portions of the overall ITS. One effort at SAE, for example, is addressing the interface that carries transmitted traffic information from a receiver to an on-board navigation system. This work does not pre-suppose the kind of wireless technology used to deliver traffic information to the vehicle. This could take place via digital cellular or conventional two-way radio or area-wide broadcast or from roadside beacons. It does not presuppose the type of navigation device that will be on board the vehicle. It could be a full-scale route guidance product that uses traffic information to calculate optimal routes, a map display system that highlights congested roads, or a voice unit that simply reports congestion to the driver. However, standardizing this interface will allow the industry to proceed in multiple directions for communications and for navigation, as dictated by the marketplace, without communications product developers having to worry about navigation product development or vice versa.

Address performance requirements

Performance standards are those that dictate what a product or process must accomplish and how good and how fast its results must be, but they do not specify how the product or process must go about producing such a result. For example, a braking performance standard might specify the maximum time allowed to bring a car to a halt from 30 miles per hour (mph). However, it would not specify the technology for doing this job, thereby allowing for both drum and disc brakes, or whatever new brake technology might appear later on. In ITS, electronic toll system procurements often specify performance requirements (e.g., speed and reliability of reading a toll tag on a vehicle traveling at perhaps 65 mph), although these specifications have not yet proceeded to national standards.

The point is that performance requirements and performance standards encourage technology producers to find better, cheaper ways of meeting the desired goal. In contrast, a standard that specifies a product must be designed in a particular way, employing particular materials or particular internal mechanisms, immediately brings innovation to a halt and may unduly favor the proprietary approaches of one vendor over another.

Challenge: accelerating the process

Some important steps have already been taken by the ITS standards community to help facilitate and speed the development of ITS standards. Notable among these are the national ITS architecture program and the funding that the U.S. DOT has been providing to SDOs to encourage broader participation in domestic and international standards efforts and to engage contractors to assist with the research and drafting work of standards writing committees. Both of these programs originated as recommendations from ITS America that were accepted, refined and funded by the U.S. DOT.

Architecture program deliverables are expected to result in the fast-tracking of particularly high-priority standards that will encourage national ITS interoperability. Broadening the base of participation will assist in building lasting consensus. Contractor support will help reduce the elapsed time to get standards written, considered and approved.

There will undoubtedly be other opportunities to accelerate ITS standards development that we can hope the community will identify, define, fund and implement. It is important that new acceleration efforts continue to focus on opportunities for eliminating real delays and bottlenecks. However, such efforts must not scrimp on the time genuinely needed for technologies to mature before standardizing begins nor on the time the industry needs to thoughtfully consider the best standardizing approach. Otherwise the result will be inadequate and unattractive standards that will impede, rather than advance, the industry.

Challenge: harmonizing domestic and international standards efforts

North America got a somewhat late start in developing ITS standards relative to Europe, and it faces several problems in working toward international ITS standards. The first is that with its head start, Europe is sometimes ready to propose draft standards before other parts of the world have had much chance to think about the issues. This results in a situation of discomfort, at least, that the draft standards may not adequately reflect the needs of other world regions.

Second, as previously observed, starting earlier does not always lead to the best standards, especially when technology is in flux. There has been a tendency in Europe, given the pressure of EU directives, to standardize ahead of deployment, sometimes with mixed results. Third, governments outside of North America have generally been supportive of international standards efforts earlier and on a larger scale. Many of the experts sent from other countries are, in effect, full-time paid consultants whose job is to move standards forward. The recent support for both domestic and global standards-making from the U.S. DOT is a genuine breakthrough that will certainly help to level the playing field, but there is a lot of catching up to do.

North America in particular needs to walk a careful line that (1) recognizes the very real pressures that (particularly) Europeans are under to get standards written and on the books, but (2) does not allow itself or the international standards process to be steamrolled by these pressures. In general, the most effective mechanism for creating and maintaining a level playing field is a robust domestic standards programs that can offer well-thought-out positions and draft standards to the international community.

Challenge: getting standards adopted and used

Standards are just so much wrapping paper unless they are broadly adopted and used by the community. The keys to making standards a living part of the industry include:

- Safeguarding the consensus process and keeping it broad, so that buy-in is developed as the standard is being developed
- In areas other than safety and public welfare, using regulatory powers to install standards only as a last resort—but not being afraid to exercise this last resort where there is a clear need
- Observing the rules for keeping standards abreast of current technology, in the manner outlined above

In addition, standards will only be adopted if people and organizations know about them. Each SDO takes responsibility for publicizing its own standards, especially because publishing and selling copies of the standards is a significant SDO revenue source. However, in a multidisciplinary field like ITS, information about standards must cross disciplines. This is clearly a job for ITS America.

A separate issue, still open, is the role ITS America should take (if any) in endorsing particular ITS standards. Some people believe that ITS America should simply get the word out on all ITS-relevant standards but not actively endorse any. Some people believe that ITS America should endorse and promote all ITS standards, or at least particularly important ones. Some believe that ITS America should work with public agencies to develop a handbook for ITS, in which standards appropriate to particular kinds of deployment are identified and recommended. Political complications arise when there are multiple standards relating to the same subject, a circumstance that is certainly conceivable, especially if both domestic and international standards are included. Ultimately, this issue will have to be resolved by ITS America's board of directors and the organizations that comprise ITS America's membership.

Conclusion

Standards-making in general, and ITS standards-making in particular, is a frustrating, maddening and intensely political activity; but one that is also a fascinating and absolutely essential part of making industry and technology work. The importance of ITS standards has been recognized by all sectors of the economy, even to the extent of receiving mention in the legislation that funds much ITS work.

Standards-making is interesting in part because it is directly on the front lines of the technology that people care about and because it is conducted by people who feel passionately about their work. If you have a role in ITS technology—as a vendor, as a deployer, or as a user—you have a stake in ITS standards.

Endnote

1. ITS America is a public–private partnership dedicated to the advancement of ITS.

BY Jerry L. Pittenger • Vice President, ITS Systems •
Battelle Memorial Institute

DEPLOYING ITS

Introduction

For over 10 years transportation professionals from the public sector, private sector and academia have been working together to analyze intelligent transportation system (ITS) concepts and technologies. A host of alternative architectures were studied to determine how best to deploy ITS. Hundreds of stakeholders, who would be directly affected by the national ITS architecture, were involved in the architecture development process. Operational tests were performed with various degrees of success, but from this work it is conclusive that significant benefits can be achieved through deployment of ITS technologies. The results of many of these operational tests have been evaluated by the U.S. Department of Transportation's (U.S. DOT's) ITS Joint Program Office, and evaluations are available on the web at <www.its.dot.gov/eval/eval.htm>.

A careful look reveals that effective ITS solutions have been made possible through technologies introduced by the computerized information age. We are now able to collect, analyze, control, or take other pertinent action using data or information that never have been available previously. Technological advances in sensors and data collection devices provide information almost instantly to allow real-time analysis by decision support systems and responsive actions that are fast enough to actually help control final outcomes in our transportation systems.

However, these new abilities afforded to our transportation systems do not come without a price. Deployment lessons to date have shown that ITS system deployments are complex and require skills that, traditionally, have not been required in implementing transportation systems. For example, road builders are now including design specifications to install fiber optic communications systems into their deployment plans. Surveillance systems are using radar devices, acoustic devices and intelligent cameras. The complexity of the systems has increased the up-front investments in money, time and people, thus demanding that work be done right the first time. Learning from our mistakes is important, but also costly.

Much can be learned from other technology-affected disciplines and associated deployments that have occurred in this country. For example, in the 1960s computers were introduced as a way to collect, analyze and convert data into information. Early systems were focused primarily on business applications but soon found their way into the engineering departments. We are all aware of the incredible pace that computer technologies have evolved into every aspect of our lives. One of the first engineering applications was Computer Integrated Manufacturing. Engineers found that they could track and control manufacturing operations never dreamed possible. Knowing what was going on in the operations allowed inventories to be reduced and raw materials to be delivered exactly when needed (e.g., just-in-time concepts). New computer-aided design methods were developed that shortened design times, tooling and production from years to months. But with all of these technological developments and applications came many hard lessons. There were hundreds of systems that functioned as designed only to find they solved the wrong problems. Many deployments were plagued with large cost and schedule overruns that were not discovered until late in the projects. Projected benefits were often never realized due to unexpected high-maintenance requirements. This was costly and caused serious setbacks for many system deployments. The people responsible for developing the systems were often viewed as the enemy and management lost trust in their estimates and performance; but people learned. Emerging out of the chaos came new engineering methods to provide order to the deployment process. Many structured engineering methods were introduced by several well-known authors and practitioners.[1,2,3] Most of these new engineering methods are based on sound engineering practices that have existed for many years in other engineering disciplines. With several different deployment methods available, people have spent much time looking at alternative methods to determine what approach might be best in their environment. Clearly, no single system development approach is best. Experience has determined that it is less important which methodology is used, but extremely important that a methodology is used. Experience has also shown that it is important to keep in mind that the end objective is to deploy a functional system that solves a targeted problem and not the exercise of the methods.

Whatever engineering methodology is selected, the methods used should be thoroughly understood by all parties involved in the deployment. This is important because the structured tools are most often used as a communications tool between the customers' and developers' technical teams. To not understand the methods will decrease the understanding of the system being designed and implemented. This can be a fatal and expensive flaw in deployment work.

The development life cycle

In deploying ITS, all engineering development methods share a common life cycle consisting of basic engineering steps (figure 21–1) that must be performed independent of the tools used. It is essential to give each step outlined in figure 21–1 adequate attention to reduce risk and to help insure successful development, deployment, operation and maintenance of the ITS systems. The process is not linear step-by-step from top to bottom; it is an iterative process that results in revisiting previous work throughout the entire life cycle. It is beyond the scope of this book to define a cookbook approach for ITS deployment. The objective is to provide an overview of what must be done, leaving all of the "how" issues to others.

The following sections discuss each of the development life-cycle steps. Note that there are separate comprehensive texts written on almost every step (e.g., definition, design, testing, training, installation). When appropriate, references are included to identify where more detailed information can be accessed. ITS deployments are usually not easy, and no cookbook approach exists. Unique differences will exist for each application. The cast of characters is always different, and the transportation system modes and operations have unique features. However, careful design and deployment of ITS systems can be accomplished efficiently and effectively, and large benefits can be derived that will advance your multimodal transportation systems to help meet the demands for today and future years.

Build the project team

The project team should be carefully selected. ITS deployment projects are complex, and the right skills are necessary to insure success. This fact has been clearly recognized by the U.S. DOT and has resulted in their prioritized Capacity Development Program. In the past, civil engineers, traffic engineers, transit engineers and highway construction teams dominated project teams working on transportation deployment programs. These disciplines are still extremely important and will continue to be key capabilities needed to build and maintain our transportation systems. However, other disciplines needed to deploy ITS include system integrators and system engineers software and computer hardware engineers, control system engineers, communications engineers, and a host of other disciplines depending on the application being addressed. Table 22–1 summarizes some of the ITS expertise needed on a project team.

Figure 21–1. ITS deployment life cycle.

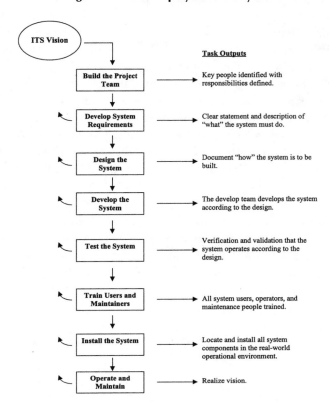

However, trying to identify every capability that will be needed at the start of any ITS project is impossible. It is necessary to complete much of the early system definition and design to understand what skills are going to be necessary for system deployment.

The key person that must be identified early is the project manager. This person should have extensive experience managing large programs with a successful performance record in related developments. The person must be able to communicate with people and inspire a vision and direction that can be understood and accepted by the team. The correct selection of the project manager can be the difference between a success or a failure. The project manager should be given flexibility to assemble a team of people that he or she is confident in and able to work with. Good interpersonal skills must exist to accomplish the project goals efficiently and effectively. The ability of the team to work together cannot be overemphasized.

Other key individuals that must be brought onto the team early are those experienced in developing system requirements and translating those results into system designs. System requirements define what the system must do. The system design defines how the system is to be constructed to meet the system requirements. All of these life-cycle steps require trained individuals with specific skill sets to clearly define what and how the ITS system is to be constructed. These people are usually senior-level staff that have experienced developing systems that are similar to the one being constructed. People who can visualize and document system requirements and develop a design that can deploy all requirements are valuable resources that are not plentiful. These people tend to be visionaries with diverse experience to recognize and identify system requirements and solutions.

The customer purchasing the system also most identify the right people to represent their interests in system development. For example, if the system being developed contains extensive software, the customer should have an experienced software engineer to communicate with and track the progress of the development team. Likewise, ITS systems often contain a host of different communications systems. The customer should have someone representing them who understand communications technologies and issues. The customer often procures these skills by hiring a system development manager to represent their interests. Lack of understanding and ability to communicate and review the work being done by the development team is one of the major pitfalls in ITS system development. Lack of communications often results in the development of perfectly functioning systems that solve the wrong problems. The customer must work closely with the development team as a partner. Without their involvement, the customer finds the problems and mistakes after the system has been implemented. The later a problem is discovered, the more costly the fix in terms of money and time.

Depending on the application, there are other people that can be important in an ITS deployment project. For example, contracting officials many times can have an influence on system deployment strategies through contracting procedures. Neighboring jurisdictions might influence system deployments if systems operations require interfaces. Careful consideration should be given early to the real stakeholders that is key to the success of the system being developed.

Table 21–1
ITS Deployment Team Capabilities

Expertise	Comment
Project management	Maintain project guidance and control. Provide focus on the project objective and motivate performance and success.
Transportation domain expertise	Insure that systems deployed are compatible with existing transportation systems and infrastructure. Ability to communicate with transportation professionals.
Functional requirements	All involved must clearly understand how the system is to perform. They must understand the vision.
System designers	Select the experienced and creative people for this part of system development.
Computer engineering	Computer hardware and software expertise.
Communications	Extensive capabilities in communications technologies used to deploy the system. Communications can include fiber, wire and/or wireless, data and/or video.
Systems engineering	System engineers have the ability to bring together multiple technologies to solve problems.
Sensor expertise	The status of systems can now be monitored by sophisticated sensors to collect data that was never before available.
Control system capabilities	Computer systems allow for automated control of systems with or without human intervention

Develop system requirements

It is essential to carefully define exactly what the system being developed is required to do before considering system designs to specify how the system will be built. All too often, projects proceed forward without a detailed and clear understanding of system functionality and performance requirements. System requirements can take several forms. Many terms are used such as functional requirements, performance requirements, software requirements and even terms including system or functional specifications. Even though there are subtle differences between these requirements, all have the objective to define requirements for some aspect of the system. This discussion puts all requirements into the broad category of system requirements. Comprehensive books have been written on this topic alone.[4,5] Any competent system integrator will understand the importance and process for developing system requirements. Like many phases of the development life cycle, there are different methods that can be used to accomplish the development task for system requirements. Use a proven method for which your developer can show previous experience and success.

Note that the developing system requirements is an iterative process. System requirements can also involve prototype systems to be built. A prototype is a throwaway system that is quickly developed to experiment with functional alternatives or to merely show the buyer what the system might do. It is essentially a mock-up of a subsystem or component that allows the user and developer to see what the final version might look like. Another popular way to review system requirements is to write the user guide(s) for the system before the system is built. Users such as operators relate well to user guides and can critique system requirements by reviewing these documents.

As the system requirements are developed, reviews or walk-throughs should be held where all parties involved carefully review the results. Be involved and provide the right people to participate as needed. At the end of the requirements definition step, a final review should be performed where all stakeholders must approve the specifications to insure agreement as to what should be built.

Design the system

Once system requirements have been completed, the work should focus on designing the system. The design will specify and define "how" the system will be built. For example, the system design determines how the system database structures, communications systems, and system interfaces are built. Several valid and effective methodologies exist for doing designs.[6,7]

Most design teams use some form of structured and top-down design methodology. Structured refers to a process that is methodical and has a set of rules. This allows for completeness and consistency and serves as a communications tool among the development team. Top-down refers to starting with the overall system and breaking it into manageable deployment pieces. Top-down structured design methods also have proven to help insure completeness of the design.

The system design should include a logical design and a physical design. The logical design focuses on the logical interfaces and data flows in the system that is being developed. It should be based on the functional requirements. The logical design will focus on functions to be performed by the system and respective data that must flow between the functions. A logical design is not concerned with where the functions reside within the overall system (i.e., what computer system), what functions reside together on a single computer, or what communications media are used to transmit data between functions. Figure 21–2 provides an example of a logical design extracted from the national ITS architecture. The physical design determines how the hardware and communications systems are configured in the system and where functions are located. The physical design maps the logical functions into a hardware or real world infrastructure. Figure 21–3 provides an illustration of a typical physical design extracted from the national ITS architecture.

Figure 21–2. Logical architecture diagram.
Source: The National ITS Architecture, Version 3.0
(Washington, D.C.: U.S. Department of Transportation, 1999).

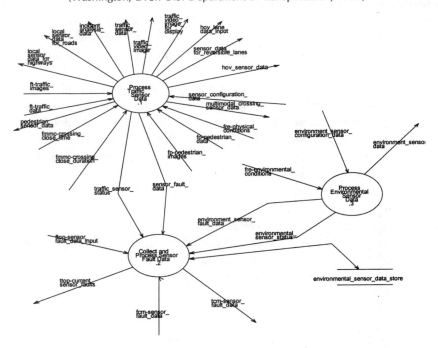

Figure 21–3. Physical architecture diagram.
Source: The National ITS Architecture, Version 3.0
(Washington, D.C.: U.S. Department of Transportation, 1999).

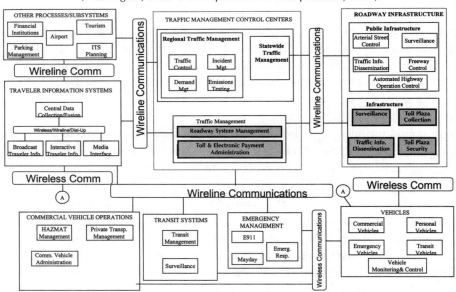

Accompanying the logical and physical design materials is a data dictionary. The data dictionary defines the data used by the system. Each data flow may actually be a data packet that consists of several individual data elements. However, a data flow may also be a single data element. Each data dictionary should include a set of rules to allow interpretation by the user.

The physical design also allows the construction of a system architecture diagram that shows graphically the physical layout and design for the system being built. Figure 21–4 illustrates an architecture diagram for an automated traveler information system. This simple diagram is an excellent communications tool to describe the overall system.

Figure 21–4. System architecture diagram.
Source: The National ITS Architecture, Version 3.0
(Washington, D.C.: U.S. Department of Transportation, 1999).

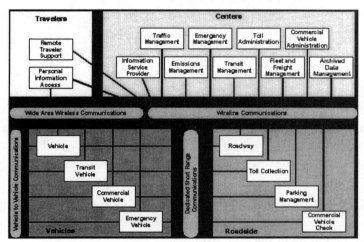

As with previous life-cycle steps, the design materials should be reviewed throughout the process at regular intervals as the design progresses. Design work can be reviewed using design walkthroughs. The walkthroughs should involve key stakeholders and users of the system being developed. It is imperative that everyone agree on the designs to insure that the correct system is being developed. Over the years, hundreds of systems have been developed that perform exactly as designed only to find that they solve the wrong problems. Complex systems are too costly to have to redo!

Once the design is completed and approved by all parties, the design documentation should be put under strict configuration control. Configuration control tracks and manages changes. The process only allows well-documented and approved changes to be incorporated. An audit trail is carefully maintained to allow both the developers and buyers to trace the history of development changes. The configuration control system provides a way to control change and provide any justification for contractual modifications if they become necessary. Changes made to approved designs are the largest cause for additional funding requests and expanded schedules.

Develop the system

System development is the life-cycle step where the system is constructed. System development work should not be creative. The work should focus on purchasing all equipment, computer hardware and computer software necessary to deploy the system according to the approved design. At this point in a deployment project, all of the creative decisions have been made and approved in the design process. The development team should deploy each part of the system exactly according to the design specifications. During the development work, errors in the design will be discovered. Design modifications should be submitted as design request changes and incorporated only by exercising the procedures defined for the configuration control system.

The system test team must work closely but independently of the system developers. As the system developers complete unit testing, they transfer the subsystem to the integration team who controls the master build step for the overall system. As each subsystem is integrated, testing is performed to insure system integrity. If problems are discovered, the subsystem is returned to the development team with documented error reports. The entire integration process is complicated by the fact that introduction of new subsystems can uncover system errors in other subsystems that may have previously been accepted.

After all subcomponents are integrated, a final system test is performed at completion of system development according to the system test plan. It is recommended that a separate test team be assigned the responsibility for execution of the system test plan. Oftentimes the buyer will want to execute their own tests to insure they get what they ordered.

Test the system

Testing the system as it is deployed is key to success. It is important to carefully plan what tests are to be run at each step of the deployment process. Before system deployment, test plans should be developed to verify system operation and to insure that each component as well as the integrated system accurately deploys the approved system design. Testing should be requirements-based and evaluate the system from various aspects such as functionality, performance (i.e., speed), reliability and security. Each test plan should consist of the following three components:

1. A detailed definition of all inputs (i.e., data or electrical) required for module operation
2. The process to be executed to exercise system functionality
3. A clear and detailed definition of the expected results

Each modular component in the system should be tested individually before being integrated into the larger system. This process is referred to as unit testing. When modular components are verified to work properly, they are integrated with the larger master system. In this process, integration test plans are used to insure that defined interfaces work and the overall integrity of the system is not compromised. The system is deployed piece-by-piece and tested at each step. At the end of development, the final test is a system test that exercises the system and compares results with the functional specifications and designs.

The test plans should be detailed and exercise each path of designed functionality expected to be encountered by the system or subsystem being tested. Testing should not attempt to prove that a system works under normal conditions but rather that the system operates under all possible conditions. The system should be stressed during testing to evaluate the systems dynamic performance. Is the system being tested able to operate in abnormal conditions when presented an environment or data that is not expected?

Testing will find problems. In the deployment schedule, allow time for problem fixes as part of the testing process. Some will be simple while others will be complex and require substantial rework. As the system is tested, all problems are documented and submitted to the development team for response in the form of an explanation of the results obtained or a documented system revision plan along with an estimated cost and time for completion. The buyer can decide what changes are needed immediately or what might be delayed so as not to affect the overall deployment schedule. The buyer should expect that the test team will generate several of these problem reports. A reasonable number of reports is not an indication as to the quality of the job performed. Complex systems do not get deployed without discovering problems along the way.

Train users and maintainers

Adequate training for users and maintainers is essential for system success. No short cuts here! Training system users and maintainers is often done before and during system installation. Do not try to operate and maintain an ITS system in the field before adequate training. System users and maintainers should have been included as part of the development team so that they understand the system requirements and how the system should operate. Training can come in many different forms ranging from classroom time to on-the-job mentoring. The system developers often do the training, but this deserves a word of caution. Many system developers are poor trainers, but the professional trainers working with the development team are often effective. In fact, getting the professional trainers involved early in the system development process is recommended to gain familiarity and understanding.

Training is a time-consuming and critical part of any system deployment. The system is designed and built to accomplish a set of functional capabilities and solve specific problems. The system must be used and maintained as designed to obtain the most benefit from the system.

System maintenance is often overlooked in the life-cycle costs of an ITS system. Maintenance of a complex system can range from 10 percent to 20 percent of the development costs per year to keep the system in operation. Plan for these costs and train adequate staff to provide the services. These services can usually be provided by the developer under contract, or internal people can be trained. Also, maintenance costs should include fees for annual maintenance of off-the-shelf product purchases. It is not uncommon for software suppliers to charge 10 percent of the purchase price per year for software products. This includes operating systems, applications packages and hardware. You will want to pay these fees to maintain the latest upgrades and maintenance for the procured systems. Many cases exist where the maintenance cost was almost ignored in considering the ongoing costs for operating the system only to discover these costs in the end.

Install the system

After the system has been thoroughly tested and verified to meet the system requirements, final installation is performed. Depending on the system, installation could include a substantial training program or a phased installation where the old system is run in parallel with the new system for a period of time. One thing for sure is that additional problem and errors will be found during and after system installation. Plan for it because it is impossible to design and develop a complex system without missing some needed functions or not realizing some installation or operational issues. The formalized life-cycle methods can only minimize the number of issues that will be discovered.

It is extremely important to keep the development team available during the early use of the system. A subset of the development team often relocates to the operational site and works with the users for the first few days, weeks, or even months depending on the criticality and complexity of the system deployed.

Also expect the users of the system to discover new functionality during initial use and respond with "wouldn't it be great if we could…" comments. The owner of the system must look at each additional feature and decide what is really needed or what can be a future enhancement to the system. The reasoning to use formalized functional definition and design methods are to minimize the number of omitted functions that can be costly to deploy late in the development life cycle.

Operate and maintain system

At this point the system is installed and tested, and users and maintenance people are trained. With careful attention to the deployment process and adequate resources, the vision as defined in the system requirements will be realized. It has been shown that benefits can be great. However, these are obtained only by using a carefully thought-out plan and process as described above.

However, do not ever plan to be finished in your ITS deployment. Good ITS systems seem to almost always uncover extensive possibilities for enhancements and improvements. New ideas will be generated by both your operational and maintenance staff to do things better. The system will probably grow over the years and the benefits and payoffs will increase. We all should count on this to happen because ITS is the future in our transportation systems for extensive improvement to meet new transportation challenges.

The real world—comments and lessons learned

Structured and systems engineering methods are important in system deployment and provide organization to a complex process. As one might expect, the methods do not allow for a cookbook system development in which the developers can merely exercise a set of rules and produce a complex working ITS system. However, developments do not have to be chaotic and risk factors can be minimized. Several ITS systems have been successfully developed and the experiences and lessons learned have been documented. This author's sacred 12 rules in system deployment are summarized as follows:

1. *Communications is essential for success.* Clear and concise communications is essential throughout the development process. At any point in time, multiple tasks will be ongoing that interact. The physical locations most likely will be at sites located hundreds of miles apart depending on the use of subcontractors or product vendors. A communications procedure and supporting tools need to be available to the development team as well as the client to exchange information and talk daily. Intranet access has helped provide project teams the tools to communicate with all participants with a need to know, as well as transmit volumes of information between the team. Commercial communications tools also help provide an audit-trail in communications that becomes useful to review the history of decisions and directions.

2. *Things will never go as planned.* Careful planning and task assignments will be done by highly qualified project managers with years of experience. However, work never goes exactly as expected! Maintain flexibility in your work to accommodate unexpected occurrences. In your plan, plan for change. Allow a (5 percent to 10 percent) contingency in budgets and schedules. Developing plans with no flexibility in tasks and schedules will result in disappointments.

3. *Deployment is hard work and will require many extra hours.* Complex projects consume the amount of time available. Independent of the time scheduled, the last few weeks or months of a project will be hectic and require extra effort. As the pieces come together, many enhancements and fixes will be identified. It is important to stick to the original project scope and make changes only necessary to implement the original functionality planned or changes that are deemed necessary to obtain a system that will be acceptable to the users. Many projects have been delayed for months trying to include all the functionality planned plus extensive enhancements identified before the development team wants to let go. A separate enhancement plan can be developed to implement desirable features in future system releases after system installation. Also, it is essential to not overwork the project team. After implementation there must be energy left for system support.

4. *Final system integration and testing cannot be done remotely.* In deploying a complex ITS system, team members are usually distributed at remote locations. Project managers or system integrators will get the request from team partners to do their integration and testing at home (i.e., remotely) in an effort to save money and avoid staff travel. The arguments presented usually focus on the availability of modern-day communications technologies and their ability to provide for operating in a decentralized mode. Carefully consider the feasibility of remote integration and testing. Experience has shown that it is usually more efficient to assemble the team at the installation site and, as a team, integrate and test. When errors are discovered, the participants can work together to resolve who has ownership of the problem and how the problem is best resolved.

5. *Develop risk scenarios and backup plans.* When the system design has been completed, a thorough risk analysis should be performed to identify the critical parts of the system (i.e., show-stoppers) that can cause major delays or system failures. Ask "what if" questions. For example, reliance on some other party to provide needed traffic surveillance data for an automated traveler information system could be a risk if the data should not be available. Likewise, reliance on infrastructure support provided by some other party could severely impede deployment if the infrastructure does not get installed when needed. For critical risks identified, develop a backup plan to mitigate the risk. In certain cases, design changes may be needed to mitigate risk or provide for contingencies (i.e., more schedule time) to minimize risk.

6. *In purchasing off-the-shelf technology, be flexible.* Functional requirements determine what off-the-shelf components—whether they be equipment, software, or packaged systems—can be used. However, when analyzing off-the-shelf alternatives be cognizant of the cost and time for custom development and retain some flexibility to accept the nonperfect system. For example, if a component meets 80 percent of the system requirements, look carefully at what must be sacrificed to allow the product to be acceptable and possibly revise the system requirements. The risk of not being flexible can cause the price or time to develop a system to double to get the last 10 percent of desired functionality. However, a word of caution is that double the price is a bargain if the last 10 percent of desired functionality is needed and critical to the success of the system. Careful judgement is required.

7. *When purchasing off-the-shelf technology, demand demonstrations.* Purchasing off-the-shelf equipment, software, or packaged systems can introduce added risks if not approached correctly. Suppliers want to sell their products, and there is the tendency to optimistically represent product capabilities to make a sale. Functionality will be mentioned that is often in development plans with the expectation that the development can be accelerated to meet your project schedule. Or the requirement for some modification will be expressed as a simple change that can be easily done due to the modular construction of their system. Be cautious. Most vendors have honest and ethical intentions, but they tend to be optimistic in their estimates. Optimism is in the nature of mankind and especially in the sales departments. It is worth the time and money to visit the suppliers' reference sites or development location to see, firsthand, what they have to sell, what is still on the drawing boards, or what the management's commitment is to provide any new capabilities or equipment to meet your ITS system requirements. Follow the sales team home to their facilities to see for yourself before making key build–buy decisions. Also, ask for customer references and talk to them. In some cases, it may be worth going to installed sites and see the product firsthand. Ask other customers questions about product performance and vendor support.

8. *Manage with help attitudes ... everyone must be successful.* In the entire ITS deployment process work in a partnership with the attitude that everyone must succeed. In any complex system, problems will be encountered. Rather than trying to strong-arm team partners to get results, try first to work with partners in trouble to help resolve issues and allow them to be successful. If project managers must result

to contractual force, the risk is high that the supplier will not work in harmony and fail to deliver anything that is not a compromise. Also, team members will recognize that the project managers with a successful attitude have their best interests in mind and will more willingly give their support and perform.

9. *Hire domain expertise and experience.* There is nothing that can beat the experience of doing it before. Try to involve people who can show direct and relevant experience to the ITS system being deployed. Pick a project manager who has a successful track record with excellent references. The depth of experience available will depend on the uniqueness of the system being deployed and technologies used. New things introduce risk and should be considered in the functional requirements and design decisions. Do not take claims as experience. Go see work previously done by the person or company and interview people who have worked with them.

10. *Recognize the profit motive of the private sector.* It is essential to recognize that private-sector partners are in business, for the most part, to make money. This fact cannot be ignored, and an environment must be set up to allow private-sector companies to succeed. Profits must be carefully and visibly protected to retain the cooperation and successful delivery of any system.

11. *Find a local person who is familiar and respected by the stakeholders to work with the developers.* An effective partnership requires positive experiences in working together and professional relationships of trust to be established. Often a project team or system integrator is not well-known to the stakeholders hired to build a system. In first meetings between the stakeholders and the development team, introductions are made. The people begin to know one another and establish working relationships. This takes valuable time, but it is a process that must occur. Simply by introducing a known person that is trusted and respected into the project development team, working relationships can be achieved in much less time. For example, a retired engineer who has been with a locale for many years can often function very effectively in this role. Meetings will begin with a discussion of family, mutual friends, or some past experiences of working together. Starting this way makes it much easier to get down to business and obtain the cooperation needed for a successful ITS deployment.

12. *Recognize that software development is a high risk.* Software development and integration is a high risk and expensive part of any project. Traditionally software developers tend to be very optimistic in developing cost estimates and schedules. Software development tends to be imprecise and riddled with uncertainties. The risks can be minimized by using good software engineering methods, but the risks cannot be eliminated. Get a proven software or computer system engineer to oversee the computer system development work. The person must understand the software development process and be able to identify the signals of software development problems.

Summary comments on ITS deployment

ITS is an exciting field that has great potential to improve our multimodal transportation systems in the U.S. field operational tests, and model deployments have provided conclusive evidence that the needed payback in terms of safety and operational improvements justify the investments. However, these applications have also resulted in the realization that deploying ITS and associated technologies is complex and expensive. New transportation engineering skills and methods are needed for ITS deployment. Fortunately, ITS deployment can be related to other engineering disciplines and benefit from respective development methods and previous lessons learned. Transportation challenges are interesting and rewarding work, and already we see people making transportation their chosen professions. People will learn quickly what it takes to deploy ITS, and benefits easily justify the investments needed. The result will be an improved multimodal transportation system in the United States that takes advantage of new technology.

Endnotes

1. Blanchard, B. S. 1990. *Systems Engineering and Analysis.*

2. Martin, J. M. 1996. *Systems Engineering Guidebook: A Process for Developing Systems and Products.*

3. Rechtin, E. 1997. *The Art of System Architecting.*

4. Grady, J. O. 1993. *System Requirements Analysis.*

5. Sommerville, I., and P. Sawyer. 1997. *Requirements Engineering: A Good Practice Guide.*

6. Whitten, J. L., L. D. Bentley, and K. C. Dittman. 1997. *Systems Analysis and Design Methods.*

7. Kendall, K. E., and J. E. Kendall. 1998. *Systems Analysis and Design.*

BY Gang-Len Chang • Professor, Civil Engineering • University of Maryland

CHAPTER **22**

EVALUATION OF ITS SERVICES

Introduction

Despite the broad consensus that intelligent transportation systems (ITS) can effectively contend with increasing traffic congestion, many responsible agencies must justify the costs as well as benefits of such investments to both policymakers and the general public. This is due in part to the fact that ITS services often involve rapidly changing technologies and different institutional arrangements that are relatively new to the community.

Diminishing resources and the increasing demand for infrastructure renovation have compounded the pressure on transportation agencies to prove the effectiveness of any deployed ITS. Thus, while ITS technologies have just evolved from their infancy to a full-scale deployment, it is imperative for the transportation community to establish rigorous evaluation procedures so as to well justify any further investment needs and receive sustained public support.

The role of evaluation

Unlike some typical "before-and-after" studies, the role of "evaluation" in ITS should not just be a "snapshot assessment" that yields a report to document the contribution of an implemented ITS service. Instead, it should function like a feedback mechanism that is fully integrated with the operations as well as maintenance of the ITS service. With such a feedback function, the operating agency can constantly monitor the performance of implemented ITS services, identify any deficiencies for timely improvement, compute the up-to-date cost/benefit ratio, and estimate their impacts to the target transportation environment.

It should be noted that a team for doing such a task typically consists of the responsible operating agency, its supervising department, and the user group (e.g., commuters). This is to ensure that the evaluation can take into account all aspects of cost and benefit, resolve the potential for conflicting priorities between different involving parties, and take full advantage of the resulting findings.

For instance, a real-time evaluation mechanism in the incident response/management system will enable the highway agency to monitor its efficiency and effectiveness after every incident response operation. The monitoring work shall include all critical tasks over the entire operation of incident management, including: the incident detection time, arrival time of the response units, incident clearance time, detour strategies and queue length during and after the incident. The total up-to-date operating cost in comparison with its resulting benefits, along with areas for potential improvement, will also be available from such a real-time evaluation module.

More importantly, any rigorous evaluation should be dynamic in nature, and constantly feed back the following information to the operating agency:

- Comparison of the actual with the anticipated system performance based on preset indicators
- Identification of the cost structure and distribution associated with various components of the implemented ITS service
- Estimate of the direct benefits resulting from the deployed ITS service and contribution of each component
- Assessment of indirect benefits and impacts to the target as well as the neighboring transportation systems due to the implemented ITS service
- Recommendations of critical areas for further improvement

It is understandable that, due to data limitations and some practical constraints, for many ITS operating agencies it may be difficult to incorporate all aforementioned functions in their initial stage of ITS evaluation. Nevertheless, efforts should be made to ensure that the evaluation be taken as part of the routine operations work of an ITS service, and be continuously conducted to feed back all essential performance-related information.

Aside from the direct product of performance efficiency and resulting cost/benefits, a rigorous evaluation work often employs extensive data and thus, offers the opportunity for the responsible agency to identify the information needed for short-term operations improvement, long-term transportation planning and area-wide environmental impact analysis. All data collected during the evaluation will enable the operating agency to develop a systemwide databank, and to arch all information associated with the target system's performance. Such information may serve not only for ITS implementation, but also for many other purposes, including environment policy design and revision of regionwide transportation plans.

Organization of this chapter

This remainder of this chapter is organized as follows: First, a review of the literature in ITS evaluation is provided, followed by a step-by-step description of procedures for evaluating individual ITS services. Next, the potential issues as well as practical constraints in performing a rigorous evaluation task area addressed. Then, an example ITS evaluation study, Chespeake Highway Advisories Routing Traffic (CHART) incident response system and concluding comments are provided.

Available literature in ITS evaluation

Despite the abundance of literature in the ITS development over the past decade, only a very few studies have focused on evaluation-related issues. Most of those were sponsored by federal agencies. Nevertheless, depending on the scope of work, one may classify existing ITS evaluation studies into different categories, as discussed in the following paragraphs.

General evaluation guidelines or framework

The core of this literature tends to identify tools and procedures for estimating various direct and indirect benefits resulting from ITS services. For instance, Volpe systems center has produced a framework for assessing the overall impacts of advanced traveler information system (ATIS) and advanced traffic management system (ATMS) services, and proposed various tools for such studies (Volpe 1995). JHK & Associates have recommended a framework for computing various ITS-related benefits (JHK & Associates 1993, 1994a, 1994b).

Along the same line but with different focus, Sierra Research Co. has developed a methodology for approximating the ITS benefits in reducing fuel consumption and emissions (Sierra Research 1993). The Federal Transit Administration has also sponsored a study to identify benefits associated with the implementation of Advanced Public Transportation Systems (APTS) (U.S. DOT 1997).

Individual ITS service or technology evaluation

Instead of providing the general concept and models for various evaluation applications, a substantial fraction of literature is focused on documenting the field testing results of individual ITS services or technologies. Examples of such studies are "Benefits of Bus Priority at Traffic Signals in Portland (Kloos et al. 1994)," "CHART Incident Response Evaluation (COMSIS 1996)," and "Estimation of Benefits of Houston TranStar (Parsons Transportation Group and TTI 1997)."

Some invaluable lessons from field operational tests have also been reported. One may find some critical operational issues and their impacts on the resulting costs as well as benefits from the following reports: "ITS Benefits, Evaluation, Costs: Results and Lessons from Minnesota Guidestar Travelink Operational Test," and "Evaluation of INFORM—Lessons Learned and Applications to other Systems (Smith and Perez 1992)." An extensive list of evaluation work along this line is reported in the references.

In review of existing literature, it is notable that "evaluation" must contain not only the typical before-and-after comparison, but also the operational efficiency and impacts to the target transportation environment and its system users. Moreover, as ITS services involve rapidly changing technologies and significantly new interactions between institutions, any rigorous evaluation must take into account the local-specific constraints, and thus, fully integrate with their operational and maintenance process.

Functioning as a continuous feedback mechanism, the evaluation work will certainly increase the efficiency of implemented ITS services and contribute significantly toward the accomplishment of the predefined deployment goals. All evaluation methods or framework proposed in the literature and hereafter can serve as the basis for development of an integrated, dynamic, and effective evaluation framework.

Evaluation framework

Despite the variety of ITS technologies and their broad application, there exists a common framework for evaluating those designed mainly for individual applications rather than for a region-wide coordination. Figure 22–1 illustrates 13 principal steps and their interrelations in such a common evaluation framework. While steps 1 to 7 are proposed to set up the basis and criteria for evaluation, the remaining 6 steps are designed to capture all resulting costs, benefits, and performance efficiency-related issues. Note that those solid lines in figure 22–1 indicate the data flows between key steps, and dash lines represent the feedback relations in the evaluation process. Each of those key steps is discussed briefly in the following paragraphs.

Set up the basis for evaluation

Step 1: identify the goals and objectives of an implemented ITS service
Due to potential tradeoffs between various system impacts, it is essential for the evaluation to start with identification of its goals and target objectives. For instance, some generally accepted goals include the improvement of "safety," "mobility," "efficiency," "productivity" and "energy as well as environment."

Figure 22–1. A flowchart for ITS evaluation.
Source: Gang-Len Chang.

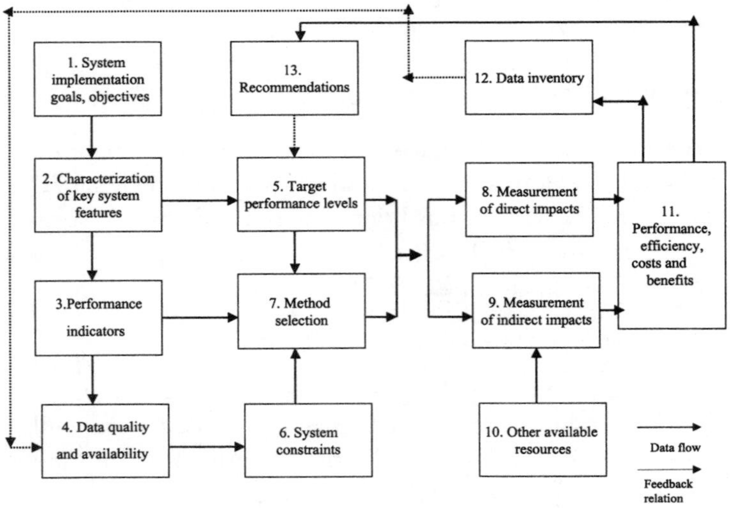

Note that the goals or objectives of different ITS services may not be consistent or compatible. For instance, the primary objectives for implementing an automatic vehicle location system (AVL) may not be for ridership increase, but for improving the efficiency of fleet operations and control. Likewise, the main function of an incident management system (IMS) is to minimize various incident impacts on highway users rather than to reduce primary highway accidents. The benefits resulting from an IMS may decrease substantially after the implementation of effective preventive strategies for safety improvement. Hence, an evaluation task cannot be conducted properly without clearly predefining the objectives or goals to be accomplished with the deployed ITS service. Those well-defined and accepted goals and objectives shall be used to guide the remaining evaluation work.

Step 2: characterize the key system features
The primary focus of this step is to establish the interrelations between the key features of an implemented system and the objectives to be achieved. A clear picture of such interrelations is essential for developing evaluation criteria and performance indicators.

For instance, on evaluating an IMS designed to minimize nonrecurrent congestion impacts, one shall first understand what detecting features it has and how it interacts with other supplemental detection systems. The performance indicators and evaluation criteria may vary significantly, depending on if it has the capability of performing automatic incident detection, or relies mainly on indirect detection module such as using messages from AVL systems or vehicle probing reports.

Similarly, an IMS, mainly for freeway incident management, may not be able to provide coordinated signal control operations during its incident detour operations. Hence, the evaluation shall focus on those available features; and assess their performance, costs, benefits and expected effectiveness or efficiency.

Step 3: establish the performance indicators
Before the assessment of performance efficiency, it is essential to set appropriate indicators for each embedded system feature. For instance, one may select the false alarm rate, detection rate and detection time as one

set of indicators for evaluating the automatic incident detection feature of an IMS. In contrast, the required dispatching headway, the average detection time and the reduction in verification time may be more appropriate than others for use in assessing its effectiveness if the IMS relies mainly on vehicle probe reports for incident detection.

Likewise, the delay per vehicle, rather than per person, may be selected as one of the performance indicators for evaluating adaptive signal control if the information about the average loading factor for buses and passenger cars is either unavailable or unreliable.

Step 4: identify the data availability and quality

The primary focus of this step is to thoroughly review the operations of the target ITS service, and to have reliable answers for questions such as "What data can be collected and have been collected?," and "Is the quality of those being collected good enough for a rigorous evaluation?"

As with the available data, one can do preliminary assessment as to whether all key functions of the implemented ITS system have been fully used or not. Furthermore, the quality of collected data, in general, can reflect if some system features may have been operated inefficiently or improperly. For instance, the traffic flow rate before an incident may not be available for some highways without adequate surveillance systems. The queue length at the onset of an incident and after its removal may not be recorded if operators are not instructed to do so.

Similarly, the fraction of flows being detoured during the incident period under various variable message sign (VMS) impacts may not be available. The development of any evaluation method shall certainly take into account both the data availability and quality. Alternative methods for indirect cost/benefit assessment may be necessary if direct performance measurements of the implemented ITS service are unreliable or mostly unavailable.

Step 5: set the target performance levels
for the ITS component under evaluation

To feed back effectively for future improvement, it is essential for the evaluation team to interact closely with the operating agency, and jointly set the anticipated performance level based on given resource limitations. The establishment of its target performance level shall be based on the differences between the originally proposed and actually implemented system features, the nationwide performance statistics of similar systems and interrelations between principal system components.

For instance, one may not expect a surveillance system to detect an incident within 30 seconds if its sensors are deployed at a spacing of one mile on freeway mainline segments. The en-route detour strategy during the incident clearing period cannot be expected to show its full effectiveness if the control center is not able to set coordinated timing plans on surface streets.

This step is also needed in response to the dynamic evolution of the transportation environment from the design of an ITS service to its implementation. Under a rapidly changing transportation environment, the performance of an existing ITS service may be enhanced by the deployment of some supplemental subsystems, or may be reduced due to some functional duplication with other technologies under operations. For instance, as mentioned previously, an IMS may not be able to effectively detour traffic during its operation period if its ATIS components (e.g., VMS, radio, and on-line Internet traffic reports) have not been ready for integrated applications.

Step 6: work within the system constraints

Both the scope of and the method for evaluation shall be designed to effectively work within the existing constraints. Examples of practical constraints include: original design deficiencies, improper field operations, insufficient preparation and training, inexperience in data collection and inventory, potential institutional barriers to uncover the entire operations and limited resources allocated for conducting the evaluation work.

The purpose of this step is to ensure that the evaluation scope set up at an early stage is achievable, and the selected methods are appropriate for producing accountable results from existing constraints. It is also intended to prevent the evaluation work from becoming just a "snapshot" of superficial cost/benefit estimation due to the existence of constraints or limitations. Instead, the emphasis of working within the current ITS environment will enable the evaluation to function as an integrated part of the ITS service's operating process. With the feedback from an effective evaluation, all system constraints or limitations may surface either concurrently or over time, and be overcome in the future through better coordination or further improvements.

Step 7: selection of methods

Depending on the data quality, availability and existing system constraints, one may select various methods for performance measurements and cost/benefit ratio computation. The selection may encompass: (1) standard statistical methods for before-and-after comparison if data are available for direct measurements; (2) semidirect estimation methods, such as using traffic simulation programs that generate estimated results based on limited measurable inputs (e.g., volume, geometry); and (3) qualitative indicators from surveys or related reports if the impacts of an implemented technology or service are indirect and not measurable.

Aside from those direct estimates, one may indirectly assess some impacts from nationwide statistics or inter-related system reports. For instance, by defining incidents incurred within one mile and 1 hour from a primary incident as "secondary incidents," one can compute the total secondary incidents from police accident reports. Using such information along with improved operations in clearing incident blockage, one can indirectly estimate the reduction in secondary incidents due to an effective incident management program.

Note that the evaluation after being through the above seven steps shall have: a set of clear goals and objectives for the implemented ITS service, a well-defined scope to guide the remaining work and in-depth understanding of practical constraints for selection of appropriate evaluation tools or methods.

Impact assessment and performance evaluation

After constructing a solid basis with the above steps, one may further proceed the evaluation through the following six steps so as to ensure that all direct and indirect impacts are included in the analysis and feed back effectively for potential improvement.

Step 8: measurement of direct impacts

Based on the selected methods and target level of performance, one shall rigorously measure all direct impacts on the users and the environment due to the implemented ITS service. For instance, direct impacts resulted from an adaptive signal control system shall include the reduction in both the maximum and average queue length, the average delay per vehicle, the fuel consumption, the average speed increase, and the average number of vehicle stops. Likewise, the reduction in incident detection time, incident response time, the total delay time and fuel consumption of highway users shall all be viewed as the direct impacts of an implemented IMS.

Step 9: measurement of the indirect impacts

Despite the difficulty in quantifying some indirect impacts, it is essential to take into account their resulting costs and benefits as much as possible with available tools and techniques, as such impacts could be as significant as those directly measurable. For instance, an effective IMS may indirectly contribute to the improvement of air quality and driving environments, to the reduction in secondary incidents and associated costs. Likewise, a reliable AVL cannot only improve the on-time performance of a transit system, but also indirectly increase its ridership. In addition, the potential security problem that increasingly plagues some transit systems may be alleviated with an AVL. Similarly, a successful bus-preemption signal system may indirectly contribute to the revenue increase as it is likely to change commuters' mode choice behavior.

Step 10: taking advantage of other available resources

As some critical data needed for evaluation of an ITS service may not be available at its initial implementation stage, one shall consider taking advantage of other related sources, and to indirectly approximate all necessary performance results. For instance, adaptive signal control systems in a neighboring state along with the discrepancies in driving behavior and traffic pattern may well serve as the basis for indirect impact assessment of a similar system. By the same token, one may employ the nationwide statistics about the similar ITS technology to project its resulting benefits and costs if all needed data were not collected up to the evaluation stage.

Aside from the indirect estimate with other available sources, a rigorous evaluation shall take into account its compound impacts on the target transportation environment due to the deployment of other ITS components. For instance, the benefits of an AVL system could be much more significant if it is integrated with adaptive signal control with priority-phasing strategies for transit vehicles. Similarly, the increasing usage of cellular phones among drivers may substantially augment the value of a communication infrastructure.

Step 11: converting the evaluation results into monetary costs and benefits

To facilitate the interactions with policymakers, it is often necessary to convert the operational improvement, and all direct as well as indirect impacts into measurable costs and benefits. For instance, both the travel time reduction and potential decrease in accidents due to ramp metering control shall all be estimated in terms of monetary savings.

Care, however, must be exercised in converting nonmonetary benefits such as the travel time savings, as a reliable estimate of "time value or cost" remains a challenging issue. To avoid potential inflation of benefits, it is essential to set a common base and adopt well-accepted procedures to transform such benefits into monetary savings.

Step 12: construction of an efficient data inventory system

It is quite likely that many currently implemented ITS services may become part of a standard ITS infrastructure in the future transportation environment. The costs as well as benefits of any individual ITS service thus, may vary substantially with the changing technologies and evolving demand patterns. One shall keep all evaluation-related data in a dynamic database so that any on-going ITS operation can benefit from the lessons of previously implemented systems and take any necessary adjustment in a timely manner. A well-organized database system can also enable the operating agency to respond to any inquiry from policymakers, and establish the interrelations between the operating cost/benefit ratio and the evolving transportation environment.

Step 13: recommendation of critical areas for potential improvement

In addition to the assessment of costs as well as benefits in typical before-and-after studies, a rigorous evaluation should compare the actual with the anticipated performance efficiency based on preset goals. For instance, a moderate improvement in the incident response time may or may not justify the total investment in the surveillance systems and related control as well as operating costs. Hence, identification of critical areas in the entire operation process for potential efficiency improvement and cost minimization shall be the core of evaluation.

Note that the steps illustrated in figure 22–1 present a general framework for integrating the evaluation as part of an ITS service. It is expected that with such an interacting process the operating agency of ITS service can benefit significantly from the constant feedback of a dynamic evaluation mechanism, and effectively operate as well as improve its deployed systems. Also note that the proposed procedures are steps that could occur in a best scenario with all potential intra- and interorganizational friction being overcome.

Potential issues in performing the ITS evaluation

Despite the broad consensus that ITS can improve the efficiency of existing transportation facilities, a rigorous evaluation of its performance and resulting costs and benefits may face resistance from some responsible operating agencies. This is often due to the fact that the benefits of an implemented ITS system may be overstated, or they cannot be fully realized as the result of insufficient preparation or planning. Thus, instead of using "evaluation" to identify necessary improvement, some responsible agencies may prefer to ignore such a need and employ only favorable data from other sources to justify its investment.

Nevertheless, performing a rigorous ITS evaluation is indeed a challenging task. Various critical issues or constraints may arise in the evaluation process and thus, affect the resulting quality. Some of these issues and constraints are discussed here.

- *Data availability.* The mechanism to collect and record the performance of an implemented ITS system often was not set up at the planning stage. For instance, some highway agencies may deploy a surveillance system that can collect only the average flow speed across lanes, not all lane-specific measurements including flow rate and occupancy that are essential for any cost/benefit analysis.
- *Data quality.* It is not uncommon to note that many ITS operators have been trained only to effectively operate the system, but not for collecting performance-related data. For instance, in responding to a severe accident, the emergency response team may fail to accurately record its arrival time and the partial and fully recovery times. Likewise, operators in the traffic control center may not recognize the need to precisely record the accident's reported time and the dispatching time of response units.
- *Data inventory.* An ITS system may be capable of collecting all needed data for both performance and impact assessment. But due to inadequate planning, much of the invaluable data, although technically available, is practically unusable. This is evidenced by the fact that there are quite rich traffic measurement data collected by many highway surveillance systems at an interval of 30 seconds, but such data are hardly used for any traffic monitoring or control applications due to the lack of an efficient data inventory system.
- *Institutional barriers.* Under some organizational structure, the agency responsible for ITS operations may not be the one initializing the planning work. Thus, the potential institutional barriers tend to discourage some responsible operators to view any evaluation attempt from a positive perspective due to the concern that some system deficiencies may be exposed in the course of analysis.

- *Selection of key parameters for benefit assessment.* Aside from the data and institutional issues, the selection of proper parameters for computing the resulting benefits is a critical task as it may significantly affect the resulting cost/benefit ratio. For instance, one of the major benefits from any ATMS is the delay or travel time reduction. Thus, depending on the adopted parameter for unit time cost (i.e., dollar per minute) an ATMS service may or may not yield an acceptable cost/benefit ratio. Researchers conducting the evaluation may be pressed to select parameters that result in an inflated cost/benefit ratio.

- *Cost allocation.* In many areawide ITS projects, it is often quite difficult to precisely allocate the large amount of indirect costs associated with their implementation. Without accounting for those incurred costs, the resulting cost/benefit ratio could be misleading. How to distinguish the routine operating costs from ITS project-specific expenses or investment thus becomes a quite sensitive issue in the ITS evaluation.

- *Methods to quantify intangible or indirect impacts.* An effective ITS system or ATMS technology may yield substantial direct and indirect benefits. For instance, the reduction in incident response and clearance time may reduce both the delay and potential secondary incidents for highway users. Transforming the secondary incident reduction into measurable benefits, however, necessitates the collection of quite detailed data and the application of appropriate statistical techniques. Thus, such benefits are often either neglected or unreliably stated due to the required efforts.

- *Adjustment to a dynamic environment.* It should be noted that due to the dynamic interaction between the users and the transportation environment, many benefits generated by an individual ITS technology or service may not be static, but they dynamically change over time. For instance, the benefit of a pre-trip information or guidance system may diminish over time after commuters develop sufficient personal travel experience under recurrent traffic conditions. Similarly, the benefits from an IMS may also be reduced if some preventive methods for safety improvement emerge to be effective. Any evaluation, failing to take into account such a potentially dynamic relation, may yield only a partial picture of the actual benefits and costs and mislead the need for further system investment.

A case study: evaluation of CHART incident response program

This section presents an example evaluation of incident response systems based on the proposed framework. The entire evaluation was conducted under numerous constraints indicated in the previous section. However, despite its deficiencies, the lessons from this evaluation could be invaluable for those conducting similar evaluation studies.

Background and scope

CHART is the highway incident management program of the Maryland State Highway Administration, headquartered in Hanover, Maryland, where the newly built and integrated statewide operations center (SOC) is located. The SOC is also supported by three satellite traffic operations centers (TOC), one being seasonal. The current network covered by CHART consists of 375 miles of freeways and 170 miles of highways, mostly on the Washington, Baltimore, Annapolis and Frederick metropolises.

The focus of this study was to assess the effectiveness of the incident management program operated by CHART. The entire evaluation consists of the following two phases: Phase-1, identification of available data and methodology; and Phase-II, assessment of the performance and the resulting benefits.

Data availability and quality

To ensure the quality and also consider the opening of the SOC in August 1995, all involved in the evaluation study decided that the analysis should be based on actual data from the operation record of CHART, rather than approximating from any other source. Thus, the 1996 incident management data were collected and used in the initial stage of evaluation.

Through a quite comprehensive review, it was found that there were two sets of 1996 incident management data available for analysis, one from the SOC and the other from TOC-3 (located at the proximity of the Capital Beltway). The SOC record contains a total of 523 incident reports for the entire 12 months in 1996. TOC-3, however, has only a total of 1,153 incidents from April to December 1996. The incident reports from TOC-4 (located at the proximity of the Baltimore Beltway) were mostly missing, and inadequate for use in the analysis.

Note that to evaluate an incident response program, one shall have, at a minimum, the following data:

- The onset time of each incident
- The receiving time of each incident report provided by drivers or automated detection systems to the traffic control center
- The departure time of the incident response unit
- The travel time and distance for the incident response unit to reach each incident scene
- The partially open time for the blocked highway facility
- The fully open time for the blocked highway facility
- The full recovery time of the entire traffic system
- The traffic flow rate and speed before, during, and after the incident
- The approximate queue distance before, during, and after the incident

As the form for recording incident-related operations was not designed to have the evaluation in mind, it naturally does not contain all the needed information. Thus, the initial evaluation was conducted under all existing constraints.

Evaluation procedures

The methodology for the evaluation was developed to take full advantage of the available data. It consisted of the following principal steps:

- Analysis of incident frequency and distribution by lane-blockage duration
- Computation of incident response rate for each operations center during 1996
- The distribution of incident clearance time by lane-blockage type
- Comparison of the average incident clearance duration with and without the incident response program
- Computation of the resulting benefits due to the implementation of an incident response program, including: assistance to drivers, reduction in driver delay, reduction in vehicle operational hours, reduction in fuel consumption and reduction in secondary incidents

Notably, due to the lack of some critical information, the resulting benefits were approximated indirectly with corridor simulation along with a calibrated statistical model. Following is a summary of the core procedures for assessing the reduction in delay, fuel consumption and vehicle operating hours::

- Randomly select 150 cases from those 1,685 incidents in 1996.
- Organize all geometric and traffic-related data for simulation analysis, including major variables such as incident duration, number of freeway lanes, the number of blocked lanes and the mainline freeway volume.
- Simulate all those 150 incidents with corridor simulation model, a corridor traffic simulation program developed by Federal Highway Administration.
- Collect all major simulation output data, including total delay and total fuel consumption.
- Simulate the identical 150 traffic scenarios, but without incidents; and collect the same delay and fuel consumption data.
- Construct a statistical functional relation between the target benefit variable (i.e., delay reduction) and key incident characteristic factors (e.g., incident duration, number of blocked lanes) based on the results of 150 simulated cases.
- Apply the above-calibrated statistical relations to the remaining 1,535 incidents; and compute the total delay time as well as the total fuel consumption.
- Apply the same procedures for estimating the reduction in emission levels.

The computation of secondary incident reduction and assistance to drivers is based directly on the statistics of the available incident reports and the accident record from Maryland Police Department.

Evaluation results

Distribution of incidents

The analysis results indicate that there were a total of 135 two-lane blockage incidents on the local roads. Most incidents on freeways were distributed along three major commuting corridors, where I-495 experienced a total of 848 incidents; and I-95 and I-270 had 105 and 183 incidents, respectively, in 1996. Thus, CHART had responded to, on average, 2.3 lane-blockage incidents per day for I-495 alone; and 0.3 and 0.5 incidents for the other two main commuting freeways.

With respect to the blockage duration, most incidents on major commuting freeways did not block the traffic for more than 1 hour. For instance, about 88 percent of incidents on I-495 were shorter than 1 hour. A similar incident pattern also exists on I-95 and I-270. There were about 80 percent of incidents on I-270 having lane blockages for less than 1 hour, in contrast to a total of 68 percent on I-95.

However, it is notable that in comparison with other highways, drivers on I-495 clearly had been caught in a long incident blockage much more often than others. For instance, there were a total of 109 incidents in 1996 on I-495 lasting over 1 hour, and about 22 of those blocking the traffic for more than 2 hours. Thus, by defining those over 1 hour as severe incidents, drivers on I-495 had experienced on average of one severe incident per three days in 1996.

In brief, it is clear that the highway network covered by CHART has been plagued by the high frequency of incidents, ranging from about 30 to 40 minutes to more than 3 hours. Nonrecurrent congestion due to incidents is apparently one of the primary contributors to the worsening traffic congestion in the entire region, especially on those major commuting highway corridors such as I-270, I-90 and I-495.

Efficiency of operations

As most data needed for analyzing the distribution of detection and response times were not available, the evaluation was focused on one of the indicators—that is, the response rate when an incident was reported.

It was found to be about 86 percent for the TOC-3 or 438 out of 532; and 99.2 percent for TOC-3 or 1,143 out of 1,153. The Maryland State Police and the local and county police were the main sources of detecting incidents for CHART.

With respect to the reduction in incident clearance duration, the average operation time for two-lane blockage incidents was 107 minutes, significantly longer than the average of 68.3 minutes for the same type of incidents managed by CHART. The improvement was found to be about 36.2 percent.

Assistance to drivers

In 1996, CHART's incident management team responded to a total of 195 incidents of relatively short duration, mostly lasting less than 1 hour and mainly for driver assistance.

Reduction in secondary incidents

All incidents that occurred within 1 hour after the primary incident, and within 2 miles, were computed from state police accident reports. The potential reduction in secondary incidents was found to be 218 based on the 36.2 percent reduction in the incident clearance time. The potential cost savings, due to the reduction of those secondary incidents, were not computed, as those were not directly measurable from the existing data.

Direct benefits

For those 1,676 recorded incidents, the total reduction in delay time was found to be 70,809,524 hours; and the total reduction in fuel consumption was about 598,406 gallons. Note that such benefits could be increased substantially if incident data on the Baltimore Beltway and those managed by TOC-4 were available for inclusion in the evaluation.

Indirect benefits such as the improvement in air quality and driving stress were not estimated due to both the data and resources constraints.

Areas for potential improvement

The results of preliminary evaluation have yielded the following recommendations for further system improvement:

- Training operators to effectively record all essential operations-related data. Many of those incident reports in 1996 were found to have a large number of either missing or incomplete items.
- Modifying the current report form to contain all vital information for improving the operations efficiency and justifying the resulting benefits.
- Continuing the performance and benefit analysis so as to best allocate the available resources and sustain the support from both the general public and state legislators.
- Evaluating the efficiency as well as cost/benefit of other components of CHART, such as the traveler information system or traffic management.
- Improving the use of freeway service patrols and optimizing their spatial distribution on freeway segments of high-incident frequency so as to reduce the incident response time.
- Installing additional surveillance sensors to share the incident detection load that is undertaken mostly through drivers' phone reports to the state and county police departments.
- Developing an incident information management system that can automate the process for storing all collected reports in a dynamic database, and generating the performance evaluation results as needed.
- Investigating the interrelations between the traffic demand patterns and the distribution of incidents so as to effectively contending with nonrecurrent congestion.

Closure

To effectively contend with ever-increasing congestion and dynamically changing traffic patterns, it is essential for any deployed ITS service to be improved and upgraded constantly. To do so, one of the most effective ways is to incorporate the evaluation mechanism in the operations process, and thereby receive feedback about its performance in a timely manner.

Nonetheless, the establishment of a rigorous evaluation mechanism demands not only on great efforts from the system operators, but also it necessitates their strong commitments to integrate the evaluation as part of their routine operations. Only by viewing evaluation from a constructive perspective can they take full advantage of its feedback and perform any necessary improvement.

In fact, with an effective evaluation mechanism, the responsible agency can have a clear picture of the resulting costs and benefits at different stages of an ITS service's life cycle. This is critical for determining whether an implemented ITS service has reached its capacity or remains to be maximized. The results of a systematical evaluation will also enable ITS operators to have a reliable assessment of the direct as well indirect impacts on both the system users and the target transportation environment.

Most importantly, with the commitment of having a rigorous evaluation mechanism in its routine ITS operations, the responsible agency may better convince the general public that it has constantly improved its system efficiency and best used all available resources. Thus, any request for further ITS-related investment may have a better chance of receiving support from policymakers and the general public.

Bibliography

Alexiadis, V. et al. 1994. "Integrated Planning/Simulation Methodology for Analysis of Traffic Management Systems." *Proceedings of the IVHS America Annual Meeting.*

Alexiadis, V., Loudon, W. 1993. *Assessment of Benefits from Implementation of IVHS User Services* (August). VNTSC report to Transportation Research Board.

American Trucking Associations Foundation. 1996. *Assessment of Intelligent Transportation Systems/Commercial Vehicle Operations User Services: ITS/CVO Qualitative Benefit/Cost Analysis.* American Trucking Associations Foundation.

Bolczak, R., "Intelligent Vehicle Highway Systems Operational Test Evaluation Guidelines," WP93W0367, FHWA, 1993.

Casey, L. 1994. *An Analysis of the Accuracy and Limitations of the IVHS Benefits Framework Simulation Model* (July). VNTSC report.

Casey, R. 1996. "The Benefits of ITS Technologies for Rural Transit." Presented at the Rural ITS Conference. Volpe Transportation Systems Center.

Chen, M. and S. Steven. 1993. *Cost Estimates for Near-term Deployment of Advanced Traffic Management Systems* (February). DOE Oak Ridge Labs.

Crescent. 1994. The Crescent Project: An Evaluation of an Element of HELP Program (February). The Crescent Evaluation Team.

Evanco, W. 1996. *The Impacts of Rapid Incident Detection on Freeway Accident Fatalities* (June). Mitretek Systems.

Farwell, R. 1996. "Evaluation of Omnilink Demand-Driven Transit Operations: Flex-Route Services." Presented at the European Transport Forum. SG Associates.

Glassco, R. et al. 1996. *Studies of Potential Intelligent Transportation Systems Benefits Using Traffic Simulation Modeling* (June). Mitretek Systems.

George Mason University. 1993. "Toward Comprehensive APTS Evaluations: Results of A National Workshop." GMU.

Haelkorn, M. et al. 1997. *Evaluation of PuSHMe Mayday System* (June). Final report.

Inman, V. et al. 1995. *TravTek Evaluation Orlando Test Network Study* (October). Federal Highway Administraiton.

ITS America. 1996. "Assessment of ITS Benefits—Results from the Field" (April). ITS America Sixth Annual Meeting.

JHK & Associates. 1992. *Proposed Analytical Framework for Modeling IVHS Benefits* (December). JHK & Associates.

Little, C., T. Liu, N. Rosenburg, D. Skinner, L. Vance. 1993. *IVHS Inventory of Models for Predicting the Emission and Energy Benefits of IVHS Alternatives* (April). VNTSC report.

Mcgurrin, M.F., and D.E. Shank, D.E. 1997. *ITS Versus New Roads: A Study of Cost-Effectiveness* (August). ITS World.

Orcutt Associates. 1984. *Evaluation Study, Buffalo Gap Road, Abilene Signal System.* Prepared for the City of Abilene, Texas.

Remer, M., T. Atherton, and W. Gardner. 1995. *ITS Benefits, Evaluation and Costs: Results and Lessons from the Minnesota Guidestar Travlink Operational Test* (November). Draft report.

Sullivan, E.C. 1990. "Estimating Accident Benefits of Reduced Freeway Congestion." *Journal of Transportation Engineering* 116, no. 2: 167–180.

Tech Environment. 1993. *Air Quality Benefit Study of SmarTraveler Advanced Traveler Information Services* (July).

Texas Department of Transportation. 1992. *Benefits of the Texas Traffic Light Synchronization Grant Program* (October). Texas DOT.

U.S. Department of Transportation. 1995. *Assessment of ITS Benefits—Early Results* (August). U.S. DOT.

Volpe Transportation Systems Center. 1996. *Benefits Assessment of Advanced Public Transportation Systems.* Volpe Transportation Systems Center.

References

COMSIS Corporation. *CHART Incident Response Evaluation* (May). COMSIS Corp.

JHK & Associates. 1992. *Inventory Models for Predicting the Emissions and Energy Benefits of IVHS Alternatives* (December). JHK & Associates.

JHK & Associates. 1993. *Modeling of IVHS Benefits—Specification for Adapting Planning and Simulation Models* (May). JHK & Associates.

JHK & Associates. 1994a. *IVHS Benefits Assessment Model Framework* (June). JHK & Associates.

JHK & Associates. 1994b. *IVHS benefits Assessment Model Framework—Program Reference Guide* (June). JHK & Associates.

Kloos, W. et al. 1994. "Bus Priority at Traffic Signals in Portland" (July). *Compendium of Technical Papers.* Institute of Transportation Engineers.

National Governor's Association and Iowa Department of Transportation. 1997. *Assessment of State Benefits and Costs from ITS/CVO Services.* National Governor's Association and Iowa DOT.

Parsons Transportation Group and Texas Transportation Institute. 1997. *Estimation of Benefits of Houston TransStar* (February). Parsons Transportation Group and TTI.

Sierra Research. 1993. *IVHS Benefits Assessment Framework Emissions and Fuel Consumption Methodologies* (July).

Smith, S., and C. Perez. 1992. *Evaluation of INFORM—Lessons Learned and Applications to Other Systems* (January). Presented at the 71st Transportation Research Board Meeting.

U.S. Department of Transportation. 1992–1993. *Assessment of Computer Dispatch Technology in the Paratransit Industry.* U.S. DOT.

U.S. Department of Transportation. 1997. *Review of ITS Benefits: Emerging Success.* U.S. DOT.

Volpe Transportation Systems Center. 1993. *Evaluation Guidelines for the Advanced Public Transportation Systems Operational Tests.* Volpe Transportation Systems Center.

Volpe Transportation Systems Center. 1995. *Intelligent Transportation Systems Impacts Assessment Results* (March). Volpe Transportation Systems Center.

BY Mark Johnson • Associate Director • ITS America

ITS AND LEGAL ISSUES—A PRIMER

Introduction

The application of intelligent transportation systems (ITS) to manage our nation's surface transportation systems necessarily implicates a full spectrum of legal issues. Many of these, such as liability, antitrust and intellectual property, are not unique to ITS in their application or effect. Other legal concerns and their resolution engender unique characteristics in the ITS arena. For example, privacy, procurement and financing fall in this second group. What follows is a primer on the several legal issues that may need to be addressed by any ITS professional.

Tort liability

A tort is an accidental or intentional harm to a person or thing. The legal concepts surrounding the assignment of fault, or liability, to a person or thing were first developed in England before the founding of the United States. In this country, most tort law is formed and enforced at the state level, with each state having a differing, but similar, set of laws and traditions. By seeking to find and assign fault, tort law is seeking to compensate the victim(s) for his or her injury in order to "make them whole."

Presently in the United States, the primary burden of the cost of vehicle accidents rests with the drivers and owners of vehicles. This is reasonable when we consider that three-quarters of vehicle accidents occur because of driver error. Consequently, when driver error (i.e., negligence) is found to be the cause of an accident, drivers (or, in reality, their insurance company) are made to pay for the resulting injury. Accidents caused by defects associated with the vehicle are assessed against the manufacturer or designer or, in addition, whoever put the defective vehicle into the "flow of commerce" where it can be purchased and used by consumers. Thus, we have two doctrines for compensation: (1) negligence and (2) products and strict liability.

For negligence, the injured person must show that he or she was owed a "duty of care" by the person causing the injury and that this "duty of care" was "breached." In other words, there must have been a failure to take reasonable precautions or actions on the part of the party who caused the injury. Damages that may be recovered include "compensatory damages" for reimbursement for actual harm: medical, economic, pain and suffering and damage to property. Moreover, "punitive damages" may be imposed where the judge or court determines that the conduct was so egregious to warrant punishment as a deterrent against similar action in the future.

Products and strict liability are relatively recent legal concepts that seek to respond to the growing complexity of products and who is in the best position to ensure that they are safe. Products liability is not concerned with the conduct of the defendant, but instead focuses on the defectiveness of the product itself. Negligence is not a factor. The law recognizes two types of defects: an error in the manufacturing process or a fundamental design defect that could create an injury. A related legal cause of action is strict liability. This theory applies to manufacturers, designers and sellers of products that, when placed in the "stream of commerce," the product is already in a defective condition unreasonably dangerous to the consumer. For example, strict liability specifies that there is a duty to supply an adequate warning against harms that are reasonably foreseeable through normal and expected uses, and even misuses, of a product.

Certain ITS applications,[1] however, break down the legal distinction between driver error and a defective product, thus making it more difficult to identify the culpable party. For example, research and deployment efforts are seeking to equip individual vehicles with devices to enhance safety. These technologies can range from a device that warns drivers of possible hazards (i.e., a car in the driver's "blind spot," to complete computer control over the vehicle). (The automated highway system research program undertaken in the mid-1990s examined possible technologies that would, in effect, "marry" the vehicle and road infrastructure whereby driver involvement, once the system is engaged, would be fully removed from the equation.) The more that the driver error can be minimized or eliminated through technology, the engineers argue, the fewer the accidents that will occur.

For the extremes on this range, warning devices and total automation, the assignment of fault is still relatively easy to do. A driver may simply ignore or not notice the warning sound or light; thus driver negligence. On the other hand, there can be no driver error where he or she gives up control over the vehicle. In this case, the owner of the "system"—the designer, system integrator or, even, the government—would likely be found at fault for an accident. (It should also be noted that such a "system" failure has the potential to result in larger accidents involving more vehicles.) A more difficult problem arises in such "interim" technologies such as adaptive cruise control (ACC). In this example, a driver would engage a system on the vehicle that would maintain a selected speed but would also ensure that a minimum distance is maintained behind the vehicle ahead. An ACC system could also maintain the vehicle within an individual lane. Under this scenario, the driver must still steer the vehicle, monitor its speed and location and can intervene at any moment to take back full control.

If an accident occurs while an ACC system is operating, it may be much more difficult to find the culpable party. Did the driver fail to monitor the system? Fail to intervene at a necessary moment? Or, did the ACC system fail to keep the established distance behind the vehicle in front, thus causing the rear-end collision? These are all questions of fact that can be sorted out in each accident; but they suggest that where more and more control of the vehicle is taken away from the driver, different and new players will be required to compensate for any resulting injuries.

Within the ITS community, tort liability has often been cited by engineers and manufacturers as preventing the development and ultimate deployment of ITS technologies, such as ACC. It is this "fear of liability," it is often claimed, that holds back the introduction of new technologies and their attendant benefits, such as improved safety, from reaching the public. Whether this "fear of liability" is holding back ITS systems such as ACC is difficult to say. Nonetheless, developers, manufacturers, insurance companies and transportation officials will need to balance the benefits of such ITS systems against the cost of compensating those who may be injured if and when these systems fail. And this analysis will have to occur individually for each new technology or advancement as it is introduced. In the United States, changes in the law are built on past experience. The ITS community will need to look at its past to help realize this balance between the benefits and costs related to any new ITS technology.

It is thought that recent experiences with the introduction of vehicle airbags may be instructive. One issue here relates to consumer expectations. When first introduced into vehicles, airbag deployments in an accident were portrayed to the public as relatively benign events, whereas in reality they are quite violent and can cause severe injuries. Lawsuits resulted against car manufacturers for these injuries despite the fact that the airbag may have saved the plaintiff's life: the public held the false, but legitimate, expectation that no injuries would result. Developers of ITS applications must be sure not to oversell what the ITS technologies and systems can actually do. Matching consumer expectations with reality may serve to minimize second-guessing in a lawsuit down the road.

Moreover, the regulatory response to unanticipated effects of airbag deployments is similarly instructive. It was discovered that children and small adults stood at risk of death from airbag deployments. In response, the National Highway Traffic Safety Administration (NHTSA) issued regulations that permit the installation and activation of cut-off switches in certain types of vehicles. These regulations, however, do not go so far as to alleviate liability running to the vehicle manufacturer or the authorized repair shop that performs the deactivation. It cannot yet be said what litigation may result where, for example, a person is injured in an accident because the airbag had been deactivated but, if it had been deployed, no injury or less severe injuries would have resulted. For ITS, the lesson here is that the U.S. regulatory structure should not be expected to provide exemptions from liability or, even at a minimum, clearly define what liability parameters technology developers will face.

ITS developers also need to realize that NHTSA, the federal transportation agency charged with ensuring the safety of motor vehicles, establishes only performance standards as opposed to design standards. Performance standards operate as minimum requirements that manufacturers must meet in order for their products to be used by the public. It is then up to the manufacturers to develop the various and competing designs that meet or exceed the government's performance standards. Satisfaction of NHTSA's[2] minimum standards does not, in and of itself, provide manufacturers with liability protection. Legal theories of product and strict liability may still be applicable.

In addition, industry on its own through market forces or through voluntary organizations may establish its own performance or design standards for ITS products. A court will want to examine adherence to such standards in each individual case as indicative of the state-of-the art and practice for the industry. But, again, adherence alone to such industry-wide standards would likely not be enough to provide exemptions from liability.

Some in the ITS community have suggested that tort law reforms at the state and federal levels are needed to alleviate many of the apparent liability concerns. Proposals have included temporary or permanent federal preemption of negligence or failure-to-warn suits for ITS products, preclusion of strict liability actions, limits on amounts and types of damages and schemes of "risk pooling" with a national fund to compensate those injured by ITS products or services. One commentator has suggested, however, that in the absence of a public perception of a "crisis" holding back the development and deployment of ITS, and all the attendant benefits in safety, tort reform to benefit ITS specifically is unlikely.[3]

Antitrust

Antitrust as a legal concept refers generally to anticompetitive behavior in the marketplace by one or more participants. Anticompetitive behavior may include a seller "tying" the purchase of one product to the purchase of an undesired product, the fixing of prices by one or more firms, or the division of a market between competitors.[4] Much of the analysis to determine if an action violates the antitrust laws turns on complex economic studies that look to actual market share, market effects, consumer perceptions and expectations, and so forth. Although there are no unique antitrust concerns attributable to ITS, practitioners in this industry need to be aware that certain business and research practices that have anticompetitive effects may result in antitrust liability.

Any collaborative effort between competitors in an industry could invite scrutiny for antitrust violations. For example, joint ventures, partnerships, industry consortiums, and even membership in a trade association, which by necessity involve cooperation and the exchange of information, may create opportunities for anticompetitive behavior, including reducing competition or restricting the members' or partners' activities in the marketplace. If, however, such collaborative organizations adopt and follow basic antitrust guidelines, the likelihood for antitrust liability may be significantly eliminated. Such guidelines may specify that competitors neither discuss nor exchange information concerning:

- Prices, price changes, pricing policies, discounts, credit or other conditions of sale
- Profits, profit margins, or cost data
- Market shares or sales territories and markets
- Allocation of customers or territories
- Selection, rejection, or termination of customers or suppliers
- Restricting territory or markets in which a company may resell services or products
- Restricting the customers to whom a company may sell
- Unreasonable restrictions on the development or use of technologies
- Any matter that is inconsistent with the proposition that each company must exercise its independent business judgment in pricing its services or products, dealing with its customers, and choosing the markets in which it will compete[5]

For ITS, antitrust concerns may also arise in research and standards-setting contexts. In 1985 and again in 1993, Congress, recognizing that private-sector cooperation in research joint ventures may be beneficial to the public, reduced the potential antitrust liability for joint ventures conducting certain research, development and production activities.[6] Congress provided that qualifying joint ventures may be ordered to pay only limited damages (i.e., only actual damages rather than the standard treble damages) if any antitrust violations are found.

Private-sector involvement in standards-setting can also be problematic. For federal government agencies (e.g., NHTSA) there can be no antitrust liability.[7] There is no, however, blanket antitrust protection for private-sector entities involved in standards-setting. Antitrust liability will not be found where such activity benefits an industry as a whole and not any individual members; thus, private-sector cooperation is seen as procompetitive.[8]

Judicial scrutiny of potential antitrust activity is most often done under the "Rule of Reason" standard. This standard requires that both procompetitive and anticompetitive effects be considered unless the activity in question, such as price fixing, is "per se" illegal.[9] Courts or enforcement authorities will use the Rule of Reason standard to review joint ventures, consortiums, or other collaborative activities between competitors.[10]

Procurement

Traditionally, the public sector has procured transportation products and services through a low-bid, competitive process. Whether it is concrete, steel rebar, or asphalt, the low-bid method has served governments well since the dawn of the interstate highway system in 1956. However, procuring ITS by means of this low-bid process has proven to be problematic.

ITS is different than steel, concrete, or asphalt. Certainly, ITS includes common pieces of equipment; but, in most cases, governments are actually buying a system comprised of state-of-the-art technology. In particular, the low-bid method for procuring software, such as to control traffic lights from a traffic management center (TMC), has been plagued by cost-overruns, misdesign, long-term maintenance failures and the basic contractor inability to provide the system as promised. Because each ITS system is often unique unto itself, the low-bid contract winner will often not be able to meet the requirements of the job.

In order to encourage competition and prevent corruption, governments have established many procurement rules that work well in the low-bid model for low-tech items. These rules, however, may impede a successful ITS procurement. Federal and state procurement rules and regulations can impose barriers by restricting what can be included in proposals and how proposals may be evaluated. Technical ability of the contractor may be the most important criterion for selection; yet regulations mandate that the contract award go to the lowest bidder. Moreover, the financial ability of a contractor to provide the long-term operations and maintenance support critical for ITS systems may not be an allowable factor for agencies to consider. Many state regulations prohibit the private contractor who designed the specifications for the project from actually bidding, thus preventing the involvement of perhaps the best-qualified contractor. Another continuing problem for ITS procurement has been the lack of technical expertise by the government agency staff. Agencies are accustomed to procuring steel, concrete and asphalt; but procuring software requires, for example, very different technical skills.

The ITS community has developed several models and recommendations for procuring ITS. Such mechanisms may include, for example, prebid conferences with potential contractors; prequalification of potential contractors where price is not considered; a "Best Value Procurement" process that first rates the technical proposal on its merits and then considers the pricing element; a requirement that the contractor present a "Proof of Concept" or other prototyping exercises, which may be paid for by the agency; and the use of existing standards and "off-the-shelf" equipment as much as possible. There is no one correct model for ITS procurement: flexibility and creativity by both the public and private sector is necessary.

The term "public–private partnership" is often used to describe the best ITS procurement practices. There is no one accepted definition of this term, or one model that has been used exclusively in practice, except to say that a public–private partnership exists where all parties, both public and private, share the costs, risks, and benefits of a project. Examples may include a "design-build-operate" contract where one contractor will design, build, and operate the project, such as a TMC, on behalf of the public agency. The contractor then will act as a systems integrator to bring all the pieces together. Tying payment by the public agency to low cost of construction and subsequent operational efficiencies will act as strong incentives to ensure quality and minimize costs if one contractor is responsible for all three phases—design, build and operation—of the project. Moreover, if there is a revenue stream arising from the project, such as through a toll, the private contractor may be willing to find its profit by access to some or all of that revenue for a period of time. (A shared resource project, discussed later in this chapter, is another form of public–private partnership.) Again, the partners' flexibility and creativity may be the only limitations.

Intellectual property

As the U.S. Constitution recognizes, ownership over patents, copyrights and trademarks incentivizes advances in technology. This concept applies equally to developers of ITS technologies and applications. However, the involvement of federal and state government funding for ITS development can create barriers to private ownership of ITS intellectual property. Therefore, a balance needs to be reached between retention of intellectual property rights by the private sector to encourage innovation with the government interest to retain these same rights where public funds supported the development of the new technology or information. Federal intellectual property law seeks to strike this balance.

The Bayh-Dole Act of 1980[11] sets forth the federal government's stand on patent rights in inventions created as part of a research effort partially or fully funded by federal monies. For inventions developed under any federal "contract, grant, or cooperative agreement," the Bayh-Dole Act strives to:

- Promote the use of inventions arising from federally supported research or development
- Ensure that the inventions are used in a manner to promote competition and enterprise
- Promote the commercialization of domestic inventions
- Ensure that the federal government obtains sufficient rights in federally supported inventions to meet the federal government's needs and to protect the public against nonuse or unreasonable use of inventions[12]

Where the private company holds ownership of the invention developed through public support, the federal government will retain a "nonexclusive, nontransferable, irrevocable, paid-up license for or on behalf of the United States."[13] The federal government, however, may not sell or lease its license in the invention for a profit. The private owner, similarly, does not have unrestricted control of the invention. He or she must make the invention available to the public within a reasonable time period and cannot intentionally hold back the invention from the marketplace. If this occurs, the federal government has "march-in" rights to force the patent owner to grant a license to a third party.[14]

The federal government will also retain similar rights in electronic data and software, including copyrights, where such items are created with public funding. The Federal Acquisition Regulations specify that the federal government holds unlimited rights in data developed pursuant to a government contract.[15] This right is negotiable, allowing the private developer to assert a copyright. For software, the federal government receives a paid-up, nonexclusive, irrevocable, worldwide license in the copyrighted software.[16]

State and local public agencies are advised to negotiate with their private contractors for long-term rights in data and software to ensure that the protected information is accessible for continued operations, maintenance and upgrade. For private contractors, however, there is a desire to retain ownership in the software so as to be able to sell or license the technology to either another private entity or another public agency. The public agency that initially supported the development of the software may want to negotiate royalty rights for such later, third-party use.

Public dissemination of trade secrets is another concern for private contractors. Specifically, private contractors do not want proprietary information made available to public agencies as part of a contract to be released to the public because of Freedom of Information (FOIA) laws. However, federal law and most states prohibit government employees from releasing such protected information, or otherwise exempt it from any required disclosure.[17]

Privacy and data protection

Without doubt, the issue that first comes to mind when the general public begins to learn about ITS is that these technologies will create a governmental "Big Brother" that will track each vehicle's movements; and can access sensitive, personal data, such as financial information. It is not to say that the public's perception is wrong or misguided; but the ITS community must respond to assuage this deeply held fear, however real or not, by educating the public on the benefits to be gained from ITS along with the privacy protections that should be built into these systems and applications.

There is no national law or policy on privacy and data protection in the United States. Instead, there is a patchwork of laws, regulations and rules at the national and state level that apply to specific activities or industries. These "sectoral" laws, such as the Driver's Privacy Protection Act[18] and the Fair Credit Reporting Act,[19] are often created in response to a tragic incident or specific egregious conduct by an industry. Only the U.S. Constitution and the Bill of Rights, which are mirrored by many state constitutions, can be said to include universal, basic privacy rights attributable to all individuals.[20] But except for the 13th Amendment, these rights apply only to actions by government officials. Even in the new Internet age, the Clinton Administration has so far not favored a national, government-driven approach; but, rather, they have encouraged the private sector to develop its own privacy and data security policies and enforcement mechanisms.[21] This industry is still too young to determine if this "hands-off" approach by the government will prove to have been best.

For ITS there seems to be three types of applications that implicate privacy and data security concerns. First, there is surveillance. This includes traffic and incident management through the use of video cameras and various types of electronic sensors on the roadway. An emerging application gaining widespread use has been automatic enforcement of traffic laws, such as red-light running. Many of these surveillance technologies can photograph a license plate or calculate a vehicle's speed at a specific time and place.

A second application, electronic toll collection (ETC), involves access to personal financial information. ETC employs dedicated short-range communications from a vehicle to a toll booth, allowing the vehicle to pass through and pay the toll electronically without stopping. In order to take advantage of this convenience, the vehicle owner must install a toll tag in his or her vehicle and establish an account with the toll authority that permits automatic payment. (ETC also raises surveillance concerns as the vehicle can be identified to have passed through an individual toll booth at a specific time.)

The third application centers on regulatory activities. For commercial vehicle operations, in particular, the hope is that ITS will allow carriers and government regulators to move to a paperless system. Enforcement of taxes, truck weight and maintenance, driver hour limitations, and the like, will all be done electronically and in real time. The private and public sectors should both realize improved efficiencies and greater overall safety. The individual truck drivers, however, may protest that this ITS application creates unacceptable intrusions on their person privacy.

In each instance where ITS is deployed, the ITS industry must strive to balance the benefits of ITS, in terms of convenience and safety, with the needs of the public to safeguard an individual's privacy. There is not one approach that is applicable in all cases, but limitations and protections can and should be built into ITS deployments. Application of this advisory list of principles, developed by the ITS industry, will go far to convince the public that this balance has been achieved:

1. *Individual-centered*—ITS must recognize and respect the individual's interests in privacy and information use
2. *Visible*—ITS will be built in a manner "visible" to individuals
3. *Comply*—ITS will comply with state and federal laws governing privacy and information use
4. *Secure*—ITS will be secure
5. *Law enforcement*—ITS has an appropriate role in enhancing travelers' safety and security interests; but absent consent, government authority, or appropriate legal process, information identifying individuals will not be disclosed to law enforcement
6. *Relevant*—ITS will only collect personal information that is relevant for ITS purposes
7. *Anonymity*—where practicable, individuals should have the ability to access ITS on an anonymous basis

8. *Secondary use*—ITS information stripped of personal identifiers may be used for non-ITS applications
9. *FOIA*—federal and state FOIA obligations require disclosure of information from government-maintained databases; database arrangements should balance the individual's interest in privacy and the public's right to know[22]

Events outside the United States may also have an effect on how ITS is ultimately deployed, both domestically and internationally. On October 24, 1998, the European Union's (EU) Privacy Directive went into effect.[23] In sharp contrast to the United States, many countries in Europe have long had national privacy and data protection laws. These national laws have not been limited to specific industries or circumstances as in the United States but seek to establish a common standard for privacy protection. Moreover, EU countries have created government watchdogs to monitor private-sector activities and, if necessary, bring enforcement actions. The EU passed its Privacy Directive in 1995 in response to the growth of electronic commerce and the ways in which personal information could be obtained, disseminated, and possibly abused.

The Privacy Directive requires all EU member nations to adopt similar national laws for the "processing of personal data" concerning data security, subjects' access to their own information, ability to correct information, registration of data collection activities, government oversight and the like. For the United States, the most problematic provision of the Privacy Directive is a limitation that personal data must not be made available to non-EU countries whose privacy laws do not "adequately" protect this information. In other words, these countries' laws do not have comparable protections to those found in the EU Directive. At present, the EU has contended that U.S. law does not meet this "adequacy" requirement. The EU has yet to enforce this provision vis-à-vis the United States in hopes that U.S. industry on its own can develop sufficient privacy guidelines and enforcement mechanisms. Regardless, any U.S. company engaged in business activities in Europe must comply with the EU Directive.

Shared resource projects for telecommunications

For state departments of transportation (DOT) and local transportation authorities, their ability to collect traffic data and process it for distribution to the public is dependent on the creation of a basic telecommunications infrastructure. This infrastructure may include, for example, loop detectors, video sensors and cameras, infra-red beacons and variable message signs all connected by a fiber optic conduit to a central management facility. The public sector, however, often lacks the resources and expertise to create this fiber optic network on its own without financial and in-kind assistance from the private sector. In response, creative state agencies have developed "shared resource" relationships with the private sector to acquire this telecommunications infrastructure. Several states have successfully employed this model, although these projects have not been met with unqualified support.

Shared resource projects involve the leverage of a publicly owned asset to attract private-sector capital and expertise. In the case of a telecommunications network for ITS, the public asset is the right-of-way along highways and secondary roads—or even along transit rights-of-way—where the fiber optic conduit is installed. The public sector needs this roadside infrastructure for ITS and other governmental purposes, but it lacks the capital and expertise to get the job done. The private-sector telecommunications industry wants access to these rights-of-way because it is a cheap and easy way to provide new telecommunications services to its customers. In return for access to the rights-of-way, the private sector will install the fiber the government needs with its own capital and effort, along with any additional capacity for resell or lease to third parties for a profit. Simply put, a shared resource project is a barter exchange premised on the complementary public–private interests in the rights-of-way.

When states begin to examine whether a shared resource project may be appropriate, there are several legal issues that first need to be assessed.[24] For example, it must be asked if the state DOT or other government agency has been given the legal authority to make available a public asset for private gain. There may be state or federal regulations, such as utility accommodation policies, that restrict or otherwise define what manner access to public rights-of-way may be given.[25] The government agency needs to determine if it may receive compensation and in what form (i.e., cash or some manner of in-kind compensation) for private use of the public rights-of-way. Another issue centers on how to value access to the rights-of-way. Historically, there has never been a market for these rights; consequently, it is very difficult for states to determine what the private sector is willing to pay and whether the public has received a fair return for its assets. Other issues include tax implications, procurement and contract structure, long-term operations and maintenance costs and liability.

Some players in the telecommunications industry have raised objections to shared resource projects as a violation of the Telecommunications Act of 1996.[26] Congress passed this law in an attempt to increase competition for telecommunications services. Increased competition, it is believed, will result in better-quality services at lower prices for the consumer. Opposition to these ITS shared resource projects centers on how the competition safeguards written into the Telecommunications Act are to be implemented.

Section 253 of the Telecommunications Act specifies that no state or local statute, regulation, or legal requirement may prohibit, or have the effect of prohibiting, any entity from providing telecommunications service.[27] The Act goes on to preserve the states' traditional role in "managing" their rights-of-way to ensure public safety.[28] Moreover, states can receive compensation from telecommunications providers for access to the states' rights-of-way if done so on a "competitively neutral and nondiscriminatory basis."[29]

What all this language means in practice, however, is an unsettled question. Recently, the Federal Communications Commission (FCC) responded to a Petition for a Declaratory Ruling[30] by the Minnesota DOT that asked the FCC to define, in essence, the states' ability to manage their highway rights-of-way where "exclusive" access to the rights-of-way is given to one entity. This entity, according to the Minnesota DOT project agreement, may then re-sell, lease, or collocate excess fiber or conduit to third parties as a "wholesaler," doing so, as the Telecommunications Act mandates, on a "competitively neutral and nondiscriminatory basis."

The FCC neither "blessed" nor preempted Minnesota DOT's agreement with the private developer. Rather, the FCC said that Minnesota DOT's petition failed to show that the agreement "neither prohibits nor has the effect of prohibiting the provision of competitive telecommunications services by certain entities. On the other hand, depending on how the Agreement is implemented, the potential competitive effects that fuel our concerns may be largely or wholly ameliorated."[31] Although Minnesota DOT has decided to go forward with the project as planned, of concern to the general ITS community is the potential "chilling" effect the FCC decision will have on other states contemplating similar shared resource arrangements and whether some sort of federal guidance is needed to provide clarification for both state DOTs and telecommunications companies.

Innovative finance

Today's financing of highway and transit projects must be done in a very different climate than when construction of the Interstate Highway System was initiated by President Eisenhower in 1956. Highway and transit construction has been financed through the collection of a national gas tax—currently set at 18.3 cents per gallon—that is then distributed back to each state according to a complicated formula worked out by Congress. The distribution is returned to the states in the form of large, often million-dollar, block grants. For each category of block grant, there are several eligible types of projects that may be funded at the discretion of the state DOT, metropolitan planning organization, or other local government authority. These state and local authorities are also required to provide their own "matching" funds, using 10 to 20 percent, to qualify for the federal contribution.

However, beginning in the early 1990s, Congress and the transportation community came to recognize that revenues from the national gas tax were not sufficient to fund all of the transportation needs of the country. In response, federal funding laws and procedures have been liberalized in order to encourage new and innovative methods for leveraging public monies, both federal and local. These changes have several goals, including giving greater authority to state and local transportation officials on how to spend federal dollars and to attract private-sector partners for both their capital and expertise. For example the Intermodal Surface Transportation Efficiency Act,[32] passed in 1991, provided new freedoms to state and local transportation officials to transfer funds between their formula block grants to match up better with local needs. The National Highway System Designation Act,[33] passed in 1995, continued to expand this flexibility but also created a new revolving fund mechanism for states, called State Infrastructure Banks (SIBs).[34] The Transportation Equity Act for the 21st Century (TEA-21),[35] passed in June 1998, includes a further evolution on these same principles. Although the SIB program was not expanded as had been proposed, Congress did create a new credit and loan enhancement program called the Transportation Infrastructure and Finance Innovation Act[36] (TIFIA). There have also been changes to the federal tax code designed to spur private-sector involvement and state and local flexibility.

Congress created SIBs in the National Highway System (NHS) Designation Act to provide states with increased flexibility in funding regional and local transportation projects. Generally speaking, the SIB law permits states, or group of states in a region, to use 10 percent of their annual federal transportation apportionment to an infrastructure bank. States can contribute their own funds to the SIB as well. The SIB is authorized to make loans to specific projects, as well as provide credit enhancements, capital reserves, letters of credit, short-term financing, and other assistance. Probably the greatest advantage of the SIB is that loan payments are not returned to the federal treasury; instead, they are deposited back into the lending SIB for second-generation loans. One caveat is that there must be an identifiable revenue stream, such as a toll, to provide security for the SIB assistance. The NHS Act created the SIB program as only a pilot; TEA-21 retained its pilot status and recapitalized four states' SIB funding. As of December 1998, 39 states had been authorized to create SIBs with total federal capitalization of $456 million. Moreover, by that date loan agreements had been signed for 54 projects to support over $2 billion in total construction.[37]

TIFIA[38] is designed to enable major transportation projects to access private financing at lower costs. If a project has the financial backing of the federal government, it is much easier to attract private capital and pay for that capital more cheaply. Based on this fact, TIFIA provides direct federal loans, loan guarantees and lines of credit to "major" transportation projects—highway, transit, bridge and rail—of at least $100 million in size. In addition, these projects must have the ability to be self-supporting through a user fee or some other dedicated revenue source. For ITS projects, the minimum threshold is set at $30 million because, as the Senate and House Conference committee recognized, ITS can provide significant capacity enhancements with limited investment.[39] TIFIA provides some $530 million in funding authority over the life of TEA-21 capped for each year ranging from $1.2 billion to $2 billion. (A later amendment to TEA-21 allows one-quarter of the discrete ITS program funding to be similar leveraged under TIFIA.[40])

For the private sector, participation in transportation projects is more attractive if they can access publicly supported, tax-exempt debt financing that otherwise is unavailable to the private sector on its own. However, the federal tax code limits the ability of private entities from receiving profits or increased project equity where public, tax-exempt financing is employed. One mechanism for the private sector is to take advantage of the Internal Revenue Service's 63–20 corporation.[41] This non-for-profit corporation allows the public and private sectors to partner for transportation projects, yet still allow the sponsoring public agency to issue tax-exempt bonds with all of their cost-saving advantages. Additional changes in the federal tax code have been proposed in the 105th and 106th Congresses that would raise the limits on using tax-exempt debt financing for privately owned and privately operated projects.

Another financing vehicle created under the NHS Act is the Grant Anticipation Revenue Vehicle (GARVEE).[42] Basically, a GARVEE permits a state to pay the costs associated with the repayment of bonds through future obligations of federal, block-grant funds. This instrument improves the cash flow of projects, particularly in the first several years of construction and operations.

The attractiveness of ITS for innovative financing is that ITS applications, such as ETC, are a cost-effective and predictable mechanism to create a revenue stream as supporting collateral. Keep in mind, however, that adding tolls to previously untolled roads, bridges, or tunnels may face strong political opposition.

Endnotes

1. This summary primarily concerns the safety benefits of ITS technologies that are attributable to the vehicle or infrastructure. It is thought that information-based ITS technologies, such as in-vehicle navigation systems or interactive kiosks for transit riders, do not pose similar liability barriers to development and deployment.

2. The U.S. Supreme Court recently decided a case that examined what liability protections are afforded by compliance with NHTSA standards. In *Geier v. American Honda Motor Co.,* 529 U.S. (2000) (98–1811), the plaintiff (Geier) was injured in an accident involving a 1987 Honda Accord. NHTSA standards in effect in 1987 required some, but not all, passenger vehicles to be equipped with passive restraints, such as air bags. In addition, the standard provided the manufacturer with a range of different restraints from which the company could choose to introduce into their products slowly over time. Geier sued Honda for her injuries, claiming that the auto company had been negligent under District of Columbia tort law for not equipping their vehicle with a driver side air bag. The Supreme Court dismissed Geier's claim, upholding the appeals court's conclusion that the NHTSA standard in question, in substance and for public policy reasons, pre-empted the state tort law claim.

3. Bagby, J. W., and G. L. Gittings. 1998. "Mitigation Litigation Barriers for Deployment of AHS and ETTM Innovation" (June). Idea Program Final Report.

4. See the Sherman Act, 15 U.S.C. §§ 1–7; Clayton Act, 15 U.S.C. §§ 12–27.

5. ITS America's Meeting Guidelines Regarding Antitrust.

6. National Cooperative Research Act, Public Law No. 98–462 (1984).

7. Office of Management and Budget Circular A-119, "Federal Participation in the Development and Use of Voluntary Standards."

8. *Allied Tube & Conduit Corp. v. Indian Head, Inc.,* 486 U.S. 501 (1988).

9. *Standard Oil Co. v. United States*, 221 U.S. 60 (1911).

10. *Northwest Wholesale Stationers v. Pacific Stationary & Printing Co.*, 472 U.S. 284 (1985).

11. Public Law No. 96–517 (1980), codified at 35 U.S. C. § 200 et seq.

12. Id.

13. Id. at § 202(c)(4).

14. Id. at § 203.

15. 48 CFR 52.227–14; 48 CFR 27.404(a).

16. 48 CFR 52.227–14(a).

17. 18 U.S.C. § 1905; see also Cal. Civ. Code 3426 et seq., Cal. Civ. Code 6254, N.Y. Pub. Off. Law 87(2)(d).

18. 13 USC § 2721 et seq. This law was enacted in response to the murder of an actress whose killer obtained her address by accessing state motor vehicle records.

19. 15 USC § 1681 et seq. This law is designed to provide certain safeguards to individuals regarding how credit reporting agencies collect, use, and disseminate personal financial information.
20. The First, Third, Fourth, Fifth, Ninth, Tenth, and Fourteenth Amendments all include privacy protections that run to individuals.

21. See "A Framework for Global Electronic Commerce," July 1997, report developed by Clinton Administration interagency group to guide public policy on development of electronic commerce).

22. ITS America's Interim Intelligent Transportation Systems Fair Information and Privacy Principles. These principles are meant to be advisory only. They may be revised or expanded as applied to specific ITS applications.

23. Directive 95/46/EC of the European Parliament and of the Council on the Protection of Individuals with Regard to the Processing of Personal Data and on the Free Movement of Such Data (Eur.O.J. 95/L281).

24. See generally: Kessler, F. W. and S. Jakubiak. 1998. "Emerging Trends and Paradigms in Shared Resource Projects" (Spring). ITS Quarterly. See also Federal Highway Administration. 1996. "Final Report: Shared Resources: Sharing Right-of-Way for Telecommunications, Identification, Review and Analysis of Legal and Institutional Issues" (April), co-authored by Nossaman, Guthner, Knox & Elliott, LLP and Apogee Research, Inc.

25. Prior to 1989, the Federal Highway Administration prohibited states from longitudinal use of rights-of-way for installation of utility facilities. See Federal Highway Administration, Highway/Utility Guide, publication number FHWA-SA-93–049 (1993).

26. Public Law No. 104–104, 110 Stat. 70.

27. 47 U.S.C. § 253(a).

28. Id. at § 253(c).

29. Id.

30. "The State of Minnesota Petition for Declaratory Ruling Regarding the Relevance of Section 253 of the Telecommunications Act to an Agreement Governing Access to State Freeway Rights-of-Way," Federal Communications Commission CC Docket 98–1 (January 1998).

31. Memorandum Opinion and Order, "In the Matter of the Petition for a Declaratory Ruling Regarding the Effects of Section 253 on an Agreement to Install Fiber Optic Wholesale Transport Capacity in State Freeway Rights-of-Way," Federal Communications Commission, CC Docket No. 98-1 (December 1999), at 4.

32. Public Law No. 102–240 (1991).

33. Public Law No. 104–59 (1995).

34. Id. at § 350.

35. Public Law 105–178, 112 Stat. 107.

36. Id. at § 1501–04.

37. Max Inman, ed., "Innovative Finance Quarterly" (Federal Highway Administration, Fall 1998).

38. Sections 1501–04 of Public Law No. 105–178 (1998).

39. "Transportation Equity Act for the 21st Century: Conference Report to Accompany H.R. 2400." Report No. 105–550. U.S. House of Representatives, 105th Congress, Second Session (1998), at 434.

40. Internal Revenue Restructuring and Reform Act of 1998, Public Law No. 105–206, § 9011(d).

41. Internal Revenue Ruling 63–20.

42. Section 311 of Public Law No. 104–59 (1995).

BY Stephen C. Lockwood • Senior Vice President •
Parsons Brinckerhoff

THE INSTITUTIONAL CHALLENGE: AN AGGRESSIVE VIEW

Introduction: institutions as an issue

As is often the case with new ideas, intelligent transportation systems (ITS) were first conceived in terms of new technologies (Mobility 2000 and Intelligent Vehicle Highway System [IVHS]). It was then embodied in a set of systems concepts (national ITS architecture); these concepts required an implementation program to support full deployment benefits (Operation TimeSaver). Only later is it apparent that changes in basic transportation policy are necessary to more fully realize the potential of ITS (management and operations [M&O]). Finally, it becomes clear that the policy itself requires adjustment in an institutional context to have the desired strategic effect.

This transition is still in its early stages. Over the past decade, ITS has been treated as a set of high-tech tools in support of conventional traffic operations and information improvements. Early deployments have been implemented on a standalone project basis, providing limited benefits on a facility-specific basis. The U.S. Department of Transportation (U.S. DOT) is tracking the rate of deployment of the basic elements of nine fundamental ITS public infrastructure elements in the top 75 metro areas (with companion rural and commercial vehicle operation [CVO] programs). The 1999 data show that only a small proportion of the nation's freeways (16 percent) have incident detection technology installed, and only about a quarter have integrated incident response programs. Only 10 percent of emergency response agencies participate in formal incident management programs. Almost none of the nation's freeway operations are interconnected with parallel arterial, and less than 3 percent of the nation's signalized intersections are operated as traffic-adaptive. Transit vehicle location technology is still limited to a quarter of fixed-route vehicles. While some basic travel condition information is available by radio in most major metropolitan areas, an average of only 12 percent of key facilities in the top 76 metro areas have route-specific data available. Levels of integration among systems are generally less than 20 percent. At the same time, private in-vehicle systems are in their infancy in the United States (as compared to Japan and Europe).

Business as usual

Experience suggests that the modest level of ITS implementation achieved to date was reached without modifying the current organizational and resource framework of state DOTs and local governments. In most cases, ITS projects have been buried in other projects or treated as special technology demonstrations. An initial round of ITS planning and programming has taken place off-line as special initiatives without challenging existing priorities. M&O and ITS have not been introduced to the formal statewide and regional planning process that have continued on a "business as usual" basis. Implementations have been dependent substantially on the creation of "virtual" institutions, which either bypass or supplement the existing institutional conventions. These informal arrangements include piggybacked project budgets, off-line planning and integration and informal institutional arrangements where stakeholder roles are based on personal relationships and middle-level staff champions. At the same time, the small number of services and the limited extent of deployment in most metropolitan areas has yielded modest local benefits. This limited, piecemeal commitment has not yet capitalized on the inherent promise of ITS.

Realizing the unique potential of ITS

The unique potential of ITS is based on a system operations dimensions that, when fully realized, distinguishes it from conventional transportation strategies and implies new institutional arrangements. Realizing this potential requires three related strategies. First, agencies responsible for transportation-related services must commit to a mission, policy and program in order to manage and operate existing facilities and to maximize customer service performance. (This mission would be a new priority for most state and local infrastructure owners.) Second, agencies must consistently apply systems engineering-based principles to the development of the basic ITS infrastructure of communications, and apply control as the basis for systems operations. Third, user services must be implemented on a consistent regionwide basis to capitalize on the reinforcing synergism of integrated multiple regional systems. The combination of these three strategies creates the potential for full exploitation of ITS through programs that would incorporate the following features:

- Strong support of an agency mission that places a high priority on improving service through real-time systems M&O, monitoring, and feedback
- Extensive deployment of a broad range of ITS systems and services to support real-time M&O, including continuous performance upgrading
- Effective integration of services on a regional basis that reflects the scale of trips and intermodal interchange
- Deliberate and systematic linkages between facility operations (supply) and information services (demand), and operationally between infrastructure and vehicle elements
- Aggressive introduction of the full range of new market-based service attributes facilitated by ITS (beyond safety, congestion and delay reduction) to include increased reliability, security, navigation and crash avoidance
- Development of direct linkages of ITS systems with closely related developments in consumer information, workplace flexibly, electronic payment systems, premium services and advances in innovative finance and project development
- Interaction with an informed consumer population energized by a whole new level of information regarding service level, options and responsibilities

Orientation and activities that support a "management-and-operations mission" are substantially at odds with the current capital improvement focus of state and local transportation, together with program, process and institutional arrangements that support it. While a program or budget line item called "ITS" may not be essential to deploying individual ITS projects, a commitment to systems M&O implies an ITS program with a variety of interrelated and mutually reinforcing services and systems. This in turn requires a systems engineering initiative, coordination of multiple stakeholders, and commitment to real-time operations. Beyond a modest threshold, increasing levels of commitment to M&O requires a formal program, organization and budget recognition that cannot be easily accommodated within the institutional status quo.

The institutional challenge

The institutional challenge, therefore, goes beyond the simple incorporation of new technologies and systems into existing programs. Substantial institutional changes are implied, starting with the adoption of new user service policy and program concepts oriented towards systems M&O by stakeholder institutions. This in turn implies adjustments in public agency roles, activities, budget and staffing, as well as new relationships with system users and private industry.

The broad institutional issue is: "To what degree are existing institutional arrangements and activities of established transportation entities—state, local, regional and private—an inhibitor to more fully capitalizing on ITS?" A second, closely related question is: "What is the nature and scope of the adjustments and innovations in the institutional setting necessary to fully realize the benefits of ITS?"

An aggressive scenario—preconditions

An aggressive scenario committed to M&O and involving an increased rate of ITS systems deployment with the characteristics described above is likely to require significant institutional changes. These changes are necessary to respond to the inherent features of an efficient approach to ITS deployment within a M&O framework. Higher levels of ITS realization as represented by the aggressive scenario; may never take place; or may evolve gradually over many years, at different paces in different settings. However, for the purposes of this chapter, it is not necessary to take a position on the future. The introduction of new concepts into an existing institutional environment can follow many paths and take place at various levels of intensity.

Realization of the potential of ITS as described above involves development of state and regional program activities that are committed to, and structured for, the provision of ITS user services through the implementation of the related systems and technologies. The required program activities in turn introduce a set of demands on institutions that underlay the enabling policy commitment, program resources and processes, and stakeholder relationships. The institutional challenges facing ITS can be described in terms of six "preconditions" or factors that should be present, including:

1. An understanding of ITS concepts, elements, strategies and the rationale for institutional change
2. An authorizing environment formalizing the mission, providing the leadership, decision-making support and organizational structure
3. New roles and relationships among various stakeholder agencies and entities necessary for effective ITS deployment and operations
4. A planning and programming process adjusted to accommodate ITS-related strategies and investments competing for available resources
5. Technology, staff and financial resources sufficient to support the deployment and operations of an ITS program
6. New public–private relationships as well as new private-sector business models responding to the specific potential of ITS

For each of these six precondition categories, table 24–1 indicates: (1) the characteristics of ITS that must be accommodated if ITS is to tap its full potential, (2) the current institutional tradition within the transportation sector and (3) the nature of institutional changes necessary to foster a high level of ITS implementation and integration. These relationships form the framework of this chapter. For the ITS characteristic in each given category, the types of challenges will be described briefly. The direction of the implied institutional adjustment is discussed, under the assumption that more fully capitalizing on ITS requires a greater commitment to systems M&O, and that incremental levels of commitment will require increasing institutional change. Each section includes a brief discussion of future prospects.

Table 24–1
Institutional Issues in ITS

IMPLICATIONS OF ITS	TRANSPORTATION INSTITUTIONAL TRADITION	INSTITUTIONAL CHALLENGE
1. UNDERSTANDING THE POTENTIAL		
a. System M&O in real time	Construction of capacity additions/preservation	Understanding the basic concepts
b. New types of user services	Limited benefits: access, congestion, safety	Being convinced of the benefits
2. AUTHORIZING ENVIRONMENT/DECISION-MAKING		
a. New customers and services	Program momentum institutionalized	Finding champions
b. Minimal construction/distributed benefits	Construction-based vested interests	Developing new constituencies
c. Condition-responsive services	Facility network for standard conditions	Redefining agency mission
d. Requires regional cooperation	Improvements controlled by single jurisdiction	Sharing regional decision-making
e. Accepts M&O responsibility	M&O subsidiary to new capacity, preservation	Organizational adjustments
f. Commitment to performance	Output in terms of lane miles of improvement	Risking mission exposure
3. STAKEHOLDER ROLES/ORGANIZATION		
a. Project development at regional scale	Coordination via individual jurisdictions	New interjurisdictional cooperation: vertical/horizontal
b. Multiple services and multiple providers	Transportation facility responsibility of public works entities	Relationships with nonpublic works entities
c. New technologies and services	Public monopoly on technology/standards	Public–private partnerships for services
d. Customer information choices	Supply–demand relationship fixed	Impacts of customer choices
4. PLANNING AND PROGRAMMING		
a. Current performance deficiencies and broader attributes	Needs defininition by standard long-term analysis	Level playing field for slating/evaluation
b. Low cost and impacts and incremental	Cost-intensive/spatially concentrated/ external impacts	Programming for incremental improvements
c. Technology-based operational coordination	Civil engineering solutions	Regional systems integration/implementation
d. Improvement depends on real-time operations	Improvement depends on designed characteristics	Planing/operations relationship
5. PROJECT DEVELOPMENT RESOURCES		
a. M&O as a new priority mission	Large backlog of facility improvement commitments	Program definition for M&O
b. Operations- and maintenance-intensive	Capital-intensive: high cost, consistent with conventional funding categories	Mobilizing funds
c. Operations and systems engineering experience necessary	Civil engineering and planning capabilities	Special staff technical capabilities
d. Private ownership of technology	Technology public and commoditized	Accommodating private capital
6. NEW PRIVATE-SECTOR ROLES		
a. Opportunity for private involvement	Private investment/products not accommodated	Mainstream public–private partnerships
b. New systems and software procurement	Construction-oriented procedures	Modify legal/administrative constraints
c. Facilitating development of research partnerships	Public sector defines/dominates program	Cooperative public–private research and development agreements
d. Regulatory issues in Intelligent vehicle implementation	Public sector imposes regulatory constraints	Accommodating new product roll-out constraints
e. Requires new forms of private–private partnerships	Individual private companies self-sufficient regarding product development	New private-sector business models
f. Private sector expands into infrastructure service	All infrastructure operations carried out by public sector	Recognize expanded private business opportunities

Public-sector focus

This chapter concentrates principally on transportation infrastructure owners in the public sector—state, local, and regional transportation agencies; and the U.S. DOT—who are charged with the responsibility for infrastructure policy, resources and other provision functions.

This is not meant to suggest that private industry "institutional issues" are not important to ITS. The dollar value of private-sector investment in ITS (largely vehicle-related services) may be an order of magnitude greater than the public infrastructure-related investment. However, most of the private-sector institutional issues are essentially commercial matters, reflecting the interplay of product development market, consumer willingness to pay, corporate investment decisions and private management risk appetite. These business decisions are not a matter of public policy, except as public-sector regulation, public acquisition and deliberate partnering affect them. Instances where public- and private-sector institutional issues intersect are included under category six.

Caveats

Two caveats should be mentioned before proceeding with this chapter. First, there is little empirical information about the current level and nature of ITS "institutionalization." Beyond raw deployment statistics for major metropolitan areas, there are no surveys of institutional policy, state or metropolitan planning organization (MPO) ITS programs, or even reliable data on current ITS funding. Second, existing case studies focus on the few states and regions that, by virtue of discretionary federal aid or extraordinary leadership, have aggressively pursued ITS deployment. These exceptions typically represent the state of the practice— often the result of extraordinary efforts of ITS champions—rather than formal institutional accommodation. By and large, the level of ITS deployment among state, regional and local transportation entities and their acceptance of systems management responsibilities is much more modest.

Institutional challenges in mainstreaming ITS

1. Understanding the potential

To the extent that effective deployment of ITS systems depends on institutional changes, the point of departure for generating institutional change to accommodate ITS is establishing a clear understanding of the potential benefits of such changes. ITS concepts and technologies are unfamiliar to many within the transportation sector and its constituents. The concepts underlying ITS, with the increased focus on management and on providing a broader range of specific users services to identifiable market segments is at odds with the principal foci of the capacity-construction tradition. Furthermore, the current piecemeal state of deployment does not produce the same type of dramatic impacts as new, major capacity improvements. Therefore, where ITS competes for resources, it is a difficult "sell" among nontechnical decision-makers and other transportation improvement stakeholders. It is difficult to make a case for devoting scarce management resources to develop the new relationships necessary to apply ITS at the scale where it is likely to be most effective.

As indicated in table 24–1, an understanding of the basic concepts of ITS and of the potential benefits are essential for improving the level of understanding of ITS. They include:

1.a.   *Understanding the basic concepts.* Real-time, regionwide systems management as a public
        responsibility and professional priority is not widely appreciated in the transportation community.
        "Operations" has typically been a secondary priority for state and local highway organizations; and
        while ITS technology is appealing, the notion of systematic incremental application of ITS application

is not well understood by naturally conservative elected officials and agency management. Furthermore, there is a natural resistance to supporting major initiatives involving untried technology and limited precedents. Even less well understood is the potential of the relationship between public infrastructure operations and emerging private traveler information and traveler assurance services. The perception that newly available ITS concepts, systems, or technology merit a change in policy or program regarding the nature of agency responsibility is not widespread.

1.b.   *Being convinced of the benefits.* Traditional transportation projects that focus on adding new capacity introduce visible changes in local accessibility and level of service (LOS). The direct benefits of some ITS improvements are much less apparent. Most published data regarding ITS benefits refer to a limited number of isolated projects or specific new installations. There is limited evidence from more integrated deployments where mutually supporting applications leverage each other. In addition, important payoffs from ITS, such as the value of improved reliability, increased security and improved traveler information are less well known; others, such as the reductions in delay from incident management, are hard to measure. Despite high cost/benefit ratios, data that are available also show that the impacts of ITS tend to be modest, widely distributed and focused on users. These features are less highly valued in the political decision arena.

Prospects

ITS is reasonably well understood as a set of technologies, packaged into specific projects. It may be expected that the interest in the obvious efficiencies and safety benefits of the high-tech features of ITS alone will continue to power a modest level of continuing deployment—both urban and rural.

However, few regions have more than a small set of improvements and the level of integration among systems is low. This "business-as-usual" low level of deployment postpones the demonstration of payoffs that are believed to be inherent in a broader commitment to ITS. Capitalizing on the leverage of broadening coverage (freeway and arterial), of the synergism among systems (operations and information), and more responsive real-time operations (incident management) requires a more rigorous commitment. Such an aggressive approach, in turn, entails resource and relationships implications that more clearly compete with other traditional options. Unless, and until, policymakers are convinced of the payoff, ITS as a significant program will not gain support.

A major professional effort is essential to educate the decision-making community on the value of the necessary institutional adjustments. This in term requires an increased understanding of the relationships between ITS as enabling technologies and systems and an operational and management program. It may be that there is a threshold of deployment that must be reached in one or more metropolitan regions before the benefits are sufficiently visible to generate the needed support. It will be increasingly important to build on early successes, by highlighting their virtues, gaining support for their extension and generalizing from their success to the justification for additional investments

2. Authorizing environment

The "authorizing environment" refers to the institutional setting where decisions are made about the allocation of scarce resources. For state, local and regional transportation agencies, the authorizing environment includes the mission, inherited policy, programmatic priorities and the legacy of public and private institutional roles. The habits and values within state DOTs, local governments and regional agencies, combined with these inherited features, constitute the "culture" of surface transportation in which new concepts such as ITS must evolve.

State DOTs, local governments, and transportation authorities view their mission as the provision of basic facility networks (construction and preservation) with a range of supporting functions relating to safety, the environment, financing, licensing and regulation. This policy is reinforced by financial reliance on legislatively determined tax funding that is typically dedicated to transportation. Despite sporadic federal aid programs encouraging focus on systems management, such as the congestion management systems required of larger metro areas with air quality problems, most state programs include only modest operational components. The principal investment priorities are construction-related; including facility improvements and the preservation and provision of new access in less-served areas.

There are several fundamental challenges encountered in altering the authorizing environment. Institutional change, in focus or in activity, requires both active inside leadership and outside support as the basis for a change in direction. As indicated in table 24–1, six key issues characterize the challenges in establishing a positive environment for new policy and program:

2.a.   *Finding champions.* Champions are crucial in the absence of established programs with influential constituencies. Ongoing transportation programs with developed stakeholder constituencies generate institutional inertia. New programs with unfamiliar characteristics, which lack established support interests, depend on articulate, well-placed supporters to lobby for agency resources and to capture and maintain a position in the resource-competitive program arena. Leadership is also necessary to convene outside stakeholders and generate constituency support. Lead agencies and lead individuals are closely related, as the latter generally requires at least tacit support from the home agency. To date, champions from a variety of institutional staff positions within transportation agencies have been very influential in moving ITS programs to an initial plateau. In several states and regions, ITS is identified with key individuals. This dependence on championship leaves ITS programs vulnerable.

2.b.   *Developing new constituencies.* Constituencies include sponsors, implementers and benefit recipients. Aside from the technical community, key supporters of conventional transportation investments are typically nonuser interests who expect to benefit directly. These supporters may include: major developers, employers, real estate business interests and construction and labor interests. Industry associations, such as ITS America and the Institute of Transportation Engineers, have provided this type of broad program support for ITS at the national, state and regional level. These constituencies, however, lack the connections and influence in the policy and program development process, wielded by traditional construction-orientated stakeholders. The short development cycle of ITS provides the opportunity to provide short-term benefits to current travelers. This more tangible benefit is somewhat offset by the more widely dispersed nature of the benefits. A major challenge to "institutionalizing" ITS at higher levels of implementation is the justification for resource diversion from a stakeholder perspective. While several states and regions (MPOs) have involved broad groups of user-stakeholders within a discrete ad hoc ITS planning process, so far there have been only limited attempts by system users, commuters, and commercial vehicle operators towards supporting a higher priority for ITS strategies.

2.c.   *Redefining the agency mission.* The traditional mission of highway and transit agencies has been dominated by output measures of facility improvement. However, the competitive value of time and reliability is stimulating increased focus in logistics and travel service on outcomes in terms of performance. The expressions of this concern are early efforts to embody performance in systems service quality terms within the formal strategic activities in state, local and metropolitan planing. At the program level, given the constraints on added capacity, system performance is increasingly being linked to improvements in M&O of existing systems. While it is still too early to draw clear conclusions, the relationships between system LOS, reliability, safety and other features related to ITS-type improvements may be expected to increase. Addition of new programs is constrained by the organizational and resource focus on competing traditional missions of access and system preservation, as well as the difficulty in reaching consensus among the larger number of stakeholders. A shift in mission priorities towards service provision will be paced by the demonstrated payoffs compared to the existing alternatives.

2.d.   *Sharing regional decision-making.* Conventional transportation programming has been evolving towards increased shared decision-making in resource allocation, especially in metropolitan areas where Intermodal Surface Transportation Efficiency Act (ISTEA) funding and planning regulations have encouraged states and local governments towards an increasingly cooperative mode. ITS reinforces this trend. First, ITS programs are incremental and multijurisdictional. They often require a joint capital commitment and, more problematically, introduce a joint operating resource commitment. As systems M&O is not typically a line item in either state or regional programs, ITS programs are now typically developed as subitems in other budgets or by special subcommittees at the regional level. This subordinate status undercuts the ability of ITS to compete for both capital and operating resources. Second, ITS projects often require actions and commitments from nontransportation entities such as police and emergency services whose budgets and priorities are entirely separate from those in the transportation services arena. There are a few mechanisms for coordinating funding across agency boundaries.

2.e.   *Organizational adjustments.* The position of systems operations responsibility within an organization varies widely among state and local government transportation agencies. In most states, operations are organized primarily at the district level, often as part of a maintenance and traffic operations unit. Many states also have a senior traffic operations manager at the headquarters level. However operations, as traditionally defined, rarely has a separate budget and until recently has been part of few state DOTs' goal statements. At the regional level, many MPOs and other regional organizations have operations, ITS, or advanced technology committees that perform a key coordination function. These suborganizations often use informal agreements and memoranda of understanding to establish the project development coordination and operation protocols necessary to proceed with ITS projects. An implementation strategy based on a new institutional mission of systems M&O would require that lines of reporting, roles and relationships within the sponsoring agencies be reoriented to align accountability with authority. The required technical and management capabilities would be assembled into units capable of managing an M&O program and development of a program or project delivery strategy.

2.f.   *Risking new mission exposure.* Program success in terms of projects completed and budgets expended are a well-understood tradition, with acceptable political risks, that deliver projects on time and on budget. Programmatically, a substantial shift towards service provision exposes its sponsors to new measures of success (or failure) in terms of real-time performance. Accepting responsibly, however circumscribed, for real-time systems operations introduces the risk that customers will begin to identify the agencies with the quality of service they are experiencing. At the same time, most systems operations involve multiple jurisdictions and multiple agencies. These arrangements can place transportation agencies in a position of apparent responsibility for aspects of ITS they do not control. Examples include the performance of the police or emergency medical service entities, or the occurrence of hazardous materials (HAZMAT). Long-lived institutions with strong in-built instincts for self-perpetuation do not easily accept such new exposure.

Prospects

At present, with very few exceptions, ITS programs exist on discretionary funds; and they are often treated as demonstrations of new technology or as special treatments for unique problems. No clear model has emerged either at the state or regional level as a promising approach to "institutionalizing" a commitment to systems M&O. Operations at the local government level are typically a fund-starved subsidiary to public works. MPOs, which lack operational authority, offer a venue for operations committees and informal communication. But only a few regional agencies have evolved congestion management systems (CMS) into more comprehensive programs; or in the case of New York City and Houston, actually developed metropolitan scale entities with important operational responsibilities. No state DOT has a funded ITS statewide program or a separate system M&O unit. Indeed there is a point of view that ITS should not have a separate program identity.

Perhaps it is too soon to expect serious consideration of the role of ITS on a long-term sustainable basis within these transportation entities. For the most part, output rather than outcomes still characterize the measures of success. At the same time, there are broader trends towards a more strategic view to outcome-oriented, customer-based, performance-driven activities. The intersection of these strategic perspectives together with ITS capabilities may influence new institutional forms

3. Stakeholder roles and relationships

Conventional transportation improvements are usually controlled by a single agency within a given jurisdiction and often confined within single jurisdictional limits. Few separate jurisdictions are typically involved. By contrast, ITS with its regional focus, intermodal potential and its operational scope requires the involvement of a wider range of players from modes, jurisdictions and agencies. Further complicating the potential roles and relationships is the potential for new roles on the part of private-sector entities providing new and usually commercialized services. In addition, transportation system users are also taking on new roles as "customers," receiving and transmitting information that can affect driver behavior and service provision. Developing new relationships for sharing and cooperation, among a varying set of participants in system deployment and service delivery, is the major coordination challenge in realizing ITS systems and services. It indicates the degree to which a range of new transportation services is no longer the separate responsibility of public works agencies. Consistent with table 24–1, the four principal dimensions of coordination among stakeholders are described below.

3.a. *Interjurisdictional cooperation.* ITS operations (for example, incident response and traveler information) ideally involve user services delivered at the scale of the user's trip regardless of jurisdictional boundaries. The regional, multimodal, capital and operational aspects of many ITS projects require cooperation and coordination at several stages in program development from planning to deployment, operations and maintenance. "Stovepiping" refers to projects developed in isolation that fail to capitalize on the systems integration potential of ITS. Typical problems that occur at any scale include overlapping authority, varied priorities, differing resources capabilities and conflicting cultures. Depending on the project's characteristics, cooperation within the public sector occurs at a set of scales that includes:

- Cooperation within agencies between planners and operators
- Cooperation within jurisdiction between modes
- Cooperation between state and local government
- Cooperation among local jurisdictions

Lack of a single program development entity for multijurisdictional ITS deployment creates the need for burdensome ad hoc arrangements on a project-by-project basis. Often, these arrangements are absent or not well executed. Defining and negotiating the approaches and arrangements is a substantial undertaking. The agencies involved must:

- Accept the impacts of operational regimes, such as diversion, that may result in some loss of jurisdictional independence
- Agree on specific condition-based protocols for actions and roles that require a commitment of resources and operational responses
- Commit to some level of real-time coordination that may involve some sharing of responsibility or even the temporary ceding control to other entities

Too often ITS projects are suboptimized, shaped by the perception of the difficulty in achieving the necessary level of coordination in project development and the desirable level of coordination in operations themselves. Relative resource availability, history of cooperation and personalities all play a major role in such perceptions. Multistate metropolitan areas, multistate intercity travel corridors and even international border crossings present additional institutional challenges for the coordination of operations, especially the legal and political authorization to pursue objectives or expend resources out side jurisdictions. Within ITS, the federal DOT has recognized these needs programmatically through its borders and corridors program and through the "priority corridors." These programs have provided an extremely effective means of building institutional relationships at the staff level, and they have facilitated technology transfer and standardization. There is also a modest degree of program standardization and real-time operational coordination. Moving beyond these actions to real-time operational coordination is a major step that may compromise individual jurisdiction control and independence for the sake of an extra-jurisdictional entity.

3.b. *Relationships with nonpublic works entities.* The slate of regional user services implies the need for transportation agencies to develop cooperative relationships with a set of other institutions whose coordinated roles are essential to improved traffic operations. These other public agencies such as law enforcement, medical and fire emergency response, HAZMAT, and commercial vehicle regulatory entities have legal jurisdiction over important activities that affect the transportation LOS. The problems of interjurisdictional cooperation and coordination described above are even greater here. To begin with, each agency will respond to a different set of priorities, which is likely to be reflected in their approach to the context where cooperation is desired. For example, very different incident management field operational protocols flow from the perspectives of police, fire and traffic operations missions. Many of these differences are reinforced in law, culture and past practice. Nonetheless, field experience suggests that concerted cooperative efforts over a period of time, including explicit accommodation of other agency's priorities, can foster improved operations. ITS technology itself has often been found to form a helpful framework for cooperative approaches. The level of cooperation developed varies considerably across states and regions in the country. Some regions have a long tradition of close cooperation that may range from polite communication to real-time information transmission, shared infrastructure and common physical facilities. Other areas appear to retain formal "stand-off" approaches. The wide variation in the level of cooperation is emphasized further in the wide variation of the traffic-related practices of the nontransportation agencies.

3.c. *Public–private sector relationships for services.* Limited public–private partnerships are needed to provide infrastructure-related services. As described in sections 5 and 6 below, formal and informal public–private "partnerships" have been developed at the level of individual projects in single regions (advanced traveler information systems [ATIS]) or even at the state level (fiber optics barter deals).

These relationships involve a single project or activities with organized commingling of resources and roles to deliver a service or share a facility. However, such project-level partnerships will constitute only a small component of a private ITS-related activity. The level of private investment in commercially based ITS, such as fleet management, in-vehicle information and control and safety systems, is expected to be three to four times greater than the total public tax-supported infrastructure-related investment. Already major private products and services are available, especially in-vehicle safety and security systems, mobile communications and traveler information.

The scale of state and regional public-sector service providers and that of national private-sector entities presents problems. National scale services require, at a minimum, some degree of region-by-region uniformity for both customer effectiveness and provider efficiency. Certain regional ITS infrastructure projects that provide support to, or are supported by, private commercial services, such as public-sector traffic information or emergency response, will need to be organized and standardized at the state and multistate level. New relationships between state and regional authorities and national information and automotive service providers or their intermediaries will have to be developed to accommodate these needs.

3.d. *Impacts of customer choices.* Travelers are playing an increasingly important role in determining the availability and quality of ITS services. A broader range of customer-driven commercial services are being offered, including roads that provide higher service levels for a fee (tolls), real-time traveler information, weather-related information and predictions, and traveler assurance or "mayday" services. The service providers are increasingly found in the private sector where options can be priced and marketed. These market-based products and services introduce a new relationship between travelers as customers and the public- or private-service providers. The rate at which service can be improved may now depend on the customer's willingness to pay rather than on public policy. Travelers are also becoming part of the service delivery chain. The effectiveness of publicly provided traveler information is directly related to consumer investment in mobile communications products. In addition, the quality of incident management is now substantially dependent on the traveler-as-informant. Incident notification is most frequently provided from N11 cellphone calls from passing or affected motorists.

This customer orientation, with its implication of market responsiveness and service options, is likely to continue to gain momentum. As more and better information on travel conditions is available and as premium services become available, travelers expectations will increasing include the notion that infrastructure should be operated and demand-responsive.

Prospects

The degree of sharing and cooperation required varies among ITS projects. A range of levels of stakeholder cooperation is visible both in the project development and project operation stages. At the project development stage, project planning and deployment cooperation requirements are clear with go/no-go implications. The focus on integration and implementation planning required within the federal aid process is clarifying these needs.

Benefits from interjurisdictional cooperation vary as related jurisdictions move up the "3-C spectrum" with increased operational communication, coordination, and consolidation. A key issue is the degree to which increasingly complex operational requirements can be met on an informal, ad hoc basis among multiple stakeholders without some legally authorized consolidation of authority. Memoranda of Understanding and other types of agreed-upon protocols provide an increased level of formality. With multiple players and multiple projects, these can become quite complex. A few MPOs have taken on limited operational roles where they are the recipients of operations-related funding (MTC) or have been used as a contracting entity because of their more flexible procurement potential. A few special entities, such as TransCom in the New York City metro area and TranStar in the Houston area, demonstrate the potential of informal reallocation and consolidation of responsibilities for regional operations. Ultimately the question that must be faced is if the full potential of ITS can be met without some kind of formal regional operating institutions such as a legislatively authorized multijurisdictional, multimodal regional ITS-related operating authority (similar to a regional transit authority). Most observers see little likelihood of the legal consolidation of operating authority in the short run.

Formal linkages between state and local agencies and private-sector stakeholders are also likely to evolve. Relationships with private service and product providers are already entering into a new phase of national consolidation. For example, state DOTs will need to develop new ways to interact with private traffic reporting services at the state and national level. At the same time the consumer market will define the direction of most of the information-based products and services. Furthermore, the increased availability and quality of real-time systems information will more clearly expose the varying quality of infrastructure operations. The threshold of acceptable LOS and system reliability may rise, pressuring state and local owner-agencies to meet improved standards of service. The accountability implied has the potential to substantially increase the travelers' expectations of improved responsiveness from infrastructure services, but also the most likely institutional arrangements for meeting them.

4. Planning and programming

Formal resource allocation takes place as part of the institutionalized statewide and regional planning and programming process. Long-range plans and multiyear improvement programs determine expenditure levels and program the steps for project implementation. To date, much of the decision-making for ITS systems deployment has largely taken place off-line, outside this planning process. In part, this reflects the "demonstration" nature of operational tests, early deployment programs, priority corridors, and model deployment initiative (MDI) projects supported by discretionary funds. It also indicates the degree to which ITS is not competing within the formal planning and programming process.

The technical processes used and the roles and relationships within the planning process have reflected this programmatic heritage. Over eighty early deployment plans have been developed using earmarked federal funds, principally focused on major metropolitan areas. These planning activities have included aspects of comprehensive service planning, involvement of a range of stakeholders, a high-level systems integration depiction and identification of follow-on projects. However their special funding has usually occurred outside a program-wide operation, add management policy, as well as exempting them from the project competition of statewide or metropolitan planing and programming. While early ITS planning efforts have included MPO and local government participation, the use of state-controlled funds and focus on upper-level networks have left this a state-dominated, project-oriented activity.

The traditional metropolitan and statewide planning and programming processes necessarily reflect the political process through the activities of involved decision-makers, the broader context of jurisdictional relationships of which this process is only one facet. The overarching issue within the planning and programming process is the degree to which the existing process provides a "level playing field" on which ITS-related projects can compete with other projects on a project merit. Table 24–1 suggests this issue has four key dimensions.

4.a.   *Level playing field in slating and evaluating investments.* The conventions of an institutionalized transportation planning process are focused on rationalizing the allocation resources among competing high-capital cost improvements based on techniques reflecting their narrow objectives, high costs, expensive implementation process, long-life cycles and major physical and environmental impacts. At the same time most MPOs have no tradition of involvement in operations-oriented projects, and MPO staff are less knowledgeable about ITS. Furthermore, the resources under MPO programming influence are scarce, particularly surface transportation programs and congestion mitigation and air quality programs, which have been very competitively sought for a wide range (and large backlog) of local government priorities.

Establishing a level playing field for the identification and evaluation of M&O improvements versus traditional capacity improvements is still a research matter, building on techniques associated with transportation systems management and CMS, and more recently the ITS deployment and analysis system. Some of the processes and methods that need to be developed and institutionalized include:

- A focus on performance-based problems with strong feedback from existing operations
- Concern for average and nonstandard conditions of incidents, weather and the like
- Measures of effectiveness for new service attributes (including reliability, security and information)
- Data on ITS benefits relating to improved traveler information or variable prices
- Discounting for varying time flow of benefits to compare ITS with major capital investments

Lack of good data for impact forecasting and evaluation will continue to be a handicap in the development of methods, although the relatively low cost and the incremental and adjustable nature of ITS improvements reduces the burden of quantitative judgments. A special challenge in the long term will be to better understand the potential of the interaction of supply operations and improved real-time systems information on travel behavior.

4.b. *Programming for incremental improvements.* The existing planning methodologies and programming practices are oriented towards large "lumpy," standalone capital improvements, often with major impacts. By contrast, specific ITS services and systems can be implemented in modest stages and then extended geographically. Software and hardware are typically upgraded with improved technology in an evolutionary manner, retaining certain components and improving others. This incremental improvement feature poses a special challenge for programming improvements in terms of single-stage projects where a multiyear program might be more appropriate unit of evaluation. Additionally, the evaluation of start-up "core" ITS investments such as communication backbones, traffic operations centers (TOCs), and basic detection and surveillance, might be understated unless their potential to support multiple future additions of high marginal value is reflected. Programming investments may, therefore, be better accomplished on a system rather than a facility basis—establishing a budget for a multiphase, multiyear program of related improvement rather than attempting to rationalize individual facility-based investments or specific stages in a larger regional program.

4.c. *Regional systems integration and implementation planning.* The convention of regional facility plans and common design standards went a long way towards insuring operational compatibility within modal networks across jurisdictional lines. ITS concepts, systems and technology introduce the more stringent demands of ITS and operational control for systems engineering and integration. First, inter-operability is required, especially among multiple vendor systems within a region (and for the few nation-scale mobility systems), across multiple jurisdiction projects, and to integrate legacy systems. Development of a systems architecture has proven to be an effective method of coordinating the large number of technical decisions among the various institutional players who may be involved. Second, implementation plans are essential to insure that ITS investments are justified by their operational value. Effective resource use implies the need to secure the involvement and commitments to operation support from the necessary range of regional systems owners and operators across modes and jurisdictions and from nonpublic works agencies. This consensus must be built around a common concept of operations and commitment of resources thereto.

"Mainstreaming" ITS requires an understanding of these two basic concepts. Furthermore, it implies the need to develop the appropriate relationship between the development of architecture and operational planning with the other key steps in planning and programming. This will require adjustments in the conventional process, including recognizing that:

- Systems integration and implementation planning require support in and of themselves—with both start up and continuing maintenance dimensions
- Systems architecture–related concepts will play an important role in identifying the logical evolution of improvements
- ITS improvements are often most effectively implemented "piggybacking" within other major non-ITS project improvements
- The data developed and information used within systems operations and specified within the architecture is extremely valuable to the overall planning

4.d. *A direct relationship between planning and operations.* The transportation planning process has historically focused on the planing, design and construction of major capital facility additions that have long implementation cycles, high costs and impacts, and which provide capacity scaled to estimated future demands over long life spans. The focus of ITS improvements is predominately on current performance through operating facilities in real time. Both of these improvement programs require their own planning and programming. However, the responsibilities for these two activities are usually quite separate, organizationally; and the activities, technology, improvement project time cycles and technical orientation of the responsible staffs are quite different.

Cost-effective capital investments through systems M&O requires that these gaps be overcome—technical and organizational. Major road and transit improvements can be specifically designed to capitalize on an aggressive systems management regime. Operations-based performance information is essential to a better-targeted capital facility planning. At the same time, significant savings can be realized through "building in" ITS improvements—piggybacking ITS component installation within major facility construction and improvement projects.

Prospects

Systems engineering is a discipline not widely available in the planning ranks of state DOTS, local government, or MPOs. As a result, much of the ITS architecture development and project planning have been carried out by operational personal principally from state DOTs and consultants, separate from the normal planning process. It is not clear the degree to which this will substantially handicap the ability of M&O investments to compete within the established planning process. In the short run, at least, special efforts will have to be made to insure that the implications of architecture for future improvements and of implementation of operational resources are integrated into the ongoing planning and programming process.

A key institutional challenge is forging the technical and programmatic linkages within the overall transportation improvement process at both the state and regional level. This may require:

- Modifying the existing planning processes to create a clear focus on short-run incremental improvements and develop articulated process links between performance and evaluation of major capital investments and the potential of M&O-oriented improvements

- Formalizing planning for M&O, recognizing the shorter time cycles and modest incremental improvement costs by creating organizational linkages between operations staff and planning staff

5. Project development resources

A resource refers to the "inputs" necessary to implement (plan, deploy, operate and maintain) ITS systems and services. These include staff expertise along with the capital and operating funds to support systems development, deployment and continuation of operations and maintenance costs.

The strong presumption of public-sector implementation has meant that shortage of public implementation resources appears to be a constraint on the rate of deployment. It is difficult to estimate the total national public resources being invested in ITS. While earmarked funds can be traced, a considerable component of ITS funding has come from flexible federal, state and local funds. In many cases, ITS improvements are combined in general transportation operations budgets or buried as components in other capital, operational, or maintenance budgets. The federal ITS expenditure level under ISTEA, when supplemented by the other eligible flexible federal aid funds as well as state and local funds, suggests an annual rate of public expenditure at about $1 billion per year or 1 percent of total capital.

Existing state and regional transportation infrastructure improvement programs take place in the context of limited funds and staff. Even where its potential is understood, ITS must compete for scarce financial and staff resources. State and regional funds are programmed on a multiyear basis. Even unfunded programs must flow through a pipeline of commitments against which any new program must compete. Funding may not be the critical scarce resource. The project development process, involving cross-agency negotiation and cooperation, is very senior and middle management labor-intensive. In an environment of agency downsizing, staff slots are limited and the required skills are increasingly scarce. The size of the national ITS program is largely a function of the number of senior ITS-oriented staff in each state DOT.

5.a. *A program definition for M&O.* Within the institutionalized transportation infrastructure development process, implementing a "system" is facilitated by definition of a program.[1] The dedication of resources at the state, local and federal level has often been framed in terms of systems completion. Network or standards are defined by the formal state and regional planing and programming process, both as functional and jurisdictional systems, and through parallel definitions of eligibility within the federal aid context. A corresponding generic definition of what constitutes comprehensive M&O program has not been developed in any jurisdiction. In most jurisdictions, individual ITS improvements are considered marginal improvements or "technology demonstrations." Few states or regions have formal, funded M&O programs that are considered major in which ITS would play a major role.

The national ITS architecture provides a template of potential services that includes a checklist for program categories and cost-effective sequences of investments from an investment leverage point of view. The hesitancy to define systems M&O performance standards and related target programs reflects finance–driven tactical reluctance on the part of agencies (federal, state and regional) as distinct from a conceptual difficulty. That ITS does not appear as a program line item in most state or regional transportation improvement projects reflects the broader reality: systems M&O is a distinct and major service responsibility; it is not widely adopted at the state or local level as a policy concept that requires a separate programmatic, budgeting, or organizational response equivalent to "preservation" or "safety."

5.b. *Mobilizing funds.* Initial deployment plans have been developed on an ad hoc basis, and few jurisdictions have estimated much less committed program level funds.

In the majority of states and metropolitan regions, ITS capital investments are typically funded as special projects, or they are combined with other major improvements. In most cases, ITS investments are considered as "special," "demonstration," or "high technology;" and they are supported with special earmarked funds. A few of the more advanced state programs have obtained special resources through discretionary federal aid such as the MDI programs or where the momentum of an early operational test has developed a strong ITS constituency. At the same time, other ITS components are conveniently combined with major improvements (such as detection or wireline communications) and buried in conventional funding. While this latter approach represents a form of "mainstreaming," it is often simply the practical recourse when explicit funding for ITS is not otherwise available. In either case, stable, long-term, program-oriented M&O programs are extremely rare.

While adequate capital is a continued challenge, a more serious handicap to mainstreaming ITS relates to operating funds. Traditional transportation improvements are capital-intensive. The "pay as you go" funding system has disconnected concepts of reserves, life cycle considerations and future operating and maintenance burdens from funding decisions. Furthermore the federal aid program on which states have depended for nearly 45 percent of capital cost has historically not been available for operations, although these constraints have now been relaxed. In contrast, the effectiveness of ITS depends on support for continuing operations and regular upgrades. Operations costs, principally staffing, are within a highway-constrained setting. Given the downsizing of state and local governments and reluctance to increase government operating costs, staff resources are a principal constraint to ITS deployment.

5.c. *Special technical staff capabilities.* Funding is not the only scarce public resource. As ITS-related programs expand, staffing is becoming a real constraint. The professional orientation in most transportation agencies has been civil engineering or planning. The personnel with operations or system engineering backgrounds are relatively rare. Additional staffing is limited by overall state policy. At the same time, the technologies on which ITS is based are part of larger information and communications industries, which are fast growing and extremely competitive. Attracting and retaining highly qualified technical staff is increasingly difficult, especially in the public sector where civil service and compensation constraints reduce management flexibility in creating satisfactory career environments. The rate of progress for many ITS programs is therefore limited by the capacity of the ITS-oriented staff. In the absence of organized ITS programs, much of the current deployment is done on an ad hoc basis, substantially dependent on the day-to-day lobbying and individual project facilitation of small ITS-dedicated staffs in state DOTs and local government. Many state efforts appear to be limited more by the small number of middle-level and senior ITS staff than lack of financial resources.

5.d. *Accommodating private capital in ITS.* Private capital can play a role in ITS infrastructure-related services development either as a private commercial enterprise or through a formal partnership with a transportation agency. The nature of this relationship is described in the next section. However, within ITS program development, formal public–private partnerships have been pursued as a source of additional or substitute investment in otherwise public ITS Infrastructure and operations. The focus of public-sector initiated commercialization initiatives through partnerships has been important in two areas. First, barter and cost-sharing arrangements have been executed for shared communication systems. For the most part these may be one-time opportunities but have provided substantial savings to ITS programs and other state activities. Legal challenges regarding the exclusive use of public right-of-way by competing communications providers have emerged and are currently in adjudication. Second, ATIS, road weather information systems (RWIS), and CVO-related information services appear to have a commercialization potential to defray costs—and perhaps earn a profit. Contractual arrangements generally involve a commingling of public and private assets and also include methods for sharing returns. These efforts are still in the early stages, and consumer willingness to pay for information and other services at a rate covering costs is still unclear. The efficient market scale of these services is a key issue. Expansion and consolidation are both underway together with service providers developing a range of alliances in search of acceptable returns. The ultimate shape and combination of these services is unclear.

Prospects

A comprehensive M&O program awaits a strong policy commitment. Such a program could be articulated at various LOS, including statewide or industry-wide standards, target thresholds, nested statewide and regional architecture and multiyear program of projects and associate resource commitments. The incremental staging and technology evolution within such a program would establish a new definition of a program appropriate to an M&O orientation.

It is not clear that the increase in capital expenditures associated with TEA-21 has unleashed an increased level of investment in ITS, reflecting the backlog competition that major facilities continue to present in the absence of a modification of state and local priorities. The current level of investment reflects both the modest priority of M&O as well as the modest influence of the champions. As indicated, the availability of capital may, however, be roughly equivalent of the organizational capacity available to spend it well.

Operationally trained leadership and staff may be the scarcest resource. Three tactics are emerging for responding to this shortage. First, a major training effort within transportation institutions is necessary. This can play an important role in filling some of the important staff vacuums. At the same time, state DOTs and local agencies (based on motives beyond ITS) are seeking more flexible employment opportunities that reflect the expectations of technical specialist in a competitive setting. At the same time, public agencies are finding that outsourcing and other forms of partnerships with private vendors are an effective strategy for accessing specialized capabilities.

6. Public–private sector issues

The concept of ITS as originally developed in the late 1980s foresaw continuation of a clear division of roles among the sectors. Provision of traffic and transit operations and system management activities relating directly to the infrastructure would be a public responsibility using tax funds. The private sector was expected to develop noninfrastructure products and services in what is expected to be a subsequent, albeit much larger, private-sector market based on direct customer sales. These were expected to concentrate on commercializable traveler information services and in-vehicle products relating to safety and control.

A wide range of private entities have interests in the ITS arena—principally from the automotive, electronic and consumer information arenas. Vendor-contractors will continue their fee-for-service activities, scaled to public investment levels. However, the level of capital investment from the private sector in in-vehicle systems and related information services is expected to be as much as one order of magnitude greater than the public investment.

The availability of resources in the private sector, which is largely internally funded, will depend on market penetration rates. Market penetration is, in turn, a function of the attractiveness and reliability of products and the consumer's willingness to pay within the very demanding national automotive products arena. Consideration of private-sector institutional issues in this private market is outside the scope of this chapter. There are, however, institutional issues arising from the intersection of the public responsibility for infrastructure M&O and the private-sector development of products and services that support or are even substituted for the public execution of those responsibilities. As indicated in table 24–1, progress in this zone of partnerships will depend on six key institutional issues:

6.a. *Mainstream public–private partnerships.* Private capital can play a role in ITS services where consumer revenues are available, either through private commercial enterprise or via formal partnerships with a transportation agency. Traffic radio is a long-standing business based on informal relationships with transportation and law enforcement agencies. Formal partnerships have been pursued as a source of additional or substitute investment in public ITS programs. These contractual arrangements generally involve a commingling of public and private assets and also include methods for sharing returns. Partnerships have focused in two areas: (1) on ITS activities where a customer revenue stream can be tapped at acceptable risks related to willingness to pay (such as ATIS, RWIS, electronic toll collection [ETC], or commercial vehicle clearance), and (2) where access to valuable public assets is available (such as public rights-of-way for shared communications facilities). The profitability of these activities is mixed. Communication resource-sharing deals have produced large one-time returns to states, but the profitability of the consumer-related investments—on a standalone basis—is unproven as the consumer willingness to pay for the quality of information available is still unclear. To date, most of the formal partnerships with private entities have been on a single local project basis. The potential of partnerships has been hampered by inappropriate procurement procedures and lack of project management experience—in both software and hardware. Costs, time frames and regulated returns in such partnerships on a local basis may be inconsistent with the economic expectations of the information systems business arena. The private-sector ability to substitute for agency M&O personnel has also been limited by an unwillingness to outsource activities that are traditionally agency-staffed.

In addition, the trend towards regional and national consolidation in these markets renders the constraints of locally based deals less viable, reducing the level of private interest in single-project partnerships. However, several ATIS ventures have the potential of being closely tied to larger non transportation information services and revenue sources that can improve their financial viability. The viability of ETC may be improved with ties into smart cards. National standardization issues relating to vehicle-to-roadside, smart cards and wireless web access are key institutional barriers to greater private interest.

6.b. *Modify legislative authorization for partnerships.* Transportation law and tradition specify an arms-length vendor relationship with the private sector as a guard against abuse. By contrast, a significant dimension of ITS relates to private sector ownership of, or involvement in, the development, finance and design of new systems and services. Capitalizing on these private resources requires partnerships between public and private entities to allow resources (assets, capital, intellectual property) to be comingled, bartered, or shared on either a competitive or exclusive basis. These types of formal or informal relationships challenge the existing legal and administrative conventions. Explicit legislative authorization may be desirable to avoid clouding otherwise promising arrangements.

The development and deployment of ITS systems is substantially dependent on the ability of the public sector to tap private technology and specialized skills of the private entities, many from outside the "transportation industry." This process has been consistently hampered by acquisition regulations and conventions based on a civil engineering tradition of sequential design-bid-construct contracts for standardized products on a competitive, low-bid basis. This practice has regularly proven inconsistent with the flexibility required in acquiring software as well as hardware, based on fuzzy specifications, with special systems integration challenges, iterative procedures and the like. Project delay, cost overruns, quality problems, complex claims and unattractive commercial risk and returns perceptions have plagued many ITS projects.

For projects and program where software and systems are involved, public agencies are more frequently turning to a range of alternative procurement approaches from outside the traditional federal acquisition regulatory process. Approaches developed in other federal agencies and at the state level for nonprofessional services accommodate scope changes and a more equitable allocation of risks between owner and vendor. Some states use nonstate agencies to conduct certain ITS procurements as a means of sidestepping constraining state regulations. Other states have begun to capitalize on common rule procedures that provide the flexibility to use negotiated scopes, cost-plus payment schemes, staged procurement and other innovations. Given the rapid changes in technology, approaches using continuing on-call service contracts are also being tried. A key challenge is the increased familiarization of public agency personnel with these options through professional capacity-building activities.

6.c. *Cooperative research and development partnerships.* While much of ITS has focused on demonstrating, refining and deploying available technology in system configurations oriented to defined user services, there have been parallel research programs to develop new technology as well. First, U.S. DOT has sponsored programs through the traditional combination of in-house and contract research focusing on traffic and transit management, human factors and crash avoidance. Second, under ISTEA, U.S. DOT embarked on an innovative long-range research program oriented towards an IVHS focusing on both safety and efficiency. In an attempt to involve the major industry players in advanced vehicle technology, the initial approach was based on the competitively procured cooperative research frame work (used in defense and aerospace), allowing a commingle of federal and private resources including maintenance of proprietary technology within a true partnership (rather than a contract) arrangement (see chapter 23). This National Automated Highway System Consortium embarked on an ambitious research and development project expected to be a continuing multiyear effort.

Despite field-level demonstrations of progress, the long-range time frame, budgetary requirements and the inflexibility of the arrangement led to the conclusion of the automated highway system program in its fourth year. The research and development focus was downscaled and narrowed to the more short-term crash avoidance and following more traditional arrangements for research (see chapter 8). The longer-term focus on major efficiency gains with related automation focus was essentially downplayed. The remaining intelligent vehicle research and development, both within the federal aid research program and within the industry, are focusing on a range of safety improvements through various information, warning and control systems.

6.d. *Accommodating intelligent vehicle rollout constraints.* More fully capitalizing on the potential of ITS will depend on the ability of private industry to develop effective products and services at an attractive cost to the consumer. This suggests a long evolutionary process, rolling out one modest upgrade after another. While this chapter focuses principally on public institutions where policy and organizational change may affect the level of ITS deployment, there are some intersections between private-sector ITS-related product markets and public policy both in the regulatory and technical areas. First, where capturing significant social benefits is at stake, public regulatory involvement in the market may be at issue. Here public policy intersects deployment of autonomous intelligent vehicle improvements around such issues as equitable access to new products, licensing, public education and liability. As new technology and products are proven, formal consideration of these issues may have to be invoked. Second, it is possible that certain intelligent vehicle products involve infrastructure as a means of reducing product costs or increasing reliability (cooperative intelligent vehicle infrastructure). The increased capabilities and reduced costs asserted for cooperative approaches bring with them a range of new costs and responsibilities for road system operators, a need for new forms of collaboration between the vehicle industry and state or local government and a host of technical demands.

6.e. *New private-sector business models.* Noninfrastructure ITS systems and services relate principally to those that may be marketed directly or indirectly to customers or those that are part of private-sector service activities. These include electronic payment systems, commercial vehicle fleet management systems, in-vehicle navigation, security and information systems and advanced vehicle control and safety systems. The deployment of these services takes place through the development of consumer markets within a competitive setting based on the customer's perception of value and willingness to pay versus price. These are obviously not public institutional issues subject to public policy, and the key barriers to deployment of these products and services are the normal conventions of private enterprise management associated with introducing new products and services to market in the corporate sector. As such, the institutional issues internal to a given business enterprise are those associated with contemporary management practice to maximize customer satisfaction and financial performance. The key issues, therefore, are those associated with a successful business such as leadership, strategic planing, customer and market focus, organization and staff development and management and process reengineering.

In the automotive industry, product development has been conducted largely within the framework of individual corporations with almost total control of product development, testing, marketing and introduction. In-house technical and financial resources were used almost exclusively to design essentially self-sufficient original equipment. The environment for ITS products and services, especially those related to the application of information of consumer information technology into the vehicle environment, requires relationships among a broader set of players than conventional in the automotive industry. It introduces the need for alliances, new partnerships among vehicle manufacturers, computer and information service and device suppliers, and telecommunications providers. A series of new institutional alliances must be developed to focus on common standards and other issues of interoperability. The success of these new relationships will be critical to the pace at which in-vehicle information products and services can be rolled out.

6.f. *Recognize expanding private business opportunities.* Outside of ITS, many state and local agencies in search of both efficiencies and outside investment have been experimenting with expanded roles for private enterprise in the delivery of facilities and services. Several forces are eroding the conventional division of responsibilities among sectors. Increasing consumer impatience with congestion is creating a demand for more aggressive M&O and related products and services. This has encouraged state and local governments to seek more effective roles and relationships with each other and private-sector entities to provide improved customer response. There is a continuing trend to directly involve private entities, such as private toll road franchises, to contract out ETC and to outsource project and construction management and total facility maintenance and operations.

Privately developed technology and consumer services entrepreneurship are likely to be an increasingly important driver of change in ITS. New technology introduces potential new service opportunities substantially independent of road-owning public agencies. Some of the services traditionally produced and staffed by public agencies may be more efficiently developed if they were procured as a turnkey service for an all-in fee—thus, eliminating a large number of public-sector procedures and costs associated with multiple service and technology procurements. The outsourcing of an entire service has been limited to ATIS where operations are expected to eventually become self-supporting (although few have) and a few isolated instances where private contractors provide operations staff for TOCs and ETC. As technologies move out of public property and facilities, and as traffic control activities become more closely integrated with traffic information, the necessity and perhaps even the possibility of complete public control will be reduced. For example, FCC's requirements for cellular 911 geo-location raise the possibility of eventual incident detection and traveler information on a network-wide basis entirely without public-sector involvement. The combinations of these expanding opportunities for private-sector involvement may be expected to encourage the evolution of ITS as a private enterprise.

Prospects

As the private side of ITS expands, both public–private and private–private relationships will be affected. Institutional relationships with the auto and electronics industry are primarily national, governed by their traditional arms-length, regulator-regulated structure in the safety and environment. However, where there is direct interface with public infrastructure, agency information or services, federal or multistate cooperation of a new type with national industries is needed. The need for national standards and protocols in areas such as N11, ETC, ATIS and "mayday" are apparent. Examples include reinforcement of standards development organization activities; consensus on common roles of public emergency service providers; common interfaces for public information input to national traveler information systems; and legal protections regarding liability, antitrust and intellectual property. Such activities are already underway with U.S. DOT encouragement (see chapter 19). However, the large number of simultaneous challenges may strain the past tradition of laissez faire evolutionary private-sector development followed by government institutionalization in these types of areas.

Similarly, changes are needed in the research relationships, both in research process and research substance. It is apparent that the public and private transportation sectors at the level of the federal government and major national corporations lack the tradition, mandate, resources and relationships to support the large-scale, long-term relationships available in other advanced technology sectors. In particular, the challenge of dealing with both precompetitive and competitive (proprietary) private technology remains unresolved. Finally, new mixes or services, such as integrated traffic information and control, will suggest rebundling project responsibilities among public and private entities that may permit cross-subsidies and private involvement in operations services. The combination of emerging private in-vehicle information and safety products together with external private traveler information and security services and increased private roles in systems operations suggest synergistic service opportunities that could change the relationship between public- and private-sector roles. Increased information about traffic conditions and increased vehicle capabilities suggest the potential of new M&O options, especially those associated with premium services, higher speeds and semi-automation. Such opportunities are likely to be of interest to major national scale corporations. This, in turn suggests:

- Nationwide suppliers will be looking for approaches that minimize their dependence on state and local relationships though standardization or relative independence from the public sector
- The owners of infrastructure (at the state and local level) are likely to have a decreasing influence on these services and how they are delivered
- As maturity in these services is gained, private enterprises will look for related paths to expand their commercial interests into a broader range of activities

Endnote

1. A system here would be a related set of improvements, the completeness of which is a significant feature of its value.

BY Chris Cluett • Senior Research Specialist •
Battelle Memorial Institute

Societal Issues in ITS

Introduction

As human beings we live our lives as members of society, and in the course of our daily activities we are faced with challenges and opportunities that are shaped by other members of society, by the natural environment, by the built environment that we create and by the technologies that we use. As social creatures, we group together into families, friendships, neighborhoods, ethnic groups, communities and nations. When we talk about society and societal issues, we are referring to people interacting in groups, and the issues and concerns that they have as they coexist in this collective, interactive way. In an evolved, complex, highly mobile society such as ours, transportation and communication play central roles in providing each member of society access to the activities and benefits that society offers. Some of the more important and obvious activities include employment, education, health care, recreation, commerce, entertainment and endless forms of social interaction. Arguably, without transportation systems, modern society and human interaction as we know it would be impossible. The focus of this chapter will be on how society and transportation affect each other and the potential role of intelligent transportation systems (ITS) in offering societal benefit.

Societal issues may seem secondary to the people responsible for the technical development of ITS products, while to members of a local citizen transportation advisory committee, societal issues may be at the core of public discourse about the potential impacts of transportation technologies on their community. An elected state transportation official may be most concerned with the cost implications of a proposed ITS system, while a local land use planner is worried about the relationship between regional population growth, sprawl, traffic congestion and what ITS might offer. We know that technologies have important effects on society, and the new ITS technologies cannot exist apart from the social environment in which they function. This social context both shapes and is shaped by the technology. We each play our role, as developer, designer, decision-maker, operator, end user, or bystander. We are a part of society, and we each have our own perspective on the advantages and disadvantages of technology. Transportation technology and society are intertwined and inseparable. Technical excellence alone does not assure the success of ITS; it is a necessary but not sufficient condition for both implementation and for public acceptance and satisfaction with the promised benefits.

This chapter seeks to understand how ITS as a set of technologies operates in the social environment, and what an understanding of the societal implications of ITS can tell us about how to implement ITS to yield greater benefits for society. Societal issues are usually labeled in a class of nontechnical issues, along with economic, legal, policy, environmental, cultural, organizational and institutional issues. Many of these topics are covered separately in this book. In this chapter, we will address a set of societal issues and explore their close interconnection with transportation systems in general and with ITS in particular. The reader is invited to review the technical discussions of ITS applications in this book and consider the implications for the many dimensions of society outlined in this chapter.

Defining societal issues

We often travel great distances from one place to another to conduct the social activities of everyday life. While as users of various forms of transportation and communication, we may take these enabling technologies for granted; we also recognize that they help define what we accept as a normal way of life in our society. We are a society composed of widely differentiated groupings of individuals, characterized by a tapestry of different life experiences, levels of education and well-being, spread out geographically in large numbers, and requiring a high degree of mobility to access the things we need and want. To a great extent transportation systems have evolved to meet the access needs of this diverse and highly mobile population, and society has itself been shaped by the evolution of our transportation systems.

There are not, surprisingly, a large number of societal issues that are intertwined in one way or another with transportation. Richardson enumerated 61 such social and economic factors, a list "not meant to be exhaustive, but rather a glimpse into some of the complexity and challenges that exist in implementing transportation systems" (1994, 5). The Societal Implications Task Force of ITS America sponsored a symposium in 1995 on alternative futures for transportation, technology and society. This symposium featured four presented papers followed by group discussion with stakeholders representing a wide range of societal constituencies, interests and perspectives. One outcome of this symposium was a report that summarized societal issues into more manageable clusters. These are listed in table 25–1 (Societal Implications Task Force 1995, 17–18).

The Federal Highway Administration's (FHWA) Office of Environment and Planning produced a reference manual on *Community Impact Assessment* in 1996 that identifies a wide range of societal impacts of transportation systems and suggests strategies for avoiding or mitigating these effects. This practical guidebook describes community impact assessment as "a process to evaluate the effects of a transportation action on a community and its quality of life. The assessment process is an integral part of project planning and development that shapes the outcome of a project. Its information is used continuously to mold the project and provide documentation of the current and anticipated social environment of a geographic area with and without the action. The assessment should include all items of importance to people, such as mobility, safety, employment effects, relocation, isolation and other community issues" (U.S. DOT, FHWA 1996, 4) The guidebook lists the major impact categories that reflect the close connections between transportation and society, and more specifically the community, as summarized in table 25–2.

Recent research has examined how ITS can be better integrated into the local transportation planning process. Many of the identified hurdles are social or institutional in nature, and current ITS programs in many different places demonstrate that these hurdles can and are being overcome. New public–private business models are being created that reflect ways of sharing information, staff and technologies to implement integrated, multimodal ITS systems. The FHWA's model deployment initiatives address public, private and commercial travel; and they are demonstrating how new institutional arrangements, enhanced ITS strategic planning at the metropolitan planning organization (MPO) level, stakeholder involvement and cooperation between the public and private sectors can create solutions to these complex societal issues.

We can capture some of the challenges with the following questions:

- How will the benefits, as well as the potential adverse impacts, of ITS be experienced by different members of society? Will society view the costs and benefits of ITS as equitably distributed?[1] To what extent will people be able to use, benefit from and pay for transportation services?

Table 25–1
Issue Clusters: Society and Transportation
Source: ITS America, reprinted with permission.

⇒ **Safety and security issues** • Concern for safety and reliability of the technology • Concern for crime and personal security in vehicles • Age and gender differences in nature and level of concern • Relationship to broader societal technology risk aversion	⇒ **Communication; collaboration; education; training** • Need for two-way communication (stakeholders learning from each other) • Coordination among technical and nontechnical actors in the ITS program • Overcoming differences in culture, orientation, background and perspective • Increasing visibility and understanding of ITS • Management of information and privacy • Social implications for transportation of information superhighway
⇒ **Providing for transportation consumers, users of ITS** • Needs of the disabled, elderly and women with young children • Focus on nondiscretionary travel requirements • Geographically disadvantaged • Being responsive to community perspectives on need and uses for ITS • Dealing with nonbelievers in technology-based solutions to transportation problems • Role of the driver and ergonomic issues	⇒ **Land use; dislocation; density** • High system costs associated with urban sprawl • Relationship between transportation, mixed Population densities and land uses • Growth of economic activity in urban periphery • Urban growth management and willingness to limit or plan for growth • Relationship between mobility and environmental sustainability
⇒ **Family structure and equity** • Single parents and one-parent households • Working women with day care needs • Implications of complex trip-chaining patterns • Aging of the population • Housing options for the elderly and effect on mobility • Need for diversity of options and alternatives • Perceived fairness of transportation options	⇒ **Access** • Accessibility of transportation facilities and services to potential users • ITS's effect on access to jobs, services, education, health care and recreation • Allocation decision-making for limited transportation resources • Needs of households that do not own vehicles • Effect of ITS costs on access • ITS technology's effect on isolation of the elderly
⇒ **Impact on nonvehicular mobility** • Pedestrians, joggers and bicyclists • Sense of community, neighborhood cohesion, social networks and quality-of-life • Intermodal efficiency	⇒ **ITS system funding, costs and benefits** • Factors influencing participation of the private sector • Management and operations costs • Timing of costs and benefits • Private- versus public-sector funding and distribution • Federal, state and local requirements; and participation • Public willingness to pay
⇒ **Public and user acceptability of ITS technology** • Perceptions of technology risks • Public attitudes and values with regard to ITS technology • Need to develop "psychological ownership" in ITS • Public role in ITS decision-making processes • Social and cultural interpretations of transportation systems	

Table 25–2
Community Impacts of Transportation
Source: Federal Highway Administration.

Social and Psychological Aspects	• Changes in population • Community cohesion and interaction • Isolation • Social values • Quality of life
Physical Aspects	• Barrier effects • Sounds • Other physical intrusions
Visual Environment	• Aesthetics • Compatibility with community goals
Land Use	• Land-use patterns • Compatibility with local plans
Economic Conditions	• Business and employment impacts • Short-term impacts • Business visibility • Tax base • Property values
Mobility and Access	• Pedestrian and bicycle access • Public transportation • Vehicular access
Provision of Public Services	• Use of public facilities • Displacement of public facilities
Safety	• Pedestrian and bicycle safety • Crime • Emergency response
Displacement	• Effect on neighborhoods • Residential displacements • Business and farm displacements • Relocation sites

- How can we anticipate the potential long-term implications of expanded ITS implementation on society? Can ITS help offset some of the undesirable effects of society's dependence on the automobile? Does ITS offer society a greater range of transportation and access options? Can we effectively mitigate some of these community impacts of transportation?
- How can ITS best meet the needs of our nation's elderly and disabled? By the year 2020, 17 percent of the population will be aged 65 or older. The Americans with Disabilities Act (ADA) makes access to public transportation for disabled individuals a national goal.
- What role might ITS technologies be able to play in creating sustainable communities well into the future? Currently, many communities are struggling with rapid population growth that threatens the quality of life of these communities. Transportation, growth and land use are closely intertwined; and the societal effects of transportation can be significant.
- Approximately 15 percent of deaths in the United States from traffic accidents are experienced by pedestrians and bicyclists. Neighborhoods can experience the negative spill-over effects of highway congestion. How can ITS address these societal issues?
- What are the characteristics of ITS technologies that engender customer acceptance? What steps can we take to make ITS more broadly beneficial and acceptable throughout society?

Society—transportation interactions and the role of ITS

Travel behavior is closely associated with the underlying structure and characteristics of the population. One way to examine the links between societal issues in ITS is to consider ongoing changes in our social structure, how those changes relate to transportation and mobility, and how ITS fits in. Characteristics of the traveling public and a better understanding of their transportation and access needs should be helpful in fig-uring out how to better deploy and adapt ITS products and services. While ITS implementation may be viewed primarily as a marketing challenge, gaining a better sense of where society is headed should allow us to avoid pitfalls and capitalize on opportunities. It should also help assure that the benefits of ITS are made available as broadly as possible across society.

Just as underlying socio-demographic changes have caused changes in travel patterns, changes in the eco-nomics of travel; the construction of new road, rail and air transportation systems; and the introduction of technologies that have enhanced transportation system performance all have contributed to societal changes. A clear example of this effect is rapid suburbanization and the ability of workers to continue to maintain sin-gle-family household residential lifestyles by facilitating the journey to work with better transportation net-works. This process has changed the locational patterns of the home and workplace, and resulted in the rise of the suburban mall, and a broad dislocation of a range of destinations that involve central daily activities, such as home–work commutes, outside-the-home child care, eating out, shopping, visiting friends and rela-tives, picking up the dry cleaning, and so on. This wide dispersal of activities requires increases in personal travel; and the complexity of routing and scheduling of such trips, coupled with relatively low-density subur-ban settlement patterns, puts lower-impact public transportation at a substantial competitive disadvantage with the personal automobile.

Let's examine some of the societal changes that we already know are having a significant effect on transporta-tion and travel behavior. The pervasiveness of these changes in society, and their obvious implications for transportation, suggests their particular relevance for the potential for ITS.[2] Sandra Rosenbloom states this position strongly, suggesting that "to marginalize these issues is not simply to *risk* the success of ITS systems and approaches—it is to guarantee their *failure*. Without a recognition of the implications of these profound societal changes, most ITS user services will themselves address only a marginal proportion of the needs of only a marginal proportion of American families" (1995, 2). These issues are outlined below and discussed in more detail in the sections that follow.

- The aging of the population, characterized by growing numbers and proportions of elderly, changing patterns of elderly driving and mobility and health service implications of the elderly
- Changing household and family structure, characterized by increasing numbers of households, smaller households, single-parent households, working mothers with young children and aging parents to care for and a changing dependency ratio, such that in the future there will be fewer persons in the working age groups between 16 and 65 years to support the increasing number of elderly
- Changing patterns of work, characterized by dual-income households, increasing female labor force participation, flextime and telecommuting and changing commute and multipurpose travel patterns
- Urban population growth, congestion, sprawl and their effect on community sustainability
- Rapid increases in vehicle ownership, person-miles traveled and number of trips
- Recent and rapid advances in communications and information technology and the explosive potential of the Internet; the increasing uses of these new technologies are influencing how businesses operate and the ways in which individuals travel and shop

Population aging

The ongoing increases in the numbers and proportions of the elderly American population is one of the more widely known and understood demographic phenomenon. As the baby boom generation grows older, experiencing as they have later ages of marriage and childbearing and smaller family sizes, and as health care for the elderly continues to improve, more and more people and higher portions of the overall population are living to older ages. Demographic projections indicate that this will continue. The trend presents a number of important societal challenges, and many of those have transportation implications.

Because women continue to experience a longer life expectancy than men, a larger share of the elderly are now and will in the future be women, with a large proportion of these women living alone. In addition, the mobility of the elderly population decreases as they age, and as their health and mobility decline, they depend increasingly on others, particularly immediate family members, for care. Rosenbloom points out that "while the elderly as a whole are increasingly more affluent, women and people of color have not shared proportionately in these favorable changes. Moreover, women comprise the largest component of the very old—those with the most need for services" (1995, 19).

The ability to remain independent and mobile are central values for the elderly. The elderly remain heavily dependent on the personal automobile for their travel, and the numbers of drivers 65-years-old and older will at least double over the next 30 years. Also, older drivers will be taking more trips and driving more miles than they do now (Burkhardt and McGavock 1999). While they tend to be aware of the decline in their driving effectiveness and safety, they generally believe that they can compensate for those deficiencies by driving less, carefully choosing their routes, driving primarily during the day and other strategies intended to lessen their perceived risk of being in an accident. Unfortunately, accident statistics indicate just the opposite. Elderly drivers are increasingly likely to experience accidents and personal injury. Over the next 30 years the number of fatalities can be expected to increase three- to four-fold, given no change in automobile fatality rates experienced today. From a societal standpoint, this is a daunting prospect. Considerable attention is being given to how ITS can help support driving functions for the elderly and make their driving safer, along with other strategies to address this looming problem. As pointed out by Burkhardt and McGavock, the costs to society go well beyond the tragedy of lost lives to "include the increasing isolation of our oldest citizens and the loss of their potential contributions to our society" (1999, 20).

The elderly will place increasing demands on the delivery of health care and social services in both metropolitan and rural areas. A recent Transportation Research Board (TRB) study notes that "although access and mobility are very important to the delivery of health and social services, there is very little interaction between transportation policy making and health and welfare policy making" (1997, 12). The TRB report goes on to note that state transportation agencies and MPOs are under increasing pressure to address the needs of those who lack personal mobility and access to these service providers, as well as to potential employers.

An estimated 15 percent of all licensed drivers in the year 2000 will be over the age of 65, and as the baby boomers continue to age, this percentage will rise. The implications of increasing physical impairments, vision and hearing loss, and slower reaction times are some of the more obvious issues. A more difficult societal issue "which needs to be addressed by individuals, families and licensing authorities is restrictions on the use of vehicles by the elderly and revocation of licenses when certain levels of incapacity are reached" (Richardson 1993, 10). Holding on to their license, their right to independent mobility, is both materially and symbolically important to the elderly. How then should we make judgments about their right to drive? And what role might ITS play in addressing some of the problems presented by the aging process? Examples range from crash avoidance systems to heads-up display and night vision enhancement to in-vehicle route guidance systems.

Changing household and family structure

A long-term trend in the United States of declining household size reflects families having fewer children now than they used to, many fewer families with large numbers of children, increases in persons living alone and in nonfamily households, an increase in single-parent households, and older persons living alone. The average household size has declined from 3.4 in 1950 to 2.6 in 1990. A higher rate of increase in the number of households compared with the overall rate of increase in the size of the population has contributed to increases in trip making. Between 1969 and 1990, all households increased in number by 49 percent, while one-person households increased 109 percent (U.S. DOT 1992, 6). The Nationwide Personal Transportation Survey (NPTS) reports that "between 1969 and 1990 the number of households, drivers, workers, and vehicles grew at a much faster rate than the population" (U.S. DOT 1992, 7).

Furthermore, single-parent households, especially when that parent is a woman, have higher poverty rates than other household types. Many of these women live in central city housing and have to commute to jobs in the suburbs, often not adequately served by public transportation. On average, these poor households find they have to spend a greater share of their limited income on transportation than other households. Because these women are struggling to hold down a job and raise their children on their own, they have to make more person-trips than households with a spouse who can share these responsibilities.

Changing patterns of work

The combination of increases in the labor force, particularly the rapid rise of female labor force participation, has had profound effects on transportation patterns. There are a large number of women with children, particularly small children, who are working. Whether these women are members of a dual-income household or are single-working parents, their transportation needs are characterized by complex trip segments that include travel to work, the babysitter, the grocery store, the shopping mall, friends and elsewhere. The traditional suburban home-to-central-city-and-return commute of a one-worker household has changed dramatically. Many more trips are now "chained" to include these other needs, families have more than one wage earner requiring separate transportation, and jobs and residences are much more widely dispersed throughout our metropolitan areas. Commute patterns now go in every direction and pretty much throughout the day.

The NPTS reports that the number of males employed in the labor force increased 32 percent between 1969 and 1990, while the number of employed females increased 99 percent (U.S. DOT 1992, 6). In two-wage earner households, men still tend to commute longer distances to work and women tend to retain primary responsibility for childcare. Their travel schedules are more constrained than for men, given their combined job, family and household maintenance responsibilities. As a result they tend to travel shorter distances to work and be less likely to get by without a personal means of travel.

More employers are offering and employees are demanding flexibility in their working hours. This includes full-time working arrangements that may be organized into four 10-hour days a week; or part-time working arrangements that can be organized in a wide variety of ways to accommodate the needs of the employee and the employer. Workers whose work hours have some measure of built-in flexibility are better able to respond to information about congestion or problems along the alternative commute routes. By delaying arrival or departure timing, they may be able to avoid these problems altogether. For them, Advanced Traveler Information Systems (ATIS) is potentially of much greater value than for commuters who must adhere to a rigid schedule.

Modern telecommunications, including the telephone and wireless systems, fax, computer and the Internet, create the ability for people to substitute these forms of information-exchange for personal trips. This can serve to curb demand for travel. Examples include telecommuting from home one or more days of the week, electronic commerce over the Internet, catalog shopping and distance-learning via television. Telecommunications also can serve to induce additional travel, thereby offsetting the gains in demand reduction and trip substitution. The greater geographic dispersion of individuals and the places where their work is directed that is made possible by telecommunications also creates a greater need to service these disparate locations. New economic and social relationships are likely to be created that call for face-to-face interactions, leading to more travel. The pervasiveness of wireless telecommunications and cellular technology make the conduct of business from any place at almost any time much easier. Workers' cars become office-like, and being caught in traffic congestion may offer productive work opportunities. If the individual can be more productive on the road, then additional travel may be encouraged (or at least less discouraged). The net effects of telecommunications on travel behavior is difficult to assess at this time; but the interconnectedness between social behavior, communications technologies and travel are quite real. It is important to anticipate the range of possible societal effects as we deploy ITS information technologies.

Changing urban form

The defining characteristic of our major metropolitan areas for the past 50 years has been suburbanization, a spreading outward from city cores that has been fueled by population growth and made possible by the automobile, freeways and public transit systems. Suburban growth can be expected to continue even further out from their central cities, creating new-edge cities, though constraints of land availability will moderate these trends in the future. Travel in this setting will involve even more complex trip patterns than today. The traditional commute from suburb to central city and back has been supplemented with suburb-to-suburb trips and reverse commuting patterns that have led to peak commute periods that last for hours in the morning and afternoon, and in some locations blend into almost unabated congestion throughout the day. Urban sprawl is both a cause and an effect of the expansion of transportation systems. However, the general lack of concentrations of high-density settlements in the suburbs, outside of the edge city centers and along major arterials, makes it difficult to plan for and finance public transportation systems to adequately service these areas. A result of these trends has been a decline in transit use.

This pattern of urban growth "brought the majority of our nation's population into the middle class" (APTA 1996, 5), but not without a variety of societal problems. These include environmentally damaging sprawl, large urban infrastructure support costs, auto dependency, extended periods of traffic congestion, loss of prime agricultural land, increased urban air pollution, and high dependency on international oil. The Mobility for the 21st Century study observes that "one of the most important developments weakening our sense of community is the loss of the human scale in the physical environment as development is geared more toward automobiles, roads and parking spaces than toward walkable communities where neighbors can meet and interact" (APTA 1996, 6).

An important social consequence of these urban dynamics is a tendency to concentrate the poor and racial minorities in the older core areas of these large cities. Because many of the job opportunities are in the suburban areas surrounding these central cities, it usually falls to the transportation system to come up with "innovative ways to connect able core workers to suburban opportunities" (Hodge, Morrill and Stanilov 1995, 23). This presents a serious social equity problem for the urban poor who cannot afford and may not have access to an automobile, and who live in parts of the city not well served by public transportation systems. The gap between the mobility patterns of the general population and those whose mobility is constrained is growing wider. These disadvantaged groups include low-income, elderly, recent immigrants, physically handicapped and people of color. "As we transition welfare recipients to work, we need to closely examine how these workforce entrants will not only get to an increasingly suburbanized job market, but also how they will accomplish their family responsibilities and household maintenance activities" (U.S. DOT 1997, 32). Solutions to these urban structural problems will likely call more for institutional rather than technical insight.

Land use patterns that have accompanied suburbanization, including residential neighborhoods built around cul-de-sacs, spatial separation of homes from businesses, busy arterials and strip developments, discourage alternatives to the automobile, such as walking and bicycling. Urban sprawl, transportation and societal well-being are closely intertwined. One writer contends that "sprawl erodes civil society—the human glue of democracy. It aggravates social and economic inequality and frays community cohesiveness. Sprawl makes owning a car a necessity of life, which can transform a low income into a poverty income" (Durning 1996, 27).

Transportation equity issues also are raised with members of society who may have physical, mental, or learning disabilities that may severely limit their mobility options. How the benefits and opportunities of access and mobility provided by our transportation systems are distributed across all members of society is a central societal and equity issue. The ADA provides some of the legal underpinnings that require such measures as wheelchair access to public transportation facilities. The replacement legislation for the Intermodal Surface Transportation Efficiency Act of 1991 (ISTEA) is called TEA-21 (Transportation Equity Act for the 21st Century). TEA-21 lists a variety of requirements for project funding, including a strong commitment among stakeholders, that reflects the desire for the benefits of federal ITS funding to be available equitably for all those who stand to be affected.

Changing travel patterns

Changes in labor force participation over the past several decades, along with rising incomes, have fueled increases in vehicle ownership and amount of travel. However, many of these forces have largely run their course. The numbers of young people who arrive at driving age each year have declined since 1980 as a function of marriage and childbearing patterns. The rapid increases in female labor force participation experienced since the 1960s has leveled out; and while there will continue to be many female drivers, the high past rates of growth will not be seen again for some time. A high percentage of both men and women are licensed drivers. Where we are still experiencing increases in licensing is with the elderly, especially elderly women. Depending on age, women drive 30 to 40 percent fewer miles compared with men the same age, but the gap between men's and women's driving continues to close (U.S. DOT 1997, 23).

Cars are made better now and last longer than they used to. The average age of the vehicle fleet is increasing and vehicle ownership is now available to a wider income segment of society. Pisarski points out that in the aggregate there are now more vehicles available in households than there are licensed persons to drive them (1992, 12). Racial minorities, particularly in cities, experience lower vehicle ownership than the rest of the population. However, evidence from the NPTS suggests that the lower income and minority groups continue to show greater increases in vehicle miles traveled than the rest of the population.

Current travel data show us how important social motivations are in determining our predominant travel patterns. Family and personal business dominates personal travel, including shopping, running errands and dropping off and picking up others; followed by social and recreational travel, with the commute to work as the third most frequent trip purpose (U.S. DOT, 11). Work-related trips account for less than 18 percent of trips and less than 23 percent of person-miles traveled. Not surprisingly, women make about two-thirds of all the weekday pickup and dropoff trips.

Psycho-social aspects of travel

The social dimensions of people's travel experiences as discussed previously are closely connected with our psychological responses. Traffic congestion has come to characterize the commuting, and much of the non-commuting, driving experience in our major metropolitan areas. While many drivers and passengers choose the automobile as their preferred mode of transportation, they decry the unpleasantness of the congested commute experience in no uncertain terms. It wastes time, costs money and raises stress levels. As we are now made acutely aware from daily news reports, stress can manifest itself not only in personal discomfort, but also in the publicly dangerous form of road rage and aggressive driving that raises safety risks for everyone. If ITS can enhance throughput and efficiency, it is argued, then an indirect benefit should be a reduction in overall stress levels among drivers. The availability of real-time, pre-trip and en-route traffic information offers travelers a measure of control over their travel experience, within the bounds of the flexibility of their work time requirements. Studies that have examined how drivers make choices when faced with unusual congestion and given the availability of timely information about the nature of the congestion indicate high proportions are willing to change some or all of their planned routes, the timing of their trip, or even postpone the trip to a different time. While ITS planners and proponents are hopeful that the net effects will include travel time savings, it is very hard to demonstrate whether this actually occurs. What does seem apparent is that drivers are more comfortable with good information than without, and many drivers are willing to trade off somewhat longer trip times for a possibly shorter trip time that also includes higher levels of uncertainty and greater stress. A related finding is that drivers prefer trip times that are predictable, rather than many trips that are shorter than normal with a lot of uncertainty about longer than normal trips mixed in. Interest in trip predictability is increasingly salient in business, as reflected in concepts such as just-in-time delivery, that is heavily dependent upon being able to predict how long each trip will take.

Opportunities and challenges

This chapter has provided a broad brush look at societal issues in transportation and some of the underlying social forces that help shape the environment in which we all engage in various forms of travel. Over the past several decades, some aspects of our transportation experience have improved and some have worsened. The automobile manufacturers are producing safer, more reliable vehicles now. Vehicle emissions are greatly reduced and cars can run free of maintenance for longer periods of time. But urban congestion is more pervasive in space and time, frustration levels with the transportation experience are generally greater, and we ask ourselves whether there is an end in sight to the effects of increasing demand for travel in the face of inadequate supply of facilities, both private and public, to accommodate the demand. Can we expect to be able to achieve sustainability in our transportation and communities that reflects a quality of life we desire and that we can expect to be enjoyed by future generations?

The good news is that there is some evidence that we are approaching saturation in levels of travel and that stabilization is occurring in such key trends as growth of licensed drivers and personal vehicle availability, suggesting exaggerated predictions of ever-increasing congestion and gridlock are overblown. However, the NPTS concludes "persons may be able to drive only one vehicle at a time, but it appears that they want to drive it more often and for longer distances" (U.S. DOT 1997, 1–48). While the NPTS analyses suggest that we may be approaching travel saturation, other social and economic factors also need to be considered. "Real income growth, changes in the relative cost of travel, roadway congestion levels, changes in the male's role regarding household travel responsibilities, and concepts such as telecommuting all may influence the timeframe for reaching saturation" (U.S. DOT 1997, 1–50). So while the jury is still out, the forces that have served for the past 50 years to exacerbate the adverse societal effects of road travel seem to be abating. This should offer us a measure of control over these effects, and ITS technologies provide many of the tools that can help.

ITS does not represent a radical departure from the historical evolutionary path of our automobile-based transportation system in this country. In that sense, ITS is not a new paradigm for travel, but it does represent a new way of thinking about how to address the societal issues raised by the constraints imposed on our current system—namely, the cost, land use and public acceptability issues associated with new roadway construction as a way of addressing increasing congestion and reduced access.

Success for ITS alone will not resolve the safety, congestion, energy and environmental or mobility problems we continue to face in our transportation systems. ITS represents an opportunity to squeeze new efficiencies out of an often inefficient transportation system, to increase predictability and smooth out some of the variability in traffic flows. But in the face of powerful economic, demographic and social forces pushing vehicle miles of travel higher and further concentrating vehicle use in our urban areas, coupled with equally strong fiscal and land use constraints, ITS may have limited, measurable[3] system performance effects. Ironically, the very gains in efficiency that are achieved may induce additional latent demand for travel that was heretofore held back by the perceived unpleasantness of congested travel. The societal benefits of ITS as discussed in this chapter will likely emerge as some of ITS's most valued benefits—a greater sense of control and predictability over the often chaotic urban driving experience, a better use of people's valuable time and a renewed sense of peace of mind brought by knowing that informed choices are now available through ATIS technologies.

ITS mostly offers new traffic system management improvements and creative demand management approaches. Strategies range from better information for drivers that can help them avoid adverse conditions, to information for transit riders that encourage mode shift. The Internet is being used more and more extensively as a way of providing up-to-the-minute travel information to computer users. Wireless communications, cable television, closed circuit television, handheld computers, automated telephone systems, autoPC, and in-vehicle navigation devices are all being introduced in the marketplace in an effort to help improve travel efficiency and to help reduce the stress of travel. At the same time, ITS technologies are improving the transportation system infrastructure, providing automated signal control, ramp metering, the capability to automate variable pricing structures, coordinated lane reversal strategies, and emergency and system management capabilities. New and somewhat exotic modes of transport are being considered that may substitute for longer distance driving, such as Maglev and other rapid rail. Automated highway systems for longer distances are possible, but they are not likely to be practical or widespread for quite a while. Coupled with technology solutions are policy strategies, such as urban growth management; transit-oriented development; neo-traditional urban designs that seek to collocate residences, places of work and shopping in order to reduce the need for vehicular travel; and congestion or value pricing that offer incentives for changes in travel behavior. Each of the technology and policy approaches has important social and behavioral dimensions. Public acceptance and willingness to pay for these solutions is critical to their ultimate success.

Many members of the ITS community acknowledge that societal aspects of ITS, and of transportation systems generally, are vitally important to the future success of ITS. We recognize that public and institutional acceptance lies at the foundation of our ability to market and implement ITS technologies. But these technologies are new, and public awareness of ITS is still limited. While it was recognized early on that the public sector, and in particular the federal government, would have to shoulder the major share of the burden to fund the early development and testing of ITS technologies in the market place, the future success of these programs will lie with the private sector's ability to invest and market ITS products to customers. It will also depend on state and local transportation planner's and policymaker's willingness to include ITS projects into their transportation plans and accord them a high enough funding priority. Finally, these agencies will need to bring the public on board. This will take active promotion and education, coupled with a public involvement approach to early deployment efforts, in order to achieve public buy-in and to better assure that the developers and implementers understand what the public wants out of ITS.

From a societal perspective, the challenges and opportunities are abundant. Private manufacturers are scrambling to bring to market traveler information and system integration products that will enjoy widespread customer acceptance. With many products just coming out of development and into the market place, competition to find the "breakthrough" products is intense. While early adopters are eager to experiment with innovative ITS products, the traveling public and many state and local transportation agencies are taking a wait-and-see approach, wary of new unproven ITS technologies. The diffusion of new technologies always takes time, but future ITS innovations that are sure to follow these early steps will diffuse more rapidly and become accepted more easily. We do not yet know whether and how much the public will be willing to pay. And when ITS use becomes widespread, we do not know how traveler behavior might be affected. Cell phones have allowed drivers trapped in today's ubiquitous urban congestion to be more productive. Will ITS have a similar effect? If ITS provides for better informed, less stressful travel, will that translate into system-wide travel time savings or congestion reduction? Maybe to some degree, but the social and psychological benefits of a more relaxed travel experience will likely predominate. What are the social characteristics of people and places that lead some areas to adopt ITS more readily and fully and others to lag way behind? More complete answers to these kinds of societal and behavioral questions will help shape the future course of ITS technologies and define their enduring benefits.

Acknowledgment

The author would like to thank Daniel Berler, Rob Puentes, Barbara Richardson and Y.B. Yim for reviewing this chapter and providing helpful comments.

References

American Public Transit Association. 1996. *Mobility for the 21st Century: A Blueprint for the Future* (October). APHA.

Albers, W. A., B. C. Richardson, P. F. Waller, and S. P. McAlinden. 1994. "Societal and Institutional Issues in IVHS Planning." Paper presented at the 1994 Society of Automotive Engineers Annual Congress and Exposition, Detroit.

Bernstein, S. 1993. "Imagining Equity: Using ISTEA and the Clean Air Act" (December). *Environment & Development.* American Planning Association.

Branch, K., D. A. Hooper, J. Thompson, and J. Creighton. 1984. *Guide to Social Assessment: A Framework for Assessing Social Change.* Social Impact Assessment Series, No. 11. Boulder, CO: Westview Press.

Burkhardt, J., and A. McGavock. 1999. "Tomorrow's Older Drivers: Who? How Many? What Impacts?" Paper presented at the Transportation Research Board, 78th Annual Meeting, Washington, D.C., January 10–14.

Durning, A. T. 1996. "The Car and the City: 24 Steps to Safe Streets and Healthy Communities" (April). *Northwest Environment Watch,* no. 3. Seattle, WA.

Johnson, E. W. 1993. *Avoiding the Collision of Cities and Cars: Urban Transportation Policy for the Twenty-first Century.* The American Academy of Arts and Sciences and The Aspen Institute.

Pisarski, A. E. 1992. *Travel Behavior Issues in the 90s* (July). Office of Highway Information Management, U.S. Department of Transportation.

Rosenbloom, S. 1995. "The Deployment of Intelligent Transportation Systems: Implications for Working Women and Elderly Travelers." Paper presented at the Alternative Futures Symposium on Transportation, Technology, and Society, Washington, D.C., March 13.

Richardson, B. C. 1995. "Societal Issues in Intelligent Transportation Systems: What Are They? Why Are They Important? What Can We Do About Them?" Paper presented at the ITS America Annual Meeting, Washington, D.C., March.

Richardson, B. C. 1994. "Socio-Economic Issues and Intelligent Transportation Systems." Paper presented at the National Policy Conference on Intelligent Transportation Systems and the Environment, Arlington, VA, June 6–7.

Richardson, B. C. 1993. *Symposia on Critical Issues in Traffic Safety.* Final report. American Iron and Steel Institute and the University of Michigan Transportation Research Institute.

Societal Implications Task Force. 1995. *The Alternative Futures Symposium on Transportation, Technology and Society* (May 30). Proceedings of a symposium sponsored by SITF, ITS America, Washington, D.C., March 13.

Transportation Research Board, National Research Council. 1997. *The Future Highway Transportation System and Society: Suggested Research on Impacts and Interactions.* Washington, D.C.: National Academy Press.

U.S. Department of Transportation, Federal Highway Administration. 1997. *Our Nation's Travel: 1995 NPTS Early Results Report* (September). U.S. DOT, FHWA.

U.S. Department of Transportation, Federal Highway Administration. 1996. *Community Impact Assessment: A Quick Reference for Transportation* (September). U.S. DOT, FHWA.

U.S. Department of Transportation. 1994. *Nontechnical Constraints and Barriers to Implementation of Intelligent Vehicle-Highway Systems* (June). A Report to Congress. U.S. DOT.

U.S. Department of Transportation, Federal Highway Administration. 1992. *1990 Nationwide Personal Transportation Survey: Summary of Travel Trends* (March). U.S. DOT, FHWA.

Van Hattum, D., and L. W. Munnich, Jr. 1994. "IVHS and Public Participation: Challenges, Opportunities and New Models for Cooperation." Paper presented at the National Policy Conference on Intelligent Transportation Systems and the Environment, Arlington, VA, June 6–7.

Wachs, M. and M. Crawford (Eds.). 1992. *The Car and the City: The Automobile, the Built Environment, and Daily Urban Life.* University of Michigan Press.

Waller, P. F. 1994a. "IVHS and Social Policy." Paper presented to IVHS America, 4th Annual Meeting, Atlanta, GA, April. Ann Arbor, MI: University of Michigan Transportation Research Institute.

Waller, P. F. 1994b. "The Social Costs of Transportation: Social and Community Impacts." Paper presented to the FHWA Colloquium on the Social Costs of Transportation, Washington, D.C., December.

Endnotes

1. Equity is a central concept that reflects the intent of the Transportation Equity Act for the 21st Century. Equity basically refers to fairness and justice (and not necessarily equality) in how costs and benefits are distributed across a population, which in the final analysis is a value judgment that usually gets addressed in a political context. Therefore, broad public participation in important transportation decisions is needed to assure that equity for all interested, or potentially affected, persons is adequately addressed. It is useful to consider the distribution of transportation's costs and benefits across members of society, over geographic space and over time across generations.

2. These societal changes, coupled with the special obligation of public-sector transportation organizations to serve the broad public interest, create a greater sense of salience of these issues for the public sector.

3. Measuring the system impacts of ITS, such as reductions in travel times, is fraught with difficulties, given the many factors other than ITS that also affect system performance and are difficult to control in the analysis.

BY James A. Bunch • Senior Principal,
ITS Planning • Mitretek Systems

ITS AND THE PLANNING PROCESS[1]

Introduction

As seen throughout this text, the implementation of intelligent transportation systems (ITS) provides an opportunity for significant improvements in transportation system efficiency, productivity, convenience and safety. These potential benefits, increasing constraints on expanding capacity and the federal shift from ITS research to ITS deployment through conventional funding channels all point to the need to integrate ITS into the overall transportation decision-making and planning process. Increasingly, ITS is also being seen as one of the prime elements in the operations and management (O&M) of transportation systems of the future.

Recognizing this, a number of pioneering regions and planning organizations have begun to incorporate ITS into parts of their planning processes (Mitretek 1999b, Deblasio et al. 1998, Siwek 1998, AMPO 1998). The federal government is also helping develop methods and techniques. Some highlights are:

- San Francisco's metropolitan planning organization (MPO), the Metropolitan Transportation Commission, has developed a regional management strategy supported by the Systems O&M Committee that focuses on management of the transportation system operations and uses ITS as a key component. System management is reflected in the region's overall goals and throughout its planning process (Dahms and Klein 1998).
- In Chicago, the Chicago Area Transportation Study has become a facilitator and coordinator between its myriad of operating agencies as well as the private sector. It established the Advanced Technology Task Force, which includes in its mission statement "to prepare a long-range vision and medium- and short-range plans ... for the development and integration of ITS in the transportation system serving Northeastern Illinois." The task force was responsible for the region's strategic early deployment plan for ITS (Zavattero and Smoliak 1996).
- In Washington D.C., the Metropolitan Washington Council of Governments (MWCOG) has developed a new vision, goals and objectives to "use the best available technology to maximize system effectiveness" (Meese 1998).
- Maricopa County (Phoenix), Arizona, has developed a mutlilayer approach to incorporate ITS into its programming and budgeting process for development of the Transportation Improvement Program (TIP). This process includes development of Candidate Assessment Reports, Design Concept Reports and TIP Design Projects (Fowler 2000).
- The state of Florida is in the process of finalizing its ITS Planning Guidelines Manual, providing a consistent set of procedures for incorporating ITS into plans across the state.
- The U.S. Department of Transportation (U.S. DOT) has developed and maintains an extensive web-accessible database of ITS benefits and costs and has funded the development of new tools for ITS assessment such as the ITS Deployment Analysis System (IDAS).

Despite the potential benefits and the pioneering efforts just discussed (as well as many others), there are still considerable challenges in mainstreaming ITS. The primary challenges include the conceptual and practical differences between ITS strategies aimed at the O&M of the transportation system and the conventional facility and service improvements aimed at capacity–system expansion, which have been the traditional focus of the planning process. Another hurdle that is often cited is the lack of data and techniques for predicting the benefits, costs and effects of ITS strategies versus traditional solutions and the difficulties with evaluating "integrated" alternatives. Finally, the differences in the traditional roles, professional knowledge and perspective, language and institutional responsibilities between the ITS operations and planning communities must also be overcome (Mitretek 1999b).

This chapter is concerned with how ITS strategies fit into the overall transportation planning and decision-making processes for an area to develop integrated solutions that best meet the area's goals and objectives: addressing traditional needs as well as emerging concerns. It places ITS decisions and project development in the broader context of overall transportation decision-making. It consequently takes a different perspective from the rest of the document. The goal of this chapter is not to promote ITS deployment. Rather, its goal is to describe how ITS may be included in the transportation decision-making process in the development of a balanced future system (including a mix of traditional, ITS and O&M elements and other policy decisions).

Transportation planning and decision-making: expanding the boundaries

In order to address ITS and O&M, the definition of transportation and decision-making must be expanded to support all transportation-related decisions that determine what the future transportation system will be, its characteristics and how it will operate. Thus, transportation planning and decision-making go beyond the federally defined transportation planning processes and its associated documentation requirements. Figure 26–1 illustrates the federal planning documentation process and some of the decision-making elements important to ITS that lie outside of them. Integrating ITS and other operational considerations into the planning process requires extending consideration beyond the federally defined transportation plan (long-range plan [LRP]), state transportation improvement programs (STIP and TIP), metropolitan transportation improvement programs, air quality conformity analysis, corridor studies and congestion management systems (CMS) and the projects they involve. Many, if not most, ITS projects emerge from locally funded decisions and systems and are not included in the federal, state or MPO planning process. Other projects may be advanced as short-term operational improvements and are perceived to be the prerogative of the owner or operator of the system. Increasingly, the private sector is also involved in providing ITS and other services critical to the performance of the transportation system.

Broadly defined, transportation planning involves all the components of the system—operational planning, public–private participation, locally funded decisions, communications system, day-to-day operations, maintenance and system management decisions and their effects. It no longer consists of capital and infrastructure projects only, but also addresses operating strategies and how they change the performance relationships of the transportation system itself. Transportation planning must now be concerned with the combined set of actions (infrastructure, ITS and O&M and policy) that best meet the region's goals and objectives in a cost-effective manner. The actions fall into three categories that interact:

1. managing transportation supply (transportation infrastructure and services and their operations),
2. managing travel demand (information, pricing, alternative modes, TDM policies), or
3. managing the environment (urban form, zoning, mixed-use incentives).

Figure 26–1. Transportation planning and decision-making.
Source: Mitretek (2000).

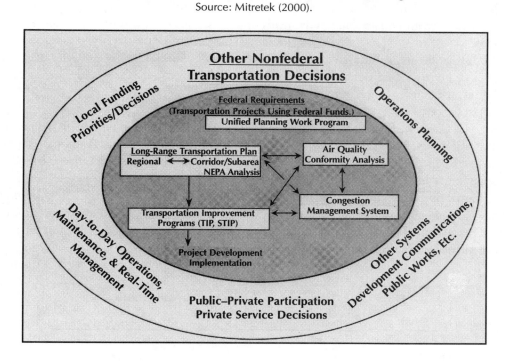

Each alternative definition is some combination of these three types of actions (see ITE 1998 for a more complete discussion). For example, congestion on a freeway can be reduced (at least temporarily) by adding additional capacity. It may also be addressed by a combination of demand (mode shift and pricing incentives) and land use policies. ITS can assist in directly managing both transportation supply and demand. It can also support policies that manage the environment and land use.

Also, more than ever, as ITS systems are implemented and integrated into the transportation system, the decisions made today affect the decisions that can be made tomorrow. Today's system operations and ITS enable what new systems may be built upon them. More importantly, they also change the operational relationships (e.g., capacity and delay associated with a specific traffic volume) and travel behavior, which then changes what infrastructure and other systems may be needed in the future. Consequently, planning and programming can no longer focus primarily on the long-range system and how it performs, assuming today's operating characteristics and relationships. Planning requires a new emphasis on determining the best development and operation paths for the future system.

The challenge: ITS and O&M versus traditional transportation improvements

Traditional solutions to transportation problems and the analyses that support them have tended to focus on long-term facility and service improvements to meet capacity constraints arising during a typical day. Because they focus on the peak congestion conditions and major infrastructure investments, these solutions and analyses have typically minimized or not addressed the following:

- The effect of operational strategies and improvements. Current operations are usually assumed.
- The effect of nonrecurrent demands, incidents, or other unusual occurrences. Major facilities are usually not designed to accommodate unusual demands or events. Analyses focus on meeting average conditions.
- Lack of information about the system, its current condition and the choices a traveler may have in making his or her trip. Traditional analyses assume equilibrium conditions where travelers fully know their choices, their travel times, costs and other characteristics.

In integrating ITS into transportation planning the conceptual and historic gap between operations and planning must also be overcome. This gap occurs along a number of dimensions including temporal, geographic scale and budgeting and funding. Figure 26–2 and table 26–1 highlight a number of these contrasts. Traditional operations issues and decisions are quick to implement (within a budget cycle), relatively low cost (within annual operating and maintenance budgets), usually independent with only localized impacts, passive (signage, fixed-signal timing, printed transit schedules) and assume that the transportation system infrastructure is constant. They have been procedure-oriented, aimed at operating the most efficient system in response to current conditions.

Figure 26–2. Traditional operations and planning versus ITS.
Source: Mitretek (2000).

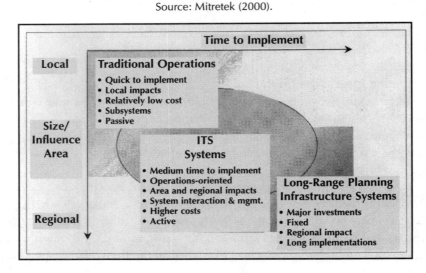

On the other hand, transportation planning decisions have been focused on expanding and modifying the facilities and services to meet long-term system performance and needs under average conditions, and they have been mostly project-oriented. The resultant projects typically assume the system will continue to operate as it does currently, are very costly with regional impacts both geographically and to the transportation system's operations and will take years to plan and implement. The planning process traditionally has been focused on meeting federal funding requirements and other regulations (e.g., CMS, TIP, LRP, National Environmental Protection Act [NEPA] and air quality conformity). Consequently, planning and operations decisions have been carried out in their own worlds with different perspectives, staff, policy makers, support organizations and time horizons.

ITS has characteristics of both traditional roles—operations and planning. ITS is both operations-oriented and aimed at managing the overall system. It usually takes several budget cycles to implement and may be

Table 26–1
Contrasts between ITS and O&M and Traditional Planning
Source: Mitretek (1999b).

	Traditional	ITS/Operations
Orientation	- Major capital facility (build/perserve) - "Build" - New capacity/service expansion - Solves, recurrent or "average" conditions - Aimed at capacity, LOS, and safety	- Systems operations & service provision - "Do" - Efficient Mgt & Op. of existing system - Response to variation in conditions - Solves different problems reliability, security, incident response
Temporal	- Problems of tommorow - Forecast driven - Long-term, multi year implementation - One time decisions - Static once in place - Fixed, predictable technology & characteristics	- Problems of today - Response to current conditions -Short term immediate implementation - Continuous, incremental - System evolves through feedback - Rapidy changing technology and characteristics
Costs /Funding	- Medium/high Major Capital Facility - Low/medium operations & maintenance - Federal aid context & requirements	- Low/medium Capital/infrastructure - Major life cycle operations costs - Often implmented using local funds
Implementors	- Public Agency - Const. ind., real estate, current users	- Public and private partnership - High tech. ind., small current constit.
Other Attributes	- Stand alone - Separable - Facility based - Low/medium technology - Capital, service improvements - Major construction - Visible & permanent	- Piggyback on other projects - Connected through communications - System based, core central systems - Advanced Technology - Non capital services, processes - Minor to no construction - Often hard to see

too expensive to fund through traditional operating budgets. It requires coordination and is not independent or separable. It may need cross-political and other jurisdictional boundaries to be effective. It begins to have "regionally significant" effects. Good system planning and coordination is therefore important to successful ITS implementation. ITS by its very nature is also active, with real-time feedback between performance measurement and O&M decisions. Thus, with the advent of ITS, bridging the gap between operations and planning becomes crucial.

The changing context of planning and decision-making towards mainstreaming ITS and O&M

New problems, new solutions

The environment within which transportation decisions are made has changed dramatically since the traditional planning process was developed 40 years ago. There is increasing recognition that "we cannot build our way out of congestion." Revolutionary advances in communications and technology will have large but unpredictable effects on transportation. Our concept of a transportation agency's role has changed—turning it from construction to service delivery. Transportation planning needs to adapt accordingly. Some of the more important issues are discussed in the following sections.

Growing and changing transportation demands

With growing economies, urban areas are facing continued rapid growth in travel over the next 20 or more years. Travel patterns are changing as well—suburb-to-suburb and off-peak travel are growing more rapidly than travel in general. It will be difficult to meet this demand with new infrastructure alone. Indeed, many transportation agencies acknowledge that there are limits to their ability to increase the capacity of the existing system because of:

- limited funding for capacity expansion;
- lack of available rights-of-way, making capacity expansion more costly and disruptive; and
- environmental concerns and public opposition to some projects.

Those who recognize these constraints understand that transportation agencies must pay greater attention to managing the existing system more effectively, in order to squeeze more mobility from existing system. ITS can provide a tool for managing existing resources more effectively.

Growing effects of disruptions

As congestion grows, the system is likely to become even more congested and fragile, subject to breakdown as incidents and other inevitable disruptions occur. These disruptions are now almost routine—causing over 50 percent of urban travel delay. Added to this is the continuing reconstruction and maintenance activities associated with the aging infrastructure.

Changing concerns of decision-makers and the public

State and local governments are being charged with finding new ways to deliver services more efficiently, focusing more on outcomes and less on inputs and outputs. These efforts stem in part from the pressure of budget deficits, but more broadly from a desire to make government more effective. Meanwhile, with growing uncertainty about the future—in part a result of the technological revolution—there is a natural inclination to make small incremental changes to the existing system rather than massive, costly and disruptive investments in new infrastructure. Long-range plans become less relevant in this environment. Planners are charged with helping decision-makers reach informed, short-term decisions while preserving options for the long term.

There is also growing interest in ensuring the safety of the transportation system. While capacity expansion is often justified in terms of safety improvements, there is a more immediate desire to make the system safer today, not years in the future.

New service attributes required

The service orientation of the U.S. economy is raising customer expectations—both passenger and freight—for a broader range of performance and service options. As society moves further into the information age, instant knowledge of the system and its conditions is becoming expected.

There is increasing evidence that travelers are willing to accept some level of congestion and delay, provided that this delay is reasonably predictable. This suggests the need to consider strategies that keep travelers informed, in real time, of how the system is performing at any given point in time. If such systems could be put in place, travelers will become less frustrated and more willing to accept the limits on the system.

Private-sector entry into transportation services

Private industry is increasingly offering transportation-related products and services. These range from privately owned and operated facilities to new technologies such as smart cards and in-vehicle information systems. These services and their effects need to be incorporated into—and perhaps facilitated by—the transportation decision-making process.

Summary of the history of ITS decision-making and planning

The development of ITS and its adoption into transportation decision-making and planning is an ongoing and evolutionary process. In large measure, ITS and operational decisions have occurred outside the federally mandated transportation planning process. In large part, ITS and operational decisions have generally been made by system owners and operators—state DOTs, transit operators, local jurisdictions, toll road and parking authorities and the like—as part of the day-to-day management of their systems. These efforts have typically been outside the federally mandated planning documentation (funded either locally or through special project funds). However, there is a growing history of incorporating ITS and system management issues into federal transportation planning. This is briefly discussed in the next section (Mitretek 1999b).

Pre-Intermodal Surface Transportation Efficiency Act

In the 1960s and 1970s there were at least two federal initiatives to try to bring system O&M decisions into the transportation planning process. The first of these was the TOPICS (Traffic Operations Improvements to Increase Capacity and Safety) program. In the mid-1970s, the Federal Highway Administration (FHWA) and Federal Transit Administration (FTA) issued regulations calling for the MPO to develop a transportation system management (TSM) element as part of their regional transportation plans.

While both the TOPICS program and TSM addressed real problems in cost-effective and coordinated ways, neither fulfilled its promise of integrating operations and planning. In reality, highway and transit operational improvements continued to be made as a part of each operating agency's "best business practices."

Intermodal Surface Transportation Efficiency Act

The pace of change accelerated greatly under the Intermodal Surface Transportation Efficiency Act of 1991 (ISTEA). Title VI, Part B of ISTEA (the Intelligent Vehicle-Highway Systems Act of 1991) established a national program "to research, develop and operationally test intelligent vehicle-highway systems and promote implementation of such systems…." The program is now called the "ITS program" to stress its multimodal nature.

Some of ISTEA's key features affecting planning and ITS—and the federal response to those ISTEA provisions—included the following:

- *Strengthened planning process.* Statewide transportation planning became a requirement and the role of MPOs was enhanced. A fiscal constraint requirement was established in metropolitan areas, helping to foster efforts to make better use of existing transportation systems.
- *Management systems.* ISTEA required the states to establish six "management systems" to improve O&M of the highway, transit and intermodal systems. (The management systems were later made voluntary.)
- *Major investment studies.* As part of the metropolitan planning regulations issued pursuant to ISTEA, FHWA and FTA required corridor level studies of transportation alternatives where major investments—such as significant increases in capacity or service—were deemed to be necessary to solve long-range transportation problems.
- *Dedicated funding for ITS.* ISTEA authorized $659 million over six years for ITS-related activities. At least $500 million of this authorization was to be used for an "Intelligent Vehicle Highway System Corridors Program" to develop and implement technology.
- *Early deployment planning.* To jumpstart ITS deployment, FHWA and FTA provided grants to state and local governments for the development of early deployment plans (EDPs). A five-step process tended to be followed for EDP development:

  1. Data collection and survey
  2. User services plan
  3. ITS architecture
  4. Strategic deployment plan
  5. Recommendations

With dedicated funding for deployment and EDP development in place, the federally mandated planning process associated with the normal federal-aid highway and transit programs was viewed by many ITS advocates as being largely irrelevant to ITS. Getting ITS strategies adopted as a part of metropolitan and statewide plans and programs was seen as merely a procedural step that had to be satisfied before funds could be released for ITS deployment. The real decisions on ITS occurred outside the traditional planning process. A review of the EDP planning process stated: "The Early Deployment Program is a first step in the necessary planning for a well-integrated regional ITS. ...It is also clear that planning for ITS as a standalone effort is of limited effectiveness. ITS planning should be integrated within the traditional regional transportation planning framework" (Smith et. al. 1995).

- *Technical methods.* U.S. DOT concurrently has undertaken significant research and development activities to produce the necessary tools for planning ITS and incorporating ITS into more traditional planning. The Travel Model Improvement Program and the Transportation Analysis and Simulation System (TRANSIMS) effort, for example, are developing a new generation of demand models with the capability to estimate the benefits of ITS. A number of manuals have been produced on ITS and planning.
- *Mainstreaming.* As the ISTEA authorization period drew to a close, U.S. DOT recommended that special funding for ITS be discontinued and that ITS be "mainstreamed" into the normal federal aid program structure.

While these activities were occurring at the federal level, very real progress was continuing at the state and local level to plan and deploy ITS. A number of metropolitan areas established task forces and other mechanisms to improve the coordination between long-range facility planning and operations planning and between the disparate operations planning of different modes and jurisdictions. ITS strategies are being considered as part of long-range planning studies. Planning goals and objectives are being broadened to include operational considerations. Nevertheless, the overall integration of planning and ITS still is the exception rather than the rule.

Transportation Efficiency Act for the 21st Century

The Transportation Efficiency Act for the 21st Century (TEA-21), enacted in 1998, continued and built upon the ITS programs from ISTEA while seeking to mainstream ITS into the normal federal-aid programs. Key features of TEA-21 include:

- *Emphasized O&M planning.* O&M was highlighted as one of the seven planning factors to be considered at both the statewide and metropolitan levels.
- *Consistency with the national ITS architecture.* TEA-21 requires federally funded ITS projects to be consistent with the national ITS architecture and with applicable standards and protocols. FHWA and FTA issued interim guidance in October 1998.

O&M planning factor

TEA-21 consolidated the issues that must be considered in local and statewide transportation planning[2] for federal funding into seven broad factors. It added and emphasized the following O&M factor: "f) promote efficient system O&M."

This factor continues a long-term policy trend towards promoting efficient management of the nation's transportation system. Work is currently under way to develop rules and guidance to build O&M orientation into both the planning and project development processes with the appropriate documentation to accommodate federal oversight. At a minimum, this continued shift towards O&M moves the emphasis in the planning process from long-range needs to a more balanced approach incorporating short- and mid-term needs and their decisions and effects. More information on the O&M activities can be found at the FHWA Operations website, <http://ops.fhwa.dot.gov>, and at the Systems Management and Planning website, <http://plan2op.fhwa.dot.gov>.

Based on these developments there is a growing understanding of what consideration of the O&M planning factor in transportation planning means. Consequently, while the details of the final O&M guidance are still being developed, the characteristics of a process that considers O&M can be highlighted:

- Consideration of efficient O&M of the transportation system in regional goals and objectives found at all levels of the process.
- Expansion of the participants in the process to include those that operate the system and others interested in and affected by the O&M of the transportation network. These include the traffic and transit system operators, emergency service and police, fire and communications representatives, as well as the private service providers of ITS and other services.
- Orientation towards service delivery and performance feedback as a central feature of the process.
- Explicit definition of how the system operates in the short, medium and long range including the relationships between congestion and system performance and response to nonrecurrent "events" such as accidents, weather conditions or service disruptions.
- Consideration of the full life cycle costs and benefits of each element of the transportation system including the costs of implementation, operations and maintenance or preservation.
- Balance the near-term management of the system and time stream of operations improvements with longer term capital investments and system expansion.

ITS becomes a central element in the O&M of the future transportation system because it provides for the identification of changing conditions (surveillance), communication (information) and response (control) as the conditions vary. The collection and analysis of ITS data also provides for the critical feedback from current operations to planning and the definition of the future system, its operations and performance.

Regional consistency with the national ITS architecture

TEA-21 also requires ITS projects funded with Highway Trust Fund dollars to conform to the national ITS architecture and standards.[3] As the ITS program moves into the deployment phase, major steps are being taken to facilitate national compatibility and interoperability. As discussed in chapter 19, the national ITS architecture is a common framework for the design and implementation of ITS. The architecture consistency[4] policy development aims to integrate these systems engineering tools (architecture and standards) with the transportation planning and project development processes. The U.S. DOT has developed both an Interim Guidance and a Draft Final Policy to implement the legislation. The Interim Guidance reflects comments from the transportation industry including federal, state, local and private sector transportation stakeholders.

The Interim Guidance is "guidance" and not a final rule; it therefore focuses on recommendations and not requirements. It has two main components: (1) planning level and (2) ITS project level recommendations and requirements. Planning level considerations are recommendations that should be followed. At the project level, ITS projects that affect regional integration must (shall) be evaluated for architecture consistency and institutional and technical integration. A "recommended approach" is also provided in the Interim Guidance as a way of meeting its requirements.

Planning level

The Interim Guidance Section IV.B concerning "ITS Considerations in Transportation Planning" states the following:

> Statewide and metropolitan planning activities should include consideration of the efficient O&M of the transportation system. This should include the regional implementation and integration of ITS ser-

vices and development of a regional ITS architecture(s), as appropriate. Regional consideration of ITS should address:

(a) the integration of ITS systems and components,
(b) inclusion of a wide range of stakeholders,
(c) flexibility in tailoring ITS deployment and operations to local needs,
(d) electronic information sharing between stakeholders and
(e) future ITS expansion.

A recommended approach that lays the ground work for the Final Policy on ITS and planning considerations is also provided as part of the Interim Guidance.

Project level
Transit ITS projects may either be "ITS projects that affect regional integration" or "other ITS projects." Once a project is determined to affect regional integration, it must be evaluated for institutional and technical integration with transportation systems and services within the region, and consistency with the applicable regional ITS architecture and national ITS architecture. Based on the evaluation, recipients must take appropriate actions to ensure the project development:

(a) engages a wide range of stakeholders,
(b) enables the appropriate electronic information,
(c) facilitates future ITS expansion and
(d) considers the use of applicable ITS standards.

While ITS projects that do not affect regional integration do not have to be evaluated, it is recommended that the same processes be followed.

The Interim Guidance remains in effect until the Final Policy is adopted. It is anticipated that the Final Policy will be adopted in late 2000 or early 2001. More information on the Interim Guidance is available at the ITS website, <http://www.its.dot.gov/aconform/aconform.htm>.

The Draft Final Program Architecture Consistency was released in the *Federal Register* on May 26, 2000. Planning level consistency is addressed in an update of the FHWA and FTA Joint Planning Rule. Project level consistency is addressed by the FHWA in the ITS Architecture and Standards Rule and by the FTA through the *Federal Register* request for comment. A few important points are discussed in table 26–2. Keep in mind that these points may become outdated as changes are made in response to comments.

Evolving framework for the planning and decision-making process, and ITS and O&M

An integrated process is one where ITS and O&M strategies are considered on an equal basis with traditional elements of the transportation system. As seen from the previous discussion, however, developing an integrated process is much more than simply merging ITS options in the traditional planning process. It requires that both the traditional planning process and the ITS deployment process evolve. An integrated process must (Mitretek 2000):

• include ITS, O&M, system preservation and infrastructure and capital expansion tradeoffs in a single process;

Table 26–2
Major Points of the Draft Final Policy on National ITS Architecture Consistency
Source: Summarized from Mitretek (2000).

- Focus is at both the planning and project stages.
- Policy would be phased in over time.
- At the planning level, the metropolitan and statewide planning processes shall include the development of an ITS integration strategy. The ITS integration strategy shall be documented within the transportation plan and shall:
  — include participation of multiple stakeholders including operating agencies, transit, highway and public safety and motor carrier agencies as appropriate;
  — identify existing and future ITS systems planned by relevant stakeholders in a region;
  — define key system functions and information sharing between participants;
  — include roles and responsibilities for developing, operating and managing all components of the system;
  — include a policy agreement on interoperability, standards and operations; and
  — identify major ITS projects, regional ITS initiatives and projects that affect national interoperability.
- The ITS integration strategy shall also assist in meeting the metropolitan and statewide goals and objectives found within the planning process and use the national ITS architecture as a resource for its development.
- At the project level an ITS regional architecture shall be developed for implementing the ITS integration strategy and guide the development of specific projects and programs. For significant regional projects it shall include:
  — concept of operations addressing the roles, responsibilities and agreements for operations and funding to support the effort; and
  — conceptual design describing the system function requirements, interface and information exchange requirements, key standards used and a prioritization and phasing of the steps for implementation.
- ITS projects must also be developed through a systems engineering process and show a clear linkage to the ITS integration strategy.
- ITS projects shall use ITS standards that have been adopted by the U.S. DOT through rulemaking.
- ITS projects should use existing standards that are tested.

- incorporate the performance of the system in both average and unusual conditions in the decision-making process, and include the continual performance feedback and re-alignment of the system as time moves forward;
- balance the near-term management of the system to meet ongoing operational issues and concerns with long-term regional objectives;
- account for the system orientation and interconnectivity of ITS and other operational strategies as well as localized impacts;
- be incremental and address the path of development, life cycle and development cycles of both operations and ITS (primarily) near-term to mid-term and long-term system expansion and needs;
- account for rapid technological development and penetration; and
- address the effect of private-sector provision of ITS services.

As planning and decision-making evolves into an integrated planning process it must change in three key ways:

• new orientation on path of development from near-term to far-term,
• incorporate new components needed for ITS and O&M and
• merge traditional and ITS deployment planning functions

New orientation on path of development, near-term to far-term

Foremost in evolving into a new integrated process is bridging the gap between ITS and O&M and infrastructure planning in their focus on different timeframes and system feedback. Figure 26–3 provides a comparison between traditional planning focused on the long range and the integrated planning process aimed at defining a development path and time stream of actions. Planning has typically focused on major investment decisions and the long-range "snapshot" of the infrastructure and transportation services (e.g., transit routes and frequencies) for the horizon year. Often, supporting policies and programs needed to implement the alternative are also included in the definition (e.g., transit-supportive zoning and mixed-use development requirements around transit stations). Typically, only the single horizon year forecasts and analysis are carried out, and all operating characteristics and policies are implicitly assumed to remain constant.

Introducing ITS and active management and performance feedback into transportation planning bridges the gaps between the ITS operations and planning, and it transforms what alternatives are and how they are created. First, because continuous performance feedback can actually change what is feasible or possible in the future, the full incremental development path should be defined. Figure 26–3 shows the effect of this feedback on the development path. Active management of the system allows the system to be adjusted for efficiency and effectiveness at each point in time. As performance monitoring takes place, incremental changes can be made to the transportation system and its O&M. This in turn alters the range of possible alternatives to consider and may alter travel patterns, land use and nonrecurrent conditions, which in turn alters the needs and deficiencies as time goes on. The result is likely to be a future system that is much different than the one derived from the traditional planning process.

This new focus on system performance and the ability to alter it changes how the system develops and leads to the new iterative process shown in figure 26–4. Features of this process include:

• System performance is continuously assessed against goals, objectives and criteria.
• It is based on the feedback cycle of operations, measurement and assessment (operations planning). It is much more focused on the problems of today and managing, preserving and operating the current system and its assets.
• Problems that cannot be solved through management of the system are carried forward to the next timeframe and set of decisions. Mid-term decisions become much more important. If mid-term resources and management are not an answer, long-term solutions and infrastructure changes are examined.
• It assumes continual communication and feedback between each timeframe. Long-range and regional visioning and planning sets goals and objectives that provide the context for the shorter timeframe decisions.
• At the same time, operations goals and objectives and estimates of system performance must come from the operations world to the planning world. At each stage of development the principles of operations (how the system will operate) and the operating performance characteristics must be assessed and incorporated into the system plans.

Figure 26–3. Conceptual comparison of traditional and integrated planning.
Source: Mitretek (2000).

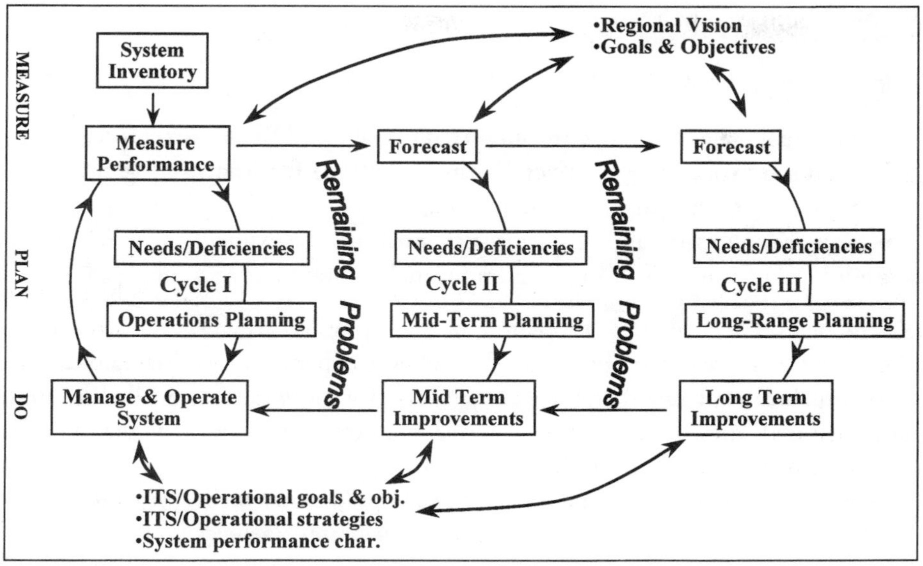

Figure 26–4. Cycles in the integrated planning process.
Source: Mitretek (2000).

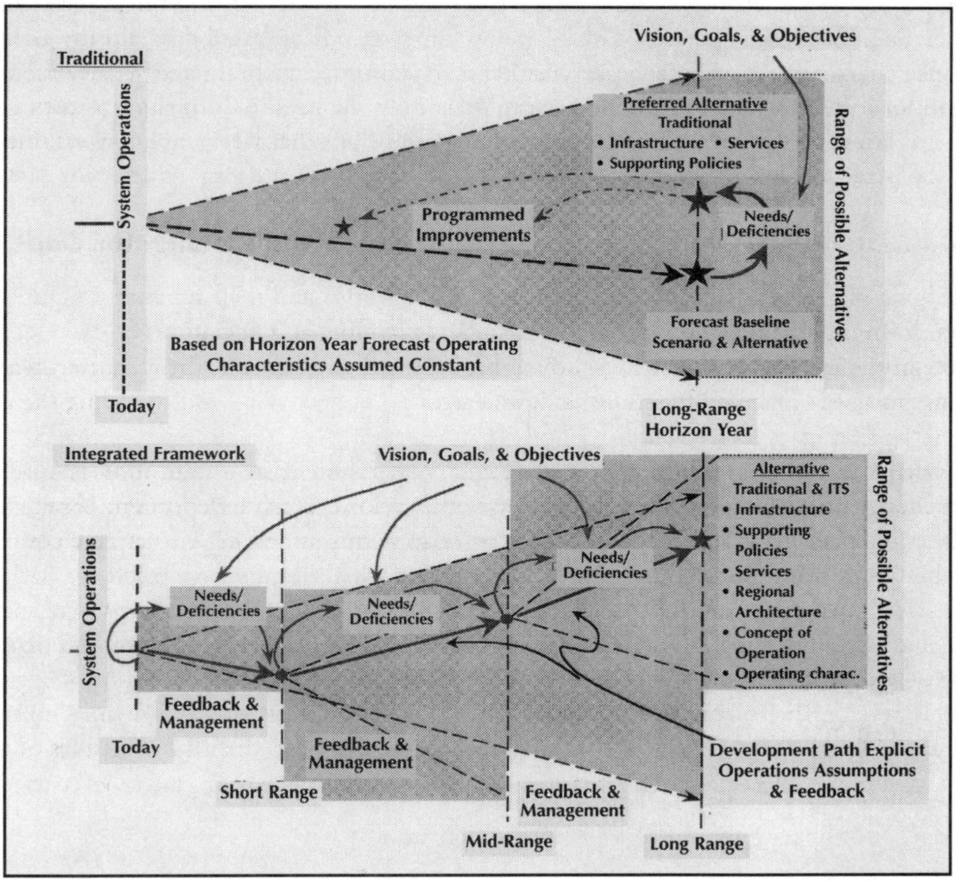

- It is incremental and based on a time path of choices.
- The process identifies not only a horizon year system, but also shows how that system will evolve and function during the intervening years.

Incorporate new components needed for ITS and O&M

As also shown in figure 26–3, planning now includes traditional and ITS infrastructure and transportation service components and their supporting policies. With the advent of ITS, operating characteristics within the transportation network are changing and regional "management" of the system is becoming possible. Consequently, operating assumptions and characteristics must now be explicitly addressed, and planning now encompasses adding ITS and O&M into the traditional components and the development of the following:

- *Regional architecture (data flows and functions).* ITS services depend on the flow and use of information to and from surveillance in the field, control centers, control mechanisms and the field and the public. A regional architecture specifies the information flows, subsystems and functions that are necessary to implement the desired services (both traditional and ITS).
- *Concept of operations including public–private assumptions (who is responsible for what).* The concept of operations addresses the roles and responsibilities of participating agencies (and departments if deemed necessary) in order to implement, operate and maintain the desired transportation system (both ITS and traditional components). It includes the necessary agreements between parties as well as the allocation of resource and cost responsibilities. It also includes the roles of the public and private sector.
- *Operating principals and characteristics (how the system will perform).* Explicit assumptions regarding the operating principals and characteristics of the system and how it will perform under different conditions must be made for each time period. With ITS, how the system is operated now directly affects these performance characteristics. For example, whether a system uses uncoordinated versus coordinated signals and how the coordination takes place can drastically change the throughput speeds at the same volumes and hours on arterials. Thus, performance relationships that were implicitly assumed must now explicitly be made to capture the predicted changes in ITS and other decisions affecting operations.

Merging of the traditional and operations, ITS deployment planning functions

Last is the merging of the traditional and operations and ITS worlds and their functions. Figure 26–5 shows this transition: from the current state-of-the-practice where planning and operations co-exist separately, to the state-of-the-art where ITS deployment planning begins to take on some of the characteristics of traditional planning, to a set of merged functions and processes.

A traditional barrier in communications, perspective and cooperation exists in transition phase I. Often, the only real interchange between the planning and operations worlds is each's independent observation of the system. Planners observe and validate their processes to existing operations. Operators take the infrastructure and services that result from the planning process and operate what they are responsible for within it.

In transition phase II, pioneering and state-of-the-art processes have begun to carry out ITS deployment planning. Steps in a typical ITS deployment planning process are:

- Stakeholder identification
- Needs and deficiencies analysis
- Select user services and develop ITS concepts plan
- Define concept of operations and regional integration strategy

Figure 26–5. Transition phases toward the integrated process.
Source: Mitretek (2000).

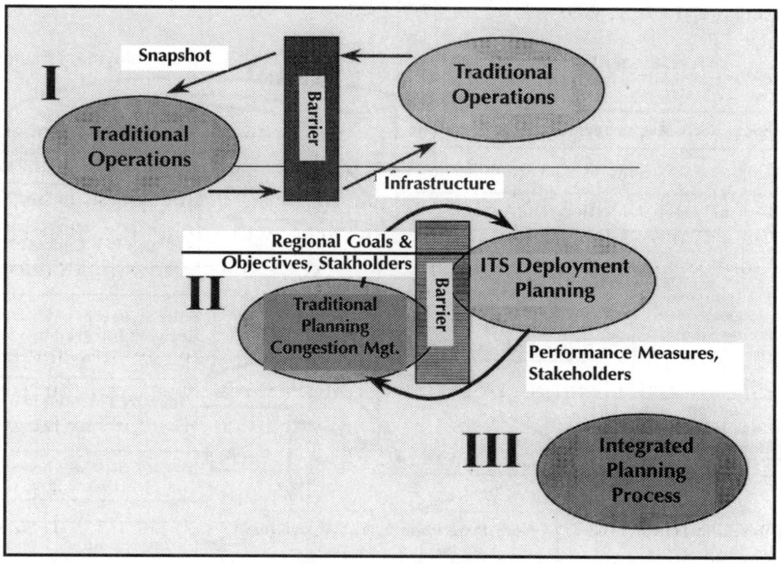

- Identify potential projects
- O&M planning
- Implement, operate, monitor and evaluate
- Feedback

This by its very nature has had to begin to address the issues raised by ITS and O&M bridging the operations and planning worlds. Because of the timeframe and budgets required to implement ITS, a new emphasis on the mid-term system is generated. Because of the system-wide nature of ITS, coordination begins to occur between operators and system performance is incorporated into the operations decisions (i.e., system-wide management versus operating individual components). The developing ITS deployment process stresses this "coordination" and "integration" among ITS stakeholders and operators (see the Professional Capacity Building Program course notes in NHI 1998).

The importance of being consistent with the regional planning process goals and objectives is also recognized, and as shown in the figure these are incorporated into the analysis. However, this communication is often only one way. Regional goals and objectives are used to develop the ITS strategies for deployment. O&M goals are rarely fed back into the overall planning process, nor are combined ITS, management and infrastructure options and their tradeoffs examined. In addition, a number of links between the two processes are needed for their integration. These are shown in figure 26–6.

Lastly, in transition phase III the links are made between ITS and traditional planning, and the functions are merged. Figure 26–7 shows these integrated functions and some of the technical and process issues that each must address. These functions and how they are carried out in the integrated planning process are examined briefly in the next two sections.

Figure 26–6. Links needed between traditional and ITS deployment planning.
Source: Mitretek (2000).

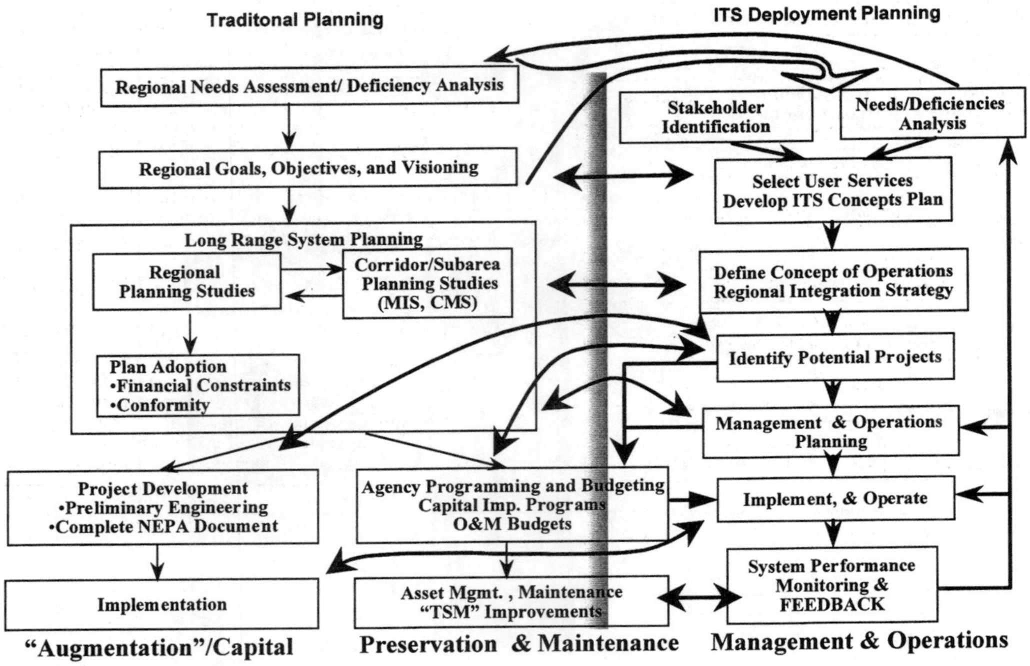

Developing a regional structure for integrated decision-making: institutional and organizational issues

Institutional roles and coordination, legal issues and new ways people will come together to provide services all affect how ITS and O&M may be integrated into transportation planning and decision-making. In fact, the institutional and organizational issues may be much harder to overcome than the technical. Re-orienting institutions from capital construction and maintenance to ongoing O&M is discussed at length in another chapter of this text. This section therefore focuses on the institutional and organizational issues associated with planning and resource allocation for the future. Figure 26–7 shows five components associated with institutional and organizing issues and organizing for integrated planning: stakeholder identification, institutional relationships, public–private roles, ways to organize and concept of planning.

Stakeholder identification

Expanding the stakeholders to include ITS and operations providers has been discussed. This must continue to combine the stakeholders from traditional planning with ITS and operations as well as users, communications providers and nontransportation entities. ITS providers and operators need to become part of the planning process and provide representatives to the MPO and its committees. Likewise, new constituencies concerned with the operation of the transportation system need to be brought in.

Figure 26–7. Integrated planning functions.
Source: Mitretek (2000).

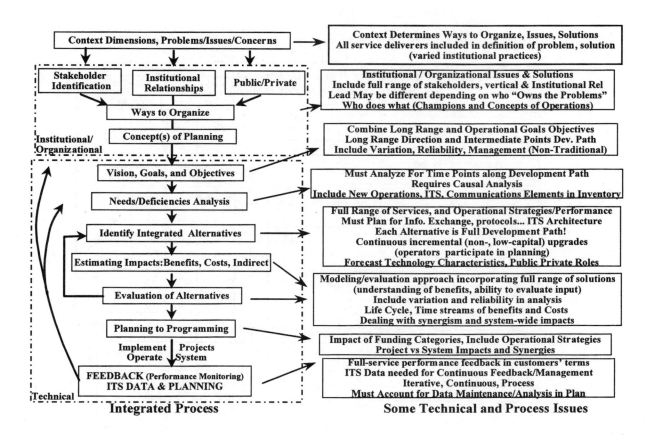

As potential ITS user services are identified, specific agencies and groups may also need to be contacted and brought into the decision-making process. Table 26–3 provides an initial screening by category of ITS user service of stakeholders that may have interest (See Ertico 1998 and Transcore 1998 for additional stakeholder lists).

Institutional relationships

It is difficult to bring in new actors and participants. One must show them why they should participate and the interconnections to their goals and objectives. New institutional relationships must be forged to merge traditional planning with ITS and operations. These include the vertical relationships within agencies as well as the horizontal ones across agencies. Internally, institutions must re-orient from capital versus operational structures that tend to promote "building" the infrastructure. Externally, MPOs and other planning organizations must adopt operational and continual time-stream planning, and operations must learn to understand the long term.

Vertically, cooperation between state and local government and regional agencies has always characterized regional planning and programming and, in some instances, actual service provisions (transit authorities).

The concept of integrated operations emphasizes vertical interdependence. Much of the promise of advanced traffic management, for example, depends on integrated freeway and arterial operations that require close cooperation between state DOTs and local governments.

Table 26–3
Initial Identification of Stakeholders for Various ITS User Services
Source: Cambridge Systematics (1998).

Potential Stakeholders	ATMS	ATIS	APTS	EMC	AVC	EPS	CVO	RR
Federal Transportation Agencies	o	o	o	o	o	o	o	o
Federal Environmental Agencies	o	o			o			
FDOT	X	o	o	o	o	o	X	X
MPOs	X	X	X	o	o	o	o	X
Local Transportation Agencies	X	X	X	o	o	o	o	X
Transit Operators	o	o	X	o	o	X		o
Police Departments	o		o	X			X	o
Fire Departments	o			X			o	
Emergency Management	o			X				
Toll Agencies						X		
Public Health Agencies	o			o				
Motorists	X	o		o	X	X	o	X
Transit Riders	o	o	X	o		X		
Bicyclist/Pedestrians	o	o	o	o				o
Private Paratransit Services	o	o	X			o		
CVO	o					o	X	
Motorist/Transit Rider Assoc.	o	o	X	o	X	X	o	o
CVO Industry Groups	o					o	X	
Traffic Reporting Services	X		o					
Major Traffic Generators	o	X	o				o	
Private Industry	o	o	o	o	X	o	o	X
Key: X Primary Participant				o Secondary Participant				

Horizontal cooperation refers to the need for transportation agencies and other transportation-related service providers (such as law enforcement and emergency services) to move towards closer cooperation. The existing degree of independence and differences in motives can place an absolute cap on the ability to improve certain key transportation services. At the same time, improved joint response to roadway incidents and the opportunity to share information and communication infrastructure provides motives for collocation, joint program development and shared policies among transportation and nontransportation agencies, both of which may have on-system responsibilities.

Public–private roles and planning

The private sector must be included in the decision-making process to develop lasting concepts of operations. A conscience analysis must be made to decide on the role of the private sector within the new relationships. What should the public's position be on private-sector provision of public services?

New relationships are also needed with private-sector players who act as providers of services or ITS infrastructure on a commercial basis. There is already a range of experience with informal relationships between private service providers and various state and local transportation agencies, particularly in the traveler information and incident response area. A new challenge to planning could emerge as private-sector players take on increasingly important roles in the delivery of ITS services, such as in-car information and safety services requiring integration with infrastructure or public information.

If public–private partnering is to be successful, these perspectives must be overcome and both parties must come to a mutual understanding of the role that they play. They must develop (Bower 1999):

- Shared goals
- Trust
- Understanding of the partnership
- Flexibility
- Shared risk

There is relatively little experience in how to integrate coordinated private-sector service delivery into a public institutional service delivery process. Issues associated with private-sector partnership are becoming better understood but still need to be further explored. These relationships are discussed in chapter 24.

Ways to organize

How to organize the integrated process depends on an area's context, jurisdictions, problems, issues and existing institutional roles. The MPO does not necessarily have to be the leader for all components or functions of the system such as ITS or operations.
Much of the literature and parallel research focus on MPO-centric models of planning that support the federal process. In fact, several other approaches exist and may be more appropriate under different conditions (Mitretek 1999b), such as:

- Standalone single agency and implementer planning and implementation
- MPO-centric coordination
- State-centric coordination
- New regional operations organization

TRANSCOM in the New York and New Jersey regions is an example of an ad hoc organization that helps manage the transportation system and crosses both state and MPO boundaries. Houston's Transtar is a similar organization (see Brigs 1999 for a complete discussion). Recently, Dallas, Texas, has also created a unique organization of organizations (the North Texas Regional Comprehensive ITS Program spearheaded by Dallas Area Rapid Transit) to coordinate over nine different ITS strategic plans and programs that have been developing in the region.

Which structure to choose for planning depends largely on an area's local context, history and the issues that it faces. Rural areas will likely be incorporated into the state plans and also may need to participate in interurban corridor organizations such as the I-95 Coalition. A new organization that focuses on ITS and systems operations is likely to form if the boundaries of the existing operating and planning organizations do not match the impact area and need for coordination of the transportation system and ITS services. An MPO or existing operating agency in coordination with the MPO may lead the technical development of ITS where their areas match the system boundaries. Technical expertise and resources to develop and update the ITS and operations strategies must also exist within the lead organization.

Concept(s) of planning

The concept of planning is to decision-making what the concept of operations is to maintaining and operating the overall system. It defines the relationships and responsibilities required to carry out the integrated planning process as it evolves. Therefore, it recognizes that institutional arrangements and levels of cooperation also evolve over time in response to the changing system. Elements of the concept of planning include:

- Identification of roles and responsibilities for the new components of planning (e.g., integration strategy, regional architecture, operations characteristics).
- Identification of new organizational structures and relationships that may be needed to match geographic and modal leadership to the problem and impact area of the system and its operations.
- Memorandum of understanding and other agreements on both the decision implementing and operating responsibilities for the system.
- Development path of institutional arrangements and planning and operating roles.

A key factor in creating the concept of planning is matching the leadership and responsibilities for each function to the problems and primary ownership. The participants must see and understand what cooperation and integration will bring them. Also, as the development path of the transportation system evolves so should the decision-making and other organizations that support it. No transformation occurs overnight. Therefore, an incremental organizational path and plan should be developed to match the changes in the system.

Technical functions in integrating ITS and transportation planning

This section provides a brief discussion on each of the technical functions in the integrated planning process described earlier. These include:

- Defining goals, objectives and measures of effectiveness
- Analyzing existing conditions and system performance
- Identifying integrated alternatives
- Estimating the costs, benefits and effects of these alternatives
- Evaluating the alternatives
- Programming and budgeting the development path
- Providing feedback and the role of ITS data

Each of these and how they need to evolve in the integrated planning process is discussed next. However, prior to the discussion of each function, a number of crosscutting issues and concepts that affect all of the functions are examined.

Crosscutting technical issues

There are three over-arching technical issues that affect the integrated planning process at all levels: (1) architecture, (2) geographic scale and (3) timeframe. ITS depends on communication and the interplay between a number of electronic devices and protocols if it is to function at all. Therefore, there are a number of different components such as the communications backbone that are necessary to provide ITS, but they provide no direct service to the transportation system or traveler. More importantly, a systems architecture is needed to ensure that the system will function once it is implemented. In addition, planning can occur at a number of different geographic scales—from the project and site level, to a corridor, metropolitan, or interurban level (figures 26–8 and 26–9).

Figure 26–8. ITS architecture components.
Source: Mitretek (2000).

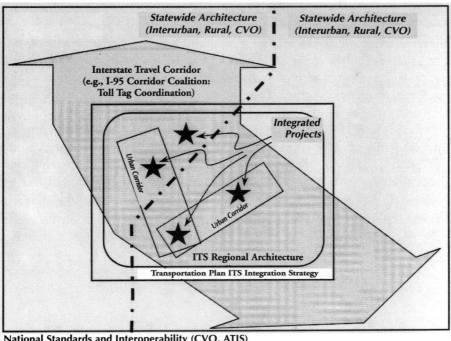

Figure 26–9. Physical architecture (transportation and communication layers).
Source: U.S. Department of Transportation (1999).

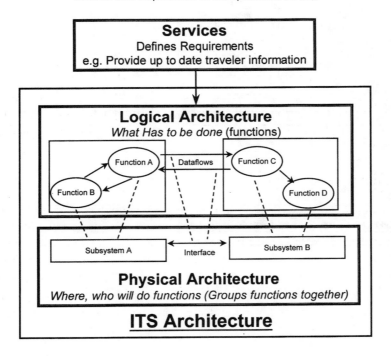

Each ITS user service has both localized and system impacts. The relationship between the two shared resources and the need for future coordination all determine the logical geographic scale for planning each service and component. For example, ramp meters each have very localized impacts that control the entry to the freeway at their location. They may even cause traffic to divert to local streets. However, their primary function is to provide corridor-wide freeway control minimizing conflicts at entry and avoid congestion due to excessive traffic at downstream locations. If they are controlled at a traffic management center (TMC), they may also need to be coordinated with other corridors to provide savings in the shared use of central systems (and staff) and system-wide integration. They should be planned, therefore, at the corridor or region-wide level.

Table 26–4 lists the categories of ITS strategies, based on the national ITS architecture and the geographical scales at which these strategies are most likely to be considered as alternatives in planning. Strategies that are planned at one geographic scale may be implemented incrementally, starting with a smaller geographic area, perhaps on a pilot basis. In such cases it is important that the initial project be compatible with the larger system that is envisioned for the long term.

Table 26–4
ITS Strategies and Geographical Scale Of Planning
Source: Mitretek (2000).

	Public/ Private	National	Statewide	Metropolitan/ Regional	Corridor/ Subarea	Municipality/ Local Government	Project
Remote Access							
Remote Traveler Support	Public/Private	X	X	X			
Personal Information Access	Private						
Centers							
Information Service Provider	Public/Private		X	X			
Traffic Management	Public		X	X	X	X	X
Emissions Management	Public		X	X			
Emergency Management	Public			X	X	X	
Transit Management	Public/Private			X		X	
Toll Administration	Public/Private		X	X	X		X
Fleet and Freight Management	Public/Private		X	X		X	
Commercial Vehicle Admin.	Private	X	X				
Vehicles							
Vehicle	Private	X	X				
Transit	Public/Private			X		X	
Commercial	Private	X	X				
Emergency	Private			X		X	
Roadside							
Roadway	Public		X	X	X	X	X
Toll Collection	Public/Private		X	X	X	X	X
Parking Management	Public/Private			X		X	
Commercial Vehicle Check	Public	X	X				

It is important to also mention that systems and their architectures nest at each geographic level. Figure 26–10 provides an illustration of how higher level requirements from national, interstate or statewide ITS architectures may influence the development of regional plans (or vice-versa) in order to ensure interoperability or exchange of information. Figure 26–10 also illustrates how project and corridor level architectures and alternatives interact. One important part of ITS architecture development at all levels of detail is to examine how geographically separate projects and corridors may need to be coordinated for sharing of information or ITS services. If the ITS projects in the figure were traffic signal systems for example, and if their coordination was not considered during implementation, then it is likely that they would not be able to communicate or coordinate within the urban corridors or the region.

Figure 26–10. Geographic intercoordination of ITS services and architecture.
Source: U.S. Department of Transportation (1999).

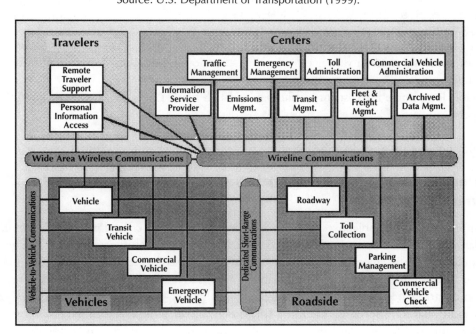

Timeframes and uncertainty

Decision-making is also carried out for different time periods—short, medium and long—which in the past have often been independent. The gap in time perspectives between traditional planning and ITS and O&M is one of the main challenges that must be overcome in integrating the two. Major capital investments take many years to plan, design and construct, so a long planning horizon is appropriate. Shorter timeframe ITS and O&M decisions provided a host of low capital and operational opportunities that long-range planning studies may overlook. While low cost and operational improvements may not be the solution in the long term, they may offer more immediate benefits. Ideally, the planning process will lead to decisions on a time stream of staged improvements that correspond to changes in travel and technology over time. Consequently, the integrated process evolves from focusing on a single (or set of) horizon year(s) to focusing on the time stream of actions. However focusing on the complete development path also presents challenges.

Tradeoffs between short- and long-term decisions along the development path or alternative development must be evaluated in the planning process. This calls for determining the time stream of benefits and costs and discounting future impacts to their present worth. Discounting must account for the time-value of money and the uncertainty of future benefits as well.

Incremental improvements along the path and their impacts on travel behavior and system performance must also be "fed back" into the analysis of the future system. This requires incremental forecasting and evaluation, which increases the burden of already overloaded staffs.

Lastly, uncertainty is inherent in any forecast and the uncertainty becomes greater the further in the future one looks. This is particularly true when rapidly changing technology is involved. Uncertainty should be acknowledged and addressed as part of the process. Approaches for dealing with uncertainty include:

- Planning for the long term is often performed in less detail than planning for the short term and focuses on the significant differences among the alternatives.
- Estimates of costs and benefits may be provided as a range of values.
- Use scenario analysis to test a variety of "what if?" scenarios and develop "robust" solutions that make sense within a range of "alternative futures."
- Use available long-range forecasts of technology and ITS market penetration developed by ITS and other experts.

The technical functions are now described keeping these overarching issues in mind.

Incorporating ITS and O&M into regional goals and objectives and measures of effectiveness

Identifying appropriate goals, objectives and performance measures is a critical part of developing a balanced integrated planning process that incorporates ITS, O&M and traditional improvements. The goals and objectives should reflect the emerging trends and concerns discussed earlier that focus attention on more efficient O&M of the system (increased system variability and nonrecurrent events and conditions, new attention on customer satisfaction, increased lack of information). They should also still include the concerns addressed in traditional transportation planning (these typically include: accessibility, mobility, economic development, quality of life, environment, safety and security, operational efficiency, system condition and performance—see Cambridge Systematics 1999). It is important that they reflect the values and concerns of the region in question. Goals aimed at "increasing ITS deployment" are not recommended.

Adding new goals addressing the increased concern for efficiency and management of the system to the regional planning process is important to shift the emphasis from infrastructure-oriented planning to a more balanced approach. Several pioneering regions around the country have already begun this process. San Francisco, California, has adopted a regional management strategy (Dahms and Klein 1999). The Washington, D.C. area has also recently updated its vision for its area to include the goals, objectives and strategies listed in table 26–5 (MWCOG 1998).

Table 26–5
Example of ITS-Related Goals, Objectives and Strategies
Source: Metropolitan Washington Council of Governments (1998).

Policy Goal 3: The Washington metropolitan region's transportation system will give priority to management, performance, maintenance and safety of all modes and facilities.

Objectives:
1. Adequate maintenance, preservation, rehabilitation and replacement of existing infrastructure.
2. Enhanced system safety through effective enforcement of all traffic laws and motor carrier safety regulations, achievement of national targets for seatbelt use and appropriate safety features in facility design.

Strategies:
1. Factor life-cycle costs into the transportation system planning and decision-making process.
2. Identify and secure reliable sources of funding to ensure adequate maintenance, preservation and rehabilitation of the region's transportation system.
3. Support the implementation of effective safety measures, including red light camera enforcement, skid-resistant pavements, elimination of roadside hazards and better intersection controls.

Policy Goal 4: The Washington metropolitan region will use the best available technology to maximize system effectiveness.

Objectives:
1. Reduction in regional congestion and congestion-related incidents.
2. A user-friendly, seamless system with on-demand, timely travel information for users and a simplified method of payment.
3. Improved management of weather emergencies and major incidents.
4. Improved reliability and predictability of operating conditions on the region's transportation facilities.
5. Full utilization of future advancements in transportation technology.

Strategies:
1. Deploy technologically advanced systems to monitor and manage traffic and to control and coordinate traffic control devices, such as traffic signals, including providing priority to transit vehicles where appropriate.
2. Improve incident management capabilities in the region through enhanced detection technologies and improved incident response.
3. Improve highway lighting, lane markings and other roadway delineation through the use of advanced and emerging technologies.
4. Establish a unified, technology-based method of payment for all transit fares, public parking fees and toll roads in the region.
5. Use public–private partnerships to provide travelers with comprehensive, timely and accurate information on traffic and transit conditions and available alternatives.
6. Use technology to manage and coordinate snow plowing, road salting operations and other responses to extreme weather conditions and to share with the public assessments of road conditions and how much time it will take to clear roadways.
7. Use advanced communications and real-time scheduling methods to improve time transfers between transit services.
8. Develop operating strategies and supporting systems to smooth the flow of traffic and transit vehicles, reduce variances in traffic speed and balance capacity and demand.
9. Maintain international leadership in taking advantage of new technologies for transportation, such as automated highway systems and personal rapid transit.

Performance measures are used to measure how the system performs with respect to the adopted goals and objectives, both for ongoing O&M of the system and the evaluation of future options. They should (Cambridge Systematics 1999):

- Be measurable
- Be forecastable
- Be multimodal
- Clear to decision-makers
- Comparable across time
- Geographically appropriate
- Measure multiple goals
- Reflect attributes that are controllable
- Relevant
- Provide ability to diagnose problems

More information on evaluation is presented in chapter 22.

Initial conditions analysis

The initial conditions and deficiency analysis determine the problems and issues that both O&M and future alternatives must address. Traditionally, "needs" have been identified and measured in order to support the major investment and infrastructure decisions of the future. The emphasis on major capacity improvement within the federal aid program placed importance on long-range (20+ year) forecasts of future needs consistent with the long implementation periods and life spans of capital-intensive improvements. The existing and planned transportation system (infrastructure and traditional services such as transit) is assessed for its ability to address long-term demand and other issues (air quality), and projected deficiencies are identified and alternatives developed to respond to the deficiencies. The existing and planned transportation inventory is usually well known because of the past and ongoing planning activities.

Extending the traditional approaches in initial conditions analysis and needs and deficiency identification to encompass the integrated planning framework (ITS, O&M and infrastructure) suggests the following changes:

- Incorporating short-term need estimation methods into the process.
- Extended inventory development:
  (a) Infrastructure (e.g., roads, transit, ITS and operations equipment such as traffic signals, detectors and surveillance equipment, variable message signs [VMS], highway advisory radio [HAR])
  (b) Services and their coverage areas (e.g., transit, ITS, traffic systems)
  (c) Communications (e.g., data flows—if they exist—communications infrastructure and capabilities)
  (d) Operating principals and guidelines (e.g., the rules used to run each component of the system, the concepts of operations between parties).
- Definition of "problem" in broader stakeholder terms—reliability regarding incidents, peak versus off-peak and freight versus passengers.
- Developing information on time stream of needs—immediate needs versus 5- to 10-year needs versus long-term needs.
- Need for more performance data for both recurrent and nonrecurrent conditions as part of the assessment.
- Imperative to look behind the performance deficiencies to identify causes.
- Greater sharing of performance data among agencies and with stakeholders.

This leads to the following steps as part of the integrated process needs analysis (Mitretek 2000):

- *Extended inventory development*
  — Infrastructure (e.g., roads, transit, ITS and operations equipment such as traffic signals, detectors and surveillance equipment, VMS, HAR)
  — Services and their coverage areas (e.g., transit, ITS, traffic systems)
  — Communications (e.g., data flows—if they exist—communications infrastructure and capabilities)
  — Operating principles and guidelines (e.g., the rules used to run each component of the system, the concepts of operations between parties)
- *Existing conditions and performance analysis*
  — Measures of effectiveness refinement (must fit data collection and projection capabilities)
  — Collecting data on existing performance
  — Reliability
  — Satisfaction
  — ITS as a data collection tool
  — Typical analyses:
    • Travel time studies
    • Incident and accident analysis (e.g., impact, duration, cause)
    • Bottleneck and delay analysis (e.g., recurrent, nonrecurrent)
- *Deficiency analysis*
  — Compare conditions with goals and objectives
  — Typical versus atypical conditions
  — Engage stakeholders for priority assessment
  — Output existing (time point) deficiencies
- *Causal analysis*
  — Critical point, flow and operations analysis
  — Travel demand patterns
  — Reliability and variability analysis (including incidents)
  — Typical versus atypical conditions
- *Forward and backward pass for future needs and deficiencies*
  — Future system definition (sketch level)
  — Projecting future conditions (travel and unusual conditions)
  — Projecting future performance

The deficiency analysis and its causal evaluation provide the basis for developing and evaluating the future alternatives and selecting a preferred development path. This becomes an iterative process and performance evaluation and feedback to the O&M of the system is continually performed.

Defining alternatives

Transportation planning can be considered as the process to support all transportation-related decisions that determine what the future transportation system will be, its characteristics and how it will operate. Defining, evaluating and selecting alternatives for the future is, thus, at the very core of transportation planning and decision-making. Consistent with this view of planning an "alternative" is (Mitretek 2000):

A set of linked/inter-related infrastructure investment, operations and maintenance actions to implement, operate and maintain the transportation system and services over the planning horizon (today to the long-range horizon year).

In order to bridge the operations and infrastructure planning worlds and recognize the importance of performance feedback in the system, an alternative describes one "development path" of decisions leading to a future system. It describes not only what the transportation system will be (infrastructure and services), but how to get there from today. Alternative development is an iterative process that includes both re-assessment of needs and deficiencies and evaluation of incremental impacts as the time period under analysis progresses.

As a reminder, incorporating ITS and O&M expands the components that must be identified for an alternative, including:

- Infrastructure (ITS and traditional components)
- Transportation services (ITS and traditional components)
- Regional architecture (data flows and functions)
- Concept of operations including public–private assumptions (who is responsible for what)
- Operating principals and characteristics (how the system will perform)
- Supporting policies and programs (public policy and regulation)

An alternative, thus, includes each of the aforementioned elements and balances the use of ITS and traditional strategies to best meet the region's goals and objectives and overcome the needs and deficiencies of the system. Some issues concerning the alternative definition are discussed in the next sections.

Deficiencies to integrated alternatives: the importance of causal analysis

Alternatives are derived from problems. However, since ITS and O&M provides new possibilities, simply identifying the symptoms (i.e., the identified needs and deficiencies) is no longer sufficient to develop integrated balanced solutions. As in the field of medicine, the extent and cause of the illness must be understood in order to identify the correct cure. The needs and deficiencies, therefore, need to be organized in ways that help identify balanced options and then their underlying causes examined. One suggested classification of needs and deficiencies is by geographic area, occurrence, incidence and goal area.

System performance is the result of the interplay and interaction between:

- Environmental conditions and factors (e.g., weather events such as snow, rain, fog; terrain; topography)
- System physical characteristics (e.g., connectivity, geometry, capacity)
- System operating characteristics (e.g., signal timing, ramp meters, toll and fare collection, high-occupancy vehicle [HOV] strategies, reliability, response times)
- Vehicle and driver operating characteristics (e.g., acceleration and deceleration, driver response, emission rates, miles per gallon, capacity)
- Perceptions and available information about the system (e.g., perceptions on travel times and costs by mode, safety, security and reliability; gaps between perceived and actual conditions)
- Land use and development patterns and characteristics (e.g., urban form, density, type of use)
- Desire for travel or type of travel behavior (e.g., route, trip time, mode, destination and number of trips)

A qualitative evaluation of the contribution of each of these factors should be made for each of the identified needs and deficiencies. Only then can the balanced set of ITS and traditional strategies be developed in response.

Building integrated ITS and traditional solutions

How should ITS and traditional elements be combined to the specific goals and objective deficiencies and needs identified in the deficiency analysis? It is recommended that this be carried out in two steps. First, a rough high-level screening of potential ITS user services should be made: matching the problems and causes with user services that may contribute to a solution. This should be based on the causal analysis and use as a resource many of the ITS toolboxes and cost/benefit databases now available. As an example, table 26–6 shows how ITS strategies potentially influence travel behavior and might be used if the causal analysis identified shifts in behavior as contributing factors to the system problems.

Table 26–6
Traveler Response to ITS
Source: Cambridge Systematics (1997).

ITS Categories	Traveler Responses				
	Route Diversion	Temporal Diversion	Mode Shift	Destination Change	Change in Demand
Traffic Signal Control	X		X		
Freeway Management	X	X	X	X	X
Transit Management	X	X	X		
Incident Management	X	X	X	X	X
Electronic Fare Payment			X		
Electronic Toll Collection	X	X	X		
Railroad Grade Crossings	X				
Emergency Management	X	X			
Commercial Vehicle Ops.	X	X		X	
Regional Multimodal ATIS	X	X	X	X	
System Integration	X	X	X	X	X

Second, the level of each and how it should be combined with improvements and policies should be determined. Once potential ITS user services are identified, specific market packages to implement them and how they can be combined with traditional elements must be explored. Ways that ITS can be combined are:

1. No ITS (ITS is nonresponsive or another response is chosen)
2. ITS as a standalone or primary response
    (a) To meet traditional goals, objectives and needs
    (b) To meet emerging goals, objectives and needs
3. ITS as a component of another element or secondary response
    (a) Supportive/integral
    (b) As mitigation

As a standalone or primary element, ITS can be included to meet traditional goals and objectives such as improvements in travel time, efficiency and emissions reduction. Coordinated signal systems to reduce delay (travel time) and frequent stops (emissions) are an example. ITS may also be included to respond to emerging goals such as improved reliability, customer satisfaction and safety. Incident management and HERO[5] services and real-time mutlimodal advanced traveler information systems (ATIS) may meet these needs. Again, it is the causal analysis that helps find the balance between the traditional and ITS elements and how they are combined. It provides an understanding of the interactions between transportation supply, demand and environment (land use), which result in the problem and how management of each may lead to a solution. As stated, ITS and traditional elements may be combined to help support each. As an example, table 26–7 provides a comparison between conventional and advanced systems approaches for another set of typical problems. This table should not be interpreted as presenting two either/or options (conventional and advanced systems), but rather as pointing out some of the considerations and tradeoffs to make when developing an integrated option. In today's world, both will usually be needed.

Table 26–7
Conventional Versus Advanced System Approaches to Selected Problems
Source: U.S. Department of Transportation, ITS Architecture Implementation Strategy (December 1999).

Problem	Solution	Conventional Approach	Advanced Systems Approach	Supporting Market Packages	Considerations
Traffic Congestion	Increase roadway capacity (vehicular throughput)	• New roads • New lanes	• Advanced traffic control • Incident Management • Electronic Toll Collection • Corridor Management • Advanced vehicle systems (Reduce headway)	• Surface Street Control • Freeway Control • Incident Management System • Dynamic toll/parking fee management • Regional Traffic Control • Advanced vehicle longitudinal control • Automated highway system	*Conventional* • Environmental constraints • Land use and community resistance • High cost of construction *Advanced* • Near-term services yield modest benefits • Latent demand effects
	Increase passenger throughput	• HOV Lanes • Car Pooling • Fixed route transit	• Real-time ride matching • Integrate Transit and Feeder Services • Flexible route transit • New personalized public transit	• Dynamic Ridesharing • Multimodal coordination • Demand Response Transit Operations	• Privacy and personal security
	Reduce demand	• Flex Time Programs	• Telecommuting • Other telesubstitutions • Transportation Pricing	• Dynamic toll/parking fee management	• Significant component of demand relatively inelastic
Lack of Mobility and Accessibility	Provide User-Friendly Access to Quality Transportation Services	• Expand Fixed Route Transit and Paratransit Services • Radio and TV Traffic Reports	• Multimodal pre-trip and en-route traveler information services • Respond Dynamically to Changing Demand • Personalized Public Transportation Services • Common, enhanced fare card	• Interactive Traveler Information • Demand Response Transit Operations • Transit Passenger and Fare Management	*Conventional* • Declining ridership *Advanced* • Interjurisdictional cooperation • Standards
Disconnected Transportation Modes	Improve Intermodality	• Inter-agency agreements	• Regional Transportation Management Systems • Regional Transportation Information Clearinghouse • Disseminate multimodal information pre-trip and en-route	• Regional Traffic Control • Multimodal Coordination • Interactive Traveler Information	*Conventional* • Often static and/or slow to adapt as needs change *Advanced* • Existing system incompatibilities • Standards
Severe budgetary constraints	Use existing funding efficiently	• Existing funding authorizations and selection processes	• Privatize Market Packages • Public-private partnerships • Barter right-of-way • Advanced Maintenance Strategies	• Transit maintenance	• Market uncertainties make private sector cautious • Telecommunications deregulation makes right-of-way barter a near-term opportunity
	Leverage new funding sources		• Increased emphasis on fee-for-use services		• Equity
Transportation following emergencies	Improve disaster response plans	• Review and improve existing emergency plans	• Establish emergency response center (ERC) • Internetwork ERC with law enforcement, emergency units, traffic management, transit, etc.	• Emergency response • Incident Management System • Emergency Routing	*Conventional* • Interagency coordination challenges *Advanced* • Interagency coordination challenges • Standards
Traffic accidents, injuries, and fatalities	Improve safety	• Improve roadway geometry (increase radius of curvature, widen lanes, etc.) • Improve sight distances • Traffic signals, protected left-hand turns at intersections • Fewer at-grade crossings • Driver training • Sobriety check points • Lighten dark roads to improve visibility/better lighting • Reduce speed limits/post warnings in problem areas	• Partially and fully automated vehicle control systems • Intersection collision avoidance • Automated warning systems • Vehicle condition monitoring • Driver condition monitoring • Driver vision enhancement systems • Automated detection of adverse weather and road conditions, vehicle warning, and road crew notification • Automated emergency notification	• All AVSS Market Packages • Intersection collision avoidance • In-vehicle signing • Vehicle safety monitoring • Driver safety monitoring • Driver visibility improvement • Network surveillance • Traffic information dissemination • In-vehicle signing • Mayday Support	*Conventional* • High costs • Human error is primary cause *Advanced* • Mixed results for initial collision warning devices • Relatively slow roll-out for AVSS services anticipated
Air Pollution	Increase transportation system efficiency, reduce travel and fuel consumption	• More efficient conventional vehicles vehicle emissions inspections • Promotion of alternatives to single-occupant vehicle travel • Increased capacity to reduce vehicle delay • Regulation	• Remote sensing of emissions • Advanced traffic management to smooth flows • Multimodal pre-trip information • Telecommuting • Other telesubstitutions • Transportation Pricing • Alternative fuel vehicles	• Emissions and environmental hazards sensing • Surface Street Control • Freeway Control • Regional Traffic Control • Interactive Traveler Information • Dynamic Toll/Parking Fee Management	*Conventional* • Increasing demand can offset initial benefit of added capacity. • Regulations, inspections are unpopular and onerous *Advanced* • Increasing demand can offset efficiency improvements

Incremental implementation and enabling ITS technologies

Understanding the incremental nature of ITS and the phasing of improvements is also an important consideration when creating the development path for an alternative. Traditional infrastructure and other improvements can function (for the most part) when implemented, irrespective of other elements. Vehicles can travel over completed roadway segments. This is not the case with ITS services. ITS is just that: systems. As systems, different components enable others to function through communications. They cannot operate independently. Thus, it matters when different ITS components or market packages are implemented.

Uncertainty and technological change

ITS and communications technologies are advancing by leaps and bounds every year, making it difficult to forecast what will be available in the future and the level at which it will be deployed. Unforeseen ten years ago was the explosion of the web and the Internet, the ubiquitous use of cell phones and the emerging wireless market, the popularity of electronic toll collection (both from the users' and operators' perspectives) and the growing use electronic enforcement for red light running. Each of these as well as other advancements are reshaping the use of ITS today and into the future. Given this advancement, ITS and O&M planning (e.g., early deployment plans, ITS strategic plans) are typically only carried out in a 5-to 7-year timeframe. In fact ITS professionals have repeatedly stated that they could not make predictions concerning ITS beyond 5 years in the future (Mitretek, 1999b). However, to meet federal requirements and to make long-range decisions, transportation planning must extend at least out to the 20-year horizon required for the transportation plan. At a minimum the mid-range technology forecasts, strategic plans and regional architecture analyses that the ITS community is comfortable with should be incorporated into the development path.

Analysis and evaluation methods

In the past the meaning of "evaluation" and "estimating impacts" varied depending on the world one came from: either operations or planning. Operations see evaluation as ongoing performance measurement of the systems they operate and manage. Estimating impacts involves ongoing measurement of the before and after conditions caused by the changes in the system operations that they introduce. Planners on the other hand see evaluation as examining future alternatives in order to make an informed choice. Estimating impacts involves making predictions of the differences in performance between alternatives before they are implemented, in order to assist in deciding when they must be made.

The integrated planning process combines both of these perspectives. It is performance-oriented using the performance measures chosen to reflect the region's vision, goals and objectives to evaluate an alternative. Starting with current conditions and the needs and deficiencies analysis, it implements and monitors the O&M of the system through feedback as time progresses. It must also predict the changes in performance into the future for the development path of each alternative. This results in a *time stream of impacts* (changes in performance) consistent with the time stream of actions found in the development path.

Figure 26–11 shows that an alternative's performance at any one time is the result of the interplay between the supply of transportation, the demand for transportation and the environment. Estimating affects the benefits and costs of an alternative, concerns determining how the alternative changes the transportation supply, and involves calculating the change in the use of the resultant system. A key element of this process is accounting for the feedback between the use of the system, its performance characteristics and the demand for travel. External impacts to the environment and society such as changes in safety (accidents), air quality, equity and land use must also be estimated from the alternative's implementation and use. Finally, the chosen performance measures are calculated.

Estimating the impacts of integrated alternatives combining ITS, O&M and traditional elements requires that the influence each have on the system be accounted for consistently. ITS provides information to both system operators and users. Following is a discussion of the overarching evaluation issues that should be incorporated.

New relationships
Incorporating ITS and O&M introduces new changes between alternatives in operating conditions and travel behavior that previously remained constant. If the impacts of these strategies are to be properly captured, then the analysis techniques must be updated to reflect these new dimensions. For example, traditionally, travel networks used in analyses are validated to reflect both travel times and volumes under current operat-

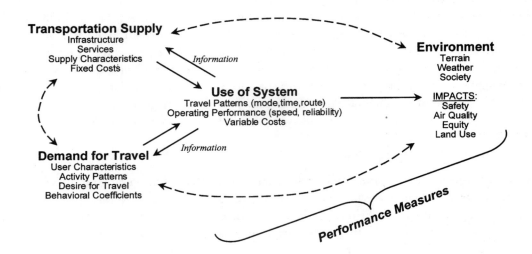

Figure 26–11. Transportation supply, demand and impacts.
Source: Mitretek (2000).

ing conditions. The volume-to-speed functions are then held constant for future analyses. This presumes that the operation of the system remains the same. If it changes with, for example, the introduction of coordinated signals then it will no longer be valid.

Time streams of impacts
Because the alternative consists of the complete development path, the time stream of both benefits and costs must now be incorporated. This requires the use of life cycle costing as well as estimating when benefits occur. Discounting of future impacts and costs to allow comparisons between changes that occur today versus those that take place 10 or 15 years from now must also be incorporated.

Uncertainty
The uncertainty of technological advancements and the costs and impacts of new services create new issues when considering ITS and O&M. The rate at which new technologies will be embraced by the marketplace, as well as how travelers will respond to technological innovation, may be difficult to predict. The economic life of a particular new technology will be hard to forecast as well. Strategies for dealing with uncertainty include: carrying out sensitivity and risk analysis on key assumptions to assist in developing "robust" alternatives, using conservative assumptions, or applying additional discounting to future impacts as a reflection of their uncertainty.

Wide range of criteria
ITS has different characteristics and creates different system responses than traditional transportation improvements. These include measures such as increased reliability, customer satisfaction and improved information. These may be difficult to value and put in a monetary cost/benefit analysis. It may also be important to show the tradeoffs and improvements in these new dimensions to decision-makers so they can see how the performance between options varies.

New stakeholder groups and distribution of impacts

ITS and operations have very different constituencies and stakeholders than those traditionally involved in transportation planning. The distribution of both the costs and impacts may also be very different from traditional facility-oriented options. Consequently, the analysis may need to show how the integrated alternatives affect these new constituencies as well as the public in general.

Figure 26–11 shows the interaction for carrying out the transportation or travel demand and impact analyses. Other analyses that are important in the overall evaluation are the cost and financial analyses. While details cannot be described here, a brief overview of each is provided next.

Transportation and travel demand analysis

The previous discussion provides some insight into the data and analysis needs for capturing the transportation system performance effects of ITS and O&M strategies in a combined analysis with traditional transportation alternatives. Some of the key features that are required are (Mitretek 1999a):

- Ability to model both traditional and ITS strategies
- Incorporation of data on incidents and other factors that induce variability in traffic conditions
- Ability to model the effect of nonrecurring factors on the transportation system performance
- Ability to model the state and availability of real-time surveillance information
- Ability to model traveler response to real-time information on network conditions
- Ability to model the response of the transportation system to incidents or other changes from average, expected conditions
- Ability to model the operational efficiencies of ITS improvements under average, expected conditions
- Ability to assess the combined effects of ITS services implemented together

How to incorporate those features depends on the level of detail needed, resources (time, staff skills and cost) and the point in the decision-making cycle being addressed. Approaches vary by coverage and level of detail, complexity and ease of use, and their internal causal relationships and ability to capture integrated solutions.

A thorough discussion of all possible analytical approaches is not covered here. However, it is important to keep in mind the general types of techniques that apply. Analytical techniques and tools used in planning studies generally fall into the following major categories (presented in general order of increasing complexity and data requirements):

- Performance measurement and extrapolation
- Impact databases, toolboxes and qualitative assessment
- Sketch planning techniques
- Planning models
- Simulation models
- Combined planning and simulation methods
- New paradigms in travel forecasting

Performance measurement and extrapolation

Today's operating agencies often rely on the "test it and see" approach. System evaluation and feedback into the O&M of the transportation system is one of the main goals of the evolving process. Thus as more ITS, operational strategies and surveillance and performance analysis are incorporated into standard practice, knowledge of the system's response to conditions will grow. Incremental change, based on current conditions, can then rely less on models and other external methods and more on actual observations of the system. Ongoing evaluation and performance measurement is described in depth elsewhere in this textbook.

Impact databases, toolboxes and qualitative assessment

These provide valuable insights in the early stages of alternative development and the exploration of elements for the integration strategy. Their applicability is based on the assumption that the regions and systems are similar and will provide similar results. They rely on previous experience or expert judgment. These assessments are used everyday by project managers in selecting the candidate projects for further investigation and making quick evaluations. Some sources of information are as follows:

- ITS cost and benefits databases
  — *Intelligent Transportation Systems Benefits: 1999 Update* (Proper 1999)
      <http://www.its.dot.gov/eval/Analyses/Analyses_BenefitsAndCosts.html>
- ITS-transit impacts matrix (Mitretek Systems 2000),
  <http://www.mitretek.org/its/aptsmatrix.html>
- Congestion management and ITS toolboxes
  — *A Toolbox for Alleviating Traffic Congestion and Enhancing Mobility* (Meyer 1998)
  — *ITS Rural Toolbox for Rural and Small Urban Areas* (Castle Rock, Black and Veatch 1999)
  — *Technology in Rural Transportation "Simple Solutions"* (Castle Rock 1997)
  — *Improving Transit With Intelligent Transportation Systems* (Smith 1998)
- Other ITS handbooks
  — *ITS Planning Handbook: Intelligent City Transport* (ERTICO 1998)
  — *ITS Handbook '99* (World Road Association 1999)
  — *Integrating Intelligent Transportation Systems within the Transportation Planning Process: An Interim Handbook* (Transcore 1998)

Sketch planning techniques

Generally, straightforward parametric or spreadsheet analyses provide an approximation of potential impacts and may rely on historical data. These are often used when there is a large number of options to evaluate, the impacts are localized, or the individual projects are relatively small. They are also used to screen an initial set of alternatives to likely candidates for further study. They may also be used to calculate adjustments to the inputs of planning and simulation models. Two recent tools developed by the U.S. DOT to support ITS analysis are the Screening for ITS (SCRITS) sketch tool and the IDAS.

SCRITS is a spreadsheet sketch tool that can be used for estimating the user benefits and screening ITS options (SAIC 1999). It provides daily analysis only for 16 different types of ITS. The user inputs baseline data and then SCRITS estimates changes in vehicle hours traveled, vehicle miles of travel, emissions, vehicle operating costs, energy consumption, number of accidents and user economic benefit. It does not estimate system operating or capital costs. Information on SCRITS can be found at the FHWA website: <http://www.fhwa.dot.gov/steam/scrits.htm>.

IDAS is a new tool designed to assist public agencies and consultants in integrating ITS in the transportation planning process. It is designed to work as a post-processor of regional planning models using their networks and trip patterns as inputs (Cambridge Systematics and ITT Industries 2000). It comes with an extensive ITS benefits library for comparison of expected impacts, an ITS cost and equipment database and its analytic procedures with default impact settings. ITS components considered by IDAS fall into one of seven categories:

1. Multimodal traveler information systems
2. Arterial traffic management systems
3. Incident management systems
4. Freeway management systems
5. Advanced public transportation systems
6. Electronic payment systems
7. Commercial vehicle operations

IDAS estimates the impacts on both costs and benefits at the system and user level. Changes in network performance may engender impacts in assignment, mode choice, temporal choice and induced and foregone demand. These impacts are then fed through a range of impact assessment modules, which identify travel time and throughput, energy, emissions and noise and safety impacts. Nontraditional measures used to capture the unique characteristics of ITS include changes in travel time reliability, transit service reliability and enhanced safety and security. Costs of ITS deployments are constructed with implicit cost-sharing arrangements identified internal to the software. For example, a new TMC need not be constructed for each ITS component deployed—IDAS automatically assumes shared costs through an integrated deployment. Benefits are converted to dollar figures and cost/benefit ratios of particular alternatives can be displayed within an alternatives comparison module. IDAS also allows risk and uncertainty analysis to be performed on many of the assumptions and inputs.

Planning models

Models that forecast average (steady-state) travel and transportation demand and associated impacts over a given time period (e.g., daily, peak period) typically use some variant of the four-step method (i.e., trip generation, trip distribution, mode split and assignment) with inputs from demographic and land-use projections. These tools are used to capture long-range impacts of transportation system changes at the regional level. They are also often used with refinements and additional detail for corridor and other more focused studies. They may be combined with sketch techniques and post-processors to analyze the impacts of ITS. ITS impacts that affect the overall capacity and performance of each facility are coded into the transportation network. Examples include the impact of coordinated signal systems, electronic toll and fare cards, HOV and advanced transit management improvements. Other shifts in behavior such as response to ride share programs or transit security can also be integrated into the regional models to determine their network impacts. Lastly, route diversion may be studied using special mode runs (see module 10 of the NHI 1999). It is difficult, however, to capture the impacts of nonrecurring conditions or traveler information in regional models.

Simulation models

These models explicitly represent the movement of vehicles, traffic flow and their interaction with the network through time (e.g., signals are explicitly modeled). They can represent unusual incidents in the system or the availability of information to specific travelers and are consequently being used with more frequency to examine ITS strategies. Ramp metering, signal priority schemes, HOV analyses and incident response are particularly appropriate. Because they must track vehicles by time, however, they typically do not have the capacity to represent complete regions in their analyses. They are consequently used more often for corridor and project operational and design analyses. Simulation tools may provide key inputs to a project's design and operation that cannot be addressed using other tools. Examples of simulation tools include macroscopic tools such as CORFLO, FREQ, TRANSYT-7F, SATURN and CONTRAM; and microscopic tools such as CORSIM and INTEGRATION (see NHI 1999 for a summary of these tools).

Combined planning and simulation methods

Combined planning and simulation methods interconnect planning and simulation models in an attempt to capture both recurrent and nonrecurrent conditions in the analysis. They still are encumbered by the network limitations of the simulation systems they use, but they are particularly useful in corridor or subarea analyses of integrated ITS and traditional improvements. These combined approaches can be implemented as one-way linkages with the regional models providing inputs to the simulation studies, or as two-way linkages with feedback between the two systems. The I-64 Corridor Major Investment Study carried out between Richmond and Norfolk, Virginia, used the former (Rush and Penic 1998). Mitretek Systems developed the Process for Regional Understanding and Evaluation of Integrated ITS Networks (PRUEVIIN) analysis framework for a Seattle Case Study using the latter (Mitretek 1999).

PRUEVINN is a two-level modeling framework developed to capture the overall travel impacts of ITS and operational improvements to the transportation system, the response to time-variant conditions (both recurrent and nonrecurrent) and the impact of improved information. At the first level, the analysis of overall travel patterns and the systems response to average and expected conditions are addressed in the traditional regional model system. Outputs from the regional analysis must be interfaced with the more detailed second-level simulation analysis. This level captures the time-variant and operational details of the transportation system using a subarea travel simulation system. At this level the detailed traffic operations, queuing, and build-up and dispersion of demand is captured and the accuracy of the traveler's information on the system can also be represented. Another key element in capturing the impacts of ITS is the representative day scenario analysis to represent nonrecurrent conditions. Lastly, feedback is carried out to ensure that the impacts to expected conditions estimated in the subarea simulation are reflected in the regional analysis.

The PRUEVINN Seattle Case Study found that the Single-Occupancy Vehicle Capacity Expansion alternative with the greatest capacity under average conditions diverted regional traffic, which caused it show no improvements over the TSM option when the variations in conditions and incidents were introduced. Key attributes of how an alternative might perform under expected travel conditions could not have been predicted using only the regional model (Mitretek 1999a).

New paradigms in travel forecasting

New travel analysis tools that combine regional forecasting with simulation and activity analysis are now under development. TRANSIMS is a longer range travel forecasting model reformulation and development project being carried out by Los Alamos Laboratories for the U.S. DOT. It will be based on a traveler's activity patterns throughout the day and use simulation techniques to model ITS and other transportation system elements. TRANSIMS' first release is now complete and ready for testing, however, ITS capabilities are not yet available. It is expected that these features will be added sometime during mid-2000. The Dynamic Traffic Assignment (DTA) program also represents the road network and individual vehicle movements in detail. It is focused on developing real-time predictive control strategies for traffic operations. Currently, the DTA models such as DynaMIT developed by the Massachusetts Institute of Technology have been used extensively for research and development, but they are not available for general application.

Environmental and other impact analyses

Environmental and other impacts include changes in:

- Emissions
- Energy
- Noise
- Safety (accidents and fatalities)
- Social equity

These impacts are the result of the interaction between the transportation network and travel demand and behavior (figure 26–11) and are consequently analyzed using post-processing of the outputs of the transportation and travel demand analysis. Again, the methods for estimating these impacts must now reflect how ITS and O&M changes the system. This should include changes to operating relationships as well as the occurrence of unusual or special events. Examples include developing new "modal" emissions models that capture changes in high accelerations and decelerations and accident models that use volume-to-capacity ratios or number high accelerations and decelerations to estimate crashes (NHI 1999).

Cost analysis

Costs for each integrated alternative must also be estimated. Agencies have less experience with implementing ITS and hence have less experience with how to estimate their capital, operations and maintenance costs. Because the operations and maintenance requirements for ITS are typically higher and more uncertain than those of traditional construction projects, funding for ongoing operations and maintenance is a major concern for agencies that decide to implement ITS. The issues associated with conducting consistent cost analyses across all elements of an integrated alternative are examined in the following sections.

Life cycle costs

One of the issues is estimating the life cycle costs to implement and operate all elements (ITS and O&M as well as traditional). While a growing database of ITS implementation and O&M costs is developing and is available at the federal ITS website, <http://www.its.dot.gov/eval/Analyses/Analyses_BenefitsAndCosts.html>, life cycle costs for traditional elements may still be difficult to come by.

Economic life of ITS and communication elements

The economic life affects how the project is discounted and the replacement need when estimating life cycle costs. The typical design life of roadway projects is 20 years, and rail structures may have up to a 100-year design life. Because of rapid advancements and early obsolescence, technology elements have much shorter lives—as low as 3 to 5 years (PB Farradyne 1999). PCs, for example, rapidly become obsolete and parts and software become difficult to maintain. Communications systems may also quickly be replaced. When comparing costs the economic life assumptions should always be examined. Also, the need to upgrade should be incorporated into the alternative design.

Shared costs, cost allocation and cost breakdown structure

Whether costs are shared among different ITS services and how they are allocated between roadside and center systems can have a significant effect on how costs are reported. If the national ITS cost database is to be used, then it is important to understand where and how it allocates costs. More importantly, because ITS is relatively new there is no standard cost breakdown structure to use to allocate costs consistently. Often, reported costs become a function of the budget structure found in the operating agencies and the historic distribution of responsibilities. Thus, labor costs for system operations may be reported in maintenance budgets or vice-versa (Daniels and Starr 1996). TMC costs may be separate or allocated to the services they support.

Need for causal costing methods

In the past, many cost estimating methods have calculated O&M costs as a percentage of capital costs. This is fine for fixed facilities where there is a history of experience and cost factors are well known. However, it is fraught with problems when evaluating advanced technologies. Every attempt should be made to develop cost build-up models based on logical cost factors such as hours of operation and full-time labor equivalents. This may also be important when allocating shared center costs among services.

User costs for ITS services

Because some ITS strategies (such as ATIS) involve consumer purchase of equipment or services, alternatives that depend on such decisions must address these costs somewhere in the analysis. This issue is nontrivial because assumptions must be made about the costs and number of users (or market penetration). These costs should be treated as a user dis-benefit rather than a cost, because cost is generally defined as public agency costs. In addition, because the private sector is expected to play a big role in the delivery of ATIS services, the treatment of private-sector service provider costs is another issue to be addressed. One way to handle this may be through keeping the actual costs to the private sector internal to the cost analysis system by estimating user fees as the cost transfer mechanism. This in turn is a way to address the user costs.

Uncertainty of emerging technology costs

With any developing technology there is a natural adjustment in costs as it reaches wide market penetration. Fax machines, computers and cell phones are examples where prices have dropped beyond all past expectations as advancements have been made and they have become ubiquitous in society. Predicting future costs of ITS products is therefore difficult at best. Where possible, national forecasts and experts should be used.

Financial analysis

The requirement that plans and TIPs be financially constrained and address the maintenance and preservation of the overall transportation system was introduced as part of ISTEA and continued in TEA-21. As ITS and operations become more significant this requirement takes on additional importance, because the systems must both be implemented and operated.

The financial analysis can provide a feasibility check on the ITS assumption and other operations assumptions in the development path. Yet, it also presents challenges. The fact that a market analysis might need to be done as part of the study is clearly one of the challenges. Many of the issues related to public–private partnering have implications for the financial analysis and decision-making framework because many other stakeholders and decision-makers (including the private-sector equipment manufacturers and information service providers) dictate the overall viability of the defined alternative. For example, if dynamic route guidance is planned and the assumption is that it is delivered using the private sector, the viability of the alternative requires decisions on the part of the individual consumers to purchase the equipment and service, the private sector to offer the service and the public sector to share traffic conditions information with the private sector. Some financial analyses might assume that the public and private sector trade data on traffic conditions, to their mutual benefit, while others might assume that the information flow is more one-sided, with a potential need to include the expected value of the information into the analysis.

Other issues concern the leasing versus purchase of communications and other infrastructure and services, and the obsolescence of equipment and technology. Of course, as operating becomes a more significant budget element for stakeholders that traditionally did not have significant operating expenses, the funds must be identified and programmed as part of the financial analysis and programming or budgeting process.

Planning to programming

Once the development path and overall integrated time stream of activities is defined, projects and ongoing operations must still be programmed to match budget categories and availability of funds, implementation schedules and areas of responsibility. In the traditional planning process this is the role of the TIP program and operating or implementing agency operations, maintenance and capital budgeting. The integration of ITS and O&M and the integrated "systems" perspective that they bring raises new issues in these processes including:

- Incorporating operations and maintenance activities into the process. Once systems are implemented they must be maintained.
- Incorporating performance orientation, deficiency analysis and performance standards. The new measures of performance and reliability need to be included in the programming weights.
- How to capture system benefits and synergy of individual projects and how to program for incremental improvements (piecemeal versus integrated systems).
- Enabling technologies and the phasing of interdependent ITS systems.
- The indivisibility of many ITS systems and the need to "bundle" components in order for them to function or to obtain their full benefits.
- The impact of private-sector involvement, resource sharing and the leveraging of funds. Often, long-term guarantees are needed to minimize risks and obtain agreements that leverage public contributions. These are difficult to incorporate into an incremental budgeting process.

There are several approaches that are being used to address these issues and develop an integrated ITS, O&M and infrastructure programming process, including assignment to specific funding categories, developing a hierarchy of system needs and funding priorities and incorporating new programming criteria and weights.

Assignment to specific funding categories

The selection and prioritization of projects is often tied to funding categories. Under ISTEA, ITS was often funded using special ITS research and deployment funds including the ITS Priority Corridor and Metropolitan Model Deployment programs. This has changed under TEA-21, which aims at mainstreaming ITS projects but also provides for more flexible funding. To allocate projects to funding, different criteria and processes are used depending on the category of funds and different agencies that may have decision-making responsibility.

ITS projects may be funded under a wide range of federal highway and transit programs authorized in TEA-21. For example, National Highway System and Surface Transportation Program (STP) funds may be used for infrastructure-based ITS capital improvements and Congestion Management and Air Quality (CMAQ) funding may be used to implement ITS strategies that improve traffic flow and reduce emissions. The operating costs for traffic monitoring, management and control facilities and programs are potentially eligible under the federal-aid highway program as well. Advanced public transportation sytem projects are eligible for capital funding under the federal transit programs. To receive these funds, ITS projects must compete with other needs. Tradeoffs between ITS and other projects are made through the state and regional programming processes. Often, ITS and O&M are pre-allocated to a specific funding category. For example, in the past, ITS projects for the Houston, Texas region were funded using CMAQ funds (Mitretek 1996).

In addition, TEA-21 provides approximately $1.3 billion in contract authority for ITS as follows:

- Research, training and standards development . . . .$603 million
- Accelerated integration and interoperability . . . .$482 million
- Commercial vehicle infrastructure deployment . . . .$184 million

Pre-allocating projects to funding categories may make programming easier, however, it may also limit opportunities and tradeoffs or integration with other traditional improvements.

Hierarchy of system needs and funding priorities

Another approach that is growing in popularity comes from "asset management" and the philosophy that existing systems must be maintained and preserved before new expansions are implemented. This approach establishes a hierarchy of system needs and funding priorities. Washington State provides an example where the transportation commission has established the following hierarchy of needs as guidelines for funding (Jacobsen 1999).

- Maintenance
- Traffic operations
- Preservation
- Safety improvement
- Mobility improvement

Funds are allocated first to maintenance needs, then traffic operations, and so forth. This ensures that the existing system will be maintained and operated efficiently. ITS services contribute to all of the categories.

New programming criteria and weights

TIP projects in a financially constrained environment are usually subject to some kind of evaluation process using common criteria. Such criteria typically include:

- Cost
- Urgency
- Impact on level of service or congestion
- Air quality impact
- Support of land use

Scoring methods used often provide extra credit for noncapacity improvements or projects with an efficiency impact. An important aspect of mainstreaming is to develop criteria that respond to the unique features of O&M improvements such as their short-term, cost-effective implementation and their ability to respond to nonstandard conditions. These include both quantitative and qualitative criteria sensitive to system reliability, customer satisfaction and contribution to system management and performance. Quantitative measures should be based on the system performance measures defined earlier in the process. Qualitative measures can include the contributions to the National Architecture Consistency requirements and system integration; the system versus local impacts, cost sharing opportunities, ability to operate and training needs for advanced systems; and other factors.

The Phoenix MPO has developed a rating point system for comparing ITS with non-ITS projects (CUTR 2000). As shown in table 26–8 the system is based on assessing five characteristics for each project. A maximum of 100 points is awarded to each project and the projects are then ranked.

Table 26–8
Example of Programming Weights: Phoenix
Source: Center for Urban Transportation Research (2000).

Category and Measure	Points
Deployment Priority Addresses all needs of entire area = 30; most needs in at least ½ area = 20; a few needs in less than ½ area = 10. Plus 5 points if project addresses special event needs or high traffic generator.	35
Congestion/Integration 0 to 25 points based on resulting VMT/lane-mile ratio (0 for lowest, 25 for highest). Projects for which VMT estimates are unavailable are scored by ITS subcommittee.	25
Cost Factor 0 to 15 points based on VMT/cost (0 for lowest and up to 15 for highest). Projects for which VMT estimates are unavailable will be scored based upon project cost only.	15
Jurisdiction Match 0 to 10 points based on extent of matching funds from federal and/or state (0 for no match and up to 10 points for highest federal match.	10
ITS Steering Committee Ranking 0 to 15 points based upon subjective decision of the ITS subcommittee.	15
Total	**100**

ITS data and feedback to planning and decision-making

The importance of ITS data and their feedback to planning and other "secondary" uses have recently been recognized by the addition of the Archived Data User Service (ADUS) in the national ITS architecture (U.S. DOT 1999). Unless the data exist to support the performance-based measures and the continual monitoring and feedback, capturing the O&M focus brought by ITS to the planning process becomes difficult. Data are needed to assess the effect of the ITS systems as well as the performance of the overall system and its response to conditions. Obtaining the information from traditional data collection methods, however, is costly if not impossible. A recent U.S. DOT strategy paper also placed "collection and use of data" as one of three key conditions in bringing ITS solutions into the metropolitan transportation planning process (Deblasio et al. 1998).

Feedback of the continual performance of the system into the planning and decision-making processes allows the system to evolve through small steps and midcourse corrections rather than discontinuous major investments. Feedback through monitoring the performance of the system also allows the decision-making process to see the effects of the decisions made and then respond. This is in marked contrast with traditional planning and its focus on the long-range forecasts of conditions and developing major investments to meet these conditions. ITS provides a source of continuous data that must be transformed into the "information" and performance measures used in the feedback process. ITS data has the potential to supplement or replace many of the data needs found in both the traditional planning process and integrated framework. Table 26–9 provides some potential uses of ITS data and a comparison with current data sources for both planning and O&M functions found in the integrated process. ITS also provides a source of information for the shorter range O&M functions of the integrated framework. It provides a means to evaluate both ITS and non-ITS programs and their combinations. Some current examples of feedback and the use of ITS data are provided in table 26–10.

Table 26–9
Uses of ITS Data for Planning and O&M
Sources: Mitretek (2000).
Margiotta, "ITS as a Data Resource: Preliminary Requirements
for a User Service" (1998, table 2.1).

Stakeholder Group	Application	Method or Function	Collection and Use of:	
			Current Data	ITS-Generated Data
MPO and State Transportation Planners	Congestion Management Systems	Congestion Monitoring	Travel times collected by "floating cars:" usually only a few runs (small samples) on selected routes. Speeds and travel times synthesized with analytic methods (e.g., HCM, simulation) using limited traffic data (short counts). Effect of incidents missed completely with synthetic methods and minimally covered by floating cars.	Roadway surveillance data (e.g., loop detectors) provide continuous volume counts and speeds. Variability can be directly assessed. Probe vehicles provide same travel times as "floating cars" but greatly increase sample size and areawide coverage. The effect of incidents is embedded in surveillance data and incident management systems provide details on incident conditions.
	Long-Range Plan Development	Travel Demand Forecasting Models	Short-duration traffic counts used for model validation. O/D patterns from infrequent travel surveys used to calibrate trip distribution. Link speeds based on speed limits or functional class. Link capacities usually based on functional class.	Roadway surveillance data provide continuous volume counts, truck percents and speeds. Probe vehicles can be used to estimate O/D patterns without the need for a survey. The emerging TDF models (e.g., TRANSIMS) will require detailed data on network (e.g., signal timing) that can be collected automatically via ITS. Other TDF formulations that account for variability in travel conditions can be calibrated against the continuous volume and speed data.
	Corridor Analysis	Traffic Simulation Models	Short-duration traffic counts and turning movements used as model inputs. Other input data to run the models collected through special efforts (signal timing). Very little performance data available for model calibration (e.g., incidents, speeds, delay).	Most input data can be collected automatically and models can be directly calibrated to actual conditions.
Traffic Management Operators	ITS Technology	Program and Technology Evaluations	Extremely limited; special data collection efforts required.	Data from ITS provide the ability to evaluate the effectiveness of both ITS and non-ITS programs. For example, data from an incident management system can be used to determine changes in verification, response and clearance times due to new technologies or institutional arrangements. Freeway surveillance data can be used to evaluate the effectiveness of ramp meters or HOV restrictions.
	Operations Planning	Pre-Determined Control Strategies	Short-duration traffic counts and "floating car" travel time runs. A limited set of predetermined control plans is usually developed mostly due to the lack of data.	Continuous roadway surveillance data make it possible to develop any number of predetermined control strategies.
		Predictive Traffic Flow Algorithms	Extremely limited.	Analysis of historical data form the basis of predictive algorithms: "What will traffic conditions be in the next 15 minutes?" (Bayesian approach).

Stakeholder Group	Application	Method or Function	Collection and Use of:	
			Current Data	ITS-Generated Data
Transit Operators	Operations Planning	Routing and Scheduling	Manual travel demand and ridership surveys; special studies.	Electronic fare payment system and automatic passenger counters allow continuous boardings to be collected. Computer-aided dispatch systems allow O/D patterns to be tracked. AVI on buses allows monitoring of schedule adherence and permits the accurate setting of schedules without field review.
Air Quality Analysts	Conformity Determinations	Analysis with the MOBILE Model	Areawide speed data taken from TDFs. VMT and vehicle classifications derived from short counts.	Roadway surveillance provides actual speeds, volumes and truck mix by time of day. Modal emission models will require these data in even greater detail, and ITS is the only practical source.
MPO/State Freight and Intermodal Planners	Port and Intermodal Facilities Planning	Freight Demand Models	Data collected through rare special surveys or implied from national data (e.g., commodity flow survey).	Electronic credentialing and AVI allows tracking of truck travel patterns, sometimes including cargo. Improved tracking of congestion through the use of roadway surveillance data leads to improved assessments of intermodal access.
Safety Planners and Administrators	Safety Management Systems	Areawide Safety Monitoring; Studies of Highway and Vehicle Safety Relationships	Exposure (typically VMT) derived from short-duration traffic and vehicle classification counts; traffic conditions under which crashes occurred must be inferred. Police investigations, the basis for most crash data sets, performed manually.	Roadway surveillance data provide continuous volume counts, truck percents and speeds, leading to improved exposure estimation and measurement of the actual traffic conditions for crash studies. Incident management can identify unreported crashes. ITS technologies also offer the possibility of automating field collection of crash data by police officers (e.g., GPS for location).
Maintenance Personnel	Pavement and Bridge Management	Historical and Forecasted Loadings	Volumes, vehicle classifications and vehicle weights derived from short-duration counts (limited number of continuously operating sites).	Roadway surveillance data provide continuous volume counts, vehicle classifications, and vehicle weights, making more accurate loading data and growth forecasts available.
Transportation Researchers	Model Development	Travel Behavior Models	Mostly rely on infrequent and costly surveys: stated preference and some travel diary efforts (revealed preference).	Traveler response to system conditions can be measured through system detectors, probe vehicles or monitoring in-vehicle and personal device use. Travel diaries can be embedded in these technologies as well.
		Traffic Flow Models	Detailed traffic data for model development must be collected through special efforts.	Roadway surveillance data provide continuous volume counts, densities, truck percents and speeds at very small time increments. GPS-instrumented vehicles can provide second-by-second performance characteristics for microscopic model development and validation.

Table 26–10
Examples of ITS Data and Planning
Sources: Mitretek (2000); Mergel (1998); Flannery (2000);
Transportation Research Board, ADUS presentations (2000).

- *Freeway Performance Evaluation in Puget Sound Region, Washington.* Loop detector data have been used to monitor congestion patterns, including variability in speeds and travel times.
- *Minneapolis—St. Paul, Minnesota Traffic Management Center Database.* Reports of travel in the A.M. peak and volumes by time of day for freeway segments. The data are available through a data management system and are used extensively by planners. The data are also used to adjust ramp meters.
- *Traffic Statistics in Chicago, Illinois.* Freeway management system data are archived and have been used to produce an "atlas" of traffic statistics for the Chicago area and other summary reports on system performance. While the electronic version of the data is still not user friendly, the reports are used extensively by planners at the MPO and throughout the region.
- *Transit system management in Portland, Oregon.* Portland's Tri-Met uses passenger count, vehicle location and event data to assist in updating schedules, set transit priority and system planning. Caused a 62% to 77% change in on-time performance and 36% in bus spacing (reliability).
- *Phoenix, Arizona System Performance.* The freeway management system data are being used to track the start and duration of congestion, HOV versus main-lane use, truck volumes and to develop volume-delay relationships.

Despite its potential, ITS data have been looked at with some suspicion by the planning community. The primary reason for this is that it is in fact different and does cause new challenges and issues to be addressed if it is to augment traditional sources (Mergel 1998, Margiotta 1998, Turner et al. 1999). These issues are discussed next and include data content and coverage; data quality control and error checking; data management and storage; data visualization and analysis; access, ownership and privacy; and roles and responsibilities.

Data content and coverage

In San Antonio, Texas, the automatic vehicle identification system provides travel times for the regional CMS. However, portions of the CMS network are not covered because the MPO was not consulted on where the field locators would be located (Mergel 1998). Likewise, in Minneapolis, Minnesota, the TMC will be able to collect data every 30 seconds across the region, yet could not provide ramp meter delay information to the MPO in a timely fashion because the loop detector placement required was not part of the original design (Mergel 1998). Planners must be aware of the existence and potential uses of the ITS data and provide input into its collection or else it may not meet their needs. This requires an ongoing dialog.

Data quality control and error checking

One of the main concerns with ITS data raised by planners is the lack of reliability and comparability with traditional sources. Data collected for operational use is often concerned more about detecting existing conditions and unusual events than accuracy of any one particular data point. Also, planners do not recognize that the data is often in rawer form than they are used to and requires additional quality control and error analysis. Detectors are often down for brief periods or report suspicious information. For example, traffic detector data from San Antonio's Transtar for October 1998 showed that "good" data was provided 76.5%, "suspect" data 1.0% and "missing data" 22.5% of the time (Turner 2000). Therefore, the sources of data must be understood by planners and the data collectors must work with users to ensure that the information for potential errors is identified, reported and corrected.

Data management and storage

ITS data collected for 24 hours a day, 360 days a year can quickly take up megabytes of storage. Whether all of the ITS data, aggregation or summaries or both are stored, the length of storage and data-retention cycles (all data for a year, daily summaries for 5 years, monthly and annual information permanent) and the information about the data (meta-data) are all important issues that affect how the data can be used and by whom. What data is saved routinely and what capabilities are added to save additional information by special request also need to be addressed. Different users have very different needs and wants that must be taken into account. For example, planners may want hourly volumes on a roadway by day and also annual weekday statistics (both by hour and daily), while traffic simulators would like 20-second or smaller "occupancy" and volume data by lane for specific days to validate their models. How these questions are answered affects the costs of maintaining the information and is one of the main functions of the dialog between stakeholders to resolve. Database maintenance and upkeep must also be budgeted and planned for. This includes maintaining past archives and backups, updating formats, keeping relationships and file locations current and other tasks. It may require more than one full-time staff to carry out.

Data visualization and analysis

The amount of data and information provided by ITS sources also makes it difficult to understand and use. Planners want information, not raw data. Therefore, data must be transformed in ways that make them humanly understandable. This is especially true if the new information on system variation and unusual events captured by continuous measurement is to become part of the overall planning process. Figure 26–12 provides one example of data visualization from Seattle, Washington (Ishimaru and Hallenbeck 1999). Other displays can show the likelihood of an incident or unusual congestion occurring, as well as weather and variations in volumes or travel times throughout the year.

Access, ownership and privacy

These issues must be resolved and should be part of the overall plan. If a policy is developed prior to public issues and concerns are being raised, especially regarding privacy, there is a much greater chance of avoiding both controversy and potential legal issues.

Roles and responsibilities

Roles and responsibilities for data collection, maintenance and quality control and use must also be established as part of the concept of operations of the overall ITS system. How costs and revenues are allocated may become important issues, especially when the data collection and data users are not the same.

Thus, with the use of ITS data and feedback of performance to the O&M of the system, the process and development path is continually updated. As conditions change, the short-, mid- and long-term operations and overall plan evolve to meet them.

ADUS

ADUS was added to the national ITS architecture (version 3.0) in October 1999 (U.S. DOT 1999). Its purpose is to provide the technical foundation within the national ITS architecture on the use of ITS data for secondary sources such as feedback to transportation planning and O&M of the system within the integrat-

Figure 26–12. Example of travel time variation along a corridor.
Source: Ishimaru and Hallenbeck (1999).

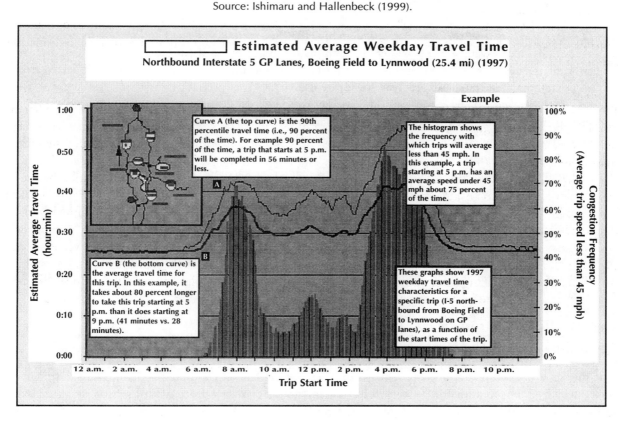

ed framework. Implementation of ADUS and the ITS data used for planning should therefore be considered as part of the development of the regional integration strategy and regional ITS architecture to meet TEA-21's architecture consistency requirements.

Within the national ITS architecture, ADUS defines the information flows and functions required when someone is considering saving and using ITS data. A new center subsystem, Archived Data Management System (ADMS), has been defined as part of ADUS. Five major functions are defined that are carried out as part of ADUS:

1. *operational data control* function to manage operations data integrity;
2. *data import and verification* function to acquire historical data from the *operational data control* function;
3. *automatic data historical archive* function for permanently archiving the data;
4. *data warehouse distribution* function, which integrates the planning, safety, operations and research communities into ITS and processes data products for these communities; and
5. *ITS community interface* function, which provides the ITS common interface to all ITS users for data products specification and retrieval.

The architecture also provides three different market packages to help in the implementation of ADUS at the local and state levels:

1. *ITS data mart (market package).* A focused archive that houses data collected and owned by a single agency, district, private-sector provider, research institution or other organization. This focused archive typically includes data covering a single transportation mode and one jurisdiction that is collected from an operational data store and archived for future use.
2. *ITS data warehouse (market package).* This market package includes all the data collection and management capabilities provided by the ITS data mart and adds the functionality and interface definitions that allow collection of data from multiple agencies and data sources spanning across modal and jurisdictional boundaries.
3. *ITS virtual data warehouse (market package).* This market package provides the same broad access to multimodal, multidimensional data from varied data sources as in the ITS data warehouse market package, but it provides this access using enhanced interoperability between physically distributed ITS archives that are each locally managed.

Within the functions and market packages the architecture now has defined many subfunctions and details to help areas think through their specific applications. Therefore, it is a very useful resource when planning for the use of ITS data.

Connections to traditional planning requirements for analysis and documentation

The process and documentation requirements to meet existing federal planning regulations and the changes introduced by TEA-21 must still be met within the integrated planning process. This section describes where in the integrated process the federal requirements may be met.

While the integrated process re-orients the planning process and expands its focus to include ITS, it is the result of an evolving response to changing conditions rather than a replacement of existing practice. This is explained next in a brief review of the typical process and products needed to meet current federal planning regulations. Also, migrating to the integrated process is needed in order to address the TEA-21 and O&M planning factor and national ITS architecture consistency requirements.

Figure 26–13 provides one common depiction of the transportation planning process as envisioned in the FHWA and FTA regulations.[6] The required products of this process are the metropolitan and statewide transportation plans (LRP) and the metropolitan and statewide transportation improvement programs (TIP and STIP). Other important products include the State Implementation Plan for Air Quality (SIP), CMS and special studies. The activities carried out as part of the process typically have a long-range focus and are aimed at producing the LRP and TIP.

A number of other requirements must also be considered in developing the LRP, TIP, STIP and other products of the traditional planning process. Plans must be financially constrained to reflect funds reasonably expected to be available over the time period they cover. Public participation and collaborative decision-making have also become central elements required in developing the federal products (NARC 1995). This includes both public and private participants and becomes extremely important in expanding the process to include ITS and O&M stakeholders. "Environmental justice" aimed at examining the effects of federal investments on the human health, economic and social effects on minority and low-income communities is of rising importance (Wiener 1997) and must be incorporated into any future planning process.

Figure 26–13. Traditional transportation planning process and federal requirements.
Sources: Modified from National Transit Institute, PBQD (1995); Transcore (1998).

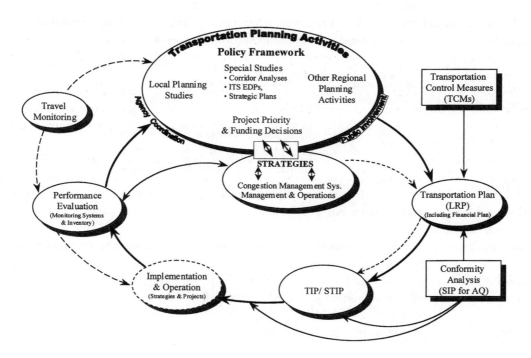

Intermodalism and the connection between transportation and land use planning must be considered and will affect the analysis of ITS in the process.

Figure 26–13 also highlights the similarities between the traditional federally oriented process and the integrated planning process. Most importantly, both are cyclic and continuous in nature. Conceptually, however, the traditional process starts with the establishment of the long-range needs, goals, objectives and LRP. The TIP and STIP programs are derived and implemented. Performance evaluation may then occur and is fed back into the planning activities (this cycle is in bold in figure 26–13). Other cycles shown connect the short- and mid-range development of CMS plans and congestion strategies with the LRP, TIP, STIP and the travel monitoring programs to the planning process. Again, this process has traditionally been focused on the long term and the performance monitoring and travel monitoring feedback have been relatively infrequent because of data collection costs and processing requirements.

The integrated process re-orients the elements of figure 26–13 focusing first on the short-term and then spiraling out to the mid- and long-term issues and solutions. The process shifts the emphasis and order of activities rather than creating new efforts. Thus, it is an evolution of the existing process rather than a replacement. The documents and products needed to meet federal regulations are still created, but when and how they are produced and what they include has changed.

The rest of this section briefly looks at each of the federally required products of the planning process and describes where they fit and some of the issues that may arise as they are developed within the integrated planning process. The federal products and documents are presented because they are the primary focus of many current practitioners and activities.

CMS

CMS is one of six "management systems" (plus a traffic monitoring system) originally required by ISTEA. CMS and its development process is the conceptual forerunner of both the integrated planning framework and the O&M planning factor of TEA-21. As stated in the final management system rule:

> An effective CMS is a systematic process for managing congestion that provides information on transportation system performance and on alternative strategies for alleviating congestion and enhancing the mobility of persons and goods to levels that meet state and local needs (FHWA and FTA 1996).

ITS has always been seen as an integral part of the CMS strategies and their development (FHWA 1998, ITE 1997). A key factor is that ITS provides the opportunity to develop and apply *regional strategies* to manage the system, not just localized or facility-oriented ones. Despite this, a review of CMS systems and ITS by the Volpe Transportation Systems Center found (Deblasio et al. 1997):

- CMS do consider ITS alternatives, but as individual projects and not in the context of a regional framework or system.
- Better coordination is needed between the developers of CMS and ITS and the agencies responsible for each.
- Although CMS is potentially an effective mechanism for incorporating ITS into the metropolitan planning process, broader coordination is needed through all of the planning activities and products.

The integrated planning process is designed to overcome these deficiencies.

TIP and STIP: metropolitan and statewide

TIPs are short-term documents that prioritize and program the list of federally funded projects that are to be carried out for each year that they cover (FHWA and FTA 1993). Both the metropolitan and Statewide improvement programs must cover a minimum of 3 years and be updated at least every 2 years. Both programs must be financially constrained by year to resources that are reasonably expected to be available during that period. They can cover more than 3 years (typically 5- to 6-year programs are developed), but they must also extend the project prioritization and financial analysis to cover the additional years. The projects within the TIPs and STIPs must be consistent with the appropriate LRP. Metropolitan TIPs must also meet national air quality conformity requirements and be consistent with the SIP. The STIP includes without modification each of the MPO TIPs within its jurisdiction.

In the Final Policy Notice of Proposed Rulemaking for Architecture Consistency, the ITS integration strategy lays out the overall components for ITS and O&M for the future and is part of the LRP documentation. Regional architectures provide more specific detail and prioritization or phasing of the ITS components. Their relationship to the integration strategy is in many ways equivalent to the TIP, STIP and LRP relationship. Yet, the regional architecture is currently defined to be part of project development and is not represented anywhere in the LRP, TIP or STIP requirements. In the integrated process the TIP and STIP do, however, need to be closely coordinated even if no formal requirement exists to do so.

Metropolitan and statewide transportation plans (LRP)

The metropolitan and statewide transportation plans (LRPs) are the main federally required products documenting an area's transportation planning and decision-making process for federal funding. They both must address at least a 20-year planning horizon. The plans must incorporate consideration of the major elements of transportation planning as defined by ISTEA and TEA-21, including: the major planning factors, air quality conformity process, financial plans and constraints, public involvement, management systems input, project level corridor and subarea evaluations, NEPA analyses and ITS architecture conformity (Siwek 1995, FHWA and FTA 1996). Metropolitan transportation plans include "both long-range and short-range strategies and actions that lead to the development of an integrated intermodal transportation system that facilitates the efficient movement of people and goods" (FHWA and FTA 1993). Definition and analysis of projected travel demand of people and goods, adopted CMS strategies, pedestrian and bicycle facilities, system preservation measures, interaction with land use plans, transportation enhancement activities and major transportation investments must be included. Detail must be sufficient to provide for cost analysis, air quality conformity and financial planning. They must be updated at least every 3 years in areas with air quality concerns and every 5 years in attainment areas. Statewide transportation plans on the other hand must reflect the associated metropolitan plans, but they can be developed at a higher "policy" level. Statewide plans are updated as appropriate.

The ITS integration strategy must be developed and included in the LRP. The integrated process brings its development into the overall planning process versus it being a separate activity with its own goals and objectives, stakeholders and solutions.

Corridor and subarea alternative development (formerly Major Investment Study) and NEPA

TEA-21 eliminated the Major Investment Study requirement introduced by ISTEA for analysis of transportation improvements in corridors and subareas. Corridor alternatives analysis is now to be integrated into the planning and NEPA analyses. Options being considered by the U.S. DOT for this were presented in March 1999 (FHWA and FTA 1999) and are now being finalized. Despite the removal of a formal separate requirement, determining what is the best integrated transportation solution (ITS, O&M and infrastructure) in a corridor is still an important element of the planning process. Corridor analysis often requires more detail and closer examination of options than the overall system analysis performed as part of the LRP. Issues associated with introducing ITS into corridor analyses have been examined elsewhere (Mitretek Systems 1999, Rush and Penic 1998, Transcore 1998).

Carrying out corridor and subarea analysis within the integrated process raises the same issues that were presented in the TIP and LRP discussions. The alternatives must now include development of the full evolution of improvements over time in the corridor. Operations of the system and changes in the performance relationships must be made explicit. Full life cycle costs, benefits and ways to tradeoff near- and far-term impacts and costs must be used.

Air quality conformity and the SIP

ISTEA linked transportation planning with meeting the requirements of the 1990 Clean Air Act Amendments. It requires that areas that do not meet the National Ambient Air Quality Standards (NAAQS) or are designated as "maintenance" areas must show that their LRPs and TIPs are in conformance with the SIP. The SIP establishes how the state will attain the NAAQS and includes the development of transportation control measures in ozone and CO nonattainment areas. The MPO must make the conformity determinations concerning the TIP and LRP (see Siwek 1995 and Transcore 1998 for additional summaries of the air quality conformity requirements and transportation planning).

The integrated planning process does not significantly alter how and when the air quality conformity determinations need to be made within the planning process. TIP conformity is carried out as part of the TIP development and LRP conformity is carried out as part of the LRP development.

Remaining challenges and initial actions toward integrated planning

Challenges

There are a number of remaining challenges that must be overcome as the standard practice evolves toward the integrated framework.

Final policy on architecture consistency and planning

The TEA-21 Final Policy for Architecture Consistency and the joint FHWA and FTA Planning Rule for Metropolitan and Statewide Planning are still under review and comment. Their effect and how the requirements for incorporating an integration strategy and regional architecture in planning and project development are still undetermined. Consequently, no one knows what good practice for these requirements is and what will suffice. Yet, these are the first actual regulations calling for mainstreaming ITS. Case studies, "model" efforts and dissemination of good practice are needed once the policy is adopted.

New organizations and public–private partnerships

New organizations aimed at managing the overall transportation system, integrating and coordinating ITS services and developing ITS architectures are carrying out many near- to mid-term planning and programming functions. As we move to the integrated planning process that merges near- and mid-long term planning, how these organizations interact with traditional planning and the roles and responsibilities of both the new and old organizations are evolving. Likewise, actual working models of sustainable public–private partnerships and the role of the private sector in future transportation are still undetermined. The National ITS Program Plan's vision assumes a growing role of independent service providers and the market in provision of services. What remains to be seen is whether these services will actually develop, and if they develop whether they will do so in a way that is consistent with the overall management of the transportation system and fulfillment of a region's goals and objectives.

Data revolution (costs, models and uses)

New technology is revolutionizing the storage and analysis of data, and ADUS has been developed in response. However, there are virtually no cases of integrating ITS data and the new techniques for data warehousing, fusion and mining into the standard practices of planning. Questions remain regarding how to maintain the volume of data and its quality over time, and the costs of different ADUS market packages and the comparability between ITS collected data and data collected from traditional means. More importantly, ITS data provide new information on variability of the system and customer satisfaction. New uses of the continuous information and how it may transform the planning and decision-making process remain to be seen.

Predicting technology

Predicting the new innovations in technology and its costs will be a perennial issue if ITS is to be fully incorporated into mid- and long-range planning. Equally important are predictions of market penetrations of technologies and services once they are deployed. Most ITS specialists are hesitant to predict the future beyond 5 to 7 years. Yet, 20-year forecasts are needed. In order to provide consistency in regional forecasts and avoid duplication of effort by local and state agencies across the country, a national baseline forecast may be needed.

Synergies of integrated systems

While examples of individual ITS implementations, their costs and benefits and analysis methods are growing rapidly, little is known still about the effects of integrated systems. These may defy simple sketch methods and require incorporating the use of information and response to variability and nonrecurrent incidents in the overall regional travel forecasting tools. The U.S. DOT Metropolitan Model Deployment Initiative has provided a beginning on collecting and analyzing information on integrated deployments. However, this is only a beginning and more information and tools for evaluating integrated ITS, as well as combined ITS and traditional solutions, are needed.

Putting it all together (no one is there yet)

There are a growing number of areas that are beginning to incorporate ITS into their planning processes and have included various aspects of the integrated planning process described here in their procedures. San Francisco, California; Chicago, Illinois; Washington, D.C.; Houston, Texas; Albany, New York; and others all are on their way in the evolution. However, no area has fully refocused its process on O&M and the development path or incorporated variation and ITS into their analysis techniques. This will come with time. There are, however, a number of initial actions that can be taken.

Initial Actions

In the meantime a number of initial activities and strategies can be used to assist in the transition from current practice to the integrated planning process (Mitretek 2000).

Initial assessment of regional context (problems, issues and concerns)

Does the region have World I or World II characteristics? Does it have relatively low congestion and stable conditions; or is it experiencing system failures due to congestion, an inability to expand capacity and high variation in conditions? Are there other conditions and issues such as a high percentage of unfamiliar travelers (tourists) that need information on the system? This assessment will help establish who may need to be part of the process, what the focus of the transition may be and when or how it may need to take place.

Establish advocacy and leadership

Several studies have found that "champions" are the key to bringing ITS projects through the deployment process (Deblasio et al. 1998, ITS America 1996), and to incorporating ITS and O&M in general into an integrated planning process. Also crucial is tying the advocacy and ownership to where the problems and issues are within the area. As the new process evolves the leaders must "own" both the solutions and the problems that they are aimed at overcoming.

Aim at crossing boundaries (communication and coordination across modal, geographic and institutional boundaries)

A recent Volpe study (Deblasio et al. 1998) found that this improved communication across artificial barriers in the system is crucial for developing a system-wide operations perspective and bringing ITS into the planning process. System-wide committees and task forces might be established, for example, to unite stakeholders from different jurisdictions as well as the new operations and ITS stakeholders.

Plan for incremental changes in the process as well as implementation of ITS systems

Organizations and decision-making processes do not change overnight. Change typically occurs incrementally. ITS services and systems can be implemented in modest stages and then extended geographically. Software and hardware are typically upgraded with improved technology in an evolutionary manner, retaining certain components and improving others. This incremental improvement feature can pose special challenges for programming ITS. The benefits of "core" start-up ITS investments—such as communication backbones, traffic operations centers, basic detection and surveillance—might be understated unless their potential to support multiple future additions of high marginal value is reflected.

Begin to develop new performance-oriented measures and collect data to support them

Key to the integrated process is the use of performance-oriented measures that reflect the user's perspective on how well the system operates. A key step in this outcome-driven approach is the use of deficiency analysis, with performance measured either against current conditions or against locally defined standards or benchmarks. Performance-oriented measures do little unless the data exist to support them. Data collection should start now no matter what stage of transition the area is in.

Move towards full definition of every project

The integrated process hinges on including all aspects of a project in its analysis. Redefining what is required to describe a project or a future system alternative can begin now. This should include not only the system infrastructure and associated costs, but also the ITS and management strategies, operations and maintenance costs, and the phasing and schedule of changes to the system.

It is also important to look at the direct strategic connections and synergies that combined infrastructure, ITS and O&M strategies offer. Major road and transit improvements can be specifically designed to capitalize on an aggressive systems management regime. At the same time significant savings can be realized through "building in" ITS improvements—piggybacking ITS onto major facility construction and improvement projects.

Move towards a system view of planning

ITS concepts, systems and technology are most effective when applied at the regional scale. The goal should be to achieve interoperability across jurisdictional boundaries, across modes and among multiple vendor systems within a region. A regional systems architecture can be an effective tool for coordinating the large number of technical decisions among the various institutional players who may be involved. Second, implementation plans are often useful for ensuring commitments to operation support from the necessary range of regional systems owners and operators. A systems perspective therefore becomes important in reflecting the true benefits and costs of ITS and O&M.

Begin to develop new analysis methods

Existing planning analysis methods predict average conditions and the traveler response to infrastructure and capacity improvements. Planners should start developing new approaches that reflect variation in system performance. A special challenge in the long term will be to understand how system capacity and improved real-time systems information interact to influence travel behavior. Equally important is developing methods to account for the full life cycle of costs and benefits when comparing future system alternatives. Some attributes of the needed analysis techniques are:

- a focus on performance-based problems with strong feedback from existing operations;
- concern for average and nonstandard conditions of incidents, weather and so forth;
- measures of effectiveness for new service attributes (including reliability, security and information);
- data on ITS benefits relating to improved traveler information or variable prices; and
- discounting for varying time flow of benefits to compare ITS with major capital investments.

Develop awareness and train staff

As the role of ITS and O&M grows, the technical expertise of staffs involved in both planning and operations must increase as well. Training is available on a number of ITS topics through the PCB. Specific course details can be found at the PCB website: <http://pcb.volpe.dot.gov/>. Other training is also provided through state and local governments, universities and ITS vendors (see the PCB website for indexes of these courses in your area).

Endnotes

1. This chapter is a summary of *NCHRP 8–35: Incorporating ITS into the Transportation Planning Process.* Unless otherwise noted all figures, tables and concepts are derived from the NCHRP project. In addition to the author, key contributors include Don Emerson, Steven Lockwood, Erin Bard and Don Roberts. The chapter also draws on previous pioneering efforts concerning integrating ITS into transportation planning, including: *Transportation Planning and ITS—Putting the Pieces Together* (Siwek 1998) and *Integrating Intelligent Transportation Systems with the Transportation Planning Process: An Interim Handbook* (Transcore 1998).

2. Section 5206(e) of TEA-21.

3. Sixteen metropolitan and 23 statewide planning factors required under Section 134, statewide and metropolitan planning and program of ISTEA (FHWA and FTA 1993).

4. TEA-21 language calls for "conformity" with the national ITS architecture and standards. U.S. DOT's incremental, phased approach to implementing this provision is better reflected by the use of the term "consistency" with the national ITS architecture. For our purposes, these two terms are considered to be synonymous.

5. HERO is a type of Incident Management Service where people report accidents and incidents, or non-tow vehicles drive the corridor with simple emergency equipment (e.g., jump start, flat fixing).

6. The interested reader can learn more details about the federal transportation process and its history by consulting the following references (especially FHWA and FTA 1993, Siwek 1995 and 1996, Weiner 1997, Mickelson 1998, Transcore 1998 and ITE 1999).

References

Association of Metropolitan Planning Organizations.1998. *Special Edition: Systems MPOs and Intelligent Transportation, MPO Monitor* (September/October). Washington, D.C.: AMPO.

Briggs, V. 1999. "New Regional Transportation Organizations." *ITS Quarterly* (Fall). Washington, D.C.: ITS America.

Bower, B. 1999. "Institutional Issues in Mainstreaming ITS" (January). Presentation to the Annual Transportation Research Board Conference, Washington, D.C.

Cambridge Systematics, Inc. 1998. *Florida Department of Transportation ITS Planning Guidelines* (Fall), Internal Drafts. Cambridge, MA: Cambridge Systematics, Inc.

Cambridge Systematics, Inc. 1999. *Multimodal Transportation: Development of a Performance-Based Planning Process—Performance-Based Planning Manual Preliminary Draft.* Washington D.C.: National Cooperative Highway Research Program, NCHRP Project 8–32(2), National Academy Press.

Cambridge Systematics and ITT Industries. 2000. *ITS Deployment Analysis System User's Manual* (January). Prepared for Oak Ridge National Laboratory and Federal Highway Administration. Oakland, CA: Cambridge Systematics and ITT Industries.

Castle Rock. 1997. *Technology in Rural Transportation "Simple Solutions."* Report for Turner-Fairbank Highway Research Center, Federal Highway Administration. McLean, VA: Castle Rock.

Castle Rock, Black and Veatch. 1999. *ITS Rural Toolbox for Rural and Small Urban Areas.* Albany, NY: New York State Department of Transportation.

Center for Urban Transportation Research. 2000. *First Draft: ITS Planning Guidelines Manual* (March). Prepared for the Florida Department of Transportation. Tallahassee, FL: CUTR.

Dahms, L., and L. Klein. 1998. "The San Francisco Bay Area's Approach to System Management." *ITE Journal* (December). Washington, D.C.: Institute of Transportation Engineers.

Daniels, G., and T. Starr. 1996. "Guidelines for Funding Operations and Maintenance of Intelligent Transportation Systems/Advanced Traffic Management Systems." *Transportation Research Record 1588.* Washington, D.C.: Transportation Research Board.

Deblasio et al. 1997. *A Review of Metropolitan Area Early Development Plans and Congestion Management Systems for the Development of Intelligent Transportation Systems* (September). For U.S. DOT, ITS Joint Program Office, Volpe National Transportation Systems Center, Cambridge, MA.

Deblasio et al. 1998. *Strategies for Incorporating ITS Solutions into The Metropolitan Transportation Planning Process* (December). For U.S. DOT, ITS Joint Program Office, Volpe National Transportation Systems Center, Cambridge, MA.

ECONorthwest and Parsons, Brinckerhoff, Quade and Douglas. 1995. *Least-Cost Planning: Principles, Applications and Issues* (September). For FHWA Office of Environment and Planning, Washington, D.C.

ERTICO ITS City Pioneers. 1998. *ITS Planning Handbook: Intelligent City Transport.* Brussels, Belgium.

Federal Highway Administration and Federal Transit Administration. 1993. "Statewide Planning: Metropolitan Planning: Final Rule." *Federal Register* (October 28). Washington, D.C.

Federal Highway Administration and Federal Transit Administration. 1996. "Management and Monitoring Systems: Final Rule." *Federal Register* (December 19). Washington. D.C.

Federal Highway Administration and Federal Transit Administration. 2000. "23 CFR Parts 450 and 1410, 49 CFR 613 and 621 Statewide Transportation Planning; Metropolitan Transportation Planning; Proposed Rule." *Federal Register* (May 25). Washington, D.C.

Federal Highway Administration and Florida DOT in Association with Teach America Corporation. 1998. *Congestion Management Systems INTERACTIVE CD-ROM: Version 1 Prototype.* Washington, D.C.

Flannery, A. 2000. *DRAFT ITS Data Archiving Five-Year Program Description* (March). Washington, D.C.: Mitretek Systems for the FHWA Office of Highway Information Management.

Fowler, T. and B. Ward. 2000. *Mainstreaming ITS into A Regional Transportation Program* (March). Paper presented at ITS America's Annual Conference, Boston, MA, May 2000.

Haigler Bailly. 1999. *Assessing the Emissions and Fuel Consumption Impacts of Intelligent Transportation Systems* (February). Washington, D.C.: U.S. Environmental Protection Agency Office of Policy.

Humphrey, T. 1995. *Synthesis of Highway Practice 217: Consideration of the 15 Factors in the Metropolitan Planning Process.* Washington, D.C.: National Cooperative Highway Research Program, National Academy Press.

Institute of Transportation Engineers. 1999. *Transportation Planning Handbook,* 2nd Edition. Washington D.C.: Prentice-Hall.

ITS America. 1996. *ITS Action Guide: Realizing the Benefits.* Washington, D.C.: ITS America.

Ishimaru, J. and M. Hallenbeck. 1999. *Flow Evaluation Design Technical Report.* Seattle, WA: Washington State Transportation Center for WSDOT.

Jacobsen, L. 1999. *Mainstreaming ITS, Operations and Management into the Planning Process* (April). Presentation at ITS America Annual Conference. Washington, D.C.

Lindley J. A. 1986. *Quantification of Urban Freeway Congestion and Analysis of Remedial Measures.* Washington, D.C.: Federal Highway Administration.

Lockwood, S. 1999. *Mainstreaming Management, Operations and ITS into The Planning Process.* Conference on Refocusing Planning for the 21st Century, February 1999, Washington, D.C.

Margiotta, R. 1998. *ITS as a Data Resource: Preliminary Requirements for a User Service* (April). Washington, D.C.: Federal Highway Administration.

Meese, A. 1998. *Inside View of ITS at a Metropolitan Planning Organization.* Paper presented at the North American Travel Monitoring Exhibition and Conference, Charlotte, N.C.

Mergel, J. 1998. *The Capability of ITS to Provide Systems Performance Data: Draft Final Report.* For FHWA Office of Environment and Planning, Volpe National Transportation Systems Center, Cambridge Massachusetts.

Metropolitan Washington Council of Governments. 1998. "The Vision." Vision statement adopted by the Transportation Planning Board on October 21, 1998, Washington, D.C.

Meyer, M. 1998. *A Toolbox for Alleviating Traffic Congestion and Enhancing Mobility.* Washington, D.C.: Institute of Transportation Engineers.

Mickelson, R. P. 1998. *Synthesis of Highway Practice 267: Transportation Development Process.* Washington, D.C.: National Cooperative Highway Research Program, National Academy Press.

Mitretek Systems. 1996. *Incorporating ITS into Transportation Improvement Planning: Phase 1* Final Report (June). Washington, D.C.: U.S. Department of Transportation.

Mitretek Systems. 1999a. *Incorporating ITS into Corridor Planning: Seattle Case Study—Final Report* (August). Washington, D.C.: U.S. Department of Transportation.

Mitretek Systems. 1999b. *NCHRP 8–35: Incorporating ITS into the Transportation Planning Process Interim Report* (August). Washington, D.C.: National Cooperative Highway Research Council of the Transportation Research Board.

Mitretek Systems. 2000. *NCHRP 8-35: Incorporating ITS into the Transportation Planning Process: Integrated Planning (O&M, ITS, Infrastructure) Draft Practitioners Guidebook* (June). Washington, D.C.: National Cooperative Highway Research Council of the Transportation Research Board.

National Association of Regional Councils. 1995. *Working Together on Transportation Planning: An Approach to Collaborative Decision-Making* (May). Washington, D.C.: FTA Office of Policy.

National Highway Institute. 1998. Course #13602: "Deploying Integrated Intelligent Transportation Systems—Metropolitan." Course slides. Washington, D.C.: NHI.

National Highway Institute. 1999. Course #15260: "Advanced Travel Demand Forecasting." Course notes. Washington, D.C.: NHI.

PB Farradyne. 1999. *Florida Statewide ITS Strategic Plan: ITS Cost Analysis Issue Paper.* Tallahassee, FL: Florida Department of Transportation.

Proper, A. 1999. *Intelligent Transportation Systems Benefits* (May). Washington, D.C.: Mitretek Systems for the Federal Highway Administration.

Rush, J., and M. Penic. 1998. *Integrating ITS and Traditional Planning-Lessons Learned: I-64 Corridor Major Investment Study.* Washington, D.C.: Prepared for the Federal Highway Administration by Parsons Brinckerhoff Inc. and SAIC.

SAIC. 1999. *User's Manual for SCRITS, SCReening Analysis for ITS* (January). Washington, D.C.: Federal Highway Administration, Office of Traffic Management and ITS Applications.

Sarah J. Siwek and Associates Transportation and Environmental Consulting. 1995. *A Guide to Metropolitan Transportation Planning Under ISTEA: How the Pieces Fit Together* (July). Washington, D.C.: Federal Highway Administration, Office of Environment and Planning.

Sarah J. Siwek and Associates Transportation and Environmental Consulting. 1996. *Statewide Transportation Planning Under ISTEA: A New Decision-making Framework* (October). Washington, D.C.: Federal Highway Administration, Office of Environment and Planning.

Sarah J. Siwek and Associates Transportation and Environmental Consulting. 1998. *Transportation Planning and ITS: Putting the Pieces Together* (June). Washington, D.C.: Federal Highway Administration, Office of Environment and Planning.

Smith, B. L. et al. 1995. *Final Report: Evaluation of the ITS Planning Process.* Charlottesville, VA: Virginia Transportation Research Council for Federal Highway Administration.

Smith, H. 1998. *Improving Transit with Intelligent Transportation Systems* (December). Washington, D.C.: ITS America.

Turner, S. M., W. L. Eisele, B. J. Gajewski, L. P. Albert and R. J. Benz. 1999. *ITS Data Archiving: Case Study Analyses of San Antonio TransGuide® Data* (August). College Station, TX: Federal Highway Administration, Texas Transportation Institute.

Turner, S. M. 2000. *Archived ITS Data: Data Quality Issues* (January). Paper presented at the 2000 Transportation Research Board Annual Meeting, Washington. D.C.

Transcore. 1998. *Integrating Intelligent Transportation Systems within the Transportation Planning Process: An Interim Handbook* (January). Washington, D.C.: Federal Highway Administration, Office of Traffic Management and ITS Applications, and Office of Environment and Planning.

Transportation Research Board. 1999. *Conference on Refocusing Planning for the 21st Century Breakout Session Summaries* (February), Washington, D.C.

U.S. Department of Transportation. 1995. *National ITS Program Plan.* First Edition, Volumes I and II (March). Washington, D.C.: U.S. DOT and ITS America.

U.S. Department of Transportation. 1999. *The National ITS Architecture: A Framework for Integrated Transportation into the 21st Century Version 3.0* (December). Washington, D.C.: U.S. DOT, <http://www.odetics.com/itsarch/>.

Virginia Department of Transportation. 1996. *Virginia's Intelligent Transportation System (ITS) Interim Tactical Plan* (August). Richmond, VA: Virginia DOT.

Weiner, E. 1997. *Urban Transportation Planning in the United States: An Historical Overview,* 5th Edition (September). Washington, D.C.: U.S. Department of Transportation, Technology Sharing Program.

World Road Association (PIARC). 1999. *ITS Handbook.* Washington, D.C.

Zavattero, D., and A. Smoliak. 1996. "Local ITS Deployment and Consensus Building: The Metropolitan Planning Organization's Role in ITS Development in the Chicago Region." *ITS America Annual Conference Proceedings.* Washington, D.C.: ITS America.

BY Thomas Horan • Executive Director •
Claremont Information and Technology Institute,
School of Information Science,
Claremont Graduate University

ENVIRONMENTAL ISSUES

Introduction: transportation and environmental sustainability

A brief history of transportation and the environment

The relationship between transportation, technology and the environment is long standing. In the early 1920s, the car was first viewed as an improvement over the horse-polluted city environment. By the early 1930s, interest in an Interstate Highway System grew as a means to help get cars and trucks out of the mud. But, as automobile ownership grew and the Interstate system manifest itself across the country, the environmental impacts became pronounced. While advances in vehicle and construction technologies brought the mobility to an unprecedented percentage of the population, it did so at the expense of many social, environmental and community amenities.

Indeed, while the Interstate system advanced considerably from its enactment in 1950, there were a number of concerns surrounding its inception.[1] Critics such as Daniel Patrick Moynihan and Lewis Mumford contended that, especially in urban areas, the Interstate system would adversely affect local communities.[2] Still, as chronicled by Tom Lewis, the Interstate era propelled ahead, buoyed by a growing economy, high federal match ratios and a national consensus around most of the Interstate objectives.[3] Over a 30-year period some 40,000 miles of Interstates were constructed, and even many more arterials. Increases in the manufacturing methods of automobiles made the auto affordable to most Americans, and the economy came to benefit and rely upon the surface transportation system. In short, automobile transportation came to be the mobility backbone of the nation's economy.

This highway-centered emphasis of the Interstate era remained firmly rooted in urban transportation planning until 1991, when the federal Intermodal Surface Transportation Efficiency Act (ISTEA) fundamentally altered U.S. transportation policy.[4] ISTEA made unprecedented efforts to balance traditional transportation policy objectives (i.e., mobility) with nontraditional objectives such as neighborhood economic development, environmental quality and the preservation and enhancement of areas of cultural and aesthetic value. In doing so, ISTEA reflected the profound influence that a set of principles often labeled as "sustainability" or "sustainable communities" have had—and will continue to have under the Transportation Equity Act for the 21st Century (TEA-21)—on the transportation sector.[5]

Taking place alongside the policy revolution that ISTEA and TEA-21 have engendered in transportation is a second, more fundamental societal revolution: the shift to an information society. The fundamental elements of economic production, distribution and consumption are being affected by this revolution; and the range of impacts is at this point only dimly understood. These impacts include changing spatial locations or what and where goods are produced, the rise of electronic and just-in-time distribution systems to deliver goods and services and a changing profile of where and how citizens work and play.

It is against this backdrop of paradigm shifts in transportation and information that intelligent transportation systems (ITS) are being deployed. Understanding the background is important, as it will generate the priorities and consequent system designs for communities throughout the United States. As other chapters in this volume have already provided an overview about both ITS and information technology advances, this chapter will proceed with a brief review about the environmental element—sustainability—and then enter into a more detailed review of ITS impacts and deployment issues relative to environmental quality.

Sustainability: origin, concept and application

What is the origin of the term "sustainability," and what does it mean? The first question—the term's origin—is easier to answer. It first appeared in the 1970s as "sustainable development," and it was widely circulated among environment and development professionals with the 1980 publication of the World Conservation Strategy.[6] A 1987 United Nations-sponsored report entitled Our Common Future—also known as the Brundtland Commission report—popularized the term and provided its most widely known definition: "Sustainable development is development that meets the needs of the present without compromising the ability of future generations to meet their own needs."[7] Other international documents have since elaborated on the term—most notably Agenda 21, the action plan adopted at the 1992 United Nations Conference on Environment and Development (known as the Rio Conference or Earth Summit).

More difficult than identifying the origin of sustainability is determining what the concept means. At least seventy definitions of sustainable development are now in circulation, and several variants of the term—sustainable communities, livable communities, livability and others—are used to describe roughly the same construct.[8] The sustainability concept thus remains ambiguous, and it is particularly difficult to translate into practical action; as Ruttan correctly notes, the popularity of the Bruntland definition stems in part from it being "so broad that it is almost devoid of operational significance."[9] And the term is indeed popular: hundreds of international conferences, professional meetings and scientific associations have used sustainability as the theme of their gatherings within the last decade.

Conceptual ambiguity notwithstanding, the U.S. transportation sector (or at least segments of it) is increasingly embracing sustainability as a meaningful policy guide, and the appearance of the term "sustainability" in mainstream policy circles in the 1990s is a notable development. The Institute of Transportation Engineers (ITE), one of the oldest and largest associations of transportation professionals, made "Transportation and Sustainable Communities" the theme of its annual international conference in both 1997 and 1998. Even President Clinton, in announcing his Administration's 1997 proposal for national transportation legislation, stated that his proposal would "build a bridge to sustainable communities that can last and grow and bring people together over the long run."[10]

Yet these references to sustainability leave unanswered the most vexing problem associated with the concept, whether applied to transportation or other policy sectors: policy prescriptions that invoke sustainability are often more poetic than practical. Defining sustainability in relation to transportation requires an analysis of how the concept can be applied to the decisions that policymakers confront every day. Perhaps the best and most tangible way to discuss its application is to highlight the elements of TEA-21—the nation's new federal transportation law—that illustrate the potential to move from sustainability principles toward practice. Indeed, ISTEA and TEA-21's vision of sustainability is a holistic policy approach to transportation that seeks to balance social, economic and environmental objectives with the traditional goal of mobility; and in this sense it represents the opportunity (though not the requirement) to move toward more sustainable practices in areas such as ITS.

Sustainability in practice: TEA-21 and a holistic approach to transportation

Several policy elements of ISTEA and its successor, TEA-21, provide important policy parameters for deploying ITS in a manner consistent with sustainability concepts. These policy dimensions include: (1) explicit listing of nontraditional policy goals to be considered in as part of holistic transportation policymaking, (2) provision of strong financial and procedural incentives to carry out these nontraditional goals and (3) guidance for mainstreaming ITS into the transportation planning and programming process.

On the first item, TEA-21 calls for transportation planners and engineers to balance traditional transportation goals (i.e., moving people and goods) with numerous nontraditional goals through a device known as "planning factors." Transportation projects that receive federal funds must be included in a comprehensive metropolitan transportation plan analyzed for how it will affect or be affected by each of the seven factors listed in table 27–1.

Table 27–1
Metropolitan Transportation Planning Factors Under TEA-21
Source: U.S. Department of Transportation, Overview of TEA-21
Provisions (Washington, D.C.: GPO, 1998).

- Support the economic vitality of the metropolitan area, especially by enabling global competitiveness, productivity and efficiency
- Increase the safety and security of the transportation system for motorized and nonmotorized users
- Increase the accessibility and mobility options available to people and for freight
- Protect and enhance the environment, promote energy conservation and improve the quality of life
- Enhance the integration and connectivity of the transportation system, across and between modes, for people and freight
- Promote efficient system management and operation
- Emphasize the preservation of the existing transportation system

In spite of a longstanding policy direction in favor of planning, the history of U.S. transportation shows that federal laws that merely list issues policymakers should consider may do little to ensure that these issues are considered; and if they are considered, that they are actually followed.[11] So beyond simply listing the importance of policy goals other than mobility, TEA-21 provides the financial and procedural incentives to integrate the nontraditional goals into the transportation policymaking process. In many instances, including the Congestion Mitigation and Air Quality Improvement program (CMAQ) and Transportation Enhancements program, TEA-21 provides even stronger financial support than originally under ISTEA. These two programs will be provided more than $13 billion over the six-year life of TEA-21 to implement the nontraditional goals articulated in the planning factors.[12]

Reinforcing the more integrated, multidimensional policy approach encouraged by the CMAQ and Enhancements programs are two provisions for community-building and preservation. An example of this new ethos can be found in Section 1221 of TEA-21; it provides the U.S. Department of Transportation (U.S. DOT) with $120 million over the six years that can be granted to state, local and regional agencies that partner with nonprofits, private-sector interests and each other to bring together transportation and land use decisions. The program, called the Transportation and Community and System Preservation Pilot Program, offers planning grants and "implementation grants" to fund cross-cutting research. This program may be useful to fund community-based demonstration projects that use information technologies to help communities create systems to make transportation and land use decisions that help result in sustainable communities. A second provision, Assess to Jobs, provides $500 million for innovative Welfare to Work programs that aim to achieve a better match between the location of jobs and the accessibility of those jobs to people who need and want them.[13]

Beyond dedicating money for programs, TEA-21 also continues ISTEA's gains in mandating greater involvement of both metropolitan planning organizations (MPOs) and the public as ways to reinforce a holistic policy approach that balances economic, social and environmental elements. TEA-21 continues the important role ISTEA initiated for involving MPOs in transportation decision-making.[14] MPOs in all urbanized areas with populations exceeding 50,000 are responsible for devising short- and long-term transportation investment plans, for selecting which transportation projects to fund within their jurisdiction, and for ensuring that transportation investments are consistent with state air quality improvement plans. Being regional organizations composed in part of local elected officials, MPOs are considered closer to the communities they serve than either federal or state transportation agencies. Yet at the same time, MPOs are not constrained by artificial city or county boundaries, thus enabling them to better manage the de facto boundaries of a regional transportation system (i.e., the entire metropolitan area). This, at least in theory, makes MPOs well positioned to balance the multidimensional "quality of life" concerns of particular communities with the entire region's interest in an efficient transportation system.[15]

ISTEA increased public involvement in transportation policymaking in several ways: public review and comment is required at all "key decision points;" the public involvement process must be inclusive, involving those "traditionally under-served by existing transportation systems;" and a process is required "for demonstrating explicit consideration and response to public input."[16] TEA-21 continues all these policies. ISTEA's public participation requirements have profoundly democratized what was once the highly insular, "top-down" transportation planning process; and many public agencies believe that transportation policy decisions are "better" as a result.[17]

Finally, TEA-21's holistic policy approach to transportation is evident in the activities of federal transportation agencies charged with implementing it. The U.S. DOT's "National Partnership for Transportation and Livable Communities," for example, builds, according to former Secretary of Transportation Federico Peña, "on the principles embodied in ISTEA ... [by stressing] the connection between transportation and community livability." In addition, the Federal Transit Administration (an agency of the U.S. DOT) is pursuing a "Livable Communities Initiative" in which it provides grants to grass-roots transportation projects that improve the social, environmental, and economic conditions in communities.[18] Besides funding actual projects, these U.S. DOT activities are playing a role in shifting the nation's transportation policy culture to one that embraces ISTEA's holistic policy approach.

The upshot of ISTEA and TEA-21's reforms is that better transportation—meaning improved connectivity between places—is just one of several standards used to judge the comparative value of alternative transportation strategies. And into this framework comes a parallel requirement to mainstream ITS. In reauthorizing the ITS Act, the clear congressional intent was to mainstream ITS into the overall planning and programming processes outlined above. In comparison to the ISTEA era of testing, planning and specially funded deployment, ITS is moving into an era of mainstreamed deployment, therefore ITS decision-makers need to understand how ITS can be integrated into this broader agenda. As the 21st century unfolds, U.S. transportation policy is structured to serve numerous social, environmental and economic goals in ways that it was not for most of this century. The multidimensional policy approach ushered in by ISTEA and TEA-21 reflects one of the critical lessons learned in the era of Interstate highway construction: too much emphasis on making places easier to pass through will tend to create places where no one wants to be.

The next section explores the potential link between the emerging generation of transportation tools—information technologies and in particular ITS—and a holistic transportation policy focused on the creation of more livable communities. That is, it addresses how these factors combine with the mainstreaming of ITS to enhance the need to think about the community integration of ITS.

ITS and sustainable communities

ITS and sustainable communities: visions and paradoxes

In 1996, former U.S. Secretary of Transportation Federico Peña gave a speech expressing his vision of what the transportation system would look like in the year 2000 and beyond. He stated that he saw a future in which "many of the improvements to the transportation system will rely on the ability of private firms and public agencies to gather, process, analyze and disseminate information."[19] Peña's vision was of an information-intensive transportation system, a system in which performance improvements would depend on the quantity and quality of information rather than on more and wider highways. Vice President Gore has recently reasserted the role of technology and transportation in producing livable and smart communities. In announcing the Smart Growth initiative, he stressed the interlinkages of transportation and community; the initiative also incorporates innovative technology (especially planning technologies like geographic information systems [GIS]) in achieving these goals.[20]

That an aggressive ITS program arrived as part of ISTEA raises important policy questions. Will ITS—conceived and designed by transportation engineers largely in the pre-ISTEA era—reflect the more traditional emphasis on moving traffic as quickly as possible? Or will ISTEA's and TEA-21's placed-based principles serve to guide ITS investments? Opinion on this question, at least among environmental analysts, is decidedly mixed. One cautiously optimistic analyst argues that, if properly directed, "ITS could be the most important enabling technology driver in decades for reform and progress in American transportation, winning for our citizens sustainable high-wage jobs, reduced traffic delay, more livable communities and a healthy environment."[21] By contrast, others view ITS unequivocally as an environmental and social Pandora's Box. Despite promising a more efficient transportation system, such analysts often argue that "A principle objective of [ITS]—to minimize total vehicle-hours of delay—has little in common with the social imperative of reducing the environmental impacts of driving."[22] Another critique of ITS goes even further: "The past 150 years [have seen] new transportation technologies stretch the envelope of urban development, raising per capita fuel consumption, consuming farmlands and open space and dirtying air basins...The so-called Intelligent Transportation System stands to worsen this state of affairs by orders of magnitude."[23]

While some evidence exists for either side in this debate, there is a more centrist position. As this author and several colleagues have outlined elsewhere, there are indeed theoretical links between ITS and a more sustainable transportation system.[24] Whether these links materialize in practice, however, will depend on how the technologies are deployed. On the one hand, if ITS deployments remain outside of ISTEA and TEA-21's policy framework, then it is possible to envision scenarios in which ITS facilitates an even more "auto-centric" culture and magnifies transportation-related problems such as air pollution and suburban sprawl. On the other hand, placed within the appropriate policy framework, ITS may be harnessed in ways consistent with ISTEA and TEA-21's placed-based approach to transportation. Properly designed, ITS can contribute to livable and smart communities. To do so requires an understanding of both traditional supply and demand approaches, as well as innovative uses outside of the demand and supply paradigm. These are addressed next.

Links between specific ITS elements and environmental sustainability

The potential link between ITS and more sustainable transportation stems from ITS' ability to create a transportation system rich in information, or what might be called an information-intensive transportation system. An information-intensive transportation system raises two prospects. First, it means using information instead of new lanes, roads and highways as a way to increase the capacity of the transportation system. In this sense, ITS "substitutes information for stuff," resulting in capacity enhancements that use fewer material resources, consume less open space and reduce the noise and community disruption related to new roads. ITS thus supports an underlying premise of sustainability thinking: that the earth's resource base has limits, that some of those limits are being approached, and therefore, sustainable development depends on accommodating economic growth while consuming fewer resources.[25]

Beyond potentially substituting for physical elements of the transportation system, the information ITS provides may also enhance the system's performance. Critical in the TEA-21 era, however, is that "enhanced performance" be defined broadly to include greater traffic efficiency and a reduction in the transportation system's negative externalities. ITS can contribute to this broader notion of enhanced performance by providing information that allows for greater operational control of the transportation system. Achieving more control of the system, in turn, increases the opportunities to address specific purposes, including broad social, economic, and environmental goals.

Table 27–2 illustrates ITS applications that facilitate greater control of the transportation system by channeling information to system managers and users. "Remote sensing," for example, can generate emissions data and assist air quality officials in targeting "gross polluters."[26] Another example is "congestion pricing," or charging drivers a fee that varies with the level of traffic on a roadway. Congestion pricing conveys information (in the form of price signals) that alerts drivers to the overall social and environmental costs of driving, making them aware that driving imposes external costs while encouraging more environmentally benign travel behavior.[27]

Overview of emission impacts

The principal near-term concern is with mobile emission impacts. Air quality is a particularly controversial issue within the ITS and the environment debate. The national ITS program asserts that ITS deployments will reduce a wide array of harmful pollutants. In fact, a recent official report cited studies in which ITS technologies measurably reduced emissions of carbon monoxide (CO), hydrocarbon (HC) and nitrogen oxides (NOx). Analysts disagree, however, over the net effects of ITS on emissions, as certain ITS applications could increase emissions by encouraging more travel. This section presents evidence and arguments on both sides of this issue, specifically: (1) studies that indicate that ITS technologies could reduce vehicle emissions, (2) speculation that ITS-facilitated increases in highway capacity could increase vehicle miles traveled (e.g., spur "latent demand" for highway use) and ultimately worsen air quality and (3) the analytic limitations in emission modeling that casts uncertainty over the entire ITS-air quality debate.

Table 27–2
ITS-Generated Information and Sustainability
Source: T. Horan, D. Dittmar and D. Jordan, "ISTEA and The New Era of Transportation
Policy: Sustainable Communities for a Federal Initiative," in D. Mazmanian and
M. Kraft, *Toward Sustainable Communities: Transition and Transformations in
Environmental Policy* (Cambridge, MA: MIT Press, 1999, p. 253).

ITS CATEGORY	APPLICATION	FLOW OF INFORMATION	CONTRIBUTION TO SUSTAINABILITY
Traffic Management	—Traffic signal synchronization	—traffic information to traffic managers allows re-timing of signals to optimize traffic flow	—reduces energy usage and emissions related to "stop-and-go" traffic and congestion
	—Incident detection	—incident (i.e., freeway accident) information to traffic managers allows faster emergency response, re-timing of ramp meters, and the like	—reduces energy usage and congestion-related emissions
Traveler Information	—Pre-trip traveler information	—traffic information to traveler allows for shift in travel time, route or mode	—reduces energy usage, congestion-related emissions and the number of trips and single-occupancy vehicles (SOV)
	—En-route traveler information	—traffic information to driver allows shift in route	—reduces energy usage congestion-related emissions
ETTM	—Congestion-sensitive road tolls (i.e., congestion pricing)	—information to drivers (in the form of price signals) that relays full social and environmental costs of driving	—reduces energy usage and emissions by reducing number of trips and SOV, reducing congestion, and perhaps encouraging less auto-dependent land use patterns (i.e., less sprawl)
Emissions Management	—Remote sensing of emissions	—vehicle emissions information to drivers or air quality managers	—aid in targeting "gross polluters" (10 percent of vehicles responsible for roughly 50 percent of emissions)
APTS	—Demand-responsive transit services	—information to transit managers and transit riders on supply/demand/status related to transit	—reduces emissions and energy usage by encouraging use of transit; helps create more equitable distribution of transportation services to under-served populations (i.e., handicapped, elderly)

Studies indicate that ITS technologies reduce emissions by providing information relevant to both supply-side and demand-side emission reduction strategies. "Supply-side" strategies seek to improve traffic flow by increasing the capacity of the transportation system. The goal is to reduce congestion-related emissions. Studies show that supply-side improvements, such as coordinating traffic signals and installing on-ramp meters and management systems on freeways, modestly reduce emissions (e.g., 10 to 15 percent reductions in CO). Electronic toll collection (ETC)—which allows drivers to pay road fees without stopping at toll booths—is another supply-side strategy; and studies show that ETC at toll booths reduces hydrocarbon emissions by up to 83 percent "per affected mile." A problem with supply-side enhancements, however, is that they may increase vehicle speeds and result in higher NOx emissions.

"Demand-side" strategies take a different approach to emissions reduction. Instead of increasing highway capacity, demand-management strategies attempt to reduce vehicle travel, either by reducing the vehicle miles of travel (VMT), the number of vehicle trips, or the number of single occupant vehicles (SOVs). The goal is to lower overall demand on the transportation system. Such strategies include both transportation control measures (TCMs) and road pricing.[28] TCMs are the traditional demand-side strategy, and ITS technologies such as advanced traveler information systems (ATIS) and advanced public transportation systems (APTS) can facilitate such strategies. The accumulating evidence, however, is that TCMs provide only marginal reductions in air pollution. For example, the General Accounting Office estimated that TCMs in the Los Angeles Basin reduced HC and CO emissions by less than 2 percent, and by no more than 5 percent for any region studied.[29]

The limited effectiveness of TCMs leads many to conclude that road pricing offers a more promising approach to demand management.[30] Pricing strategies may, in fact, provide four to eight times more emissions reductions than traditional TCMs.[31] One controversial pricing strategy—congestion pricing—could generate significant revenue, and one study showed that congestion pricing fees of about $0.10 to $0.15 per mile could reduce travel during that period by 10 to 15 percent.[32] Despite these potential benefits, congestion pricing faces considerable political resistance, as such programs are often perceived as imposing disproportionate costs on less affluent drivers or as a "tax increase."[33]

The conclusion drawn from this discussion is that empirical and speculative studies alike indicate that ITS technologies reduce vehicular emissions under certain scenarios. Some analysts, however, propose alternative scenarios under which ITS could worsen air pollution. These scenarios often raise the issue of "latent demand."

Latent demand and emissions modeling

"Latent demand" refers to "the additional, unanticipated vehicles that appear on roads because people switched routes, modes, or travel times; or because they decided to take trips they had previously not taken. Latent demand is present when congestion is severe enough to deter people from taking trips using their most preferred routes, modes, or times of day...."[34] The concern is that some ITS applications, particularly automated highway systems (AHS), would effectively increase highway capacity which, in turn, could lead to more driving by unleashing latent demand for highway use. More driving would increase vehicular emissions, and an increase in highway capacity might encourage continued expansions in suburban development (e.g., "sprawl").

Concerns over latent demand, however, rest upon a great deal of analytic uncertainly. An extensive Transportation Research Board report on the effects of highway capacity increases on travel and emissions concluded that context plays a critical role:

> On the basis of current knowledge, it cannot be said that highway capacity projects are always effective measures for reducing emissions and energy use. Neither can it be said that they necessarily increase emissions and energy use in all cases and under all conditions. Effects are highly dependent on specific circumstances, such as the type of capacity addition, location of the project in the region, extent and duration of preexisting congestion, prevailing atmospheric and topographic conditions and development potential in the area.[35]

The debate over latent demand and ITS is further complicated by the lack of knowledge about how reductions in congestion affect emissions. Empirical studies indicate that such reductions vary widely. Advanced traffic signal coordination and incident detection, for example, log impressive emissions reductions due to smoothed traffic flow. One such system, the Automated Traffic Surveillance and Control (ATSAC) system in Los Angeles, California, reduced traffic delay by 20 percent and emissions by 10 percent.[36] ATIS systems provide similar though less pronounced emission reductions, yet it remains unclear whether such emission reductions last over time as market share increases.[37]

Not surprisingly, the myriad of uncertainties in this area underscore the need for improved emission modeling techniques. ITS technologies, by making dramatic changes in "average" driving conditions, make average speed-based emission factor models such as the U.S. Environmental Protection Agency's (EPA's) MOBILE5 and California's EMFAC7F inadequate tools for estimating the related environmental impacts. Imprecise emissions models could cause considerable problems, especially if (or when) ITS deployments face legal challenges on environment grounds. A recent review by the EPA found that, although modeling developments had improved the likelihood that ITS impacts of traffic flow and related emission profiles could be calculated, there were still significant limitations in detected regional impacts.[38] For this reason a series of modeling packages are being developed by the U.S. DOT.[39]

Sample impacts of ITS impacts

The most reliable assessments have been at the project level and focused on air quality and emission impacts of specific ITS technologies. With respect to the ITS technologies highlighted in this chapter, previous research indicates that they generally reduce emissions, although caveats apply to each technology or its application or both.[40] Table 27–3 presents a quick "snapshot" of select findings from previous studies on the environmental impacts of these technologies and applications. Though it is not a comprehensive list, it provides sample findings from several key studies and evaluations that are often used as the basis for impact assessments in the environmental area.[41]

A recent DOT review of findings—including several noted in table 27–3—concluded that the environmental benefits will be positive but mixed " In general, all ITS services have shown some positive benefit. Negative benefits are usually outweighed by other positive impacts. For example, higher speeds and improved traffic flow result in increases in nitrous oxides, however other emission measures, fuel consumption, travel time, and delay, are reduced."[42] For example, DOT concluded that traveler information can have a small positive effect on emissions, citing results from the Boston SmarTraveler ATIS program.[43] The interesting finding to note here from the SmarTraveler evaluation was that although the emission reductions were estimated to be significant for participating travelers, only a small proportion of the total number of trips in the metropolitan area were expected to be affected, and hence, the system-wide benefits were small.

Similarly, large emission reductions can be achieved at individual electronic toll facilities; however, the overall benefit (on a corridor- or system-wide basis) is dependent on the frequency of toll plazas. A report by the Clean Air Action Corporation[44] estimated the average emission reductions to be 72 percent for CO, 83 percent for HC, and 45 percent for NOx, per mile of impacted operation. However, this is based on the assumption that the distance involved in the average barrier toll transaction is only 0.55 miles. Hence, the reductions, although large, are highly localized and may be insignificant at the network level. The Clean Air Action Corporation estimates are based on a study of the Muskogee Turnpike in Oklahoma, Asbury Plaza on the Garden State Parkway in New Jersey and Western Plaza on the Massachusetts Turnpike.

Perhaps the most frequently assessed localized impacts are in the area of advanced traffic systems management (ATMS). Adaptive traffic signal coordination has significant potential for providing energy and environmental benefits. The ATSAC program reported a 13-percent reduction in fuel consumption and a 14-percent reduction in vehicle emissions.[45] Similarly, the City of Abilene ATSC system estimated a 6-percent reduction in fuel consumption, 10-percent reduction in HC emissions, and a 13-percent reduction in CO emissions. In contrast, NOx emissions were estimated to increase by 4 percent.[46]

Table 27–3
"Snapshot" Overview of Studies on the Environmental Impacts of ITS Technologies.
Sources: S. Shaheen, T. Young, D. Sperling, D. Jordan and T. Horan, *Identification and Prioritization of Environmentally Beneficial Intelligent Transportation Technologies* (Berkeley, CA: California PATH, 1998).
U.S. DOT, *Intelligent Transportation Systems Benefits: 1999 Update* (Washington, D.C.: Government Printing Office, 1999).

Study	Environmental Impact Findings	Evaluation Method	Caveat
TRAFFIC SIGNAL COORDINATION			
Abilene, Texas Signal System (International ITS Information Clearinghouse 1995)	-Fuel consumption: -5.5% -CO emissions: -12.6% -HC emissions: -9.8% -NOx emissions: +4.2%	N/A	-May increase vehicle speeds and result in higher NOx emissions. -Supply-side enhancements that increase highway capacity may induce travel demand.
Automated Traffic Surveillance and Control (ATSAC), Los Angeles Area (Los Angeles Department of Transportation 1987)	-Fuel consumption: -12.5% -CO emissions: -10.3% -HC emissions: -10.2%	-Emissions impacts calculated using factors obtained from EPA's MOBILE1. -Fuel consumption impacts obtained from TRANSYT-7F.	Same as above
ATSAC, Los Angeles Area (Los Angeles Department of Transportation 1994)	-Fuel consumption: -13.1% -Emissions: -13.6% -Also predicted city-wide ATSAC implementation to result in the following over 15-year period: ▶ CO emissions: 8,650 tons (-13.6%) ▶ ROG emissions: 1,432 tons (-20%) ▶ NOx emissions: 2,022 tons (-13%) ▶ CO_2 emissions: 1,005,461 tons (-13%)	-Emissions impacts calculated using model developed at Texas A&M in 1992. -Fuel consumption impacts obtained from TRANSYT-7F.	Same as above

Study	Environmental Impact Findings	Evaluation Method	Caveat
SCOOT, Toronto (Siemens Automotive 1995)	-Fuel consumption: -6% -CO emissions: -5% -HC emissions: -4%	N/A	Same as above
IN-VEHICLE ROUTE GUIDANCE			
Comprehensive Automobile Traffic Control System, Tokyo, Japan (Kobaysahi 1979)	-Fuel consumption: -3% to -7% -CO emissions: -6.5% -HC emissions: -6.2% -NOx emissions: -0.4%	-Conducted in 30-square-mile area with 103 intersections. -Route guidance provided to 300 vehicles with two-way communication capability. -Emission impacts calculated using simulation models. -Fuel consumption impacts calculated using "the relationship between gasoline consumption and vehicle speed."	-May increase vehicles speeds and result in NOx increases. -Supply-side enhancements that increase highway capacity may induce travel demand.
FREEWAY INCIDENT DETECTION			
Institute of Transportation Engineers (1989)	-Estimates decreases of 10 to 42 percent in travel delays resulting from traffic congestion attributable to accidents, thus leading to reduced congestion-related emissions.	N/A	-Increased vehicle speeds may increase NOx emissions. -Supply-side enhancements that increase highway capacity may induce travel demand.

Table 27–3 (continued)

Study	Environmental Impact Findings	Evaluation Method	Caveat
PRE-TRIP ATIS			
SmartTraveler (SmartRoute Systems 1993): provides travelers with real-time, location-specific traffic and transit information by telephone	Estimated 1999 emission reductions ranges as follows: ▸ CO emissions: -2,726 to -7,338 kg per day ▸ VOCs emissions: -270 to -726 kg per day ▸ NOx emissions: -14 to -26 kg per day	-Emission impacts calculated using EPA's MOBILE5a emission model. -Study calculated emission impacts by predicting impacts on VMT and speed resulting from expected changes in travel behavior and avoided delay.	-Must gain market share to have significant impact on travel behavior.
PRICING (ETC/Automatic Vehicle Identification)			
National Research Council, TRB (1994)	-Congestion pricing fees of about $0.10 to $0.15 per mile could reduce travel during that period by 10 to 15 percent.	N/A	-Formidable political obstacles. -Various concerns about "equity:" -Those most likely to be negatively impacted may be from a broad spectrum of lower- and middle-income working households least able to make changes in their driving schedules (Giuliano 1994). -Congestion pricing might negatively affect economic activity in areas where it is implemented (Hodge 1995).

Study	Environmental Impact Findings	Evaluation Method	Caveat
Marshall (1994)	-Metropolitan Transportation Commission in the San Francisco Bay Area estimates that raising the Bay Bridge toll from $1 to $3 (excluding low-income drivers) during the morning rush hour would reduce traffic by seven percent and, consequently, reduce emissions.	N/A	Same as above
REMOTE SENSING			

Booz, Allen, Hamilton (1998)	-Could assist in targeting "gross polluters" (those 10 percent of vehicles that account for over 50 percent of ozone-forming emissions).	Comparative Analysis of Three Remote Sensing Tests	Raised multiple issues contributing to implementation difficulties:
			
			-Technological problems
			  * misidentifies some vehicles as super-emitters
			  * currently limited to single-lane traffic
			
			-Privacy issues
			
			-Equity: tends to affect the poor disproportionately

These modest impacts have continued to provide the DOT with sufficient data to espouse environmental goals for ITS; the most recent version being derived from the National ITS Deployment Strategy.47 However, achievement of these results will be very dependent on local circumstance. Moreover, many ITS projects and assessments to date have not fully explored innovative new linkages with transit, planning and community development. While such applications may depart for the traffic operations focus of early ITS, they indeed embody the fuller range of goals articulated under ISTEA and TEA-21.

Toward sustainable ITS deployment

Recent and future directions

Drawing conceptual links between ITS and principles of the sustainable communities epoch is one thing. Making those links in practice is another. Such links appear to be occurring in some cases: Minnesota's DOT, for example, initiated a Sustainable Transportation Initiative to implement ITS programs consistent with sustainability principles. And the federal ITS program—having symbolically embraced a more holistic, less highway-focused approach by changing its name in 1994 from "intelligent vehicle highway systems" to "intelligent transportation systems"—continues to list environmental quality as an important goal.48

Yet, federal spending priorities tell a somewhat different story. According to a Congressional Budget Office (CBO) report, only $5.6 million—totaling 1.2 percent of federal ITS funds obligated through 1994—went to projects in which environmental concerns were the primary motive. This compares with $304.6 million (65.3 percent of federal funding obligated through 1994) spent on travel and traffic management projects. These data led the CBO to conclude that:

Among the objectives (for the ITS program) set for by the Congress, the one that seems to have received the least attention is the environment. Although some of the travel management projects could benefit the environment, how they might do so is not entirely clear because short-term reductions in traffic and congestion could lead to greater numbers of vehicles on the road, resulting in even greater pollution.49

The CBO report rightly points out that funding for ITS projects does not necessarily represent an "either-or" scenario between promoting environmental goals versus those related to mobility. Nevertheless, as noted above environmental analysts continue to be wary about how ITS investments will ultimately worsen pollution by encouraging more driving. These concerns often point to continuing federal support of AHS, or more recently AVI, as evidence that the philosophy guiding ITS investments remains rooted in the Interstate era.

Not surprisingly, efforts to apply ITS to broader, holistic applications have been decidedly mixed. Their theoretical links to sustainability notwithstanding, ITS technologies in fact grow out of a traffic operations focus on traffic mobility. And as discussed earlier, the ultimate effects ITS will have on the transportation system—and on society more generally—will depend on how the technologies are applied. This raises an immediate question: How can ITS technologies be applied to the surface transportation system in a manner that enhances sustainability? This section addresses this question by highlighting how ITS and related information technologies can be better integrated into ITS deployment.

The ability of ITS to promote a more sustainable transportation system will depend in part on stronger linkages being made in four areas: (1) use in robust community planning, (2) innovative uses in systems operation, (3) broader connections to telecommunications and (4) new use relating to access to jobs. Each of these dimensions will be touched on here, including applicable systems, examples, and policy connections (table 27–4).

Table 27–4
Dimensions for Advancing ITS for Sustainable Deployment
Source: *Wired to Go: The Information Age Hits the Streets*
(Minneapolis, MN: Humphrey Institute, 1998).

	APPLICABLE SYSTEMS	CASE EXAMPLE	POLICY CONNECTION
Comprehensive Planning	GIS Systems	Lake Street GIS mapping of citizen perceptions and traffic performance	Citizen Participation, Smart Growth, Operational Performance
Innovative Operations	Automatic Vehicle Identification Systems Remote Sensing APTS	Seattle area demonstration of multimodal systems	Alternative Mode, Facilitation, Livability, Trip Reduction
Connections to Telecommunications	ATIS Systems Telework Systems	Minnesota promotion of telework and e-enriched communities	Livable Communities, Trip Substitution
Connections to Social Equity	APTS Systems Systems	St. Mary's county use of GIS to link jobs, people, and access to transportation	Welfare to Work, Jobs Access

Comprehensive systems planning

The new policy dimension is to link ITS technologies to a broad agenda for community development and preservation. Community development can have several dimensions—economic, environmental and social. No matter which dimensions those deploying transportation and technology hope to address, however, community development can only be successful if it addresses the specific needs and conditions of a community as expressed by those within that community. This suggests two guidelines for the community development process: that it be inclusive, involving a diverse array of stakeholders from all segments of the community; and that it be adequately informed, meaning that every effort be made to understand what these community stakeholders perceive as their community's strengths and weaknesses.

It is this kind of inclusive, informed community development process that can be found in the planning and analysis of Minneapolis' 29th Street Corridor Project, also known as the Lake Street project. Using funding from ISTEA, the 29th Street Corridor Project is rehabilitating an abandoned rail corridor into a multipurpose greenway that will serve as an alternative transportation corridor (e.g., walking, biking), as a recreational amenity, and possibly as a catalyst for the economic revitalization of the area. To analyze the benefits the Greenway project could bring, and assess how residents of the neighborhoods adjacent to the Greenway perceive the project, a recent project led by the University of Minnesota (in collaboration with the author) used GIS to analyze the travel behavior and community perception of Greenway-area residents.[50] In addition to exploring the political dynamics of an ISTEA-funded transportation project attempting to achieve numerous goals that transcend transportation, this analysis also showcased how GIS could be used to improve the quality of public participation in the policymaking process. This entails developing benchmarks for sustainability and then applying these benchmarks to specific locales. These benchmarks can include "hard" environmental impacts—such as emissions and land-use—and "soft" environmental impacts—such as mode-share and community perceptions.

Innovative systems operations

On a general level, linking ITS into a greater systems operations point of view is key to having ITS support existing communities and systems. The focus on near-term operations is consistent with TEA-21's emphasis on preserving the existing system. Recent attention has turned to spatial differences within existing regions in how the transportation system functions. For example, first-ring suburbs appear to be a critical juncture in facilitating compact regional development—improving with operation of these "in-between" places can enhance their attractiveness to business and residents alike.[51] The deployment of ATMS and ATIS systems that enhance these communities can enhance their access and competitiveness—all of which can be part of a community strategy toward smart growth.

Such an approach would be more multimodal in nature. An example of such an approach is the transit system in the greater Seattle, Washington area. Developed out of their model deployment initiative, the Busview program allows King County transit riders to obtain real-time bus tracking information via the web. In essence, this provides the transit equivalent to the increasing popular traffic condition updates available over the Internet by providing transit riders up to date information on specific buses.[52]

More aggressive steps are underway in other regions to use automatic vehicle identification to promote congestion pricing. Regardless of ongoing scholarly debates about the equity of congestion pricing, the public generally believes that pricing schemes may unduly burden certain populations. As a result, public officials have generally refrained from advocating such a policy. It is within this politically charged context that the pricing issue comes to the fore in the case of New York's Tappan Zee Bridge. Some groups (and even some political leaders) are now considering congestion pricing (especially for commercial trucks) as a viable option for the Tappan Zee Bridge, and the electronic infrastructure that would enable such pricing—ETC—is now in place on the bridge to collect conventional tolls.[53] On the west coast, the recent completion of the SR-91 evaluation has provided demonstrable proof on the positive public acceptance that congestion pricing can enjoy if it is linked to tangible service gains. A second implication, however, is that congestion pricing as a strategy needs to be considered within the context of an entire transportation approach—for example in the case of SR-91, may have reduced high-occupancy vehicle travel—presenting a policy dilemma that will need to be addressed as new high-occupancy toll lanes are considered.[54]

Linkages to telecommunications

Telecommunications and transportation must, first and foremost, be linked within a comprehensive planning process. All too often, however, transportation and telecommunications planning occurs in separate forums:

> ...Public forces [are] at work that encourage or restrict the evolution of both transportation and telecommunications systems. Rarely, however, are these two functions considered jointly and comprehensively. ...Regulators [of these two systems], set up in different agencies, rarely consider the implications of their decisions for the entire transportation system or the entire telecommunications system—let alone their inter-system implications.[55]

The need for integrated planning in these areas is particularly important due to the uncertain nature of how telecommunications may affect the transportation sector. Until now, most of the research on the transportation-telecommunications relationship has focused on the relatively narrow question of whether telecommunications might substitute for travel (i.e., eliminate trips).[56] Applications such as telecommuting, teleconferencing and various forms of teleservices (e.g., on-line shopping, banking) have been widely mentioned in relation to the "substitution hypothesis."[57] What this research has shown, however, is that the substitution hypothesis only hints at the complexity of the transportation-telecommunications relationship. Depending on the circumstances, telecommunications can replace, generate, or modify trips, as well as have second-order consequences for land use that ultimately influence travel patterns.[58]

The complex, context-specific relationship between telecommunications and transportation has several implications for urban planners. Perhaps most of all, it should dispel any notion of telecommunications as a "magic bullet" for the problems of urban transportation. Indeed, there is no reason to assume that the inter-action between transportation and telecommunications will necessarily create synergies that reduce traffic congestion, address transportation-related environmental problems, or positively contribute to various factors influencing urban quality of life. Such synergies are likely to result, instead, from policymakers actively coordinating transportation and telecommunications strategies to achieve a variety of goals, whether it be reducing the number of automobile trips or making urban areas more livable. For urban communities, then, the key to realizing the full spectrum of benefits from the transportation-telecommunications relationship is likely to be the formal and innovative integration of transportation and telecommunications planning.

The issue of formally integrated transportation and telecommunications planning is being pursued in the telework program in Minnesota. In addition to sponsoring telework centers, the Minnesota DOT is actively working with communities to design electronic enriched (e-enriched) communities that allow for telework and other forms of community exchange. For example, as part of a master plan revision for the city of Lino Lakes, a technology review was conducted in conjunction with a new urbanist approach to community redesign—a design the stresses pedestrian travel, live–work arrangements and trip substitution for cultural amenities. While the impact of such smart communities on transportation can be difficult to assess, the direction is clear—there is considerable community and community interest in using technology to enhance "livability," and ITS trip substitution services will need to be considered in this context. This linkage will lead to consideration of how to create vibrant and livable communities using telecommunications technology and in a way that is consistent with regional and "smart growth" plans.

Linkages to social equity

TEA-21 contained a major Access to Jobs provision. This section (3037) recognized the relationship between the adequacy of the transportation system and the economic gains of individuals and communities. ITS needs to be cognizant of how deployment priorities are not only affecting the natural environment, but also the urban social environment. For example, ATMS systems that emphasize throughput through arterials in low-income communities, especially without attention to developing systems that advance transit usage or other operational improvements for residents of those communities, run the risk of community conflict over such systems. Several innovative elements can be developed in support of Access to Jobs. A recent Federal Register notice states: "Localities are encouraged to implement innovative approaches to service management such as the establishment of regional mobility managers or transportation brokerage activities, application of GIS tools, implementation of ITS including customer trip information technologies, the integration of automated regional public and human service transit information scheduling and dispatch functions, vehicle position monitoring systems and electronic fare cards."[59] These functions can be aimed at a variety of areas and groups; the inner city; and first-ring suburban and rural communities as well as a variety of transit dependent groups, including an increasingly elderly population. For example, in St. Mary's County, Maryland, the Department of Social Services is using GIS software to guide the connection between the locations and transport of welfare recipients and new jobs.[60]

Summary and conclusions

This chapter has reviewed the myriad of connections between ITS and the physical and social environment as suggested by the term "sustainable communities." This connection is best understood by first understanding the overarching goals of the transportation system: to assist in producing vibrant, livable and environmentally-responsive communities—what have been labeled as "sustainable communities." Within this context, ITS can be seen as having a number of elements that can support the planning and operation of transportation systems, and the connection with other telecommunications advances in the community. Following is a discussion of several policy and system design implications that derive from this review.

Focus on how ITS technologies can help create quality places, rather than just facilitate movement from place-to-place

The most promising examples of ITS deployment are those in which transportation technologies were part of comprehensive strategies focused on using transportation policy to create quality places—the unique areas where people live, shop, work and participate in community life. This is a far broader approach to ITS and other transportation-related information technologies than one that focuses solely on mobility or facilitating the movement of people and goods from place-to-place. In Santa Monica, for example, the city's Downtown Urban Design Plan is a comprehensive effort to use transportation investments to improve the quality of a particular place (in this case, downtown Santa Monica). The plan seeks to make downtown Santa Monica more pedestrian- and transit-oriented through various infrastructure and aesthetic improvements that include widening sidewalks, converting several one-way streets to two-way, creating a Transit Mall at the very center of downtown that will form a high-profile hub of the city's transit service, planting trees along sidewalks, and adorning downtown streets with public art. Information technology is contributing to the plan by providing several open-air information kiosks in the transit mall area to provide real-time transit information and trip planning services. Within this context, the use of global positioning systems and ATIS technologies supports the advancement of the "big-blue bus" as a viable transport mode for Santa Monica—it does not replace the use of a "smart corridor" but expands it to be a smart and livable corridor.

Deploy ITS technologies within the context of a broad definition of "accessibility" and community sustainability

The first recommended activity is to develop new ways to measure accessibility. Now when transportation planners and policymakers are considering options to relieve congestion, address the economic needs of their communities, and pursue development that is efficient and affordable, they have no tools to compare place-based transportation decisions with traditional flow and mobility transportation policies.

The way in which accessibility is defined can have important policy implications.[61] For example, one way to consider accessibility is roughly akin to mobility— "the ease of connection between places." This definition stresses connectivity: the ability of an area's transportation and telecommunications system to connect people to places and opportunities. Yet another conception of accessibility—as "the ability of people to benefit from places and services"—highlights the qualities of place: the ability of an area's transportation technologies to provide connectivity and, just as importantly, to create places that are more livable and attractive. It is this second definition of accessibility that spawns projects like the Lake Street Greenway in Minneapolis, in which a transportation project is simultaneously an urban recreation project, an economic development project and perhaps a setting in which Lake Street-area residents might develop closer community ties and a stronger sense of place.

Public participation is critical when developing measures and indicators of sustainable communities. Demonstration projects would be undertaken to work with communities to decide what indicators should be used to measure increased accessibility and higher quality of life in a community. If communities had tools to measure their success, then it would be help spur the use of these tools all across the country.

Maximize connections to a broad array of information and digital technologies that can enhance sustainable communities

Finally, this new era in transportation policy highlights the need for new tools consistent with TEA-21's holistic approach, and it is this niche that ITS and other information technologies are poised to fill. Perhaps the most central theme of this chapter is that ITS—as currently defined—contains several but not all of the broad sweep of the digital technology advances that will affect the shape, form and sustainability of communities. What first started out as a traffic management approach to enhancing arterial signal coordination must now be seen as part of a constellation of technological approaches available to communities. ISTEA and now TEA-21 provide the policy guidance for how these technological approaches are to be weighed. As noted at the outset of this chapter, they are to be considered as part of a balanced transportation approach that gives priority to maintaining the existing system and doing so in a manner that balances economic, environmental and social goals. Within this broader context, there is an enhanced role for use of the data and methods (GIS) in community planning, there is a broader array of services that can be considered (use of trip-substitution technologies), and there is a greater emphasis of a full multimodal approach.

The overarching goal, therefore, is not ITS for traffic mobility, but rather ITS and other digital technologies for sustainable communities. "Community design" refers to community development through both physical and social infrastructure. ISTEA spurred a wave of new thinking about transportation's contribution to community design, and much of this new thinking has manifested in efforts to create more livable communities. TEA-21 will continue to support this new thinking. While differing in their specifics, livable communities' initiatives tend to emphasize the revitalization of traditional downtown cores as a center for entertainment, commerce and social interaction. This can involve the creation of a more pedestrian-friendly atmosphere, re-arranging downtown traffic circulation and improving transit services, as well as mixing residential and commercial land uses. Ideally, this approach can serve numerous economic, social and environmental goals. ITS has an opportunity to contribute to this creative and vital new approach to developing transportation systems. It is a larger challenge than staying on the streets, but a challenge that is in keeping with the increasingly broad responsibility every sector has—including transportation, education, housing—in maximizing community vitality and gain.

Acknowledgments

This chapter draws upon a series of studies undertaken by the author in collaboration with several colleagues. First and foremost, the author acknowledges the substantial contribution of Daniel Jordan to the development of several of the thoughts, facts and conclusions contained in this chapter. Some of the sustainability concepts were summarized in an article by Horan, Dittmar and Jordan (see endnote 5). The author also acknowledges the support and use of findings from two studies. Several ITS policy and sustainability components are drawn from the "Wired to Go" study, conducted with funding from the U.S. DOT and in partnership with the Humphrey Institute, Claremont Graduate University and the Surface Transportation Policy Project (see endnote 24). The author also acknowledges the support of the Minnesota DOT, the ITS Joint Programs Office and the Office of Congressman Sabo in providing support and guidance for the project. Additional data on ITS impacts on environment are drawn from the "Identification and Prioritization of Environmentally Beneficial Intelligent Transportation Technologies" study, conducted for the California

PATH program in partnership with the University of California Davis (see also endnote 24). The author gratefully acknowledges the contribution of Susan Shaheen and her colleagues at U.C. Davis in the compilation and synthesis of the environmental impacts data. Any errors remain the responsibility of the author.

Endnotes

1. Leavitt, H., 1970, *Superhighway—Superhoax,* New York: Doubleday & Company; Kay, J.; 1998, *Asphalt Nation: How the Automobile Took Over the Nation, and How We Can Take It Back,* New York: Random House.

2. See Mumford, L., 1963, *The Highway and the City,* New York: Mentor Books; and Moynihan, D. P.; 1960, "New Roads and Urban Chaos," *The Reporter 22,* no.8: 13–20.

3. Lewis, T., 1999, Divided Highways: Building the Interstate Highways, Transforming American Life, New York: Penguin Press.

4. For commentary on the significance of ISTEA, see Dilger, R., 1992, "ISTEA: A New Direction for Transportation Policy," *Publius, The Journal of Federalism;* For the politics involved in Congress' passage of ISTEA, see Gifford, J., Horan, T., and White, L., 1994, "Dynamics of Policy Change: Reflections on 1991 Transportation Legislation," Transportation Research Record 1466 (December).

5. See Horan, T., Dittmar, H., and Jordan, D., 1999, "ISTEA and the New Era of Transportation Policy: Sustainable Communities for a Federal Initiative" in Mazmanian. D. and Kraft, M., eds, *Toward Sustainable Communities: Transition and Transformations in Environmental Policy.* Cambridge, MA: MIT Press.

6. International Union for the Conservation of Nature, 1980, *World Conservation Strategies,* Geneva: IUCN.

7. Brundtland Commission (World Commission on Environment and Development), 1987, *Our Common Future,* New York: Oxford University Press.

8. Munro, D., 1995, "Sustainability: Rhetoric or Reality?" in Tryzyna, T., ed., *Sustainable World: Defining and Measuring Sustainable Development,* Sacramento, CA: International Center for the Environment and Public Policy and The World Conservation Union, 27–35.

9. Ruttan, V. W, 1993, "Sustainable Growth in Agricultural Production: Poetry, Policy and Science" (February), Department of Agriculture and Applied Economics, University of Minnesota. Staff Paper, 91–47.

10. Clinton, W.S., 1997, Remarks on the Rollout of NextTea, Washington, D.C., March 12.

11. Regulations following the Federal-Aid Highway Act of 1962, for example, also included a list of issues to consider in planning transportation investments, many of which were analogous to those listed in ISTEA's planning factors mandate (e.g., land use, "social and community-value factors"). Yet observers generally agree that the 1962 Act made little difference in practice, as federal and state transportation projects remained narrowly focused on highway construction and traffic efficiency. (See Morehouse, T., 1971, "Artful Interpretation: The 1962 Highway Act," M. N. Danielson, Ed., *Metropolitan Politics: A Reader,* Second

Edition; and Rose, M., 1990, *Interstate: Express Highway Politics, 1939–1989,* Revised Edition, Knoxville, TN: The University of Tennessee Press.

12. Summarized in Horan, T., Dittmar, H., and Jordan, D., 1999, "ISTEA and The New Era of Transportation Policy: Sustainable Communities from a Federal Initiative" in Mazmanian, D., and Kraft, M., eds., *Toward Sustainable Communities: Transitions and Transformations in Environmental Policy,* Cambridge, MA: MIT Press.

13. See U.S. Department of Transportation, 1998, *Overview of TEA-21 Provisions,* Washington, D.C.: Government Printing Office.

14. Often referred to as "councils of governments," MPOs are diverse, often organizationally complex entities that differ in size, technical capabilities and degree of political independence. The roughly 339 MPOs designated under ISTEA (the number of MPOs changes as population changes) are generally alike in being intergovernmental organizations with representatives from the jurisdiction's state, regional and local governments. All MPOs derive their authority under federal transportation planning mandates, but some possess additional state-conferred powers to address other regional issues such as growth management.

15. Lyons, W., 1994, *The FTA-FHWA MPO Reviews—Planning Practice Under ISTEA and the CAAA* (January), John A. Volpe Transportation Systems Center, U.S. Department of Transportation.

16. This and the other referenced public involvement provisions are found in ISTEA's implementing rules, 23 CFR 450.212 et seq.

17. For example, one study found that MPOs believe that more public involvement produces "better" policy decisions in that "[transportation] plans and programs are more reflective of the public's transportation needs and hence enjoy broader and stronger public support" (GAO 1996, 19).

18. Peña, F., 1996, quoted in "Building Livable Communities Through Transportation," Washington, D.C.: U.S. Department of Transportation, 1996, vi.

19 Peña, F., 1996., Remarks Prepared for Delivery at the Transportation Research Board Annual Meeting, Washington, D.C., January 10.

20. Gore, A. , 1999, Remarks As Prepared for Delivery: Livability Announcement, Washington, D.C., January 11.

21. Replogle, M., 1995, "Intelligent Transportation Systems for Sustainable Communities," in Hennessey, T., and Horan, T., eds., National Conference on Intelligent Transportation Systems and the Environment: Conference Proceedings (June 6–7), Virginia: The Institute of Public Policy, George Mason University, 53–59.

22. Gordon, D., 1992, "Intelligent Vehicle/Highway Systems: An Environmental Perspective," in Gifford, J., Horan, T., and Sperling, D., eds., *Transportation, Information Technology, and Public Policy: Institutional and Environmental Issues in IVHS, Proceedings: A Workshop on Institutional and Environmental Issues,* Asilomar Conference Center, Monterey, California, April 26–28, Fairfax, Virginia: The Institute of Public Policy, George Mason University, 9–27.

23. Cervero, R., 1995, "Why Go Anywhere?" *Scientific American* (September), 93.

24. For example, see Jordan, D., and Horan, T., 1997, *Intelligent Transportation and Sustainable Communities, ITS Quarterly 5,* no. 3.; Shaheen, S., Young, T., Sperling, D., Jordan, D., and Horan, T., 1998, *Identification and Prioritization of Environmentally Beneficial Intelligent Transportation Technologies,* Berkeley, CA: California PATH; Humphrey Institute, 1998, *Wired to Go: The Information Technology Hits the Streets,* Minneapolis, MN.

25. The phrase "substituting information for stuff" is taken from Robert B. Shapiro, chairman and CEO of Monsanto Company. In a 1997 interview published in a Harvard Business Review article entitled "Growth Through Global Sustainability," he underscored the indispensable role of information in promoting sustainable development: "Using information is one of the ways to increase productivity without abusing nature...A closed system like the earth's can't withstand a systematic increase of material things, but it can support exponential increases of information and knowledge. Sustainability and development might be compatible if you could create value and satisfy people's needs by increasing the information component of what's produced and diminishing the amount of stuff" (p. 882).

26. "Remote sensing" refers to technologies that can measure the exhaust emissions from vehicles as they pass a roadside detector.

27. See National Research Council, Transportation Research Board, 1994, *Curbing Gridlock: Peak-Period Fees to Relieve Traffic Congestion.* Special Report 242. Washington, D.C.: National Academy of Sciences.

28. TCMs are defined in the 1988 California state Clean Air Act as "...any strategy to reduce vehicle trips, vehicle use, vehicle miles traveled, vehicle idling, or traffic congestion for the purpose of motor vehicle emissions." The 1990 federal Clean Air Act lists 16 TCMs that state sand localities can include in their transportation plans. These include traffic signalization improvements, ridesharing and carpooling programs, and high-occupancy vehicle lanes. Market-based measures such as congestion pricing, though consistent with this definition of TCMs, are not considered traditional TCMs, so this paper makes the distinction between TCMs and pricing.

29. U.S. Congress, General Accounting Office, 1993, *Urban Transportation: Reducing Vehicle Emissions with Transportation Control Measures,* Washington, D.C.: U.S. Government Printing Office.

30. University of California at Los Angeles Extension, Public Policy Program, 1992, Annual Symposium Series on the Transportation, Land Use, Air Quality Connection, *Summary of Proceedings: The Role of Pricing and Market-Based Strategies* (October 20), Los Angeles, CA.

31. Burbank, C., 1995, "ITS and the Environment" (Spring), Public Roads; Shank, D., 1995, *Benefits Summary* (March 29), Washington, D.C.: Mitre Corporation.

32. National Research Council, Transportation Research Board, 1994, *Curbing Gridlock: Peak-Period Fees to Relieve Traffic Congestion,* Special Report 242, Washington, D.C.: National Academy of Sciences.

33. For a discussion of the politics and equity see Rom, M., 1994, "The Politics of Congestion Pricing," in *Curbing Gridlock: Peak Period Feed to Relieve Traffic Congestion,* Special Report 242, Transportation Research Board, 280–299. Also, Giuliano, G., 1994, "Equity and Fairness Considerations of Congestion Pricing."

Curbing Gridlock: Peak Period Fees to Relieve Traffic Congestion, Special Report 242, Transportation Research Board, p. 250–279.

34. Kanninen, B., 1995, "Intelligent Vehicle/Highway Systems (IVHS): Economics and Environmental Policy." In Hennessey, T. and Horan, T., eds, National Policy Conference on ITS and the Environment Conference Papers, Arlington, VA, June 6–7, Fairfax, Virginia: The Institute of Public Policy, George Mason University, 341–352.

35. Transportation Research Board, 1995, *Expanding Metropolitan Highways: Implications for Air Quality and Energy Use,* Special Report 245, Washington, D.C.: National Academy Press.

36. City of Los Angeles Department of Transportation, 1994, "Automated Traffic Surveillance and Control (ATSAC) Evaluation Study" (June), Los Angeles, CA.

37. Horan, T. A., Hempel, L., and Bower, M., 1995, *Institutional Challenges to the Development and Deployment of ITS/ATS Systems in California* (May), Berkeley, CA: California PATH.

38. U.S. Environmental Protection Agency, 1998, *Assessing the Emissions and Fuel Consumption Impacts of Intelligent Transportation Systems,* Washington, D.C.: EPA.

39. Mitretek, 1999, Modeling and Simulation Workshop, Washington, D.C., January 9.

40. U.S. Department of Transportation, 1999, *Intelligent Transportation Systems Benefits: 1999 Update,* Washington, D.C.: U.S. Government Printing Office, available at <http://www.mitretek.org/its/BeneCost.nsf/frm/RptHome?OpenDocument>.

41. For a recent summary, see Miller, C., 1999, "A Discussion of Intelligent Transportation Systems Environmental Impacts" (February), *ITE Journal,* Washington, D.C.: Institute of Transportation Engineers, 85–89.

42. U.S. Department of Transportation, 1999, *Intelligent Transportation Systems Benefits:1999 Update,* Washington, D.C.: U.S. Government Printing Office, available at: <http://www.mitretek.org/its/BeneCost.nsf/frm/RptHome?OpenDocument>.

43. Tech Environmental Inc., 1993, "Air Quality Benefit Study of the SmarTraveler Advanced Traveler Information Service" (July), Boston, MA.

44. Clean Air Action Corp., 1993, "Proposed General Protocol for Determination of Emission Reduction Credits Created by Implementing an Electronic Pike Pass System on a Tollway" (December), *Study for the Northeast States for Coordinated Air Use Management.*

45. City of Los Angeles Department of Transportation, 1994, "Automated Traffic Surveillance and Control (ATSAC) Evaluation Study" (June), Los Angeles, CA.

46. Orcutt Associates, 1994, "Evaluation Study, Buffalo Gap Road, Abilene Signal System," prepared for the City of Abilene, Texas.

47. ITS America, 1999, *National ITS Deployment Strategy,* Washington, D.C., July, Interim Final Draft.

48. See Hennessey, T., and Horan, T., eds., 1995, *National Conference on Intelligent Transportation Systems and the Environment: Conference Proceedings* (June 6–7), Washington, D.C.

49. U.S. Congressional Budget Office, 1996, *High-Tech Highways: Intelligent Transportation Systems and Policy* (October), Washington, D.C.: 44.

50. Humphrey Institute, 1998, *The Midtown Greenway: A New Model for Sustainable Urban Communities* (February), Minneapolis, MN.

51. For a summary of the first-ring suburb issue, see Morrish, W., 1999, "Repositioning the 1945–65 Suburb: Summary of a National Conference," Minneapolis, MN: The Design Center.

52. See Dailey, D., and MacLean, I., 2000, *Busview: An APTS Precursor and Deployed Applet* (June), Seattle, WA: University of Washington.

53. Summarized in Replogle, M., 1998, "ITS and Traffic Management in the NY I-287 Corridor: Conflict and Collaboration," in Humphrey Institute, 1998, *Wired to Go: The Information Age Hits the Streets,* Minneapolis, MN, 44–70.

54. See Sullivan, E. ,1998, "Evaluation of the SR-91 Fastpass System," Final report prepared for the California Department of Transportation.

55. Schuler, R., 1992, "Transportation and Telecommunications Networks: Planning Urban Infrastructure for the 21st Century," *Urban Studies 29,* no. 2: 298.

56. There are dozens of such studies, but P. Mokhtarian (1990, "A Typology of Relationships Between Telecommunications and Transportation," Transportation Research A , 24A 3) and I. Salomon (1986, "Telecommunications and Travel Relationships: A Review," Transportation Research A, 20A 3) offer the most comprehensive reviews of the literature as well as useful conceptual frameworks for analyzing the trans-portation-telecommunications relationship.

57. Analysis of the potential of telecommunications to substitute for travel began in earnest with J. Nilles, F. Carlson, P. Gray, and G. Hanneman (1976, *The Telecommunications-Transportation Tradeoff: Options for Tomorrow,* New York: John Wiley and Sons), and it has continued since then (i.e., SCAG 1996). For highly optimistic endorsements of the substitution hypothesis in what are often labeled "futuristic" works, see Toffler, A., 1981, *The Third Wave,* New York: William Morrow; and Negroponte, N., 1995, *Being Digital,* New York: Alfred A. Knopf.

58. Again, Mokhtarian (1990, "A Typology of Relationships Between Telecommunications and Transportation," Transportation Research A , 24A 3) and Salomon (1986, "Telecommunications and Travel Relationships: A Review," Transportation Research A, 20A 3) provide the best reviews of the evidence on this topic.

59. U.S. DOT, 1998, "Job Access and Reverse Commute, Notice." *Federal Register 63,* no. 215 (November 6).

60. For a review see Chen, D., 1998, "Getting Smarter About Low Income Mobility: Can Intelligent Transportation Technologies Improve Basic Accessibility to Jobs," in Humphrey Institute, 1998, *Wired to Go: The Information Age Hits the Streets,* Minneapolis, MN, 71–81. Also, Public Technology, 1998, *Roads Less Traveled: Intelligent Transportation Systems for Sustainable Communities,* Washington, D.C.: Public Technology.

61. For a discussion of these definitions, see Horan, T. and Jordan, D., 1998, "Integrating Transportation and Telecommunications Planning in Santa Monica," *Journal of Urban Technology,* Vol. 5. No. 2, 1–20.

User services document what ITS should do from the user's perspective. Broad ranges of users are considered, including the traveling public as well as many different types of system operators. Thirty user services formed the basis for the National ITS Architecture development effort. Two new services, Highway Rail Interface and the Archived Data user services, were added to the original list of services. These user services were jointly defined by the U.S. Department of Transportation and ITS America with significant stakeholder input. New or updated user services may be added to the National ITS Architecture over time.

1. **Pre-trip Travel Information**—Provides information to assist travelers in making mode choices, travel time estimates and route decisions prior to trip departure. It consists of four major functions: (1) Available Services Information, (2) Current Situation Information, (3) Trip Planning Service and (4) User Access. Information is integrated from various transportation modes and presented to the user for decision-making.

2. **En-route Driver Information**—Provides drivers with information while en-route, which will allow alternative routes to be chosen for their destination. Driver information consists of two major functions: (1) Driver Advisory and (2) In-vehicle Signing. The potential decrease in traffic may also provide benefits in highway safety, reduced air pollution and decreased congestion.

3. **Route Guidance**—Provides travelers with directions to selected destinations. Four functions are provided: (1) Provide Directions, (2) Static Mode, (3) Real-Time Mode and (4) User Interface.

4. **Ride Matching and Reservation**—Provides travel users with information on rideshare providers. Three major functions are provided: (1) Rider Request, (2) Transportation Provider Services and (3) Information Processing. This will also include a billing service to the providers.

5. **Traveler Services Information**—Provides travelers with service and facility data for the purpose of assisting prior to embarking on a trip or after the traveler is underway. The functions that are included in this capability are Information Receipt and Information Access. This will provide the traveler with a "yellow pages" type of capability.

6. **Traffic Control**—Provides the capability to efficiently manage the movement of traffic on streets and highways. Four functions are provided: (1) Traffic Flow Optimization, (2) Traffic Surveillance, (3) Control Function and (4) Provide Information. This will also include control of network signal systems with eventual integration of freeway control.

7. **Incident Management**—Identifies incidents, formulates response actions and supports initiation and ongoing coordination of those response actions. Six major functions are provided: (1) Scheduled Planned Incidents, (2) Identify Incidents, (3) Formulate Response Actions, (4) Support Coordinated Implementation of Response Actions, (5) Support Initialization of Response to Actions and (6) Predict Hazardous Conditions.

8. **Travel Demand Management (TDM)**—Generates and communicates management and control strategies that support and facilitate the implementation of TDM programs, policies and regulations. It consists of two major functions: (1) Increase Efficiency of Transportation System and (2) Provide Wide Variety of Mobility Options.

9. **Emissions Testing and Mitigation (ETAM)**—Provides state and local governments with the capability to enhance their air quality control strategies. The ETAM will provide both wide area and roadside emissions monitoring. Information gleaned from ETAM will be used by TDM in the traffic management center to mitigate pollution and may be provided to enforcement agencies to compel offenders to comply with standards.

10. **Highway–Rail Intersection (HRI)**—Provides functions to control highway and rail traffic in at-grade HRIs. Two subservices are supported: Standard Speed Rail Subservice, which is applicable to light rail transit, commuter rail and heavy rail trains with operational speeds up to 79 miles per hour (MPH); and High-Speed Rail Subservice, which is applicable to all passenger and freight trains with operational speeds from 80 to 125 MPH.

11. **Pre-trip Transit Information**—Allows travelers to access a range of multimodal transportation information at home, work and other major sites where trips originate. These systems provide timely information on transit routes, schedules, transfers and fairs; and intermodal connections to rail, ferry, or other transportation systems.

12. **En-route Transit Information**—Provides travelers with real-time transit and high-occupancy vehicle information allowing travel alternatives to be chosen once the traveler is en-route. It consists of three major functions: (1) Information Distribution, (2) Information Receipt and (3) Information Processing. This capability integrates information from different transit modes and presents it to travelers for decision-making.

13. **Personalized Public Transit**—Provides flexibly routed transit vehicles to offer more convenient customer service. Small publicly or privately operated vehicles provide on-demand routing to pick up passengers who have requested service and deliver them to their destinations. Route deviation schemes, in which vehicles leave a fixed route for a short distance to pick up or discharge passengers, is another way of improving service.

14. **Public Travel Security**—Creates an environment of safety in public transportation. This service provides systems that monitor the environment in transportation stations, parking lots, bus stops and on-board transit vehicles; and it generates alarms, either automatically or manually, when necessary. This improves security for both transit riders and operators. Transportation agencies and authorities can integrate this user service with other anticrime activities.

15. **Electronic Payment Service**—Allows travelers to pay for transportation services by electronic means. Four functions are provided: (1) Electronic Toll Collection, (2) Electronic Fare Collection, (3) Electronic Parking Payment and (4) Electronic Payment Services Integration.

16. **Commercial Vehicle Electronic Clearance**—This service will enable transponder-equipped trucks and buses to have their safety status, credentials and weight checked at mainline speeds.

17. **Automated Roadside Safety Inspection**—Facilitates roadside inspections by allowing real-time access at the roadside to the safety performance record of carriers, vehicles, and drivers. It also automates as many items as possible of the manual inspection process. It would, for example, allow for more rapid and accurate inspection of brake performance at the roadside. Through the use of sensors and diagnostics, it would efficiently check vehicle systems, driver requirements and ultimately driver alertness and fitness for duty.

18. **On-board Safety Monitoring**—Provides monitoring and warnings of safety problems. Of primary importance is to inform the driver, as soon as possible, of any problem that has been detected. Of secondary importance is notifying the carrier of detected safety problems. Last in importance is the notification of appropriate enforcement agencies.

19. **Commercial Vehicle Administrative Processes**—Consists of 3 subservices: (1) Electronic Purchase of Credentials, (2) Automated Mileage and Fuel Reporting and Auditing and (3) International Border Electronic Clearance.

20. **Hazardous Material Incident Response**—Provides immediate description of hazardous materials to emergency responders. It provides enforcement and response teams with timely, accurate information on cargo contents to enable them to react properly in emergency situations.

21. **Emergency Notification and Personal Security**—Provides for the faster notification of travelers involved in an incident.

22. **Emergency Vehicle Management**—Provides public safety agencies with fleet management capabilities, route guidance and signal priority or preemption for emergency vehicles.

23. **Longitudinal Collision Avoidance**—Helps prevent head-on, rear-end, or backing collisions between vehicles, or between vehicles and other objects or pedestrians.

24. **Lateral Collision Avoidance**—Prevents collisions when vehicles leave their lane of travel.

25. **Intersection Collision Avoidance**—The Intersection Collision Avoidance service warns drivers of imminent collisions when approaching or crossing an intersection or railroad grade crossing that has traffic control (e.g., STOP signs or a signal). This service also alerts the driver when the proper right-of-way at the intersection or grade crossing is unclear or ambiguous.

26. **Safety Readiness**—Provides warnings about the condition of the driver, the vehicle and the roadway.

27. **Vision Enhancement for Crash Avoidance**—Improves the driver's ability to see the roadway and objects that are on or along the roadway.

28. **Pre-crash Restraint Deployment**—Anticipates an imminent collision and activates passenger safety systems before the collision occurs, or much earlier in the crash event.

29. **Automated Vehicle Operation**—Provides a fully automated, "hands-off," operating environment.

30. **Archived Data User Service Description**—This user service will provide an ITS Historical Data Archive for all relevant ITS data and will incorporate the planning, safety, operations and research communities into ITS. It will provide the data collection, manipulation and dissemination functions of these groups, as they relate to data generated by ITS. The ITS Historical Data Archive will function as a data warehouse or repository to support stakeholder functions.

• A •

Acceptance Testing—A formal process to validate that a system meets all of its requirements.

Advanced Driver and Vehicle Advisory Navigation Concept (ADVANCE) Project—Was launched in 1991 as a major test of dynamic in-vehicle route guidance systems in the Gary-Chicago-Milwaukee corridor.

Advanced Public Transit Systems—Apply ITS technology to the needs of public transit, including fixed-route systems, as well as route deviation and demand-responsive modes.

Advanced Rural Transportation Systems (ARTS)—A collection of ITS technologies applied to the rural environment.

Advanced Traveler Information Systems (ATIS)—Disseminate information to the traveling public over a variety of distribution channels, including cable television, digital broadcasts, the Internet, kiosks and personal hand-held devices.

Advanced Vehicle Control and Safety Systems (AVCSS)—Focus on crash avoidance by enhancing driver performance. AVCSS include advanced collision avoidance systems and the automated highway system.

Architecture Flow—A grouping of data flows from the logical architecture that originates at a sub-system and ends at another in the physical architecture.

• C •

Commercial Vehicle Operations (CVO)—Improve motor carrier safety and productivity by improving and targeting inspections; and reducing paperwork through electronic transactions, weigh-in-motion and automatic vehicle technologies.

Communications Layer—One of three layers defined by the National ITS Architecture. The communications layer includes all of the communications equipment (e.g., wireline and wireless transmitters and receivers) and the information management and transport capabilities necessary to transfer information among entities in the transportation layer.

Compatibility—Means that adjoining devices or systems can work together cooperatively (or at least without interfering with one another), and that a variety of similar (if not identical) components can be substituted for one another. Devices can be connected to one another without the need for special interfaces.

Component—One of the parts that makes up a system. A component may be hardware or software and may be subdivided into other components.

Congestion—A freeway condition where traffic demand exceeds roadway capacity.

Congestion Strategy—A strategy that optimizes corridor operations to minimize the spread of congestion.

Council of ITS Standards—A council established by ITS America to coordinate the standards-setting efforts in the United States. It includes representatives from American National Standards Institute, Institute of Electronics and Electrical Engineers, Society of Automotive Engineers, American Society of Testing and Materials, Electronics Industries Association, NAB, National Electronic Manufacturers Association, Telecommunications Industry Association, Institute of Transportation Engineers and American Association of State Highway and Transportation Officials.

• D •

Data Dictionary—(1) A collection of the names of all data items used in a software system, together with relevant properties of those items; for example, length of data item, representation and so forth. (2) A set of definitions of data flows, data elements, files, data bases and processes referred to in a leveled data flow diagram set.

Data Flow Diagram—A diagram that depicts data sources, data sinks, data storage, and processes performed on data as nodes and logical flow of data as links between the nodes.

Data Structure—A physical or logical relationship among data elements, designed to support specific data manipulation functions.

Dedicated Short-Range Communications (DSRC)—Short-range communications devices that are capable of transferring high rates of data over an air interface between mobile or stationary vehicles and normally stationary devices that are either mounted to structures along the roadway or are hand-held.

Design Requirement—A requirement that specifies or constrains the design of a system or system component.

Design Specification—A document that describes the design of a system or component. Typical contents include system or component architecture, control logic, data structures, input/output formats, interface descriptions, and algorithms. (See IEEE Std 610.12-1990.)

Diversion—A strategy for diverting traffic that optimized corridor operations in response to corridor incidents.

• E •

Electronic Toll and Traffic Management (ETTM)—Uses automatic vehicle identification (AVI) to electronically collect tolls, enabling vehicles to pay tolls with less delay at tollbooths.

Electronic Toll Collection (ETC)—Advanced toll collection systems using transponder/toll plaza telecommunications devices such as AVI or ETTM systems.

• F •

Faster and Safer Travel Traffic Routing and Advanced Controls (FAST-TRAC)—An Oakland County, Michigan field test of advanced traffic management systems and ATIS.

Functional Requirement—A requirement that specifies a function that a system or system component must be able to perform.

Functional Specification—A document that specifies the functions that a system or component must perform. Often a part of the requirements specification.

• G •

Geographic Information System (GIS)—A computerized data management system designed to capture, store, retrieve, analyze and report geographic and demographic information.

Global Positioning System (GPS)—A government-owned system of 24 earth-orbiting satellites that transmit data to ground-based receivers. GPS provides extremely accurate latitude and longitude ground position in WGS-84 coordinates. However, for U.S. strategic defense reasons, deliberate error (called selective availability) is introduced into the code that is provided for civilian users.

GSM—The standard for digital cellular adopted by European cellular operators. Provides a mobile transport platform that can be used for ATIS or other ITS data transmissions.

• H •

High-Occupancy Vehicle (HOV)—Any vehicle, bus, van, or car with multiple riders. An HOV lane refers to a roadway lane reserved for use by HOVs, expressways, arterials and collectors.

High-Occupancy Toll Lane (HOT Lane)—Single-occupancy vehicles pay a fee to use an HOV lane.

Highway Advisory Radio (HAR)—A traffic information broadcasting system used in the United States. Drivers are alerted to tune their car radios to a specific channel in order to receive transmitted information.

• I •

IDEA Program—Transportation Research Board Program to support product innovation and development.

Institute of Electrical and Electronic Engineers (IEEE)—A standards development organization.

Incident—An occurrence in the traffic stream that causes a reduction in capacity or abnormal increase in demand such as accidents, stall vehicles, spilled loads, or special events.

Intermodal Surface Transportation Efficiency Act (ISTEA)—Public Law 102-240, Dec. 18, 1991. The ISTEA of 1991 provided the primary federal funding ($151B) for all surface transportation programs in the United States for the 6-year period during 1992–1997. This legislation includes the Intelligent Vehicle-Highway Systems Act of 1991 (Title VI, Part B.)

Intelligent Transportation Infrastructure (ITI)—A communication information system that will integrate traffic, transit and emergency service components already in place in cities and rural communities.

Intelligent Transportation Systems (ITS)—People using technology in surface transportation to save lives, time and money and improve the quality of life. Some examples of ITS are electronic payment systems that allow vehicles to pay tolls on roadways without performing an actual cash or token transaction or slowing their passage greatly, traffic management systems that can help determine the location and seriousness of an interruption in traffic and options to clearing it, automatic vehicle location systems that can locate a vehicle through cellular systems even if the driver does not know his or her location in an emergency, and collision-avoidance sensing systems that have helped some trucking companies reduce preventable accidents by up to 75 percent—because they can "see" smaller vehicles in what once were "blind spots."

Interfaces—Connections between systems or subsystems.

Interoperability—The ability of systems to provide services and accept services from other systems and to use the services so exchanged to enable them to operate effectively together (ISO TC 204-Doc. N271).

• K •

Kiosk—Computer terminal display located in a public area such as a shopping center airport or office complex, giving real-time traffic information for the purpose of trip or route planning. May also include information on services, facilities and the like.

• L •

Latent Demand—Refers to the additional, unanticipated vehicles that appear on roads because people switched routes, modes, or travel times, or because they decided to take trips they had previously not taken.

Layer—A breakdown or stratification of the physical architecture comprised of the transportation layer and communications layer.

Logical Architecture—Defines the activities or functions that are required to satisfy the user services. Identifies system functional processes and information flows grouped to form particular transportation functions. These processes are then broken down into subprocesses and into process specifications (also called "p-specs").

LORAN-C—A land-based radio navigation system operated by the U.S. Coast Guard as a public service. This hyperbolic system uses signals broadcast from land-based radio towers.

• M •

Market Packages—Represent slices of the physical architecture that address specific services like surface street control. A market package collects together several different subsystems, equipment packages, terminators and architecture flows that provide the desired service.

Measure of Effectiveness (MOE)—The quantified variables derived from traffic measurements that measure the improvement in traffic operations. Common MOEs are total travel time, total travel, delay, average speed, accident rate and throughput.

Message Sets—Define how a particular function or parameter is defined and described, and what the allowed ranges are for each parameter (or object).

Metropolitan Model Deployment Initiative—Showcases the measurable benefits of taking an integrated, region-wide approach to managing transportation and providing traveler information services.

Modem—A device that converts serial digital data from a transmitting terminal to a signal suitable for transmission over a telephone line to a receiving terminal.

• N •

National Highway Traffic Safety Administration (NHTSA)—A branch of the U.S. Department of Transportation (U.S. DOT) that focuses on safety and standards.

National ITS Architecture—Provides a framework for designing transportation systems that implement the full set of 30 ITS user services. The architecture defines the functions that must be performed, the subsystems that provide these functions and the information that must be exchanged to support these user services.

National Program Plan—Jointly developed by the U.S. DOT and ITS America with substantial involvement from the broader ITS community. The purpose of the plan was to guide the development and deployment of ITS. It includes detailed descriptions of the ITS user services that provide key background information for the user service requirements included in the National ITS Architecture documentation.

Navigable Database—A digital street map database containing sufficient detail and scope to support driver and vehicle guidance applications (e.g., the generation by computer of a high-quality driving route between two stated addresses).

Navigation—The determination of the vehicle's position and direction of travel, using information provided by GPS or another internal position device and computerized maps.

• O •

Object-Oriented Analysis (OOA)—Attempts to define object classes associated with the objects and the relationship between different objects and classes in the systems problems domain. OOA attempts to understand the problem domain and what the systems' responsibilities are for the problem domain.

Operation Time Saver—A U.S. DOT initiative to create and deploy a national intelligent transportation infrastructure within 10 years.

Outsourcing—Turning over a function in part or in full to a third-party contractor.

• P •

Performance—The ability of a system or subsystem to perform its functions.

Performance Evaluation—The technical assessment of a system, subsystem, or component to determine how effectively objectives have been achieved.

Performance Specification—A document that specifies the performance characteristics that a system or component must possess.

Physical Architecture—Provides a physical representation (though not a detailed design) of the important ITS interfaces and major system components. It provides a high-level structure around the process and dataflow defined in the logical architecture.

Position—The latitude, longitude and altitude of a point on the surface of the earth.

Preemption/Priority Systems—Preempt control of normal signal timing plans to provide priority for selected transit vehicles, emergency vehicles and for approaching trains at signals adjacent to railroad grade crossings.

Process Specification—Elemental functions that must be performed to satisfy user service requirements. The lowest level of functional hierarchy.

• Q •

Quality Assurance (QA)—(1) A planned and systematic pattern of all actions necessary to provide adequate confidence that an item or product conforms to established technical requirements. (2) A set of activities designed to evaluate the process by which products are developed or manufactured.

• R •

Ramp Metering—Regulates the number of vehicles entering the freeway over a given time interval so that demand does not exceed capacity.

Recurrent Congestion—Types of congestion that are routinely expected at predicable locations during specific time periods.

Requirement—(1) A condition or capability needed by a user to solve a problem or achieve an objective. (2) A condition or capability that must be met or possessed by a system or system component to satisfy a contract, standard, specification, or other formally imposed documents. (3) A documented representation of a condition or capability as in (1) or (2).

Requirements Specification—A document that specifies the requirements for a system or component. Typically included are functional requirements, performance requirements, design requirements and development standards.

Risk Analysis—An analysis of potential critical risks that may delay or prevent the deployment of ITS technologies, and recommends mitigation plans that will eliminate or reduce these risks.

• S •

Selective Availability—A technique of deliberately introducing inaccuracy into GPS broadcasts for civilian use.

Server—(1) A computer providing a service, such as shared access to a file system, a printer, or an electronic mail system to LAN users. Usually a combination of hardware and software.

Smart Card—An electronic information carrier system that uses plastic cards about the size of a credit card with an imbedded integrated circuit that stores and processes information.

Specification—(1) A document that describes in a complete, precise, verifiable manner, the requirements, design, behavior, or other characteristics of a system or system component; and, often, the procedures for determining whether these provisions have been satisfied.

Standards Development Organization (SDO)—Organizations that manage the development of standards in specific areas.

Stolen Vehicle Recovery System (SVRS)—Application of AVI and automatic vehicle location technology with nonroute-specific radio navigation tracking systems to locate and track stolen vehicles.

Subsystem—A secondary or subordinate system within a larger system.

Sydney Coordinated Adaptive Traffic System (SCATS)—One of several forms of adaptive traffic control systems with the ability to change the phasing and timing strategies and signal coordination within a network to meet variations in demand.

System—A collection of components organized to accomplish a specific set of functions.

• T •

Test Phase—The period of time during which the components of a hardware or software product are evaluated and integrated, and the product is evaluated to determine whether or not requirements have been satisfied.

Topologically Integrated Geographic Encoding & Referencing (TIGER) Files—Computer-based map files created for the Census Bureau in support of the 1990 census.

Transportation Control Measures—Strategies to reduce vehicle trips, vehicle use, vehicle miles traveled, vehicle idling, or traffic congestion for the purpose of motor vehicle emissions.

Transportation Demand Management (TDM)—Policies and strategies are aimed at reducing vehicle demand by developing and encouraging modes of travel other than the single-occupant vehicle. Also known as "travel demand management."

Travel Technology (TravTek)—A public–private partnership involving the City of Orlando, the Florida DOT, Federal Highway Administration (FHWA), General Motors and the American Automobile Association. An operational test that provided motorists with traffic congestion information, motorist services (yellow pages) information, tourist information and route guidance information.

• U •

Urban Traffic Control System (UTCS)—A real-time traffic-responsive traffic control system originally developed by the FHWA.

User Services—User services document what ITS should do from the user's perspective. A broad range of users are considered, including the traveling public as well as many different types of system operators. Thirty user services formed the basis for the National ITS Architecture development effort.

User Service Bundles—A logical grouping of user services that provides a convenient way to discuss the range of requirements in a broad stakeholder area.

User Service Requirements—A decomposition of each user service into fundamental needs.

• V •

Validation—The process of evaluating a system or component during or at the end of the development process to determine whether it satisfies specified requirements. (See IEEE Std 610.12-1990.)

Variable Message Sign (VMS)—Signs that electronically or mechanically vary a display as traffic conditions warrant. Also referred to as changeable message signs or dynamic message signs.

Vehicle Navigation and Information Systems (VNIS)—Smart cards applications for vehicles and route guidance, and vehicle location and traffic information displays onboard cars and trucks. Uses map databases and ETTM technology.

Vehicle-to-Vehicle Communication—Dedicated wireless system handling high data rate, low probability of error and line of sight communications between vehicles. Advanced vehicle services may use this link in the future to support advanced collision avoidance implementations, road condition information sharing, and active coordination to advanced control systems.

Verification—(1) The process of evaluating a system or component to determine whether the products of a given development phase satisfy the conditions imposed at the start of that phase. (2) Formal proof of program correctness. (See IEEE Std 610.12-1990.)

Verification & Validation—The process of determining whether the requirements for a system or component are complete and correct, the products of each development phase fulfill the requirements or conditions imposed by the previous phase, and the final system or component complies with specified requirements.

• W •

Walk Through—A static analysis technique in which a designer or programmer leads members of the development team and other interested parties through a segment of documentation or code, and the participants ask questions and make comments about possible errors, violation of development standards and other problems.

Wide Area Wireless Communications—A communications link that provides communications between an untethered user and an infrastructure-based system. Both broadcast (one-way) and interactive (two-way) communications services are grouped into wide area wireless communications in the architecture. These links support a range of services in the architecture including real-time traveler information and various forms of fleet communications.

Wireline Communications—A communications link serving stationary sources. It may be implemented using a variety of public or private communications networks that may physically include wireless (e.g., microwave) as well as wire-line infrastructure. Both dedicated and shared communications resources may be used.

• A •

AAL—adaption layer

AASHTO—American Association of State Highway and Transportation Officials

ACC—adaptive cruise control

ADIS—advanced driver information systems

ADSL—asymmetrical digital subscriber line

ADVANCE—Advanced Driver and Vehicle Advisory Navigation Concept

AHS—automated highway system

AMS—American Meteorological Society

ANSI—American National Standards Institute

APC—automatic passenger counters

APS—automatic protection switching

APTS—advanced public transportation system

ARTS—advanced rural transportation systems

ASTM—American Society of Testing and Materials

ATA—American Trucking Association

ATIS—advanced traveler information systems

ATMS—advanced traffic management systems

ATSC—Automated Traffic Surveillance and Control

AVCS—advanced vehicle control systems

AVI—automatic vehicle identification

AVL—automatic vehicle location

AWIPS—advanced weather interactive processing system

• B •

BPR—Bureau of Public Roads

BRI—basic rate interface

• C •

CACS—comprehensive automobile communication system

CAD—computer-aided dispatch

CALTRANS—California Department of Transportation

CBI—constant bit rate

CBO—Congressional Budget Office

CCD—charge couple device

CCDV—contracted cell delay variation

CCTV—closed circuit television

CDPD—cellular digital packet data

CEN—Comité Européen de Normalisation

CHART—Cheaspeake Highway Advisories Routing Traffic

CIR—committed information rate

CLEC—competitive local exchange carrier

CLP—cell loss priority

CMAQ—Congestion Mitigation and Air Quality Improvement

CMM—Capability Maturity Model

CO—central office

COTS—commercial-off-the-shelf

CPE—customer premise equipment

CS—convergence sublayer

CSO—Council of Standards Organizations

CTA—Chicago Transit Authority

CV—commercial vehicle

CVIEW—CV information exchange window

CVISN—commercial vehicle information systems and networks

CVO—commercial vehicle operations

• D •

DACS—digital access cross-connect switch

DDS—digital data service

DGPS—differential global positioning system

DMS—dynamic message sign

DMV—Department of Motor Vehicles

DOTs—departments of transportation

DR—dead reckoning

DSL—digital subscriber line

DSP—digital signal processing

DSRC—dedicated short-range communication

DTA—dynamic traffic assignment

• E •

ECO—Employee Commute Options

EDI—electronic data interchange

EFT—electronic funds transfer

ERGS—electronic route guidance system

ERP—enterprise resource planning

ETAM—emissions testing and mitigation

ETC—electronic toll collection

ETTM—electronic toll and traffic management

EU—European Union

• F •

FCC—Federal Communications Commission

FDM—frequency division multiplexing

FHWA—Federal Highway Administration

FMS—freeway management system

FOIA—Freedom of Information Act

FOS—fiber optic shuttered

FRS—frame relay service

FSS—frequency selective service

FTA—Federal Transit Administration

• G •

GARVEE—Grant Anticipation Revenue Vehicle

GEO— geo-stationary earth orbit

GFC—generic flow control

GIS—geographic information system

GM—General Motors

GOES—geostationary earth satellites

GPS—global positioning system

• H •

HAR—highway advisory radio

HAZMAT—hazardous materials

HEC—header error check

HEO—highly elliptical orbit

HRI—highway–rail intersection

HSSC—high-speed subcarrier

HUFSAM—Highway Users Federation for Safety and Mobility

• I •

IAG—Interagency Group

IDIS—integrated driver information system

IEC—International Electrotechnical Commission

IEEE—Institute of Electrical and Electronics Engineers

IFTA—International Fuel Tax Agreement

ILD—inductive loop detector

ILEC—incumbent local exchange carrier

IMS—incident management system

INS—inertial navigation system

Interstate 4R program—Interstate resurfacing, restoration, rehabilitation, and reconstruction program

Interstate system—also known as the National System of Interstate and Defense Highways

IRP—International Registration Plan

ISDN—integrated services network

ISP—information service provider

ISO—International Standards Organization

ISTEA—Intermodal Surface Transportation Efficiency Act

IT—information technology

ITE—Institute of Transportation Engineers

ITSA—Intelligent Transportation Society of America

ITU—International Telecommunications Union

ITS—intelligent transportation systems

IVHS—Intelligent Vehicle Highway Systems

IVI—intelligent vehicle initiative

IXC—Interexchange Carrier

• J •

JIT—just-in-time

JPO—Joint Program Office

• K •

kbps—kilobit per second

KPA—key process area

• L •

LATA—local access transport area

LAN—local area network

LCD—liquid crystal display

LEC—local exchange carrier

LED—light emitting diode

LEO—low earth orbit

LOS—level of service

• M •

M&O—management and operations

Mbps—Megabit per second

MDI—model deployment initiative

MEO—medium earth orbit

MMIC—millimeter-wave monolithic integrated circuits

mph—miles per hour

MPO—metropolitan planning organizations

• N •

NAHSC—National Automated Highway System Consortium

NAL—network access line

NASA—National Aeronautics and Space Administration

NCAR—National Center for Atmospheric Research

NCDC—National Climatic Data Center

NEXRAD—next generation weather radar

NGSO—nongeostationary orbiting

NHS—National Highway System

NHTSA—National Highway Traffic Safety Administration

NITI—national intelligent transportation infrastructure

NPTS—Nationwide Personal Transportation Survey

NRC—National Research Council

NT1—network termination and supply module

NTCIP—National Transportation Communications for ITS Protocol

NWS—National Weather Service

• O •

OC-1—optical carrier level 1

OEM—original equipment manufacturer

OFCM—Office of the Federal Coordinator for Meteorology

OMCHS—The Office of Motor Carriers and Highway Safety

• P •

PAS—passing aid system

PATH—Partners for Advanced Transit and Highways

PCS—personal communications service

PDA—personal digital assistants

PLCP—physical layer convergence protocol

PMD—physical medium dependent

POP—point of presence

POTS—plain old telephone service

PRI—primary rate interface

PT—payload type

PVC—permanent virtual channel

• Q •

QOS—quality of service

• R •

RAD—rapid application development

RBDS—radio broadcast data standard

RBOC—Regional Bell Operating Company

RDS—radio-data system

RF—radio frequency

RFID—radio frequency identification

R&D—research and development

RWIS—road weather information systems

• S •

SAE—Society of Automotive Engineers

SAFER—safety and fitness electronic records

SAR—segmentation and reassembly

SEI—Software Engineering Institute

SDO—standards development organizations

SOC—statewide operations center

SONET—synchronous optical networking

SPS—standard positioning service

STS-1—synchronous transport signal level 1

SVC—switched virtual circuits

• T •

TAG—technical advisory group

TEA-21—Transportation Equity Act for the 21st Century

TC—technical committees

TCC—transit control center

TCIP—Transit Communications Interface Profiles

TCM—transportation control measure

TDM—transportation demand management

TIA—Telecommunications Industry Association

TIFIA—Transportation Infrastructure and Finance Innovation Act

TMC—traffic management center

TOC—traffic operations center

TRB—Transportation Research Board

TSC—Transit Standards Corsortium

TSM—transportation system management

TTI—Texas Transportation Institute

• U •

UNI—user network interface

U.S. DOT—United States Department of Transportation

UTCS—urban traffic control system

• V •

VAMS—value-adding meteorological services

VAN—vehicle area network

VBR—variable bit rate

VCI—virtual channel identifier

VDOT—Virginia Department of Transportation

VICS—Vehicle Information and Communication System

VIP—video image processors

VLU—vehicle logic unit

VMS—variable message sign

VMT—vehicle miles of travel

VPI—virtual path identifier

VT—virtual tributaries

• W •

WAN—wide area network

WASHCOG—Metropolitan Washington Council of Governments

WDM— wavelength-division multiplexing

WFO—weather forecast offices

WG—working groups

WIM—weigh-in-motion

WMATA—Washington Metropolitan Area Transit Authority

A